1,000,000 Books

are available to read at

www.ForgottenBooks.com

Read online
Download PDF
Purchase in print

ISBN 978-0-282-34893-9
PIBN 10848591

This book is a reproduction of an important historical work. Forgotten Books uses state-of-the-art technology to digitally reconstruct the work, preserving the original format whilst repairing imperfections present in the aged copy. In rare cases, an imperfection in the original, such as a blemish or missing page, may be replicated in our edition. We do, however, repair the vast majority of imperfections successfully; any imperfections that remain are intentionally left to preserve the state of such historical works.

Forgotten Books is a registered trademark of FB &c Ltd.
Copyright © 2018 FB &c Ltd.
FB &c Ltd, Dalton House, 60 Windsor Avenue, London, SW19 2RR.
Company number 08720141. Registered in England and Wales.

For support please visit www.forgottenbooks.com

1 MONTH OF FREE READING

at

www.ForgottenBooks.com

By purchasing this book you are eligible for one month membership to ForgottenBooks.com, giving you unlimited access to our entire collection of over 1,000,000 titles via our web site and mobile apps.

To claim your free month visit: www.forgottenbooks.com/free848591

*Offer is valid for 45 days from date of purchase. Terms and conditions apply.

English
Français
Deutsche
Italiano
Español
Português

www.forgottenbooks.com

Mythology Photography **Fiction** Fishing Christianity **Art** Cooking Essays Buddhism Freemasonry Medicine **Biology** Music **Ancient Egypt** Evolution Carpentry Physics Dance Geology **Mathematics** Fitness Shakespeare **Folklore** Yoga Marketing **Confidence** Immortality Biographies Poetry **Psychology** Witchcraft Electronics Chemistry History **Law** Accounting **Philosophy** Anthropology Alchemy Drama Quantum Mechanics Atheism Sexual Health **Ancient History Entrepreneurship** Languages Sport Paleontology Needlework Islam **Metaphysics** Investment Archaeology Parenting Statistics Criminology **Motivational**

THE ANCIENT AND NOBLE FAMILY

OF THE

SAVAGES OF THE ARDS

WITH SKETCHES OF ENGLISH AND AMERICAN BRANCHES
OF THE HOUSE OF SAVAGE

Compiled from Historical Documents and Family Papers, and Edited by

George Francis Armstrong

G. F. A.

With Illustrations of Arms,
Mansions, Ruins of
Castles, and

Ancient Sites & Monuments
connected with the
Family

"All hail the flower of Ulster!"—BARBOUR (A.D. 1375).

London:
MARCUS WARD & CO., LIMITED, FARRINGDON STREET, E.C.
AND AT BELFAST AND NEW YORK
1888

"The nobilitie of those Inglishemen [Anglo-Normans] wich came in at the conqwest, is much to be extolled and noted, wich being to souch an interprise but a few in nomber, how valiauntly & circumspectlye ded thei procede! and agayne, after what soarte thei made fortresses, and inhabited as thei went! what travayle, what paynes, what diligence usid thei therin! Thei sought neither for delicate fare, neither desired thei to lye in walled townes, uppon soft beddes, but pursued their enemies, untill thei had banyshed theym: for, if thei had don the contrarie, as souldiers do now a dayes, thei had neiver achived their purpus. Albeitt, it is to be thoght that the desier of wynnyng landes to ther posteritie chainged payn unto pleasur.—A MEMORIALL or a NOTE for the wynnyng of Leynster, too be presented too the KYNGES MAJESTY and his Graces most horable COUNSAYLE." (*Calendar of State Papers*, A.D. 1537. Henry VIII.)

PREFATORY NOTE.

HE Editor of the following compilation has edited it because there was no one else forthcoming to do so. He disclaims all ambition to figure as a genealogist; there is no rôle for which he is less qualified by either tastes or ability.

His collaborators, equally with himself, repudiate also all intention of putting together a work to attract purchasers or court the criticisms of the Press. The work has assumed a semi-public form simply because without some sort of public announcement and agency it would be unlikely to find its way to the numerous and scattered members, connections, and friends of the SAVAGE family, who would regret, if it existed, that they did not possess copies of it.

The Editor must apologise to those into whose hands it may fall for any inaccuracies they may discover in it. It is probable that, on the whole, it is a more accurate family-history than most that lay claim to accuracy; because it aims at nothing more than the discovery and statement of bare truth. But in some cases the Editor has been obliged to take quotations from authorities second-hand; and for the exact verbal accuracy of these excerpts, particularly when they happen to be clothed in mediæval or legal dog-Latin, he cannot absolutely vouch. He has not dared to "correct" where he is unfamiliar with any recognised standard of perfection. And yet he has been supplied with such quotations by competent copyists, and he is satisfied that any errors that may have occurred in transcription are of slight consequence. He would add that the scantiness of public documents relating to certain periods of the SAVAGE family-history has rendered it impossible in some instances to obtain information which may hereafter be quite accessible, when State Papers still lying out of reach of the ordinary reader have been calendared and printed.

No attempt has been made to treat the history of the English and American branches of the SAVAGES with fulness, and the compilers are aware that the list of American branches in particular is incomplete.

The Editor's warm thanks are due and are cordially tendered to the following ladies and gentlemen who have afforded him most valuable aid:— The Right Rev. the Lord Bishop of Down & Connor (Dr. Reeves); the Rev. George Hill, the very able Editor of *The Montgomery Manuscripts* and Author of *The Macdonnells of Antrim*; the Rev. Classon Porter, of Larne; the obliging officials of the Record Office, Dublin; the Librarian and Assistant-Librarian of the Royal Irish Academy; Colonel H. J. Savage, of Southsea, present representative of the SAVAGES OF ARDKEEN; Lieut.-General Andrew Nugent, of Portaferry House, present representative of the SAVAGES OF PORTAFERRY; Francis Walker Savage, Esq., of Springfield, Gloucestershire, one of the few living English representatives of the Savages of Clifton, Cheshire (Earls Rivers), who generously placed at the Editor's disposal his numerous notes and his beautiful sketches of SAVAGE mansions and monuments in England, and rendered him all manner of assistance; Francis W. Eveleigh Savage, Esq., to whose indefatigable researches the book owes perhaps the most essential portion of its contents; Mrs. M. E. Armstrong, whose sketches of SAVAGE relics in the Ards have furnished the subjects of many

PREFATORY NOTE.

of the woodcuts; Arthur Nugent, Esq., of Quintin Lodge, Leamington, who contributed many reminiscences and information of various kinds touching the SAVAGES of Ulster; Thomas Vesey Nugent, Esq., of Merrion Square, Dublin; Colonel John Vesey Nugent; Mrs. Savage, of Rochester, Kent; Mrs. Thomas English, of Woolwich; the Hon. Judge Savage, U.S. Consul at Belfast; Richard Savage, Esq., of Stratford-upon-Avon; John R. Savage, Esq., of Philadelphia; Miss Savage, of Town Malling, Kent; Mrs. Chauncey Lyttleton Savage, of Philadelphia; Mrs. Clifford Lloyd; Miss Minnie Savage; William R. Young, Esq., of Galgorm Castle, Co. Antrim; the Rev. Hugh Stowell, Rector of Ardkeen; Thomas Shaw, Esq., J.P., of Kirkcubbin; Charles H. Brett, Esq., of Belfast; Mr. James Shanks, of Ballyfoundra; Charles Murray, of Portaferry, than whom no one is more familiar with the topography and traditions of the Ards; and lastly to the Messrs. Marcus Ward & Co., for several interesting items of information, and for much other help and hearty coöperation.

Two other names are sorrowfully remembered of two eminent antiquarians to whom the Editor owed much, but who have unhappily passed away during the revision and printing of the book; and he can only record with a sigh his obligations to his late lamented friends, Sir Samuel Ferguson, poet, novelist, and archæologist; and Richard Caulfield, Esq., LL.D., Editor of the Corporation Records of Cork, Youghal, and Kinsale, and other valuable works.

June, 1888.

CONTENTS.

	PAGES
PREFATORY NOTE,	vii.-ix.

INTRODUCTION.

Eminence of the SAVAGE family in France, England, and Ireland. Their connection with the history of the English power in Ulster for seven hundred years. Aim of the Compilation. Interest of the subject, both local and general, ... 1–5

CHAPTER I.
THE NAME "SAVAGE."

Its origin and meaning. Arms of SAVAGE. Charges like those of the House of Anjou. Their symbolism. The Crest of the SAVAGES of ARDKEEN, and what it typifies, ... 6, 7

CHAPTER II.
THE SAVAGE FAMILY IN NORMANDY, BURGUNDY, AND ENGLAND.

The Norman Stem and Burgundian Branch. Their Norman home. LE SIEUR LE SAUVAGE arrives in England with William the Conqueror. Settlement in Derbyshire. English branches. SAVAGE of ROCK SAVAGE, Cheshire, the EARLS RIVERS; Earlier Kent Branch—SAVAGE of BOBBING COURT; SAVAGE of ELMLEY CASTLE, Worcestershire; SAVAGE of BROADWAY; SAVAGE of TETBURY, Gloucestershire; SAVAGE of BLOXWORTH, Dorsetshire; Later Kent Branch—SAVAGE of BOUGHTON MOUNT; SAVAGE of TACHBROOKE, Warwickshire. American Branches—SAVAGE of MASSACHUSETTS; SAVAGE of SAVAGE'S NECK, . . 8–117

CHAPTER III.
THE SAVAGES OF THE ARDS.—SAVAGE OF ARDKEEN *(Main Line)*.

THE SAVAGES LORDS OF THE ARDS, LECALE, &c.—Arrival of WILLIAM (afterwards BARON) LE SAVAGE in Ulster with DE COURCY (afterwards EARL of ULSTER). Settlement in the Ards. Ardkeen Castle, A.D. 1180. Portaferry Castle. Church of St. Mary of Ardkeen, the burial-place of the ARDKEEN SAVAGES. The BARON SAVAGE succeeded by his son SIR ROBERT SAVAGE. *Prest* granted to SIR ROBERT SAVAGE at Carrickfergus Castle by KING JOHN. Succeeded by his son SIR HENRY LE SAVAGE. Dominican Friary at Newtownards said to have been founded by the SAVAGE family during his lifetime. Succeeded by his son HENRY LE SAVAGE. HENRY LE SAVAGE succeeded by SIR ROBERT SAVAGE, living A.D. 1300. Eminence of the Family at this time. SAVAGES oppose invasion of Edward Bruce. HENRY SAVAGE a hostage for his brother SIR ROBERT in Dublin Castle. WILLIAM SAVAGE commanding the army of Ulster. Death of Edward Bruce. Extension of the SAVAGE power in Ulster. Vigorous warfare of SIR ROBERT SAVAGE. SIR ROBERT appointed by the King Sheriff of Coulrath, Seneschal of Ulster, and Warden of the Marches. Confirmed by the King in possession of Manors in Antrim representing nearly half the modern county. EDWARD SAVAGE Constable of Carrickfergus Castle. Narratives of SIR ROBERT SAVAGE and his son HENRY. Lissanoure Castle. SIR ROBERT succeeded by his son HENRY, LORD SAVAGE, a Baron by Writ. ROLAND (Raibilin) SAVAGE's encounter with Hugh O'Neill. EDMUND SAVAGE,

CONTENTS.

Seneschal of Ulster and Warden of the Marches. JORDAN SAVAGE. HENRY, LORD SAVAGE, succeeded by SIR ROBERT (FitzJordan) SAVAGE. SIR ROBERT appointed Sheriff of the Ards. Marries Christiana, daughter of John Macdonnell, Lord of the Isles, and granddaughter of Robert II., King of Scotland. Warfare with the Irish Chiefs of Ulster. PATRICK SAVAGE, Seneschal of Ulster, and his brother RICHARD, treacherously murdered by the Irish Chief MacGilmore. Vengeance of the SAVAGE family. King Henry IV. grants JOHN, son of RICHARD SAVAGE, the Guardianship of the Peace, A.D. 1401. Henry V. grants EDMUND, son of EDMUND SAVAGE, late Seneschal, the "Liberties of Ulster." Conflicts with the Irish. Great defeat at Ardglass of the O'Neills and their allies by the SAVAGES, assisted by the English of Dublin. The SAVAGES established as Lords of Lecale. Their Castles at Ardglass. SIR ROBERT (FitzJordan) SAVAGE succeeded by ROBERT SAVAGE, LORD of LECALE, also called LORD of ARDKEEN. ROBERT succeeded by PATRICK SAVAGE, LORD of LECALE, &c. Treachery of the Whites of Dufferin. Alliances of the Irish Chiefs. The SAVAGE power in Lecale temporarily shaken. PATRICK SAVAGE succeeded by SIR ROLAND SAVAGE. SIR ROLAND appointed Seneschal of Ulster by Edward IV. Question of the identity of SIR ROLAND SAVAGE with "JANICO" SAVAGE. Appeal to the King by the abbots and people of Down to aid the SENESCHAL SAVAGE in his efforts to hold the English territories of the North against the O'Neills and the Irish hordes. SIR ROLAND, LORD of LECALE and in MOYLINNY in Antrim, one of "the English noble folk who make war and peace for themselves." Important State Paper urging the King to assist SIR ROLAND SAVAGE and his kinsmen to reconquer the territories lost by the English. SIR ROLAND SAVAGE succeeded by RAYMOND ("Ferdorough Mac Seneschal") SAVAGE, LORD of LECALE and of ARDKEEN. Difficulties of RAYMOND's position. Confirmed by the Lord Deputy in the Lordship of Lecale. Contest between RAYMOND and his kinsman ROLAND SAVAGE for precedence in the Little Ards. They refer the question to the Lord Deputy and Council. Final division of the Upper Ards between ROLAND of PORTAFERRY and RAYMOND of ARDKEEN, and Treaty between them. Attempt of Queen Elizabeth to plant the Lower Ards under Smith. RAYMOND SAVAGE protects Smith's followers. Ardkeen Castle temporarily in the hands of the Queen's Government. Letter from Capt. Brett, written from Ardkeen Castle. RAYMOND succeeded by his nephew FERDOROUGH SAVAGE, LORD of ARDKEEN. FERDOROUGH succeeded by HENRY SAVAGE, LORD of ARDKEEN, High Sheriff of the Co. Down, A.D. 1634. HENRY confirmed in possession of the Castle and Manor of ARDKEEN by James I. Intermarriages with the O'Neills and the Nevins, Lairds of Monkrodden. Plantation of the Great (or Lower) Ards by the Montgomeries. Pictures of the life and society of the Ards in the 17th century. Rebellion and massacre of 1641. Freedom of the Ards from the disturbances. William Montgomery's account of HENRY SAVAGE of ARDKEEN. HENRY succeeded at ARDKEEN by his eldest son, JOHN SAVAGE, High Sheriff of the Co. Down, A.D. 1663. His marriage. Succeeded at ARDKEEN by his son CAPT. HUGH SAVAGE, an officer in the army of William III. HUGH wounded at the Boyne and at Aughrim. Confiscation of the lands of members of the SAVAGE family who had sided with James II. Description of the Ards in the lifetime of CAPT. HUGH SAVAGE. Montgomery's Account of "The Two Ancient Families of the SAVAGES" (ARDKEEN and PORTAFERRY). Old dwelling-house at Ardkeen Castle demolished, and new House of Ardkeen built. CAPT. HUGH SAVAGE's will. Genealogical table of his descendants. SAVAGE of ROCK SAVAGE (BALLYGALGET). SAVAGE of GLASTRY. HUGH succeeded at Ardkeen by his son FRANCIS SAVAGE, High Sheriff of the County Down, A.D. 1732. Intermarriages with the Lucases of Castleshane. FRANCIS SAVAGE Colonel-Commandant of the Ards Regiment of Volunteers in 1760. His will. Genealogical table of his descendants. Marriage of his daughter MARY with FRANCIS SAVAGE of GLASTRY. Succeeded at ARDKEEN by his son CHARLES SAVAGE, High Sheriff of the Co. Down, A.D. 1770. Intermarriages with the Prices of Hollymount and Saintfield. Hollymount becomes the property of the SAVAGES of ARDKEEN. Genealogical table of FRANCIS SAVAGE of ARDKEEN's descendants. Intermarriage with the Baylys of Norelands. Descent maternally of the Meredyths, Baronets, from the SAVAGES of ARDKEEN. CHARLES SAVAGE succeeded at Ardkeen by his son FRANCIS SAVAGE, of ARDKEEN and HOLLYMOUNT, High Sheriff and M.P. for Co. Down. Mrs. Delany and Hollymount. FRANCIS SAVAGE and the Irish House of Commons. Intermarriage with the Butlers, Earls of Carrick. CLAYTON BAYLY, heir to the ARDKEEN Estates, representative maternally of the SAVAGES of ARDKEEN, assumes the name of SAVAGE. Lady HARRIET SAVAGE marries Col. Forde of Seaforde. Ardkeen lands sold to Mr. Harrison. FRANCIS SAVAGE of Hollymount and Ardkeen succeeded in the representation of the SAVAGES of ARDKEEN in the male line by Major-General SIR JOHN BOSCAWEN SAVAGE, K.C.B., K.C.H., of BALLYGALGET (ROCK SAVAGE, Co. Down). SIR JOHN BOSCAWEN SAVAGE's services. Anecdotes. Genealogical table of SIR JOHN BOSCAWEN SAVAGE's descendants. Succeeded by his eldest son Lieut.-General HENRY JOHN SAVAGE. LIEUT.-GENERAL SAVAGE's services, &c., Genealogical table of his descendants. Succeeded by his son COL. HENRY JOHN SAVAGE, present representative of the SAVAGES of ARDKEEN in the male line. COL. SAVAGE's services. His children, &c., ... 118-243

CHAPTER IV.

SAVAGE OF ARDKEEN (continued).—SAVAGE OF BALLYGALGET, EARLIER LINE.

ROLAND SAVAGE of BALLYGALGET, an officer in Queen Elizabeth's army, uncle of HENRY SAVAGE of ARDKEEN, builds the Castle of BALLYGALGET and the Castle of KIRKISTONE. Intermarriage with the Magennises, Lords of Iveagh. Genealogical table of ROLAND SAVAGE's descendants. ROLAND SAVAGE, M.P. for Newry. Captain SAVAGE, an officer in his kinsman Magennis's Regiment, on the side of James II., taken prisoner by Capt. Hunter at Killyleagh Castle. Confiscation of the property of the SAVAGES of BALLYGALGET for siding with James II., ... 244-251

CHAPTER V.

SAVAGE OF ARDKEEN (*continued*).—SAVAGE OF KIRKISTONE CASTLE.

KIRKISTONE CASTLE described. Intermarriage with the family of M'Gill. WILLIAM SAVAGE of KIRKISTONE, High Sheriff of the County Down. Picturesque Story of the Monks of Drumnacoyle. KIRKISTONE CASTLE and the Montgomery family, its present owners, · · · · · · 252-256

CHAPTER VI.

SAVAGE OF ARDKEEN (*continued*).—SAVAGE OF BALLYGALGET (ROCK SAVAGE)—LATER LINE.

Founded by PHILIP SAVAGE, second son of CAPT. HUGH SAVAGE of ARDKEEN. Intermarriage with the Cramers and with the Echlins of Ardquin. ROCK SAVAGE (BALLYGALGET) House and Demesne. Narratives. Genealogical table of PHILIP SAVAGE's descendants. MAJOR SAVAGE and the rebels of '98. Intermarriage with the Lushingtons, &c. MARMADUKE COGHILL SAVAGE. FRANCIS SAVAGE of GLASTRY. SIR JOHN BOSCAWEN SAVAGE succeeds his nephew HENRY SAVAGE at BALLYGALGET. Demolition of ROCK SAVAGE (BALLYGALGET) Mansion. The BALLYGALGET (ROCK SAVAGE) family become the representatives of the ARDKEEN family in the male line, in the person of SIR JOHN BOSCAWEN SAVAGE, · · · · · · · · · · · 257-268

CHAPTER VII.

SAVAGE OF ARDKEEN (*continued*).—SAVAGE OF GLASTRY.

Doubly SAVAGE of ARDKEEN. FRANCIS SAVAGE of GLASTRY, High Sheriff of the Co. Down, marries his first cousin Mary, daughter of FRANCIS SAVAGE of ARDKEEN. Her beauty. Genealogical table of FRANCIS of GLASTRY's descendants. FRANCIS SAVAGE, his son. COLONEL CHARLES SAVAGE. CAPT. HENRY SAVAGE of FRINDSBURY. Young CHARLES SAVAGE, his gifts and early death. FRANCIS SAVAGE of GLASTRY is succeeded by his son, the REV. HENRY SAVAGE of GLASTRY, Incumbent of Ardkeen. Genealogical table of the REV. HENRY SAVAGE's descendants. Succeeded at GLASTRY by his eldest son, FRANCIS SAVAGE, J.P., Barrister-at-Law. RAYMOND SAVAGE killed by a fall from his horse. FRANCIS SAVAGE of GLASTRY succeeded by his brother EDWARD SAVAGE. Intermarriages with the Willingtons and with the Armstrongs. EDWARD SAVAGE originally designs his nephew EDMUND ARMSTRONG, the Poet, as his heir. Is succeeded by his only daughter, SARAH J. A. SAVAGE. Her early death. JANE SAVAGE (MRS. E. J. ARMSTRONG). GEORGE FRANCIS ARMSTRONG, representative of his uncle EDWARD SAVAGE of GLASTRY, · · · · · · · · · 269-286

CHAPTER VIII.

SAVAGE OF ARDKEEN (*continued*).—MONUMENTS, EPITAPHS, &c., OF THE ARDKEEN FAMILY IN THE ARDS.

SAVAGE Monuments in the Ards. The old Church of Ardkeen. Vaults of the SAVAGES of ARDKEEN. The peasantry and the old Ballygalget Graveyard. Epitaphs. Story of the GLASTRY Tomb, · · 287-295

CHAPTER IX.

SAVAGE (NOW NUGENT) OF PORTAFERRY.

Contest of ROLAND and RAYMOND SAVAGE for precedency again referred to. Difficulty still in deciding the question of seniority. Intermarriage with the Macdonnells, Earls of Antrim. SAVAGE of PORTAFERRY addressed by the Lord Deputy as "LORD SAVAGE." Letter from ROLAND SAVAGE to the Earl of Sussex, Lieut.-General of Ireland, asking for support against his Irish enemies. Genealogical table of ROLAND's descendants. SAVAGE of BALLYVARLEY. SAVAGE of BALLYMADUN, Co. Dublin. ROLAND succeeded at Portaferry by PATRICK, LORD SAVAGE. LITTLE ARDS mentioned in A.D. 1586 as inheritance of the LORDS SAVAGE. Spenser's allusion to the SAVAGES of the ARDS. O'Daly's satirical account of the Ards. Their reduced state at this time. The LORD SAVAGE aids the Crown during the disturbances of 1599. Intermarriage with the Plunket family. PATRICK succeeded at PORTAFERRY by his son, ROLAND, LORD SAVAGE. Lord Deputy Chichester tries to get him to marry his daughter. Intermarriages with the Russells of Rathmullen and the O'Haras of Antrim. Weekly market at Portaferry granted to ROLAND SAVAGE. ROLAND succeeded at PORTAFERRY by his brother CAPTAIN PATRICK SAVAGE. Confirmatory Grants of the lands of PORTAFERRY and other lands to PATRICK SAVAGE by CHARLES I. State of the Ards in

xiv. CONTENTS.

PAGES

PATRICK's lifetime, and of PORTAFERRY and the CASTLE, described by Montgomery. Intermarriage with the Montgomeries, Viscounts, Lords of the Great Ards. Genealogical table of PATRICK SAVAGE's descendants. Intermarriages with the Wiltons, O'Neills, Barts., &c. Succeeded at PORTAFERRY by his son HUGH SAVAGE. Montgomery's account of HUGH. His strength. His wit. His misfortune. Succeeded at PORTAFERRY by PATRICK SAVAGE, formerly of Derry in the Ards. Montgomery's account of him, and of the Ards. Genealogical table of his descendants. Intermarriages with the Prices of Saintfield, Halls of Narrow-Water, &c. PATRICK is succeeded at Portaferry by his son EDWARD SAVAGE. Succeeded by his uncle JAMES SAVAGE. JAMES is succeeded at PORTAFERRY by his son JOHN SAVAGE. JOHN is succeeded by his brother ANDREW SAVAGE. Intermarriage with the Nugents of Dysart (family of the Earls of Westmeath). ANDREW is succeeded at PORTAFERRY by his son PATRICK SAVAGE, High Sheriff of the Co. Down. Arthur Young's description of Portaferry. Intermarriage with the Halls of Narrow-Water. Genealogical table of PATRICK SAVAGE's descendants. Succeeded at PORTAFERRY by his son ANDREW SAVAGE, High Sheriff of the Co. Down, who assumes the name of NUGENT and claims the Barony of Delvin. Intermarriage with the Veseys, Viscounts de Vesci. Genealogical table of ANDREW (SAVAGE) NUGENT's descendants. Intermarriages with the Stronges, Barts., of Tynan Abbey; Verners, Barts.; Maxwells, Lords Farnham; Brookes, Barts., of Colebrooke; Tisdalls of Charlesfort; Heads; Pitts, &c. ANDREW NUGENT succeeded at PORTAFERRY by his eldest son, COL. PATRICK JOHN NUGENT, High Sheriff of the Co. Down. Genealogical table of COL. PATRICK JOHN NUGENT's descendants. Intermarriages with the Langhams, &c. COL. NUGENT succeeded at PORTAFERRY by his eldest son, Lieut.-General ANDREW NUGENT, present representative of the SAVAGES of PORTAFERRY, - 296-324

CHAPTER X.

SAVAGE OF PORTAFERRY (continued).—RELICS, EPITAPHS, &C.

The Shrine of St. Patrick's Hand. Old Cathedral of Down, ancient burial-place of the SAVAGES of PORTAFERRY. Epitaphs at Templecraney, at Ballytrustan, at Ballyphilip. Arms of SAVAGE and MONTGOMERY at Portaferry House. Arms of NUGENT in Downpatrick Cathedral, ... 325-331

CHAPTER XI.

SAVAGE OF PROSPECT.—PROSPECT BRANCH OF THE SAVAGES OF THE ARDS.

HENRY SAVAGE, Lieutenant in the Saintfield Regiment of Volunteers, 1760. Intermarriage with the Gillespie family. Major-General Sir Robert Rollo Gillespie. Genealogical table of HENRY SAVAGE's descendants. Intermarriages with the Nixons, Cottnams, Johnstons, Halcotts, Lloyds, Beauclerks, Lawleys, Dawsons, Murdocks, Wolesleys, Macdonalds, Vicomtes de Coux, Hamiltons, Youngs of Galgorm Castle, Lanyons, &c. Clifford Lloyd. HENRY SAVAGE succeeded by his eldest son Lieut.-Col. PATRICK SAVAGE. LIEUT.-COL. SAVAGE's services. Intermarriage with the Millers of Ballycastle. LIEUT.-COL. SAVAGE succeeded by his son, CAPT. HENRY SAVAGE, Royal Engineers. CAPT. HENRY SAVAGE succeeded by his nephew WILLIAM HENRY SAVAGE, present representative in the male line, ... 332-337

CHAPTER XII.

THE SAVAGE FAMILY AT CARRICKFERGUS.

Carrickfergus Castle. The Constableship and the SAVAGE family. The Shrievalty and Mayoralty and the SAVAGE family. Savage property at Carrickfergus. Humble descendants, ... 338-343

APPENDICES, ... 345

List of Illustrations.

	PAGE
PORTAFERRY HOUSE, seat of the SAVAGES—now NUGENTS—OF PORTAFERRY, *Frontispiece.*	
Crest of SAVAGE (*ancient*),	6
Crest of SAVAGE assumed from Danyers,	6
Crest of SAVAGE OF ARDKEEN,	6
Arms of the SAVAGES,	6
Ruins of ROCK SAVAGE, Cheshire, ancient Seat of the SAVAGES, EARLS RIVERS,	8
Arms of Meynill and SAVAGE,	14
Arms of SAVAGE quartering Danyers,	19
Tomb of THOMAS SAVAGE, Archbishop of York, in York Minster. (Ob. 1508),	22
Monument in the Savage Chapel, Macclesfield, to the Right Hon. THOS. SAVAGE, EARL RIVERS, &c., ob. 1694. The two altar-tombs are supposed to be those of Sir JOHN SAVAGE, ob. 1615, and Sir THOMAS, his son, ob. 1635,	25
Tomb of SIR JOHN SAVAGE, of Clifton, Knt., ob. 1528, and of his Wife, the Lady Elizabeth, daughter of Charles Somerset, Earl of Worcester, in the Savage Chapel, Macclesfield. (The slab with the cross marks the burial-place of GEORGE SAVAGE, father of Bishop Bonner),	32
Monument of SIR JOHN SAVAGE, of Clifton, Knt., ob. 1597, and of the Lady Elizabeth, his Wife, ob. 1570, in the Savage Chapel, Macclesfield,	37
Portion of BEESTON CASTLE, Cheshire, seat of the SAVAGES OF BEESTON,	39
Ruins of HALTON CASTLE, Cheshire, ninety years ago,	47
Arms of SAVAGE, with Supporters,	61
The Savage Chapel, Macclesfield, Cheshire, burial-place of the SAVAGES of Cheshire (EARLS RIVERS), founded by THOMAS SAVAGE, Archbishop of York, circ. 1501,	63
ELMLEY CASTLE, seat of the SAVAGES of ELMLEY CASTLE,	75
ELMLEY CASTLE (north-east view), seat of the SAVAGES OF ELMLEY CASTLE,	83
Tomb of GILES and WILLIAM SAVAGE, of ELMLEY CASTLE, in the Savage Chapel, at Elmley,	85
TETBURY CLOSE (front), seat of the SAVAGES OF TETBURY,	92
Arms of Estcourt,	93
TETBURY CLOSE (from the grounds), seat of the SAVAGES OF TETBURY,	98

	PAGE
Portrait of MAJOR THOMAS SAVAGE (*from an old painting*),	109
Portrait of SAMUEL PHILLIPS SAVAGE,	111
ARDKEEN CASTLE HILL, Co. Down, site of the ancient stronghold of the SAVAGES OF ARDKEEN, with CHAPEL (to the left), and portion of Strangford Lough,	118
Ruins of LISSANOURE CASTLE, Antrim residence of SIR ROBERT SAVAGE, now the property of the Macartney family,	138
CASTLE at ARDGLASS known as "KING'S CASTLE," residence of the SAVAGE family in Lecale. (From an old woodcut),	154
KILCLIEF CASTLE, Co. Down, for a time the stronghold of the FitzSimons branch of the SAVAGES,	173
SKETRICK CASTLE, off the western shore of Strangford Lough, an ancient stronghold of the SAVAGES OF ARDKEEN,	182
Last remaining fragment of the ancient CASTLE OF ARDKEEN, on the summit of Ardkeen Castle Hill (1884),	202
KNOCKDHU, Co. Down, site of BALLYGALGET CASTLE and ROCK SAVAGE HOUSE,	244
KIRKISTONE CASTLE, formerly the seat of the SAVAGES OF KIRKISTONE,	252
Ruins of the old Church of Ardkeen, burial-place of the SAVAGES OF ARDKEEN CASTLE,	257
GLASTRY HOUSE, Co. Down, formerly seat of the SAVAGES OF GLASTRY,	269
Tomb of the SAVAGES OF GLASTRY, outside the Old Church of Ardkeen,	287
Ruins of PORTAFERRY CASTLE, ancient stronghold of the SAVAGES OF PORTAFERRY,	296
QUINTIN CASTLE (restored), held by the Smiths under the SAVAGES OF PORTAFERRY, now owned by the Anketell family,	304
Keep of PORTAFERRY CASTLE, from the gardens of PORTAFERRY HOUSE,	319
Ruins of the Old Cathedral of Downpatrick, ancient burial-place of the SAVAGES OF PORTAFERRY,	325
Ruins of Templecraney Church, later burial-place of the SAVAGES OF PORTAFERRY, with part of the pleasure-grounds of PORTAFERRY HOUSE,	332
CARRICKFERGUS CASTLE,	338
Arms of COCK,	377

List of Maps.

Rough tracing of Section of Map in State Paper Calendars of Henry VIII.'s reign, Hibernia, 1567—Rough tracing of Section of Map in State Papers of Henry VIII., Section of Ortelius' Improved or New Map of Ireland, ... } *To face page* 174

Ancient Drawing of the Town of Carrickfergus, ... *To face page* 340

INTRODUCTION.

F the ancient and noble Norman family of SAVAGE—or, as the Normans wrote it, LE SAUVAGE—the first who came into these kingdoms passed from Normandy into England with the army of the Conqueror, A.D. 1066, and settled in Derbyshire. From Derbyshire the SAVAGE family branched out into several English counties; and from Derbyshire, in 1177, they established themselves in Ireland in the person of WILLIAM SAVAGE, one of the twenty-two Knights who fought by De Courcy in the subjugation of Ulster, and subsequently one of the Ulster Palatine Barons.

In England the SAVAGES became the owners of extensive estates, held high offices, contracted noble alliances, distinguished themselves at decisive political conjunctures, amassed great wealth, attached themselves to successive monarchs, were advanced to various dignities, and the VISCOUNTS SAVAGE and EARLS RIVERS transmitted royal blood to their descendants. The family contributed its share of illustrious men to the state, to arms, to the church, to literature. Their names are found among the Crusaders, among the warriors knighted at the Siege of Caerlaverock, among the Knights and Esquires who fought at Agincourt. Sir Arnold Savage, in Henry IV.'s time, was twice Speaker of the English House of Commons; Sir John Savage, commanding the left wing of Richmond's army at the victory of Bosworth Field, helped very materially to establish the House of Tudor on the English throne; Thomas Savage, in the following reign, was Bishop of Rochester, of London, and ultimately Archbishop of York; and the world of letters has been enriched

B

from the SAVAGE stock by the poet Richard Savage,[1] the poet Walter Savage Landor,[2] and the poet Alfred Lord Tennyson.[3]

In Ireland their sphere of activity was narrower than in England, but their position relatively was no less eminent. Assisting in the Ulster conquest, WILLIAM LE SAUVAGE won with his sword lands which for over seven hundred years have remained in the possession of his posterity. As a Palatine Baron he helped to lay in that valuable province the foundations of the supremacy

---

[1] Richard Savage, born 1698, was, as is well known, the natural son of Richard Savage, 4th Earl Rivers, by Anne, Countess of Macclesfield.

[2] Walter Savage Landor represented maternally the SAVAGES OF TACHBROOKE, in Warwickshire; and though his biographer, Mr. Forster, has not traced this branch of the SAVAGES to the Cheshire stock, there cannot be any doubt of their descent therefrom. Indeed, there were strong marks of affinity to the race in Landor himself. Landor's pride in his SAVAGE blood was carried beyond all reasonable bounds. Readers of his biography will remember Mr. Forster's story :—"I had, on one occasion, the greatest difficulty in restraining him from sending a challenge to Lord John Russell for some fancied slight to the memory of Sir Arnold Savage, Speaker of Henry the Seventh's First House of Commons [Forster is here curiously inaccurate in his dates]; yet any connection beyond the name could not with safety have been assumed."

[3] Lord Tennyson's descent from the SAVAGES was thus set forth in the public prints at the time of his elevation to the peerage :—"The Laureate's descent from John Savage, Earl Rivers (from which stock came Johnson's friend), implies descent from the Lady Anne, eldest sister of Henry IV., and so from sixteen English kings—namely, the first three Edwards, Henry III., John, the first two Henrys, William the Conqueror, Edmund Ironside, Ethelred the Unready, Edgar the Peaceable, Edmund I., Edward the Elder, Alfred, Ethelwulf, and Egbert. But Edward III. was the son of Isabella, daughter of Philip the Fair, King of France, who descended from Hugh Capet and nine intervening French kings, among whom were Robert II., Philip Augustus, Louis VIII., and St. Louis. The last is not the only saint who figures in this splendid pedigree. The mother of Edward II. was Eleanor, daughter of Ferdinand III., King of Castile and Leon, who was canonised by Clement X. Again, through the marriage of Edmund of Langley, Duke of York, with Isabel, daughter of Peter the Cruel, Mr. Tennyson descends from Sancho the Great and Alphonso the Wise. Other crowned ancestors of the poet are the Emperor Frederick Barbarossa and several Kings of Scotland, notably Malcolm III., and 'the gracious Duncan,' his father. In truth, the Shakespearean gallery is crowded with portraits of his progenitors—e.g., besides those already mentioned, John of Gaunt, Edmund Mortimer Earl of March, Richard Earl of Cambridge, Richard Plantagenet 'the Yeoman,' Edmund Beaufort Duke of Somerset, Lord Hastings (of the reigns of Edward IV. and Richard III.), and Lord Stanley. Mr. Tennyson is not only descended from the first Earl of Derby, and that third earl with whose death, according to Camden, 'the glory of hospitality seemed to fall asleep,' but from the 'stout Stanley' who fronted the right of the Scots at Flodden, and whose name in Scott's poem was the last on the lips of the dying Marmion. 'Lord Marmion,' says Scott, 'is entirely a fictitious person;' but he adds that the family of Marmion, Lords of Fontenay in Normandy, was highly distinguished, Robert de Marmion, a follower of Duke William, having obtained a grant of the castle and town of Tamworth. This Robert's descendant, Avice, married John, Lord Grey of Rotherfield, one of the original Knights of the Garter, whose great-granddaughter became (in 1401) the wife of John, Lord D'Eyncourt, another ancestor of Mr. Tennyson's, whose uncle, the Right Honourable Charles Tennyson, many years Liberal Member for Lambeth, assumed the name of D'Eyncourt by royal licence."

of England. In the accounts of successive conflicts with the Irish of the North the names of his descendants figure conspicuously for centuries. As time went on, by conquest and by royal gift the possessions of the SAVAGES OF THE ARDS increased until they became the lords of territories wider than those of any other Ulster feudatories. They were summoned to Parliament, and as Barons by Writ-of-Summons were known as the LORDS SAVAGE. By one English monarch after another they were entrusted with the foremost offices in the district. From time to time, as Seneschals of Ulster and Wardens of the Marches, they swayed the North and held it against the enemies of England. At the direst moment of danger and depression, when the inhabitants of the little English colony of Ulster were threatened with destruction at the hands of the Irish swarms, it was round the SENESCHAL SAVAGE that they rallied, it was to his "faithful liegeman" the SENESCHAL SAVAGE that they prayed the King to send succour for their preservation. The descendants of almost all the other Anglo-Norman conquerors of Ulster—the Mandevilles, Jordans, Chamberlains, Copelands, Martels, Ridals—were swept away or rendered utterly powerless. The SAVAGES still held their ancient inheritance in the ARDS, unsubdued. In them, as a recent Irish antiquarian truly states, "all the English interest centered." It is hardly an exaggeration to assert that, but for the bravery, the determination, and the tenacity of the SAVAGES at moments of supreme danger, the Northern Province might have been brought completely under Irish control, and with that subjection the whole current of Ulster history might have been changed. They often held the gap, and held it alone. They helped prominently to hand on the possession of Ulster from the first conquest in 1177 to the final "Settlement" of the Seventeenth Century.

But loyal at heart to their kings as the SAVAGES OF THE ARDS undoubtedly were, they were not always permitted to be so in act. It was the old story. The loyalist in Ireland was frequently sacrificed in those early centuries by blundering or dishonest rulers just as he is at present. Unsupported by the arm of England, he stood face to face with the implacable enemies of England. If his territory should be invaded, if his cattle should be driven off by the combined forces of neighbouring Irish chieftains, he seldom obtained protection or redress. With his dependants, his own little army, he had to fight his own battle as best he could. If it did not suit the policy, or the convenience, of the Lord Deputy to defend the King's liege against the King's enemies, he was declared to have made war on his own authority, and was treated as a rebel —perhaps to the personal aggrandisement of the Lord Deputy himself. On one occasion the SAVAGES were reported to be amongst the "English noble folk" who were in rebellion against their monarch, and a portion of their territory of LECALE passed into the hands of the then Deputy, the Earl of Kildare. When Anglo-Norman Ulster became completely separated from the Pale, the SAVAGES and their few allies were practically isolated. Pressed upon on all sides but the sea by the Irish hordes, under the leadership of their old enemies the O'Neills, in alliance with their rivals the Bissetts and Macdonnells of Antrim, they gradually lost their once firm grasp of their outlying possessions. But in the LITTLE ARDS they were immovable. Tradition states that when the O'Neills and their confederates, under the famous Shane, attempted the invasion of that corner of the SAVAGE estates, and laid siege to the Castle of ARDKEEN, they were driven back by the SAVAGES with such effect that they never ventured to undertake the same enterprise again.

Unlike their English kinsmen, the SAVAGES of the ARDS were not courtiers. Had they been less independent and less stiff-necked, had their chiefs ingratiated themselves with the Monarchs or their Irish Deputies, it is possible that neither the abortive attempt of Smith to occupy the LOWER ARDS, nor the successful efforts of Montgomery to plant the same territory, would have been sanctioned and supported, the former by Elizabeth, the latter by James and Charles. It is possible that to them might have been granted the mission entrusted to others, that they might have been reinstated in all they had lost, that they might have become once more, and continued to this day to be, the most powerful, as they are unquestionably the most ancient, of the English families of Ulster.[1]

It is of the fortunes of the Irish branches of the SAVAGE family only that the Editor of the following pages has attempted to preserve any minute record. A brief preliminary sketch of the English branches has been deemed necessary as introductory to the main portion of the narrative; for the English and Irish branches never forgot their consanguinity; even until within comparatively recent times their representatives corresponded as "cousins;"[2] and the feeling

---

[1] They are at present represented in the ARDS by Lieut.-General ANDREW NUGENT of PORTAFERRY, whose grandfather, ANDREW SAVAGE, Esq., of PORTAFERRY, assumed the name of NUGENT. Their kinsmen, the Russells of Killough, now represented by Thomas John, Count Russell, of Quoniamstown and Ballystrew, Co. Down, are alone coeval with them.

[2] "My father," writes Mr. Thomas Vesey Nugent, January 29, 1881, "had often shown me a letter from Lord Rivers, dated some time towards the end of the 17th century, addressed to Rowland or Patrick Savage (I forget which), commencing 'My dear Cousin,' and requesting him to procure some falcons or hawks from the Isle of Man. This letter was quite legible, but the paper was in a very dilapidated condition. I am certain that it is not now in existence." And Mr. Arthur Nugent writes:—"Among the papers at Portaferry there was a letter from the first Lord Rivers, whose name was Savage, addressed to a Mr Savage, of Portaferry, thanking him for some hawks, and asking him to send him some more. He addressed him as '*My dear Cousin*.' I have often heard my father

of kinship is as lively, and its recognition as general, amongst the members of the Irish and English branches to-day as it was in the days of their ancestors. But a full history of the SAVAGE family in England must be left to some other pen; and the writer who attempts it will find the State papers and other public records teeming with information about them. The present Editor has contented himself with putting together, in as orderly a manner as other and discordant occupations would permit, a considerable mass of information concerning the ULSTER family which had come into his hands, and which appeared to him well worthy of preservation in some kind of permanent form.

The memoirs of a family that has taken an active part in the history of an important portion of our empire for seven hundred years, cannot but be interesting and precious to its members and to all who are connected with it by blood or by friendship; and it is for these that this compilation is principally intended. But it may perhaps be found to have a wider interest, as throwing, indirectly, some light on a period of Anglo-Irish history which has yet to be thoroughly investigated, and in which lie the germs of political problems with which we have still to grapple.

---

mention it. The letter concluded with the words, '*Your Cousin*, RIVERS.'" (*Letter to* EDITOR.) The letter was preserved with care by the late Mr. Andrew Nugent (Savage), of Portaferry House, being "very old, quite yellow, and falling to pieces." It appears that the Isle of Man hawks were considered of superior breed, and the proximity of the ARDS to the Island suggested the request.

Crest of SAVAGE (ancient).   Crest of SAVAGE assumed from Danyers.   Crest of SAVAGE of Ardkeen.

CHAPTER I.

THE NAME "SAVAGE."

N its older Norman-French and Anglo-Norman forms, *Le Sauvage* and *De Sauvage*, its Latinized equivalents *Salvagius* and *Silvaticus*, its English spelling *Savage* and *Savadge*, and its Irish distortion *Mac-i-Tavishe*,[1] this surname occurs frequently as an eminent one from very early times. When first borne as a surname, *Le Sauvage* signified, probably, not the *ferocious*, but the *Forester*, as distinguished from the inhabitants of fortified towns.[2]

THE ARMS OF SAVAGE.

The armorial bearings of the family of SAVAGE—*six lioncels rampant sable, three, two, and one, armed and langued gules, on a field argent*—symbolize the forest life and warlike character of their Norman forefathers, and are remarkable as being the same charges, with a difference of tinctures, as those of William, Earl of Salisbury, surnamed Longespée, son of King Henry II. by the Fair Rosamond, which latter bearings some heralds believe to have been derived from the Royal House of

Arms of the SAVAGES.

---

[1] The ARDKEEN family were known just as often amongst the Irish under the name of *Mac Seneschal*, from so many of their Chiefs having held the office of Seneschal of Ulster under the English Kings.

[2] Subsequent to the Norman Conquest, when fortified places became numerous in England, those who preferred the natural defence of the woods to stone walls were called by the Anglo-Normans *les Sauvages*. It will be remembered that the surname was bestowed by the Normans

Anjou.[1] The crest, *a lion's jambe, ppr., rising out of a ducal coronet, or* (for which in later times the SAVAGES, LORDS OF ARDKEEN, substituted *a mermaid rising out of the waves, ppr.*, to symbolize their lordship over Lough Strangford, or numerous islands in that spacious arm of the sea), was also indicative of the same free warrior-life.

---

upon the brave and powerful Eadric, and in this connection Mr. Freeman (in his *History of the Norman Conquest*) interprets it as the "Wild;" but his references to the word subsequently, bear out our remarks in the text. Speaking of the heroic strife of the Saxons, he says—" But it was not in the towns only; every defensible spot, woods, marshes, mouths of rivers, were all seized upon and strengthened in readiness for an attack. Men thought it shame to dwell at such times under the shadow of a house. The wild men, the *Savages*, as the mocking tongues of the Normans called them, dwelled of their own choice in tents and lurking-places, lest their strength should grow rusty among the comforts of their own roof-trees."—(Freeman, *Norman Conquest*, vol. iv., p. 187.) And in a foot-note on the same page he quotes—" Plures in tabernaculis morabantur; in domibus, ne mollescerent, requiescere dedignabantur, unde quidam eorum a Normannis *silvatici* cognominabantur."

[1] See *English Heraldry*, by Charles Boutell, M.A. In the arms of William, Earl of Salisbury (surnamed Longespée), the field is *azure*, and the *six lioncels rampant, three, two, and one,* are *or*. Geoffrey of Anjou bore the *lions rampant* on his shield. Was not Tortulf, the founder of the House of Anjou, also surnamed *The Forester*?

Mr. Boutell writes—"The Lion was in high favour with the most noble and powerful Barons of England—the Bohuns, Longespées, Fitz-Alans, Lacies, Percies, Seagraves, and such as they." And again—"The fine Shield of WILLIAM LONGESPÉE, Earl of Salisbury, son of Henry II. and FAIR ROSAMOND, . . . is supposed to have been assumed and borne by the Earl on his marriage with the daughter and heiress of D'EUREUX, when in right of his wife he succeeded to the Earldom of Salisbury: but this theory does not rest upon any solid foundation, since it would be very difficult to show that the Shield with the six lioncels was certainly borne, on his armorial ensign, by the father-in-law of Earl William. Also, if a Shield charged with an escarbuncle and many lioncels, which has been assigned to GEOFFREY Count of ANJOU, was really borne by the Founder of the House of PLANTAGENET, Earl WILLIAM LONGESPÉE may have derived his own shield from his paternal grandfather."—*English Heraldry*, pp. 83 & 192.

Ruins of ROCK SAVAGE, Cheshire, Ancient Seat of the SAVAGES, EARLS RIVERS.

CHAPTER II.

THE SAVAGE FAMILY IN NORMANDY, BURGUNDY, AND ENGLAND.

SECTION I.—THE NORMAN STEM AND BURGUNDIAN BRANCH.

EW authentic particulars, probably, can be gathered at this late date concerning the early history of the SAVAGE family in Normandy or elsewhere prior to the tenth century. "There was one of this name," writes Carew in a marginal note in *The Book of Howth*, "who was one of the Knights of the Round Table;" and among

"The goodliest fellowship of noble knights
Whereof the world holds record"

we do undoubtedly find the names of Sir Dodinas le Savage, Sir Pinell le Savage, and Sir Balan le Savage.[1] But the family of SAVAGE will hardly care to claim these phantoms as their ancestors. The archives of the ancient and noble family of DE SAUVAGE, Lords of Montbaron, were destroyed in a fire that

---

[1] It is interesting to find Lord Tennyson, in his poem of *Balin and Balan*, assigning to the Knight Le Savage the arms of those SAVAGES, EARLS RIVERS, to whom his own descent is traced—

" . . . This rough beast upon my shield,
Langued gules, and tooth'd with grinning *savagery*."

occurred in the Château de Montbaron in June, 1615. This branch of the SAVAGES had extended at a remote period into the province of Burgundy, and the French genealogists thus write of them:—" C'est une ancienne et noble famille d'extraction originaire de Bourgogne, sur les confins du Nivernois. Les anciens titres ayant été brûlés dans un incendie arrivé le 15 Juin, 1615, dans la maison seigneurale de Montbaron, on ne peut remonter la filiation qu'à Claude de Sauvage, qui épousa, par contrat passé le 3 Août, 1552, Marguerite de la Croix, fille de Philbert, Écuyer, Seigneur de Ramilly, de Palmasse et du Tremblay. Par ce contrat il lui fut accordé la Terre et Seigneurie de Montbaron dans la paroisse de Cervon." [1]

What remained of the titles, referring to the later history of this branch, were, when the above was written, principally in the archives of the Château de Saint-Thibault. But the destruction of the earlier records is a bar to further genealogical research in this direction.

The *Norman* home of the SAVAGE family, however, is presumed to have been in the neighbourhood of Avranches; the first of the family to come to England was THOMAS LE SAUVAGE—"LE SIEUR LE SAUVAGE"[2]—who arrived with the Conqueror, and whose name appears in the lists of the Normans who survived the Battle of Hastings; and the first settlement of the SAVAGE family in England was at Scarcliffe, in Derbyshire.[3]

SECTION II.—THE DERBYSHIRE AND CHESHIRE HOUSE—SAVAGE OF SCARCLIFFE AND STAINESBY, IN DERBYSHIRE, AND OF CLIFTON (ROCK SAVAGE), IN CHESHIRE—THE EARLS RIVERS.[4]

LE SIEUR THOMAS LE SAUVAGE, born in Normandy, living in 1066, was succeeded by JOHN SAVAGE, ESQUIRE, who was living prior to the year 1090. In the latter year his name appears in connection with Derbyshire along with

---

[1] Extrait du *Dictionaire de la Noblesse*, par De la Chenaye-Desbois et Badier, &c.

[2] See *Histoire Générale de la Normandie*, par M. Gabriel de Moulin. Extrait des noms des Seigneurs Normands qui se trouvaient à la conquête d'Angleterre, de l'histoire et chronique de Normandie, imprimée à Rouen. See also Bromton's *Chronicle*, Fox's *Monumenta*, and Towers' *Essay on Surnames*, p. 277.—"'Out of ye ancient Chronicles of England touching the names of other Normans wh. seemed to remain alive after ye battle [of Hastings] and to be advanced in ye signiories of this land, Thomas Savage last in ye list.' Taken from John Fox's copy called 'Ye Roll of Battle Abbey.' Fox does not mention it as such, but says he took it out of 'ye annals of Normandy in French.'"—*MS. note of Francis Walker Savage, Esq., of Springfield, Gloucestershire.*

[3] See Ormerod's *Cheshire*. See also Beamont's excellent *History of Halton Castle and Norton Priory*, p. 106—a work from which the Editor has ventured to make extensive extracts.

[4] The principal authorities for the particulars of this sketch of the Derbyshire and Cheshire house of the SAVAGES are, (1) a copy of the grand pedigree of the LORDS SAVAGE drawn out by

that of Peveril[1] and that of Roger de Burun, ancestor of the Lords Byron of Rochdale.[2] JOHN LE SAVAGE was succeeded by

ADAM LE SAVAGE, whose name, according to the Heralds, appears in a deed of this period, but without date.[3] This ADAM LE SAVAGE was father of

ROBERT LE SAVAGE, of Stainesby, Co. Derby, who was father of

JOHN LE SAVAGE, Lord of Stainesby, who was succeeded by his son,

SIR GEFFREY LE SAVAGE, of Stainesby, Knt. This SIR GEFFREY LE SAVAGE,

the Heralds in the year 1631, and described upon the engrossment itself as "The Genealogie of the Right Honorable Sir Thomas Savage, Kt., Viscount Savage of Rock Savage in the County of CHESTER, diligently and seriously collected and faithfully reduced out of Ancient Deeds, Evidences, Inquisitions, and Matters of Record from his Rt. Worthy and Noble Ancestors, with their Descents, Matches, Coats Armorial, and Achievements of Honour; as also of his Noble Issue and Offspring unto the present year of our LORD, 1631, and the Seventh Year of the Reign of our Sovereign LORD CHARLES by the Grace of GOD King of Great Britain, France, and Ireland, Defender of the Faith, &c. Matriculated, depicted, set forth for the perpetual memory thereof to Ensuing POSTERITY;" (2) an Abstract of the Pedigree of the Family of SAVAGE from the College of Arms; both of them placed in the hands of the Editor by Francis Walker Savage, Esq., of Springfield. But the footnotes will show that many other authorities have been consulted.

[1] Of the Peverils, so celebrated through the enchantment of Scott's *Peveril of the Peak*, the following account from Banks is not without interest :—"Ranulf Peverel at the general survey held sixty-four lordships in several counties, and reputed the progenitor of several families of the same name; for having married Maud, daughter to Ingelric, a noble Saxon, one of the most celebrated beauties of the age (who had been a concubine of William Duke of Normandy), not only the children he had by her, but that very William, begotten on her by the said duke before the Conquest, had the name of Peverel. Which William, the 2d of the Conqueror's reign, had the custody of the Castle of Nottingham; and in the time of Stephen was one of the chief commanders at the battle of Northallerton. William, his son, is mostly memorable for having poisoned Randolph earl of Chester; when, fearing the severity of Henry II. for so foul a crime, [he] fled away (though it is said he turned monk to avoid being hanged), and his lands were seized; which, after being in the crown for some years, were at last given to John, the King's son; but some came to the family of Ferrers, with Margaret, daughter and heir of the said William, particularly Higham, since called Higham-Ferrers, in the County of Northampton. Hamon Peverel is next mentioned, as the eldest son of the aforesaid Ranulph, and one of the barons to Roger de Montgomery, Earl of Shrewsbury. His wife was Sybil, daughter and heir to Gerard de Tournay."—Banks: *Extinct and Dormant Baronage of England*, vol. i.

[2] *Burun*, or *Byron*. "Of this name there were two who lived in the time of William the Conqueror ; viz., Ralph, who held eight lordships in Nottinghamshire and five in Derbyshire; and Erinsius, who had thirty-two lordships in Yorkshire and twenty-eight in Lincolnshire. From Ralph descended Hugh, to whom succeeded Roger de Burun, whose barony was given by King John to William Briwer; after which time no further mention of him or his posterity is made. But from him is said to be derived the family of the present lord Byron, now flourishing amongst the peers of the realm."—Banks : *Extinct and Dormant Baronage of England*, vol. i.

[3] Original pedigree of the EARLS RIVERS.

of Stainesby, married Letice, daughter of Sir Henry de Arderne (otherwise Arden), Knt., and so became connected with Warwickshire by an alliance with the family from which Shakespeare in later years maternally descended. Sir Henry de Arderne (or Arden), "by his deed in writing," according to Dugdale,[1] "gave the manor of Baginton [in Warwickshire] in Frank marriage at the Church dore, with Letice his daughter, unto GEFFREY SAVAGE the day that he married her. In whose line it continued till towards the later end of H. 3 time; but then, by an heir female, devolved to Ednesoure, . . . from whom it shortly went unto Herthull till R. 2 time, and then was passed to Sir Wm. Bagott by Sir Ric. de Herthull, Kt. . . . Of the first GEFFREY SAVAGE," adds Dugdale, "this is all I find, viz., that he is mentioned in the Sheriff's account of 5 H. 2, as also that 31 H. 2. Thomas de Arden had suites with him for two hides of land in this county; and that he had issue Helias and Geffrey." SIR GEFFREY LE SAVAGE, who appears to have died A.D. 1190 (1 Ric. 1), was, by his wife Letice (née Arden or Arderne), the father of

I. JOHN, subsequently Lord of Stainesby, to whom we shall presently revert.
II. Helias, of whom Dugdale writes—"12 H. 2 [1165-6] the E. of Warwick, having the manor of Badsley Endsor in his hands, past it to Helias, the son of Geffrey Savage: which Helias died without issue (as I guess), for it appears that the same Earl confirmed it to Geffrey Savage, Brother of the said Helias, and his heirs, to be held by the service of one Knight's fee." And again, in connection with the lands of Pooley, Dugdale writes—"Pooley. This, as a member of Polesworth, did anciently belong to the Marmions of Tamworth Castle; and being originally given by Marmion to Burdet in Fee Ferme, for the Rent of xs. yearly, was soon after granted from Burdet to Sauvage, as appears from a confirmation made from Geffrey Sauvage to William Burdet in 10 H. 3, which passages from Marmion to Burdet, and Burdet to Sauvage, were about King Stephen's time; for Osanna, then Abbesse of Polesworth, with the consent of her fellow Nunns, granted to Helias, the son of Geffrey Sauvage, a chapell here, but without service, as also a chapell yard; in consideration whereof he gave to that convent the inheritance of four acres of the best Meadow ground in this Village, promising to pay yearly during his life xiid. upon S. Edith's altar, on the day of her Festivall: and bequeathed his body, wheresoever he should

---

[1] See *Antiquities of Warwickshire*, by Sir William Dugdale. London, 1730.

depart this life, to be buried in the church at Polesworth. Which agreement was so made in the presence of Roger de Clinton, then Bishop of the Dioces. But this tenure in Fee Ferm did not long continue; for it is evident that Robert Marmion (whom I take to be the man that first granted it to Burdet) did, in consideration of x marks in the nature of a Fine, and the yearly payment of a Sore Sparhawk to himself and his heirs, release the said xs. annuall Rent unto Geffrey Sauvage (brother and heir of the said Elias). And, moreover, that the said William Burdet acquitted to Sir Philip Marmion all his right in the Homage and services of William le Salvage (successor to the before specified Geffrey) for these lands in Povele; which from thenceforth were held immediately of the Marmions, by the service of the said Sore Sparhawk, or 2s. to be paid at the Feast of S. James the Apostle, in the nature of a Socage tenure."

III. Geffrey; "which second Geffrey," writes Dugdale, "gave to the monks of Stoneley 2 parts of his Mill, called Partford Mill, with the Sute thereto, due from his tenants of Hull and Wotton; and was also a benefactor to the nuns of Polesworth, granting unto them in Robert de Weston, his bondman, with his issue. But it seems he was in some disfavour with K. Ric. 1., for in 7 of his reign [1195-6] he gave 50 marks pro habenda benevolentia Regis: in which year he came to an agreement with Tho. de Ardern concerning the Manoor of Wotton. About the beginning of K. John's time [1199] I find that Henry de Armentiers impleaded him for a Kt.'s Fee here, in his absence, when he was beyond sea in the K. Service,[1] for which

---

[1] We may as well quote what further Dugdale tells us about Wotton:—P. 268. "Wootton was held in the Conqueror's time by Roger de Montgomerie, but he and his posterity lost all for their Rebellion, and being in the hands of K. H. 1 was, inter alia, given to Geoffrey de Clinton, who upon his foundation of the priory at Kenilworth, gave thereunto the church of this town, an 1 hyde of land. Which grant of his had been greater, but that he reserved part of the woods to be afforested to enlarge his Park of Kenilworth: but the rest Geffrey Salvage had, and very probably by the grant of the same Geffrey, it being a whole Kt's fee, who had much ado to hold it, as it seems; for in 2. Ric. 1, Richard de Frevill, then Lord of Wolston, impleaded him for it. And in 7. Ric 1. he was constrain'd to come to an Agreement with Tho. de Arderne about it, who then levyed a Fine thereof to him. Nay in 2. John Henry de Armentiers had suits with him for it; who claimed it in right of Isabell his grandmother; alledging that she was seized thereof in H. 2. time; and that by David de Armentiers, her son, it so descended to him the said Henry. Whereunto Geffrey answered, that being in K. service beyond sea, he had protection; for which he paid Fine at his

he had afterwards tryall by battail. . . . In 6 John [1204-5] it appears that being surety for Will. de Hardreshill to the Jews of Northampton, of whom the said Will. had borrowed a large sum of money, he was distrained for that debt, and thereupon necessitated to complain to the K. to whom he gave a fine of x. marks that the said Will. might be compelled to pay it himself. In 5 H. 3, [1220-1] he was joyn'd in commiss. with other persons of quality in this county to be one of the Justices for taking an assize of novel disseisin, which Philippa Marmion had brought against Rob. Marmion the younger touching her dowrie of such lands as Rob. Marmion her husband dyed seized of in Tamworth and Middleton." This said Geffrey Savage died in 1222, and was succeeded by his son

1. Geffrey ("the 3d"), who paid his relief and did homage "for half a Kt.'s Fee being held [by his father] of the King in this county; which Geffrey," Dugdale continues, "in 12 H. 3 [1227-8] was with Hugh Despenser in the K. army, for which cause the Sheriff had commanded to respight those demands he made of him (this being the time when Ric. E. of Cornwall, the K. brother, with divers of the Barons put themselves rebelliously in armes)." This 3d Geffrey Savage married Petronill, daughter of Hugh le Despenser, and dying in 1231 (15 Henry 3), left, with two daughters, Lucia and Philippa (of whom more presently), three sons, viz.,

    Geffrey (a 4th Geffrey), who succeeded his father, and who at his father's death was a ward in custody of his grandfather Hugh le Despenser. This Geffrey died without issue, 34 H. 3. [1249-50];

    Robert, and

    William, who succeeded his brother Geffrey, and whom Dugdale describes as "William Sauvage, sometime Lord of Pooley," and of whom he writes—"William le Savage his Brother, then Rector of the Church of Newton, in this County, became heir to the estate, and doing his Homage had livery of all his lands

---

passage, to the end he might not be impleaded in his absence; whereupon he was then discharged. But it seems that did not end the business; for upon a full Agreement betwixt them, where it appears that the said Geffrey allow'd him a third part of the said Kts fee, there is mention made that they had a trial by Battle for it."

held of the K. in capite. . . . Which William had a brother called Robert, who, being Steward to the Nuns of Polesworth, gave certain rent issuing out of the lands of Freseley for maintenance of the Knights belonging to the Chapel of our blessed Lady in that monastery, by reason of his purpose to be buried there; for so I find he was; as also Petronill his mother; and that there was a speciall indulgence of xx days penance afforded by Brandanus B. of Ardagy in An. 1253 (37 H. 3) to all those of what dioceses whatsoever that should say three pater-nosters and as many aves for the health of his the said Rob. &

Arms of Meynill and Savage.

Petronill's souls. This William the parson overlived his said brother Robert, and was a further benefactor to these Nuns, giving them all such mess. lands and rents which the same Rob. held in Fresele and Dodenhale with his part of that land where the Chappel beyond St. Edith's well in Povele wood was built, to the end, that out of the profits thereof a mark of silver should be yearly paid; viz.—half at the anniversary of the Lady Petronil his mother and the other at the anniversary of the before-mentioned Rob. Savage his brother; as also a stone of wax for the lights at Mattens in the said Monastery; and dyed in 43 H. 3. [1258-9] seized of large possessions in this shire; and in the counties of Wigorn, Staff., Leic., & Derb., leaving Thos. de Ednesoure, the son of Tho. de Ednesoure by Lucia his sister, and Philippa, then the wife of Hugh de Meynill, his other sister, his heirs."[1] "Which said Tho. & Hugh had livery

---

[1] Of this Philippa de Meynill, *née* Savage, Dugdale elsewhere relates—"Philippa, . . . who with Robert de Mortimer the abbot of Stoneley & prior of Kenilworth, in 7 E. 1.

of these lands, doing their homage in 44 H. 3; whereupon the possession of this Manor went with Ednesoure, Menill having of Savage's lands in this county Newton before mentioned."

This first SIR GEFFREY SAVAGE, of Stainesby, Knt., is presumed to have been also, by his wife Letice de Arden (or Arderne), the father of

see p 199

    IV. SIR WILLIAM SAVAGE, KNT., *afterwards* BARON LE SAVAGE, *one of the twenty-two Knights that accompanied De Courcy, afterwards Earl of Ulster, in the invasion of Ulster in 1177, and founder of the ancient and noble family of the* SAVAGES OF THE ARDS, *of the history of which the main portion of this work is to treat.*

Sir GEFFREY LE SAVAGE, of Stainesby, was succeeded in the lordship of Stainesby by his son,

    JOHN SAVAGE, of Stainesby, living in 1208, who was father of

        JOHN SAVAGE, *of whom presently as Lord of* STAINESBY, *and ancestor of the* SAVAGES, EARLS RIVERS; SAVAGES *of* ELMLEY CASTLE; SAVAGES *of* TETBURY, &c.; and of

        SIR ROGER SAVAGE, KNT., *founder (according to the Rivers pedigree) of the* KENT *branch of the* SAVAGES, *of the history of which we shall treat below under the head of* "SAVAGE OF BOBBING COURT."

JOHN SAVAGE, of Stainesby, dying, was succeeded at Stainesby by his first-named son,

    JOHN SAVAGE, of Stainesby, who married Agatha, daughter and heiress of Henry St. Andries, by whom he had a son and successor,

        SIR THOMAS SAVAGE, of Stainesby, Knt., living 29 Edward I. (1300-1), who was succeeded by his son,

        SIR ROBERT SAVAGE, of Stainesby, Knt., 41 Edward III. (1367-8), who married Amicia, daughter and heiress of Thomas Walkington, by whom he had a son and successor,

        SIR JOHN SAVAGE, of Stainesby, Knt., "in lief 49 Ao. Edward III." (1375-6). He married Margaret, daughter and heiress of Sir Thomas Danyers (otherwise Daniers and Daniels), Knt., de Bradley (who afterwards married Sir Peter Leigh, of Lyme, Cheshire). By this marriage Clifton, in the County of Chester, came

---

[1278-9] held this Wotton & Hull with the Crosse-Grange, for 1 Kts. Fee. Which Philippa had here at that time 12 servants holding 1 yard land at will, & giving aid at the feast of S. Michael at the lord's pleasure, with 4 cottyers and 3 freeholders which held half a yard land by certain rent, fealty, and suit of court, twice a-year; as also a Court Leet & assize of bread & beer by the confirmation of K. H. 1."

into possession of the SAVAGE family. The history of the removal of the elder branch of the SAVAGES into Cheshire is as follows :—The manor of Chedle belonged to a family of that name in the 12th century. A grandson of the then possessor, Sir Roger, left two daughters, one of whom, Clemence, married William de Bagaly, and had issue a daughter and heiress, Isabel, who married T. Daniell (otherwise Danyers). The daughter and heiress of Daniell (or Danyers), Margaret by name, married about 49 Edward III. the above named JOHN SAVAGE for her second husband. Clemence, one of the co-heiresses of Sir Roger de Chedle, had Clifton and divers lands in Chedle by inheritance, which descended to his grand-daughter Margaret, and JOHN SAVAGE in right of his wife thus became Lord of Chedle. Of Clifton we read in Ormerod—" This town or place (for here is only a mannor-house with the demain-lands thereof) hath its name from the cliffs or broken rocks therein. It is now at this day commonly called ROCK SAVAGE, since the structure of that sumptuous building erected there by SIR JOHN SAVAGE, Anno Domini 1565; 7 Elizabethæ."[1] . . . Further on, Ormerod describes the situation of the future principal seat of the SAVAGES. " The situation is remarkably fine. Halton Castle rises behind; at one side is the estuary of the Mersey; and the Weever, also an estuary, descends in front to its confluence with the first-named river. Over the Weever is a fine view of Frodsham and the Welsh hills, Overton Scar and Hellesby Tor closing up one side of the picture, while the richness of the Lancashire shore makes a fine contrast on the other. Many of these features in the landscape would have an additional charm to the eye of a Norman chieftain from the strength which they added to his fortress; and the beauty of the scenery as well as the difficulty of access were increased by a deep ravine under the mansion, still dark with oaks and tangled with briars, through which a small brook forces its way from Halton to the Weever."[2] The SAVAGES had also a seat (an earlier one) at Frodsham. Banks *(Dormant Peerage)* describes the SAVAGES OF CLIFTON as "an ancient family whose chief seat for many ages was at the Castle of Frodsham in Cheshire, and partly at another noble house built of later time at Clifton on the opposite side of the River, called ROCK SAVAGE." Sir JOHN SAVAGE (the 1st of Clifton), by his wife Margaret (*née* Danyers, otherwise Daniell), had issue,

    I. JOHN, of whom presently as heir to his father, and his successor in the Lordship of Clifton, &c.

    II. William.

---

[1] Ormerod: *Cheshire*, vol. iii., p. 526.   [2] Ormerod, vol. iii., p. 530.

III. Arthur, who married and had issue a son,
   John, of Edwall, Co. Derby (the elder), "in lief 1 Ed. IV.," who married and had issue (with a 2nd son, John), a son,
      Thomas, of Edwall, Esq. This Thomas Savage, of Edwall, married ——, daughter of Robert Eire, of Hilton, and had issue, John, of Edwall, ob. 39 Eliz., who married Alice, daughter and heiress of Humphrey Stafford, Esq., of Eyam, and had issue Humphrey, who married Jane, daughter of Edward Barber, Esq., and, dying before his father, by her left issue, Humphrey, of Edwall, Co. Derby (1 James I.), who was father of another Humphrey Savage, who was living in 1630.
IV. Roger.
V. George.
I. Petronel, married to Reginald Leigh of Blackbrook.
II. Elizabeth, married, *1st*, to Sir John Macclesfield; *2ndly*, to Randle Manwering, of Carengham.
III. Isabella, a nun.
IV. Margaret, married to John Dutton, Esq., 2nd son of Sir Piers Dutton, 6 Henry V., afterwards heir to Sir Piers his father.
V. Dowse, married to Sir Henry Bold, of Bold, Knt.
VI. Mary, married to John Leigh, of Boothes.
VII. Lucy, married to Hamlet Carrington.
VIII. Maud, married to Sir John (Thomas?) Booth, of Barton, in Lancashire, Knt.
IX. Ann, married to Charles Noel, of Dalby, Esq.
X. Eleanor, married to Jofrey Warberton, of Arley, Esq.
XI. Blanch, married to Thos. Carrington, Esq.
XII. Dorothy, married to Robt. Needham, of Sherington, Esq.

SIR JOHN SAVAGE, the 1st of Clifton, died in 1386. He was succeeded by his eldest son,

SIR JOHN SAVAGE, of Clifton, Knt., who was knighted at the Battle of Agincourt (1415). He married Maude, daughter and heiress of Sir Robert Swinnerton, Knt., of Barrow, County of Chester, and of Rushton, Comford, and Austenfield, County of Stafford.[1] It is probable that this SIR JOHN

---

[1] Sir Robert Swinnerton's ancestor, Sir Roger Swinnerton, was made a banneret by Edward III., to whom the King (in part of three hundred pounds' worth of land, for the supporting of the state of a banneret for life) had given all the lands which belonged to

was the JOHN SAVAGE whose brilliant tilting at the tournament held at Inglevere, near Calais, in May and June, 1390, has been described in one of the most delightful chapters of Froissart's *Chronicle* (Chapter xiii.). During the truce between England and France, three French Knights held a tournament at Inglevere, and defended the lists, for thirty days, against all comers, from England or elsewhere. Their names were Sir Boucicaut the Younger, the Lord Reginald de Roye, and the Lord de Saimpè. "On the 21st May, as it had been proclaimed, the three Knights were properly armed, and the horses ready saddled, according to the laws of the tournament. . . . The King of France," Froissart tells us, "was present at these jousts. Being young, and desirous of witnessing extraordinary sights, he would have been much vexed if he had not seen these tournaments. He was therefore present at the early part and latter end of them, attended by the lord de Garencieres; but both so disguised that nobody knew of it, and they returned every evening to Merquise" [a town in Picardy, four leagues from Calais]. . . . "The ensuing day, Wednesday, was as fine as the foregoing, and the English who had crossed the sea to take part in or view the tournament, mounted their horses at the same hour as on the preceding day, and rode to the place appointed for the lists, to the delight of the French, who were rejoiced to see them. It was not long after their arrival that an English Squire, a good tilter, called JOHN SAVAGE, a squire of honor, and of the body to the Earl of Huntingdon, sent to touch the shield of Sir Reginald de Roye; the Knight answered, he was ready and willing to satisfy him. When he had mounted his horse, and had his helmet buckled and lance given to him, they set off at full gallop, and gave such blows on the targets that, had the spears not broken, one or both must have fallen to the ground. The course was handsome and dangerous, but the Knights received no hurt, though the points of the lances passed through the targets and slipped off their side armour. The spears were broken almost a foot from the shaft, the points remaining in the

Hugh le Despenser, Earl of Winchester, in the counties of Stafford and Chester, and after by his charter, dated at Nottingham, 16 Julii (8 Ed. III.), 1334. . . . He gave also little Barrow to him and his heirs by another charter, dated at Westminster, 25 Septembris, 8 Edward III. . . . And these were confirmed to Robert de Swynerton, 13 Dec. 2 Rich. II., 1378. Which Sir Robert Swynerton, Banneret, died 13 Ed. III. After whose death Robert Swynerton, Clerk, possessed the same as son and heir; which Robert died mense Junii 23 Edward III.; after whose death Sir Thomas Swinnerton, Knight, as brother and heir of Robert, possessed the same lands; which Sir Thomas died mense Decembris 35 Ed. III.; after whose death, Sir Robert Swinnerton, his son and heir, enjoyed them and left them to this Maude, his daughter and heir.—*From an "Abstract from the Pedigree of the Family of Savage, from the College of Arms," in possession of Francis Walker Savage, Esq., of Springfield.*

shields, and they gallantly bore the shafts before them as they finished their career. The spectators thought they must have been seriously wounded, and the French and English hastened each to his companion, whom, to their joy, they found unhurt. They were told that they had done enough for that day, but JOHN SAVAGE was not satisfied, and said, '*He had not crossed the sea for only one tilt of the lance.*' This was reported to Sir Reginald, who replied, 'He is in the right, and it is but just that he should be gratified either by me or one of my companions.' When they had rested themselves awhile, and received new lances, they began their second course, each aiming well at the other; but they failed from the swerving of their horses, to their great vexation, and retired to their posts. Their lances, which they had accidentally dropped, were given to them, and they set off in their third course. This time they hit on the visors of their helmets, and by the force and crossing of their lances, both were unhelmed as they passed. The tilt was much applauded for its correctness and vigour. When returned to their posts, the English told JOHN SAVAGE that he had very honourably performed, and that it was now time for him to make way for others to tilt as well as himself. He complied with this, and, laying aside his lance and target, dismounted, and rode on a hackney to witness the performance of others." This SIR JOHN SAVAGE, instead of the arms which had always heretofore been borne by his family, viz., ar., six lioncels sa., took his mother's arms, ar., a pale fusillée sa., and for crest

Arms of SAVAGE quartering Danyers.

a unicorn's head, couped, ar., which she granted him to bear after the death of her father, 3 Henry V. (1416).[1] SIR JOHN SAVAGE held the distinguished office of Seneschal of Halton Castle, the royal fortress near his own manor of Clifton. "On the 11th June, 10th Henry VI. (1432), SIR JOHN SAVAGE, another soldier then Seneschal of Halton, was commanded to receive from Randle Brereton, sheriff of Cheshire, the bodies of Richard de Whelock and George de Wevre, and to keep them safely in the Castle of Halton until

[1] Sir John Savage, great-grandson of Sir John, K.G., who died at Boulogne, "again took for his arms, ar., six lioncels sa., and for his crest a lion's jambe, sa., erect out of a ducal coronet or, which coat was afterwards always borne by his family."—Lee's *Tetbury*, p. 231.

they should be discharged by due course of law [Ches. Recog. Rolls]. These persons were probably ordinary offenders sent to prison to await their trial. What was their offence, or before whom they were tried, and what was the result, we may know when the palatine records have been indexed. In the meantime we may conjecture that they were brought to trial either before the Justice of Chester, who until the time of Henry VIII. held at least three courts every year, or before the court of Quarter Sessions, which was held four times a-year. The Justice of Chester was often some nobleman of rank, who was paid a salary of £100 a-year, and did his work by deputy. In 1432, Humphry, Duke of Gloucester, the 'good Duke Humphry,' was Judge of Chester, and SIR JOHN SAVAGE often aided as his deputy. Coming down to a little later period than this, we find Humphry Stafford, Earl of Buckingham, and of four other earldoms—Hereford, Stafford, Northampton, and Perch—filling the office of seneschal of Halton and Widnes. At this time, therefore, the office seems to have been one of great dignity."[1] This SIR JOHN SAVAGE died in 1450. He was succeeded by his eldest son,

SIR JOHN SAVAGE, of Clifton, Knt., who married Elizabeth, daughter of Sir William Brereton, of Brereton, Knt.,[2] and by her had issue,

    I. JOHN, Knt., of whom presently as successor to his father in the Lordship of Clifton.

    I. Eleanor, married to Sir Piers Leigh, of Lyme, Knt.
    II. Elizabeth, married to John Leake, of Sutton, Co. Derby.
    III. Helein, married to Peter Warberton, of Arley, Esq.
    IV. Ann, married to Sir Roger Pilkington, Knt.
    V. Margaret, married to Sir Edward Trafford, of Trafford, Knt.
    VI. Katherine, married to Thomas Leigh, of Adlington, Esq.

SIR JOHN SAVAGE was succeeded at Clifton by his eldest son,

SIR JOHN SAVAGE, of Clifton, "Senior," Knt., who married Katherine, daughter of Sir Thomas Stanley, afterwards Lord Stanley, and sister of Sir Thomas Stanley, afterwards Earl of Derby, and who by her had issue,

    I. JOHN, "Junior," Knt., of whom presently as heir apparent to his father of the Lordship of Clifton.

---

[1] Beamont: *Hist. of the Castle of Halton and the Priory or Abbey of Norton* (Warrington, 1873), pp. 94-5. Sir John Savage's immediate predecessor in the Seneschalship was William Harrington, who had borne the King's banner at Agincourt.

[2] The Breretons were an eminent family in Cheshire. Several of them also were Seneschals of Halton Castle.

II. Thomas, Bishop of Rochester, 1492, thence translated to London, 1497, thence to the Archbishoprick of York, 1501; died 1508, his body being buried in York Minster, his heart at Macclesfield, in Cheshire, where he built a chapel at the side of Macclesfield Church, known as the SAVAGE CHAPEL, and where he intended to have made a college. He appears to have been the "Thomas Savage, Esq., doctor-of-laws," who (along with John Weston, prior of St. John's in England; Master John Gunthorp, dean of the Cathedral Church of Wells; Master Christopher Urswyk, the King's almoner, and Master Henry Aynesworth, also a doctor-of-laws) was appointed in March, 1488, "to treat for truce or perpetual peace with the most illustrious Ferdinand, King of Castile and Leon, and the most serene and noble princess his wife, the lady Isabella, or the ambassadors or deputies;" who was appointed by the King in the same year to negotiate a peace with the King of Portugal (1488, 4th H. VII.— "Appointment of Thomas Savage, doctor-of-laws, and Richard Nanfan, Knight, to be commissioners and envoys from the King of England, with authority to treat with the King of Portugal, or his duly authorized commissioners, for a firm and lasting peace and friendship between the two Kings and their subjects"); and to whom was entrusted (again in association with Sir Richard Nanfan) a still more interesting commission—on the 11th December of the same year— viz., the negotiation of a marriage between Prince Arthur and Katherine of Arragon.—"Commission to Thomas Savage, doctor-of-civil-laws and Chancellor of the Marches, and Richard Nanfan, a Knight for the King's body, to treat with the councillors and commissioners of the King of Castile, Ligeoun, Aragon, and Sisilia, and his queen-consort, for a perpetual league and friendship between them and the King of England; and also for the espousal and marriage between the King's son, Arthur prince of Wales, duke of Cornwall, and earl of Chester, and Katerine, one of the daughters of the said King and Queen of Castile, &c.; with powers to make terms respecting the provisions and dowry of the princess, the time and mode of her passage to England, and her establishment and treatment in the said country;" and on whom, 8th December, 1490, the King conferred a "grant for life, in consideration of good service and other matters, of an annuity of six marks sterling, out of the issues of the manor of Bridcroft in Bamwith, in the honor of Pountfret, parcel of the duchy of Lancaster, co. York; which manor has come by forfeiture into the King's hands, and has been annexed to the said honor."[1] ARCHBISHOP SAVAGE was noted, amongst other things, for his hospitality and his love of the chase, as the following passage from Doran's *Saints and Sinners* amply illustrates :—" Up York there was no lack of Archbishops who held that appetite was an excellent thing to get and get rid of. There was one exception perhaps in the person of Savage, who, after filling the Sees of Rochester and London, was translated to the Archbishoprick of

Tomb of THOMAS SAVAGE, Archbishop of York, in York Minster. (Ob. 1508.)

York, 1501-7. He made the whole province, as well as the hospitable county from which his province takes its name, especially indignant at his not appearing to be enthroned. He sent his fool, John Goose, to amuse the household, and a deputy to go through the enthronization with maimed rites. This, however, might have been endured if it had been followed by the usual feast. York had already found solace in the funeral baked meats of one Primate by thinking of the inauguration cheer of his successor; but there was no feast on this occasion, and the orthodox appetites as well as the thirsty claimants to be guests were profoundly scandalized. . . But Yorkshire soon forgave the man, for he made up for his inaugurating shortcomings by feasting half the county. The frank people then readily pardoned him for neglecting his professional duties, since

---

[1] See *Materials for History of Henry VII.* (Master of the Rolls Series.)

he kept the county alive and musical with the tongues of the Archiepiscopal hounds."[1] "The Archbishop was buried at York Minster in a splendid altar-tomb under a canopy, the body being above ground, his heart in the SAVAGE CHAPEL at Macclesfield, Co. Chester. After the great fire at the Minster, his tomb was much injured, and in the course of restoring it the body was found rolled in sheet-lead, and so retaining the outward form in a degree. Beneath this were several layers of sear-cloth, and, on these being removed, the Verger told the writer of this note that the body was discovered in the most perfect state of preservation, and that there was three days' growth of beard on the face (as hair continues to grow after death). He said he shook hands with His Grace, and that his hand was as plump as his own. The body was carefully re-wrapped in its enclosures, and again entombed."[2]

III. Sir Humfrey, Knt.
IV. Sir Laurence, Knt.
V. James, Archdeacon of Chester.
VI. Sir Edmund, Knt., who fell at Flodden Field in 1513. "Men of Chester bore a distinguished part in the battle of Flodden Field, 1513. It was particularly fatal to the burgesses of Macclesfield, several of whom, with their Mayor, Sir Edmund Savage, were left dead on the field."[3] Sir Edmund Savage married Mary, daughter and heiress of William Sparke of Surrey, and widow of Roger Legh del Ridge, Macclesfield, Co. Chester, and had issue a son,

    Sir Edmund, knighted by the Earl of Hertford at Leith, Scotland, in 1544. "The Earl of Hertford, after a victory obtained over the Scots, 1544, knighted at Leith about 60 officers who had accompanied him, one-third of whom were of the most distinguished families in Cheshire, among whom was Sir Edmund Savage, whose father fell at Flodden Field." (Lysons.)

VII. SIR CHRISTOPHER, Knt., *founder of the families of* ELMLEY CASTLE, BROADWAY, *and* TETBURY, *of which we shall treat hereafter under* "SAVAGE OF ELMLEY CASTLE," "SAVAGE OF BROADWAY," *and* "SAVAGE OF TETBURY."

---

[1] Doran's *Saints and Sinners*, vol. ii., p. 10.
[2] MS. note of Francis Walker Savage, Esq., of Springfield.
[3] Lysons: *Magna Britannia*, vol. ii., p. 308.

VIII. William.
IX. George.
X. Sir Richard, Knt.
  I. Elizabeth, married to Sir John Hampden, of Hampden, Knt.
  II. Alice, married to Sir William Brereton, of Brereton, Knt.

SIR JOHN SAVAGE, "Senior," of Clifton, died 22nd November, 11th Henry VII., 1495, aged 73, having survived his eldest son,

  SIR JOHN SAVAGE, of Clifton, K.G. In 1484, this SIR JOHN SAVAGE, "Junr.," and eight of his brethren were made freemen of Chester, SIR JOHN SAVAGE being then Mayor (*Vale Royal of England*, p. 188). The brethren are there ranked as follows :—1, Sir John Savage, Jun.; 2, James; 3, Lawrence; 4, Edward, for Edmund; 5, Christopher; 6, George; 7, William; 8, Richard; 9, Homfrey. This SIR JOHN SAVAGE was a very distinguished soldier. He commanded the left wing of Richmond's army at the Battle of Bosworth Field, his uncle, Thomas, Lord Stanley, afterwards Earl of Derby, commanding the right,[1] and he was very instrumental, together with Lord Stanley, in raising Richmond to the throne as Henry the VII., and in thus establishing in his person the Tudor dynasty. For his services Henry VII. conferred many favours upon him. He made him a Knight of the Garter, and bestowed upon him manors and offices. Henry VII. "per literas suas patentes, datas 7 die Martii, 1 Hen. VII., 1485, memoria reducens diutina et laudabilis servitia, nec non probitatem actusque strenuos intimi dilecti militis nostri Johannis Savage junioris, quem, tam in armis quam in moribus et consilio, florere dinoscebatur; qualiterque idem Johannis cum multitudine copiosa suorum fratrum, consanguineorum, sevientium, amicorum benevolorum, ad sua grandia costus et onera, personæque suæ pericula multimoda, in servitio nostro in conflictu et prælio contra magnum adversarium nostrum Ricardum tertium tunc nuper regem Angliæ prætensum, cæterosque suos complices et fautores, quam contra alios rebelles et proditores nostros contra nos hostiliter guerram levantes, etc. Concessimus eidem Johanni castrum et manerium de Gresley et Kimbley in comitatu Nottinghamiæ, et

---

[1] "It would appear from this letter [*Paston Letters*, vol. ii., p. 156] that the different corps of which the royal army was composed wore the liveries of their respective lords and chiefs. The colour of the coats worn by Sir William Stanley's retainers at the Battle of Bosworth was red—   'Sir William Stanley, that noble Knight,
    Ten thousand red-coats that day had he.'—*Song of the Lady Bessy*.
In the same contemporary poem we read of
    'Sir John Savage' fifteen hundred white hoods,
    For they will fight and never flee.'"
                  See Jesse's *History of King Richard III.*, p. 292.
The "white" of the "white hoods" probably corresponded with the *argent* of the Savage shield.

Ehelston in comitatu Derbiæ, ac mineram carbonum, etc.; quæ fuerunt Johannis Domini Zouche; ac etiam maneria Elineton-Holmesfield in comitatu Derbiæ; et maneria de Granby et Sutton in comitatu Nottinghamiæ; et manerium de Shepeshed in comitatu Leycestriæ,[1] ac maneria de Sutton-Hubybunderell, alias dictum Hobbadler, et Watton, alias Wotton, Croston, Endeborne, in comitatu Salopiæ; quæ fuerunt Francisci Lovell militis, nuper vice-comitis Lovell; habendo prædicto Johanni Savage, et hæredibus masculis de corpore (Lib. D. pag. 171, v. The original among the evidences at Rock Savage. Anno Dmi. 1669)."[2] "The

Monument in the Savage Chapel, Macclesfield, to the Right Hon. THOMAS SAVAGE, Earl Rivers, &c., ob. 1694. The two altar-tombs are supposed to be those of Sir JOHN SAVAGE, ob. 1615, and Sir THOMAS, his son, ob. 1635.

manor of Ilkeston (Tilchestune) was granted," says Lysons, "on the attainder of John Lord Zouch, as a partizan of Richard III., by Henry VII., in 1485, to SIR JOHN SAVAGE, of whose descendant, SIR THOMAS SAVAGE, it was purchased in 1608 by Sir John Manners, ancestor of His Grace the Duke of Rutland, who is now [1817] the present proprietor."[3] Of the manor of Holmsfield Lysons writes

[1] "His grandson, Sir John Savage, sold Shepeshed to Thomas Duport, Esq., in 1572."—Nichol: *Leicestershire*.
[2] "Abstract from the Pedigree of the Family of Savage, from the College of Arms," &c.
[3] Lysons: *Derbyshire*, p. 192.

—" This manor belonged to the Deincourts when the Survey of Domesday was taken, and continued in that family till the death of William Deincourt in the reign of Henry VI. One of his sisters and co-heirs married Sir William Lovell; on the attainder of his son Francis Lord Lovell, in the reign of Henry VII., this manor was granted to SIR JOHN SAVAGE. It is now [1817] the property of the Duke of Rutland, whose ancestor purchased it of the SAVAGE family in 1586."[1] And of Elmton—" The manor of Elmton belonged to Walter Deincourt when the S. of D. was taken; and it continued in that family till the death of William Lord Deincourt in 1422. Ralph Lord Cromwell, who married one of his sisters and co-heirs, died seised of this manor in 1454; his sister and heir brought it to Sir William Lovell. On the attainder of Francis Lord Lovell, in 1485, it was granted to SIR JOHN SAVAGE."[2] In addition to these tokens of his gratitude the Monarch conferred other favours upon SIR JOHN. "Feb. 16, 1488. 'Grant in survivorship to JOHN SAVAGE, Junr., a Knight for the King's body, and his son, JOHN SAVAGE, Esq., of the following offices:—The office of Steward of the town or manor with the custody of the park and lodge of Tewkesbury, co. Gloucester; the office of Steward of the manor or lordship of Elmsley, co. Worcester; the office of Constable or Keeper of the castle, park, lodge, and warren at Elmsley; the office of the chase of Croslawade, co. Worcester; the office of Sheriff of Worcestershire; the office of Stewardship of the lordships or manors of Erlscrombe and Weirpedil, co. Worcester, and of Whittington, Chadworth, and Sidney, co. Gloucester.' This grant is made on surrender of the patent 21 Sept. 1 Henry VII., granting, for life, to Richard Nanfan, an Esquire for the King's body, several of the above offices."[3] In 1489, Dec. 10, SIR JOHN SAVAGE, Knt., is one of those to whom are addressed Commissions of the Peace of Oyer and Terminer, in the Co. of Gloucester. "This SIR JOHN," says Ormerod, "was slain at the Siege of Boloigne, in France, 8 Hen. VII., 1498 [? 1492] in the life-time of his father. See Stow in eodem anno. He was a valiant man and an expert soldier, and was made a Knight of the Garter by Henry Seventh."[4] Lord Bacon gives the following

---

[1] Lysons: *Derbyshire*, p. 134.
[2] Lysons: *Derbyshire*, p. 157.
[3] *Materials Illustrative of the Reign of Henry VII.*, p. 245. It is added in parenthesis— "A marginal note, on the patent roll made 20 July, 13 Hen. VIII., records that John Fyneux, Knt., Chief Justice of the King's Bench, in obedience to a writ of certiorari, made return that the said JOHN SAVAGE, Sen., Knt., and John Savage, Junr., Knt., had pleaded guilty to an indictment charging them with certain offences, and had delivered up the above patent to be cancelled."—Given at Grenewiche, P.S. No. 133. Pat. p. l. m. 10 (17).
[4] Ormerod: *Cheshire*, p. 527.

account of the manner of his death:—"[The King] and his army, the fifteenth of October, removed from Calais, and in four days' march set him down before Boloign. During this siege of Boloign, which continued near a month, there passed no memorable action nor accident of war; only SIR JOHN SAVAGE, a valiant captain, was slain, riding about the walls of the town to take a view." *(History of Henry VII.)* SIR JOHN married Dorothy Vernon, only daughter of Sir Ralph Vernon, of the family of Vernon, Lords of Haddon, &c., ancestors of the Barons Vernon, and by her had issue,

    I. SIR JOHN, of whom presently as successor to his grandfather in the lordship of Clifton, &c.

    I. Alice, married to Sir William Brereton, of Brereton, in Cheshire, Knt.

    II. Felicia, married to Robert Milwood, of Eaton, in Derbyshire, Esq.

    III. Ellen, married to John Hawarden.

    IV. Maude, married to Sir Robert Needham, of Shenton, in Shropshire, Knt.

[SIR JOHN SAVAGE, K.G., had also a base son,

    George Savage, Parson of Davenham,[1] who himself had several base children, viz., by a daughter of —— Winslow,

        1. John Winslow, Archdeacon of Middlesex;

        2. Elizabeth, married to —— Clayton, of Shelwall, in Cheshire;

    by a daughter of —— Dyes, of Barrow, in Cheshire,

        1. Randle Savage, of the Lodge;

        2. Margaret, married to —— Hayes, of Litley, in Aston-juxta-Pickmore;

    by Elizabeth Frodsham (first, or subsequently, married to one Edmund Bonner, "a Sawyer with Mr. Armingham")—

        Edmund Bonner, Archdeacon of Leicester, and afterwards twice Bishop of London—the notorious Bishop Bonner. Bonner's illegitimacy has been doubted. "Strype tells us that his contemporary, Nicholas Lechmore, one of the barons of the exchequer, had found evidences among his family papers that

---

[1] Probably this is the "George Savage, Clerk," to whom, in 1488, the following grant was made by Henry VII.:—Feb. 4, 1488, 3 H. VII.—"Grant, for life, to George Savage, clerk, of the custody of the hospital called the 'Spittelhous de alto pecco,' between the towns of Hope and Castleton, Co. Derby (in the King's gift by reason of the duchy of Lancaster), with all the lands, tenements, and profits, &c., of the office; the grantee to celebrate there, by himself or deputy, four times a year, mass and divine service for the King's good estate, and for the souls of the dead founders of the hospital."—See *Materials for a History of Henry VII.* The flat slab with the crozier, represented in the woodcut on p. 32, marks the resting-place of this George Savage, parson of Davenham.

Bonner was born in lawful wedlock."[1] Be this as it may, there seems to be no reason to doubt the current account of his parentage. In an old, odd, and amusing Pedigree of the Bishop, which lies before us,[2] some reference is made to certain Worcestershire lands of the SAVAGES which he had in his possession, and it seems that his mother, shortly before his birth, was sent out of Cheshire to the care of SAVAGE OF ELMLEY CASTLE in that county, where Bonner was born. *Afterwards*, according to this account, his mother was married to Bonner the Sawyer. "This George Savage," runs the story, "was the bastard son of SIR JOHN SAVAGE, Knight of the Garter. The which Georg was made priest and became parson of Davenham, in Cheshire, and after begatt Edmund Savage (whom we call Edmund Bonner) of the body of Elizabeth Frodesham, who died at Fullham in K. E. 6 tyme, when Bonner was prisoner in the Marshallsey [for not recognising the right of supremacy of the Regent Somerset and the Council over the Church], who gave notwithstanding for her mourning coates at her death. . . . The Earle of Warwick's lands in Worcestershire (he being attainted of Treason) were given to the second SIR JOHN SAVAGE, which was Elmley, Sudley, Bushly, Hadly, Rydmarkly. Hadly, Elmly, and Sudly had every one a castle and a park, and Bushly and Rydmarkly had both parks and no castle. Now, when it fell into the King's hands by the death of Pansfoote, then Edm. Bonner did change lands in Essex with the King for Bushly and Ridmarkly, the which two towns are now in the tenor and occupation of one Searle and Sheaphed. Searle is cossen to Bonner, and hath Bushly. Sheaphed was brother-in-law to Bishop Ridley and hath Redmarkly. And furthermore the said Shephed hath condempned Bonner in the Guild Hall for Bishop Ridley's goods which amounted to 400£ in a nisi

---

[1] See *Dictionary of National Biography*, article "BONNER, or BONER, EDMUND," contributed by Mr. James Gairdner.

[2] Copied from the old Coddington book of pedigrees compiled at the Visitation taken in 1566 by William Flower Norroy, and also the Visitation of Cheshire taken by William Flower, alias Norroy, King-of-Arms, and Robert Glover, Somerset Herald, his Marshal, 1580, corrected and added to by Richard St. George Norroy in 1613.

penis, since the Queenes reign that now is."[1] The character of Bonner, who was at least a man of marked and recognized ability, has been, without doubt, painted blacker than it deserved. As Mr. Gairdner, in his article on the Bishop in the *Dictionary of National Biography*, justly says, referring to the number of martyrs for whose deaths he has been held responsible—"That Bonner condemned these men is certain; that he took a pleasure in it, as Foxe insinuates, is by no means so clear. It may be that he did not protest as he might have done against the severity of an inhuman law. A victim himself to the injustice of puritanism in the days of King Edward, he saw tendencies destructive to the commonwealth in the opinions which he condemned, and rough remedies were but the fashion of the times. Still, though his functions were merely judicial, the revulsion of feeling created by these repeated severities extended to their agents, and there is no doubt that Bonner was unpopular." Mr. Gairdner rightly insists that Bonner was controlled by the Queen, who in her turn was governed by Philip and the cruel *régime* of Spain. He is also of opinion that the true Bonner was a very different person from the Bonner of popular fancy and tradition. "Sir John Harrington, who was quite a boy when Bonner died, says that he was so hated that men would say of any ill-favoured fat fellow in the street, that was Bonner. This, however, tells us little of the real character of the man. The special merit by which he rose was that of being an able canonist, quick-witted and ready in argument. From some recorded anecdotes, it would appear that he had a quick temper also, and was given to language that now-a-days would certainly be called unclerical. A number of his sharp repartees are preserved by Harrington, which show that he was a man of lively and caustic humour,[2] rather than the cold-blooded monster he is commonly supposed to have been."]

SIR JOHN SAVAGE, K.G., as we have seen, was slain at the Siege of Boulogne, 1492. He was succeeded by his eldest son,

---

[1] From a copy in possession of Francis Walker Savage, Esq., of Springfield.

[2] This description of him shows that he had inherited at least some SAVAGE traits with which we shall become familiar.

THE SAVAGES OF THE ARDS.

SIR JOHN SAVAGE, of Clifton, &c., Knt. (knighted about 13 Henry VII.). He was Sheriff of Worcestershire 24 years together from the death of his father. He was styled "Sir John Savage, the Elder," 12 Henry VIII. He married Ann, daughter and heiress of Raufe Bostock, of Bostock, in Davenham parish, Esq., and had issue,

I. SIR JOHN, of whom presently as successor to his father in the lordship of Clifton, &c.
II. Edward.
III. George.
IV. Lawrence, married ——, daughter and heiress of Randal Egerton, of Walgrave, and had issue,
  1. John, who married ——, daughter and heiress of——, and had issue, Sir Arthur, Knt. The Right Hon. Sir Arthur Savage, Knt., of Rhebane, Co. Kildare, Ireland, M.P., was a distinguished soldier. He took a prominent part in the military operations of England against the Irish in the reign of Queen Elizabeth, having about 2,000 men under him, and fought at the Battle of the Curlew Mountains, 15th August, 1599.[1] "In 1614, Sir Arthur Savage, Knight and Privy Councillor (previously distinguished in the war in Munster), obtained a grant of various castles, rectories, houses, mills, woods, lands, tithes, &c., in the Counties of Cavan, Mayo, Galway, Limerick, Tipperary, Kerry, Cork, Clare, Kildare, Wicklow, Meath, Roscommon, and Dublin, as well as in the City of Dublin."[2] He married, and, dying 13th March, 1633, left issue,
    Sir Thomas, Knt., his successor.
    William, who married, and, dying 4th December, 1634, left three daughters, co-heiresses,—
      Sarah, 5 years and 2 months of age at her father's death;
      Jane, aged 4 years at her father's death. She married Henry Borrowes, ancestor of Sir Erasmus Dixon Borrowes, of Gilltown, Co. Kildare.

---

[1] An Arthur Savage, in 1585, was appointed Lieutenant to Captain Henshaw at Carrickfergus. It was possibly this Arthur Savage.
[2] Dalton: *King James's Army List*.

Frances, aged 10 months at her father's death. She married Sir Lawrence Parsons, of Birr Castle, and by him was ancestress of the Earls of Rosse. (*See under* "Rosse, Earl of," Burke's *Peerage and Baronage*).

V. Richard.
VI. Robert.
VII. Thomas.

I. Ann, married, about 1533, to Henry, Lord Berkeley, of Berkeley Castle, Co. Gloucester. (*See* Stow.) "This Lady Berkeley was held in great reverence by this family, as she not only, after she had been left a widow, recovered the estates belonging to the family which had been sequestered by the King, but also sold her dower-house to obtain money to re-roof the castle with lead, as it had fallen into a sad state of disrepair. There is a fine portrait of her by Holbein, published in 'Holbein's Portraits;' and in the great window of the hall at the Castle the SAVAGE arms are emblazoned amongst the other noble descents. The lead on the roof at this present day is the same she placed there."[1] The following notice of the Lady Berkeley (Ann Savage) appears in the text of the work entitled "Holbein's Portraits":—"The Lady Berkeley was Ann, daughter of SIR JOHN SAVAGE. . . . She was the second wife of Thomas Lord Berkeley, whose Lady, Mary Hastings, daughter of the first Earl of Huntington, had died without issue. Lord Berkeley, dying on the 15th of September, 1534, left her a young widow, with a daughter, Elizabeth, then under one year old, who became the wife of Thomas Butler, tenth Earl of Ormonde, and pregnant of a son, afterwards Henry, eleventh Lord Berkeley. Her character, which probably deserved a better fate, is nearly buried in oblivion. She was a wise, honest, and spirited manager for her infant children, under circumstances which, especially in her time, rendered such a conduct highly difficult and delicate. William, Marquis of Berkeley, having died without children, and on ill terms with his brother, Maurice, great-grandfather to this lady's husband, settled his Castle of Berkeley, with its appendant barony, on King Henry VII. and his issue male; on failure of which, he willed it that they should

---

[1] From MS. notes by Mr. Francis Walker Savage of Springfield, lent by Mr. Savage to the Editor.

revert to his right heirs: that failure occurred by the death of Edward VI., and the immediate restitution of the estates to the youthful lord appears to have been chiefly owing to the prudence and care of his mother." From her descend the Lords Berkeley, of Berkeley Castle.

SIR JOHN SAVAGE died "2 Martii, 19 Henry VIII., 1527," having survived his wife. (She had had a brother, William Bostock, but he died and she became sole heiress.) SIR JOHN was succeeded by his eldest son,

Tomb of SIR JOHN SAVAGE, of Clifton, Knt., ob. 1528, and of his Wife, the Lady Elizabeth, daughter of Charles Somerset, Earl of Worcester, in the Savage Chapel, Macclesfield. (The slab with the cross marks the burial-place of GEORGE SAVAGE, father of Bishop Bonner.)

SIR JOHN SAVAGE, of Clifton, &c., Knt., who married Elizabeth, daughter and heiress of Charles Somerset, Earl of Worcester. "This SIR JOHN SAVAGE [in some fray] killed one John Pauncefote, Esq., whereupon he and his father both were indicted for murder, and arraigned in the King's Bench, this SIR JOHN SAVAGE the younger as principal, and SIR JOHN SAVAGE the elder as accessory, who confessed the fact, but upon mediation of Cardinal Wolsey and Charles Earl of Worcester, the King's Chamberlain, they were pardoned by the King, paying four thousand marks, and covenanting that they would not come into the counties of Worcester or Chester during their lives without the King's licence under his Great Seal, Privy Seal, or Privy Signet, as appears by the indenture made the 24th day of November, 12 Henry VIII., 1520. (Lib. D., p. 179—the original now remaining amongst the evidences at Rock Savage, 1669.) But, after, the King, under his Great Seal dated 12 Junii, 16 Henry VIII., 1524, gave liberty to this SIR JOHN SAVAGE the younger, to go, ride, or dwell in any place either in Worcestershire or Cheshire (Lib. D., p. 172)." "What were the circumstances of the case we are not informed, but, as the consequences which followed it were not capital, it is but charitable to suppose that their crime was unpremeditated, and only arose out of one of those sudden affrays so common in those unsettled times."[1] SIR JOHN SAVAGE ("the Younger," of whom we now treat), by his wife the Lady Elizabeth, daughter of the Earl of Worcester, had issue,

I. SIR JOHN, Knt., of whom presently as successor to his father in the lordship of Clifton, &c.

II. Henry.

I. Margaret, married to Sir Richard Bulkeley, Knt.

SIR JOHN SAVAGE died "27 Julii, 20 Henry VIII., 1528, aged 35 years" (his widow afterwards "married William Brereton, of the Bedchamber to Henry VIII., beheaded for matters touching Queen Anne, 17 May, 1536, 28 Henry VIII."—Stow.—He was younger son of Sir Randle Brereton of Malpass.) SIR JOHN was succeeded by his elder son,

SIR JOHN SAVAGE, of Clifton, &c., Knt., who at his father's death was aged 3 years and 9 months. This SIR JOHN married Elizabeth, daughter of Thomas Manners, Earl of Rutland, about 1 Edw. VI. (1547-8). In 1550 Richard, Bishop of Coventry and Lichfield, guaranteed to this SIR JOHN SAVAGE, Knt., the manor of Tarvin, reserving the yearly rent of £31. "This SIR JOHN assumed for his proper coat six lions sable, and the lion's paw erected sable for his crest; now one by quartering Daniel's [Danyers'] coat therewith among others, which before was borne as his proper coat." . . . "The virtuous Lady Elizabeth died at Frodsham, dii Mortis 8 dii Augusti, 1570, 12 Elizabethæ (Lib. D., page 180)." After whose death he married, 2ndly, Elinour, widow of Sir Rd. Peshull of Beaurepaire, in Southamptonshire, and daughter of John Cotgrave, Esq., 14 Eliz., 1572. "Which Elinour had given unto her by the will of Sir Richd. Peshull, her former husband, all his lands in Bromley, Beaurepaire, Stratfield Say, Stratfield Mortimer, Terges, Basingstoke, Chinham, Tadley, Pamber, Silchester, Sherborne Monachorum, Sherborne St. John, Sherborne Cowdray,

---

[1] Beamont: *History of Halton Castle, &c.*, pp. 106-7.

Stovington, Dene, Bradley, and Berdenstock and Clack, Cowick, and Basing, in the counties of Southampton and Wiltshire; which lands SIR JOHN SAVAGE settled on his younger son Edward, and on his heirs by Polyxena, daughter of William le Gries, of London, Gentleman, and of Katherine his wife, natural sister of the said Dame Elinour. . . . This SIR JOHN SAVAGE, of Clifton, built the new fair house at Clifton, Anno Domini 1565, 7 Elizabethæ, which was afterwards called ROCK SAVAGE. He first writ himself of Rock Savage 17 Eliz., and so by little and little sometimes of Clifton and sometimes of Rock Savage to the 21 Eliz. But afterwards he constantly writ himself of Rock Savage, which his posterity have ever since retained."[1] Of the building of this new mansion of Rock Savage, Clifton, Beamont writes:—"In 1565, Queen Elizabeth's early days, Clifton, the family manor-place, having fallen into decay through age, SIR JOHN SAVAGE rebuilt it in a more stately style, and gave it the new name of Rock Savage, which has almost ever since supplanted Clifton as the name of the township. It has been said that the Queen honoured the builder by laying the first stone of the new house, and that she afterwards visited him at it, but there appears to be no foundation for either of these traditions, for in none of her Majesty's royal progresses do we find that she ever came so far north as Rock Savage. After the building of the new house at Rock Savage, Clifton was deserted, and at that hour it was said she remained like an aged matron, well contented to go to her grave, having seen in her lifetime her daughter advanced to such a height of honourable dignity.[2] What the new house of the SAVAGES was," continues Mr. Beamont, "may be gleaned from this description, written by a contemporary, who says:— 'We next behold the magnificent fabric of Rock Savage overlooking the waters and goodly marshes round about the skirts of it, and so contrived is the situation that from the lower meadows there is a fine easy ascent upon the face of the house, which as you approach it still nearer, as is the nature of true beauty, fills the eye with more delight; and to see now the late additions of delectable gardens, orchards, and walks, would make one say it longs to be the abode of so honourable a master as it doth service to.'"[3] Ormerod was of opinion that "a comparison of Rock Savage with the house at Brereton will leave little doubt that SIR JOHN SAVAGE and his son-in-law Sir William Brereton employed the same architect in the erection of their sumptuous fabrics." The name of the architect does not seem to have come down to us. SIR JOHN SAVAGE was

---

[1] Abstract from the College of Arms, &c.
[2] An old author, quoted in Greswell's *Runcorn*.—Beamont.
[3] See Greswell's *Runcorn*, p. 24.—Beamont.

seven times Sheriff of Cheshire,—in 1560, 1565, 1570, 1573, 1574, 1579, 1591; and three times Mayor of Chester,—in 1569, 1574, and 1597. "In 1 and 2 Philip and Mary, and also in 4 and 5 of the same reign, SIR JOHN SAVAGE was Seneschal of Halton. On the 20th April, 2 Elizabeth (1560), when an inquisition was taken after the death of James Merbury, SIR JOHN is again mentioned as filling the same office, and he still held it in 1570, when he is again mentioned."[1] By his 1st wife, Elizabeth, daughter of the Earl of Rutland, he had issue,

I. John, born 1548, who died in infancy.

---

[1] Beamont: *Halton Castle*, p. 99. Mr. Beamont also gives the following narrative in connection with the history of this SIR JOHN SAVAGE as Seneschal of Halton Castle:—"We have already seen Halton occasionally used as a prison for malefactors; but in the year 1579 its proud castle, once the chief seat of the constables of Cheshire, and which had given thrones to its possessors, declined from its former high estate, and became transferred into a prison for recusants, and SIR JOHN SAVAGE, its constable and seneschal, was ordered to receive such of this class of sufferers for conscience' sake as should be sent there. At this time it appears to have been thought necessary to repress with a strong hand offenders of this kind, and accordingly, on the 3rd June of the following year, a letter from the Privy Council was received by the Ecclesiastical Commissioners at Chester, which gave them to understand that the penalties on recusancy were to be increased. The tender knees of the reformed faith, as yet but feeble and tottering, required to be strengthened, and Halton, of which SIR JOHN SAVAGE was governor, was deemed a proper place for receiving such persons as either wavered in adopting the reformed faith or obstinately resisted it. The Privy Council also directed the Commissioners to select some fit and godly person—a spiritual person or teacher was probably intended—who should take charge of them, and the prisoners were to have for their diet the same allowance that was made to prisoners of the same kind in the Fleet Prison in London. Amongst those who habitually absented themselves from Church and other places of public worship, and conscientiously adhered to the Roman Catholic faith, was Sir John Southworth, the representative of a long line of knightly ancestors. Sir John, who had obstinately refused to attend Church, and had kept a Seminary Priest, one James Cowper, in his house at Samlesbury, not long after the queen's accession was summoned with others to sign his submission to Her Majesty, but he would only comply so far as to sign an undertaking not to maintain or countenance others in their recusancy. In other respects he was loyal to the Queen, and afterwards, when a general muster of arms and armed men in Lancashire was made, Sir John furnished his quota of two light horse, two corselets, two coats of plate, two pikes, two long bows, two sheaves of arrows, two steel caps, and one caliver (the weapon which Falstaff bade Bardolph put into Wart's hand), and one morion. In 1579, when an order was made that the leading Lancashire recusants should be imprisoned, Sir John Southworth, and Campion, the Jesuit, who had visited at his house, were amongst the number. To what place Campion was first sent we do not know, but Sir John was sent, and possibly Campion with him, to Halton Castle, this same fortress, where his kinsman, Henry Southworth, who, as has been mentioned, died in the still stronger fortress, the Tower of London, had been born. Sir John Southworth, who was among the first of those sent to Halton, was courteously received by his brother Knight, SIR JOHN SAVAGE, the Seneschal, who, no doubt, compassionate the condition of a prisoner committed to his charge for conscience' sake. To his keeper's great relief, on the 22nd July, 1581, the prisoner was ordered to be removed from Halton."

II. Sir John, Knt., of whom presently as successor to his father at Rock Savage (Clifton).

III. Thomas, born 1556, who died young.

IV. Edward, Constable (under his father, the Seneschal) of Halton Castle, 1592; born 1560; married Polyxena, daughter of William de Gries, of London, Gentleman, and had issue,
   1. Sir John, of Beaurepaire, Knt.

V. Francis, born 1562, who died young.

I. Margaret, born 1549, married to Sir William Brereton, of Brereton, in Cheshire, "afterwards Baron of Laghlin in Ireland, who built the fine new house at Brereton for Sir Laurence Smith, of Atherton, in Cheshire, marrying Jane, the mother of this Sir William Brereton. They granted the body and wardship of this William Brereton to this Sir John Savage, who thereupon married his daughter to him, with 1,000 marks portion, dated 24 Januarii, 4 Eliz., 1561 (Lib. D., page 178)."

II. Elizabeth, born 1552, married to Thomas Langton, Baron of Newton, in Lancashire, 1580, who was divorced from Margaret Sherborne, his wife, by sentence of the Consistory of York, 25 Junii, 1580.

III. Elinour, born 1557, married to Sir Henry Bagnal, son and heir of Sir Nicholas Bagnal, Knt., Marshall of the Queen's Army for Ireland, 1577[1]—"one thousand pounds portion." Afterwards she married Sir Sackville Trevor.

IV. Mary, born 1563, married to Sir Richard Milles, in Hampshire.

[*Note.*—A pedigree, in the Harl. MS. 1165, Fo. 93[b,] of the family of Hitchcock of Preshute, Wilts, records a marriage between Thomas Hitchcock of Preshute and *Mary, 4th* daughter of Sir John Savage, of Clifton, by Elizabeth, daughter of Thomas Manners, Earl of Rutland. By Thomas Hitchcock she was mother of
   1. Richard Hitchcock.
   2. Thomas Hitchcock.
   3. John Hitchcock, married Elizabeth, daughter of John Stile, of Marlboro', Co. Wilts., and had issue,
      John Hitchcock, of Preshute, in Co. Wilts., who married Bridget, daughter of Edmd. Hungerford, of North Stanten, Esq.]

---

[1] The Bagnal family became identified with Newry, Co. Down, and had an interesting history in connection with Irish affairs.

V. Frances, born 1567, married to Thomas Wilkes, in the County of Surrey, Esq.

SIR JOHN SAVAGE (who had no issue by his 2nd wife) died on the 5th December, 1597, aged 73, and was buried at Macclesfield, 24th January, 1598. He was succeeded by his eldest surviving son and heir,

SIR JOHN SAVAGE, of Rock Savage (Clifton), Knt., afterwards Baronet, Constable and Seneschal of Halton Castle, Mayor of Chester, 1607, and Sheriff of Chester also the same year. Sir JOHN SAVAGE was created Baronet (being the nineteenth from the institution of the order) 29th June, 9 Jacobi, 1611. He married Mary, one of the daughters and co-heiresses of Richard Allington, Esq., deceased, about the 18 Elizabeth (1575), and had issue,

Monument of SIR JOHN SAVAGE, of Clifton, Knt., ob. 1597, and of the Lady Elizabeth, his Wife, ob. 1570, in the Savage Chapel, Macclesfield.

I. John (aged 3 years in 1580), who died young.
II. THOMAS, of whom presently as the 1ST VISCOUNT SAVAGE, and as successor to his father at Rock Savage and in the Baronetcy.
III. John, murdered in 1609 by Ralph Bathurst, who, being arraigned for the murder and refusing to plead, was sentenced to the *peine forte et dure*, and was pressed to death on 13th July in the same year.

IV. Richard.
V. William. (All these four last-named sons were living 42 Eliz., 1600.)
VI. George.
VII. Philip.
   I. Grace, married to Sir Richard Wilbraham, of Woodhay, in Cheshire, Knt. and Bart. She survived her husband, and died at Chester, 1662.
   II. Elizabeth, married, 1st, to Thomas Manwaring, "who then waited on her father," and was younger son of Manwaring of Martin Sands, nigh Over, in Cheshire, and had issue. She married, 2ndly, Sir Ralph Done, of Dudden in Cheshire, descended from the Dones of Athinton.

[This SIR JOHN SAVAGE had also an illegitimate son known as John Savage, of Barrow.]

SIR JOHN SAVAGE died in 1615, and was buried at Macclesfield on Friday, the 14th July of that year, in the night-time. He was succeeded by his eldest surviving son,

SIR THOMAS SAVAGE, of Rock Savage, Bart., afterwards VISCOUNT SAVAGE of Rock Savage. He was created VISCOUNT SAVAGE by King Charles I., 6th of November, 1626. "Jane, sister and heiress to Sir Wm. Cordell, Master of the Rolls, and Lord of Long Melford in Suffolk, gave by her will to SIR THOMAS SAVAGE Long Melford with other lands in Suffolk, dated 15 Julii 1602. She was widow of Richard Allington, and grandmother to Sir THOMAS SAVAGE." LORD SAVAGE, when SIR THOMAS, stood high in King James I.'s favour, and "on the baptism of John his son and heir, on the 31st December, 1606, Henry Prince of Wales honoured him by being the child's godfather, and presented him, instead of the usual gossip's spoons, with a quantity of silver plate, which was of more value and far more useful *(Issues of the Exchequer, 300)*. In 1617, the King returning from Scotland to London passed through Lancashire and Cheshire on his way. . . . [On the 21st of August] he proceeded to Rock Savage, where he was received in fitting state by its owner, SIR THOMAS SAVAGE. After partaking of the goodly repast prepared for him and his suite, his Majesty, attended by his host, hunted and killed a buck in Halton Park. . . . Halton . . . had been visited by Edward II. after the death of Thomas of Lancaster, and this visit of King James I. was the second royal visit with which Halton and its old castle had been honoured."[1] LORD SAVAGE was Chancellor of the Queen's Court at Westminster,

---

[1] Beamont: *Hist. of Halton, &c.*, pp. 108–9.

1634. He married Elizabeth Darcy, eldest daughter and co-heiress of Thomas Lord Darcy, afterwards Viscount Colchester, and Earl Rivers,[1] and by her had issue,

I. JOHN, of whom presently as his successor.
II. Sir Thomas, Knt., who married Bridget, widow of Sir Edward Somerset, K.C.B., fifth son of Edward Somerset, Earl of Worcester, and daughter and heiress of William Whitmore of Leighton, in Wirrall, in the County of Chester, Esq., by Margaret, his wife, sister and heiress of Sir George Beeston, of Beeston, in Cheshire, and daughter of Sir Hugh Beeston. From this marriage descended the SAVAGES OF BEESTON, in Cheshire. The Hon. Thomas Savage, of Beeston

Portion of Beeston Castle, Cheshire, seat of the SAVAGES OF BEESTON.

Castle, by his wife Bridget (*née* Whitmore), grand-daughter of Sir Hugh Beeston, had issue—

Darcy Savage, of Beeston Castle and of Leighton, Esq.[2]

Elizabeth Savage, married to Marmaduke, 2nd Lord Langdale, and had issue *(inter alia)*,

---

[1] "After the Widvile family, that of Darcy was the next which bore the title [of Earl Rivers], whereto Thomas, son of John Lord Darcy, of Chich, was advanced the end of Charles I., with remainder, for default of issue-male, to his son-in-law, Sir Thomas Savage, who also by the same patent was created Baron and Viscount Savage of Clifton (alias Rock Savage) in Cheshire."—Banks: *Dormant Peerage*.

[2] Beeston subsequently passed to the family of Mostyn, by marriage of Bridget, only daughter and heiress of Darcy Savage, Esq., to Sir Thomas Mostyn, Bart.

Elizabeth,[1] married to Sir Hugh Smithson, of Stanwick, Bart., by whom she had issue,

Hugh Smithson, who died unmarried in his father's lifetime.

Langdale Smithson, who married Philadelphia, daughter of William Revely, Esq., of Newby Wisk, Co. York, and, predeceasing his father, left an only son,

Hugh Smithson, successor to the Smithson Baronetcy, who married Lady Elizabeth Seymour, the heiress of the Percys, Dukes of Northumberland, and on the death of his father-in-law, Algernon Seymour, Duke of Somerset, "succeeded to the manors limited to him, obtaining in the same year an Act of Parliament to allow himself and his Countess to assume the surname and arms of Percy. His lordship was installed Knight of the Garter in 1757, and was created *Earl Percy* and *Duke of Northumberland* in 1776." From him descends the present Duke of Northumberland. (*See* Burke: *Peerage and Baronetage.*)

III. Francis, baptised (in London?) June 5, 1608.
IV. James, baptised August 13, 1609, died without issue.
V. Henry, baptised Feb. 26, 16—.
VI. William, died without issue.
VII. Robert, died without issue.
VIII. Charles, whose daughter Mary married Jeremy Thoresby of Leeds.
   I. Jane, baptised May 26, 1607, married to John Pawlet, Lord St. John, 1622, afterwards Marquis of Winchester, a conspicuous loyalist in the reign of King Charles the First, "who withstood in his magnificent castle of Basing, in Hampshire, an obstinate siege of two years against the rebels, who levelled it to the ground, because in every window was written *Aimez Loyauté*. He died

---

[1] "This lady herself derived descent from the ancient Percys thus:—John, Lord Neville, married Maud de Percy; his eldest son by whom, Ralph, 1st Earl of Westmoreland, left a daughter, Cecilia, who married Richard, Duke of York, whose daughter by the said Cecilia, Anne, had by her 2nd husband, Sir Thomas St. Leger, Knt., a daughter, Anne, who married George Manners, Lord Ross; and her daughter, Lady Elizabeth Manners, having married SIR JOHN SAVAGE, Knt., was great-grandmother of ELIZABETH SAVAGE, daughter of the HON. THOMAS SAVAGE, of Beeston Castle, Cheshire; which ELIZABETH married Marmaduke, 2nd Lord Langdale, and was mother of Lady Smithson."—Burke: *Peerage and Baronetage.*

in 1674, and was buried in the Church of Englefield in Berkshire,"[1] where on his monument is an admirable epitaph in English verse written by Dryden.[2] Jane, Marchioness of Winchester, died in her 23rd year in giving birth to her second son. Her virtues and accomplishments have been immortalized by Milton in his well-known ode entitled "An Epitaph on the Marchioness of Winchester,"[3] written by him in 1631, when at Christ's Church,

---

[1] Dr. J. Warton.

[2] *Epitaph written by Dryden*

"ON THE MONUMENT OF THE MARQUIS OF WINCHESTER.

"He who in impious times undaunted stood,
And 'midst rebellion durst be just and good;
Whose arms asserted, and whose sufferings more
Confirm'd the cause for which he fought before,
Rests here, rewarded by an heavenly prince;
For what his earthly could not recompense.
Pray, reader, that such times no more appear:
Or, if they happen, learn true honour here.
Ask of this age's faith and loyalty,
Which to preserve them, Heaven confined in thee.
Few subjects could a king like thine deserve;
And fewer such a king so well could serve.
Blest king, blest subject, whose exalted state
By sufferings rose, and gave the law to fate.
Such souls are rare, but mighty patterns given
To earth, and meant for ornaments to heaven."

[3] *Milton's* "EPITAPH ON THE MARCHIONESS OF WINCHESTER.

"This rich marble doth inter
The honour'd wife of Winchester,
A Viscount's daughter, an Earl's heir,
Besides what her virtues fair
Added to her noble birth,
More than she could own from earth.
Summers three times eight save one
She had told; alas! too soon,
After so short a time of breath,
To house with darkness and with death.
Yet had the number of her days
Been as complete as was her praise,
Nature and Fate had had no strife
In giving limit to her life.
  Her high birth, and her graces sweet,
Quickly found a lover meet;
The virgin quire for her request

Cambridge. It is believed that there was a Cambridge-collection of verses on the death of this accomplished lady; and, "I may further observe," writes Todd, "that there is an Elegy on this occasion at end of 'La Dance Machabre, or Death's Duell, by W. Colman, 12mo, p. 68, entitled *An Elegie vpon the Ladie Marshionesse of Winchester, daughter to the right honourable Thomas Lord Savage,*' &c., consisting of twenty lines." T. Warton supposed that it was Milton's acquaintance with the family of Lord Bridgewater, for whom he wrote *Comus*, that led to his writing this Epitaph; for, says he, "our marshioness was the daughter of Thomas lord viscount Savage, of Rock Savage, in Cheshire; and it is natural to suppose, that her family was well acquainted with the family of Lord Bridgewater, belonging to the same county. . . . And afterwards we find some of that family intermarrying with this of the marquis of Winchester. . . . Mr. Bowle remarks," adds Warton, "that her death was celebrated by Sir John Beaumont and Sir W.

> The god that sits at marriage feast;
> He at their inviting came,
> But with a scarce well-lighted flame;
> And in his garland, as he stood,
> Ye might discern a cypress bud.
> Once had the early matrons run
> To greet her of a lovely son,
> And now with second hopes she goes,
> And calls Lucina to her throes;
> And, whether by mischance or blame,
> Atropos for Lucina came;
> And with remorseless cruelty
> Spoil'd at once both fruit and tree :
> The hapless babe, before his birth,
> Had burial, yet not laid in earth ;
> And the languish'd mother's womb
> Was not long a living tomb.
>   So have I seen some tender slip,
> Sav'd with care from winter's nip,
> The pride of her carnation train,
> Pluck'd up by some unheedy swain,
> Who only thought to crop the flower,
> New shot up from vernal shower ;
> But the fair blossom hangs the head
> Side-ways, as on a dying bed,
> And those pearls of dew, she wears,
> Prove to be presaging tears,
> Which the sad morn had let fall

Davenant." He further tells us that "in Howell's entertaining Letters there is one to this lady, the Lady Jane Savage, Marchioness of Winchester, dated Mar. 15, 1626. He says, he assisted her in learning Spanish : and that Nature and the Graces exhausted all their treasure and skill in 'framing this exact model of female perfection.' He adds, 'I return you here the Sonnet your Grace pleased to send me lately, rendered into Spanish, and fitted from the same ayre it had in English, both for cadence and feete,' &c." Dr. J. Warton remarked with truth, "It was a singular lot, both of husband and wife, to have received the honour of being celebrated by two such poets." The Marchioness of Winchester left issue,

Charles, afterwards 1st Duke of Bolton.

II. Dorothy, baptised March 3, 1614, married to Lord Andover, son and heir of the Earl of Berkshire (Thomas Howard).

III. Elizabeth, married to Sir John Thimbelby, of Irnham, Lincolnshire.

On her hastening funeral.
  Gentle Lady, may thy grave
Peace and quiet ever have;
After this thy travel sore
Sweet rest seize thee evermore,
That, to give the world encrease,
Shorten'd hast thy own life's lease.
Here, besides the sorrowing
That thy noble house doth bring,
Here be tears of perfect moan
Wept for thee in Helicon;
And some flowers, and some bays,
For thy hearse, to strew the ways,
Sent thee from the banks of Came,
Devoted to thy virtuous name;
Whilst thou, bright Saint, high sitst in glory,
Next her, much like to thee in story,
That fair Syrian shepherdess,
Who, after years of barrenness,
The highly-favour'd Joseph bore
To him that serv'd for her before.
And at her next birth, much like thee,
Through pangs fled to felicity,
Far within the bosom bright
Of blazing Majesty and Light:
There with thee, new welcome Saint,
Like fortunes may her soul acquaint,
With thee there, clad in radiant sheen,
No Marchioness, but now a Queen."

IV. Anne, married to Robert Brudenell, of Stonton, in Northamptonshire, 2nd Earl of Cardigan, April 20, 1661.
　　V. Katherine, a nun at Dunkirk in 1666.
　　VI. Henrietta-Maria, married to Raufe Sheldon, of Beeley, in Gloucestershire, Esq.

"While Viscount Savage was in London, probably attending upon his duties as the Queen's Chancellor, he was seized with an illness, of which he died on the 16th of December, 1635. . . . The Viscount's body was conveyed to the family burial-place at Macclesfield, and on its way through Congleton these entries in the Corporation books show that it was treated with marked respect:—

	s.	d.
'Mending Rood Lane against the coming of Lord Savage's corps	1	6
Sugar, 6 lbs.; cloves, 1 oz., at the entertainment	11	0
There was a horse-load of wine and many other items, particularly		
Four links to light	5	0'

On the same day on which the Viscount was laid in earth, his mother, Lady Mary Savage, of Bostock Hall, was also borne to the grave, and laid probably in the same tomb with her son in the family burial-place, the Savage Chapel at Macclesfield."[1] LORD SAVAGE was succeeded by his eldest son,

　　SIR JOHN SAVAGE, BART., second VISCOUNT SAVAGE, who succeeded to the EARLDOM of RIVERS, in right of his mother, in 1639. "Lady Elizabeth Savage, daughter of Thomas Darcy, Lord Darcy of Chiche, and Earl Rivers, and widow of THOMAS SAVAGE, 1st VISCOUNT SAVAGE, was created on 21st April, 1641, Countess of Rivers for life.[2] Her ladyship died in 1650, when the title became of course extinct." (Burke: *Extinct and Dormant Peerage*.) "There were certain articles drawn for this JOHN's marriage with Anne Compton, daughter of William, Earl of Northampton, 16 Julii, 1649; but it did not take effect." He married, *1st*, Catherine, daughter of William Parker, Lord Morley and Lord Monteagle, of Horneby Castle, in Lancashire. "Besides the castle of Halton, of which he was at the same time castellan, seneschal, and constable, as well as lessee, he had another residence, the sumptuous house of Rock Savage, with its splendid views of wood and water, hill and champaign. The prospects which dawned on him at his father's death were fair and bright. Almost from his birth he had enjoyed the favour of royalty. The lines had fallen to him 'in pleasant places,' and he was married to a noble lady of a rank equal to his own,

---
[1] Beamont, pp. 111, 12.
[2] William Ryley, Bluemantle, certifies the death, on the 25th February, 1639-40, of Thomas Earl Rivers, at his residence, Winchester House, New Broad Street, London, and his interment at Chick, St. Osyth, Essex.—*Cal. State Papers, Doncaster*, Charles I.

Catherine, daughter of Lord Morley and Monteagle, the peer to whom was addressed the memorable letter which led to the discovery of the Gunpowder Treason. But these prospects, so bright, were too fair to last. Gloom and darkness were on the way, and the days were hastening on

> When hard words, jealousies, and fears
> Set men together by the ears.

. . . It would seem from this entry in the Congleton books in 1638—'Banqueting stuff for Lord Savage, £2 : 0 : 0'—that the Corporation, still loyal to the house of SAVAGE, had been entertaining his lordship. In 1642, when the sword of the great Civil War was first drawn and the scabbard thrown away, the Earl found 'he had fallen on evil days and evil tongues.' Bound to the King by every motive of duty, loyalty, and gratitude, he cast in his lot with such of those nobles and gentry as at the outset of the struggle subscribed to find forces for his Majesty's service, among whom his name appears as engaging himself for a force of 30 mounted horse. But he and his family sent officers as well as men to serve the King, and Thomas Savage, who appears as a lieutenant-colonel in Colonel Osborne's regiment, was probably his near relation.[1] His opponents, not unnaturally, perhaps, taking umbrage

[1] Minutes transacted at Whitehall, May 5, 1639.—" Letter to Viscount Savage, that the Lords being acquainted by the Earl of Dorset that he and his brother have many occasions which require their presence in town this term, their Lordships give way to their coming up."—*Cal. State Papers*, Charles I.

There was a SIR EDWARD SAVAGE living at this time, and taking an active part in the service of the King, whose name appears in the State Papers more than once in association with that of LORD SAVAGE (EARL RIVERS), and who must have been a very near relative of the Earl's, either a cousin or a nephew. He seems to have been a man of influence, and rather a favourite with members of the Royalist party. On June 11, 1639, he writes from "the Camp at Birks" to Sec. Windebank:—"I being with my best friend the good Duke when he wrote lately to you, and sent you the copies of the Scots' petition and letter sent by them to the Lords' house, with his Majesty's answer thereunto, hath commanded me now to let you know he has not news enough to write himself to you, whom heartily he loves, but that this day the Earl of Rothes, the Earl of Dunfermline, Lord Loudon, whose name is Campbell, Sir William Douglas, Sheriff of Teviotdale, and Alexander Henderson, who was Moderator at the last Assembly in Scotland, are now at the Lord General's tent with the rest of our privy councillors here, who are appointed by his Majesty to hear the Scots' grievances and to parley for a peace, which I pray God may be concluded for our Master's honour and safe return to Whitehall, that I may tell you some true Scotch stories that we have met withal in these parts, which, to speak truth to our gracious Master, many of the Scots have foresworn I believe."

On the 10th July following (1639), Edward Nicholson, writing from Westminster to Sir John Pennington, mentions, at the close of a long letter, that the King has conferred on this Edward Savage the honour of Knighthood :—" P.S.—The King made, I hear, 10 Englishmen Knights in the North, whereof Mr. Hill, James Thynne, son of Sir Thomas Thynne, Mr. Grenville, and *Ned Savage* were four."

In the following December, we find the same SIR EDWARD SAVAGE sending a petition of his

at his proceedings, scrupled not to say hard things of him. Amongst others they said, as a parliamentary paper of July, 1642, informs us :—'The LORD RIVERS gives out many scandalous speeches against us, and strives by all the means he can to set the whole country against us.' [Hist. of the Siege of Manchester, p. 11.] Confidence amongst neighbours being now thrown aside, suspicion took its place, while trade was interrupted, and scarcity and want seemed almost at the door. On the 30th December, 1642, the County of Chester, availing itself of a seeming lull, tried to avert the storm from its borders by meeting and entering into a convention of neutrality at Bunbury; but this peaceful movement was annulled and set aside by the Parliament. Meanwhile the King's commissioners of array, not disposed to remain indifferent to the distractions of the neighbourhood, issued public notice to all soldiers not to seize or take up horses or property without authority, on pain of being heavily punished for such offences. It has been said that on the 21st February, 1643, Sir William Brereton[1] seized both the castles of Halton and Beeston on behalf of the Parliament; but as respects Halton, this is a mistake. It is true that after the failure of the Bunbury convention Sir William seized on Beeston Castle; but its rival castle was already in the possession of EARL RIVERS, who gave it a governor, and threw into it a sufficient garrison, and as a royal castle should hoist the royal colours, so these now floated over the old walls of Halton; and while sentries kept the gate, the portcullis was probably renewed, the warder resumed his place on the high turret, pikemen and musketeers, in half or whole armour, patrolled the courts, and some time elapsed after this before Sir William Brereton made any attempt to wrest the castle from its owner. . . . One of the worst consequences of these disturbed times was the separation it caused between those who, being nearest neighbours to each other, ought to have

---

VISCOUNT SAVAGE's in favour of one Thomas Cheshire, a dependant of the LORD SAVAGE, who was seeking an appointment. Both letters are interesting :—
"1639, Dec. 3. John Viscount Savage to Sir John Heydon"—
"I presume to importune you on behalf of Thomas Cheshire, a servant of mine, concerning the Minister's place for Trinity Minories, now vacant and at your disposal. What favour you shall show him herein I shall acknowledge as shown to myself, and be obliged to requite it in the like or any other way." *(Seal with Arms.)*
SIR EDWARD's recommendation is as follows :—
"Dec. 3. Sir Edward Savage to Sir John Heydon."
"Mr. Cheshire, the bearer hereof, was of Brazenose College in my time, and was held to be a very good scholar. Since that time he has approved himself an honest man, and painful in his vocation, and no doubt worthy of your favour, to whose nobleness I commend him, and leave him at your disposal." *(Seal with Crest.)*

[1] The Brereton family, as we have seen, were closely connected by intermarriage with the SAVAGES.

been the best friends. EARL RIVERS at Halton and the Brookes at Norton, the two nearest neighbours, espoused opposite sides in the struggle, and were directly opposed to each other. Colonel Henry Brooke, the then head of the house at Norton, was appointed by Parliament a commissioner for raising the assessment they had ordered, and he was afterwards for four years their high sheriff of Cheshire; and Major Peter Brooke, an active Parliamentarian commander, who, in January, 1643, was elected a member of what was afterwards called the Long Parliament, for the borough of Newton, was Colonel Brooke's brother. But, on the other hand, Edward Bridgman, Esquire, who had married

Ruins of Halton Castle, Cheshire, ninety years ago.

Dame Eleanor Brooke, their mother, was a zealous royalist, and suffered much in that cause. . . . Domestic or country-house sieges seem to have been a distinguishing feature of our great civil war. Besides Norton, apparently the first instance in the neighbourhood, the houses at Crowton, Biddulph, Withinshaw, and, above all, Lathom, were thus attacked. But now the Parliament had higher aims in view, and towns and cities became their objects of attack. At the end of March, 1643, Wigan was invested and fell before their arms, and the turn of Warrington came next. . . . The fall of so important a place, so near to Halton Castle, necessarily filled with alarm the little band of defenders of the fortress. They remounted their guns, secured their outposts, redoubled their watch and ward, and made such preparation as they could to resist the coming storm. Impressed with the importance of the occasion, and that the Castle might be better prepared for defence, EARL RIVERS, on the 24th June, 1643, appointed Captain Walter Primrose governor of the castle and commander of the forces within it. It soon appeared that all these preparations had not been made too soon. . . . No royal chronicler like the industrious Burghall has left on record the particulars of the siege at Halton, or has told us the exact date when it began. We may suppose, however, that when the siege of Warrington ended, the troops, flushed with victory, would be anxious for more work, and would demand to be led to Halton. Certain it is that no long time elapsed after Warrington fell before a besieging force appeared before Halton Castle, and summoned it to surrender, and that, on the summons being refused, they made their approaches before the place in military form. No plan of these has come down to us, but probably the plan adopted at Pontefract was that adopted at Halton. Lines were drawn around it, and a series of forts planted in the most advantageous positions to command it. While the siege continued, the castle chapel, which stood just outside the walls, 'was demolished and totally destroyed.' [*MS. Petition of the Inhabitants of Halton after the Restoration.*] Once begun, the siege was steadily pressed on for several weeks, but towards the middle of July, 1643, the defenders, beginning to experience some want of provisions, listened to terms of parley, and on the 22nd July, 1643, the castle was surrendered on honourable conditions, and Sir William Brereton entered and took possession of it in the name of the Parliament. That the garrison had well performed their part appears from the account given by one of the enemy, who, in relating the surrender of the castle, tells us, with a lingering sense of spleen, that it would have fallen sooner if the garrison had not received supplies through the treachery of some of the Parliamentary commanders. Early in the following year (1644) Prince Rupert arrived in the neighbourhood, and his renown as a fiery warrior naturally filled the enemy with alarm; it was no longer safe for any small forces of the Parliament to keep the field. On the 18th March, the force which was besieging Beeston, hearing of his approach, raised the siege hastily and withdrew to Chester. But that which filled the enemy with alarm, as might be expected inspirited and emboldened the king's friends. Halton again opened its gates to Colonel Fenwick, the new governor, and a party of Royalists, who now entered it and again hoisted the royal standard, had their quarters beaten up by the garrison at Warrington, probably to divert the prince's attention. In the month of June of the same year, when the prince was meditating his attack upon Liverpool, and the enemy's forces were drawing towards that place for its relief, some of them, on the 15th June, attempted to pass over the river at Haleford, within sight of Halton Castle, but they were met and defeated, and taken prisoners by two of Goring's regiments, under Blaickston; Sir William Davenant, the poet, was with the enemy on this occasion. Early in July, when Rupert had left the neighbourhood, and was on his way to the fatal field of Marston, Halton, no longer supported by the influence of his name, again succumbed to the enemy, and the royal flag was once more hauled down. . . . Once more in the power of the Parliament, which had now reduced to submission most of the neighbouring garrisons, Halton Castle was easily kept by the small force which Sir William Brereton had thrown into it; but Rock Savage, its near neighbour, was no longer a pleasant or a safe residence for EARL RIVERS, its noble owner. It had suffered at the hands of the soldiery during the siege of Halton, and the ruin then begun had afterwards proceeded at so rapid a rate that at length the proud pile, reared so recently at so much cost, was no longer a fit home for its owner, and he deserted it, and removed to Frodsham Castle." . . . The Parliamentarians, in their triumph, now began to inflict what punishment they could upon the SAVAGE family. "On the 9th February, 1646," continues the historian of Halton Castle, "a council of war assembled at Warrington, at which Colonel Henry Brooke, Sir William Brereton, Sir George Booth, Sir Thomas Stanley, Roger Wilbraham, Henry Delves, Philip Mainwaring, and Robert Dutton, Esquires, were present, when an order was issued, and shortly afterwards obeyed, for dismantling Beeston Castle, and we can hardly doubt that a like order was then issued respecting the Castle of Halton, Colonel Brooke's formidable neighbour. On the 1st October, 1646, the names of JOHN, EARL RIVERS, and THOMAS SAVAGE were struck out of the commission of the peace for Cheshire by order of the Parliament. The cavaliers were now made to feel the iron heel of conquest. They had suffered in their persons; they were now to suffer in purse. A series of questions had been freely circulated, for the purpose of ascertaining the degree of each man's delinquency. The answers had been obtained, and now, as a consequence,

> Nobles and Knights, so proud of late,
> Must fine for freedom and estate.

Fines were now exacted according to the measure of each man's malignancy, and the money was employed either in furthering the triumphant cause or in rewarding its friends. As might be expected, EARL RIVERS and his family suffered heavily in this way. He was fined £1,110; his mother, the Dowager

Countess, £100; Thos. Savage, Esq., of Emling [Elmley] Castle, £1,487; Thos. Savage, Esq., of Beeston, £557; and Thomas Savage, gentleman, of Barrow, £70. . . . In the lull, before the outburst of the civil war, forty noblemen and others had joined in declaring their full belief that the King had no design to make war upon the Parliament, and that he would use a constant and firm endeavour towards the settlement of the true Protestant religion, the just privileges of Parliament, the liberty of the subject, and the law, peace, and prosperity of the Kingdom. It was the concluding passage of this declaration which was echoed by the words, *Relig. Prot.—Leg. Angl. Liber. Par.*, which afterwards appeared on the royal coins, and have since proved a puzzle to some antiquaries. Amongst those who signed this declaration was JOHN, EARL RIVERS. . . Not very long after the signing of the above declaration, a furious mob entered the house of his mother, the Dowager Countess, who lived near Colchester, and after destroying her furniture and curiosities, worth £40,000, would, if she had not secured her safety by flight, have done her further violence, for no better reason than that she was a Roman Catholic. When war seemed no longer to be avoided, the King associated EARL RIVERS with Lord Strange in his Cheshire commission of array, but in this capacity the EARL proved of little use, in consequence of his co-religionists, the Roman Catholics, having been previously disarmed. But his being named for this employment, and his joining those noblemen and others who came forward with offers of troops for the King's service, led to his being one of those who were especially excepted when a power was given to the Earl of Essex to pardon certain delinquents and others. The EARL, still bent on peace, was one of those who, at a later period, appealed to the Lords of the Privy Council in Scotland to stay the intended invasion of England. Although his share in those various actions resulted in no benefit to his Majesty, it caused him to be classed as a delinquent, a recusant, and a malignant, and greatly increased the amount of the fines on his sequestration." . . . "The triumph of the Parliament party was now complete. EARL RIVERS, the Castellan, Constable, and Seneschal of Halton, had lost his office; his castle was dismantled, and Rock Savage was roofless. He retired to his seclusion at Frodsham, to live in quiet and wait for better times; but those times he was not to see, for anxiety and care had made him prematurely old, and on the 10th of October, 1654, he died at Frodsham Castle in the prime of life. The same night the castle was set on fire and burnt down. The incendiary who kindled the flame probably intended it to be the EARL'S funeral-pile, but, if so, he was disappointed, for the body was rescued from the fire, and two days afterwards it was buried with due honour in the Savage Chapel at Macclesfield." JOHN, EARL RIVERS,

by his first wife, Catherine, daughter of the Lord Morley and Monteagle, had issue,
I. THOMAS, VISCOUNT SAVAGE, of whom presently as successor to his father.
II. John, living 1666, who died without issue.
III. Richard, who married Alice, the widow of John Barneston, of Cherton, and daughter and heiress of Thomas Trafford, of Bridge Trafford, in Cheshire, and by her had issue,
    JOHN, living in 1666, of whom hereafter as inheritor of the family honours.
I. Elizabeth, married to William, Lord Petre.
II. Jane, married, *first*, to George Bridges, Lord Chandos, by whom she had issue, two daughters; *secondly*, to Sir William Sidley; and *thirdly*, to George Pitt, of Stratfieldsay, Herts. Her grandson by the last, George Pitt, Esq., was created Baron Rivers in 1776. This Lady Jane Savage was thus ancestress of the Pitts, Barons Rivers, and of Alfred, Lord Tennyson, the present Poet Laureate.[1]

---

[1] The following extracts exhibit the genealogy of the Pitts, Barons Rivers, and their descent from the SAVAGES, EARLS RIVERS. They also exhibit the descent of Alfred, Lord Tennyson, from the SAVAGES:—

Sir William Pitt, eldest son of John Pitt, Clerk of the Exchequer in the reign of Queen Elizabeth, was also a principal officer in the Exchequer in the reigns of Queen Elizabeth, James, and Charles I. He was knighted at Newmarket, in 1618, and died in 1636, and was buried at Stratfieldsaye, in Hampshire.

Edward Pitt, his eldest son, was father of John, his fourth son, whose son, George Morton Pitt, of Twickenham, in Middlesex, died in 1756, leaving an only daughter and heir, Harriet, married to Lord Brownlow Bertie, brother to Peregrine, Duke of Ancaster.

George Pitt, eldest surviving son of Edward, married Jane, eldest daughter of John Savage, Earl Rivers, widow, first, of George Bridges, Lord Chandos (who, to the exclusion of his own family, left her Sudeley Castle and all his estates, which she carried to this last husband); and, secondly, of Sir John Shelley, Bart. [We quote from Banks, but evidently he is in error here.] By his wife Jane, daughter of John, Earl Rivers, this George Pitt had issue,
    I. GEORGE, of whom presently as successor to his father.
    I. Jane, married to Christopher Hildyard, of Kelstern, Co. Lincoln, grandson and heir of Henry Hildyard, who intermarried with the Lady Ann, eldest daughter of Francis Leke, 1st Earl of Scarsdale and Baron d'Eyncourt of Sutton, and by him had issue,
        Dorothy Hildyard, married to George Clayton, of Grimsby, Co. York, by whom she had issue,
            Elizabeth Clayton, married to Michael Tennyson, of Preston, Co. York, son and heir of Ralph Tennyson, Esq., of Preston, Co. York, by whom she had issue,
                George Tennyson, Esq., of Bagons Manor and Usselby Hall, who inherited the Clayton Estates in 1794. He married Mary, daughter and heiress of John Turner, Esq., of Caistor, Co. Lincoln, and by her had issue,
                    I. The Rev. George-Clayton Tennyson, of whom presently.

III. Catherine, married to Sir Charles Sidley, brother of Sir William, by whom she had issue an only daughter,

 II. The Right Hon. Charles Tennyson, of Bagons Manor and Usselby Hall, who assumed in 1835 the surname of D'Eyncourt.
 I. Elizabeth Tennyson, married to Matthew Russell, Esq., of Brancepeth Castle, Co. Durham, M.P.
 II. Mary Tennyson, married to John Bourne, Esq., of Dalby.

The Rev. George-Clayton Tennyson married Elizabeth, daughter of the Rev. Stephen Ffytche, Vicar of Louth, Co. Lincoln, and died in the lifetime of his father, having had issue,

 I. Frederick Tennyson, co-heir of the Earls of Scarsdale, who married Maria Gulliotta.
 II. Charles Tennyson, in Holy Orders, who married Louisa Sellwood, and who assumed the additional surname of Turner.
 III. *Alfred Tennyson, Poet Laureate, born 1809, created Baron Tennyson, 1884.* Lord Tennyson married Emily, daughter of Henry Sellwood, Esq., and has issue.
 IV. Horatio Tennyson, who married Charlotte, daughter of Dudley C. Cary Elwes, Esq.
 V. Septimus Tennyson.
 VI. Arthur Tennyson, who married Harriet West.
 I. Mary Tennyson, married to Allen Ker, Esq.
 II. Emily Tennyson, married to Captain Jesse.
 III. Matilda Tennyson.
 IV. Cicilia Tennyson, married to Edmund Lushington, Esq.

Mr. George Pitt died in 1676. He was succeeded by his eldest son,

GEORGE PITT, who died in 1734, and was buried at Stratfieldsaye. He married Lora, daughter and heiress of Audley Grey, Esq., of Kingston, in Dorsetshire, who was his second wife, and died in 1750; their issue was four sons and five daughters. John, the second son, was of Encombe, and was father of William Morton Pitt, of Kingston, Esq., who married Miss Gambier, and had an only daughter, Anne, who married Charles, Viscount Marsham, son and heir-apparent to the Earl of Romney.

GEORGE PITT, of Stratfieldsaye, was the eldest son of the aforesaid George, by his first wife, Lucy, daughter of Thomas Pile, Esq., widow of Laurence Lowe, of Shaftesbury, Esq. He married Louisa Bernier, and had two daughters and four sons, whereof James and Thomas, the youngest two, died S.P.

SIR WILLIAM AUGUSTUS PITT, the second son, was K.B., and a general in the army, who married Mary, daughter of Scroope, Viscount Howe, and died in 1809, S.P.

GEORGE, first LORD RIVERS [of this family], was the eldest son, and having been ambassador to Spain, in 1770, was, by letters patent, May 20, 1776, created Baron Rivers of Stratfieldsaye, in the county of Southampton, with limitation to the heirs male of his body; after this, he obtained a further creation of the title of Baron Rivers, of Sudeley Castle, in Gloucestershire, with the remainder severally, to his brother, Sir W. A. Pitt, K.B., and in default of issue male, then to the male issue of his daughter by Peter Beckford, of Stapleton, in Dorsetshire, Esq., March 16, 1802. His lordship married Penelope, daughter of Sir Henry Atkins, of Clapham, in Surrey, Bart., and had issue, GEORGE, his successor, and three daughters, *viz.*, first, Penelope, who

Catherine Sidley, mistress to King James II., by whom she was created Countess of Dorchester for life. "After the dissolution of her connection with the King, she married Sir David Colyear, Earl of Portmore.[1]

IV. Mary, married to Henry Killigrew, Esq., Groom of the Bedchamber to James, Duke of York.

V. Frances, who died young.

married Edward, Earl Ligonier (from whom she was divorced), and was remarried to Captain Smith; second, Louisa, wife of the aforesaid Peter Beckford, Esq.; third, Marcia, baptized April 14, 1756, married James L[ane] Fox, Esq.

GEORGE, second LORD RIVERS on his father's death in 1803, died unmarried, in July, 1828, when the barony of Rivers of Stratfieldsaye expired; and he was succeeded in that of Rivers of Sudeley Castle by his nephew, HORACE BECKFORD, son of his sister Louisa, before mentioned. *See* Banks: *Dormant and Extinct Peerage of England*, vol. iv., appendix, p. 41.

[1] The following account of the Sidley (or Sedley) family is extracted from Burke's *Extinct Baronetage*:—

"This family (of very great antiquity in the County of Kent) was anciently seated at Romney Marsh, where there are lands now called Sidley's and Sidley's Marsh; they built afterwards, *temp.* Edward III., a mansion house at Scadbury, in Southfleet, in the same county.

"II. SIR JOHN SIDLEY, Sheriff of Kent, 19 James I., who married Elizabeth, daughter and heir of the celebrated Sir Henry Savile, founder of the astronomical professorship at Oxford (was warden of Merton College, in that university, and provost of Eton), and had issue,

HENRY, his heir.

WILLIAM, successor to his brother.

CHARLES, who inherited as fifth baronet.

He died 13th August, 1638, and was succeeded by his eldest son,

"III. SIR HENRY SIDLEY, who died unmarried in 1641, and was succeeded by his brother,

"IV. SIR WILLIAM SIDLEY. Of this gentleman, Anthony Wood states, 'that when he was a young man, he lived very high in London, with his friend Richard Dormer, esq., of Rousham in Oxfordshire (whose wife was Anne, one of the daughters of Charles Cotterell, master of the ceremonies), and they endeavoured who should outvie each other in gallantry and in splendid coaches.' He married Lady [Jane] Savage, daughter of John, Earl Rivers, and relict of George Lord Chandos, but by her ladyship (who married after his decease George Pitt, esq., of Strathsfieldsaye) had no issue. He died in 1656, and was succeeded by his brother,

"V. Sir Charles Sidley, born in 1639, distinguished for his wit and gallantry. As a critic, too, he was so much admired that he became a kind of oracle among the poets, and no performance was approved or condemned until Sir Charles Sedley had given judgment. King Charles used to say, that nature had given him a patent to be Apollo's viceroy. After a long course of profligacy and extravagance, Sir Charles began to apply himself to politics, and sat in several parliaments for the borough of Romney. He took an active part in promoting the Revolution, which at first excited astonishment, as he had received many favours from James II.; but these had been cancelled by an intrigue which the monarch carried on with his daughter, afterwards created COUNTESS OF DORCHESTER. This elevation by no means gratified Sir CHARLES, and on being asked why he appeared so warm for the

EARL RIVERS married, 2ndly, Mary, daughter of Thomas Ogle, Esq., by whom he had issue,
 I. Peter.
His Lordship, dying, as we have seen, in 1654,[1] was succeeded by his eldest son,
 THOMAS, 3rd EARL RIVERS. "The Restoration" (we again take the liberty of quoting from Mr. Beamont's account of the SAVAGE family in his *Halton Castle*), "though it had brought back the King, and restored to the SAVAGES their possessions, did not immediately bring them into this neighbourhood. Their castle at Halton was a ruin, Rock Savage was almost in the same state, and their castle at Frodsham had perished by fire. THOMAS, VISCOUNT SAVAGE, who, on the death of his father, the late EARL, had succeeded as third EARL RIVERS, having no longer a Cheshire home, removed his residence to London. Halton, however, being once more his own, he appointed his constable to take charge of the prison, his steward to administer his affairs, and his bailiff to execute processes at the castle as before. His family had suffered much for their constancy in the King's cause, but the new EARL, who was no bigot, showed that when there was good reason he was open to conviction, and had courage to change his opinions. In 1680, when the Duke of York's devoted adherence to Popery gave rise to a cry through the country to exclude him from the throne, and a struggle between the court and the popular party began, and ran so high that liberty seemed to be in danger, EARL RIVERS cast in his lot with the popular party, and in 1682, when the Duke of Monmouth made a progress through Cheshire to aid the cause of the exclusionists, EARL RIVERS, and his eldest son, LORD COLCHESTER, though they were not implicated in any of the rival plots which were the spawn of those unquiet times, joined the duke and received him as a guest at Rock Savage, which had now been repaired and restored. For taking part in this proceeding LORD COLCHESTER was prosecuted by the grand jury at Chester Assizes, on the 17th September, 1683, and ordered to find sureties of the

Revolution, he is stated to have replied, 'from a principle of gratitude; for since his majesty has made my daughter a countess, it is fit I should do all I can to make his daughter a queen.' He married Catherine, third daughter of John, Earl Rivers, and had by her an only daughter,
 CATHERINE, mistress to James II., by whom she was created COUNTESS OF DORCHESTER for life. After the dissolution of her connection with the King, she married Sir David Colyear, Earl of Portmore.
Sir Charles married, secondly (whilst his first wife was living), Catherine Ayscough, of Yorkshire, by whom he had a son, SIR CHARLES SIDLEY, Knt., who *d.v.p.*, leaving by Frances, his wife, third daughter of Sir Richard Newdigate, a son CHARLES, created a Baronet in 1702. Sir Charles Sidley died 20 August, 1701, when the title became extinct."
 [1] "This John, Earl Rivers, sold Long Melford, in Suffolk."

peace. In June, 1684, when, at the instance of the Duke of York, an order was given by the Secretary of State to the Lord Lieutenants to seize all guns and muskets that might be found in the possession of persons not qualified by law to hold them, we may be sure that the order was rigidly carried out at Halton and Rock Savage, where the Duke of York was known not to be in favour. But this inquisition discouraged neither EARL RIVERS nor LORD COLCHESTER. . . . About the year 1693, EARL RIVERS sustained a severe loss in the death of his eldest son, LORD COLCHESTER. . . . The next year, EARL RIVERS, whose own death was probably accelerated by grief for that of his son, died at the age of 67. He was buried in the family burial-place at Macclesfield, leaving behind him the character of a modest patriot, who, while he had welcomed the revolution of 1688, had mixed but little in public affairs, remembering the early misfortunes of his house in the cause of Charles I."[1] THOMAS, 3d EARL RIVERS, by his wife Elizabeth, daughter of Emanuel, Lord Scrope, of Bolton, Earl of Sunderland, had issue,

    I. THOMAS, VISCOUNT COLCHESTER, heir apparent to the EARLDOM of RIVERS and the ROCK SAVAGE estates. This young nobleman gave great promise of an eminent and useful career. Like the EARL RIVERS, his father, he was a strong supporter of William of Orange, and on the arrival of that Prince in Exeter, in 1688, we find that LORD COLCHESTER, then a lieutenant in Lord Dover's troop of guards, was the first Nobleman who waited upon him with an offer of his service. LORD COLCHESTER married Maria, daughter of Charles, 6th Earl of Derby, and by her had issue,

        1. Charlotte-Catherine, who died without issue.

    II. RICHARD, of whom presently as successor to his father in the EARLDOM.
    I. Elizabeth, who died without issue.
    II. Annabella, who married Lord Erasmus Norwich, of Brampton, in the Co. of Northampton, and died without issue.

His Lordship married, *secondly*, the Lady Annabella Bertie, daughter of the Right Hon. Robert, Earl of Lindsey, Baron Willoughby of D'Eresby, Lord Great Chamberlain of England, but by her had no issue. LORD RIVERS, dying, as we have seen, in 1694, was succeeded by his second and only surviving son,

    RICHARD, 4th EARL RIVERS. "Upon the death of THOMAS, Earl RIVERS, in 1694," writes Mr. Beamont, "his eldest son, LORD COLCHESTER, having died before him without male issue, the RIVERS title and estates, including the family

---

[1] Beamont: *History of Halton Castle*, pp. 127-129.

interest in the ancient castle of Halton, devolved upon RICHARD, VISCOUNT SAVAGE, his second and now only surviving son, who thereupon became EARL RIVERS. Although the castle now no longer possessed its old importance, or was a fit place of residence for the family, the SAVAGES had still their old home, Rock Savage, in the same neighbourhood, which they had now restored and made once more habitable, as formerly. . . . RICHARD, EARL RIVERS, the new owner of Halton, following the example of his late brother, took an active part in public affairs, in the conduct of which, and in the military profession which he had adopted, he showed equal ability and skill. . . . On the 3d December, 1705, when the Duke of Argyle—

'Argyle, the state's whole thunder born to wield,
And shake alike the senate and the field'—

was raised to the rank of an English peer by the title of Earl of Sundridge, the office of introducing him by his new title to the House of Lords was assigned to EARL RIVERS. . . . In the year 1707, when the nation determined to support the claims of the House of Austria to the Crown of Spain, in opposition to the House of Bourbon, and an army of 13,500 men was despatched to Spain, the Queen appointed EARL RIVERS to command it. The EARL sailed with the forces, and safely disembarked them at Alicant about 8th February, but there being some conflict between his commission and that of Lord Galway as to which of them was to command in chief, the two generals came to a timely agreement, and in order to prevent detriment to the service, EARL RIVERS generously yielded up the chief command to Lord Galway, and soon afterwards returned to England. By this timely concession EARL RIVERS escaped the discredit of being present in the disastrous battle and defeat which the allies sustained afterwards at Almanza. . . . In 1709, EARL RIVERS, who stood high in the royal favour, was sworn of the Privy Council, and in the following year the Queen sent him as her minister and plenipotentiary to Hanover, with instructions to satisfy that court that the Protestant succession was of all things the object which the Court of England had most at heart—a task which, in the face of the hundred addresses presented against it, all of which had been most graciously received, was one of considerable difficulty, requiring great adroitness and skill. On 1st January, 1712, EARL RIVERS was appointed Master-General of the Ordnance, an office for which he was eminently qualified, and he brought to its discharge the large amount of skill and experience which he had acquired by his long service. . . . RICHARD, Earl RIVERS, was the father, and Anne, Countess of Macclesfield, was the mother of SAVAGE the poet. SAVAGE was born 10th

January, 1698, and soon afterwards the Countess, by Act of Parliament, was divorced from her husband, the Earl of Macclesfield, and married to Colonel Brett. EARL RIVERS, who was anxious to make the best reparation in his power by acknowledging his base son as his own, became his sponsor at the font, and called him RICHARD SAVAGE, after himself. A few years afterwards, while the son was still young, the EARL, lying on his death-bed, and being minded so far as he could to make him further reparation for the injustice of his birth, sent anxiously to the Countess of Macclesfield to find him, and when he was falsely assured by her that he was dead, he left to another person the legacy of £6,000 which he intended for him, and thus the mother robbed the child of what might have made him independent. . . . In 1714 (or, according to Dr. Johnson's account, in 1712) the EARL's busy career drew to a close, and on the 14th December in that year he breathed his last."—*Beamont.* By his wife, Penelope, daughter of Roger Downes, of Wardley, in the County of Lancaster, Esquire, his LORDSHIP had issue an only daughter,

I. ELIZABETH, of whom presently.

[By Anne, Countess of Macclesfield, his LORDSHIP had issue, as we have seen, Richard Savage, the Poet. The life of this remarkable and unfortunate man of genius is well known from Dr. Johnson's masterly biographical sketch, the best of the celebrated *Lives of the Poets.* Johnson (who derived his information chiefly, no doubt, from Savage himself) lays considerable stress on the earnest efforts of EARL RIVERS to make some provision for his son, which were baffled by the inhuman Countess of Macclesfield. Richard Savage, we know, came very near being appointed Poet Laureate. In 1743 he was confined for debt in the Newgate at Bristol, where he was treated by Mr. Dagg, the Keeper of the prison, with great humanity, being supported by him at his own table without any certainty of recompense. "His friends made several attempts to effect his release, but after six months' incarceration, he was seized with a sickness which proved mortal, and he died July 31st." He was buried at the expense of the Keeper in St. Peter's Churchyard, Bristol, adjoining the gaol, August 2, 1743, near the south stair. A small marble tablet was erected by an admirer of his genius some years ago on the south side of St. Peter's Church, close to his supposed grave. In family histories the pourtrayal of appearance and character are always interesting. Let us quote here Dr. Johnson's description of Richard Savage. "He was of middle stature, of a thin habit of body, a long visage, coarse features, and melancholy aspect; of a grave and manly deportment, a solemn dignity of mien, but which, upon a nearer acquaintance, softened into an engaging easiness of manners. His walk was slow, and his voice tremulous and mournful. He was easily excited to smiles, but very seldom provoked to laughter. His mind was in an uncommon degree vigorous and active. His judgment was accurate, his apprehension quick, and his memory so tenacious that he was frequently observed to know what he had learned from others in a short time better than those by whom he was informed; and could frequently recollect incidents, with all their combination of circumstances, which few would have regarded at the present time, but which the quickness of his apprehension impressed upon him. . . . He had the art of escaping from his own reflections, and accommodating himself to every new scene. . . . His judgment was eminently exact, both with regard to writings and to men. The knowledge of life was indeed his chief attainment; and it is not without some satisfaction that I can produce the suffrage of Savage in favour of human nature, of which he never appeared to entertain such odious ideas as some, who perhaps had neither his judgment nor experience, have published either in ostentation of their sagacity, vindication of their crimes, or qualification of their malice. His method of life particularly qualified him for conversation, of which he knew how to practise all the graces. He was never vehement or loud, but at once modest and easy, open and respectful; his language was vivacious and elegant, and equally happy upon grave and humorous subjects. . . . His temper was, in consequence of the dominion of his passions, uncertain and capricious; he was easily engaged and easily disgusted; but he is accused of retaining his hatred more tenaciously than his benevolence. He was compassionate both by nature and principle, and always ready to perform offices of humanity; but when he was provoked (and very small offences were sufficient to provoke him), he would prosecute his revenge with the utmost acrimony till his passion had subsided. . . . A kinder name than that of vanity ought to be given to the delicacy with which he was always careful to separate his own merit from every other man's, and to reject that praise to which he had no claim. He did not forget, in mentioning his performances, to mark every line that had been suggested or amended: and was so accurate as to relate that he owed *three words* in 'The Wanderer' to the advice of his friends.

... When he loved any man, he suppressed all his faults; and when he had been offended by him, concealed all his virtues: but his characters were generally true, so far as he proceeded; though it cannot be denied that his partiality might have sometimes the effect of falsehood. In cases indifferent, he was zealous for virtue, truth, and justice: he knew very well the necessity of goodness to the present and future happiness of mankind; nor is there perhaps any writer who has less endeavoured to please by flattering the appetites or perverting the judgment."[1]

His LORDSHIP left also, by Mrs. Colydon, an illegitimate daughter,

Bessy, who, Sir B. Burke tells us, "had a fortune of £60,000, and married Frederick, Earl of Rochford."[2]]

His LORDSHIP was succeeded by his cousin,

JOHN SAVAGE, a Catholic priest, who never assumed the family honours. "JOHN SAVAGE," says Mr. Beamont, "to whom the title had descended on the death of his cousin the late EARL, acting under a deep sense of the obligation of his sacred calling, for which we must honour him, or leaning secretly to the fortunes of his fallen master James II., declined to take the title that belonged to him, preferring to remain in a private station, and when he died without issue in 1728, the title of EARL RIVERS became extinct. In the meantime, Halton Castle, Rock Savage, and the rest of the large estates of the family, passed to, and were enjoyed by, EARL RICHARD'S daughter and only child,

[1] Johnson: *Life of Savage.*
[2] *Family of the Earls of Rochford*—

"William Henry Nassau de Zuleistein, the founder of the English honours of this family, was son of Frederick, a natural son of Henry, Prince of Orange, grandfather of King William, and consequently he himself first cousin of his said Majesty. [He was the 1st Earl of Rochford.] ...

"Frederick, third Earl of Rochford, who led a retired life, and died at his house in Great Queen Street, Lincoln's-Inn-Fields, June 18, 1738. He married Bessey, daughter of Richard Savage, Earl Rivers, and had issue two sons; first, William Henry, his successor; and secondly, Richard-Savage-Nassau, who married Elizabeth, daughter and heir of Edward Spencer, of Rendlesham, in Suffolk, Esq. (widow of James, Duke of Hamilton); and by her had issue a daughter, Lucy, who died unmarried, and two sons, viz., William-Henry, hereafter mentioned, and George.

"William-HENRY, fourth Earl of Rochford, was employed in several embassies to the Courts of Turin, Paris, and Madrid, was for some time principal Secretary of State for the Northern and afterwards the Southern department, and was also a Knight of the Garter. He married Lucy, daughter of Edward Young of Dunford, in Wiltshire, Esq., but died without issue, 1781, and was succeeded by his nephew,

"William Henry, fifth Earl of Rochford, son of his brother Richard [Savage] Nassau, who was then deceased."—Banks: vol. iv., Appendix.

"ELIZABETH, COUNTESS OF BARRYMORE, wife of James, fourth Earl of that name. While Lord and Lady Barrymore inhabited Rock Savage," continues Mr. Beamont, "that fine old house saw some of its palmiest days. They repaired and enlarged the house, added to it large stables and outhouses, and kept up the family honour with its accustomed hospitality, and more than its usual splendour. The COUNTESS, however, did not long survive her acquisition of the estate, for, though she outlived JOHN SAVAGE, she died before the Earl, her husband, leaving to succeed her an only child,

"The Hon. PENELOPE BARRY, who, about the year 1730, married the Hon. James Cholmondeley, second son of George, second Earl of Cholmondeley, then a major in the army. In 1731 her husband became a lieutenant-colonel. Having seen much service in the interval, he served in the campaign in Flanders in 1744, and the next year he served and distinguished himself at the battle of Fontenoy. Upon the news of the Pretender's victory at Prestonpans, Colonel Cholmondeley, now a brigadier, was despatched in command of two regiments to Scotland, where he greatly signalised himself at the battle of Falkirk, when he and General Huske are said to have saved the fortunes of the day."[1] . . .

"General Cholmondeley died at Rock Savage on the 13th October, 1775, and his wife, the owner of Rock Savage, survived until 1786, and then died at the same place, leaving her great estates to her husband's nephew, George James, Earl, and afterwards Marquis, of Cholmondeley. After her death, Rock Savage, being deserted, fell to ruin, and so rapid was its decay that a gentleman who was born in the house lived to follow a pack of hounds through its ruins in pursuit of a fox. . . . The Castle of Halton necessarily suffered somewhat from the desertion of Rock Savage and the withdrawal of its noble proprietors from the neighbourhood; but though over its walls the ivy now waves instead of the banners of Fitz Nigel, Lacy, or Plantagenet, the old ruined fortress has associations which Rock Savage has not, and its story may be fitly concluded in the reflections of an American traveller:—'To see every day the walls on which our forefathers, ages ago, patrolled in armour, or from which they aimed the crossbow, to walk and study and repose habitually under their shadow, to have always, in sport and in toil, in sorrow and in joy, such monuments of time and history about one; how ought it not to refine and mature the character, and make a man feel his place between two eternities, and inspire him to live well the short and evil day in which, if ever, what he does for futurity must be done quickly and with might.'"[2]

[1] Beamont: *Halton Castle*, &c., pp. 134-5.
[2] Beamont: *Halton Castle*, p. 142. The concluding quotation is from Coxe's *Sketches of England*.

ARMS OF SAVAGE OF ROCK SAVAGE.

The arms of the SAVAGES of SCARCLIFFE, STAINESBY, and ROCK SAVAGE (CLIFTON) were originally, argent, 6 lions (or lioncels) sable, armed and langued gules; the crest, a lion's jambe armed gules, rising out of a ducal coronet or. As we have seen, however, in 1416 the then SIR JOHN SAVAGE, of Clifton (Rock Savage), assumed his mother's arms, the arms of Danyers, ar., a pale fusillée sa., and for crest, a unicorn's head, couped, ar., "which she granted to him to bear after the death of her father." But his descendant and representative, SIR JOHN SAVAGE, of Clifton (Rock Savage), who died in 1597, reassumed for his proper coat the six lions sa., and for his crest the lion's jambe, erect out of a ducal coronet or.

The arms of the EARLS RIVERS, however, who represented also the Darcys of Chich, displayed numerous quarterings, and the following is a full list of them as emblazoned in the Grand Pedigree, temp. Charles I. :—

Arms of SAVAGE, with Supporters.

SAVAGE.

1. Savage.
2. Walkington.
3. Danvers (or Danyers).
4. Bagaley.
5. Vernon, Baron de Shipbrook.
6. Malbank, Baron de Namptwich.
7. Swinnerton.
8. Pinchester, Cobham and Pagnell.
9. Bostock.
10. Earl of Chester.
11. Venables.
12. Dutton of Dutton.
13. Minshull.
14. Allington.
17. Gardener.
18. Middleton.
19. Cordal of Milford.
20. Smith.

DARCY.

1. Darcy of Henton.
2. Bartram of Motford.
3. Fitzlangley.
4. Harleston.
5. Wanton.
6. Bardwell.
7. Pagnell.
8. De Voloignes.
9. Check of South Check, Suffolk.
10. Glanville of Boxhom.
11. Blundel.
12. Darcy.

The supporters of the SAVAGE shield are, Dexter, a falcon billed, or; Sinister, an unicorn argent. These supporters are interesting, for, according to Sir Bernard Burke, Ulster King-of-Arms, the SAVAGES of Cheshire are one of the few distinguished houses that, as commoners, are by prescriptive right entitled to use supporters to their coat of arms.[1]

The Motto of the Cheshire SAVAGES is, *A te pro te.*

MONUMENTS OF THE SAVAGES OF ROCK SAVAGE IN THE SAVAGE CHAPEL AT MACCLESFIELD.

Ormerod[2] tells us that Thomas Savage, Archbishop of York, who was a native of Macclesfield, and who died in the year 1508, either founded or projected the foundation of a College of secular priests or canons; as we cannot find any reference to the charter of foundation, or any other records connected with the College, it is probable that his intentions were never fulfilled. Smith, writing in 1585, speaks of the College as built, and adjoining the church on the south side, but adds that the steeple thereof was not fully finished. The Chapel, which remains, is connected with the parochial chapel to which it forms a south aisle, and has been the burial-place of the SAVAGE family. The Chapel formerly communicated with the Church by a door which, when Ormerod wrote, had been built up. The entrance is on the west side under a turret of three stories. "Over the door is a projecting window, in the lower part of which are carved the arms of England, placed between those of the See of York, impaling *argent* a pale lozenge *sable* (SAVAGE ancient) on the left hand, and the coat of SAVAGE quartered with those of ARCHBISHOP SAVAGE'S successive Sees [Rochester, London, and York] on the right. The entrance is enriched with various other shields and gothic ornaments. On the outside of the Chapel is an ancient monument much more worn, in which that prelate's heart is said to be deposited. ARCHBISHOP SAVAGE'S chapel is now [1810] the property of the Earl of Cholmondeley."[3]

The most remarkable monuments in it are those of SIR JOHN SAVAGE (father of the Archbishop), who died in 1495; Sir JOHN SAVAGE, who married the Earl of Worcester's daughter, and died in 1528; SIR JOHN SAVAGE, K.G., who built the manor of ROCK SAVAGE, was seven times Sheriff of Cheshire, three times Mayor of Chester, and died in 1597; and THOMAS SAVAGE, Earl Rivers, who died in 1694; the latter has the effigies of the Earl in white

---

[1] See *Landed Gentry, Corrigenda (Early Edition).*
[2] Ormerod: *Cheshire,* pp. 738–9.
[3] Ormerod.

marble by Staunton. The following are the details of the principal SAVAGE monuments at Macclesfield, as described by Lysons, Ormerod, and others :—

MONUMENT OF SIR JOHN SAVAGE, WHO DIED IN 1495.

"Under an open arch on the south side of the Chancel in Macclesfield Church [St. Michael's] is the monument of SIR JOHN SAVAGE, Knt., and Katherine, his wife, daughter of Thos. Lord Stanley, and Sister of Thos. 1st Earl of Derby. It is an altar-tomb, with the effigies of a Kt. and his lady.

The Savage Chapel, Macclesfield, Cheshire, burial-place of the SAVAGES of Cheshire (Earls Rivers), founded by THOMAS SAVAGE, Archbishop of York, circ. 1501.

He is represented bare-headed, in plate armour, with scalloped elbow-pieces, gorget, and shirt of mail, and collar of roses; under his head are his helmet and lambrequin without the crest, and a dog at his feet. The lady has the reticulated head-dress and veil of King Edd. IVth. reign; the former has 'Ihs' in text-hand within each mesh. On the altar-tomb are shields, supported by Knights and Ladies, on which are the arms of ARCHBISHOP SAVAGE, and the families of Savage, Stanley, Vernon, Latham, &c."[1]

MONUMENT OF SIR JOHN SAVAGE, WHO DIED IN 1528.

On the south side of the Savage Chapel at Macclesfield is an altar-tomb with the effigies of a Knight and his Lady. He appears in plate armour with

---

[1] *See* Lysons: *Magna Britannia*, vol. ii., p. 450.

a collar of SS. on, a lion at his feet, she in the angular head-dress of Henry 8th reign, and a little dog at her feet. On the lower part of the tomb are figures of knights and ladies carved in bas relief. The following inscription was formerly [in 1584] on an arch over this monument:—" Sir John Savage, wh. was made Kn.t in the wars of . . . wh. died the 26 day of July in the year 1528, and lady Eliz.th his wife daur. of . . . which Lady Eliz.th died day . . . Ano. Dni. . . ."[1]

Ormerod tells us of this Sir John and his wife—" Sir John Savage of Clifton, Knight, stiled the younger, 12 Henr. 8th, son and heir of Sir John, married Eliz.th daur. and heir of Charls. Somerset, Earl of Worcester," &c.

(*See woodcut on p. 32.*)

MONUMENT OF SIR JOHN SAVAGE, WHO DIED IN 1615.

"In the Savage Chapel," writes Hanshall, "on the south side of Macclesfield Church, under two arches in the north wall, are altar-tombs, with the effigies of two Knights in alabaster; one of them is represented in plate-armour, bare-headed, with his helmet and crest, a unicorn's head, for a pillow, and a lion at his feet. The arches are enriched with crockets, &c. In the pediments are shields with the ancient arms of Savage, ar., pale fusillée sa., and the crest a unicorn's head erased.[2] On the lower part of the tomb are blank shields held by angels."

This is supposed to be the monument of the SIR JOHN Savage who died in 1615. It is again described, with a slight variation in the details, by Ormerod:—

"On the north side of ARCHBISHOP SAVAGE's Chapel are two altar-tombs, placed under obtuse gothic arches opening into the church as well as the chapel. On the first is the recumbent alabaster figure of a warrior in plate armour, his head resting on his helmet and his feet on a dog, a chain suspended round his neck, the countenance very aged. In the centre niche of the tomb below is a coat much defaced impaling Savage ancient."[3]

(*See woodcut on p. 25 for this and succeeding monument.*)

---

[1] *See* Hart: *Miscellanies*, 2151 fol., 82 p.

[2] The "ancient" arms are not the ancient arms of the SAVAGES, but those of Danyers, which had been assumed by them and afterwards dropt for the true "ancient" arms, the 6 lioncels, &c.

[3] Ormerod: *Cheshire*, vol. iii., p. 368. Again the arms alluded to as "ancient" are those of Danyers, assumed by Sir John, the 2nd of Clifton.

MONUMENT OF ——— SAVAGE.

"On the second is another recumbent alabaster figure of a warrior in plate armour; the face has a much more youthful expression than the last. His collar is composed of S.S., and the hilts of his sword and dagger richly studded. His head rests on a helmet with the family crest, and his feet on a lion. In niches at the side of the altar-tomb below are figures of angels supporting blank shields. Over the arches are mouldings ornamented with crockets and finials, and the arms of SAVAGE between two unicorns' heads."—*Ormerod.*

MONUMENT OF THOMAS SAVAGE, 3rd EARL RIVERS.

At the east end of the Chapel, where the altar formerly stood, is a splendid monument of THOMAS SAVAGE, 3rd EARL RIVERS, "who died in 1694. This monument has the effigy of the Earl by Staunton, with this inscription :—'Here lyeth the body of the Right Hon[le.] Thomas, Earl Rivers, Viscount Colchester, and Savage of Rock Savage, Baron Darcy, of Chich, who died the 14th day of Sept[r.], 1694, at his house in G[t.] Queen's Street, within the Parish of St. Giles in the fields, in the County of Middlesex, and was interred the 14th day of October following, in the 67th year of his age. He married two wives, the 1st was the Lady Eliz[th.] Scrope, one of the three co-heirs of Emanuel the Right Hon. the Earl of Sunderland, Baron Scrope of Bolton and Lord President of the King's Council in the north, by whom he had issue, the Right Hon[l.] Thos. Viscount Colchester deceased, who married the Lady Charlotte Stanley, the eldest dau[r.] of the Right Hon[l.] the Earl of Derby, Baron Stanley, Lord of Man and the isles, but left no issue male, and the now Right Hon[l.] Richard Earl of Rivers, Viscount Colchester and Savage of Rock Savage, Baron Darcy of Chich, Lieut. of the County Palatine of Chester, as also custos rotulorum of the same County Palatine, Lieut.-General of Horse under his Most excellent Mat[ie.] and Capt. of the 3d troop of Guards, and the Lady Eliz[th.] and Annabella Savage yet living, with several other children who died young. His 2nd wife was the Lady Annabella Bertie, dau[r.] of the now Right Hon[l.] Robert Earl of Lindsey, Baron Willoughby of D'Eresby, Lord G[t.] Chamberlain of England, L[d.] Lieut. of the County of Lincoln and custos rotulorum of the parts of Holland, Kesteven, and Lindsey, in the said county, and one of the Lords of his Majesty's most Hon. Privy Council. She survived him, and is now living and never had any issue.'"[1]

"On the opposite side is a large mural monument occupying the recess of the altar. Above a large altar-tomb is a recumbent figure in a flowing robe and large wig, under a canopy supported by four marble Corinthian pillars, over

---

[1] Lysons: *Cheshire*, p. 461.

which are the arms and crest of SAVAGE, with the supporters, a falcon billed or, and a unicorn argent. Over the pillars are also the EARL'S arms impaled with those of his wives. Over the figure is inscribed—

'Here lyeth the body of the
right honble Thomas, Earle Rivers,
viscount Colchester, and Savage of Rock Savage,
baron Darcy, of Chich, who died
the 14th Day of September, 1694.
&c., &c., &c.'"

MONUMENT OF ROGER LEGH AND HIS WIFE.

"On the east wall near the Earl Rivers' monument is a brass plate with the effigies of Roger Legh, who died in 1506, and his 6 sons, above which is the figure of a mitred ecclesiastic kneeling at an altar under which is the following inscription :—'This pardon for saying V. pater nostr. V. aves and a creed is XXVI thousand years and XXVI days pardon.' Beneath the monument is this inscription :—'Orate pro animam Rogeri Legh et Elizh. uxoris suæ qui quidem Rogeris obiit III. die novembris 1506. Elizh. vero obiit V die Octobris A.D. 1489 quor.' On a label issuing out of the man's mouth was, 'In die judicii libera nos, Domine,' and from the woman's, 'A damp. liba nos, Dom.'"[1]

MONUMENTS OF MEMBERS OF THE SAVAGE FAMILY UNKNOWN.

"In the centre of the south side of the Chapel," says Ormerod, "is an arch with an altar-tomb, closely resembling those on the north side, from which the figure has been removed, and a smaller arch nearer the entrance also without a figure."

MONUMENT OF SIR JOHN SAVAGE, WHO DIED IN 1597.

"At the west end of the Chapel is a large mural monument consisting of an altar-tomb on which are the figures of an armed knight and his lady, and of a female sitting at their feet; over them is a circular arch, in front of which are two pillars terminating in pyramids. The arch is surmounted with two figures and the arms and supporters of SAVAGE."

"This SIR JOHN SAVAGE, whose monument is above described, was son and heir of SIR JOHN SAVAGE and the Lady Elizabeth Savage, daughter of Charles Somerset, Earl of Worcester, and married Elizabeth, daughter of Thomas

---

[1] Lysons: *Cheshire.*

Manners, Earl of Rutland, about 1st Edward 6th, 1547. . . . He built the magnificent house at Clifton, and called it Rock Savage."—*Ormerod.*

"Within the arch," writes Ormerod, "there are three tablets, the first of which is inscribed—

'Memoriæ Sacrum
viri clarissimi, prudentissimi, piissimiq. D.
Joannis Savagi, equitis aurati, antiqua
Savagorum gente oriundi, de tota republica
Castriensi et Hamptoniensi optimè meriti, 5to Decemb.
anno 1597°, ætat. 74, in dolorem consanguineor^m
et bonorum omnium vita functi. Thomas
Savagus miles et baronettus, majore filio
nepos, in uxorem duxit Elizabetham filia
Thomæ baronis Darcie de Chich prima',
et per eam favore principis indulgentiori
existens sorte thalami et affinitate cineri
in successione proximus isti honori, pietatis,
ergo singularis, hoc posuit monumentum.'

"On the other tablets are the following verses :—

'Cum fermè octavum finisset maxima lustrum
   Imperii princeps Elizabetha sui,
Et gelidum bis ter lustrasset luce Decembrem
   Sol, nondum occiduis præcipitatus aquis,
Divino jussu arripitur Savagus ad astra;
   Nunc sacro Abrami nobilis umbra sinu
Duodemus miles successivè hicce Johannes,
   Familia ex illa, nominis ejus erat.
Mater erat comitis, comitis conjux quoq; nata,
   Ex illo dena prole beata parens;
Mascula cujus erat par æqua, at tres obierunt,
   Et tantum inventi jam superesse duo,
Nempe, Johannis major eques auratus, et alter
   Edwardus titulum qui tenet armigeri.
Feminei sexus numero quoq; quinque fuere,
   Quæ de prædictis prodierant thalamis :
Prima Breretoni natarum militis uxor,
   Margareta, ipso nomine gemma fuit;
Waltoniensq; Baro duxit Langtonis Elizam;
   Cessit Bagnoliis Ele(a)nora toris;
Militibus Millo ac Weero, nupsere sorores,
   Maria et Francisca, utraq; fausta viro.
Hanc habuit prolem generosi stemmatis hæres
   A victore suos qui numerabat avos.
Bis ter functus erat Comitis Vice; ter quoque Major
   Quem dubiis legit Castria rebus erat.

> Justicia, Hospitium, cum prompta ad munera dextrâ
> Hic monumentum illi firmius ære struunt:
> Mortuus is cum Savagis majoribus ejus
> Macclesfeldensi conditur æde sacrâ.
> Dixit Aristoteles fælicia saxa deorum
> . . . . quibus sacris thura fuere rogis
> . . . . bus insunt clausa virorum
> . . . . b . . . beata suis.'"

SECTION III.—THE EARLIER KENT BRANCH—SAVAGE OF BOBBING COURT.

The KENT branch of the SAVAGES of SCARCLIFFE and STAINESBY became eminent at a very early period.

In Hasted's *History of Kent* the earliest mention of this branch of the family is in connection with Bobbing Manor, near Milton, in that County, which Manor, according to Leland, belonged to the Molynes before it came to the SAVAGES. "The paramount manor of Milton," says Hasted, "claims over this parish, subordinate to which is the manor of Bobbing, the mansion of which, called Bobbing Court, was the ancient residence of the family of SAVAGE, or LE SAUVAGE, as they were called in French, who were of eminent account, and possessed good estates in this part of Kent." And again Philipott writes—"Bobbing, in the Hundred of Milton, was the ancient seat of the illustrious Family of SAVAGE."[1]

SIR ROGER SAVAGE, son of JOHN SAVAGE of Stainesby, was, according to the Pedigree of the EARLS RIVERS, quoted above, the founder of the Bobbing Court family. SIR RALPH LE SAVAGE Hasted states to be "the first owner of the manor whom he has met with." SIR RALPH SAVAGE was a Crusader, and was present with King Richard I. at the Siege of Askalon in Palestine.[2]

Edward I. summoned, by his writs dated 8 February, in the 1st year of his reign (1272), at Dover, several of the gentry and their wives in the several counties of Bucks, Bedford, Essex, Sussex, Hertford, and Kent, to be present at his and his Queen's coronation at Westminster, on the Sunday next after the feast of St. Valentine the Martyr; and amongst those of Kent appear ROGER LE SAUVAGE and his wife, and RANDOLPHUS LE SAUVAGE (a later

---

[1] Philipott: *Villare Cantianum*, p. 81.

[2] His name occurs in the list of Crusaders prefixed to Bohn's Edition of Wiffin's translation of the *Jerusalem Delivered* of Tasso. In the *Chronicles of the Monastery of Melsa*, temp. 1152, "Sir Ralph Salvage" is mentioned as giving a grant of the lands of Mellescroft, &c., to the Abbey. The Editor of the Chronicles, however, says that this "Salvagius" stands probably for *Salvayne*, though it is written "Salvage" in the MS.

RALPH) and his wife. This later RALPH is mentioned again in 1275 as Assessor, in Co. Kent, "of the fifteenth granted by the Prelates, Earls, Barons, and others in the Kingdom."[1]

In the 23d year of Edward I. (1283), JOHN LE SAUVAGE obtained a grant of free-warren for his lands in Melstid and other places, in the County of Kent; and in the same year JOHN LE SAVAGE was Commissioner of Array in the Co. of Kent.

In 1297 (temp. Edward I.), ROGER LE SAVAGE, of the same Kent family, was summoned to perform military service in person in Flanders,—the muster to be at Sandwich on the 24th November of that year.[1]

In 1298, the above-named JOHN LE SAVAGE, stated by Hasted to have been grandson of the first RALPH, was *locum tenens* for the Captain of the Cinque Ports, and in the same year he was summoned from Kent "to perform military service in person against the Scots,"—the muster to be at York on the 25th May.[1] "Yelsted, formerly called Gelleshed," writes Hasted, "is a manor of this parish (Stockbury), which was formerly part of the possessions of the noted family of SAVAGE, who held it of the family of Auberville, as the eighth part of one Knight's fee. JOHN DE SAVAGE, grandson of RALPH DE SAVAGE, . . . obtained a charter of free-warren for his lands here in the 23d year of Edward I." "The manor of Owne," says Ireland, in his *History of Kent*, "generally styled in ancient records 'the manor of the court of Owne,' is situated on the edge of the marshes of Kimsley Downe, at a small distance eastward from the manor of Grovehurst. This manor, in the reign of Edward I., was in the possession of the family of the SAVAGES, one of whom, JOHN LE SAVAGE, in the 23d year of that Prince, had a grant of free warren and other liberties in his manor of One, near Middleton." "The manor of Warden," again, as Hasted tells us, "in the reign of Edward I. was in the possession of the family of SAVAGE OF BOBBING (*Rot. Cart. ejus an.* No. 6). Brothers Ralf Pritelwelle and John de Tanet, then Treasurers of Christ Church, Canterbury, by their indenture, dated anno 1292, 21 Ed. I., demised to farm to JOHN SAUVAGE, the marsh of Warindone in Shepye, and its appurts., with the feeding of 100 sheep and one ram thereon, to hold for eight years at the rent of 45s. per annum for the three first years, and 50s. for the subsequent five years. The seal appendant has on it this coat of arms, viz., on a cross 4 eagles; over it an escutcheon—on a chief 3 lions rampant. The legend—S. Johannis Savvage. Apogr. Surrenden library (vol. 2, p. 667)."

---

[1] *See* Parl. Writs and Writs of Military Summons.

In 1299, we are told by Hasted, RALPH DE SAVAGE'S (*i.e.* the first RALPH'S) descendants, SIR JOHN DE SAVAGE, SIR THOMAS DE SAVAGE, of Bobbing, and SIR ROGER DE SAVAGE, were with King Edward I., with many other gentlemen of this county, at the siege of Carlaverock in Scotland, and were all honoured there by that Prince with the Degree of Knighthood.

SIR ROGER LE SAUVAGE, Knt., according to Hasted, possessed the manor of Bobbing Court in the next reign, that of Edward II., and in the 5th year of it obtained to him and his heirs free-warren and other liberties for his lands in Bobbynges, Middleton, Borden, Newenton, and Stokebury (*Rot. Cart. ejus an.* N. 47). ROGER DE SAVAGE in 5 Edward II. (1311-12) had a grant of liberties for his demesne lands at Yelsted. During his lifetime, in 15th and 16th Edward II. (1321-2, 1322-3), SIR RALPH SAVAGE was Sheriff of Kent, and in the 8th, 11th, 12th, and 13th years of the same reign, the same SIR RALPH was Knight of the Shire for that County, as was also a JOHN SAVAGE in the 12th of the same reign (1318-19). "King Edward III. in his 12th year (1338-9) directed his writs to the Bishop of Rochester, Roger de Northwode, the Prior of Rochester, the Abbot of Boxley, Thomas de Cobbam, Stephen de Cobbam, Philip de Pympe, Stephen de Ashburie, Humphrey de Northwode, and RALPH DE SAVAGE, reciting that the Island of Shepey would soon be invaded by the enemy's fleets, and, being desirous to prevent the same, he commanded them to send and have ready their men-at-arms and archers, according to the quantity of land and tenements which each of them possessed in the Island." "Rushindon, formerly called Rossingdone, in the island of Shepey, is a manor which in the reign of Henry II. seems to have been in the possession of that Prince, who gave it to the Church of the Holy Trinity, now Christ Church, Canterbury, £15 rents in Rissendon, and other places in this neighbourhood, after which it came into the possession of the family of SAVAGE." . . . "In a book for collecting the aid for making the Black Prince a Knight, in the 20th year of K. Edw. III., the estate of S<u>t.</u> Helens, a reputed manor in Barming, is thus entered, viz., Certain lands and tenements, called Seynt-helyns—Of LORA SAVAGE, and her parceners, with the Prioress of S<u>t.</u> Helens, for half a knight's fee, which William Payserer, Thomas de Hardres, and the said Prioress held in East Barmelyng of the Earl of Gloucester. In Mr. Petyt Fœdary of Kent's Book it is thus noted:—Formerly divided into three parts, of which one part lately belonged to the said Prioress, another part was escheated, and then (temp. Hen. VIII.) those two parts were in the hands of Thomas Reve, and the third part belonged as was said to the Rectory of Barming."[1] . . . "At the

---

[1] Hasted, vol. ii., p. 251, note.

making the Black Prince a Knight," Hasted states elsewhere, "the heirs of JOHN SAVAGE then paid respective aid for this manor [of Milstid] as one Knight's fee." SIR ROGER SAVAGE married Clarice, daughter of the Lord Delaware, and by her had issue a son and successor,

SIR ARNOLD SAVAGE, KNT., of Bobbing Manor, who married Margerie, daughter of Lord Poynings. This SIR ARNOLD SAVAGE was Lieutenant of Dover Castle (temp. Richard II.). As Sheriff of Kent in the time of Richard II., he is described by Hasted:—"ARNOLD SAVAGE, of Bobbing-Court, near Sittingbourne, where he had a castellated house, was a Sheriff in the 5th year, and was a man of great note in his time. His arms were argent, 6 lioncels sable, as they now stand on the roof of Canterbury Cloysters, and in several churches in this county."[1] . . . "In the 28th year of K. Edward III. Thomas, son of James Tracy, died seised of the manor of Tracies, with its appurts. in Newington, by the service of finding, together with the manor of Lucy, one man and one horse, with a sack and a pack, viz., each by the moiety of the said service, for the carrying of the King's kitchen utensils as far as Wales, for his war there, whensoever and as often as it should happen. Soon after which this family became extinct here, and the manor came into the possession of the family of SAVAGE, for it appears by the escheat rolls that SIR ARNOLD SAVAGE, of Bobbing, in this County, Knt., died seised of it in the 49th year of King Edward III., holding it by the like service."[2] The manor of Bapchild Court, Ireland states, was anciently part of the possessions of the family of the SAVAGES seated at Bobbing Court, one of whom, ARNOLD (whom he erroneously calls the son of SIR *Thomas* SAVAGE), died possessed of it in the 49th Edward III.[3] By his wife, the above-named Margerie, daughter of Lord Poynings, SIR ARNOLD SAVAGE had issue a son and successor,

SIR ARNOLD SAVAGE, of Bobbing Court, Knt., LL.D., P.C. This SIR ARNOLD SAVAGE was one of the most distinguished Englishmen of his day,—"a man," as Hasted says, "of eminent repute." In the 25th year of Edward III. (1351–2), according to Hasted, he was a Knight of the Shire for the County of

---

[1] Hasted, vol. i., p. lxxxv.

[2] Hasted adds in a footnote:—"The service in this roll is recorded somewhat different from the above-mentioned. It seems as follows:—Arnold Savage, Chr., held at the day of his death, in his demesne, as of his fee the manor of Tracy of the King in capite, by the service of finding one man, with an horse, a sack, and a pack, for the carrying of the wooden furniture, *vessellamenta lignea*, with the King, whenever he, by reason of the war, should pass with his army into Wales, for 40 days, at the King's cost, in food and drink for the said man and horse." (Vol. ii., p. 558.)

[3] Ireland: *Hist. of Kent*, vol. iv., p. 71.

Kent, and in the 29th of the same reign (1355-6) he was constituted one of the Conservators of the Peace for that County. In the 47th Ed. III. (1373-4), we read that ARNOLD SAVAGE, a Doctor-of-Laws, was one of the negotiators between France and England at Bruges. In the 5th and 9th years of Richard II.'s reign he was Sheriff of the County of Kent. In the latter year "he, among others of good rank, attended John of Gaunt, King of Castile, in his voyage to Spain. In the 13th year of Richard II. he served in Parliament as Knight-of-the-Shire for Kent. In the 16th year of Richard II. he was made Constable of Queenborough Castle, being the third in succession since the first appointment to that office. In the next reign, that of Henry IV., he was chosen Speaker of the House of Commons twice,—viz., in the Parliaments of the 2nd and 5th years of it, and was likewise one of Henry IV.'s Privy Councillors." (Philipott, p. 81; Cott. Records, pp. 404, 425.) He is the SIR ARNOLD SAVAGE celebrated by Walter Savage Landor in the *Imaginary Conversations*,[1] and after whom Landor named his own eldest son. His conduct as Speaker in 1401 is thus eulogised in the *Chronica Monasterii S. Albani*:—"Post Epiphaniam convenit universa regni nobilitas ad Parliamentum celebrandum, in quo quidem Parliamento Dominus Ernaldus Savage constitutus est militum Parliamentalium Prolocutor; qui tam diserte, tam eloquenter, tam gratiose, declaravit communitatis negotia, præcipue ne de cætero taxis gravarentur, aut talliagiis, quod laudem ab universis promeruit ea die."[2] SIR ARNOLD married Joane, daughter of —— Eckingham, by whom he had issue, a son, ARNOLD, and a daughter, Eleanor. He died Nov. 29, 1410, and was buried in the South Chancel of the Church of Bobbing, where his wife also was interred. He was succeeded by his only son,

SIR ARNOLD SAVAGE, of Bobbing Court, Knt. In the retinue of Henry V. at the Battle of Agincourt (A.D. 1415) we find SIR ARNOLD SAVAGE, Knt.; and the name, Sir Harris Nicholas tells us, occurs both in the Sloane MS. 6400, and in the Norman Rolls. Also at the Battle of Agincourt was present, in the retinue of Sir Raulf Shyrley, MONR. JOHN SAVAGE, Chlr.; and the name of SIR JOHN SAVAGE, Knt., is amongst the "Names of Persons entitled to the Ransoms of the French Prisoners, between the 3rd Henry V., 1415, and the 8th Henry VI., 1430"—

"Ao. 7 Hen. V., 1419-20.

---

[1] "Henry IV. and Sir Arnold Savage."

[2] *Chronica Monasterii S. Albani. Annales Henrici Quarti, Regum Angliæ*, p. 335. (Master of the Rolls Series.) In the same year the *Chronica* mention a "Johannis Savage, Prior of Wymundham."

"SIR JOHN SAVAGE, Knt. ('one of those either mentioned in the Roll of Arms or known from other evidence to have been in the battle')."[1] This SIR JOHN SAVAGE appears to have been Sir JOHN of Clifton, and thus there seem to have been two branches of the SAVAGE family represented on the great battle-field of Agincourt. It was either this SIR ARNOLD SAVAGE or his father that was one of the executors of the poet Gower. From the description, "a near relation of the Cobhams," it would seem that it was this one. "It appears from the poet's will, preserved at Lambeth, that two at least of Gower's four executors were Kent men, and one of them SIR ARNOLD SAVAGE, a near relation of the Cobhams."[2] This ARNOLD SAVAGE of Bobbing Court married Katherine, daughter of Roger, Lord Scales,[3] and died without issue, March 25, 1420. He was buried in the north chancel of Bobbing Church, where his wife was buried beside him. He was succeeded at Bobbing Court by his sister and heiress,

ELEANOR SAVAGE, married, *1st*, to Sir Reginald Cobham, Knt., and, *2ndly*, to William Clifford, son of Sir Lewis Clifford, K.G., of Clifford's Castle, Herefordshire (who was younger son of Roger, Lord Clifford). On the decease of his wife's brother, SIR ARNOLD SAVAGE, and of his widow, who held the manor of Bobbing in dower at her death, in the 16th Henry VI., William Clifford became entitled to Bobbing Court; and in the same year he also died. "In the 16th of Henry VI.," writes Hasted, "William Clifford, Esq., Sheriff of the County [of Kent], died seised of the manor of Sutton, leaving issue by ELEANOR his wife, sister and sole heir of ARNOLD SAVAGE, of Bobbing, in this County, Esq., two sons, Lewis and John, the latter of whom was ancestor to the present Rt. Hon. Hugh, Lord Clifford, of Chudleigh, in the Co. of Devon."[4]

ARMS OF SAVAGE OF BOBBING COURT.

The arms of SAVAGE OF BOBBING COURT were, as we have already seen, the same as those of the SAVAGES of STAINESBY, in Derbyshire, of CLIFTON (ROCK

---

[1] See *The History of the Battle of Agincourt*. By Sir Harris Nicholas.
[2] *Archæologia Cantiana*, vol. vi., p. 87.
[3] "Roger Scales (Baron), . . . who, the 4th Richard II., upon that insurrection under Jack Straw, was one of those eminent persons whom the rebels seized and compelled to march along with them. The 5th of Richard II., he was by inquisition found one of the co-heirs to William de Ufford, Earl of Suffolk, and having been summoned to Parliament, from 49th of Edward III. to the 9th Richard II. inclusive, d. the next year; leaving Joane, his wife (daughter and heir of Sir John de Northwoode), surviving." Banks adds in a note, "She had a daughter Catherine, who married Sir Arnold Savage, of Kent; her mother was Catherine, daughter and co-heir of Sir John de Aspal, Knight."—*See* Banks: *Extinct and Dormant Peerage, &c.*
[4] Hasted: *Hist. of Kent*, vol. ii., p. 412.

SAVAGE), in Cheshire, and of the ARDS, in Ulster. The arms of ARNOLD SAVAGE, who married Marjorie, daughter of Lord Poynings, are described above, in the passage quoted from Hasted, "argent, 6 lioncels sable, as they now stand on the roof of Canterbury Cloysters, and in several churches in this county." Philipott (p. 81, Pedigree of SAVAGE, Vista. Co. Kent, 1575) states that "the SAVAGES bore for their arms, Argent, 6 lions rampant sable, 3, 2, and 1." The seal of SIR JOHN SAVAGE, of Kent, has also been described above—"On a cross 4 eagles; over it an escutcheon, on a chief 3 lions rampant. The legend, S. Johannis Savvage."

The names of SIR JOHAN SAVAGE and SIRE ROGERO SAVAGE are inscribed in the roll of arms compiled between 1308 and 1314, in the reign of Edward II.:—" Les noms et les armes à Bannarez de Engleterre—Kent: Sir Johan Savage de Ermyne od le chef de azure iij lioncels de argent. Sir Roger Sauvage de Argent a vj lioncels de sable."

MONUMENTS, &C., OF THE SAVAGES OF BOBBING COURT.

Kilburne, in his *Topographie or Survey of the County of Kent*, 1659, writes— "In the Church of Bobbing were interred an Esquire of the family of Clifford, and several Knights of the family of SAVAGE (most of which persons were so interred above 200 years since)."—p. 31.

Ireland (*Hist. of Kent*, 1829) states that "in the north Chancel of Bobbing Church, dedicated to St. Bartholomew, are several ancient gravestones of the families of the SAVAGES and the Cliffords, many of which are entirely stripped of their brasses."[1]

In the windows of St. Margaret's Church, Canterbury, were formerly these arms,—Clifford impaling SAVAGE.[2]

In the windows of the Chapter House of Canterbury Cathedral, which were formerly much enriched with painted glass, were the arms of Lord Ros and his wife, SIR ARNOLD SAVAGE, Sir Thomas Erpingham, &c.[3]

We also read in Hasted that the arms of SAVAGE were emblazoned in the windows of Wickhambreux Church; and that "in one of the windows of Milton Church was formerly the figure of a man kneeling, with the above coat, only the lions placed 3 and 3, and underneath, 'Orate paia [pro (?)] Wi Savage Armigi.'"

Also in some of the arches of the two aisles of the Church of St. Margaret-at-Cliffe, near Dover (written in the Survey of Domesday, "S. Margarita"), were the arms of SAVAGE.

---

[1] Vol. iv., p. 113.
[2] Hasted: *History of Canterbury*—(2 vols, 1801)—vol. i., p. 231.
[3] *Id.*, vol. i., p. 515.

SECTION IV.—THE WORCESTERSHIRE BRANCHES—SAVAGE OF ELMLEY CASTLE.

Direct from the Cheshire family branched the SAVAGES of ELMLEY CASTLE, of whose history a good deal is to be learnt from an excellent lecture by the Rev. Hugh Bennett, M.A., Vicar of Elmley, and late Fellow of Worcester College, Oxford, entitled *Passages from the History of Elmley Castle*.[1] The manner in which the grand old Castle of Elmley came into the hands of the SAVAGE family has been already partly explained. But we will here follow Mr. Bennett.

"Among the chief supporters of Henry VII.," writes Mr. Bennett, "was SIR JOHN SAVAGE, of Rock Savage, in Cheshire. He commanded the left wing of King Henry's army at the Battle of Bosworth Field. This SIR JOHN SAVAGE was killed soon afterwards at the siege of Boulogne, in France. But to his son,

ELMLEY CASTLE, seat of the SAVAGES OF ELMLEY CASTLE.

another SIR JOHN SAVAGE, the King gave the Earl of Warwick's lands in Worcestershire. These lands were Elmley Castle, Bushley, Hanley, and Redmarley." To him succeeded his son, that SIR JOHN SAVAGE who, as we have seen, lost these lands in consequence of his implication in the unfortunate affair of Pawlet's homicide. After this, King Henry VIII., in 1545, *granted* the Elmley Castle estate to another member of the same family, a SIR CHRISTOPHER SAVAGE, who was Esquire of the Body of the King, "and to him they have descended by inheritance to the MR. SAVAGE of our own days [1865]."[2] In

---
[1] Printed at Worcester in 1865.
[2] *Elmley Castle*, by H. Bennett, M.A., &c., pp. 16, 17. Mr. Bennett appears to have been wrongly informed in stating that the Elmley Castle estate was *sold* to Sir Christopher Savage by Henry VIII. The Charter (still preserved) from Sir William Herbert, Knt., on behalf of the Serene and Excellent Prince, King Henry VIII, in the 36th year of his reign, *grants* to CHRISTOPHER SAVAGE, and the heirs of the said CHRISTOPHER, the manor and Castle of Elmley, with all its members, in

Gough's *Camden*, vol. ii., we read—" Hamley [in Worcestershire] is from Upton a mile *in dextra ripe Sabrinæ*, a mile above Upton, a slite shotte from Severn. It is an uplandish towne. The castelle standeth in a park at the west part of the towne. SIR JOHN SAVAGE, and his father and grandfather, lay much about Hamley and Theokesbyri, as Keepers of Hamley. The earls of Gloucester were owners of the Castel, and lay much there. Mr. Cometon [Compton] clean defaced it in his time, being Keeper of it after SAVAGE.—*Leland.*" Rudder tells us that CHRISTOPHER, son of SIR JOHN SAVAGE, of Clifton (Rock Savage), Cheshire, was granted by Henry VIII., about A.D. 1544, the estates of Elmley Castle, in Worcestershire."[1] "It is pretty certain that the Castle itself," says Mr. Bennett, "was destroyed somewhere about this time, *i.e.*, in the reign of Henry VII. or Henry VIII.," it being part of the policy of those kings to weaken the nobles by demolishing their great strongholds before allowing the confiscated estates to pass out of their own hands. "Not long afterwards, the house which is now called Elmley Park [or Elmley Castle] was built, and I have no doubt that many a stone of the old castle was used up in it."[2] The old Chantry of the Blessed Virgin Mary of Elmley was suppressed the very year after CHRISTOPHER SAVAGE came into possession of the ELMLEY estate; but it would appear that under the SAVAGES the Parish Church of Elmley was restored; and about this time, it is supposed, the SAVAGES built, or at least enlarged, the Chapel at Elmley, where their monuments are. On the ancient pedestal of the font of the Church of Elmley a new bowl was placed at the restoration of the Church. "On the eight sides of this bowl are carved various devices, some of which curiously illustrate the history of the Church. The easternmost side bears a representation of the five wounds of our Saviour; the westernmost has the Fleur-de-lys (the lily), which was the emblem of the Virgin Mary, to whom the Church was dedicated. Others bear the Tudor Rose, the Portcullis (another Tudor emblem), the Ragged Staff (the old badge of the Earls of Warwick), and, I think, some devices which appear in the arms of the SAVAGES. . . . It is plain that the date is sufficiently marked as being the time of the Tudor kings and the SAVAGES."[3]

We shall now follow in genealogical form the history of the SAVAGES of ELMLEY CASTLE.

CHRISTOPHER SAVAGE, Esq., of Elmley Castle, and of Upton in the Co. of Gloucester, son of Sir Christopher Savage, of Upton, Knt., by his wife Ann,

---
the Co. of Worcester, &c., &c. This charter, with the seal of Sir W. Herbert attached, is now in the possession of Mr. F. W. SAVAGE, of Springfield.

[1] Rudder: *History of Gloucester*, p. 732. (?)
[2] Bennett: *Elmley Castle*, pp. 16, 17.   [3] *Id.*, p. 20.

daughter of Sir John Stanley, of Elford, Knt., and grandson of Sir John Savage, of Clifton (Rock Savage), Co. of Chester, married Anne, daughter of Sir Richard Lygon, Knt. (of the family of Lord Beauchamp), and died seised of the manors of Ashton-sub-Edge, Broad Campden, Barrington, and Westington, in the County of Gloucester. In the 36th year of his reign Henry VIII. granted him, as we have just seen, the estates of Elmley Castle, in the County of Worcester. By his wife, Anne Savage (*née* Lygon), MR. CHRISTOPHER SAVAGE had issue,

 I. FRANCIS, of whom presently as successor to his father.
 II. George, Archdeacon of Gloucester and Rector of Segrave, who obtained the Manor of Walton from his father-in-law, George Turvile, Esq., and by purchase. He married Anne, daughter of the said George Turvile, Esq. (*ob.* 1552), grandson of Sir William Turvile, of Aston, and by her had issue,
  1. George, of Walton-on-the-Wold, Leicestershire, Esq., who married Mary, daughter of William Tracy, Esq., of Toddington House, Co. of Gloucester.

MR. CHRISTOPHER SAVAGE was succeeded by his eldest son,

FRANCIS SAVAGE, Esq., of Elmley Castle, who married Anne, daughter of William Sheddon (or Sheldon), of Borley's Court, Co. of Worcester, and had issue,
 I. WILLIAM, of whom presently as successor to his father at ELMLEY CASTLE.
 II. ANTONY, of Broadway, Co. of Worcester, *of whom hereafter as ancestor of the* SAVAGES OF BROADWAY *and of the* SAVAGES OF TETBURY.
 III. Walter, married ——, daughter of —— Smith, Esq., of Crobet, Co. of Sussex.

MR. FRANCIS SAVAGE, of Elmley Castle, was succeeded by his eldest son,

WILLIAM SAVAGE, Esq., of Elmley Castle, Justice of the Peace and Quorum, &c. During his lifetime Queen Elizabeth visited Elmley Castle and slept there as his guest. "In the year 1575," writes Mr. Bennett, "I find that Queen Elizabeth slept at Elmley Castle on Saturday and Sunday, August 20th and 21st. She was on her way from Worcester, and came 'through Battenhall Park, by made ways, with a great train both before and behind.' On the Monday, the Mayor and Aldermen of Worcester, with a large company of nobility, attended the Queen on horseback from Elmley to the borders of the county, on her way to Sudeley. She probably went down Kersoe Lane. . . . WILLIAM SAVAGE, to whom there is a monument in the Savage Chapel [at Elmley], was probably living at the Park at that time. It was he who purchased the Chantry and Manor of Elmley Castle from Queen Elizabeth. . . . It seems to have been barely the landed estate which was [granted] by Henry VIII. The family of SAVAGE, according to Nash, were noted for their hospitality."[1] Mr. WILLIAM SAVAGE, of Elmley Castle, married Anne, daughter, and one of the co-heiresses, of John Knottesford, Esq., of Great Malvern, and by her had issue,

> I. SIR JOHN, KNT., who married Dorothy, daughter of Sir Henry Poole, of Superton, Co. of Gloucester, Knt. "No. 6 Bell," of the peal of bells belonging to Elmley Church, Mr. Bennett states, bears the following inscription:—"GOD Save our King. April the 7th, Anno 1620. Sur John Savedge, William Mansill, John Smith, C.W."
> II. GILES, of whom presently as successor to his father at Elmley Castle.
> I. Mary, married to Sir Thomas Estcourt, Knt., of the family of Estcourt of Estcourt, Co. of Gloucester, who was knighted by James I., Nov. 17, 1807. He was M.P. for Gloucestershire, and died at Cirencester, of the plague, whilst on his return from attending Parliament.[2]

MR. WILLIAM SAVAGE, of Elmley Castle, died 1616. He was succeeded at Elmley Castle by his second son,

GILES SAVAGE, Esq., Lord of Elmley Castle, Justice of the Peace and Quorum, High Sheriff of the Co. of Worcester, 1626, who married Katherine,

---

[1] Bennett: *Elmley Castle*, p. 21. "A worthy family in Cheshire, who, since their settlement in this County [Worcestershire], have been dignified with the highest offices, and remarkable for their hospitality."—Nash: *Worcestershire*, vol. i.

[2] Sir Thomas Estcourt and his widow, Dame Mary Estcourt, daughter of WILLIAM SAVAGE, Esq., of Elmley Castle, were buried at Shipton Moyne Church, where is the following inscription on the monument erected to his memory:—

> "Vita introitus Mortis. Mors Æternitatis.
> Death followeth life, life death; when men should die,
> Their buriale is a new nativitie.
> Then, gentle reader, call not this a tomb,
> But of a second life the happy womb.

"Here rest the bodies of Sr. Thomas Estcourt, of the Manor of ESTCOURT, in Shipton Moyne, in this County, Knight; and of Dame MARY, his wife, the daughter of WILLIAM SAVAGE, of Elmley Castle, in the County of Worcester, Esq. He was a pillar of this Country, and much honored and beloved for his Wisdome and Hospitality: he lived religiously, and (in his return from Parliament, being then one of the Knights for this County) died at Cirencester, the 4th of July, Ao. Dni. 1624.

"In whose memory his aforesaid wife caused this Monument to be erected.

> "Thy hour-glasse is first run, and there remains
> In mine but a small part of falling graines;
> Thou wer't my leader to this hallowed place,
> And I came after, though with slower pace;
> My voyage done, here I my rest will take,
> And in this bed sleepe with thee and awake."

(Given in a footnote by Mr. Lee in his *History of Tetbury*, p. 199.)

daughter of Richard Daston, Esq. ("Justice Daston.") On the monument erected by Mrs. Katherine Savage in the Savage Chapel at Elmley "are two Latin lines [probably inscribed by her children], to this effect:—'Reader, build your own monument while you live, unless fortune has given you as good a wife.' . . . She lived to the age of 84, and was buried at Malvern, where there is, or was, a very elaborate Latin inscription to her memory, beginning with—'Stop, stranger, a little while; it will be worth your while to know what lady is buried here.' Mention is then made of her family, and of her being the wife, 'equally loving and beloved,' of GILES SAVAGE, of Elmley Castle; that she remained a widow forty years; 'in household matters she was like Solomon's mother of a family; in almsdeeds like another Dorcas; in acts of religion a very Anna. She exchanged mortality for immortality on the longest day of the year, 11th June, 1674. Elmley has her effigy (together with those of her husband and children);[1] Heaven has her soul; the sepulchre possesses her body; her survivors and posterity have her example,' with more to the same effect."[2] By his wife (this exemplary lady) MR. GILES SAVAGE had issue,

I. THOMAS, of whom presently as successor to his father.
II. William, who was buried at Elmley Church, and whose effigy is on the same tomb as that of his father and mother.[1]
III. Giles.
IV. John, who, according to the inscription on his father's monument in the Savage Chapel at Elmley, "died in the same year as his father" (1631).[1]

MR. GILES SAVAGE died 31st January, 1631, and was buried in the Savage Chapel at Elmley.[1] He was succeeded by his eldest son,

THOMAS SAVAGE, Esq., of Elmley Castle. "In the time of the Civil Wars between Charles I. and the Parliament, Elmley, like Worcester, was on the side of the King. Mr. SAVAGE of Elmley is described as a 'staunch Royalist,' and no doubt the village went along with him. Evesham, under Col. Dingley, was on the side of the Parliament, and it requires no great flight of imagination to suppose that there may have been now and then a skirmish in the Vale between parties from Evesham and the Elmley men under MR. SAVAGE. When Parliament gained the upper hand, MR. SAVAGE suffered for his loyalty; he was fined in the first instance in the sum of £1,500, but he afterwards effected a composition with the Commissioners who were appointed to settle with 'delinquents,' whereby it was agreed that he should pay £60 a-year for three lives to the Vicar of Elmley, and that his fine should be reduced to

---

[1] See hereafter, under "Monuments of the SAVAGES OF ELMLEY CASTLE."
[2] Bennett: *Elmley Castle*, p. 26.

£1,100. It was rather a dear composition for him, but probably he preferred to make this use of his money to simply paying it over to the support of Cromwell or the Parliament. In 1651 was fought the Battle of Worcester, between Charles II. and Oliver Cromwell, and with this battle is connected a tradition which has great interest for us at Elmley. The chief fighting took place at Sidbury. The present West Midland Railway passes through the field of battle just before it enters Worcester. At that time there was a gateway at the entrance of the city, through which the street passed. When the King's army was routed, his soldiers fled as fast as they could into Worcester, pursued by Cromwell's cavalry, and the King himself was very near being taken there; but just at the time some one drew a load of hay into the gateway, and blocked up the entrance so that horsemen could not enter. The King, who was a very short distance before his pursuers, rode up to the gateway, dismounted, and crept under the hay into the town, leaving his horse outside. As soon as he was within the walls, a cry was made to find another horse for the King, and a loyal gentleman of Sidbury [one of the SAVAGES, it is said] turned out his own horse at once ready saddled, on which the King mounted, and fled away through St. Martin's Gate, and so to Boscobel. All this is matter of history; but . . . according to the common belief of Elmley, handed down from father to son, the man who so promptly blocked up the gateway with his load of hay, and saved the King's life, was an ancestor of Mr. Moore [of Kersoe] . . ; and the land at Kersoe, which has long been in his family, was given to this ancestor as a reward for this very service. Whether it was given by the King himself, after his restoration, is not known. Charles II. was not famed for acts of gratitude of this kind, and I think it quite as likely to have been given by that same loyal MR. SAVAGE who had already fought and suffered so much in the King's behalf, and given, perhaps, in the joy of his heart when the King came back to enjoy his own again."[1] (We shall have yet to describe some curious relations between the descendants of this Mr. Moore and the last representative of the SAVAGES OF ELMLEY CASTLE that held the Elmley estates.) MR. THOMAS SAVAGE married Mary, daughter of Sir Thomas Storrs, of Bardolph, Co. of Norfolk, and by her had issue,

I. THOMAS, of whom presently as successor to his father.

1. Mary, married to John Willis, Esq., of Fen Ditton, Co. of Cambridge.

Mr. THOMAS SAVAGE died subsequent to the year 1655. He was succeeded by his son,

---

[1] Bennett: *Elmley Castle*, pp. 21, 22. Mr. Bennett adds in a footnote—"Mr. Savage was imprisoned in Worcester Gaol in 1655, but for what offence against the ruling powers I do not know."

THOMAS SAVAGE, Esq., of Elmley Castle, who married Margaret, 2nd daughter of Sir Philip Woodhouse, of Kimberley, Co. of Norfolk, M.P. for Thetford in the Restoration Parliament, by his wife Lucy, daughter of Sir Thomas Cotton, Bart., and Margaret his wife, daughter of Lord William Howard, of Naworth Castle, Cumberland. (Sir Philip Woodhouse was ancestor of the present Earl of Kimberley.) MR. SAVAGE by this marriage had issue,
    I. THOMAS, of whom presently as successor to his father.
    I. Anne, married to Sam. Bracebridge, Esq., of Lindley, Warwick.
    II. Lucy, married to Thomas Adderley, Esq.
    III. A daughter, married to —— Reed, Esq., of Lugardine.
MR. THOMAS SAVAGE was succeeded by his son,
THOMAS SAVAGE, Esq., of Elmley Castle, Sheriff of Worcester, 1694, who married Ann, daughter of ——, and had issue,
    I. THOMAS, of whom presently as successor to his father.
Mr. THOMAS SAVAGE died 1694. He was succeeded by his only son,
THOMAS SAVAGE, Esq., of Elmley Castle. He married Elizabeth, Countess of Coventry, widow of Thomas, first Earl of Coventry, and daughter of "Captain Richard Graham, who had fought for King Charles I." This Mr. THOMAS SAVAGE, Mr. Bennett tells us, was a great benefactor of the Church in the parish of Elmley. "It was he who built the present vicarage house. In the registry of Worcester there is a terrier, dated 16th September, 1714, and signed by Prideaux Sutton, vicar of Elmley, and by Henry Ward and Joseph Terreitt, churchwardens, which gives an account of the property at that time belonging to the vicarage. The first thing mentioned is 'a good vicarage house, built by THOMAS SAVAGE, Esq., in exchange for a very old one.' . . . In 1723 the same MR. SAVAGE gave £200 as a benefaction to augment the vicarage of Elmley."[1] By his wife Elizabeth, Countess of Coventry, Mr. SAVAGE had issue,
    I. A son, who died without issue.
    II. A son, who died without issue.
    I. ELIZABETH, of whom presently as heiress to her father.
    II. Mary, married to Thomas Coventry, Esq.
    III. ——, married to Philip Monoux.
On the death of Mr. THOMAS SAVAGE without male issue, the Elmley property was divided between his three daughters, co-heiresses. The eldest daughter,
ELIZABETH SAVAGE, of Elmley Castle, married William Byrche, LL.D., of Leacroft, Staffordshire, Chancellor of Worcester, and ultimately became heiress to the Elmley estates. Dr. Byrche, by his wife Elizabeth (*née* SAVAGE), had issue,

---
[1] Bennett: *Elmley Castle*, p. 27.

I. THOMAS BYRCHE, who assumed the name of SAVAGE, and of whom presently as successor to his father and mother, and representative of the family of ELMLEY CASTLE.

I. Elizabeth Byrche, married to John Perrott, Esq., and had issue,
1. Thomas, who died without issue.
1. Mary, who died without issue.

II. Jane Byrche, married to Robert Clavering, Esq., of the old family of Clavering, of Callaly Castle, Co. of Northumberland,[1] and had issue,
1. ROBERT CLAVERING, who assumed the name of SAVAGE, and of whom presently as successor to his uncle, Mr. THOMAS BYRCHE SAVAGE, and representative of the SAVAGES OF ELMLEY CASTLE.
1. Jane, who died without issue.
2. Dorothy, married, 1797, to the Rev. Jos. Jekyall Pye, and died without issue.

MRS. BYRCHE was succeeded by her eldest son,

THOMAS BYRCHE SAVAGE, Esq., who assumed the name of SAVAGE in 1748, by Act of Parliament, when the Elmley estates were settled on him. He married Dorothy, daughter of Thomas Kynnesby, Esq., of Loxley Hall, Co. of Stafford (she married, 2*ndly*, Ralph Adderley, Esq.), and died, 1776, without issue. At his death his property was divided. He left his estates to his widow for life, and, on her death, to ROBERT CLAVERING, son of his younger sister, Jane, and, on failure of issue, to Thomas Perrott, son of his elder sister, Elizabeth, with remainder to his nieces, Jane Clavering and Mary Perrott, with remainder to his own right heirs for ever. The remaining portion of the estate was left by MR. BYRCHE SAVAGE to his nephew, ROBERT CLAVERING, the son of his younger sister, Jane. MR. BYRCHE SAVAGE was succeeded by his nephew,

ROBERT CLAVERING SAVAGE, Esq., of Elmley Castle, who married Miss Barlow, sister of the wife of Baron Parke, afterwards Lord Wensleydale, and had issue,

---

[1] Sir Bernard Burke gives the following account of this family of Clavering:—"This family, from which sprang the Vescis, Lords of Alnwick, the Lacis, Earls of Lincoln, the Eures, Lords Eure, in the male line, and the Altons and many other eminent houses in the female, entered England under the banner of THE CONQUEROR; and the gift of numerous estates marked the services which they subsequently rendered to his cause. The family is a scion of the great house of De Burgh, and it originally bore that surname; but from the time of HENRY I. until that of EDWARD I., when commanded to take the designation of CLAVERING, from an estate in Essex, the head of the family assumed for surname the Christian name of his father, with the addition of FITZ."—Burke: *Landed Gentry*, under "CLAVERING OF CALLALY."

I. ROBERT CLAVERING SAVAGE, of whom presently as successor to his father, and representative of the SAVAGES OF ELMLEY CASTLE. MR. ROBERT CLAVERING SAVAGE died 1829. He was succeeded by his only son, ROBERT CLAVERING SAVAGE, Esq., of Elmley Castle, who died 1866, without issue. This MR. ROBERT CLAVERING SAVAGE was the last of his race that ever owned the Elmley Castle estates. He was very little of a SAVAGE by blood or by character. His mother survived her husband 20 years, and resided at Elmley Castle in much state. At her death, as the House was not entailed, she directed by will that it should be sold, as she desired to leave everything she could away from her son, who was of an eccentric and not very reputable character. But he, by his great-uncle's will, inherited the Park and large landed estates. "After the sale of the old House of Elmley Castle and the Park,

ELMLEY CASTLE (north-east view), seat of the SAVAGES OF ELMLEY CASTLE.

CLAVERING SAVAGE, who lived in London and Paris, often came to stay with his tenant, Mr. Moore (the descendant of the person of that name who helped to save the life of Charles II. by stopping the gate at Worcester with a hay-cart—*see p. 80*), at Mr. Moore's old farm; and he built large stables on his land, and there kept a stud of some dozen horses. His life, both in London and in Paris, was spent in dissipation and low debauchery, and as he grew older he seemed to grow more wicked; and such a hatred did he conceive of all his family that he determined to realise all his property and convert it into bank notes, which he intended to live on, and, when near his death, to burn what might remain. He therefore went one day to his friend Moore, and told him that he (Moore) *must buy the estate.* Of course Moore replied that it was not in his power to do so; but MR. SAVAGE said he had arranged all that, and directed him to go to Worcester, to a certain person whom he named, assuring him that he would there find the means. This Moore accordingly did. The person to whom he had been directed provided the money, and the estate passed into his hands, but was sold immediately after for a much larger sum, Moore receiving the surplus. The estate was sold under the title of "Elmley Park," and in the name of Mr. Moore (who of course only did what Mr. SAVAGE requested him to do), and so escaped the notice of those interested in the matter. By entail it must have passed to the SAVAGES OF TETBURY, who, however, did not know of the transaction for many years after. CLAVERING SAVAGE did not live long after to enjoy his bank notes, as he died at his house in London in a fit, and, fortunately, did not accomplish his purpose of burning the remnant of them. As there was no will, and the property having become personal, it had to go to next of kin, and it was placed in the hands of Mr. Arthur Smyth, Queen's Proctor, until letters of administration should be taken out, which was done by the deceased's mother's sister, Lady Wensleydale, widow of Baron Parke, for herself and her sister, Miss Barlow, an old lady of (it is said) over 100 years of age. She left her portion of the property to a Mr. Williams, an adopted son. Lady Wensleydale left her share to her daughter, married to Mr. W. Lowther. The amount of property handed over came to £88,500 in bank notes, and £30,000 in debentures; and there was also a fine service of plate, and an extraordinary amount of clothing. His two pair of carriage-horses and his favourite cob remained in possession of the stable-keepers, but the cob began to miss his master after the first week, and, refusing all food, died. This cob was the only thing in the world that the wicked old man expressed any regard for. It is curious that, just before the estate was sold, he spent a considerable sum in restoring the fine old tombs and monuments in the Savage Chapel of Elmley Church, which adjoins the Castle; which shows what an extraordinary disposition was his—great pride in the old family of which he was such an unworthy descendant, yet by his act of selling the property depriving the present representatives of the chance of reviving some of its former glories."[1]

[1] From some MS. notes by Francis Walker Savage, Esq., of Springfield, to which Mr. Savage appends the following:—"This notice of Robert Clavering Savage has been compiled from notes taken from conversations with the Vicar of Elmley, and from correspondence with Mr. Arthur Smyth, Queen's Proctor, of 55 Warren Street, Fitzroy Square, London, who administered to the property of the late R. C. Savage in 1860.—FRANCIS W. SAVAGE."

MONUMENTS OF THE SAVAGES OF ELMLEY CASTLE.

The following descriptions of the SAVAGE monuments at Elmley are taken from Mr. Bennett's *Lecture on Elmley Castle* and Nash's *Worcestershire*:—

"In the Savage Chapel [at Elmley] the monuments of the SAVAGES appear to have been all erected at the same time. The figures are those of William Savage, and of his son Giles, together with that of Giles Savage's wife and five children, four kneeling at the feet of their father and mother, and one little one in the mother's arms. The inscription over William Savage is—'Here lies William Savage, Esquire, Justice of the Peace and Quorum, father of Giles, who married Anne Knottesford, daughter and one of the co-heiresses of John Knottesford, by whom he had four sons and twin daughters, of which daughters Mary married Thomas Estcourt, soldier, and died 7th August, 1616. The souls of the just are in the hand of God.' The inscription over Giles Savage is—'Here lies Giles Savage, Esquire, son of William Savage, Esquire, Lord of Elmley Castle, Justice of the Peace and Quorum, High Sheriff of the County of Worcester, who died 31st January, 1631. In whose memory his most loving wife, Katharine, daughter of Richard Daston, Esq., *placed near* [referring to her effigy on the monument], together with her four sons, Thomas, William, Giles, and John

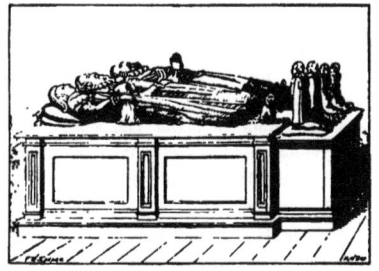

Tomb of Giles and William Savage, of Elmley Castle, in the Savage Chapel, at Elmley.

(of whom John, the youngest, died in the same year with his father), and a beloved little daughter, born after his death, *whom she embraces in her arms* [this also refers to the effigies on the tomb], had this monument erected as a pledge of her faithfulness and obedience.' On the other side of the monument are two Latin lines to this effect—'Reader, build your own monument while you live, unless fortune has given you as good a wife.'"[1]

Of the same interesting monument Nash writes:—"In this chapel [the north chapel of Elmley Church] is a very handsome tomb for William Savage, Giles his son, and his wife Katherine, holding in her arms a new-born child; under the men's feet lions; under the woman's reindeer's head with neck erased, Argent, attired Or, and pierced through the neck with an arrow Or, feathered Argent, upon a wreath Or and Gules.

[1] Bennett: *Elmley Castle*, p. 25.

"Over William Savage his shield with these arms:

" 1. ar. 6 lioncells rampant sa., *Savage.*
2. ar. a pale fusillé sa., *Savage of Malvern.*
3. ar. a cross fleuretté sa. [*Swinerton*].
4. ar. 3 escocheons in fesse between as many mullets gules.
5. ar. on a fesse az. 3 garbes or, *Peverell.*
6. barry wavy of six, ar. and az., a saltire or.
7. sa. a fesse humet ar., *Bostock.*
8. ar. 2 bars az., *Hilton.*
9. quarterly ar. and gules, in the 2d and 3d a fret or, *Dutton.*
10. az. a crescent and star in chief ar., *Mynshull.*
11. gules, a chevron between 3 martlets ar., *Walkinton.*

Crest, a lion's paw sable, armed gules, out of a coronet or."

The superscription :

"'Hic jacet Gulielmus Savage, armiger, justiciarius pacis et quorum, pater Egidii, qui duxit Annam Knotesford, filiam et unam ex coheredibus Joh'is Knotesford, fervientis ad arma, ex qua quatuor genuit filios et gemellas filias, quarum Maria nupsit Thome Estcourt militi, et obiit 7 Augsti, A.D. 1616. Justorum animæ in manu Dei sunt.'

"Below, on the right hand, six lionceaux sable, *Savage.*

"On the left, or, two pallets gules, Knotesford.

[A cross engrailed ar., an annulet of the field, arms of *Knightly.*]

"Over Gyles and his wife are the same arms: the crest, on a wreath ar. and sa., an unicorn's head erased ar., attired or.

"'Hic jacet Egidius Savage, armiger, filius Gulielmi Savage armigeri, dom'us de Elmley-castle, justiciarius pacis et quorum, suprefectus comitatus Wigorn, qui diem clausit supremum 31 Januarii A.D. 1631. In cujus memoriam amantissima ipsius conjux Katherina fillia Ricardi Daston armigeri juxta posita una cum quatuor filiis, Thoma, Gulielmo, Egidio, Johanne, quorum Joh'es minimus natu obiit 13 Aug. œdem quo pater anno, et dilecta filiola quam post obitum ipsius est enixa et utrisque ulnis amplectitur, hoc monumentum fidelitatis et obedientiæ ergo extrui curavit.'

"Underneath this on the right hand, argent, six lionceaux sable, *Savage.*

"On the left, gules, on a bend, or, three mullets sa., *Daston,* quartering or, a fesse wavy between six billets sa., *Dumbleton.*

"On the right side of the monument, these lines:

'Lector, sepulchrum vivus edifica, tuum
Fortuna sic non conjugam dederit parem.'

"At their feet, four sons praying."[1]

"The next in order," writes Mr. Bennett, "is that of Mrs. Mary Savage, on the floor of the chancel. She was the wife of Thomas Savage, the son of Giles and Katherine, of whom I have just spoken. According to Nash's pedigree of the Savages, she must have lived to see the marriage of her son, her grandson, and her great-grandson, all of whom were named Thomas Savage. It was either her husband or her son that fought for Charles I., and her great-grandson who married the Countess of Coventry. The inscription in the chancel records that though she was of so great age, she laboured under no infirmity of disease, and at last seemed rather to breathe away her life than to die. She died in 1708, aged 84."[2]

Of this monument Nash gives the Latin inscription:—

"In the chancel, on a flat stone—'M. S. Maria uxor Thomæ Savage armigeri, filia Johannis Hare de Stow in com. Norf., Baronetti, cujus si pietas, liberalitas, cunctæque virtutes redere potuissent immortalem, nunquam hoc saxum condidisset reliquias. Obiit Novembris 13, anno Domini 1708, et ætatis. 84. Sed quamvis tam multis annis provecta, nulla morbi infirmitate laborans, tam subito et levi flatu spiritum emisit, dixisses illam non expirasse sed obdormisse.'"[1]

"I come now," writes Mr. Bennett, "to the monument of the Earl of Coventry. The inscription is too long to give you the whole of it, but the history is this:—He succeeded his nephew as Baron Coventry, and became the first *Earl* of Coventry in the reign of William III. His wife was Winifred, the daughter of Pierce Mount Edgecombe, Esq., of Devonshire. By her he left two sons, Thomas and Gilbert. For his second wife he married Elizabeth Graham, daughter of Captain Richard Graham, who had fought for King Charles I. By this marriage he greatly offended his two sons, either because they thought her below him in rank, or because (as I imagine) she was a young lady and he an old man, and they did not approve of their father forming such a marriage in his old age. He had no children by her. After his death his young widow caused this monument to be erected, intending to place it at Croome, and the inscription records that 'after her own death she wished her body to be buried *here*, with her most beloved husband;' and at the end of the inscription on the *pedestal* spaces are left for the day and the year of her own death to be filled in. When the monument was ready, her stepson, 'the most worthy heir of his father's honours' (as he is called in the inscription), refused to allow his stepmother to erect it at Croome; and he himself placed a stone

---

[1] Nash: *Worcestershire*, vol. i., p. 386.   [2] Bennett: *Elmley Castle*, p. 26.

there to his father's memory with these words :—' Here lieth the body of Thomas, the first Earl of the family of Coventry, who departed this life, July 15, 1699, aged 70.' In the meantime the Countess Dowager had married THOMAS SAVAGE, Esq., of Elmley Castle, and by his order it was brought here. You may find this stated in English on the south *side* of the pedestal. She appears to have married MR. SAVAGE within a year of the Earl of Coventry's death, and of course before the monument was finished. As wife of MR. SAVAGE she had a daughter, christened at Elmley in April, 1701, and several children afterwards. She died at Elmley, and was buried here, the entry in the register being as follows :— 'The Right Hon. Elizabeth, Countess Dowager of Coventry, wife of THOMAS SAVAGE, Elmley Castle, Esq., buried April 10, 1724.' The inscription on the Earl of Coventry's monument was not filled up, and there is no other monument to her memory."[1]

SECTION V.—THE WORCESTERSHIRE BRANCHES *(continued)*—SAVAGE OF BROADWAY.

From the SAVAGES OF ELMLEY CASTLE branched the SAVAGES OF BROADWAY.

ANTONY SAVAGE, Esq., designated "of Broadway," 2nd son of FRANCIS SAVAGE, ESQ., of Elmley Castle (*see ante*, p. 77), married Elizabeth, daughter of John Hall, Esq., of Idlecote, Co. of Warwick, and had issue,

 I. RICHARD, of whom presently as successor to his father.
 II. Ralph, who married, and had issue,
   1. Walter.
   2. John.
   3. Francis. [*Query*—Is this the Rev. Francis Savage who married Joyce, daughter of Thomas Cooper, of Powick, in Worcestershire (which Joyce was married, 2*ndly*, to John Blencowe, Esq., of Marston St. Lawrence), and whose daughter,
    Mary, was married to Thomas Blencowe, eldest son of the above-named John Blencowe, and died in 1678, leaving issue a son,
     —— Blencowe, of Marston St. Lawrence ?]
   4. Antony.
   1. Elizabeth.
 III. Charles, " of Tetbury," Co. of Gloucester, married, in 1663, Elizabeth, daughter of Antony Abington, of Dowdeswell, Co. Gloucester (she died 1663), and died 1652, aged 62 years, having had issue,

---

[1] Bennett: *Elmley Castle*, pp. 26, 27.

1. William, "of Tetbury," D.L. and J.P., Co. of Gloucester, married, *1st*, Mary, daughter of W. Bird, Esq., of Wootton-under-Edge; *2ndly*, Jane, daughter of —— Parkney, of Bashall; and, *3dly*, Elizabeth, daughter of —— Cottle. He died 1661, aged 59 years, having had issue,

    Charles, "of Tetbury," who married Elizabeth, daughter of Thos. Harris, of Colarch, and died in 1750.
    William, "of London," æt. 24 in 1682.
    Mary.
    Anne.
    Elizabeth.

2. Abington.
3. Antony.
4. John.
1. Anne.
2. Elizabeth.

IV. Antony, "of Broadway."
V. FRANCIS, of Tetbury, *of whom hereafter as ancestor of the* SAVAGES OF TETBURY.
VI. John, 1647.
VII. John, who married Philippa, daughter of George Gifford, of the County of Bucks.

I. Katherine, married to John Abington, Esq., of Dowdeswell, Co. of Gloucester.

MR. ANTONY SAVAGE, of Broadway, was succeeded by his eldest son,

RICHARD SAVAGE, Esq., of Idlecote, Co. of Warwick, baptised 1582, married Milicent, daughter of William Moulton, of Todinham (she died 1629), and had issue. He was succeeded by his son,

WALTER SAVAGE, Esq., of Broadway, Co. of Worcester, baptised 1605, æt. 21, 3 Car. I.; married, 1627, Mary, daughter of —— Wheeler (she died 1658), and had issue,

I. WALTER, of whom presently as successor to his father.
II. Thomas, "of London," born 1629, died 1690.
III. John, born 1630.
IV. Richard, born 1630.
I. Ann, born 1630, married to John Priest Sheldon, Esq.
II. Milicent, born 1634.

MR. WALTER SAVAGE died Oct., 1640. He was succeeded by his eldest son, WALTER SAVAGE, Esq., of Broadway, baptised 1623; married, 1647, Elizabeth, daughter and heiress of Edmund Skinner, Esq., of Ledbury, Co. of Hereford (she died 1668), and had issue,

  I. Walter, born 1649, died 1650.
  II. Edward, born 1650, died 1651.
  III. WALTER, of whom presently as successor to his father.
  IV. John, born 1653.
  V. Philip, born 1662.
  VI. William, born 1662; married, 1684, Ann, daughter of William Hobday, Esq., of Broadway (she was born 1665), and died 1727, having had issue,
    1. Henry, Vicar of Broadway, born 1697, died 1771.
    2. John, died 1704.
    3. George, born 1704, died 1770.
    4. Walter, born 1706, died 1750 without issue.
  VII. George, born 1666; married, 1698, Elizabeth, daughter of William Hodges, Esq., of Gloucester, and had issue,
    1. Thomas, Vicar of Standish, Co. of Gloucester, born 1699, married Elinor, daughter and heiress of Thomas Barrow, Esq., of Field Court, Co. of Gloucester (she died 1762), and died 1760, having had issue,

      George, of Middle Hill, Co. of Worcester, born 1742, died 1790, without issue.

      Martha, born 1758, died 1760 (?)

      Eleanor, co-heiress, born 1740; married, 1762, to John Wogan, Esq., of Weston, Co. of Pembroke, and had issue, John Wogan, Thomas Wogan, Eleanor Wogan, married to Thomas Roberts, Esq., and Susannah Wogan, married to Thos. Stokes, Esq.

      Anne, born 1745, married to Sir Thomas Crawley-Boevey, Bart., of Flaxley Abbey, Co. Gloucester, and was ancestress of the present Baronet.

      Elizabeth, married to Edward Jones, Esq., of Thingley Corsham, Co. of Wilts.

      Margaret, married to John Mills, Esq., of Gloucester, and had issue one child.

    2. Nathaniel.

1. Anne, married to Thomas Mee, Esq., of Gloucester, and had issue one daughter,
Elizabeth Mee.

I. Mary.
II. Joyce, born 1657, married to Nicholas Webb, Esq.
III. Edith, died without issue.

MR. WALTER SAVAGE died 1706. He was succeeded by his eldest surviving son,
WALTER SAVAGE, Esq., of Broadway, born 1651; married, 1681, Sarah, daughter of Richard Skippe, Esq., of Pennington, Co. of Hereford (she died 1732), and had issue,

I. WALTER, of whom presently as successor to his father.
II. George, born 1634, died 1699.
I. Sarah, died 1723.
II. Ann, born 1686, died 1739.

MR. WALTER SAVAGE died 1712. He was succeeded by his elder son,
WALTER SAVAGE, Esq., of Broadway, born 1683; married Cicilia, daughter of Thomas Oldys, Esq., of Tingeworth, Bucks (she is buried at Broadway), and died in 1718 without issue.

Middle Hill, Broadway, was long the residence of the Broadway branch of the SAVAGE family. It was subsequently sold to the late Sir Thomas Phillipps, the eminent antiquarian.

SAVAGE MONUMENT IN BROADWAY CHURCH.

The following inscription is in the Church of Broadway:—" Memoriæ sempeterniæ mariti clarissimi Walteri Savage, armigeri, qui 35 ætatis anno præpropero nimis fato naturæ debitum, vir non minus pietate quam integritate eximius. Cum Christo qui vita est consisus sanctam resurrectionem expectat. Uxor . . . M.S. hoc fidi amoris monumentum moerens posuit Junii 24, 1640."

Arms, *Savage* empaling ar. a chief az.

(N.B.—There are the arms of Wheeler, ar. on a chief az. 3 wheels. The wheels are probably effaced, or were overlooked by the historian.)

This Walter Savage of Broadway was the son of Richard Savage, son of Anthony Savage, of Broadway. *(MS. note by Mr. Francis Walker Savage.)*

SECTION VI.—THE GLOUCESTERSHIRE BRANCH—SAVAGE OF TETBURY.

From the ELMLEY CASTLE branch of the SAVAGES OF ROCK SAVAGE branched also the SAVAGES OF TETBURY, in Gloucestershire. It is worth while noting that we find in the *Historia et Cartularium Monasterii Gloucestriæ* the name SAVAGE occurring in connection with that County early in the 13th, and in the 14th, century. We meet with Geoffrey Savage, a Justice; William Savage, a Canon of Cirencester; and Robert and William Savage, landholders. In the reign of Henry III., Robert le Savage held there the manor of Kingsholme. Of this manor we read in Gough's *Camden*, vol. i., that Henry III. granted the manor of Kingsholme, then valued at £48 a-year, to Robert le Savage, to be held by service of Doorkeeper to the King's Pantry. 32 Ed. I., Robert le Savage conveys it to John Dunlevy.[1] But the TETBURY branch

TETBURY CLOSE (front), seat of the SAVAGES OF TETBURY.

of the SAVAGES was founded by FRANCIS, grandson of the above-mentioned FRANCIS SAVAGE, Esq., of Elmley Castle, in Worcestershire, who, as we have seen, was son of CHRISTOPHER SAVAGE, of Elmley Castle, in whose person the Worcestershire family branched from the Rock Savage (Clifton) stem.

The genealogical history of the TETBURY family, briefly sketched, from FRANCIS SAVAGE, its founder, onwards, is as follows:—

FRANCIS SAVAGE, Esq., of Broadway, afterwards of Tetbury, 5th son of Walter Savage, Esq., of Broadway, and grandson of Francis Savage, Esq., of

---
[1] This name *Dunlevy* is suggestive of a connection of the Robert Savage who held Kingsholme with the County of Down, for Dunlevy was the name of the most prominent Irish Chief whom De Courcy, Savage, and their companions-in-arms dislodged from that district. But we shrink from the difficult task of pursuing the inquiry it invites.

Elmley Castle, married, in 1621, Mary, daughter of Edmund Estcourt, Esq., of Shipton Moyne, Co. of Gloucester, brother of that Sir Thomas Estcourt who, as we have seen, married Mary, daughter of William Savage, Esq., and grand-daughter of Francis Savage, Esq., of Elmley Castle—the "Dame Mary Estcourt" who erected the monument to her husband in Shipton Moyne Church (*see* note, p. 78).[1] The marriage-license of FRANCIS SAVAGE and MARY ESTCOURT, written in Latin, is still possessed by their descendants. MR. FRANCIS SAVAGE inherited the property of his aunt, Dame Mary Estcourt. (Her will is still possessed by the TETBURY family.) He also acquired considerable other property, together with the old Mansion at Tetbury, from his wife, the whole of which was devised entail to his son, JOHN SAVAGE, and his heirs. MR. FRANCIS SAVAGE, of Tetbury, like most other members of the SAVAGE family,

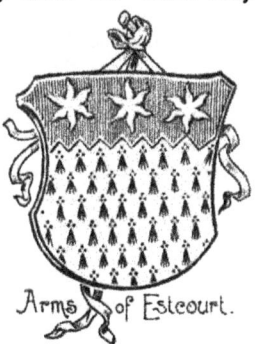

Arms of Estcourt.

---

[1] *Family of Estcourt, of Estcourt.* This ancient family, says Mr. Lee, has been settled in Gloucestershire, and been possessed of lands in the parish of Shipton Moyne, as appears by deeds at Estcourt, since 1300.

The first Estcourt mentioned in these deeds is WALTER DE LA ESTCOURT, who held an estate at Shipton in this County. He married Margaret ——, and died about 1325. He was succeeded by his son,

SYMON DE LA ESTCOURT, who married, *1st*, Margaret de la Woodemill; and, *2ndly*, Johanna——. He had four sons, WALTER, Richard, William, and John. He was succeeded by his eldest son,

WALTER DE LA ESTCOURT (living in 1373), who married Juliana ——, and was succeeded by his eldest son,

JOHN DE LA ESTCOURT, who married Alice, heiress of Beauboys, of Shipton Moyne, and Fairwood, in Dorsetshire, and thence obtained a separate estate at Shipton. (His wife survived him, and married, *2ndly*, John Wynter, of Wotton-under-Edge.) He was succeeded by his son,

JOHN DE LA ESTCOURT, who married, *1st*, Eleanor ——; and, *2ndly*, Margaret ——; and by his 1st wife, Eleanor, had issue two sons, JOHN, and William, who died without issue. He was succeeded by his elder son,

JOHN DE LA ESTCOURT, who married Elizabeth Seymour, and had issue two sons, THOMAS and Walter. This JOHN DE LA ESTCOURT obtained a pardon from K. Richard III. for some offence committed against him. He was succeeded by his elder son,

THOMAS DE LA ESTCOURT, who married, *1st*, Catherine, daughter of Richard Ellyott, Serjeant-at-Law, and, *2ndly*, Catherine, daughter of Richard Hall, and by his 1st wife had issue a son and successor,

EDMUND DE LA ESTCOURT, who married Johanna, daughter of William Button, Esq., of ——, Wiltshire, and had issue,

I. THOMAS DE LA ESTCOURT, who married Emma Ascough. He was a Welsh Judge, and a handsome monument is erected to him in Shipton Church. He was father of

THOMAS ESTCOURT, knighted by K. James I., Nov. 17, 1607, who married Mary, daughter of WILLIAM SAVAGE, Esq., of ELMLEY CASTLE.—Lee: *History of Tetbury*, pp. 196-8.

including the EARL RIVERS, its head, was a stout Royalist. Charles I. visited Tetbury in 1643, and his visit is described in the *Iter Carolinum*, an account of the King's marches from 1641 to 1643:—"Tuesday, August 8th, To Tetbury to dinner;" and on that day the King addressed an order "To all Collonells and other officers of our Army, both the Horse and ffoote," to spare Tetbury during the Civil War. This order was placed, no doubt, in the hands of Mr. SAVAGE, as the principal personage in Tetbury, and recently it was discovered by MR. SAVAGE's descendant, Mr. Francis Walker Savage, of Springfield, Westbury-on-Trym, in an old chest containing other family papers in the ancient SAVAGE Mansion of Tetbury Close.[1] MR. SAVAGE would naturally assist at the King's reception when his Majesty rested at Tetbury in 1643; and he probably took a still more prominent part as a loyal subject in the Civil Wars themselves. "During the Civil Wars," writes the Historian of Tetbury, "there appears to have been a great deal of fighting in the neighbourhood of Tetbury; and towards the end of the year 1643 the whole country was kept in a perpetual state of alarm. Both parties established themselves in every eligible spot where a castle or defensible house could be found. Colonel Massey, who commanded for the Parliament, was continually skirmishing, and kept all his adversaries on the alert. 'In the space of five months there was fighting at Berkely, Beverstone, Cheltenham, Huntley, Marshfield, Newent, Painswick, Tainton, *Tetbury*, and Wootton-under-Edge. He himself was often in extreme peril.'[2] John Corbet, a Parliamentary Preacher, in his *Historical Relation of the Military Government of Gloucester*, published in 1645, states that 'on the other side of the City (Gloucester) the enemy (the Royalists) was emboldened to erect new Governments at Tedbury and Wotton-under-Edge. Men did incite the Governour to march that way, who withall had his eye upon Beverstone Castle, newly garrison'd, and commanding the rich clothiers of Stroudwater; hither he advanced with a party of three hundred foot and four score horse. These horse sent before were so formidable to the enemy at Tedbury, that the governour, Horatio Cary, with his whole regiment, were put to flight, and dissipated with the loss of fourteen of their men slain and taken prisoners.' Afterwards he speaks of Colonel Massie attacking Malmesbury, which was defended by Col. Henry Howard, who resolutely refused to surrender when summoned by Col. Massie. 'Thereupon our foot and artillery were brought up from Tedbury, and within two houres drawn into the suburbs and lower

---

[1] A fac-simile of this order of Charles I. is given in the Rev. Mr. Lee's *History of Tetbury*.
[2] Lee: *Hist. of Tetbury*, pp. 19, 20. The quotation in the passage is from Washborn's *Bibliotheca Gloucesteriensis*, vol. ii., p. 81.

part of the towne.' The place was afterwards taken by Col. Massie.[1] Mr. Francis Savage, by his wife Mary (*née* Estcourt), had issue,
   I. Francis, baptised in 1626, died in 1636.
   II. John, of whom presently as successor to his father.
   III. Walter.
   IV. William, baptised in 1633.[2]
   V. Francis, baptised in 1636.
   VI. Thomas, baptised in 1638.
   I. Mary, baptised in 1622.
   II. Lucy, baptised in 1628.
   III. Elizabeth, born in 1629, died in 1683, aged 54 years.

Mr. Francis Savage died on the 2nd March, 1671. He was succeeded by his eldest surviving son,

John Savage, Esq., of Tetbury, baptised in 1630, who married Jane, daughter of ——, and had issue,
   I. Francis, of whom presently as successor to his father.
   II. William, baptised in 1663.
   I. Elizabeth, baptised in 1657.
   II. Katherine, baptised in 1661.
   III. Jane, baptised in 1668.

Mr. John Savage died in 1683. He was succeeded by his eldest son,

Francis Savage, Esq., of Tetbury (who, until the death of his father, resided at Severn Stoke, Worcestershire, when he removed to Tetbury); baptised in 1651; married at Dowdeswell, in 1675, Dorothy, daughter of —— Solway, Esq., of Worcester, and by her had issue,
   I. Francis, of whom presently as successor to his father.
   II. John, baptised in 1677, died in 1691.
   III. William, born in 1691, who married Sarah, daughter of J. Jenkins, Esq., of South Cerney, and died in 1775.
   IV. Charles, born in 1692, died in 1750.
   V. Walter, born in 1694.
   I. Dorothy, born in 1680.
   II. Mary, born in 1684.
   III. Jane.
   IV. Susan, born in 1690.
   V. Ann, born in 1696.
   VI. Elizabeth, married to John King, Esq.

---
[1] Lee: *Hist. of Tetbury*, pp. 20, 21.
[2] The Burial Register of Tetbury has the following entry:—"1681—Mr. William Savage, Esquire, Octob. ye 3."

Mr. FRANCIS SAVAGE was succeeded by his eldest son,

FRANCIS SAVAGE, Esq., of Tetbury, baptised, in 1676, at Severn Stoke Church, who married Abigaile, daughter of Joseph Wickes, Esq. He left to his son JOHN SAVAGE all his freehold messuages, land, and tenements, except the house and garden at Westcourt and all the land in the tything of Upton, in the parish of Tetbury, which he left to his son Francis. MR. SAVAGE, by his wife Abigaile (*née* Wickes), had issue,

- I. JOHN, of whom presently as successor to his father.
- II. Francis, of Westcourt and Upton, who married Mary ——, and died intestate in 1769, in the lifetime of his brother JOHN, leaving an only child,
    1. JOHN, of whom presently as successor to his uncle, and representative of the SAVAGES OF TETBURY.
- I. Elizabeth.
- II. Eleanor, who died 1763.

Mr. FRANCIS SAVAGE died 1740. He was succeeded by his elder son,

JOHN SAVAGE, Esq., of Tetbury, who inherited his father's property, with the exception of the house and garden at Westcourt and the land in the tything of Upton, as above stated. Mr. John Savage died in 1772, without issue. He was succeeded by his nephew,

JOHN SAVAGE, of Tetbury, in Holy Orders, Rector of Beverstone and Weston Birt, Co. of Gloucester. (The living of Weston was presented to MR. SAVAGE by the Halford family, old neighbours of the SAVAGES, between whom and the latter there seems to have been an immemorial friendship and intimacy.) THE REV. JOHN SAVAGE married Charlotte, daughter of Walter Wiltshire, Esq., of Shockerwick House, County of Somerset, and by her (who died in 1846, aged 92 years) had issue,

- I. JOHN, of whom presently as successor to his father.
- II. Francis, of Springfield, Westbury-on-Trym, County of Gloucester, born in 1790, who married Juliana, daughter of Thomas Walker, Esq., of Redland, County of Gloucester, and died in 1845, leaving issue,
    1. Francis-Walker, now of Springfield, born in 1829.
    2. Charles-Walter, born in 1830.
    1. Louisa-Walker, who died in 1845.
    2. Frances-Harriet, who was married, in 1854, to the Rev. James Heyworth, of Henbury Hill, Co. of Gloucester, and has issue a daughter,
        Mabel-Frances Heyworth.

3. Juliana-Charlotte, who was married, in 1861, to George-Frederic, son of the Rev. James Heyworth, of Henbury Hill, 5th Dragoon Guards, and has issue,
>Frederic-James Heyworth, Lieut. Scots Guards, who served with the 2nd Bat. Scots Guards in the Expedition to the Soudan in 1885, and was present in the engagements at Hashem and Temai (medal with clasp).
>Cecil-Francis Heyworth, Lieut. Royal Fusiliers.
>May-Juliana Heyworth.
>Alice-Maud Heyworth.

I. Charlotte Savage, who died in 1847, without issue. She was buried beside her mother in the vault at Tetbury.

II. Elizabeth, who died at Cheltenham in 1866, aged 88 years, and was the last member of the family buried in the SAVAGE vault at Tetbury.

III. Louisa, married to Jacob Wilkinson, Esq., of Bath; died in 1858.

THE REV. JOHN SAVAGE died at Bath on the 17th March, 1803, and was buried in the family vault at Tetbury, March 26, 1803.[1] (See his epitaph under "Savage Monuments and Inscriptions at Tetbury.") He left his house and property, situated in or near Tetbury, for the use of his widow for her life (she died in 1846), and after her death to his eldest son. He was succeeded by his eldest son,

JOHN SAVAGE, Esq., of Tetbury, who married Rachel, daughter of Robert Claxton, Esq., of the Island of St. Kitt's, W.I. (She died in 1870, aged 79 years.) MR. JOHN SAVAGE, having settled at Henleaze, in the parish of Westbury-on-Trym, and his brother, Mr. Francis Savage, at Springfield, in the same parish, after the death of his mother sold the old house of Tetbury Close, in 1850, to Mr. Joseph Woods, Banker, of Tetbury, retaining, however, much of the old lands, which are still in possession of the family. For many of the latter years of his life MR. SAVAGE resided in Bath. MR. JOHN SAVAGE, by his wife Rachel (*née* Claxton), had issue,

I. John-Claxton, who died without issue at Oxford in 1836, aged 23 years.
II. Henry, who died in infancy.
III. FRANCIS, of whom presently as successor to his father in the representation of the TETBURY family.
IV. WILLIAM, of whom presently as successor to his brother FRANCIS.
I. Maria, who died in 1842 without issue.

---

[1] "1803. The Rev. Mr. John Savage, Rector of Beverstone, March 26."—*Burial Register of Tetbury Church.*

Mr. John Savage, of Tetbury, died in 1870, aged 85 years. His widow only survived him a few hours, and husband and wife were buried together in Bathford Churchyard, the burial-place of Mr. Savage's mother's family, the Wiltshires of Shockerwick. He was succeeded by his elder surviving son,

Francis Savage, Esq., J.P., who married Caroline-Bass, widow of —— Sharpe, Esq. (She died in 1885.) Mr. Francis Savage resided many years at Bath. He died 1882, aged 68 years, without issue, and was succeeded in the representation of the Tetbury family by his only surviving brother,

William Savage, in Holy Orders, Vicar and Prior of Burcombe, Wilts., who married Ann-Hunt, daughter of the Rev. Charles Holdsworth, Vicar of Stokenham, Co. Devon. (She died 1885, without issue.)

The present male representatives of the Savages of Tetbury are the last-named Rev. William Savage, Vicar of Burcombe, and his first-cousins, Francis Walker Savage, Esq., of Springfield, Westbury-on-Trym, Co. of Gloucester, and Charles Walter Savage, Esq.

Tetbury Close (from the grounds), seat of the Savages of Tetbury.

SAVAGE MONUMENTS AND INSCRIPTIONS AT TETBURY.

We quote the following from Mr. Lee's work on Tetbury:—

"The old Church, which was pulled down in 1777 to make room for the present one, contained many valuable monuments, especially an Altar one to the great William de Braose, which was erected under the arch which separated the Chancel from the South Aisle. It, with many others, was destroyed at the time of the rebuilding of the Church; but the inscriptions on several of the monuments have been preserved in Rudder, and in some of the Parish Registers. These are given below, together with some of the most remarkable in the Parish

Church."[1] Amongst those given are the following connected with the SAVAGE family at Tetbury:—

"On the left-hand, entering the old Church, was a little Chapel, wherein stood 'a fair wall-piece and lively effigies of JOHN SAVAGE, Gent., in his sable robes kneeling.'

"In the same Chapel lyeth the body of WILLIAM SAVAGE, Esq., the father of CHARLES SAVAGE, Gent., 'a great lover of antiquity, and a studious gentleman in Heraldrie.'

"There is also another wall-piece in memory of MR. JOHN SAVAGE.

"Over MR. SAVAGE's seat, facing the pulpit, hangeth a large tablet, whereon is written in letters of gold:—

'To the happy memory of CHARLES SAVAGE, of Broadway, in the County of Worcester, Esquire, and ELIZABETH his wife, the daughter of Anthony Abington, of Dowdeswell, Esq.'[2]

"On a brass tablet let into a stone slab, in the South Cloister of the present Church, having evidently been removed from the old one, is the following inscription:—

> Hic Jacet Franciscus Savage
> Filius Gvalteri Savage de Brod-
> way in com. Wigorn. armig. qui obi-
> it 2° Die Marcii, ano. Domini 1671.
> Maria uxor ejus Filia Edmun-
> di Estcourt Gen: obiit 26°
> Die August Anno Domi. 1645."

This FRANCIS SAVAGE was the founder of the Tetbury family.

"In the old Church, on the West side, there was a monument to JOHN SAVAGE, who was represented kneeling before an Altar, and this quaint inscription upon it in capital letters:—

> 'Our bodies all received from earth, Earth must againe them keepe
> Untill the Lord shall raise them up, to life from deadly sleepe:
> Our souls aloft to Heaven shall mount, where death them cannot presse;
> Death only is a dore to us, the true life to possesse;
> Our glory here still vanishing, prone to decay, to fall,
> Shall after death be stablished, be made Angelicall.
> What then! what then![3] though SAVAGE Death our *Savage* thus hath slayne,
> Regard it not, 'tis nothing, for it was with Christ to raigne.

'JOHN SAVAGE, Gent., deceas'd the 28th Maye, Anno Do. 1608.'"

---
[1] Lee: *History of Tetbury*, p. 146.
[2] Mr. Lee's authority is Abel Wantner's *MS. Hist. of Gloucestershire*.
[3] Observe the rapture of the poet as he delivers himself of his triumphant pun upon the name SAVAGE!

In the present Church, over the Vestry door, is this inscription:—
M. S.
Joannis Savage, Arm.
Qui e vitâ cessit,
Decembris 19,
A.D. 1772.
Francis Savage, Gen.
Obiit Oct. 18, A.D. 1769, Æ. 54.
Elizabetha Savage,
Obiit Nov. 14, A.D. 1777, Æ. 69.
Eleanora Savage,
Obiit Aug. 6, A.D. 1763, Æ. 49.

On a handsome monument on the South side of the Altar:—
M. S.
Joannis Savage, A.M.
Viri innocui, probi, pii,
qui vixit annos lix.
Obiit xvii. Mart. mdccciii.

INSCRIPTIONS ON THE MONUMENTS OF THE SAVAGES OF TETBURY EXISTING IN THE PARISH CHURCH OF TETBURY IN 1857.

(Copied from Lee's "History of Tetbury," Appendix III.)

(South Cloister.)

(1) Hic jacet FRANCISCUS SAVAGE, Filius Gualtieri Savage de Brodway in Com. Wigorn, Armig. qui obiit 2° die March Ano Domini 1671. MARIA, uxor ejus filia Edmundi Estcourt, gen. obiit 26° die August, Anno Domini 1645.
J. S. 1689.
C. S. 1750.
J. C. S. 1836.
M. S. Feb. 7th, 1842.
J. S. 1803.
C. S. 1846.

(2) Here lyeth the body of FRANCIS SAVAGE, late of this place, gent., who departed this life the seventeenth day of April, in the year of our Lord 1740, aged 63 years.

(3) Underneath are interred the mortal remains of SARAH, wife of William Savage of this town, gent. who died the 19th day of July, 1767, aged 73.
WILLIAM SAVAGE, died 15th Octr. 1775, aged 84.
C. S. 1847.

(South side of East wall, on a marble slab.)

(4) M. S.
JOHANNIS SAVAGE, Arm.
Qui e vita cessit
Decembris 19,
A.D. 1772,
Ætatis suæ 63.
FRANCISCUS SAVAGE, Gen.
Obiit Oct. 17, A.D. 1769, Æt. 54.
R.I.P.
ELIZABETHA SAVAGE
Obiit Nov. 14, A.D. 1777, Æt. 69.
ELEANORA SAVAGE
Obiit Aug. 6, A.D. 1763, Æt. 49.

(5)   (South side of Altar.)
M. S.
JOANNIS SAVAGE, A.M.
Viri, innocui, probi, pii,
qui vixit annos LIX.
Obiit XVII. Mart. MDCCCIII.

(North wall of South Cloister.)
(1)   Near this tablet
Lies interred the body of
JOHN CLAXTON SAVAGE, B.A., Oriel
Coll. Oxford;
eldest son of John and Rachel Savage,
of this place, and of Henleaze,
in this County.

He died at Oxford the 20th of Jany.,
1836,
Aged 23 years.
"What I do thou knowest not now,
But thou shalt know hereafter."

(South Cloister.)
(2)   To
MARIA,
only daughter of
John and Rachel Savage,
who died at Henleaze,
February 7th, 1842,
Aged 18 years.
"The Lord knoweth those that are His."

SECTION VII.—THE DORSETSHIRE BRANCH—SAVAGE OF BLOXWORTH.

Another branch of the ROCK SAVAGE (CLIFTON) family was that of SAVAGE OF BLOXWORTH, or, as it was anciently written, *Blocksworth*.

We find in old records that the SAVAGES had some connection with the County of Dorset as early as the reign of Henry IV.; and in the *Book of the Monastery of Hyde* mention is made of John Savage, King Henry IV.'s Escheator in Dorsetshire, who, in 1404, in his official capacity seized the manor of Piddlebrenthide in that county, a manor belonging to Hyde Monastery, on a charge of non-fulfilment of the conditions of tenure. But it was in the reign of Henry VIII. that Bloxworth came into the possession of the SAVAGE family; and then, in the person of RICHARD Savage, apparently the tenth son of SIR JOHN SAVAGE, "senior," who died in 1495, but described as "*the 6th* son of the House of Rock Savage, Cheshire," the DORSETSHIRE branch of the SAVAGES may be said to have been established.

In the 38 Henry VIII. (1546-7), "this manor, advowson, and capital messuage," writes Hutchins,[1] "and a fishery at Hungerhill, parcel of the possessions of Cerne Abbey, also the site and capital mansion, rectory, and advowson of the vicarage of Tarent Monkton, belonging to Tewksbury Abbey,[2] also a portion of the tythes there, parcel of Cranborn priory, were granted to RICHARD SAVAGE and George Strangeways, gentlemen, and their heirs, for £640 17 0, to be held of the King in chief by the fortieth part of a Knight's fee. 3 & 4 Philip and Mary, RICHARD SAVAGE, of Piddle Hinton, held this manor and advowson;

---
[1] *History of Dorsetshire*, vol. i., p. 105.
[2] We have already seen in what way the SAVAGES OF CHESHIRE became associated with Tewkesbury (*vide ante*, p. 76).

THE SAVAGES OF THE ARDS.

William, his son and heir, had his livery the same year: the yearly value was £19 13 4, so that the SAVAGES seem to have bought Strangeways' right. . . . Marsh, now a farm, situate two miles north-west of Bloxworth, was in 1658 in the possession of Henry Woolfrys, sen., and Henry, his grandson, son of Henry Woolfrys, deceased, for £1,450 convey this farm, with the appurtenances, to HENRY SAVAGE and heirs. 1661, 13 Car. II., PAUL SAVAGE, of London, goldsmith, son of HENRY, &c., conveys it, then consisting of a messuage, &c., 146 acres of land with common of pasture, &c., in Bloxworth and Marsh, for £1,800, to Haviland Hiley and his heirs."

"The seat formerly of the SAVAGES, now of Mr. Pickard," writes Hutchins, "stands in West Bloxworth, and was built by SIR GEORGE SAVAGE."

The following pedigree of the SAVAGES OF BLOXWORTH mainly follows that given in Hutchins, which is extracted from *The Visitation Book, 1623, continued*. It is supplemented, however, by some information drawn from the Parish Registers:—

RICHARD SAVAGE, Esq., of Piddle Hinton and Bloxworth, 6th son of the House of Rock Savage, Co. Chester, married Agnes, daughter of —— Willis, Esq., of Piddle Hinton, and by her had issue,

    I. WILLIAM, of whom presently as successor to his father.
    II. John, who married Agnes, daughter of —— Loop, and had issue,
        1. William, who married Alice, daughter of John Compton, Esq., and had issue,
            William.
            John.
            Job.
            Mary.
            Agnes.
            Elizabeth.

Mr. RICHARD SAVAGE was succeeded by his eldest son,

WILLIAM SAVAGE, Esq., of Bloxworth, who married Petronel, daughter of Robert Welsted, Esq., of Winborn Minster, and by her had issue a son and successor,

GEORGE SAVAGE, Esq., of Bloxworth, living in 1623, who married Mary, daughter and heiress of Gervase Ashley, Esq., of Sherborn, and by her (who died 1638) had issue,

    I. WILLIAM, of whom presently as successor to his father.
    II. Richard, of Sidling, baptised in 1591, who married Dorothy, daughter of William Hardy, Esq., and had issue,
        Katherine, married to Robert Brown, Esq., of Godmanston.

III. George, baptised in 1596.
IV. George, baptised in 1600.
V. Giles, baptised in 1603.
I. Agnes, baptised in 1588; married, in 1626, to Roger Walley.
II. Elizabeth, baptised in 1594.
III. Margery, baptised in 1597.
IV. Mary, baptised in 1606.
V. Petronel, baptised in 1608.
VI. Mabel, baptised in 1610.

Mr. GEORGE SAVAGE, of Bloxworth, was succeeded by his eldest son,

WILLIAM SAVAGE, Esq., of Bloxworth, Sheriff of Dorsetshire in 1640, born in 1590. He married Joan, daughter of Richard Page, Esq., of Uxenden, Co. Wilts., by whom he had issue a son and successor,

SIR GEORGE SAVAGE, of Bloxworth, Knt., baptised in 1636, who married Anne, daughter of Thomas, son of Edward Bower, Esq., of Spetisbury, and by her had issue,

I. WILLIAM, of whom presently as successor to his father.
II. George.
III. Thomas, who married Elizabeth, daughter of ——, and had issue,
    1. Elizabeth, baptised in 1668.
IV. Page, baptised in 1668.
V. John, baptised in 1672.
VI. Galen, baptised in 1678.

SIR GEORGE SAVAGE, of Bloxworth, died 1683. He was succeeded by his eldest son,

WILLIAM SAVAGE, Esq., of Bloxworth.

The property was sold by SIR GEORGE SAVAGE to Sir John Trenchard, whose family now hold it.

ARMS OF THE SAVAGES OF BLOXWORTH IN BLOXWORTH CHURCH.[1]

In the Church. On the north wall are these coats of arms:—
1. Savage, with a fleur-de-lys G. Crest, a beast's paw erect, in a ducal coronet, O. Under the former, 2, 1, and 6. 1. Savage. 2. Az., a cinque foil Erm. in a border of the 2nd. 3. G. a crescent. O. a chief chequée Az. and A. 4. O. a fess dancette Az. between three martlets ... in a border of the 2nd. 5. Sa. a chevron Erm. between three leopards' heads. A. in surtout O. a bend vaire. 6, 1, and 4. Savage, 2 and 3. O. a bend vaire cotized O.

---

[1] Extracted from Hutchins' *History of Dorsetshire*.

On the east wall—
1. Savage imp. Az. a cinquefoil Erm. in a border of the 2nd.   2. Savage imp. O. a chevron between three martlets Az.   3. Savage imp. Sa. a chevron Erm. between three leopards' heads. A.

Over the entrance—
Savage imp. O. a bend vaire, cotized of the 1st, with Savage's crest.

SECTION VIII.—LATER KENT BRANCH—SAVAGE OF BOUGHTON MOUNT.

Kent, with which the SAVAGES were so closely associated in ancient times, became once more the county of a branch of the old family in the 17th century. This branch was an offshoot of the SAVAGES OF BLOXWORTH, and was established at Boughton Mount, Kent, by Mr. JOHN SAVAGE of Lion's Inn.

The estate of Boughton Mount came into the possession of the SAVAGE family by intermarriage with the family of Alchorne, of Aylesford. "Boughton Mount," writes Ireland,[1] "formerly called Wychden, situated on the opposite, or northern, side of Coxsheath, near the parish of Loose, in the reign of Queen Elizabeth was the property of John Alchorne, of Aylesford. His grandson, of the same name, left an only daughter, who carried this estate in marriage to JOHN SAVAGE, Gent., of Lyon's Inn. He was descended from the SAVAGES of Blexworth, in Dorsetshire, a branch of those of Rock Savage, in Cheshire."

Of Anne Alchorne, who carried this estate to the SAVAGES, we get the following genealogy in Hasted :—

JOHN ALCHORNE, purchaser of Boughton Mount, married twice. His wives were, Anne, sister of Sir Thomas Colepepyr, of Aylesford, Knt., and Alice, daughter and heiress of Richard Walsingham, of Penshurst, Gent. By the latter he had issue,

I. JOHN, of whom presently as successor to his father.
II. Edward.
III. Robert.
I. Elizabeth.
II. Agnes.
III. Mary.

Mr. JOHN ALCHORNE was succeeded by his eldest son,

JOHN ALCHORNE, ESQ., of Boughton Mount, who married Mary, daughter of Henry Crispe, Esq., and, dying in 1636, was succeeded by his son,

JOHN ALCHORNE, ESQ., of Boughton Mount, who married Mary, daughter of Thomas Aynscombe, Esq., of Mayfield, Sussex, and was succeeded by his only daughter and heiress,

---
[1] Ireland: *History of Kent* (4 vols., London, 1829), vol. iii., pp. 12, 13.

ANNE ALCHORNE, of Boughton Mount, who married JOHN SAVAGE, ESQ., of Lion's Inn.

The following genealogy of the SAVAGES OF BOUGHTON MOUNT is gathered from Hasted and Ireland:—

JOHN SAVAGE, Esq., of Boughton Mount, by his wife, ANNE ALCHORNE, of Boughton Mount, had issue,

I. RICHARD, who died, in his travels, at Prague, in Bohemia, in 1669.

II. JOHN, of whom presently as successor to his father.

Mr. JOHN SAVAGE, of Boughton Mount, died, and was succeeded by his second and only surviving son,

JOHN SAVAGE, Esq., of Boughton Mount, High Sheriff of Kent in 1726, who married ——, and had issue a son,

I. RICHARD, of whom presently as successor to his father.

I. A daughter, married to Benjamin Hubble, Esq., of Town Malling.

Mr. JOHN SAVAGE, of Boughton Mount, died 9th April, 1726. He was succeeded by his son,

RICHARD SAVAGE, ESQ., of Boughton Mount, who married ——, daughter of —— Gulston, Esq. Mr. RICHARD SAVAGE dying without issue in 1780, the seat of Boughton Mount continued to be the residence of his widow until her death, when by his will it passed to the two daughters and co-heiresses of his late sister, who had married Benjamin Hubble, Esq., of Town Malling.[1]

The following further notices occur in Hasted's *Kent*:—

The lessee of the parsonage of West Farleigh is Mr. JOHN SAVAGE; but the Dean and Chapter reserve the presentation of the Vicarage to themselves.[2]

The Rev. Culpeper Savage, A.M.

Culpeper Savage, A.M., Vicar of Town Sutton, resigned 1747.[3]

Church of Stone. Vicars. Culpeper Savage, obt. 1753. He held this Vicarage with that of Sutton Valence, which he resigned in 1747, on being presented to that of Eastry, with the Chapel of Worth, which he held with this Vicarage by dispensation.[4]

---

[1] Ireland: *Hist. of Kent*, vol. iii., p. 13.
[2] Hasted: *Kent*, vol. ii., p. 297.
[3] *Id.*, vol. ii., p. 416.
[4] *Id.*, vol. iii., p. 542. There is a "Tablet or Monument at Boughton Montchedsea of Captn. J. Alchorne and Mary his wife, daughter of Thomas Aynscomb, Esq., of Mayfield, Sussex; and also of Richard Savage, their grandson, who died at Prague, in Bohemia, 1669; also of J. Alchorne, his son, who married a Colepepper, of the Aylsford family, and died in 1636. His only daughter married J. Savage, of Lyon's Inn."—*MS. note of Miss Savage of Town Malling*.

SECTION IX.—THE WARWICKSHIRE BRANCH—SAVAGE OF TACHBROOKE.

In a letter of Mr. Robert Landor, brother of WALTER SAVAGE LANDOR, written about the year 1864, and quoted by Forster in his life of the poet, occurs the following passage:—" It seems that the family was seven hundred years old, and several notices of my brother's death repeat the same tale. *We may go back about half way, but no further;*" and Mr. Forster, in a foot-note, remarks that the reference here is to the Tachbrooke branch of the SAVAGES. LANDOR'S pride in his maternal ancestry was no doubt excessive, and it might give a little trouble to trace his descent from the main stem of the Norman family whose name he delighted to bear; but for our own part we cannot question it. Neither Mr. Forster nor Mr. Robert Landor appears to have investigated the history of the Tachbrooke branch of the SAVAGE family with any great care. Forster commits the astonishing historical blunder of calling Sir Arnold Savage, who died in 1410, "Speaker of *Henry VII.'s* first House of Commons;" and Mr. ROBERT LANDOR found no traces of the SAVAGES in Warwickshire, apparently, earlier than the beginning of the 16th century.

The name occurs in connection with Warwickshire, notwithstanding, certainly as early as the end of the 12th century; and we know in what way a branch of the Stainesby family became identified with Warwickshire at that period (*vide ante*, p. 11). In *The Parliamentary Writs and Writs of Military Summons*, we find the following record at A.D. 1282 :—" Savage, William le, dec. (Warwick), Thomas de Eadnesoure, in right of his wife and Philippa de Menill, coparceners in the inheritance belonging to the said Willielmus, acknowledge the service of half a Knight's fee. Expedition against the Welch. Muster at Rhuddlan, 2 Aug." Again, we find the SAVAGE name associated with Tachbrooke-Malory in the reign of Edward III.; for Dugdale, writing of Whitnash, says, " Sir Thomas de Haseley had issue Robert, who granted this Manour unto John, his son; from whom descended Thomas Haseley, of Whitnash, who by his Deed dated on the day of S! Lucie the Virgin, 20 Ed. 3, past it away to Tho. Savage, of Tachebroke-Malory in this county; which T. Savage had a fair estate in lands here before, purchased by John, his father, from John Malory, of Walton, in Leicestershire, descended to him the said John, from Will. Malory his grandfather. All which lands together with the said Manour did the same T. Savage, by his Deed bearing date on the feast day of the translation of S! Edward the K., 1 R. 3, grant unto Benedict Medley of Warwick and his heirs."[1]

---

[1] *The Antiquities of Warwickshire*, by Sir William Dugdale (London, 1730), p. 365.

It is not here our purpose, however, to investigate the history of the English branches of the SAVAGE family with any minuteness, and we shall content ourselves with merely quoting some passages from the life of WALTER SAVAGE LANDOR which refer to his maternal descent, and to the property inherited from the SAVAGES OF TACHBROOKE.

ELIZABETH SAVAGE, of Tachbrooke, wife of Doctor Landor, of Warwick, and by him mother of WALTER SAVAGE LANDOR, was "eldest daughter and co-heiress with her three sisters of CHARLES SAVAGE, the head of an old Warwickshire family, the bulk of whose property had been transferred to a younger branch who bore the name of Norris. The paternal fortune, not very large even before it was divided, the eldest daughter shared with her three sisters; but after her marriage to Doctor Landor, two estates in Warwickshire, Ipsley-Court[1] and Tachbrooke (clear brook), were bequeathed to her by the representatives of the Norris branch of her family, two great-uncles, very wealthy London merchants; and so much of the original land of the SAVAGES OF TACHBROOKE was thus restored. The condition of strict entail to the eldest son accompanied the bequest, as if the object were to revive so far the consideration and condition of the old family; and, Doctor Landor's perpetual estates in Staffordshire being in like manner entailed, there remained for the younger children that might be born to his second marriage, apart from any possible bequests from other relatives or prudent savings by their mother, only the succession to a smaller estate in Buckinghamshire left equally to her and her three sisters by the same Mr. Norris, after expiry of the life interest in it of another descendant of the same family, the Countess of Conyngham. This estate was called Hughenden Manor, and is now[2] the property of Mr. Disraeli."[3]

On the death of his mother, WALTER SAVAGE LANDOR became the representative of the Tachbrooke branch of the SAVAGES.

---

[1] Forster adds in a note the following account of Ipsley-Court:—" In a letter to me of August, 1852, Landor described Ipsley-Court, which with his Llanthony estate has descended to his eldest son, as having been purchased by Mr. Samuel Savage early in the last century, with some farms and a park. 'He never resided there; and his steward, the rector of the parish, took down the noble old house, leaving only the two wings, one of which my father inhabited, adding a dining-room of thirty feet or more. The whole length exceeds ninety. The opposite wing contains offices, stables, coach-houses, &c. These wings were added in the time of Charles II. Nothing can be less architectural. The views are extensive, rich, and beautiful. My father cut down several thousand pounds worth of oaks; my mother as many. It is about forty years since I saw the place; but there are still, I hear, oaks of nearly a century's growth.'"—Forster: *Walter Savage Landor: a Biography*, vol. i., p. 5, *foot-note*.

[2] 1869.

[3] Forster: *Walter Savage Landor: a Biography*, vol. i., pp. 4–6.

"WALTER SAVAGE LANDOR, Esq., of Ipsley Court, Co. Warwick, and Llanthony, Co. Monmouth, born 30th Jan., 1775; married, May, 1811, Julia, daughter of Jean Thuillier, Baron Neuveville, of Bath, a lady of Swiss extraction, and had

ARNOLD-SAVAGE, his heir.
Walter-Savage.
Charles-Savage.
Julia-Elizabeth-Savage."[1]

Mr. WALTER SAVAGE LANDOR died in 1865, and was succeeded in the representation of the SAVAGES OF TACHBROOKE by his eldest son,

ARNOLD SAVAGE LANDOR, Esq., of Ipsley Court, Co. Warwick, and Llanthony, Co. Monmouth.

SECTION X.—AMERICAN BRANCHES—SAVAGE OF MASACHUSSETTS.

WILLIAM SAVAGE, Esq., living in 1600, 5th son of SIR JOHN SAVAGE, of Rock Savage, Knt. and 1st Baronet, and brother of SIR THOMAS SAVAGE, 1st Viscount SAVAGE, of ROCK SAVAGE, is presumed to have settled at Taunton, in Somersetshire, and to have been the father of

  I. THOMAS, of whom presently as founder of the SAVAGES OF MASSACHUSETTS.
  II. A son, afterwards Dean of Carlisle.
  III. A son, name unknown, who "lived 50 miles from London."

The first-named son,

THOMAS SAVAGE, born in 1608, went out to America with Sir Harry Vane in the *Planter* in 1635 (then aged 27), and was amongst those who helped to establish the Colonies of Massachusetts and Rhode Island. The 1st THOMAS SAVAGE, writes Farmer,[2] came to Boston, N.E., in 1635. He was admitted freeman in 1636; Member of Artillery Co. in 1637, and its Captain in 1651. He represented Boston in 1654 and during the eight succeeding years, Hingham in 1663, Andover in 1671. He was Major, and at one time was Commander-in-Chief of the Forces, in the early part of King Phillip's war, in 1675. He was elected Assistant in 1680 and 1681. Drake, in his *History of Antiquities of Boston, Mass.*, tells us—"The 1st Thomas Savage came from London with Sir Harry Vane in 1635, aged 27 years. Was admitted Member of the Church, January, 1637. Married, in 1637, Faith, 'daughter of William and Ann Hutchinson,' and, for siding with his wife's mother (Ann Hutchinson), was dismissed, and driven to unite with Gov. Coddington and others in the purchase of Rhode Island, where he remained for a short time, afterwards

---

[1] Burke: *Landed Gentry.*   [2] *History of Massachusetts.*

returning to Boston." MAJOR THOMAS SAVAGE married, *1st* (as we have seen), in 1637, Faith Hutchinson, and by her (who died Feb. 20, 1652) had issue, with other children,

    I. HABIJAH, of whom presently as successor to his father in the representation of the MASSACHUSETTS BRANCH of the SAVAGES.

    II. THOMAS, of whom and of whose line we shall treat separately below.

MAJOR SAVAGE married, *2ndly*, Mary, daughter of —— Simms, and by her had issue,

    I. Ephraim, who, with his brother Benjamin, settled in South Carolina.
    II. Perez, who died in slavery among the Turks.
    III. Ebenezer, of whom nothing is known.
    IV. Benjamin, who settled with his brother Ephraim in South Carolina.
    I. Hannah, married to Benj. Gillam.
    II. Dyonesia, married to Saml. Ravenscroft, of Virginia.
    III. Sarah, married to John Higginson, of Salem, Mass.
    IV. Mary, married to Mr. Thatcher.

MAJOR SAVAGE died Feb., 1682, aged 75 years, and was buried at Boston, where a tombstone, with the arms of SAVAGE OF ROCK SAVAGE, was erected over his grave. He was succeeded in the representation of the Massachusetts branch of the SAVAGE family by his eldest son,

    HABIJAH SAVAGE, who married Harriet, daughter of Major Lyng, by whom he had issue an eldest son and successor,

    THOMAS SAVAGE, who married Mehitath Harwood, and by her had issue an eldest son and successor,

    THOMAS SAVAGE, who married Elizabeth Fowle, and by her had issue an eldest son and successor,

MAJOR THOMAS SAVAGE (*from an old painting*).

JOHN SAVAGE, who married Ann Allen (*née* Scott), and by her had issue an only son and successor,

BENJAMIN SAVAGE, who married Elizabeth Dunn, and by her had issue a son, JOHN SAVAGE, who was living in 1864.

LINE OF THOMAS SAVAGE, 2ND SON OF MAJOR THOMAS SAVAGE, FOUNDER OF THE MASSACHUSETTS BRANCH OF THE SAVAGE FAMILY.

THOMAS SAVAGE, 2nd son of Major Thomas Savage who went to America with Sir Harry Vane, was born 28th May, 1640. He became a member of the Artillery Company in 1665; was an officer in Sir William Phipps's expedition to Canada in 1691; was subsequently Lt.-Colonel of the Suffolk Regt. Lt.-Col. THOMAS SAVAGE married, in 1664, ——, daughter of Joshua Scottow, and by her had issue,

    I. THOMAS, who married Margaret Lynde, and had issue,
        1. Margaret.
        2. Elizabeth.
    II. Habijah, who married Hannah Phillips, and had issue,
        1. Habijah.
        2. Thomas.
        3. Arthur.
        1. Hannah.
    III. ARTHUR, of whom presently.
    I. Elizabeth, married to Mr. Wadworth.
    II. Faith, married to Col. Waldo.
    III. Lydia, married to Timothy Prout.

LT.-COL. THOMAS SAVAGE died 2nd July, 1705, aged 65. His son,

ARTHUR SAVAGE, born 29th March, 1680, married Faith, daughter of —— Phillips, and by her had issue,

    I. SAMUEL-PHILLIPS, of whom presently.
    II. Arthur, married Mrs. Betsy Strops, and by her had issue,
        1. Arthur.
        1. Faith.

Mr. ARTHUR SAVAGE was succeeded by his son,

SAMUEL PHILLIPS SAVAGE, "a prominent man in the stirring scenes preceding and including the War of the Revolution, which ended in the Independence of the Colonies and the establishment of the United States of America. He was President of the Board of War of the Colony of Massachusetts. He was Moderator of the public meeting in the 'Old South Church' in Boston, Mass.,

whence, after exciting speeches, a number of men, disguised as Indians, went to the wharf, where a ship lay which had just arrived from England laden with tea, and threw the cargo overboard —the well-known historical incident which goes by the name of 'the Boston Tea-Party.'" He resided at Weston, near Boston.[1] SAMUEL PHILLIPS SAVAGE married Miss Sarah Tyler, and by her had issue,
 I. William, who died in infancy.
 II. Samuel, who married Miss Hope Doune, of Wellfleet, Cape Cod, and by her had issue,
  1. Samuel.
  2. William.
  3. Charles.
  4. Elisha.
  5. John.
  1. Hope.
 III. WILLIAM, of whom presently.
 IV. Joseph, who died in infancy.
 V. Joseph, Captain of Artillery, born 12th June, 1756.
Captain Joseph Savage fought throughout the War of the Revolution, being present at various battles, among which were those of Trenton, Monmouth, and Yorktown. Subsequent to the close of the war, he commanded at West Point, and was one of the original members of the Society of the Cincinnati. He married Miss Thatcher, and left issue,
 1. Samuel-Aldridge, who married Letitia Webber, and had issue,
  Joseph-Wyndham, who was a Member of the New York Legislature, a banker, and, at the time of his death, Mayor of the City of Rahway. He married, *1st*, Caroline F. Childs, and by her had issue,
   Josephine.
   Frances.

---

[1] His portrait, painted by Copley, from which our engraving is taken, is in the possession of Mr. John P. Savage, of Frankford, Philadelphia, and is a very fine picture. Copley was born at Boston, and went to England at the breaking out of the Revolutionary War. He was the father of Lord Lyndhurst, the famous Chancellor.

Mr. Joseph-Wyndham Savage married, *2ndly*, Sarah F. Pike, and by her had issue,
>Joseph-W.
>Walter.
>John-M'Clelland.
>Charlotte.
>Lavinia.
>Letitia.
>Sarah.

Mr. Savage married, *3rdly*, Frances Parcells, by whom he had no issue.

2. George-Washington, who has been President of the New York Board of Underwriters, Judge of the Court of Common Pleas, Union County, New Jersey, and is now (1887) United States Consul at Belfast, Ireland. The Honourable Judge Savage married, *1st*, in 1849, Mary Shaffer, and by her had issue,
>George-William, a Lawyer.
>Joseph-Webber, a Merchant.
>Edward-Shaffer, a Lawyer.

He married, *2ndly*, Elizabeth C. Marbacher, and by her has issue,
>Samuel-Phillips, a Lawyer.
>John-Marbacher, Vice-Consul, U.S., at Belfast.

3. William.
4. Charles-Thatcher.
5. Phillips.
1. Sarah.
2. Lucy.

VI. Henry, an officer in the Revolutionary Army, born 18th Dec., 1758.
I. Faith, who died unmarried.
II. Jane, who died unmarried.
III. Sarah, born 27th June, 1760; married to Hon. George Thatcher.
IV. Lucy, born 11th Nov., 1761; married to Amos Biglow.

Mr. SAMUEL PHILLIPS SAVAGE's third son,

WILLIAM SAVAGE, United States Consul at Jamaica, born 14th June, 1750, married Miss Jane Cope Demetrios, of Clarendon, Jamaica, and by her had issue,

I. JOHN, of whom presently.
II. James-Roden, who died by a fall from a horse.

Mr. WILLIAM SAVAGE was succeeded by his elder son,

JOHN SAVAGE, who married, *1st*, Miss E. A. White, and by her had issue,
I. William-James-Mathias, who died without issue.
I. Ann-Jane, who died without issue.
II. Sarah, who died without issue.
III. Mary-Elizabeth, married to H. J. M'Connell, and has had issue,
    1. Henry-L. M'Connell.

Mr. JOHN SAVAGE married, *2ndly*, Miss J. A. White, and by her had issue,
I. JOHN-RICHARD, of whom presently.
I. Ellen-Emma, who died without issue.
II. Virginia-Demetrios.
III. Ella-Eliza-Tilly, married to Chas. H. Irvine, and has had issue,
    1. William-Struthers Irvine.
    2. Mathilda Irvine.
IV. Julia-Rosalia, who died without issue.

Mr. JOHN SAVAGE was succeeded by his eldest son by his *2nd* marriage,

JOHN-RICHARD SAVAGE, of Frankford, Massachusetts, who married Sally, daughter of Elkana W. Keyser, and has issue,
    1. Mahlori-Levis.
    2. John-Richard.
    1. Jeannette, married to Robert Leville.
    2. Kate-Wallace.

SECTION XI.—AMERICAN BRANCHES *(continued)*—VIRGINIA BRANCH—SAVAGE OF "SAVAGE'S NECK."

Another THOMAS SAVAGE, born in 1592, and stated to have been one of the Cheshire family, and to have come from Chester, arrived in Virginia with Captain Newport in 1607. When Newport wished to take the Indian Namontacke to England, and there show him to his fellow-countrymen, young SAVAGE consented to remain as a hostage for his safe return with the Indian Chief Powhatan. During his residence with Powhatan, who is stated to have become much attached to him, he learned the Indian language, and he acted as Interpreter in the Company's service, in which he early attained the rank of Ensign, and afterwards that of Captain. He established himself on the Eastern Shore of Virginia, on the peninsula between Chesapeake Bay and the Atlantic Ocean, probably about 1621-2, when Sir George Yardley was Governor, and Mr. John Pory Secretary.

In Mr. Pory's account of an expedition to the Eastern Shore, it is stated of CAPTAIN THOMAS SAVAGE that, "being a boy, he was left with Powhatan for Namontacke, and to learn the language, and, as this author affirmeth, with much honestie and good success hath served the publicke without any recompense, yet had an arrow shot through his body in their service." CAPTAIN SAVAGE was evidently a favourite with the Indians by whom he was surrounded on the Eastern Shore of Virginia, for about this time there was given to him from them, by their Chief Ismee Sechemee, a tract of 9,000 acres of land. This gift was confirmed by the Company, a Patent reciting the facts being issued by them, the record of which is still to be found in the city of Richmond, the capital of Virginia. This land, situated in the lower county of the Eastern Shore, Northampton, is known as "Savage's Neck," and a part of it was owned, and for some years dwelt in, by a descendant of CAPTAIN THOMAS SAVAGE, WILLIAM LYTTLETON SAVAGE, of the present generation. CAPTAIN THOMAS SAVAGE married Hannah (or Ann) ——, who survived him, and seems to have subsequently married Daniel Cugly, for in 1686, by an order of Court, JOHN SAVAGE, son of THOMAS, becomes guardian of "his sister, Margery Cugly." By his wife Hannah (or Ann), CAPTAIN THOMAS SAVAGE had issue (with other children who died young),

JOHN SAVAGE, who succeeded his father. JOHN SAVAGE was born in 1624. He attained to some distinction in the Colony, was a Magistrate, a Captain of the King's Forces, and represented his County in the House of Burgesses. He married, 1*st*, Anne Elkington, of England, and by her had issue,

 I. Susanna, married to John Kendall.
 II. Grace, married to George Corbin.

CAPTAIN SAVAGE married, 2*ndly*, Mary Robins (who survived him and afterwards married William Cowdrey), and by her had issue,

 I. THOMAS, of whom presently as successor to his father.
 II. John, born in 1673.
 III. Elkington, born in 1675.
 I. Mary, born in 1671.
 II. A daughter, unnamed when her father's will was written.

CAPTAIN JOHN SAVAGE died in 1678. He was succeeded by his eldest son,

THOMAS SAVAGE, born in 1669, who married Alicia Harmanson, and by her had issue,

 I. THOMAS, of whom presently as successor to his father.
 II. George.

I. Margaret.
II. Mary.
III. Zeribee.
IV. Sophia.

MR. THOMAS SAVAGE died in 1728. He was succeeded by his eldest son,

THOMAS SAVAGE, born about 1700. He married, in 1722, Esther, daughter of Nathaniel Lyttleton, who, on the death without issue of her brother, Southey, became the representative of the elder branch of the Lyttleton family in Virginia, and inherited the Lyttleton family estates there. By his wife Esther (née Lyttleton) MR. THOMAS SAVAGE had issue,

I. THOMAS, who died abroad, unmarried.
II. NATHANIEL-LYTTLETON, of whom presently as representative of the families of SAVAGE OF SAVAGE'S NECK, and LYTTLETON of Virginia.
I. Sarah.
II. Margaret.
III. Hannah.

MR. THOMAS SAVAGE died in 1737. He was succeeded by his surviving son,

NATHANIEL LYTTLETON SAVAGE, heir to his father's estate and that of the Lyttletons, born in 17—. Mr. NATHANIEL LYTTLETON SAVAGE was a member, with a colleague, George Savage, of the Convention from the County of Northampton which assembled on the 6th May, 1776, and framed the first Constitution of Virginia. He married Anne Reynolds, of York, and by her had issue,

I. THOMAS-LYTTLETON, of whom presently as successor to his father.
II. Nathaniel-Lyttleton.
III. William.
IV. John.
V. Joseph.
VI. George.
VII. Southey.
I. Susanna.
II. Anne.

MR. NATHANIEL LYTTLETON SAVAGE died in 17—. He was succeeded by his eldest son,

THOMAS LYTTLETON SAVAGE, born at Yorktown, Virginia, 8th January, 1760. He married, 1st, Mary-Burton, daughter of Col. Lyttleton Savage, and by her had issue,

I. NATHANIEL-LYTTLETON, who died in childhood.
1. Maria, married to Mr. Severn Eyre Parker.

II. Leah-Lyttleton, married to Mr. Harold L. Wilson.

MR. THOMAS LYTTLETON SAVAGE married, 2ndly, Margaret Teackle, and by her had issue,

    I. THOMAS-LYTTLETON, of whom presently as successor to his father.

    II. William-Lyttleton, born 5th September, 1812, studied Law with General B. Taylor, of Norfolk, and removed from Virginia to the latter city. He married, 11th June, 1840, Sarah Chauncey, daughter of Elihu Chauncey, of Philadelphia (of the old English family of Chauncey), and died 25th December, 1867, leaving issue,

        1. William-Lyttleton.
        2. Charles-Chauncey.
        3. Henry-Chauncey.
        4. Albert-Lyttleton.
        1. Henrietta-Chauncey, married to Mr. A. Charles Barclay, of Philadelphia, and has issue,
            William-Lyttleton Barclay.
            Walter Barclay.
            Henry-Chauncey Barclay.
            Mary-Savage Barclay.
            Emily Barclay.
        2. Mary-Eyre, married to Joshua Lidd Howell, of New Jersey, and has issue,
            Evelyn-Virginia Howell.

    I. Anna, born 10th February, 1797, married to George Armstrong Lyon, of Carlisle, Pennsylvania.

    II. Susan, born 3rd December, 1801, and married to Henry Park Custis Wilson, of Maryland.

    III. Mary-Burton, born 2nd April, 1804, and married to William Lyttleton Eyre, of Virginia.

    IV. Elizabeth-Upshur, born 19th June, 1806, who is now (July, 1887) the survivor, unmarried, of the children of THOMAS-LYTTLETON and MARGARET-TEAKLE SAVAGE.

    V. Eleonora (or Ellen), who was born 31st October, 1808, and died in childhood.

MR. THOMAS LYTTLETON SAVAGE was succeeded by his elder son,

THOMAS LYTTLETON SAVAGE, born 19th November, 1798. He married, *1st*, Louisa M. Mayo, and, *2ndly*, Lauretta Winder, and had issue,

    I. THOMAS-LYTTLETON, of whom presently as successor to his father.

    I. Maria, married to Mr. Fitzhugh.

MR. THOMAS LYTTLETON SAVAGE was succeeded by his only son,
THOMAS-LYTTLETON SAVAGE.

In the will of CAPTAIN THOMAS SAVAGE there appears the bequest of "a silver cup with the sign of *the Swan* pictured on it," to his son John, at the time receiving his education in England. Also, there is a small old-fashioned spoon, with the figure of *a Swan* distinctly engraved on the handle, which came from the stock of silver of a SAVAGE nearly related to the father of the late MR. THOMAS LYTTLETON SAVAGE. With the figure of *the Swan* is associated a tradition to the effect that Henry VII. granted the use of the badge of *a Swan*, as a high honour, to the Sir John Savage of Clifton who fought for him at Bosworth Field, and afterwards at the Siege of Boulogne, where, being surrounded by the enemy and refusing quarter, he was slain. This tradition has been handed down from generation to generation in the Virginia family of SAVAGE, and we give it as it has been related to us.

The Virginia SAVAGE estate was sold between thirty and forty years ago, and has passed into the hands of several successive owners.

With this brief account of the English and American branches of the SAVAGES of Scarcliffe and Stainesby, we pass to a more detailed history of the family in ULSTER, and commence with their settlement there, in the 12th century, in the person of WILLIAM, BARON SAVAGE, of the ARDS.

ARDKEEN CASTLE HILL, Co. Down, site of the ancient stronghold of the SAVAGES OF ARDKEEN, with CHAPEL (to the left), and portion of STRANGFORD LOUGH.

CHAPTER III.

THE SAVAGES OF THE ARDS.—SAVAGE OF ARDKEEN, MAIN LINE.

The Anglo-Norman Conquest of Ulster, A.D. 1177.

IN the interests of history it is to be regretted that the accounts we have received of the Anglo-Norman invasion of Ulster are so deficient in minuteness. A general outline of the movements of the daring little army under the leadership of Sir John de Courcy, and a description more or less vivid of two or three picturesque incidents, are all that have been transmitted to us. The very names of De Courcy's companions-in-arms, with a few exceptions, have been ascertained only by inference. And yet there are few more brilliant military achievements chronicled in the records of that warlike age. The main facts of the dashing expedition have been described, however, over and over again; every student of Anglo-Irish history is familiar with the gigantic figure of the hero of the Ulster Conquest; many have been captivated by the tale of the wounded Sir Amorey Tristram and the wild roses which he chose for his armorial bearings and transmitted to his descendants, the Earls of Howth; and few are unaware that the most powerful of the knights who fought by De Courcy's side and established themselves firmly in the heart of the Irish enemy in the North were Savage, Russell, and Mandeville.

With twenty-two Anglo-Norman knights and three hundred soldiers De Courcy, encouraged by Henry II., started from Dublin on the venturous invasion in the month of January, A.D. 1177. In four days the little band had reached Downpatrick. Hence, with varying successes, which have been recounted,

SAVAGE OF ARDKEEN, MAIN LINE.

probably with considerable veracity, in the *Annals of the Four Masters*, they pushed their conquest northwards till they brought, nominally at least, under Anglo-Norman dominion a tract of country corresponding roughly to the present counties of Louth, Down, Antrim, and half of Londonderry. The seat of De Courcy's Palatine "Earldom" was established by him at Downpatrick, and presently we find him exercising all an Earl Palatine's powers and privileges, and issuing charters witnessed by his various Barons.

The Anglo-Norman Conquest of Ulster, A.D. 1177.

As we have said, one of the most powerful of the Ulster Barons was SIR WILLIAM LE SAVAGE, with whom, as the first representative of the Irish branch of the SAVAGES, we commence the history of the family in Ulster.

I.—WILLIAM, BARON LE SAVAGE (BORN ABOUT A.D. 1150).

SIR WILLIAM LE SAVAGE, KNT., afterwards a Baron of Ulster, was, as we have seen, a scion of the house of SAVAGE of SCARCLIFFE, STAINESBY, and CLIFTON (ROCK SAVAGE), and appears to have been the 4th son of SIR GEOFFREY LE SAVAGE, of Stainesby, by his wife Letice, daughter of Sir Henry de Arderne (see p. 11, *supra*).

WILLIAM, BARON LE SAVAGE, born about A.D. 1150.

In most of the Anglo-Norman victories in Ulster, and in some of the defeats, WILLIAM LE SAVAGE was probably a sharer. When De Courcy offended King John, and his great rival De Lacy was empowered by the King to wrest Ulster from him and take him prisoner, and when he marched against the English in Ulster with a formidable army, WILLIAM LE SAVAGE stood firmly by his old friend and leader; and when De Courcy was brought under, the BARON LE SAVAGE was one of those whose sons became hostages for him to the King.

"The earliest mention of the Barons of Ulster" (we quote from the *Ulster Archæological Society's Journal*) "is in [a mandate] from King John, addressed to them, 6th year of his reign, stating that if they did not cause their lord, John de Courcy, to come to the King's service, as they were bound, and gave hostages to do, he, the King, would seize their hostages and estates. Lynch says these Barons were of his [De Courcy's] kindred and friends, amongst whom he made sub-infeudations of that vast territory; but unfortunately, he neither gives the writ nor the names of those to whom addressed. We, however, have from Dr. Butler *(Notes to Grace's Annals, Irish Archæological Society's Publications)*, that ROBIN, son of WILLIAM SALVAGE, was one of those hostages, and the title 'LORD SAVAGE' frequently occurs in Irish history. . . . Without resting on tradition, we have on written evidence, of the Barons of Ulster, as far as the present writer's researches reach, the Barons SAVAGE, Russell, Bisset, White, and Crolly. . . . The Palatines' power of creating Barons does not

WILLIAM, BARON LE SAVAGE, born about A.D. 1150.

appear to have been profusely exercised. Davies only mentions eleven in Ireland, though this was far short of the number; of whom two alone, the Baron Misset (correctly Bisset) and the BARON SAVAGE, were in Ulster."[1]

Of the mandate above referred to, and of the occasion of it, Banks gives the following account:—"The story of Earl John having been seized by Lacy and sent prisoner to London, and confined there in the Tower, seems controverted by a record preserved in that very Tower of London; which, if it is to be relied on, seems as if he surrendered himself to the King, and delivered hostages for his appearance within a certain time, limited even by L. J. Lacy himself. Which hostages were,[2] 'Milo, filius Johannis de Curcy, Juvenis, et ROBINUS, filius WILLIELMI SALVAGE, liberantur Roberto de Veteri-Ponte in custodia; Johannes de Curcy, filius Rogeri de Cestria, liberatur Willielmo Briwer; Walkelinus, filius Augustini de Ridal, liberatur Willielmo Boterell, vice-comiti Corunbiæ; Petrus, filius Willielmi Haket, liberatur Reginaldo de Clifton, constabulario de Dunster; Alexander, filius Willielmi Sarazin, liberatur Willielmo de Blunvill, constabulario de Corf; Johannes, filius Adæ Camerarii, et Johannes, filius Richardi, filii Roberti, liberantur Hugoni de Nevill.' Upon the King's accepting the challenge [of the King of France], he demands him of his *barons in Ulster* by the aforesaid record (a proof he was not in the Tower), viz.:—'*Rex omnibus baronibus de Ultoniâ*, &c., *qui juraverunt et obsides dederunt pro Johanne de Curcy* salutem—Mandamus vobis et vos districte summonemus quatenus venire faciatis Dominum vestrum Johannem de Curcy in servitium nostrum, unde jurastis et obsides vestros tradidistis, sicut eosdem obsides et feoda vestra diligitis: scientes quod nisi venerit in servitium nostrum infrà terminum quod ei inde a justiciario nostro statutus fuit, nos ad obsides vestros et ad feoda vestra nos capiemus. Et in hujus rei, &c. Teste domino Norwicensi apud Geitinton primo die Septembris.' Upon their assent to send him," Banks continues, "the King grants him a safe conduct. 'Rex, &c., omnibus, &c., salutem—Sciatis quod concessimus salvum et securem conductum Johanni de Curcy, et suis quos secum duxerit in veniendo ad nos et in redeundo usque ad medium quadragesimæ Anno, &c., VI°. Et in hoc rei, &c. Teste meipso apud Brehill XXI° die Octobris.' This procedure shows his [De Courcy's] confinement in the Tower to have happened upon the delivery of him to the King by his hostages; who, for his safe conduct, placed him there until the day of combat."[3]

---

[1] The settlement of the Bissets in Ulster, as will be seen, was subsequent to the Anglo-Norman invasion.
[2] Rot. Pat., anno 6 John. 1 mo. Dorso.
[3] Banks: *Dormant and Extinct Peerage*, vol. i., p. 59.

SAVAGE OF ARDKEEN, MAIN LINE.

Not long after the Ulster Conquest we find WILLIAM, BARON LE SAVAGE, a witness to John de Courcy's charter to the Prior of Down. The following are amongst the names affixed to that document:—

WILLIAM, BARON LE SAVAGE, born about A.D. 1150.

"Witness, Richard Fitzrobert, *my Seneschal;* Roger de Castria, *my Constable;* Adam, *my Chamberlain;* William and Henry Copland, William Saraceno, William de Courcy, Philip de Hasting, Simon Passelaw, WILLIAM SAVAGE, Richard de Dundonald, Reiner his brother, William Hoch, Walter de Logan, Master Walter."

Several of those whose names appear in this list of witnesses figure amongst the territorial Magnates of Ulster. Historians seem to be agreed that the conquered territory (including the modern Louth) was divided amongst the following leaders:—SAVAGE, Russell, Audley, De Gernon, Vernon, De Verdun, Clinton, Mandeville, Jordan, Stanton, Poer, Copeland, Chamberlaine, Ridal, Stokes, Passelevy, Martel, Logan, Sendal. White and Bisset are names that appear in Ulster subsequently. Many of these family-names are associated with the early English baronage; and most of the companions of De Courcy were probably scions of Anglo-Norman or English houses then or subsequently ennobled. Of the leaders enumerated, Gernon, Vernon, and Verdun (all names that have been, like that of SAVAGE, connected with Derbyshire) appear to have settled in and about Louth, the Irish *Uriel;* Russell in the south-eastern part of Lecale, at Killough; Copeland has left his name in the Copeland Isles, off the north-east coast of the County of Down; Logan was established in Antrim; Mandeville originally in Dufferin; Audley on the southern margin of Lough Coyne; and SAVAGE settled in the Ards, that fertile peninsula which extends from Belfast Lough to Ballyquintin Point and lies between the great inlet of Strangford and the Irish Sea.

There was one spot in the Upper Ards peculiarly fitted for the site of a formidable fortified castle. The elevated peninsula of Ardkeen, which juts out into Strangford Lough, three miles west-by-east of the town now known as Portaferry, had been "one of the most important strongholds of the ancient Irish, who made it a place of refuge from the violence and rapacity of the Danes, and had a large well-fortified camp protected on three sides by the sea, with extensive pastures in the rear for their cattle."[1] The peninsula, according to Lewis, was "originally called Ard-*Coyne*, from its situation on the shores of the Lake which was formerly called Lough *Coyne*." According to Harris[2] and the *Parliamentary Gazetteer of Ireland*, the name "Ardkeen"

---

[1] *See* Lewis's *Topographical Dictionary of Ireland*, article "Ardkeen."
[2] *See* Harris's *History of the County Down*.

WILLIAM, BARON LE SAVAGE, born about A.D. 1150.

signifies "high head." But the present Bishop of Down and Connor (Dr. Reeves), in his admirable *Ecclesiastical Antiquities of Down, Connor, and Dromore*, suggests a better etymology, and says that the promontory was probably so called from ᴀʀᴅ ᴄᴀᴏɪɴ, which means "the pleasant height." Its loftiest point, by the Ordnance Survey measurement, is 140 feet above the level of the Lough, by the waters of which at full tide it is surrounded on three sides. On the summit of this "pleasant height," almost immediately after the conquest of the Ards, was built the castle of the SAVAGE family known ever since its foundation as the CASTLE OF ARDKEEN. In 1180 this Castle is referred to by De Courcy in his Charter to Black Abbey, in the Ards (quoted by the Bishop of Down and Connor in the *Ecclesiastical Antiquities*), and is exempted from the payment of tithes to that Abbey. It was a large and strongly-built castle "surrounded by a rampart, and looking boldly down upon the Lake." From its summit would be visible a splendid panorama of wood and sea and mountain. Eastward the Ards—the "little hills" of Uladh—undulated away to the Channel; north, west, and south stretched the blue waters of the vast Fiord, studded with its many islands, on some of which gleamed the chapels of the early Irish saints, and bearing on its shores here and there the lately-erected castles of the Norman conquerors; while in the distance rose the lofty rock of Scrabo, and further off the blue peaks of Ulster, from Slieve Donard to Divis and Cave Hill. It has been supposed that at this time also the Castle of Portaferry was built by the BARON LE SAVAGE. This latter Castle was designed as a fortress to guard the Ards territory from incursions from across the narrow strait at the mouth of Strangford Lough—the "ferry" which gives Portaferry its name. At the south side of Ardkeen Castle Hill, not far from the margin of the Lough, a church was erected, probably at a still earlier period, and from it Ardkeen parish takes its designation. According to Bishop Reeves, the church was formerly styled "Ecclesia Sanctæ Mariæ de Ardkeene (*Cal. Canc. Hib.*, p. 131)." This church and the surrounding cemetery became the burial-place of the SAVAGES OF ARDKEEN.

In the whole of Ulster there was probably no territory better situated for purposes of defence than the Ards, and no spot in the Ards more fitted to receive a stronghold of the future lords of the district than the peninsula of Ardkeen, which bears a kind of miniature likeness to the peninsula of the Ards itself— open to land-attacks at one side only, and surrounded on all others by the sea.[1]

---

[1] The admirable defensive position of the Ards was long afterwards appreciated and described in a tract prepared by Sir Thomas Smith in relation to the settlement of that district in Elizabeth's reign, and reprinted by the Rev. George Hill in an Appendix to *The Macdonnells of Antrim*.

And it is remarkable that, during the seven hundred years that have elapsed since the Conquest, the SAVAGE family of all the Anglo-Norman settlers in Ulster has been the most successful, stable, and permanent, and, with the sole exception of Russell of Killough, is the only one of the original Anglo-Norman families in Ulster that at the present moment possesses any portion of the lands acquired with the sword at the invasion of A.D. 1177.[1]

WILLIAM, BARON LE SAVAGE, had two sons,

    I. ROBERT, of whom presently as successor to his father, and representative of the SAVAGE family in Ulster; and

    II. Thomas.

THE BARON LE SAVAGE was succeeded in the representation of the SAVAGE family in Ulster by his elder son,

II.—SIR ROBERT LE SAVAGE, KNT. (LIVING IN 1204).

In the *Calendar of State Papers*, at the date A.D. 1205, but more correctly A.D. 1204,[2] we find the following abstract of the Latin document already quoted from Banks:—

"Hostages for John de Curcy of Ulster:—

Young Milo Fitz John de Curcy ROBIN, SON OF WILLIAM SALVAGE	To be delivered in custody to Robert de Vipont.
John de Curcy, son of Roger de Chester	......Wm. Briwerr.
Wilikin Fitz Austin Augustine de Ridel	......Wm. Borerell, Sheriff of Cornwall.
Peter Fitzwilliam Hacket	To be delivered to Reginald de Clifton, Constable of Dunster.
Alexander Fitzwilliam Sarazein	To be delivered to William, the Constable of Corf.
John Fitz Adam, the Chamberlain John Fitz Richard Fitz Robert	To be delivered to Hugh de Neville.

Pat., 6 John, M. 1. dors."

The ROBIN, son of WILLIAM SAVAGE, here mentioned as ordered by King John to be delivered in custody to Robert de Vipont, along with young Milo de Curcy, son of John de Curcy, is one of the hostages to whom reference is made above in the extract given from the *Ulster Archæological Society's Journal*.

---

[1] The family of NUGENT OF PORTAFERRY, as has been before mentioned, and as shall be explained hereafter, representing *paternally* the Portaferry branch of the family of SAVAGE, still enjoys possession of a considerable portion of the old SAVAGE territories in the Little Ards.

[2] See an article on "John de Courci," by Mr. J. H. Round, in the *Dictionary of National Biography*, vol. xii.

SIR ROBERT LE SAVAGE (living in 1204). His close association with Milo, his being placed along with him in the custody of the same person, and the fact that he occupies the second place in the King's list of the hostages, are noteworthy, and seem to point to the eminence of his father, and perhaps to some blood-relationship with De Courcy. ROBIN is, of course, the diminutive of Robert—a name that frequently appears in the SAVAGE family. ROBERT LE SAVAGE may have been under age at this time. At any rate, we may assume that he was born some time about the year 1180.

The Robert de Vipont in whose custody ROBERT LE SAVAGE was placed, Banks informs us, "was in great favour with King John, and assisted the said King against his rebellious subjects." In the 12th Henry II. he held eight knights' fees of the honour of Torneys, and accounted £85 for the farm of the honour of Tickhill, brought into this family by reason of his marriage with Idonea, daughter and heiress of John de Bouilli, or Buisli. He was with the King in France; and for his services there had a grant of the castles of Appleby and Burgh, with the whole of the bailiwick of Westmoreland; which grant included the barony, though not the borough of Appleby, which before had been granted to the burgesses there. . . . By Idonea his wife . . . he had issue a son John, and a daughter Christian, who married Thomas, son of William, son of Ralph, baron of Graystock; and, dying the 12th Henry III., was succeeded by John his son and heir, who was Sheriff of Westmoreland, and died about the 26th Henry III.[1]

We may reasonably assume that ROBERT LE SAVAGE was placed either in the Castle of Appleby or in that of Burgh.

Five years later, July 10, A.D. 1210, SIR ROBERT LE SAVAGE is mentioned in the State Papers as one of several knights to whom *prests* (loans) were made by King John at Carrickfergus Castle during the King's visit to that great royal fortress of Ulster; and his name appears again as a knight to whom a *prest* was made at Dublin on "Thursday next after the Assumption." Amongst the names of the knights to whom prests were made on this latter occasion before the Earl of Salisbury and Richard de Marisco, occur those of the Earl of Albemarle, 100s. paid to Ralph Gernon, Richard de Furnell, ROBERT LE SALVAGE, William le Butiller (Butler), William de Courtenay, Henry Fitzgerald, John de Rochfort, Warin Fitzgerald, Norman d'Arcy, and 1 Knight of Flanders.

On the 22nd Dec., 1215, SIR ROBERT LE SAVAGE made with King John "a fine of 10 marks for his release"—the occasion of which does not appear.[2]

---

[1] Banks, vol. i., p. 193.
[2] See *Calendar of State Papers, Ireland*, 17–18 John 1215.

"Robertus Le Savage de Hibernia finem fecit cum Domino Rege per decem marcarum pro deliberatione sua." *Rot. Fin. T.L.*

<small>Sir Robert Le Savage (living in 1204).</small>

We find THOMAS SAVAGE, whom we conclude to be the younger son of the BARON LE SAVAGE, and younger brother of SIR ROBERT, also mentioned as one of the knights to whom prests were made at Carrickfergus in A.D. 1210.

SIR ROBERT LE SAVAGE was succeeded in the representation of the SAVAGE family in Ulster by his son and heir,

III.—HENRY LE SAVAGE (LIVING IN 1259; DIED ABOUT 1277).

In the "account of Ulster of the whole of the 45th year of King Henry [A.D. 1260–61], by Nicholas de Dunhened, the Seneschal," a fac-simile of which is printed in the Irish MSS. edited by Mr. Gilbert, HENRICUS LE SAUAGE is stated to have been fined "half a mark, because, though attached, he did not appear"—"HENRICUS LE SAUAGE dimidiam marcam quia attacheatus non venit." The occasion of this *attachment*, or summons, we have not been able to ascertain; but in the same account appears against the name of Thomas Fitzgilbert an entry of "half a mark by *plevin*[1] of the same HENRY." This HENRY was probably identical with HENRY LE SAVAGE, the son of SIR ROBERT LE SAVAGE.

<small>Henry Le Savage (living in 1259; died about 1277).</small>

In A.D. 1272, HENRY SAVAGE, "son of SIR R. SAVAGE," is mentioned in the State Papers as having been a juror, along with his kinsmen *Hugh Savage, Henry Savage of Tullaneske* (Tullacheskegh, the modern Ballyskeagh, in N.W. of Newtown Ards Parish), *Thomas Savage*,[2] and others, at an Inquisition taken at Le Finaleburn, in Twescard (North Antrim),[3] in 1272, "by Sir William Fitzwarrin, Seneschal of the Lord Edward in Ulster, as to how Sir Henry Mandevyle behaved in regard to the King, the Lord Edward, and the English of Ulster," after the Lord Edward "had made him Bailiff in Twescard."

HENRY LE SAUVAGE, we learn from the State Papers, held *in capite* of the King, 5 Knights' Fees by service of 1 Knight. In demesne also he held 18 corucates—about 2,520 acres—of land. He had many free tenants who owed suit of court in his manor.

During his lifetime, in 1244, it is stated that the SAVAGE family built a Dominican Friary at Newtown Ards. "A convent of Dominican Friars," writes Harris,[4] was settled here in the year 1244 by the SAVAGES (as it is said), in

---

[1] Security by pledge, or by pledging.

[2] He is mentioned above as a Knight who received a prest at Carrickfergus. He was probably uncle of HENRY LE SAVAGE.

[3] "The word Twescard is an anglicism of the Irish Tuaiṛceaṛt, 'the North,' and was borrowed from the natives by the English settlers, to denote the territory around Coleraine."—*Reeves.*

[4] *History of the County Down.*

which Chapters of the order were held in 1298 and 1312."[1] In De Burgo's *Hibernia Dominicana* we have the following account of this Friary :—" De Villanovano, seu Newtonensi, Cœnobio Sancti Columbæ in Dunensi, Agro Ultoniæ. Anno 1244. Apud Villam Novam, alias Newtonam, Cœnobium fuisse Ordinis Prædicatorum Anno 1244 fundatum, referunt Scriptores hucusque pro Cœnobiorum nostrorum Erectionibus laudati, de illoque extat Decretum Illustrissimi æquè ac Clarissimi Oliverii Plunkett, Archiopiscopi Armacani, et Commissarii Apostolici, cujus expressum Tenorem superius exscripsi, ubi etiam anteriorem de isto Conventu Litem, á Fratribus Minoribus moram, recensui Cœterùm Fundatoris Nomen latuit prorsùs Waræum, tàm in *Antiquitatibus Hibernis*, quàm in *Hibernicarum Rerum Annalibus.* Asserit tamen *Alimandus,* eum fuisse aliquem ex Anglicana, SAVAGEORUM Familia, quæ me Teste, adhuc opulenta viget in Territorio de Ardes, præsertim circà Pagum Maritimum de Portaferri."[2] The foundation of the Newtown Ards Friary is attributed to the SAVAGES, again, by the author of the *Histoire Monastique d'Irlande* (Louis Augustin Allemand), dedicated in 1690 to James II. of England, Marie d'Este de Modene, and James Francis Edward, "né Duc de Cornouaille" :—" Dans le Comté de Doune, á Newtowne, petit lieu sur la Côte dans la peninsule d'Ardes, qui est aujourd'hui une Isle depuis qu'on a fait une canal qui joint l'extremité septentrionale du lac de Cone avec la Baye de Knockfergus. Il y a donc à Newtowne un bien beau Couvent bati en 1244, par les SAVAGES, Seigneurs Anglois. Cette maison etoit fort considerable, et il s'y est tenu plusieurs Chapitres provinciaux. Feu M. Sanson marque Newtowne comme une Abbaye dans ses Cartes, ne prenant pas garde que ce nom n'appartient pas à des Maisons de Mandians et que lorsque les Anglois comme Speed et quelques autres ont appelé ces sortes de Couvens Abbay, c'est que leur langue donne ce nom indifféremment à toutes sortes de Maisons Religueuses, ce que la nôtre ne permet pas. Il n'y a que l'ancien Registre de l'Ordre qui fasse mention du Couvent de Newtowne, le nouveau n'en dit rien, et Fontana n'en pas non plus."[3]

HENRY LE SAVAGE died about the year 1276-7. He was succeeded in the representation of the SAVAGE family in Ulster by his son,

---

[1] Harris writes—" This Priory was, at the time of the suppression, possessed of three Town Lands, which, with the Site of it, were granted by King James I. to James Viscount Claneboys, at a rent of 13s. 4d. current money of Ireland. . . . They afterwards came by assignment to Montgomery Visc. Ardes."—*Topographia Hibernica.*

[2] See *Hibernia Dominicana*, Ed. 1762, p. 241, § xi.

[3] See also MacGeoghegan, *Hist. of Ireland.*

IV.—HENRY LE SAVAGE (BORN A.D. 1270).

This HENRY LE SAVAGE was born at the Feast of St. Lawrence, Aug. 10, A.D. 1270, and was a minor at his father's decease.

An Inquisition was made into the extent of his father's lands, &c., in March, 1276-7, at Portchaman (Bushmills), in Twescard (North Antrim), of which we find the following record (partly quoted above) in the State Papers:—
"Extent of the lands of HENRY LE SAUVAGE, made at Portkaman on Sunday next after the feast of St. Patrick, *a.r.* 5 Edward I., by John de Suckville, *Hugh Le Sauvage*[1] [no doubt a relative of HENRY, and the same *Hugh* that is mentioned above], Walter le Flemming, Thos. de Croch, &c., &c., who say that HENRY LE SAUVAGE held *in capite* of the King [Henry III.] 5 Knights' fees by service of 1 Knight; he also held in demesne 18 carucates [about 2,520 acres] of land, yearly worth in rents, mills, and other issues £55 3 4; there are free tenants who yearly owe £8 7s rent; there is nothing in villenage. HENRY, son of said HENRY, aged seven years at the feast of St. Lawrence [Aug. 10] *a.r.* 5 Edward I., is his next heir. There are many free tenants who owe suit of court in the said manor, namely, Henry de Logan, Hugh Foot, Adam, son of Elias, William de Chedisden, *Walter Sauvage*, Adam Carpenter, *Henry Salvage*,[2] Roger Bonekyl, William Fitz-Thomas, Thos. de Croch, Walter de Flemming, and Thos. de Logan." All these latter names, it will be observed, were either English or Anglo-Norman, which would seem to imply that the Irishry at this time had been either driven out of the SAVAGE estates or reduced to servitude.

On the 20th July, A.D. 1277, we find that King Edward I. committed to William Fitzwarin, the King's valet, the custody of the lands and tenements of HENRY LE SAUVAGE, deceased, who held *in capite* of the King in Ireland, to hold till the age of HENRY'S heir. Fitzwarin was to have for this guardianship 30 librates of the land of the King's gift, and he was to answer yearly at the Exchequer, Dublin, during the custody for the issues of the lands. (*Chester. Pat.*, 5 Ed. I., m. 7.)

> [Others of the SAVAGE family in Ulster, and of the SAVAGE name in other parts of Ireland, who flourished at this period, most, perhaps all of them, in the lifetime of HENRY LE SAVAGE, were—
> > *Hugh Le Sauvage*, who took part in the Inquisition above referred to (A.D. 1272).

---
[1] Probably the same Hugh as is mentioned as a juror in A.D. 1272 (see p. 125, *supra*).
[2] Perhaps the Henry Savage of Tullaneske (Ballyskeagh) mentioned in 1272.

Walter Sauvage, a free tenant of HENRY's in A.D. 1277.

Henry Savage, also a free tenant of HENRY's in A.D. 1277. This is probably the *Henry* who is mentioned, in A.D. 1282, as one of the sureties for the good conduct of the Mandevilles, Anglo-Norman neighbours, and probably kinsmen, of the SAVAGES.

Alexander Savage. In A.D. 1278, we find at the Indictment against Percival of Lucca and others for usury and clipping money the name of *Alexander Savage* amongst the jurors. He is mentioned again as a juror in A.D. 1282; and again as a witness to a deed of Richard Bagod, 18 Ed. I. (1289-90). (*See Rot. Plac.*) He was probably the father of a *William Savage* to whom we shall have to refer hereafter.

Adam Le Sauvage. In A.D. 1283 we find *Adam Le Sauvage* attorned before the King, Edward I., along with Peter Clonkard, in all pleas and plaints in the Irish Courts, by Adam Fitzjohn, Parson of Duncurry, about to go to foreign parts for purposes of study; which fact the King now notifies to his bailiffs in Ireland. This *Adam* seems to have had possessions in Connaught, and to have been seized of Ballyncorghy, Byrgyle, and Tullaghhope (34 Ed. I.). He married Idonea ———, and had three sons, *Richard Savage, Walter Savage*, and *Milo Savage*.

Geoffrey Sauvage. At A.D. 1293, Dec. 10, *Geoffrey Sauvage* appears in the *Calendar of Documents Relating to Ireland* as one of the jurors at an inquiry into the conduct of William de Vescy, Justiciary of Ireland, and the Abbot of St. Thomas, near Dublin, with regard to their taking and returning the Common Seal; and on the 4th April, 1299, the same *Geoffrey* took part in an Inquisition sped at Dublin, concerning Adam de Seynt Boys (Holywood), the Archbishop of Armagh, and the lands of Kilclogry.

Ellen Sauvage. In the same *Calendar*, at the same date (A.D. 1293), in the Roll of Receipt for Easter Term, a. I. 21, Dublin, Monday [May 4], *Ellen Sauvage* is mentioned as having the marriage of Robert Cruys of Naul.

Robert Sauvage. At Jan. 20, A.D. 1297-8, the *Calendar of Documents relating to Ireland* gives an abstract of a Royal mandate addressed from Ghent to John de Langeton, the Chancellor, touching Thomas Harald of Ireland, who had come to the King (Edward I.), to the war in Flanders, and had sworn to remain there during the King's pleasure, notifying that the King pardons to him the King's suit of peace for all transgressions committed by him in Ireland; and the Chancellor is to cause him to have letters of pardon thereupon. Similar letters were to be granted to various Magnates of Ireland who had come to the King to the war of Flanders in company with John Fitz Thomas. Among these latter who had gone to Edward I.'s war in Flanders was *Robert Savage*. Of the others, those identified with Down and Louth were John Gernon, John Chamberlain, and Roger Tuite. We have been unable to ascertain whether this *Robert Savage* was the famous *Sir Robert* who succeeded *Henry Le Savage*, and of whom the next article is to treat.

HENRY LE SAVAGE (born A.D. 1270).

William, son of Alexander Savage. In A.D. 1302, *William*, son of *Alexander Savage*, is mentioned as one of the Irish Magnates selected to attend Richard de Burgo in the Scottish War, in which Edward I. chastised the Scots from the Tweed to the Firth of Moray. In A.D. 1303, *William*, son of *Alexander Savage*, was attorned for Richard Tuite, about to set out in the service of the King in the retinue of De Burgo. In 1301, *William Savage* was witness to a Deed of Thomas de Ledwych (Rot. Plac. 29 Ed. I.). He married Catherine, daughter and co-heiress of Nicholas de Chene, or Clone. He is designated *William Le Savage of Ulster*. Of this *William Savage* we shall hear more presently.[1]

Richard Le Savage. In A.D. 1310, *Richard Le Savage* was one of those summoned to a Great Council convened at Kilkenny. Perhaps this is the *Richard Savage* who is mentioned in the *Annals of the Four Masters* as having died in A.D. 1361. If so, he must have lived to a very advanced age.]

HENRY LE SAVAGE was succeeded in the representation of the SAVAGE family in Ulster by

---

[1] There was a William Savage, of Meath, 17 Ed. II., who had a son, Walter Savage, of Meath, mentioned in 1323. William Savage, 34 Ed. I., appears as having a son James.

V.—SIR ROBERT SAVAGE, KNT. (BORN BEFORE A.D. 1300; DIED A.D. 1360).

This SIR ROBERT SAVAGE was a very celebrated knight. It is possible that he was the ROBERT SAUVAGE who, as we have seen from the *Calendar of State Papers*, served in Edward I.'s war in Flanders. He died, as we shall see, in 1360, and, if he was old enough in 1297 to have fought in Flanders, he must have been over 80 years of age at his death. In this, of course, there is nothing impossible; but, although the date of his death is well known, there is no mention of the age at which he died.

In A.D. 1315, Edward Bruce landed at Olderfleet, in Antrim, and proceeded towards Carrickfergus, with the intention of subduing the country between that place and Dublin. The Anglo-Norman lords of Ulster—the "flower of Ulster," as Barbour calls them[1]—marched out to oppose them. As Barbour narrates in *The Bruce*—

> "And forowt drede or affray
> In twa battaills took their way
> Toward Cragfergus, it to se.
> But the lords of that countré,
> Mandeveill, Besat, and Logane
> Thair men assemblyt euerilkane.
> The SAWAGES war alsua thair.
> And quhen thai assemblyt war
> Thar war well ner twenty thousand."

"At this time," writes a contributor to the *Ulster Archæological Society's Journal*, in a note appended to the above account, "the family of LORD SAVAGE was perhaps the most powerful in Ulster."[2] A great battle was fought at Rathmore, in the present Co. of Antrim, probably in and around the fine old Rath that still gives its name to that place, and the Anglo-Norman feudatories were defeated. SIR ROBERT SAVAGE probably fought at this battle.

"In 1315, Edward Bruce having invaded Ireland," writes the late Duke of Leinster in his work on the Earls of Kildare, "the King, Edward II., required the 'Magnates Hiberniæ' to sign a letter of allegiance, *and to give hostages to be kept in Dublin Castle.*"[3] This may explain why it is that in that year we find hostages for SIR ROBERT SAVAGE in the Castle of Dublin. The following extract from the *Historic and Municipal Documents of Ireland* brings this circumstance vividly before us:—

---

[1] "All hale the flowr of Ulster."
[2] *Ulster Archæological Society's Journal*, vol. iv., p. 5.
[3] *The Earls of Kildare*, p. 27.

SAVAGE OF ARDKEEN, MAIN LINE.

"PRISONERS IN DUBLIN CASTLE.

Sir Robert Savage, Knt. (born before A.D. 1300; died A.D. 1360).

"A.D. 1315.—Mayor and Bailiffs of Dublin to make payment to Henri de Badowe, constable of Dublin Castle, for the hostage of ROBERT LE SAVAGE.

"2. Memorandum quod eodem [vicesimo] die [Augusti, 1315], per ipsum thesaurarium, mandatum fuit maiori et ballivis civitatis Dublin quod de pecunia quam domino, regi, debeat tam de firma civitatis predicte et ejus arreragiis quam aliunde, sine dilacione habere faciant Henrico de Badowe constabulario castri Dublin, quinquagenta et quinque solidos octo denarios, pro vadiis HENRICI LE SAUUAGE, obsidis pro ROBERTO SAUUAGE, milite, fratre suo, a vicesimo sexto die Marcii, anno regni regis nunc nono, usque ad octavum diem Septembris, proximo sequentem, videlicet per centum sexaginto et septem dies, utroque die computato, capiendo per diem quatuor denarios." The document indicates the eminence of SIR ROBERT SAVAGE in A.D. 1315, and his fidelity to the Crown in opposition to Edward Bruce.

Of HENRY SAVAGE, the brother of SIR ROBERT, we have discovered no subsequent traces; but SIR ROBERT, as we shall see, conferred his Christian name, "Henry," upon his own son and heir.

In the same year SIR ROBERT SAVAGE'S kinsman, WILLIAM SAVAGE, of whom we have already heard (see p. 129, *supra*), was one of the Chieftains of the Army of Ulster which encamped at Swords, not far from Dublin; and an interesting petition in Norman-French, dated A.D. 1319, and printed also in the volume of *Historic and Municipal Documents of Ireland*, contains a complaint from the King's Collector and Receiver at Swords to Roger Mortimer, the Justiciary, concerning certain ill-usages on the part of WILLIAM SAVAGE'S soldiers while they were quartered there. We give the document, preceded by the Editor's abstract of it:—

"SCOTS AND ULSTERMEN AT SWORDS.

"A.D. 1319.—Randulf le Clerk, collector and receiver of the King's rent at Swords, petitions the Justiciary, Roger de Mortimer, for redress and consideration. Alleges that on first Tuesday of Lent, when the Army of Ulster was at Swords, he was seized, beaten, and robbed of Eighteen pounds of the King's money, which he had that day received; that he was held in prison during four days and nights[?]; robbed of all his corn, vessels, clothes, accounts and remittances, so that he has nothing left; and as he is of great age he prays commiseration and allowance, as well as punishment of those that had maltreated him."

"A vous, Sire, Rogier de Mortemer, justice Dirlaunde, monstre Randulf le Clerk, quỳllour de la rente le reỳ, a Swerdes, qe le primer Marsdỳ de Quaresme qant lost de Uluestre fut a Swerdes, vỳndrent WILLIAM SAUUAGE, un des

SIR ROBERT SAVAGE, KNT. (born before A.D. 1300; died A.D. 1360).

cheventeẏns du dit host, Johan de Maundeville, Richard Pijioun, e Thomas Baude, de la compagnẏe de dit WILLIAM SAUUAGE, en le vile de Swerdes, hors du clocher de la eglise de Swerdes, le dit Randulf pristrent e batẏrent et malement traiterent, e illuesques luẏ des robberent de xviii lieures desterlings de les deners le reẏ, quil anoit prest de la rente le reẏ, meisme le Marsdẏ receu, e meisme le iour les voleit auoir pae au tresorer Dirlaunde e de illuesques luẏ pristrent e enprisonerent de totes manieres des bleez, vesseaux, draps, roulles, tailles et de totes manieres dacquitaunces qil auoit du paement vers le reẏ, qe rien pur sustenance, gaignerie, vesture, ne pur evidence de acounte oue luẏ remystrent. Issint qe le dit Randoulf rien ad fors qe unement son corps, par quoẏ vous prie le dit Randulf pour Dieu a pur lalme le reẏ, depuẏs qil est nonpuẏssaunt de totes manieres de bien e de chatieux et il est meismes de grant age qe cele perte luẏ seit allowe desicome le reẏ poet auoir recoucir é instiser les persones qi luẏ derobberent, come gentz qi sount a la pees le reẏ."

The active part which WILLIAM SAVAGE took in this war was brought to a close in 1317, in which year he was slain at Drogheda. His death is noticed in Clyn's *Annales Hiberniæ* at that date—"Dominus Rogerus de Mortuo Mari, justiciarius factus, applicuit in Pascha apud Yohel, cum militibus 38, exiens de navibus fecit 2 milites; et applicans ad se dominum Johannem de Brimegham, dominum Nicholaum de Verdona, ejecit omnes de nacione et cognomine de Lacy ex Hybernia; et coegit fugere ad Scotiam in estate. Et occiduntur juxta Pontensam civitatem multi de Ultonia; quorum principalis fuit ubi de interfectis, WILLELMUS SAVAGE. Hic autem et alii Ultonienses per Scotos extra patriam suam expulsi fuerunt; et Scotos insequentes per Mediam, Legeniam, et Momoniam, non minus quasi quam Scoti preter combustionem et interfectionem populo terre dampnum intulerunt."[1]

After his temporary success, Edward Bruce was defeated and slain at Dundalk by the Englishry under Bermingham, in Oct., 1318; and about this time, we may assume, SIR ROBERT SAVAGE entered upon that vigorous warfare with the Irish the brilliant results of which have been recorded by the Dublin Annalists, by Holinshed, by Campion, and by many other chroniclers and historians.

In the 15th Edward II., ROBERT SAVAGE was one of the thirty-three *Magnates Hiberniæ* who were summoned to the service of the King in Scotland. In August, A.D. 1322, Edward II. invaded Scotland with a large army, and marched into Fifeshire; but he was obliged to return owing to want of provisions

---

[1] *Fratris Johannis Clyn Annales Hiberniæ* [*Friar John Clyn, of the Convent of the Friars Minors, Kilkenny*]. Edited by the Very Rev. Richard Butler, A.B., M.R.I.A., Dean of Clonmacnoise. Printed for the Irish Archæological Society. MDCCCXLIX. P. 13.

and forage, the Scots having laid the country waste; and on the 30th May, A.D. 1323, he concluded a truce with the Scottish King, Robert Bruce, for thirteen years. SIR ROBERT SAVAGE may not have won much glory in this inglorious campaign, but he must at least have acquired from it considerable knowledge of the military science of his time.

SIR ROBERT SAVAGE, KNT. (born before A.D. 1300; died A.D. 1360).

In A.D. 1327, the loyalty, valour, and discretion of SIR ROBERT SAVAGE received royal recognition. He was appointed by Edward II. Sheriff of the county of Coulrath—by which name the modern county of Londonderry was known until the beginning of the 17th century,—the northernmost of the counties into which the English portion of Ulster was divided. The *Patent Rolls*, 20 Ed. II. (1326), record—"Rob.' Sauvage ħeb. šilem war' in co' de Koulrath." At the same time his neighbour, John de Mandeville,[1] was appointed Sheriff of Down and Newtown, and John de Athye Sheriff of Carrickfergus and Antrim. Harris, in his *Hibernica*, Part II., *or Treatises relating to Ireland*, p. 73, gives the terms of the warrants as follow:—

"Rot. Pat. 20 Ed. 2.—

"Robert Savage has a warrant for the Office of Sheriff of the County of Coulrath of the same date [as that of John de Mandeville for the Shrievalty of Down and Newtown].

"'To have and to occupy during our pleasure; so that you be responsible to us at our Exchequer at Dublin for the issues of those counties, taking such fees as other Sheriffs in time past have used to take. We also by these presents command all Bailiffs, and other our faithful subjects of said counties, that they be obedient and answerable to you in the said office.'" (11th Sept., 20 Ed. 2,—1326.)

In A.D. 1327, Brian, son of Henry O'Neill, had fallen into SIR ROBERT SAVAGE's hands, and the latter was ordered by the King to transfer him to the custody of the Constable of Carrickfergus Castle. ROBERT SAVAGE, on the 26th April, is commanded by the King to set free Brian, son of Henry O'Neill, in his custody, "for the security of the peace, to be kept in custody by the Constable of the Castle of Cragfergus." (*Patent and Close Rolls of the Court of Chancery.*)

John de Bermingham, the conqueror of Edward Bruce, had been created Earl of Louth by Edward II., in recognition of his brilliant services. His elevation and his establishment as a new-comer in their neighbourhood had alarmed and exasperated the old Anglo-Norman seigneurs of Uriel and Ulidia (Louth and

[1] Possibly the John de Mandeville mentioned in the petition above, quoted as one of the company of William Savage at Swords in 1315.

SIR ROBERT SAVAGE, KNT. (born before A.D. 1300; died A.D. 1360).

Down)—the SAVAGES, the De Verduns and the De Gernons, who were no doubt closely allied to one another by blood,—and actual warfare ensued. "In the year 1328, John de Bermingham, Earl of Louth, his brother Pierce, and many others of his kindred, together with sixty of their English followers, were slain in a pitched battle at Balbriggan (probably Balbriggan near the northern border of Dublin County) on Whitsun-eve, 10th June, by the Anglo-Norman faction of the De Verduns, De Gernons, and SAVAGES; the cause of animosity being the election of the Earl to the palatinate dignity of Louth, the country of the latter party."[1] It is possible that SIR ROBERT SAVAGE may have taken part in these proceedings, but not probable, as he was occupied at the time in discharging a royal trust. At any rate, he must have been cognizant of the actions of his haughty and too daring kinsmen.

In A.D. 1335 (temp. Edward III.), SIR ROBERT SAVAGE, KNIGHT (*Robertus Sauvage, Miles*), and his kinsman, JOHN SAVAGE, Esquire (*Johannes de Sauvage, Armiger*), "Ulster Chiefs," were ordered, in a mandate addressed to James Butler, Earl of Ormond, to attend John d'Arcy, the Justiciary, in the King's expedition against Scotland.—*Rot. Scotiæ, in dorso, m. 36.*

SIR ROBERT SAVAGE had now had much experience of military expeditions, and had earned the reputation, which the chroniclers have perpetuated, of "an excellent soldier."

About the same time a still higher mark of royal favour was bestowed upon him by Edward III., and we find him occupying the important office of Seneschal of Ulster, with the duties of which seem to have been associated those of Warden of the Marches. SIR ROBERT seems to have been the first of a long list of Seneschals who were chosen from the family of SAVAGE.[2] "The King (Edward III.) commands William de Logan, Treasurer of Ulster, that he should acquit ROBERT LE SAUVAGE, Seneschal of Ulster, of 10 *li.*, the fees of one year, from the issues of the lands which were the property of William de Burgo, lately Earl of Ulster, which he held from the King *in capite*, being in the King's hands by reason of the minority of the Heir. Witness, Roger Outlawe, Prior, &c., locum-tenens of John D'Arcy, Cragfergus, 11 April, 8 Ed. III."[3]

---

[1] See the *Dublin Penny Journal*, March 8, 1834; note to *The Annals of Ireland*, A.D. 1328; M'Geoghegan's *History of Ireland*, &c. See also Burke's *Peerage and Baronetage*, under "Talbot de Malahide."

[2] A little bay under the Castle Hill of Ardkeen is still known as "Seneschal's Port," and is so marked on the Ordnance Map. Whether it took its name from this SIR ROBERT SAVAGE, the Seneschal, or whether it received it at a later period, we are unable to say.

[3] See *Patent and Close Rolls of the Court of Chancery.*

A few years later we find EDWARD SAVAGE (properly *Edmund* SAVAGE, who was probably SIR ROBERT'S second son) Constable of the Castle of Carrickfergus, and the power of the SAVAGE family in Ulster was now at a great height.

[margin: SIR ROBERT SAVAGE, KNT. (born before A.D. 1300; died A.D. 1360).]

"In A.D. 1342," according to the *Annals of Ireland*, "SIR ROBERT SAVAGE, KNIGHT, began to build several castles in many places of Ulster, particularly in his own manors, telling his son and heir-apparent, SIR HENRY SAVAGE, that they would thus fortify themselves lest the Irish should hereafter break in upon them, to the utter ruin of their estate and family, and to the dishonour of their name among other nations. His son answered, That wherever there were valiant men there were forts and castles, according to that saying, *Filii castramenti sunt*, the children [of Israel] encamped, *i.e.*, brave men are designed for war, and that for this reason he would take care to be among such, which would prove the same in effect as if he lived in a castle, adding that he took a castle of *Bones* to be much better than a castle of *Stones*. Upon this reply his father gave over in great vexation, and swore he would never more build with stone and mortar, but keep a good house and great retinue about him; foretelling, however, that his posterity would repent it, as indeed they did, for the Irish destroyed the whole country for want of castles to defend it."[1]

Holinshed tells the same now well-known and oft-repeated story in succincter form:—"There dwelleth in Ulster a wealthie Knight, one SIR ROBERT SAVAGE, who the rather to preserve his owne began to wall and fortifie his manor-houses with castles and piles against the Irish enemie, exhorting his heire HENRIE SAVAGE to applie that work so beneficiale for himself and his posteritie. 'Father,' quoth young SAVAGE, 'I remember the proverb—Better a castle of Bones than of Stones. Where strength and courage of valiant men are present to help us, never will I, by the grace of God, cumber myself with dead walls; my foot shall be wheresoever young blood be stirring and where I find room to fight.' The Father let lie the building and foreswore to go any further forward with it."[2]

Campion, who repeats the tale, adds his own comment:—"But yet the vaunt thereof, and such like, hath been the decaye, as usual, of the SAVAGES, as of all the English gentlemen in Ulster, as the lack of walled towns is also the principal occasion of the rudeness and wildnesse in other parts of Ireland."[3]

---

[1] Camden: *Britannica*, vol. iv., p. 495.—*The Annals of Ireland*.

[2] It has been suggested that *Bones Castle*, near Downpatrick, was the castle over which this celebrated quarrel arose, and that *it* was the last castle built by SIR ROBERT SAVAGE.

[3] Campion gives 1350 as the year in which the incident occurred.

SIR ROBERT SAVAGE, KNT. (born before A.D. 1300; died A.D. 1360).

The story figures in Thierry's *History of the Norman Conquest;* and more theory has been built upon it than has been justified by historical facts. Thierry, like Campion, holds that it indicated a general indisposition on the part of the Anglo-Norman conquerors to defend their territories with castles; and Mr. Goldwin Smith, in his *Irish History and Irish Character*, states with great inaccuracy:—"In some cases the colonists seem to have neglected building castles altogether. The family of SAVAGE in the North were driven out of their possessions by the natives owing to their having acted on the pithy maxim that 'a castle of bones was better than a castle of stones.'"[1] This was not true of the SAVAGE family, for their territories, with the exception perhaps of some of the manors conferred upon SIR ROBERT by Edward III., bristled with castles, the remains of which are to be seen to this day. Indeed this fact has been dwelt upon by other writers. William Montgomery, writing in A.D. 1702, after describing their several castles in the Ards, concludes his observations by remarking—"So that, long running risks, the SAVAGES were convinced that castles of stones were necessary to save castles of bones from being broken." And the Rev. R. Butler, in his notes to Dymmock's *Treatise of Ireland*, discusses the question in relation to the country at large:—"It sometimes happened that the settlers expressed a dislike to castle-building. Thus Campion, p. 133, states that SAVAGE OF THE ARDS, in Ulster, about A.D. 1350, declared that he preferred 'a castle of bones to a castle of stones, and, by the grace of God, would never cumber himself with dead walls.' This is not to be wondered at, in an age when these adventurers considered themselves, if not invulnerable, yet nearly invincible, and, moreover, believed that the Heavenly Host itself was arrayed in their favour against the Irish. . . . But SAVAGE'S *objection to castles was only an exception; and the policy of building them became general and long continued.*"[2]

In February, A.D. 1344, Edward III. "granted to ROBERT SAUVAGE power to treat and parley with certain felons, as well English as Irish, in the parts of Ulster."[3]

"At this time," writes M'Geoghegan in his *History of Ireland*, referring to the reign of Edward III., "ROBERT SAVAGE, a rich and powerful man in Ulster, declared war against the ancient proprietors of the lands he had usurped, and put many of them to the sword in the County of Antrim."

---

[1] *Irish History and Irish Character*, by Goldwin Smith, pp. 59, 60.
[2] John Dymmock's *Treatise of Ireland*. Published by the Irish Archæological Society from a MS. in the British Museum. With Notes by the Rev. Richard Butler, A.B., M.R.I.A. (Trim). Note, p. 21.
[3] *Patent and Close Rolls of the Court of Chancery*, 18 Ed. III., 6 Feb.

In A.D. 1347, Edward III. confirmed to this brave warrior the manors of Rath- Sir Robert Savage, Knt. more, Duntorsy, Ballencan, and Donaghty, with their appurtenances, in Ulster.[1] (born before A.D. 1300; died A.D. 1360). These manors were bestowed upon him for his services in taking the rebellious Mandeville prisoner and crushing his revolt. They appear to have lain between the sea and Lough Neagh, in the southern portion of the present County of Antrim, and between the Bann and the mountains. A portion of them was included in Mawlyn, or Moylinny, which is now the Barony of Upper Antrim and embraces the parishes of Upper Antrim, Ballycor, Donegore, Kilbride, and Rashee, together with the granges of Doagh and Naltun, a space of about 37,000 statute acres. A neighbouring townland in the parish of Donegore, called *Bally-Savage*, preserves the family name.[2] Rathmore is in the present parish of Donegore, and the manor is supposed to have comprehended a larger territory in the 14th century than the whole parish of Donegore now comprises. The "Great" Rath, the scene of Edward Bruce's victory over the Anglo-Norman chivalry of Ulster, still remains to mark the centre of this manor, and it is said that traces of an ancient castle—possibly erected by Sir Robert Savage—are still to be seen in its immediate vicinity. Duntorsy, or Drumtorsy, is represented by Killowen, and lay to the west of the Bann, at Coleraine. Donaghty, anciently Duneachdach, is represented by the modern parish of Dunaghy, including the present town of Clough, "the Clough-maghera-donaghie of the Irish." Ballencan is supposed to have lain between Armoy and Ballycastle. Near Doagh there is a townland still called Ballyharington-Savage.

The lofty conical hill on which stands the old "Moat of Donegore," which was probably used as one of the Savage outposts, is a striking object in that fruitful valley through which the river known as the Six-Mile-Water runs westward towards Lough Neagh. From its summit a magnificent view of the valley, the Antrim mountains, the broad lake, and the hills of Tyrone, greets the eye. On the long, flat-topped, cultivated hill to the north-east of it lies the townland of Bally-Savage. Both hills can be well seen from the railway which now runs from Carrickfergus Junction to Antrim. The railway from Antrim to Coleraine traverses much of the remainder of the district which constituted the royal gift of Edward III. to the Savages. It was a territory worth fighting for—extensive, fair to look upon, well situated, well watered, abounding in fertile tilth and richest pasture-lands,—worth fighting for, but difficult for a single family to hold against multitudinous foes.

---

[1] *Rot. Pat.*, 21 Ed. III., m. 1, *Tor. Lond.* Quoted by Bishop Reeves, *Ecclesiastical Antiquities*, &c., p. 281.

[2] See *Ecclesiastical Antiquities of Down and Connor*, p. 281.

THE SAVAGES OF THE ARDS.

SIR ROBERT SAVAGE, KNT. (born before A.D. 1300; died A.D. 1360).

In A.D. 1353, writes Sir Bernard Burke, "SIR ROBERT SAVAGE fought a battle against the Irish, in which 3,000 Irishmen were slain, in the Townland of Bally-Savage, in the parish of Donegore, adjoining Antrim."

He resided, according to the same authority, at the Castle of Lissanoure, near Ballymoney, on the banks of Lough Guille, in the County of Antrim, which castle, adds Sir Bernard, was founded, tradition states, by Sir *Philip* SAVAGE, in the reign of King John.[1] Tradition is clearly at fault in ascribing the foundation of Lissanoure Castle to a SIR *Philip* SAVAGE in the reign of King

Ruins of LISSANOURE CASTLE, Antrim residence of SIR ROBERT SAVAGE, now the property of the Macartney family.

John, no person of that name, as far at least as we can discover, having existed at that period. Indeed the name "Philip" does not appear in the SAVAGE family till several centuries later. It is probable, however, that the Castle of Lissanoure was built by SIR ROBERT SAVAGE himself, and it was his place of residence when discharging the duties of the Shrievalty of Coulrath.

[1] See Burke's *Genealogical and Heraldic Dictionary of Landed Gentry* (early editions), under "Nugent [orig. Savage] of Portaferry." The Castle of Lissanoure, when the Savages lost their Antrim territories, became the property of the O'Haras, who sold it in the 17th century to the Macartney family, who are its present owners. In *The Imperial Gazetteer of Ireland* (1846), we find the following account of it:—"*Lissanour Castle.* An improved and romantically situated demesne 6½ miles east by south of Ballymoney. It was the residence of Earl Macartney, and is now the seat of G. Macartney, Esq. An ancient building, a fragment of which still remains, was supplanted by the present one in 1829, and is said to have been erected by *Sir Philip Savage* in the reign of King John."

The character and sayings of Sir Robert Savage and of his son Sir Henry seem to have had a considerable fascination for the annalists and historians. Campion relates the following story of Sir Robert :— *[Sir Robert Savage, Knt. (born before A.D. 1300; died A.D. 1360).]*

"This Savage having prepared an army against the Irish, allowed to every soldier before he buckled with the enemy a mighty draught of acqua vitæ, wine, or old ale, and killed in provision for their return beef, venison and fowl, in great plenty; which divers of his Captains misliked, and, considering the success to be uncertain, esteemed it better policy to poison the cates and do them away, than to cherish a sort of caitiffs with princely food, if aught should happen to themselves in this adventure of so few against so many. Hereat smiled the gentleman, and said: 'Tush, ye be too full of envy. This world is but an inn, whereunto ye have no special interest, but are only tenants at the will of the Lord. If it please Him to command us from it, as it were from our lodging, and to set other good fellows in our room, what hurt shall it be to us to leave them some meat for their suppers: let them hardly win it and wear it. If they enter our dwellings, good manners would no less than welcome them with such fare as the country breedeth, and with all my heart much good may it do them. Notwithstanding, I presume so far upon your noble courage that verily my mind giveth me that we shall return at night and banquet ourselves with our own store.' And so they did, having slain 3,000 Irishmen."

The excellence of his table, no less than the excellence of his wit and soldiership, has found a place in history :—" Hic," says James Grace in the *Annals of Kilkenny*, "hic mensam semper splendidissimam servavit"—an hereditary characteristic which did more perhaps to impair the fortunes of his posterity than their proverbial contempt of stone defences.[1]

The *Annals of the Four Masters*, A.D. 1360, state that in that year " Sir Robert Savage (of the County Down) died." *The Annals of Ireland*, in Camden's *Britannica*, linger over his memory with affection and admiration, and again record the story of his magnanimous liberality and light-hearted courage :—

"MCCCLX., 35th of the King's reign.[2] In this year died Sir Robert Savage, of Ulster, a valiant Knight, who, near Antrim, slew in one day 3,000 Irish with a small party of English; but before the engagement he took care to give to each of his men a good dose of wine or ale, whereof he had good

---

[1] We have seen already that the English branches of the Savage family were also noted for their hospitality.

[2] More properly the 34th Edward III.

SIR ROBERT SAVAGE, KNT (born before A.D. 1300; died A.D. 1360).

store, and reserved some for his friends likewise when they came. Besides this, he ordered that sheep, oxen, venison, or fowl, both wild and tame, should be killed, and made ready to entertain the conquerors on their return from battle whoever they should be; saying, That it would be a shame if such guests should come and find him unprovided with meat and drink. It pleasing God to bless them with victory, he invited them all to supper, and rejoiced with them, giving God thanks for his success; and he said, I thank God, for that it is better thus to keep it, than to let it run waste on the ground as some advised him."[1]

The late Mr. James Wills, in his *Lives of Illustrious and Distinguished Irishmen*, writes of SIR ROBERT SAVAGE at considerable length, commenting upon the state of society in Ireland in the 14th century which his exploits illustrate:—

"SIR ROBERT SAVAGE.
"FLOURISHED A.D. 1353.

"It is perhaps the peculiar character of this period of our biography that, while it has more than the ordinary proportion of names rendered eminent by rapid rise, great actions, and weighty importance in their generation, there is comparatively little or no record of the illustrious persons who bore them;— *stat nominis umbra* might be taken for their common motto. To have a history, even in the most vague and general acceptation of the term, it was necessary not only to be famous in their day, but to be identified with the whole tissue of our national history, that the events of the age may be stated in the life of an individual. Hence it is that, while numerous names are rendered eminent by the circumstances of a long descent and wide-branching families which can trace their fortunes to the valour and wisdom of ancestors who lived in this period, we are yet obliged to confine our notices to a small selection of names, mostly within a few great families. The history of Ireland for many centuries is, in fact, little more than a history of the Geraldines and Butlers, of the De Burgos, Berminghams, and other illustrious settlers. But of the great Irish chieftains so renowned in their day . . it has been with some difficulty we have been enabled to connect some scattered notices to diversify our pages. Lives constructed regularly according to the rigid notion of biography, strictly personal in their main details, have been quite impossible even in those cases in which the materials are the most favourable. These reflections may be received as a preface not inappropriate to the scanty notice of SIR ROBERT SAVAGE. The incident it contains is highly characteristic of the age in which it occurred, and will afford the reader one of the occasional gleams of the moral and civil state of that period which should not be lost.

---

[1] See also *Carew MSS., Book of Howth.*

"'About this time,' writes Cox, 'lived SIR ROBERT SAVAGE, a very consider-
able gentleman in Ulster, who began to fortify his dwelling with strong walls
and bulwarks; but his son derided his father's providence and caution, affirming
that a castle of bones was better than a castle of stones, and thereupon the old
man put a stop to his building.' Some of the neighbouring Irish had made a
plundering expedition into the territories of this stout old Knight of Ulster;
he promptly assembled his people, and collected assistance from his neighbours,
with the intent of chastising the affront, and perhaps repairing the losses he
must have sustained. But with a cool deliberation, worthy of the warrior who
deemed that his valour needed no bulwarks, he thought it would be paying
too serious a compliment to an enemy he despised to go without his supper
on their account, and gave orders to have a plentiful supper prepared for himself
and his companions at their return from the fatigues of the day. One of the
company, not without reason, surprised at the premature provision for an event
of which his fears suggested the extreme uncertainty, observed that it was not
unlikely that his hospitable forethought might turn out for the advantage of
the enemy. SIR ROBERT replied, in the true spirit of Hibernian[1] wit, bravery,
and hospitality, that he had better hopes from their courage; but that he should
feel ashamed if his enemies even were to find his house inhospitable and devoid
of cheer. His valour was crowned on this occasion with a complete and
decisive victory, sufficient even to fulfil his son's architectural project; as by the
historian's account his party slew three thousand Irishmen near Antrim, and
returned joyfully to supper.

"The story is probable enough, though the numbers of the slain are likely
to be exaggerated; for unless some unusual accident operated in his favour,
this particular either implies a larger force than a person of less than the
highest authority could well have commanded, or the revolting supposition
that SIR ROBERT and his friends exercised their valour upon a defenceless
crowd, whom it would have been sufficient to repulse with the loss of a few
prominent ringleaders. It is pretty evident that such slaughters rarely took
place in the many encounters we have had from time to time to notice; yet
in these the chief leaders of the English were engaged with larger bodies of
the Irish, whose skill in retreat was hardly less than the skill and discipline
of the English in attack. It must be observed that such a result should have
found a more distinguished place in the history of the time.

"Of more importance is the view which such incidents afford of the dreadful
state of the country, where a slaughter, considerable enough to warrant such

---

[1] Rather *Norman*, SIR ROBERT SAVAGE probably not having a drop of Hibernian blood in his veins.

an exaggeration (if such it be), can be mentioned as a cursory incident, insufficient to call for any detail. The true horror of a state in which there seems to have been an unrestrained licence of private war on every scale, according to the means or objects of the individual, is not easily placed in the deep shade of enormity and terror which its real character demands. . . ."

[Others of the name and family of SAVAGE who flourished in Ireland at this period, and in the lifetime of SIR ROBERT, were—

William Savage, son of *Alexander Savage*, of whom mention has been made above.

Richard Le Savage. In A.D. 1310, *Richard Le Savage* was one of those summoned to attend a great Council convened at Kilkenny. This may have been the *Richard Savage* whose death is recorded in the *Annals* as having taken place in 1361.

Henry Le Sauvage, SIR ROBERT's brother, living in 1315.

John de Savage, Armiger, who was, as we have seen, one of those ordered to attend John D'Arcy, the Justiciary, in the expedition against Scotland (Ed. III.).

Edward (properly *Edmund*) *Savage*, who, as we have seen, was Constable of Carrickfergus Castle in A.D. 1340.

HENRY SAVAGE, son and heir of SIR ROBERT, of whom mention is first made about A.D. 1350.]

The *Annals of Ireland* state that SIR ROBERT SAVAGE was buried in the Conventual Church of the Friars Preachers of Coulrath (Coleraine), near the River Bann. Of this church and its monuments there appears to be no trace left.

It is stated that the townland of Ballyventra, *i.e.*, *widow's town*, was bequeathed by him to his widow. This land adjoins the parish of Donegore, Co. Antrim.

SIR ROBERT SAVAGE was succeeded in the representation of the SAVAGE family in Ulster by his eldest son and heir,

VI.—SIR HENRY SAVAGE, BARON SAVAGE (LIVING IN A.D. 1342, temp. Ed. III.; LAST MENTIONED A.D. 1382, temp. Rich. II.).

SIR HENRY SAVAGE, KNT., BARON SAVAGE, the brave but rash author of the now historical saying, "Better a Castle of Bones than a Castle of Stones," on the death of his father, SIR ROBERT, must have succeeded to very considerable domains. Lord of the Ards and of the various manors in Antrim bestowed upon his father by King Edward III., with the personal reputation of a brave and daring soldier, and inheritor of the prestige which his father had bequeathed to his family and name, he must have been the most powerful and influential of the English chiefs in Ulster. It is not too much to assume that SIR ROBERT SAVAGE had been regarded as the mainstay of the English power in the North. The name of no other great Anglo-Norman chieftain appears in the contemporary history of the northern province. In his lifetime the Irishry, who had helped to disorganise the English possessions in Ulster temporarily under Edward Bruce, had been beaten back beyond the border, and the protection of the English territory was placed practically in the hands of SIR ROBERT SAVAGE, as Seneschal of Ulster and Warden of the Marches.[1] A chieftain who was credited with having in a pitched battle slain 3,000 Irish, must at least have made his sword dreaded by the Irishry and valued by his King. And it is not surprising to find that for several generations the most important offices the Crown could bestow in the North were conferred upon members of the SAVAGE family.

HENRY, LORD SAVAGE, living A.D. 1382.

In A.D. 1374, on the 22nd Dec. (48 Ed. III.), HENRY SAVAGE, KNIGHT, was summoned to Parliament. He was thus created a Baron by Writ-of-Summons in that year.[2]

In A.D. 1375, he appears to have been fined 100/- for non-attendance. (?)

In the same year, the *Annals of the Four Masters* relate that "SENICIN [which is the same name as Jenkin and Janico] SAVAGE was slain by Mac Gennis" (of the County of Down), probably in a skirmish.

In A.D. 1375, the King granted "to Jeffrey Scholmaistre, of Cragfergus, and ROBERT SAVAGE, the office of Controller of the Great as well as the Small Customs in the ports of Craghfergus [Carrickfergus], Coulrath [Coleraine], and Down, to hold during the King's pleasure.[3]

On the 22nd January, A.D. 1377, HENRY SAVAGE was again one of the Barons summoned to Parliament, as he was once more on the 11th September, A.D. 1380 (4th Richard II.), and, for the last time, apparently, on the 29th April, A.D. 1382 (5th Richard II.).[4]

The SAVAGES held their extensive territories by sheer strength of arm and force of will. Threatened and incessantly attacked on all sides but the seaboard by the Irish chiefs and their hordes of kerns and gallowglasses, and

---

[1] The facts of the history of SIR ROBERT SAVAGE and his son HENRY, LORD SAVAGE, are sufficient to explode the current notion, propagated by Spenser perhaps, that the English families of Ulster had been quite driven out of their possessions by Bruce. Spenser indeed makes a kind of exception in the case of the SAVAGES, but clearly he was very imperfectly informed on the whole subject.

[2] See Lascelles: *Liber Hiberniæ*, and Sir Bernard Burke: *List of Dormant and Extinct Peerages of Ireland*.

[3] See *Patent and Close Rolls of the Court of Chancery*, 49 Ed. III.

[4] See Lascelles: *Liber Hiberniæ*. Barons by Summons to Parliament.

HENRY, LORD SAVAGE, living A.D. 1382. sometimes even by their old Anglo-Norman rivals, their swords were seldom in the scabbard. "This family" (the SAVAGES OF ARDKEEN), says William Montgomery, "were sore enemies of the O'Neills." The *Annals of the Four Masters* give a striking narrative of a conflict with their hereditary foes in the year 1383, which illustrates the terrible nature of the warfare of the time, and shows how little the SAVAGES could depend for aid even upon their neighbours of kindred blood :—

"In A.D. 1383, Neill O'Neill, with his sons and the chiefs of Tyrone, marched with a great force into Trian Congail [in Antrim] to attack the English, and they completely plundered and burned many of their towns. The English of the district collected together to oppose them, and Hugh O'Neill and RAIBILIN [which is the equivalent of *Ravellin, Raouline* and *Roland*] SAVAGE having encountered each other in a charge of their cavalry, they pierced each other's bodies with two violent thrusts of their spears; RAIBILIN returned to his house desperately wounded, where he was again attacked and killed by John Bissett, and Hugh O'Neill died on the third day from the effects of his wounds, and the son of John Bissett was slain by RAIBILIN's people [the SAVAGES] three days after RAIBILIN himself was slain." The encounter is said to have taken place near Carrickfergus.

This RAIBILIN, or ROLAND SAVAGE, may have been a brother of LORD SAVAGE, or his nephew, or his son. From the fact of his having taken refuge in his castle in Bisset's neighbourhood, it is apparent that the battle was fought in the vicinity of Bisset's territory (the Glyns), and it is possible that Bisset had on this occasion sided with the O'Neills from jealousy of the growing power of the SAVAGES on his flank. Nothing tended to diminish the power of the Englishry more than such private rivalries; and the swift and terrible vengeance of the SAVAGE kindred, vividly and curtly described by the Annalists, shows with what rapidity the fires of family hatred could be kindled.

Of the name *Raibilin* or *Ravellin* (which is an approximation to the Irish pronunciation) a contributor to the *Ulster Archæological Society's Journal* writes :—"Rawelyn is Raoul-ine, *i.e.*, young Raoul (Rollo), a common Christian name in Armorican France at this day. Roland, or Rowland, was the usual form in this country."[1] The name frequently appears in the SAVAGE family in the forms Rawelyn, Roland, and Rowland; but here we find it for the first time.[2]

---
[1] See *Ulster Archæological Society's Journal*, vol. IX., p. 177. Note appended to an article on "Col. Thos. Smyth's Settlement in the Ards, 1572."
[2] The Rev. George Hill, repeating the story of the encounter in his admirable history of *The Macdonnells of Antrim*, takes *Ravellin* to be the equivalent of ROBERT. Any opinion of Mr. Hill's

Of HENRY, BARON SAVAGE, we do not hear after his last recorded summons to Parliament in A.D. 1382.

[During the lifetime of HENRY, BARON SAVAGE, flourished in Ireland the following kinsmen of his name:—

Richard Savage (mentioned above). He died A.D. 1361 (the year after the death of SIR ROBERT). *The Annals of the Four Masters* record his death:—"A.D. 1361. *Cluithe an righ* (the King's game, a disease not now known) was rife throughout all Ireland, and *Richard Savage* died of it." This particular mention of him shows that he was a man of considerable note in Ireland.

Janico (Jenkin, or Sinicen) Savage. He was slain, as we have seen, by Mac Gennis, A.D. 1374. It is added in the *Dublin Annals*, "the literati were left orphans by his loss."

Robert Savage. He was appointed, as above-mentioned, a Controller of the Ulster Ports in 1375.

Roland (Raibilin or Ravellin) Savage. He was treacherously slain, as we have just seen, by John Bisset after his desperate encounter with Hugh O'Neill, in which he mortally wounded the latter, in A.D. 1383.

Edmund Savage. This *Edmund* (the same name as *Redmond*, *Emon*, *Raymond*, *Esmond*, and *Edward*) was one of the most powerful and distinguished members of the SAVAGE family at this period. He was probably a younger brother of the LORD SAVAGE, and a younger son of SIR ROBERT. King Richard II. appointed him to the offices of Seneschal of Ulster and Warden of the Marches, which had been ably filled by SIR ROBERT SAVAGE apparently till his death in 1360. In A.D. 1385 (21st Oct., 9 Rich. II.), "the King notifies that though he appointed *Edmund Savage* Senescal of the liberties of Ulster and Guardian of the Marches there, and John Rynaux Chancellor and Treasurer of the same liberties, it was not the intention of the King that the said Senescal should grant any commissions of the peace, nor that said Chancellor should seal such, nor should he present any person to any church in the parts aforesaid under pretence of his office." (*Patent*

---

on such matters is of great weight; but here we think we are safe in adopting the view of the writer in the *Ulster Archæological Society's Journal* quoted in the text.

and Close Rolls, 21 Oct., 9 Rich. II.) In the same year the King appointed "*Edward*" Savage (no doubt the same *Edmund*), Thomas Alwyn Clerk, and Richard Russell to inquire on oath, &c., concerning the sedition in Ulster. (*Patent and Close Rolls*, 6 Dec., 9 Rich. II.) The next year, 10 Rich. II., A.D. 1386, "the King grants to *Ed. Savage*, Seneschal of the liberties of Ulster and Guardian of the Marches there, 80 marks yearly." In 1389, "the King, considering the great position which *Edmund Savage*, Senescal of the liberties of Ulster, &c., holds in these parts, has granted to him the ward and marriage of Elizabeth and Marjoree, daughters and heirs of Sir Hugh Byset, on bail." (*Patent and Close Rolls*, 14th Oct., 13 Rich. II.) In this year, 1389, Margorie Bisset was married to John of Islay, known as John *Mor* Macdonnell, and by this marriage the family of the Macdonnells, afterwards Earls and Marquises of Antrim, got their footing in the Glyns of Antrim, which the Bissets, when banished from Scotland for the murder of the young Earl of Athol in 1242, purchased of De Burgo. On the 14th of October in the same year (1389) Robert Lang had been appointed Constable of Carrickfergus Castle. "Same year," M'Skimin writes, "Lang's grant was revoked, and a mandate sent to Lang, *Edmond Savage*, and William Meuve, to deliver the keys to Sir Gilbert de Malshel, nominated to the office." (See M'Skimin: *History of Carrickergus*.) In 1392-3 Edmund Savage's patent was renewed, and the following record in Norman-French appears in the volume entitled *The King's Council in Ireland, 16 Richard II*. Edited by the Rev. James Graves, A.B., M.R.I.A. :—

"III. Pro Esmond Savage.

"A Justice et Conceille notre Seigneur le Roi en Irlaund supplie *Esmond Savache*, que come le dit *Esmond* ad occupie loffice de Shenescalrie Dollestres del graunt notre Seignour le Roi par ses lettres patentz de south la tesmoignance Monsieur Johan Stanlie, Levesque de Mithe jadys Justice Dirlaund, come en les ditz lettres patentes pleinement appiert, que pleise a votre tresgraciouse seignourie grauntrer renuler les ditz lettres patentz de south votre tesmoignance, et le dit *Esmond* supplie que vous pleise luy graunter qil et ses hommes poient savement venir et realer a vous par un an sanz ascune empechement; et eusement supplie le dit *Esmond* que la commissioun que Robert Lange ad de la Constablerie de Chastelle de Cnokfergorse[1] soit renule solouk la tenure des ses lettres patentz de south la tesmoignance de Evesque de Mithe, nadgers[2] Justice notre dit Seignour le Roi en Irland; ces voilletz faire eiant regard de graunt travail et costages que le dit *Esmond* ad en le service notre Seigneur le Roi.

"INDORSACIO. Eit le suppliant novellos patentes notre Seignour le Roẏ, sous son grant seel Dirland, de effice de Seneschalcie Duluester, et aussi sauf conduyt pour luy et ses gens pour venir, demourer, sejourner et retourner de nous vers son paix sanement et sans empescheiment, par les dites lettres patentes notre Seigneur le Roẏ, en due fourme. Donne a Kilkenny, le xxvij[e] de Janver, lan notre Seignour le Roy Richard Seconde seszieme.[3]

John Savage. In the publication just quoted appears an entry of the same year (A.D. 1393), as follows:—James Carmardyn prays for a charter of pardon for the homicide of *John Savage*, who was slain by chauncemedley, and by reason of assault

---

[1] Carrickfergus.
[2] Lately.
[3] *The King's Council in Ireland, 16 Richard II.* Ed. by Rev. James Graves, A.B., M.R.I.A. Published by authority of the Lords Commissioners of Her Majesty's Treasury, &c., p. 123.

The following is the English translation of the grant:—"To the Justice and Council of our Lord the King in Ireland prays *Esmond Savache*, for as much as the said *Esmond* has filled the office of the Seneschalship of Ulster by grant of our Lord the King by his letters patent under the teste of Sir John Stanley [and] of the Bishop of Meath, formerly Justice of Ireland, as in the said letters patent plainly appears, that it may please your most gracious lordship to grant a renewal of his said letters patent, under your teste; and the said *Esmond* prays that it may please you to grant that he and his men may have power safely to come to and return [from] you for one year without impeachment; and likewise the said *Esmond* prays that the commission which Robert Lange has of the constableship of the Castle of Carrickfergus may be renewed according to the tenor of his letters patent under the teste of the Bishop of Meath, late Justice of our said Lord the King in Ireland. May it be your will to do this, considering the great labour and expense the said *Esmond* incurs in the service of our Lord the King.

"*Indorsement.* Let the suppliant have new [letters] patent of our Lord the King, under his great seal of Ireland, of the office of Seneschalship of Ulster, and also safe conduct for him and his men to come, remain, sojourn, and return safely and without impeachment from us towards his own country, by letters patent of our Lord the King, in due form. Given at Kilkenny, the twenty-seventh day of January, the sixteenth year of our Lord King Richard the Second."

made by him. Granted at the request of the Bp. of Meath, for a fine of 40/-.[1]

Jordan Savage (probably SIR ROBERT'S *third* son, and the LORD SAVAGE'S younger brother), father of ROBERT SAVAGE, of whom presently as appointed Sheriff of the Ards in A.D. 1400, and as successor to HENRY, BARON SAVAGE.]

During the lifetime of HENRY, LORD SAVAGE, in the reign of Richard II., though most of the Anglo-Irish nobles were either in a state of passive independence of the King or in active rebellion and in alliance with the Irish chiefs, the SAVAGES appear to have remained steadfast in their loyalty. The confirmation of EDMUND SAVAGE in the Seneschalship of Ulster would seem to be sufficient evidence of the cordial relations existing between them and their English sovereign. But the state of Ulster, at the same time, as an integral part of the King's dominions, was anything but satisfactory, as sufficiently appears from the "*Credentials for the Message sent to England by the Guardian of the land of Ireland, and by the Council there.*" After speaking of M'Marghe, the Irish rebel, and his alliance with the Earl of Desmond, in Munster, for the destruction of the Earl of Ormond and of the English families that are rebels ("as the Baryttes, Powers, Gerardyns, Bermynhames, &c."), these *Credentials* proceed to state that "many counties which are obedient to the law are not in the hands of the King, except the county of Dublin and part of the county of Kildare. . . .

"Item the County of Meath is a Liberty of an Earl Palatine, and given to others, and the King has nothing.

"*Item the County of Ulster is a Liberty, and given to others, and the King has nothing.*"[2]

HENRY, BARON SAVAGE, was succeeded in the representation of the SAVAGE family in the Ards by

---

[1] The following is the original:—"A Justice et Conseil notre Seignour le Roy en Irland supplie James Carmardyn, que il vous plese de votre especial grace luy granter chartre de pardoun notre dit Seignour le Roy pur la mort *Johan Savage,* le quel fut occi par chandmelle, et sa assaut desmesne, pour un aese fin eut faire a notre dit Seignour le Roy."

[2] *King's Council in Ireland,* p. 261. Wexford, Cork, and Tipperary were also "Liberties Earls Palatine;" and from Carlow, Kilkenny, Waterford, Kerry, Limerick, Connaught, and Roscommon, the King "had nothing, through default of obedience and execution of the law, and by the rebellion and the war of enemies, &c."

VII.—SIR ROBERT (FITZJORDAN) SAVAGE, KNT. (LIVING A.D. 1389, temp. Rich. II.; LAST MENTIONED A.D. 1433, temp. Henry VI.).

SIR ROBERT SAVAGE, who is last mentioned in A.D. 1433.

With the death of HENRY, LORD SAVAGE, the Barony-by-Writ which he enjoyed appears to have passed into abeyance, as for a considerable time we do not find the title "LORD" SAVAGE again indicated in historical documents. It is plain that he left no surviving male issue, for SIR ROBERT, his successor in the representation of the family, was the son of *Jordan* SAVAGE, who, we conjecture, must have been HENRY's next brother.

In A.D. 1400, Henry IV. "granted to ROBERT, son of JORDAN SAVAGE, the office of Sheriff of Arde in Ulster." The Ards were thus constituted a distinct County, and they continued so, apparently, for nearly two centuries. The following is the official record of the appointment:—

"18. R. coffiis' Robto f' JORDANI SAVAGE off' vic' de Arde in Ulton'. Dub,' 6 Ap. — p ipm loc' ten' & cons'." (*Patent Rolls*, 1 Henry IV.)[1]

From the last date at which we have found HENRY, LORD SAVAGE's name mentioned (1382) to within a few years of the appointment of ROBERT (FITZJORDAN) SAVAGE to the Shrievalty of the Ards, the most eminent member of the family, and the most eminent of the Englishry in Ulster, was EDMUND SAVAGE, the King's Seneschal, of whom some account has been given in the preceding article; and this EDMUND we think we are right in assuming to have been a younger brother of the LORD SAVAGE.

Eleven years before the noteworthy appointment by which the Ards were elevated to the dignity of a County,[2] and which was in itself a recognition by the State of the power and the deserts of the SAVAGE family, the Marshal, on the advice of the Lord Lieutenant and Constable, granted licence to ROBERT SAVAGE to marry CHRISTIANA, daughter of John Macdonnell, Lord of the Isles. The enrolment is in the Public Record Office, Dublin; and the following is extracted from the Calendar of the *Patent and Close Rolls*:—
"The Marshal, on the advice of the Lord Lieutenant and Constable, granted licence to ROBERT SAVAGE to marry Christiana, daughter of John de Isle, Lord of the Isles. Dublin, 16th Feb., 12 Ric. II." (A.D. 1389).

This marriage brought the SAVAGE family into close alliance with the Royal House of Scotland, and with some of the noblest families of Scotland and England. CHRISTIANA was granddaughter of Robert II. of Scotland, the first monarch of the Stuart Dynasty, her father, John, Lord of the Isles, having

---

[1] In 1390, the lands of Ballygalgell, in the Ards, were entrusted to Richard Russell during the minority of Roger, Earl of March and Ulster.

[2] At least we have not come upon the record of any earlier appointment of a Sheriff of such county.

SIR ROBERT SAVAGE, who is last mentioned in A.D. 1433.

married Margaret, fourth daughter of that King. Robert III., King of Scotland, the Duke of Albany, and the Earl of Buchan and Ross, were her maternal uncles; the Earl of Moray, David Lindsay, Earl of Crawford, William Douglas, Lord of Galloway, Sir John Lyon, ancestor of the Earls of Strathmore, Sir James Sandilands, ancestor of the Lords Torphichen, were her uncles by marriage; and she inherited the blood-royal of England as well as that of Scotland. Through her the descendants of ROBERT SAVAGE, if so disposed, may trace their descent from Robert II., King of Scotland, from Robert I. (Bruce), King of Scotland, from David I., King of Scotland; from Judith, niece of William the Conqueror, and through her from Robert the Magnificent, Duke of Normandy, from Richard the Good, Duke of Normandy, from Richard the Fearless, Duke of Normandy, from William Longsword, Duke of Normandy, and from Rolf, first Duke of the Normans; through David I. from Malcolm III. (Cean-Mohr), who married Margaret, sister of Edgar Atheling; and through the latter Princess from Edmund Ironside, from Ethelred II., from Edgar, from Edmund I., from Edward the Elder, from Alfred the Great, from Ethelwulf, King of Wessex, from Egbert, King of Wessex; and through Malcolm Caen Mohr from Duncan I., King of Scotland (who was murdered by Macbeth), from Malcolm II., King of Scotland, from Kenneth III., King of Scotland, and from several other Scottish Kings his predecessors.

CHRISTIANA SAVAGE'S grandfather, King Robert, died the year after her marriage with SIR ROBERT SAVAGE.

In A.D. 1407, Hugh, son of Art Magennis, Chieftain of Iveagh, an Irish enemy of the SAVAGES, seems to have received temporary protection from SIR ROBERT SAVAGE or his kinsmen, for the following passage occurs in the *Annals of the Four Masters* at that date :—"Hugh, son of Art Mac Gennis, lord of Iveagh, was expelled from his own territory by the sons of Cunladh O'Neill and his own kinsman, namely, the son of Murtagh Oge Mac Gennis, and he fled into SAVADGE'S country, whither they pursued him, but were defeated by him, and Mac Gilmore was slain."

The *Annals of Ireland* in Camden's *Britannica*, vol. iv., relate a notable story of another M'Gilmore and the SAVAGES, in the narrative of the same and following year, A.D. 1407 and 1408. EDMUND (otherwise EDWARD) SAVAGE had been succeeded in the Seneschalship of Ulster in A.D. 1398 (22 Richard II.) by PATRICK SAVAGE, who is mentioned again as Seneschal the same year as that in which ROBERT SAVAGE was appointed Sheriff of Arde (A.D. 1400).[1] At A.D.

[1] Extracted from a MS. list of Seneschals of Ulster compiled by Bishop Reeves, and kindly lent by him to the Editor.

1407 the Dublin Annalist writes:—" MCCCCVII. A perfidious base Irishman, called [Hugh M'] Adam Mac Gilmori, never christened, and therefore called Corbi, who had caused the destruction of forty churches, took PATRICK SAVAGE prisoner, forced him to pay 2,000 marks for ransom, and afterwards killed both him and his brother RICHARD." This PATRICK SAVAGE is described by M'Geoghegan in his *History of Ireland* as an Anglo-Irishman of great influence in the North. There can be but little doubt that he was PATRICK SAVAGE the Seneschal, there being no other prominent member of the SAVAGE family with the same christian-name mentioned at this period, and the office of Seneschal having been filled immediately after the date of his death by the appointment of Sir Janico Dartas, or D'Artois, who held it for several years subsequently.[1] He seems to have been captured by an ambush, or by some other treacherous surprise. For this foul murder of their kinsman the SAVAGES were not to be baulked of their vengeance, and in A.D. 1408 they caught Hugh M'Gilmore in a trap of his own setting. The *Irish Annals* proceed to state:— " MCCCCVIII. This year Hugh Mac Gilmori was slain at Cragfergus [Carrickfergus] in the Church of the Friars Minors, which he had formerly destroyed, and broke the glass windows for the sake of the iron bars, which gave admittance to his enemies the SAVAGES."

SIR ROBERT SAVAGE, who is last mentioned in A.D. 1433.

The *Annals of the Four Masters*, describing the incident from an Irish point of view, say that " Mac Gilla More was *treacherously* slain at Carrickfergus by the SAVADGES;" but the treachery was obviously on the side of the man who first received a ransom of 2,000 marks for a prisoner, and then murdered the prisoner and his brother, who had probably brought him the ransom; and there is a grimly-humorous poetic justice in the picture of the SAVAGES pursuing M'Gilmore to such a hiding-place, and entering the last refuge of the sacrilegious robber through the windows, of which he had previously destroyed the glass and stolen the iron bars.[2]

In A.D. 1411, King Henry IV. granted to JOHN, son of RICHARD SAVAGE (evidently the RICHARD SAVAGE who, along with his brother PATRICK, was murdered by M'Gilmore), "the Guardianship of the Peace concerning felonies

---

[1] Sir Janico D'Artois served as Seneschal of Ulster in 1408, 1413, 2nd 1422. He died in 1426.
[2] "[A.D.] 1407. Hugo M'Adam M'Gillamor, falsus et ethnicus inimicus in Ultonia cremavit et destruxit 40 ecclesias, et manucaptum habuit Patritium Savadg, quem crudeliter tractavit, unde vulgo appellabatur . . . et iste Hugo M'Adam M'Gillamor non diu postea petere beneficium sanctuarii compulsus, sed in ecclesia seu monasterio minorum apud Knockfergus sine misericordia et reverentia fuit interfectus, que [sic] ipse et pater antea cremaverant."—Dowling: *Annalis Hiberniæ*. These incidents form the basis of a story entitled "Corby Mac Gilmore," by the late Sir Samuel Ferguson. See *Hibernian Nights' Entertainments*. Edited by Lady Ferguson.

SIR ROBERT SAVAGE, who is last mentioned in A.D. 1433.

as well as outlaws." (See *Patent and Close Rolls*, 22 Oct., 13 Henry IV.) This JOHN SAVAGE was probably the JOHN mentioned above as being granted "licence to treat," &c., with certain persons in Ulster.

In A.D. 1414, M'Geoghegan informs us that "Jenico de Artois, who commanded in Ulster, determined to revenge the attacks which were made against the lands of Magennis; but he was completely defeated at Inor, where several of his men were killed."

In A.D. 1418, Henry V. granted to EDMUND, son of EDMUND SAVAGE, late Seneschal, the liberties of Ulster during his pleasure. (*Patent and Close Rolls*. Dublin, 26 Jan., 5 Henry V.)

We now come to a series of events in the life of SIR ROBERT SAVAGE that had considerable influence on the subsequent fortunes of the SAVAGE family in Ulster.

"In A.D. 1418" (we quote the *Annals of the Four Masters*), "a great war arose between the son of O'Neill of Claneboy and the Albanaigh (Scots), and the English of Ulidia (County of Down) and of the Route (County of Antrim.)" In this war the SAVAGES, as the English family with the largest interests at stake, took, no doubt, a leading part. But we have not found any further particular mention of SIR ROBERT SAVAGE till A.D. 1433, when he appears in alliance with M'Quillan[1] in conflict with O'Neill and the forces of his own wife's kinsman, Macdonnell of the Isles. The *Annals of the Four Masters* give the following account of the struggle:—A.D. 1433. "A great contest arose between the Tirconnellians and the Tyronians; and O'Donnell, namely Niall Garo, the son of Torlogh of the Wine, marched his forces into Dhuv Thrian (the Black District), to aid Mac Quillan; and O'Neill, that is Owen, led a force in pursuit of O'Donnell and Mac Quillan. At this time Macdonnell of Scotland came with a large fleet to aid O'Neill, and the Scots proceeded to attack the preying parties of Mac Quillan and of ROBERT SAVAGE, whom they overcame,[2] and committed great slaughter and destruction on ROBERT's and Mac Quillan's people; and such of their party as escaped from the Dhuv Thrian were mostly slain at the shallow pass of Newcastle (in the parish of Kilcoo, County of Down). After that, O'Neill, Henry his son, and Macdonnell marched their forces to Ardglass, which they burned; and Macdonnell afterwards, with his Scots, proceeded from Ardglass in their ships to Inisowen (in Donegal), while O'Neill with his party proceeded by land to coöperate with them in plundering Tirconnell. . . . Mac Quillan having been expelled from his own country by

---

[1] The M'Quillans are said to have been originally a Welsh family.
[2] That is, of course, the "preying parties," not ROBERT SAVAGE himself.

the Mac I Neills of Claneboy, was forced to take refuge in the Ardes of Ulidia (in the County of Down) with SAVAGE."

Sir Robert Savage, who is last mentioned in A.D. 1433.

Twenty years after this brush with the O'Neills and Macdonnells, the SAVAGES, still probably in the lifetime of SIR ROBERT (FITZJORDAN) SAVAGE, obtained a signal victory over the Irish, on the completeness of which there is a singular unanimity of opinion amongst the annalists on both the English and the Irish side. The following extract from the *Annals of Dublin* gives the English account of the battle and its origin:—A.D. 1453. "The O'Neills, of Clanneboy, suffered a great overthrow at Ardglass, from the SAVADGES, assisted by the English of Dublin, who had landed upon their territory. The following was the cause of their going thither:—A British (Welsh) fleet had attacked and plundered the fleet of Dublin and taken the Archbishop prisoner; the Dublin fleet pursued them as far as the North Sea, and on their return landed upon the Ardes, SAVADGE'S territory, and assisted him against his northern enemies. In this battle of Ardglass, Henry O'Neill was taken prisoner by the English; Cu-uladh, the son of Cathbarr Magennis, heir apparent of Iveagh, Hugh Magennis, Mac Cartan, and fourteen leaders of the Route (Co. Antrim), were slain. The total of the slain on the side of the Irish amounted to 520." The account given by the "Four Masters" differs very little from the foregoing, but adds some interesting particulars:—A.D. 1453. "The O'Neills of Claneboy sustained a great overthrow at Ardglass by the SAVADGES, and the English of Dublin, who, with a large fleet, pursued as far as the Northern sea a Welsh fleet, by which the shipping of Dublin had been plundered, and the Archbishop of Dublin taken prisoner; and on their return, Henry, the son of O'Neill Buighe, met the English at Ardglass; and they took him prisoner and slew Cu-uladh, the son of Cahane Magennis, heir to the lordship of Iveagh, Hugh Magennis, Mac Artan, and also fourteen leaders from the Routes [in Antrim], and their entire loss amounted to five hundred and twenty." The Editors of the *Annals of the Four Masters* give the following commentary in a note:—"The battle here mentioned was fought at Ardglass, in the County of Down, and the circumstances above narrated were as follows:—A fleet of pirates from Wales having carried off some ships from the Bay of Dublin, and having at the same time taken prisoner Tregury, then Archbishop of Dublin, and a native of Cornwall, the pirates were pursued by a fleet from Dublin, which overtook them off the coast of Down or Antrim, defeated them, and liberated the Bishop; and, according to some accounts, 520 of the pirates were slain; but according to these Annals it would appear that 520 of the Irish forces were killed by the English and the SAVADGES, who were a powerful

Sir Robert Savage, who is last mentioned in A.D. 1433. family, of English descent, settled in the county of Down, and who carried on frequent contests with the O'Neills of Claneboy and other Irish Chiefs in that county, of whose lands they got possession."

If Sir Robert Savage, Sheriff of Arde, was living in A.D. 1453, he must have been nearly eighty years of age.

Prior to this period we have not found the Savages mentioned in connection with Lecale. During the succeeding century they figure repeatedly in history as the Lords of that territory, and their estates in Ireland appear at this time to have attained perhaps their utmost magnitude. They were Lords

Castle at Ardglass known as "King's Castle," residence of the Savage family in Lecale. (From an old woodcut.)

of the Ards,[1] of the barony of Lecale, and of a great portion of the County of Antrim. On the occasion of the Battle of Ardglass, they had the good fortune, rare in their history, of receiving what ought to have been always freely tendered to them and to all the other representatives of English power in Ireland, namely, the hearty coöperation of their English brethren in their contests with the natives.

---

[1] We should note here that in 1425 the lands of "Aghene in the County of Ards, in Ultonia," were entrusted to the keeping of Galfridius Sloghtre during the minority of Richard, Duke of York, Earl of Ulster.

The principal town in Lecale was Ardglass. On Ardglass and its Castles we may quote an interesting article that appeared in the *Dublin Penny Journal* of March 30, 1833:—" In the reign of Henry VI. [Ardglass] was a corporation, governed by a Portrieve. So late as the beginning of the reign of Charles I., the duties of the Port of Ardglass were let to farm. The history of this interesting town is involved in much obscurity. The ancient family of the SAVAGES are generally supposed to have been the first colonists of the place, and the founders of most of the castles remaining here, to whom a good part of Lecale, as well as the Ardes, anciently belonged. . . . But, however this may be, it is certain that the *southern* part of Lecale originally belonged to the Magennises; and the historian of the county, Harris, from whom most of our materials are taken, is of opinion that the SAVAGES were only intruders of a rather recent time." This surmise of Harris's rather bears out the opinion above stated, that the occupation of Lecale by the SAVAGES as its *lords* dates from the " Battle of Ardglass" in 1453, or thereabouts.

Sir Bernard Burke states that the SAVAGES built seven castles at Ardglass.[1] Some of the "seven castles" of Ardglass, the ruins of which still attest their ancient strength and extent, had, possibly, other founders. Harris, however, says:—" One may judge likewise that others of them were built by the SAVAGES, to whom a good part of Lecale as well as the Ards anciently belonged."

They appear also to have held from time to time the Castle of Kilclief, the picturesque ruins of which stand on the shores of Lecale near the mouth of Strangford Lough. Of Kilclief the Fitz Simondses, or Fitz Simonses, said to have been a branch of the SAVAGE family descended from a SIMON SAVAGE, subsequently became temporarily the lords.[2]

> [During the lifetime of SIR ROBERT (FITZ JORDAN) SAVAGE, the following members of the SAVAGE family flourished in Ireland:—
>> *Robert Savage, of Carrickfergus.* He was appointed, as we have seen above, one of the Comptrollers of the Great and Petty Customs of Ulster ports in A.D. 1375. In 1402, the " King granted letters to *Robert Savage* and Thomas Sutton, burgesses of the town of Cragfergus, to send two weys of corn as well for the necessity of the Bishop of Connor as for their own." (*Patent and Close Rolls*, 6 March, 3 Henry IV.)

SIR ROBERT SAVAGE, who is last mentioned in A.D. 1433.

---
[1] *Landed Gentry.* Under " Nugent of Portaferry."
[2] " Kilclief was the head-quarters of the Fitzsymonds, who were kinsmen of the SAVAGES, having been the descendants of some SIMON SAVAGE, but they seem to have been known in 1640 as a distinct sept."—Hill: *Montgomery Manuscripts*, p. 308, footnote.

John Savage, Canon of Donylek. "The King, at the petition of JOHN SAVAGE, Canon of the house of the Blessed Virgen de Dynelek, on the part of the Prior and convent of the same House, granted to them licence to elect an Abbot in the place of Thomas last Abbot. Trym, 16 Nov., 4 Henry IV." (1402.)

Patrick Savage, Seneschal of Ulster, &c. He was, as already described, taken prisoner by Corby M'Gilmore, and after a ransom of 2,000 marks had been paid for his release, was murdered by that brigand in A.D. 1407.

Richard Savage, brother of the last-named *Patrick,* who with the Seneschal was murdered also by M'Gilmore in A.D. 1407.

John Savage, Armiger. In A.D. 1402, 12 Aug., 3 Hen. IV., he was, along with John Mirrison, granted "licence to treat with certain persons as well English as Irish in Ulster." He was probably the son of the above-named *Richard Savage,* the same *John Savage* who is spoken of in A.D. 1411 as having been granted "the guardianship of the peace concerning felonies as well as outlaws" in that year.

Nicholas Savage. The *Patent and Close Rolls* record that "*Nicholas Savage* gave 20s for the pardon of all forfeitures and fines on the security of John, son of Luke Nettervylle. Trim, 10 Dec., 9 Henry IV."

Edmund Savage, son of the late Seneschal, *Edmund Savage.* In A.D. 1418, "the King granted to *Edmond,* son of Edmond Savage, Seneschal, the liberties of Ulster, during his pleasure. Dublin, 26 Jan., 5 Henry V. (See *Patent and Close Rolls.*) How long this *Edmund Savage* held the Seneschalship of Ulster does not appear.

Thomas Savage. In A.D. 1435, a *Thomas Savage* is mentioned as a citizen and merchant of Dublin. "The King granted to Thomas Savage, citizen and merchant of Dublin, that he should not be put on the assize. 24 May, 13 Henry VI." (See *Patent and Close Rolls of the Court of Chancery.*) He may have been a kinsman of the Ulster SAVAGES.]

SIR ROBERT SAVAGE, Sheriff of Arde, the date of whose death is uncertain, was succeeded in the representation of the SAVAGE family in Ulster by

VIII.—ROBERT SAVAGE, LORD OF LECALE AND OF THE ARDS (LIVING IN A.D. 1468, temp. Ed. IV.; DIED ABOUT A.D. 1469 (?), temp. Ed. IV.).

ROBERT SAVAGE, "LORD OF LECALE," is mentioned by the Annalists in the year 1468. He is the first of the family we have found so designated.

The Baron Russell of Killough, living in A.D. 1490, is stated to have married Joanna, daughter of ROBERT, BARON SAVAGE, LORD OF ARDKEEN.[1] This ROBERT SAVAGE, of ARDKEEN, could hardly have been ROBERT, Sheriff of Arde, as the dates would not tally. He must, therefore, have been this son and successor, ROBERT SAVAGE, LORD OF LECALE.

ROBERT SAVAGE, LORD OF LECALE, &c., was succeeded in the representation of the SAVAGE family in Ulster by his son,

IX.—PATRICK SAVAGE, LORD OF LECALE AND OF THE ARDS (LIVING A.D. 1469, temp. Ed. IV.; DIED ABOUT A.D. 1482, temp. Ed. IV.).

In the year in which PATRICK SAVAGE is referred to in the *Annals*, he seems to have been very young.

In A.D. 1469, the SAVAGES, in battling with their Irish enemies, were discomfited, and on this occasion their misfortune was owing in great measure to one of those shameful alliances which were too common in the history of Ireland. White, of Dufferin, an Englishman by descent, and bound probably to the SAVAGES (like most of the Anglo-Norman chiefs of Ulster) by family ties, joined with Henry O'Neill and M'Quillan in an attempt to usurp the lordship of Lecale, and succeeded in taking PATRICK SAVAGE prisoner and in assuming the chieftainship, with their support :—"[A.D. 1469.] PATRICK SAVAGE was taken prisoner by the Whites, and Patrick White, aided by Henry O'Neill and Mac Quillan, assumed the Lordship of Leathcathail." (Quoted by Bishop Reeves, *Ecclesiastica Hibernica*.) Or, as the *Annals of the Four Masters* amplify the narrative,—"The son of SAVADGE, *i.e.*, young PATRICK, was taken prisoner by the family of White (both in the County of Down), and Patrick White assumed the Lordship of Lecale, by the aid of O'Neill, that is Henry, and of Mac Quillan; and they expelled all the SAVADGES from the territory." The last clause probably contains an Irish exaggeration; but at any rate the SAVAGES for the moment seem to have fallen back into the Ards. But the ascendency of the Whites in Lecale did not last long.[2]

---

[1] See *Montgomery Manuscripts*, p. 314, Editor's footnote. In the genealogical account of the Barons Russell, from which this reference is extracted, there is clearly an error in referring George, Baron Russell, to the reign of Henry IV., as will be seen hereafter.

[2] The Whites are said to have originally settled in Antrim. Dufferin had been previously the inheritance successively of the Mandevilles and of the M'Quillans. The family of White is now represented by the Whites of Loughbrickland.

PATRICK SAVAGE, who was living in A.D. 1482.

In A.D. 1470, Sketrick Castle, which afterwards came into permanent possession of the SAVAGES OF ARDKEEN, was taken by the O'Neills, and given in charge to M'Quillan to guard it.

In A.D. 1475, the *Annals of the Four Masters* inform us that "Felim. the grandson of O'Neill, and the son of SAVADGE (of the County of Down), were taken prisoners by Con, the son of Hugh Buidhe [Boy] O'Neill; but the son of SAVADGE made his escape from him afterwards."

That this "son of SAVADGE" was the PATRICK by whose seizure the Whites had succeeded, with the help of the O'Neills and M'Quillans, in usurping the lordship of Lecale, seems pretty clear. His escape appears to have exasperated Con O'Neill; for, seven years afterwards, he again succeeded in seizing him, and, either in vindictiveness or wanton cruelty, he put out his eyes. —A.D. 1482. "The son of SAVADGE, *i.e.*, PATRICK, was taken prisoner by Con, son of Hugh Buidhe O'Neill, who put out his eyes." (*Annals of the Four Masters.*)

Three years afterwards, as we shall see presently, the SAVAGES had their revenge for this mutilation, and probably consequent death, of their young chief.

[The following persons of the SAVAGE kindred flourished during the lifetime of PATRICK SAVAGE:—

Sir Roland Savage, Seneschal of Ulster A.D. 1482, of whom presently as Lord of Lecale, &c., and representative of the SAVAGE family in Ulster.

James Oge Savage, i.e., *young James Savage*, who was slain, as we shall see, by the sons of the Seneschal, in 1490.]

The date of the death of PATRICK SAVAGE is doubtful, but he was succeeded in the representation of the SAVAGE family in Ulster, and in the recovered Lordship of Lecale, by

SIR ROLAND SAVAGE, who died A.D. 1519.

X.—SIR ROLAND SAVAGE, KNT., SENESCHAL OF ULSTER (LIVING A.D. 1482, temp. Ed. IV.; DIED A.D. 1519, temp. Henry VIII.).

The same year as that in which PATRICK SAVAGE, LORD OF LECALE, had his eyes put out by Con O'Neill, SIR ROLAND SAVAGE was appointed Seneschal of Ulster by Edward IV. The entry in the Calendar of the *Patent Rolls* runs thus:—

"22 Ed. IV.

"℞ con' Roulandū Savage mil' [   ] libtatis sive co' Ulton'. Dub. 2. Aug."

Extracts from the State Papers, which follow, will show that Sir ROLAND SAVAGE was not only Lord of Lecale, but chief also of his kinsmen in Moylinny—that portion of Antrim which comprehended some of the manors of SIR ROBERT SAVAGE, the first Seneschal of his family, who died A.D. 1360; and we shall presently see that SIR ROLAND's son and representative, RAYMOND SAVAGE, was, after his father's death, recognised by the Lords Deputies Lord Leonard Grey and Lord Fitzwilliam successively, in indentures still preserved, as both Lord of Lecale and Lord of Ardkeen and other territories in the Ards.

Sir Roland Savage, who died A.D. 1519.

Three years after SIR ROLAND SAVAGE's appointment, the SAVAGES had their revenge for the injury inflicted on their former chief. The *Annals of the Four Masters* inform us that in "A.D. 1485, Hugh O'Neill, son of Buidhe, son of Bryan Balloch O'Neill, Lord of Trian Congail (Upper and Lower Claneboy, in Down and Antrim), having gone on a predatory excursion into Lecale, was overtaken by the English, and slain with the cast of a dart." The vigilance of the English in Lecale was probably owing to the energy and ability of SIR ROLAND SAVAGE, the King's Seneschal, who, as we have reason to believe, became the mainstay of the English in Ulster.

A quarrel arose about this time between SIR ROLAND's sons and certain of their kinsmen. Whatever may have been its origin or the object of those concerned in it, it was attended with fatal consequences. The historian of the family would fain draw the pen through the passage of which honesty compels the quotation:—A.D. 1490. "Young JAMES SAVAGE was killed by the sons of the SENESCHAL SAVAGE."[1]

SIR ROLAND SAVAGE, we shall presently see, is stated in the *Annals of Loch Cé* to have been deprived of his territory of Lecale shortly before his death by the machinations of the Earl of Kildare and the Prior Magennis; and to have been succeeded by his son EMONN, who "with difficulty was inaugurated in his place;" and the State Papers show that the name *Emonn* here is but an Irish mispronunciation and misspelling of *Raymond*, which name also appears in the forms *Redmond* and *Remund*. Now, in the State Papers (which will be fully quoted in the proper place) occurs, at A.D. 1536, this article of a treaty between RAYMOND SAVAGE and the then Lord Deputy:—

"The said Remund (*Jenico* Savage, formerly chief captain of the same nation, now being removed out of the way—*Jenico Savage quandam principali ejusdem nationis capitaneo e medio sublato*) shall have superiority, name, and preeminence of his nation and country of SAVAGE, otherwise called Lecale, as principal captain thereof."

[1] *Annals of the Four Masters.*

Sir Roland Savage, who died A.D. 1519.

Is Janico another name of Sir Roland? And are Sir Roland Savage (Raymond's father), who had been deprived of his Lordship of Lecale, and Janico Savage (the immediate predecessor of Raymond), who had been Lord of Lecale and had been "removed out of the way," one and the same person? Or had another member of the family, by name Janico Savage, usurped the Lordship of Lecale and held it between the period of Sir Roland's death (A.D. 1519) and the restoration and establishment of Raymond by the Lord Deputy (A.D. 1536)?

The objections to the supposition that Janico was one and the same with Sir Roland may be stated thus:—

1. Though *aliases* are common in Irish history, and the same person frequently appears in different documents under different names, these *aliases* are generally surnames or nicknames given, for example, to distinguish one member of a family from another, as the "fair-haired," the "dark-haired," and such-like, and not additional christian-names.

2. The name of Sir Roland Savage, Knight, being a familiar one to the English authorities, and Sir Roland having held an important public office in the King's gift, is it not likely that in an official document he would still be spoken of as Sir Roland Savage, even if he had had a second name?

3. Is it likely that the Savage family would have been left without any representative in the Lordship of Lecale from the death of Sir Roland in A.D. 1519 to the date of the indenture restoring Raymond in 1536—a space of 17 years?

As against these objections the following considerations may be urged:—

1. Is it not quite possible that Sir Roland Savage might have been *popularly* known, for some reason or another, as Janico, just as in the present day people are often called familiarly by names other than their baptismal names, and cease to be known by their true names?

2. So many years having elapsed since the death of Sir Roland, there would have been nothing peculiar in the Lord Deputy's inserting in the Indenture the name by which he was popularly known.

3. If Sir Roland had really been deprived of his possessions through the instrumentality of the Earl of Kildare, and if they had been handed over to the Prior, it is quite possible that the Lordship of Lecale might have been alienated from the Savage family for fully seventeen years.

And the following facts may be stated in direct support of the hypothesis:—

1. Raymond Savage, whom the *Annals of Loch Cé* declare to have been the son of Sir Roland, is always subsequently designated in history "the son

SAVAGE OF ARDKEEN, MAIN LINE.

of *the Seneschal*," while his *brother*, JAMES SAVAGE (father of the inheritor of Ardkeen in 1612), is called, as we shall see, the son of JENIAKE or JENKIN, well-known equivalents of *Janico* and *Jenico*, and the descendants of JAMES MAC JENIAKE SAVAGE have been always called for distinction "the race of *the Seneschal*." It is difficult to escape from the conclusion to which these facts point—that the name JANICO was really an *alias* of SIR ROLAND, the Seneschal.

<small>SIR ROLAND SAVAGE, who died A.D. 1519.</small>

2. It does not appear that any Seneschal of the name SAVAGE was appointed subsequent to the death of SIR ROLAND, A.D. 1519.

3. In a remarkable *undated* Petition of the people of Lecale and the Ards to the Throne, there is actually mentioned a Seneschal SAVAGE, named JANICO, who, as far as we can at present ascertain, must have held the office of Seneschal about the time we find it occupied by SIR ROLAND.

The preponderance of such evidence as we possess appears to us to favour the surmise that the Seneschal JANICO SAVAGE and the Seneschal SIR ROLAND SAVAGE are identical. But, however this may be, this seems to be the proper place to introduce a notice of the Seneschal JANICO SAVAGE, as to no other period, anterior or subsequent, do we find it possible to refer him.

It would appear that about this period (A.D. 1482-1494) the position of the Englishry in Ulster had become extremely critical. Few in number, and surrounded by multitudes of the Irishry, it only needed union amongst the Irish chieftains, and disunion amongst themselves, to bring them to the verge of destruction. Most of the Anglo-Norman and English families had been weakened by long warfare; some of them at this time had almost disappeared. We hear no more of the Chamberlaines, the Stantons, the Sendals, the Copelands, the Passelevys, the Ridals, the Audleys, the Mandevilles, as powerful independent families. The Whites, in Dufferin, seem to have enjoyed a doubtful kind of independence by casting in their lot with the Irish Chiefs. The Bissets in Antrim, the Russells in Down, and the SAVAGES in Down and Antrim still dominated; but even their position demanded constant fighting for its defence. The O'Neills on the western border of Antrim and the M'Quillans in the north, the O'Neill Boy family settled in Clandeboy between the SAVAGE territories in Down and the SAVAGE territories in Antrim, the Magennises on the south-western border of Lecale, the M'Cartans, the O'Flynns, and the O'Kanes, together with large levies of Scots from the Western Isles, and Welsh pirate-bands attacking from the sea—this was a combination hard for the bravest and most skilful knights to withstand, when,

Y

SIR ROLAND SAVAGE, who died A.D. 1519.

after all, they and their followers were but a handful, remote from their English kinsmen of the Pale, and unassisted by their English Sovereign.

The one military leader to whom the hardly-pressed Englishry of the North seem now to have looked for help, guidance, and protection was the Seneschal JANICO SAVAGE. Bravely and skilfully he seems to have fought against enormous odds, and gratefully and ungrudgingly his fellow-countrymen have recorded their appreciation of his untiring energy and valour.

No more interesting document in connection with the history of Ulster at this period is forthcoming than the Petition in which the English folk in Down pray their King to send succour to his faithful servant and true liegeman JANICO SAVAGE, "your Seneschal of Ulster, who has kept and defended your said country with great *aventure* daily in dread, he and his men, with great care, hunger, thirst, watching, bloodshed and many slaughters, against your said enemies mortal, and given many great slaughters and discomfitures in which his friends that were to him most succour are slain and passed unrewarded as yet."

This really important document, which we are about to quote in its entirety, seems to have been first brought to light by the late Sir William Betham, Ulster King-of-Arms, who sent what purported to be a true copy of it to the Royal Irish Academy. In the alleged "true copy" it appears that the Seneschal's name is "Janico D'Artois;" but that very eminent antiquarian, Dr. Reeves, the present Bishop of Down and Connor, shortly afterwards examined the document carefully in the Chapter House at Westminster, where it was then preserved, and discovered that the name was not Janico D'Artois, but JANICO SAVAGE. Dr. Reeves made an exact copy of its contents, and sent it to the Academy, in the transactions of which it is printed.

Some misconception also appears to have arisen about its date, no date being affixed to the document itself. By some[1] it was referred to the reign of Henry IV. But the English may be, manifestly, that of a later period. It is signed by the then Bishop of Down *and Connor;* and the union of these two Sees did not take place till A.D. 1441. But even this latter date Bishop Reeves is of opinion is too early. The style of *writing* is also that of a later period; and the Bishop, who is unquestionably the very best authority on the subject, has given it to the present Editor as his opinion that it belongs to the latter end of Henry VII.'s reign or to the earlier part of Henry VIII.'s. There is, as already stated, no record that we can discover of any JANICO SAVAGE flourishing in the reign of Henry IV.; and the English power in Ulster in that reign was not at a low ebb. But in the lifetime of SIR ROLAND SAVAGE, as

---

[1] See Mr. Hill's *Montgomery Manuscripts*, p. 314, footnote.

during some fourteen or fifteen years prior to the first mention of his appointment as Seneschal, the position of the Englishry was precarious, and the Savage family in particular were the object of repeated attacks from the Irish Chiefs and their allies. Two of the Irish Chiefs named in the document—Con O'Neill and Henry O'Neill—figure in the *Irish Annals* of this very time, and the *Irish Annals* represent them as in alliance with M'Quillan. It may have been written, as we have said, in the interval between A.D. 1482 and A.D. 1494.

Sir Roland Savage, who died A.D. 1519.

The following is a copy of the Petition as it is printed in the *Transactions of the Royal Irish Academy* (vol. v., p. 132), the representations of the seals only being omitted[1]:—

"To the Kyng our Souverain lord.

"Meekly Beseecheth your mooste Noble Hieghnesse and pre-excellent grace your humble subjects and servauntes whose seales vnto thes presentes beth affixed, with all the faithful and trewe liege peaple of Therldome of Vlster whiche some tyme was named the third mooste Rialle Erldome in Christiante and nowe in defaute of lordship and peaple with your enmyes daly destroid and under tribute constitute and thraldom ȝe graciously to considre the said thraldom and tribute with the importable werres vpon youre said liege peaple daly continued with the Bretones and with the Scottes of the oute Iles whiche beth wt Irishmen enmeyes of the land confedered that is to say wt Oneyll buy O'Kane Mcgwylyn henry Oneylle Con Oneylle Mcgynnasse McCartan and the Offlynnes which in short tyme fynally and vtterly woll destroye your said Erldome and peaple withoute that it be by youre mooste gracious hieghnesse provided to send vnto theym a certain of peaple to inhabite and to defende your said grounde other to send vnto your faithfull servant and trwe liege man Janico Savage youre Senescall of Vlster which hath kept and defende your said cuntray wt grete aventure daly in drede he and his men withe grete care hunger thurste watching blodeshed and mannys slaghtie ayens youre said Enmyes mortell and yeven many great slaghties and scomfettes in which his frendes that was to hym mooste socoure beth slayne and passed unrewarded as yet: suche fees outhir such rewarde wher with he may wage Sawdiours to resiste and to defend your said Enmyes and kepe your said countray to be sped within shorte tyme ellys your said peaple will fynally be destroied and your said countray wt youre Enmyes conquered wating daly and nyghtly

---

[1] The original is "written on a piece of parchment, five inches, seven-eighths long, and nineteen inches and a-half wide, the names of the seals being written on the straps to which the seals are attached."—*Transactions of the Royal Irish Academy*, vol. v., p. 132.

SIR ROLAND SAVAGE, who died A.D. 1519.

whanne the said Scottes of the oute Iles of Scotland with the said Irishmen confedered shal vtterly destroi them. Thiez premissez to be remembred and remedied by youre said preexcellent grace. We mekely in the reverence of Almighty Jesu which by his prophete Moises delyuered the children of Israel oute of the thraldome and bondage of Kyng pharoo besecheth in way of charite. And we duly to pray for the preseruyng of your maieste roiall. Besechyng mekely more ovir your preexcellent grace that it might please your hieghnesse to geve vnto the berers herof Thomas lambert and david Callan in the circumstance of the premissez faith and credence."

[The following are the signatures annexed to the document, with seals:—]

Sigellum Dunĕn.
[et] Conneren Epĩ.
Prioris de
Duno.

Archid̃ Dunĕn.		Abbtis de Bangor[1]
	Abbtis de Saballo[2]	
Abbtis de Ines[3]		Abbtis de Jugo Dei[4]
[No seal] Magr̃ sc̃i Joh̃is Bapte.		[No seal] S. coĩe ciuetat de Duno.
[No seal] Georgi Russhel Baronis		[No seal] Ville de Ardglasse
	Ville de Kilcleth.[5]	

The Signatories to this remarkable Petition are, as we have seen, the Bishop of Down *and Connor*, the Prior of Down, the Archdeacon of Down, the Abbot of Bangor, the Abbot of Saul, the Abbot of Inch in Lecale, the Abbot of Grey Abbey in the Ards, the Master of the Knights of St. John the Baptist, the Corporation of Downpatrick, George, Baron Russell of Killough,

---

[1] The Monastery of Bangor, in the Lower Ards.
[2] Saul in Lecale.
[3] Qy. Inch in Lecale?
[4] The Monastery of Hore Abbey, otherwise Leigh, otherwise Grey Abbey, in the Ards.
[5] Kilclief.

the town of Ardglass, and the town of Kilclief, in Lecale. All these persons and places are confined to Lecale and the Ards. It is noteworthy that no individual representing any of the old Anglo-Norman families signs it, except the Baron Russell. No member of the SAVAGE family affixes his seal to it; and this is probably attributable to the fact that JANICO SAVAGE was at once the person for whose support the petitioners pray and himself the head of the SAVAGE family.

Sir Roland Savage, who died A.D. 1519.

It does not transpire what response, if any, followed this petition, but it had probably little effect.

Whether JANICO is the same person as SIR ROLAND or not, we learn that SIR ROLAND SAVAGE found it impossible to defend his territories without undertaking wars on his own authority, and thereby incurring condemnation as "one of the English great Rebels" of Ireland.

In the *Patent and Close Rolls of the Court of Chancery*, 2 Aug., 9 Henry VII. (A.D. 1494), SIR ROWLAND SAVAGE, Knight, is mentioned in connection with Ulster; but the enrolment is, unfortunately, imperfect or obliterated. Twenty-one years later, in the reign of Henry VIII., SIR ROLAND was still living and fighting. The very valuable and interesting paper on the State of Ireland and Plan for its Reformation, dated A.D. 1515, published in the State Papers of Henry VIII.'s reign, includes SIR ROLAND SAVAGE OF LECALE, KNIGHT, amongst the "more than 30 great captains of the Englyshe noble folke, that followeth the same Iryshe ordre [as has been previously described in the document], and kepeth the same rule, and every of them maketh warre and pease for hymself, without any lycence of the King, or any other temperall person, saive to hym that is strongest and of such as may subdue them by the sword." The names of these "30 and more great captains of the Englyshe noble folke" are worth examining, and are given as follows :—

"The Errle of Desmounde, Lord of the Countye of Kerye.
The Knight of the countye Kerye.
Fitz mawryshe, of the countye of Kerye.
Sir Thomas Desmounde, Knyght.
Sir John of Desmounde, Knyght.
Sir Gerot of Desmounde, Knyght.
The Lorde Barrye.
The Lorde Roache.
The younge Lorde Barrye.
The Lorde Cowrceye.
The Lorde Cogan.

SIR ROLAND SAVAGE, who died A.D. 1519.

  The Lorde Bareth.
  The Whyt Knyght.
  The Knight of the Walle.
  Syr Geralde of Desmoundis sonnes, of the countye Waterford.
  The Powers, of the countye of Waterforde.
  Sir William Bourke, Knight, of the countye of Lymryk.
  Sir Pyers Butler, Knight, and all the Captaines of the Butlers in the countye of Kylkennye, and of the countye of Fyddert.

"Here folowyth the names of Englyshe greate rebelles in Conaght.
  The Lorde Bourke, of Connyke Ghowle (?)
  The Lorde Bourke, of Clanrykarde.
  The Lorde Bremeyeham of Aurye.
  Syr Myles Stauntons sonnes.
  Syr Jordan Dexter sonnes.
  The Lorde Nangle.
  Sir Walter Barretes sons de Tyre Auly.

"Here foloweth the names of the great Englyshe rebelles of Wolster.[1]
  SIR ROWLAND SAVAGE, of LECCHAHYLL, KNIGHT.
  Fitzhowlyn, of Tuscarde.
  Fitz John Byssede, of the Glynnes.[2]

"Hereafter folowith the names of the Englyshe capitaynes of the Countye of Meath, that obey not the Kinges lawe.
  The Dyllons.
  The Daltons.
  The Tyrreles.
  The Dedalamaris."

The same document states that at this time several English counties paid tribute to some powerful neighbouring Irish chieftains :—Co. Meath to O'Connor, £300; Co. Uriel to the Great O'Neill, £40; Co. Kildare, Co. Wexford, Co. Kilkenny, Co. Limericke, and Co. Cork, sums varying from £20 to £40 annually; the King's Exchequer 40 marks : while of the Barony of Lecale it says:—"Barony of Lecchahill, in the countye of Wolster, to the captayne of Clanhuboy payeth yerely 40£ orelles to Oneyll, whether of them be strongeist." The total amount from all the English counties that paid tribute was £740. The Ards are not mentioned as paying any tribute.

---

[1] Ulster.
[2] Now the Barony of Glenarm, in Antrim.

The writer is of opinion that most of these "English noble folk," then in effect rebels, if they were aided and backed by the King in their contests with the Irish, would loyally coöperate with their Sovereign for the establishment of order and good government in the country. [SIR ROLAND SAVAGE, who died A.D. 1519.]

Farther on, the able writer of this document recommends a reconquest by the King and "the noble folk of England and Ireland" of those parts of Ulster which had "byn conquered and inhabytyd with the Kingis subgettes before nowe," including the Baronies of *Lecale*, *Arde*, the Dufferins, Carrickfergus, Bentrye, Greencastle, Dundrum, Gallagh, *Mawlyn* [*Moylinny*], Twescard, the Glynnes, and all the "remnant lands lying betwixt the Green Castle and the river of the Banne; and the expulsion therefrom of all the Captains grown and dyscendyd of the blode and lynage of Hughe Boy Oneyll." In connection with this scheme he again gives a list of the great English "rebells" dwelling in "Wolster":—

"Sir ROLAND SAVAGE, and his Kynesmen.
The Baron Russell, and his Kynesmen.
Fitz john, Lord of the Glynnes, and his Kynesmen.
Fitzhowlyn, Lord of Tuscard, and his Kinnesmen."

And he localizes the Antrim territories of Sir ROLAND SAVAGE thus:—"The said captayne, SIR ROLAND SAVAGE, and his Kinnesmen *in the baronye of Mawlyn,*[1] *and in all the lands marching with the sayd baronye of Tuscard,*[2] *and with the baronye of the Glynnes.*" And he recommends that the Deputy should combine with "SIR ROWLAND SAVAGE and his Kinnesmen" in settling these, and conquering the neighbouring, districts.

The reasons why SIR ROLAND SAVAGE was deprived of Lecale and the manner in which he was deposed are alike obscure. It is certain that a considerable portion of the territory passed into the hands of the Earl of Kildare, and it is equally certain that the tradition of the Irish themselves attributed the establishment of the Earl's power there to his having taken the part of the Irish Magennises against the Anglo-Norman SAVAGES. We quote from Mr. Hill's *Montgomery Manuscripts* the following passage in which the question is discussed:—"[The Earl of Kildare's lands in Lecale], tradition affirms, were originally acquired by an Earl of Kildare from the family of Maginnis, in gratitude for his having protected the latter against the usurpations of the SAVAGES.—(*The Earls of Kildare*, by the Marquis of Kildare, vol. i., p. 244; Harris: *State of the County Down*, p. 22.) It is more probable, however,

---

[1] Moylinny.   [2] Otherwise *Twescard*.

SIR ROLAND SAVAGE, who died A.D. 1519. that these lands came into the Kildare family by the marriage of Gerald, the eighth Earl, with Alison Eustace, granddaughter of Sir Janico D'Artois, a noble Gascon chief, who had served as Seneschal of Ulster in the years 1408, 1413, and 1422. At his death, in 1426, it was found by post-mortem inquisition that he was in possession of 'eight messuages and five carucates of land in Bright and Rasteglas, assigned to him by John Dongan, bishop of Down; Ardglass and Ardtole, the lands of Gilberton, now Ballygilbert, the gift to him of the abbot and convent of Inch; and a carucate in Nunton, now Ballynagallagh, the gift of the prioress and convent of the blessed Mary of Down, all lying in the parish of Bright. . . . On the attainder of Silken Thomas, the tenth Earl of Kildare, in the reign of Henry VIII., his possessions in Lecale were seized into the hands of the crown, and farmed out to Sir William Brabazon;[1] and after his death, 9th July, 1522, to others. Gerald, the eleventh Earl, was restored in blood and to the family estates in 1552, being afterwards confirmed in them, by letters patent of Queen Mary, the 13th May, 1554, and a further patent, first and second Philip and Mary, 1555, to hold all which had been the inheritance of his father in use or possession at any time, by the service of one knight's fee. The lands are not set out in these patents; but it is quite apparent that from the high favour in which this Gerald stood with the sister sovereigns, Mary and Elizabeth,—receiving from the former, 28th October, 1557, a reversionary grant of the priories of Inch and Saul, of St. John, and SS. John and Thomas, and St. Patrick in Down; and from Elizabeth, in 1583, such a lease of the tithes—that any attempts on the parts of the bishops to reclaim Bright and Rossglass would have been perfectly useless.'—(Hanna's *Account of the Parish of Bright* in the *Downpatrick Recorder*.) The Ardglass estate," continues Mr. Hill, "remained in the Kildare family until the year 1808, when it was sold by the Right Hon. Charles Fitzgerald, Vice-Admiral of the Red, created Baron Lecale, to his stepfather, William Ogilvie, Esq., whose great-grandson, Aubrey De Vere Beauclerk, now possesses it."[2]

The Irish *Annals of Loch Cé* sorrowfully record SIR ROLAND SAVAGE's death in the year 1519.—[A.D. 1519.] "The son of the SAVAGE, *i.e.*, RAIBHILIN,[3] the man of greatest bounty and valour of all the Foreigners of Erinn in his own time, died, after having been expelled from his patrimony by the power of the Earl of Cill-dara (Kildare) at the persuasion of the Prior Mag Aenghasa [Magennis]; and his patrimony was quietly, prosperously held by the Prior in

---

[1] Then Lord Treasurer of Ireland; ancestor of the noble house of Brabazon, Earls of Meath.
[2] Hill: *Montgomery Manuscripts*, p. 308, footnote.
[3] Irish form of Roland.

despite of him until he died; and it would not be surprising if it was for grief on account of his territory, *i.e.*, Tricha-ced-na-soillse,[1] that he died." SIR ROLAND SAVAGE, who died A.D. 1519.
SIR ROLAND SAVAGE left issue,

   I. RAYMOND, of whom presently as his successor in the Lordship of Lecale and of Ardkeen.

   II. James, surnamed MacJeniake.

He was succeeded by his elder son,

XI.—RAYMOND SAVAGE, LORD OF LECALE AND OF ARDKEEN
(LIVING A.D. 1519, temp. Henry VIII.; DIED A.D. 1575, temp. Elizabeth).

RAYMOND SAVAGE, LORD OF LECALE AND OF ARDKEEN, who died A.D. 1575.

The *Annals of Loch Cé*, continuing the notice above quoted, state that "EDMOND [= *Redmond*, = *Remond* and *Raymond*] SAVAGE, *i.e.*, his [SIR ROLAND'S] son, was inaugurated in his place, although he did not easily obtain his patrimony." RAYMOND'S name in the original Irish of the *Annals* is spelt *Emonn*, in some State Papers it is written *Remond*, and in an Indenture of A.D. 1559 it appears as *Redmond*. Such variety of spelling and pronunciation of proper names in Ireland was quite common in the 16th and 17th centuries. As a christian-name, in what was probably its original French form, *Raymond*, it has been revived from time to time in the SAVAGE family.

RAYMOND SAVAGE held his territory of Lecale in the midst of difficulties, and he endeavoured to strengthen himself by bringing into his dominion numbers of Scottish settlers—a policy then regarded by the English government as fraught with great danger to the State. In a Report on the State of Ireland to Henry VIII., entitled "Articles and Instructions to Our Soweraine Lord the King, for his land of Irelland," and dated 1534, we have the following reference to him :—(A.D. 1534.) "Wher as now of late many of the Scottes beth entyrid into the north parts of the land of Irland in a dominion called Lekayle; wher one of your English rebels, callid SAVAGE, is lord, wher as they inhabite and dwell, which is not to be suffyryd, for many inconveniences that ther of may ensue. For in your noble progenitor Edward the Third is days, one Bruce, brother to the Scotysh King, did entyr with 10 thousand men, and ther thoght to haiv wone that north contre, and dyd inhabite there, unto such tyme that he, and all his men, by your deputie and subjectes ther, were slayn in the feld. Therfor it is expedient your deputie have commaundment to expell them from thens, les thy, in process off tyme, know the fertylite of the land, and ther draw to them more of ther name, to encres ther strenth."

---

[1] Note by the Editor of the *Annals*—"The Tricha-ced (or cantred) of the light—Lecale Barony, Co. Down."

Raymond Savage, Lord of Lecale and of Ardkeen, who died A.D. 1575.

Two years after this, the Lord Deputy, Lord Leonard Grey, recognised RAYMOND SAVAGE as chief Captain of his nation, and a compact, quoted in the *Calendar of State Papers* and in the *Carew MSS.*, was arranged between RAYMOND and the Deputy. In the *Carew MSS.* the substance of the Indenture is given with fulness and accuracy:—

"A.D. 1536, May 31. Indenture made between Lord Leonard Grey and REMUND SAVAGE, principal captain of his nation.

"(1.) He will be a faithful liege subject of the King.

(2.) He will serve the King and his Deputies with all his power, and rise up with all his men as often as he shall be called upon, in every journey and great voyage, against all rebels and enemies dwelling within a day's journey of him.

(3.) The said REMAND (JENICO SAVAGE, formerly chief captain of the same nation, now being removed out of the way) shall have superiority, name, and preëminence of his nation and country of SAVAGE, otherwise called Lecale, as principal captain of the same.[1]

(4.) He shall give to the Lord Deputy, for acquiring his favour and friendship, one hundred cows, fat and strong, and one good horse, or 15 marks of Irish money.

"Dated 31 May, 28 Henry VIII.

"Contemp. copy. Latin. P. 1."

RAYMOND SAVAGE, however, was accused again, in 1539, of encouraging the Scottish immigrants, and of refusing to pay rent (*ferme*) to the Treasurer, Sir William Brabazon. Brabazon writes to Thomas Cromwell thus:—

[A.D. 1539.] "Brabazon to Cromwell.

"I have a ferme of the King's majestie, toward that country called Lecale, where sum of the King's souldeors under me do lie, and the Scottes be dailie at warre with them. Some of the Captayns of the Scottes say they will serve no man; but what they get by the sword, that will they have. . . . I have sent unto your Lordship a letter enclosed herein, sent from Knockfergus unto a servaunt of myne lying in Lecale."

Lord Leonard Grey the same year informs Cromwell that he has made an expedition against SAVAGE, on the ground that the latter would not pay his

---

[1] The following is a copy of this portion of the original Indenture, now in the Public Record Office, Dublin, for which the Editor is indebted to the kindness of the Bishop of Down (Dr. Reeves):—" Preterea concordia est quod dictus Remundus modo exist[ens] (jenico Savage quondam principali ejusdem nationis Capitaneo e medio sublato) habebit superioritatem nomen atque preminenciam sue nationis et patrie de SAVAGE alias dicte Lecale tanquam principalis Capitaneus ejusdem, habebitque et recipiet eadem honorea commoda et proficua qualia aliquis predecessorum suorum precepit [?] et habuit temporibus preteritis."

ferme to the Treasurer. He "assembled" at Trym on the 7th October, and reached Dundalk on the 10th. He then marched with an army into Lecale and the Ards, and took eight castles, and delivered them to Brabazon to "ward." He speaks in glowing terms of the physical advantages of Lecale.

RAYMOND SAVAGE, LORD OF LECALE AND OF ARDKEEN, who died A.D. 1575.

A.D. 1539. Grey to Cromwell.

" . . . For so much as Mr. Thesourer was fermour of the Kinges countre of Lecayll, and that SAVAGE, chyeff capitayne of his nation, wolde not pay his ferme unto the Thesourer, and besydys the sayd SAVAGE browght into the sayd countre dyverse Scottys, which had myche of the sayd country in their subjection, then yt was concluded betwyxt the said Mr. Thesourer and me that we showlde have gone towardes the sayd Lecayle, and so, with the ost, we sett forward, and entered into the said countre, took all the castles there, and delivered them to Mr. Thesourer, who hath warded the same. I toke another castell, being in M'Gynous countre, called Downdrome, whych I asure your Lordeship as yt standyth ys one of the strongest holtes that ever I saw in Irelande, and most commodios for the defence of the hole countre of Lecayll, both by sea and lande; for the said Lecale ys invyroned rounde aboute by the see, and noo way to goo by lande into the sayde country, but only by the said castle of Dundrum.

"Owte of which country the sayd Scottes fled, and left mych corne, butters, and other pylfre behind them, which the ost hade. Besydys this I toke a castle that the said Scottes had, and other castles in ARD, bordering to the sayd Lecayll, which likewise I delivered to the Thesourer, in nombre all 8 castles.[1] I assure your Lordeship I have bin in manye places and countries, and yet did I never see for so myche a plesaunter plott of grounde than the sayd Lecayll, for the comodities of the lande, and diverse ilandes in the same ynvyroned with the sea, which were soon reclaymed and inhabited, the Kinges pleasure known."

Mr. Bagwell, in his excellent *History of the Tudors in Ireland*, thus deals with this invasion of Grey's:—" Foiled in [another] attempt, which can hardly be described as otherwise than treacherous, Grey determined to chastise the SAVAGES, who had refused to pay rent to Brabazon, the King's tenant in Lecale. This old English family had become quite Hibernicised, and were now bringing Scotch mercenaries into the country. Various castles were taken and delivered to Brabazon, who also took charge of Dundrum, an important stronghold belonging to Magennis, which commanded the entry to Lecale on the land side. The Scots fled, leaving corn, butter, and other rural plunder behind. Grey was much struck by the fertility of the district, which is still famous."

---

[1] There is a note by the Editor in the *Calendar of State Papers* to this effect:—"Cox gives a very incorrect narrative of this expedition into Lecale, and erroneously ascribes it to the date of May, 1538."

THE SAVAGES OF THE ARDS.

RAYMOND SAVAGE, LORD OF LECALE AND OF ARDKEEN, who died A.D. 1575.

In A.D. 1541, the SAVAGES are mentioned in R. Cowley's "Plan for the Reformation of Ireland" (*Cal. State Papers*, vol. iii.) as having "cum into the Kingis majesty;" and the fidelity of RAYMOND SAVAGE to the Crown is testified in a letter from the Lord Deputy and Council of Ireland to Henry VIII., written in the same year. He is there mentioned as one of the Chieftains who assisted with his followers in the expedition against O'Neill.

[A.D. 1541.] "The Lord Deputy and Council of Ireland to Henry VIII.

. . . . . .

"According to our former wryting to your Highnes, we have invaded the contreis of O'Neil, where we have been by the space of 22 daies, and have burnid grete parte of the same, and distroyed miche of his cornis and butters, whiche is the grete lyvinges of the said Oneil, and his followers; and have perused the grete parte of his country, and all the quarters of the   .[1] We have also slayne dyverse of his people. The said Oneil never made showe unto us of no powar, but kepte him, and his, and ther cattell in grete wooddes and fastnes, where we could not attayne them, nor yet have perfite knowlege, where they were. He persistethe still in his disobedience, but we trust in God so to provide for him that he shall be brought more baase. There mette with us, in the middes of his countrey, Odonel, with a greate bande of horsemen and galoglas, and also one Nele Connelach with his bande, with Orayly, Magnenessa, Brian Omaghor, Filome Roo, SAVAGE, Ohanlon, and dyverse other capytains of the Irissherie, who have all solemplye sworne upon the Evangelistes to do there uttermoste in your Highnes sarvice ageinste the said Oneil, and that they will never be at peace with him without the consente of us of your Counsell; and have made a solempne instrumente of the same subscribed with their hands."

In the midst of the rebellions, disturbances, and intrigues of the next twelve years, RAYMOND SAVAGE seems to have gradually lost his grasp of Lecale.

The old conflicts of the SAVAGES with the O'Neills were renewed in A.D. 1551; but on September 27 of that year the Lord Chancellor, Thomas Cusack, writing to the Earl of Warwick, mentions that the contention of SAVAGE OF ARDE and Hugh M'Neill Oge, King of Clandeboye, had been "ordered"—*i.e.*, brought to a peaceful termination.

In 1553, the Deputy St. Leger, in an Order of Council, denounced the attempts of the SAVAGES to "usurp" the castle of Kilclief, in Lecale, from the Bishop of Down and Connor. Kilclief, as we have mentioned, was identified with the FitzSimons branch of the SAVAGE family.[2]

---

[1] There is a blank in the original.

[2] Harris, writing in 1743, gives the following account of Kilclief:—"The Castle and Lands of *Kilclief* were an ancient See House and Manor of the *Bishops* of *Down;* and it was there that

In A.D. 1553 it would appear that the only territory over which the SAVAGES enjoyed absolute sway was the Upper Ards; at least they are not mentioned as Lords of Lecale or of their old Antrim territories, although they undoubtedly continued to possess portions of the former district long subsequently.

Raymond Savage, Lord of Lecale and of Ardkeen, who died A.D. 1575.

The following extracts from the "Copy of the book sent from Sir Thomas Cusack, Lord Chancellor of Ireland, to the Duke of Northumberland's Grace for the present state of Ireland," preserved in the *Carew MSS.*, gives an interesting account of those lands of Down which had formerly belonged to some of the leading Anglo-Norman lords:—

"May 8, 1553. State of Ireland.
 . . . .

"Donfrey [that is, Dufferin] whereof one John Whit[1] was landlord, who was deceitfully murdered by McRanyll Boy[2] his son, a Scot; and since that murder he keepeth possession of the said lands, by mean whereof he is able to disturb the countries next adjoining on every side, which shortly, by God's grace, shall be redressed. The same country is no great circuit, but small, full of woods, water, and good land, meet for Englishmen to inhabit.

"The next country to the same eastward is Lecaill, where Mr. Brerton is farmer and captain, which is a handsome, plain, and champion country of 10

Kilclief Castle, Co. Down, for a time the stronghold of the FitzSimons branch of the Savages.

John Ceky, Bishop of that See, publickly cohabited with *Lettice Thombe*, a married woman; for which Scandal *Swain*, Archbishop of *Armagh*, in 1441, had him served with a Monitory processe in his *Castle of Kilclief;* and there was a Chamber in the said Castle, then called the Hawks Chamber, which by Tradition of the old Natives, was the place where the Bishop's Falconer and Hawks were kept. [Visit. Bk. in Coll. Lib. of 1622.] Yet possibly this Tradition might have been taken up from the Figure of a Fowl, resembling a Hawk, carved on a Stone Chimney Piece in a Room on the Second Floor, on which also is carved in Bas Relief a Cross Patee. The Castle is yet entire, though it is covered with Thatch; it is a large Building, and the first Floor of it vaulted, has two Front Wings, in one of which is a Stair-case, and in the other a Stack of Closets. The Lands surrounding the Castle are a fine Demesne, which, with a Water Mill on them, are held from the Bishop by the Revd. *Peter Leslie*; South is a Denomination Land, called *Bishop's Court*, in Lease to Mr. Justice *Ward*, near which are *Sheepland* and *Ballykernan*."—Harris: *History of County Down*, pp. 23-4.

[1] White.
[2] Macdonnell.

Raymond Savage, Lord of Lecale and of Ardkeen, who died A.D. 1575.

miles long and 5 miles breadth, without any wood growing thereon. The sea doth ebb and flow round about that country, so as in full water no man may enter therein upon dry land but in one way, which is less than two miles in length. The same country *for English freeholders and good inhabitance is as civil as few places in the English pale.*[1]

"The next country to that and the water of Strangfourde is Arde, SAVAGE his country, which hath been mere English, both pleasant and fair, by the sea, of length about 12 miles and 4 miles in breadth, aboute; which country is now in effect for the moste part waste.

"The next country to Arde is Clanneboy, wherein is one Moriorthogh Dunelaghe, one of the Neyles, who hath the name as Captain of Clanneboy, but he is not able to maintain the same. He hath 8 tall gentlemen to his sons, and all they cannot make past 24 horsemen. There is another sept in that country of Phelym Backagh's sons, tall men, which taketh part with Hugh Mac Neill Oge, till now of late that certain refused him and went to Knockfergus. . . . . The same Hugh [O'Neill Oge] hath two castles, one called Bealefarst [that is, Belfast], an old castle standing upon a ford out of the Arde to Clanneboy, which well repaired, being now broken, would be a good defence betwixt the woods and Knockfergus."

In the MS. Council-book of Ireland, preserved in the library of the Royal Irish Academy, Dublin, SAVAGE's name appears in a list of "Yrishe Lordes and Capitaynes," who sent horse and foot to the "Hostings and Musters of the English Pale in Ireland, A.D. 1556-60. . . . SAVAGE . . . iiij Horsemen, xiiij Kerne."[2] The numbers contributed by SAVAGE on this occasion were quite equal to the average supplied by the English Barons in Ireland.

A contest now arose between RAYMOND SAVAGE and his kinsman ROLAND SAVAGE for the inheritance and captainship of their nation in what was left in the Ards of the once extensive possessions of their fathers.

Whose son this ROLAND SAVAGE was we have failed to discover after considerable research. We find no reference to him by name prior to the year 1559. That he could not have been a brother of RAYMOND's is clear from the facts that RAYMOND inherited the lordship of Lecale from his father, SIR ROLAND SAVAGE, formerly Seneschal of Ulster, and RAYMOND's descendants, the ARDKEEN family, were ever after called "the race of the Seneschal," to distinguish them from the descendants of this very ROLAND of A.D. 1559. But that he was a very near relative of RAYMOND's is indisputable.

---

[1] The English freeholders referred to, as later documents show, were largely of the SAVAGE kindred.
[2] See "National MSS. of Ireland," Part iv. 1, Appendix v.

Sections of Ancient Maps, showing SAVAGE Territories in Down.

The feud, however, between the rival claimants to the disputed territories in the Little Ards about the middle of the 16th century seems to have been protracted and bitter, and both parties were fully alive to its ruinous consequences to their kindred and country. ROLAND and RAYMOND, accordingly, finally agreed to request the Lord Deputy and Council to arbitrate, and in A.D. 1559 (first year of Queen Elizabeth's reign) they appeared before their Lordships, and prayed them to "put a quiet and loving end" to their differences. The result was that the Upper Ards were divided pretty evenly between them, and each was to be "Captain of his Nation" within his own dominion. The enrolment of the Treaty thus established is amongst the Patent and Close Rolls in the Record Office, Dublin. A very imperfect abstract of it is given in that very imperfect and slovenly compilation known as "Morrin's Calendar." Morrin gives the first half of its contents, and leaves on the reader's mind an utterly erroneous impression of its terms and meaning. We have seen and read the document in the Public Record Office, and the following is a copy of the *terms* of the "Treaty":—

A.D. 1559.   From the Patent and Close Rolls, 1st Elizabeth.   Membrum 26.

"Treaty between ROLAND and REDMOND SAVAGE, and their kinsmen: reciting that contention had arisen amongst them for the inheritance and chieftainship of their nation; and, having appeared before the lord Deputy and Council, declaring the losses and injuries they sustained, and having prayed their lordships to put a quiet and loving end to their differences, for the greater wealth and commodity of their country, it was ordered and adjudged that ROLAND SAVAGE should be captain of *his nation and freeholders having rightful inheritance in the lands of Ballyncontowne, in the Ards, Tullagharnan, Ballydowe, Tewesities, Ballentonragh, Ballynbentlyng, Ballyngrenagh, Ballyfannor, Ballywored, Tolnecrewe, Ballywlake, Ballywarter, Tolocraffeere, Knockavillar, Ballyharvan.* And also the said REDMOND for his part shall have the expenses as Captain upon all such of his nation or freeholders as have or ought to have a rightful inheritance in those lands following: ——[1]*kstown, both Ballycranes* [i.e., *Ballycranemore and Ballycranebeg*]*, Cookestown, Irishtown, Ballylisbane,* ARDKYNE, *Ballyward, Ballygalget, Ballycoller, Ballyniskinny, and Tullomayle.*"

It does not appear that this document confers any actual right of *precedence* upon one party or the other. Each was to have the rights of Captain of his Nation within his own territory as now defined. Circumstances, however,

---

[1] The first letters of the word are blotted in the original enrolment. The name is probably Kirkistown, though the first blotted letter seems like a C.

tended subsequently to give precedence to ROLAND and some of his successors, as will be seen hereafter.[1]

We now come to the inauguration of a new policy in Ulster, and fresh vicissitudes in the history of the SAVAGE family.

Thomas Smith, son of Sir Thomas Smith, Queen Elizabeth's secretary, having been granted by the Queen a portion of the Lower Ards, which had fallen into the hands of the O'Neills, landed at Strangford on the 31st August, 1572, and, writing to Burghley from Down, on the 10th September, he states that Sir Brian M'Felim O'Neill would not part with one foot of the land. He (Smith) had referred the matter to the Lord Deputy, and had withdrawn his soldiers from Newtown in the Ards to Ringhaddy in the Dufferin.

On the 10th October, Turlough Lynagh (O'Neill) writes to the Lord Deputy and Council, demanding that Mr. Smith may not be permitted to inhabit in the lands of Sir Brian M'Felim. On the 14th of the same month, Malbie, writing to the Lord Deputy, states that Sir Brian M'Felim has taken all the prey, and fired the towns, *and that* HENRY SAVAGE *has been slain by his special appointment;* and that the abbeys of Newtown (stated, as we have seen above, to have been founded by the SAVAGES), Bangor, Moville, Holywood, and others, have been burned. It would appear from this that HENRY SAVAGE had been favourable to the scheme of colonisation of the Great Ards by Smith and his men.

"Whatever English adventurers may have thought of Thomas Smith and his pamphlet, there was nothing in the movement which could possibly be pleasing to the Irish. The Norman family of SAVAGE has from early times enjoyed dominion in the Ards, and their title to considerable estates in the southern half had been acknowledged in 1559. It was evidently not intended to interfere with them, and so they seem to have favoured Smith's enterprise." So writes Mr. Bagwell. The position of the SAVAGES, however, was now one of extreme difficulty and danger. Those of them whose lands lay in the southern portion of the Upper Ards, being farther removed from their powerful enemies the O'Neills, needed neither the vigilance nor the diplomacy that were required of the LORD OF ARDKEEN and his dependants, whose territories stretched along the borders. RAYMOND SAVAGE, LORD OF ARDKEEN (or, as he is generally called in the correspondence of this time, FERDORAGH MAC SENESCHAL—*i.e.*, the dark-faced son of the Seneschal, or *Edmond* SAVAGE[2]), adopted apparently a double game. It was indeed difficult for any Anglo-Irish chief at this period to know

---
[1] This question will be somewhat more fully discussed under "SAVAGE (now NUGENT) OF PORTAFERRY.

[2] The English correspondents had probably followed as closely as they could the pronunciation of the name RAYMOND which was current amongst his Irish neighbours.

with whom to ally himself. The governing powers were themselves constantly playing a double game and games of fast-and-loose with the Anglo-Irish; just as at the present period the loyal inhabitants of Ireland are first sacrificed by the Government for its political ends, then taunted for not taking their own protection into their own hands, then fallen back upon for support in trying emergencies, and then once more cast aside, defrauded and despoiled. RAYMOND SAVAGE probably foresaw that Smith's expedition would prove abortive, and that, for a time at least, his neighbour, Sir Brian M'Felim, would triumph. His sympathies were probably with Smith, for he proved himself a friend and protector to Smith's broken followers in the course of the next year, 1573. His tendencies were possibly not disloyal; but it must have been perfectly clear to him that the Government which had recently confiscated his neighbour's lands, and had taken every excuse to deprive his father and himself of their patrimony, might, if not now frustrated, speedily put its hand upon the remnant of his wide ancestral estates; which indeed, shortly afterwards, it temporarily did.

_{RAYMOND SAVAGE, LORD OF LECALE AND OF ARDKEEN, who died A.D. 1575.}

On the 10th September of the same year, Essex wrote from Carrickfergus to the Privy Council, announcing his arrival there with a small company. On the 29th of September, the Queen wrote from Greenwich to the Lord Deputy about giving commission of general Captaincy in all Ulster to the Earl of Essex, and concerning a Commission to mark a boundary-line between the Smiths and the Earl of Essex. On the 20th October, Essex informed the Privy Council from Carrickfergus that he had taken 400 of Sir Brian M'Felim's kine and slain 40 of his men; and that there was news that Thomas Smith, Mr. Secretary's son, was slain in the Ards by Irishmen of his own household, whom he much trusted.

After this murder of Thomas Smith, RAYMOND SAVAGE took his unfortunate followers under his protection, and led them into a place of safety in his own territory. Essex, writing to the Privy Council from Carrickfergus on the 28th October, states that "the Baron of Dungannon, More, and Malbie, with horse, sent to the relief of Cumber, were stayed at the ford at Belfast." Essex had marched to their aid. Cumber had been burnt. *Mr. Smith's men had been "conducted into the Little Ardes by* FERDOROUGH SAVAGE." There had been a skirmish with Sir Brian M'Felim and all his power, and 100 had been slain. Norreys and Malbie had had their horses shot, but both had been rescued. The rebels would never offer any fight but upon great advantages.

It is manifest that the LORD OF ARDKEEN was now not in antagonism with the party Smith's men represented. Two months later, however, he was actually engaged with the O'Neills in opposing Essex. "The Irish," wrote Essex to

2 A

RAYMOND SAVAGE, LORD OF LECALE AND OF ARDKEEN, who died A.D. 1575.

the Queen on the 2nd November, "assert that the war is not the Queen's." This belief had taken hold not only of the Irish but also of the soldiers under Essex's own command. The majority of the people of the North seemed to look upon his enterprise as a private one, as in effect it was; and Essex began to feel that his extraordinary position was becoming perfectly untenable. On the 2nd November he writes to Burleigh, offering, if the Queen should like to take up the whole enterprise, to serve with 100 horse, and take a portion but double that of the private adventurers.

Meanwhile, the leaders of the Englishry in the Ards had almost to a man given their support to the O'Neills, evidently with the impression that their own territories might be now best preserved against the encroachments of adventurers like Essex by helping to establish the O'Neills firmly on their borders. "The Irish," Essex declares, "expected that he (Essex) would return to England, and leave the government of the country to Sir Brian M'Felim." On the 2nd December, 1573, Essex, in his Instructions to Mr. John Norreys and Edward Waterhouse on their going over to Court, makes the following statement:—"All the freeholders and inhabitants of the Ardes be gone out and joined in rebellion with Nele Mac Bryan Fertoughe, especially FERDOUROUGHE MAC SENESCHALL and the rest, saving SAVADGE, chief of that name [evidently ROLAND, of Portaferry], Denys Smythe, and JAMES MAC JENIAKE SAVAIGE [RAYMOND'S brother, sometimes also surnamed *Ferdorough*], which Denis Smyth and JAMES SAVAIGE, under colour of keeping in, doe more hurt by sending victualls and intelligence unto the rebels than the rebels themselves can do."

In the difficult circumstances in which RAYMOND SAVAGE was now placed, he seems to have had recourse to divers practices which the Government regarded as treasonous. From a very interesting letter of Jerome Brett, written to Lord Fitzwilliam on the 8th January, 1574 (to which our attention has been most obligingly drawn by Mr. Charles H. Brett, of Belfast), it would appear that he had assumed to himself some time previously the right of coining money and of making peace and war without warrant. He is also accused of having been implicated in the murder of White (probably of the Dufferin family), and of another Englishman named Browne. Brett states that he had received the Deputy's pardon for all offences, "treason against her Majesty's person and coining of money excepted." Since receiving that pardon, however, and very lately, he had committed sundry felonies and treasons, as in aiding and receiving Sir Bryan's men that were hurt by the English host; in taking prisoners and releasing them; in making peace and war; and in harbouring and protecting "a notorious traitor and murderer" named Patrick Hazard.

Either on account of RAYMOND's "treasonous practices," or in order to hold the Upper Ards in check, or for both reasons, the Castle of Ardkeen had been seized some time before the 1st January, 1574, and a garrison had been placed in it under command of Jerome Brett, who, in connection with Smith's enterprise, had been commissioned to overawe the inhabitants of the Ards.

RAYMOND SAVAGE, LORD OF LECALE AND OF ARDKEEN, who died A.D. 1575.

Meanwhile, the LORD OF ARDKEEN had evidently taken up his quarters near the opposite shores of Lough Strangford, possibly in another of his formidable strongholds, the Castle of Scetrick on the Island of that name.

Jerome Brett, in the letter above alluded to, states that RAYMOND SAVAGE had come to the country of which he had the government (viz., the district about Ardkeen), "to be entertained for 12 horsemen and 40 kern," saying that he was from the Earl of Essex, offering him many courtesies, and expressing much regret that Brett had not more forces at his disposal. Brett regarded his movements with suspicion, and calls his expressions of sympathy "crocodile's tears." By the killing of White, Browne, and others, he says, "he hath received such entrance as it is very hard to keep him from bytinge of such shepe." Brett's belief evidently was that he was endeavouring to circumvent him, and by some sudden stroke to regain possession of Ardkeen Castle and drive the garrison out of his territories. It is quite possible that Brett may have been right in some of his surmises; but it seems more probable that he was in error, for in Essex's instructions to Waterhouse, written prior to the date of this letter, he states that he had taken RAYMOND SAVAGE into his protection. Brett, however, was of opinion that his suspicions were justified by an incident which soon afterwards followed.

On the 7th of January, at night, RAYMOND SAVAGE crossed over Strangford Lough by boat, with twenty-six foot soldiers, and sent round some sixteen horsemen by land. He placed himself and his men in sundry advantageous positions, and lay in concealment, it would seem, till near daybreak. Then he suddenly caused the "prey" (the cattle) of the town of Ardkeen to be "raised," supposing (Brett believed) that he (Brett) would be the first man that would attempt to rescue the prey, and that RAYMOND would thus find a ready opportunity of capturing or slaying him. RAYMOND's party, however, as they "lay in their barke," were discovered by Brett's subordinate officer Mr. Storeys and his men, and Storeys immediately shot off a falcon.[1] SAVAGE's followers then declared that they had only come to ask for the assistance of Brett's foot soldiers, to aid them in making "a prey" (or foray) elsewhere.

---

[1] A falcon was a large cannon, carrying 25 lbs. shot.

Raymond Savage, Lord of Lecale and of Ardkeen, who died A.D. 1575.

Whatever may have been SAVAGE's intention, it does not appear that he incurred any further displeasure of Government. He had already, as we have said, allied himself with Essex, when Essex had been transformed by the Queen from a private adventurer into the royal Governor of Ulster; and he is stated to have accepted the command of a company under that Earl.

In 1575 Sir Henry Sydney, the new Viceroy, officially intimated that he had taken into protection EDMONDE (*i.e.*, RAYMOND) SAVAGE, *alias* FERDOROUGH MAC SENESCHAL.

RAYMOND SAVAGE, Lord of Ardkeen and of Lecale, had attained a good old age when he died. His life had been eventful. He had struggled hard to retain possession of the territories which his ancestors had so valiantly acquired, and so valiantly defended against overwhelming numbers for four hundred years; and amongst the men of his generation he must have been distinguished by some conspicuous virtues, for even the Irish chroniclers go out of their way to praise the hereditary enemy of their people; he was, say the *Annals of Loch Cé*, "the man of greatest humanity and bounty of all the foreigners of Erinn, although" (which was but too true) "he was injured regarding his property."

RAYMOND (FERDOROUGH MAC SENESCHAL) SAVAGE died in 1575. He was succeeded in the representation of the family by his nephew, the eldest son of JAMES (FERDOROUGH MAC JENIAKE) SAVAGE, viz., by

Ferdorough Savage, Lord of Ardkeen, who died A.D. 1602.

XII.—FERDOROUGH SAVAGE, LORD OF ARDKEEN (DIED JUNE 15, 1602, temp. Eliz.).

This FERDOROUGH SAVAGE, and his brothers JANICO (or, as the Irish called him, *Shenikin-a-bui*, or Janico the Fair-visaged) and ROLAND, the founder of the earlier Ballygalget branch of the SAVAGES, were all Royalists.

It would appear that JANICO still retained some portion of the old family possessions in Lecale, for in the year in which he is stated to have died (A.D. 1602) JENKIN BOY SAVAGE was "pardoned" for some alienation of lands in that Barony.[1]

Montgomery states that FERDOROUGH and his next brother JANICO were killed in an encounter with the O'Neills in the County of Antrim. The place of their death is said to have been Clogney Castally, in the County of Antrim, and the date, June 15, A.D. 1602.

---

[1] See *Patent and Close Rolls*, 45 Eliz., mem. 8.

FERDOROUGH SAVAGE was succeeded in the representation of the family and in the possession of Ardkeen Castle and Manor by the eldest son of his brother JANICO (JENKIN, or SHENIKIN-A-BUI, who had married Geyles ——, who, as his widow, resided at Grenagh), viz., by

XIII.—HENRY SAVAGE, ESQ., OF ARDKEEN, HIGH-SHERIFF OF THE COUNTY OF DOWN (BORN Feb. 22, 1588, temp. Eliz.; DIED 1655, temp. Commonwealth).

At the death of his father JANICO, HENRY SAVAGE was a minor, aged 14 years, 3 months, and 21 days, and he was placed under the guardianship of his surviving uncle, ROLAND SAVAGE, Esq., of Ballygalget Castle, a "soldier in Queen Elizabeth's wars," who was pensioned for his services and his "maims" therein.[1]

In the Patent Rolls, 3 James I. (1605), occurs the following grant:—" To ROWLAND SAVAGE was granted on the 22nd October of the said year, for a fine of 40s., the wardship and custody of HENRY SAVAGE, son and heir of JENKIN SAVAGE, late of Ardchin, Co. Down, gent., and grandson and heir of FERDOROUGHE MACJENIAKE SAVAGE, deceased, at a rent of £5; retaining thereout £3 10 for the maintenance and education of said HENRY, as hereinafter mentioned."

During HENRY SAVAGE's minority new colonies of Scots were established in the Great Ards and Claneboy,—those of Sir Hugh Montgomery and James Hamilton; and the descendants of the settlers under Montgomery still speak the Ayrshire dialect of their forefathers.

At an Inquisition made at Newry, on the last day of March, 1617, it appeared that "HENRY SAVAGE, of ARDKEENE, within the Co. of Downe, and his assigns, was and is seised and possessed, in fee, of the castles, lands, and tenements hereafter mentioned, that is to say, the Castle, towne, and lands of Ardkene, contayning 1 towneland, the towne and land of Ballilissbane 1 towneland, Cokestowne, al' Ballicokerie, 1 towneland, Irishtowne, al' Balligalagh, 1 towneland, Ballycrannymore 1 towneland, Ballycrannybegg 1 towneland, Krewe ½ a towneland, Ratalla ¼ of a towneland, Downe ¼ of a towneland with a freshwater lough, Ballycoller 1 towneland, Ballyvickenny 1 towneland, Tullymayly 1 towneland, Ballyward 1 towneland, the Castle and land of Skaterick, the iland of Ranish called the Calfe-iland, the Trashnagh-iland, the iland called Iland-roee, the iland called the Partan-iland, the iland called Iland-dromond, the two Mynisses, the iland called the Grass-iland, the iland called Inishe-an-royne, the Iland conolly, all which are lying and being in the Co' of Downe. The same

---

[1] See *Calendar of State Papers*.

are holden of the King that now is *in capite* by Knight's service." Most of the townlands here named, it will be remembered, correspond with the territories confirmed to Raymond Savage in A.D. 1559. Liberty was also granted to Henry Savage to hold a Court Baron within the limits of the town of Ardkeen.

[margin note: Henry Savage, Esq., of Ardkeen, born A.D. 1588; died A.D. 1655.]

The old struggle for precedence and priority on the part of the Portaferry branch of the family seems to have renewed itself on this occasion; for Roland Savage, of Portaferry, son and heir of Patrick, called Lord Savage, laid claim, without success, to the entire of Henry's castles and lands. One Henry Owen Savage, whose parentage we have not ascertained, also claimed the Ardkeen estates on some untenable ground; and Sir James Hamilton, Knight, the new owner of Claneboy, attempted to set up a claim to some of the islands, but in vain. The Lord Bishop of Down desired that the right of the

Sketrick Castle, off the western shore of Strangford Lough, an ancient stronghold of the Savages of Ardkeen.

said Bishop, as in right of the Church, and the right of the Glebe lands of the parish Church of Ardkeen, might be saved unto him. The Bishop of Down here referred to was Robert Echlin, the founder of the family of the Echlins of Ardquin and Echlinville. He had been consecrated in 1613. He became possessed by Bishop's lease of the lands of Ardquin and Castleboy, said to have been originally Savage property, some of which is stated to have been granted to the Church as an expiatory offering by a Chief of the Savages in Roman Catholic times.[1] His family continued to flourish in wealth and importance

---

[1] In the Appendix to Harris's *History of the County Down* we read:—To the Account of *Abbacy* or *Ardquin* add,—Seven Town Lands (being Bishop's Lands) about Ardquin, leased to Mr. *Echlin*, are said to have been given to the Church by *Savage* of *Portaferry*, as an expiatory Devotion, when all *Ireland* was Popish." This is probably not historically accurate.

for generations in the Ards, and, as will appear hereafter, became connected with the SAVAGES of Portaferry and Ardkeen by several intermarriages.[1]

HENRY SAVAGE, ESQ., OF ARDKEEN, born A.D. 1588; died A.D. 1655.

In or about the year 1628, HENRY SAVAGE married ELLIS (or ALICE) NY NEILE, the widow of Con O'Neill, the former lord of Claneboy and Great Ards. Of this ELLIS NY NEILE, Mr. Hill, in the valuable notes to his edition of the *Montgomery Manuscripts*, gives the following account :—" The *Inquisition* of 1623 states, 'We find a lease of Con O'Neale's to Ellis Neal his wife, and Hugh Boy O'Neale his son, of the lands of Ballycarngannon (in Drumbo parish), Bressage (in Saintfield parish), and Crevy (in Drumbo parish), dated the 1st of June, 1616, for 101 years, at 8 shillings rent during said Con's life, and after his decease his wife to give as much to his heir during her life, and after her death, yielding 20 shillings to his heir, out of every of the said townlands. And we find the said Con did by indenture, dated 2nd December, 1616, make a conveyance of said lands unto Lord Claneboy and Sir Moyses Hill, who have been in possession thereof ever since.' These terms are described in our copy as '*not in the Manuscript*' from which it was transcribed. Ellis Nyneil was a namesake in full of the first Countess of Antrim, and was most probably related to her. She was the second wife of Con O'Neill, as their son Hugh was only five years of age in 1616. Ellis was not old at the time of Con's death, for in 1628 she remarried with HENRY SAVAGE, of Ardkeen. She died in the following year. Her son, Hugh Boy O'Neill, must have died young, as the author [Montgomery] mentions that Daniel was old Con's only surviving offspring. The name *Ellis* is now sometimes written *Alice*, and the form *Nyneil*, used in the text, implies that the lady was the daughter of an O'Neill, most probably one of the many chieftains this race furnishes."[2]

William Montgomery, who frequently conversed with his relative Mr. HENRY SAVAGE in the latter's old age, says :—" The said HENRY told me that the two first Viscounts Montgomery and Hamilton offered him five thousand pounds sterling if he would sell his wife's (the said Ellis) jointure to them, which had been happy for him, because she died about a year after their marriage."

Some years after the death of his wife Ellis Ny Neile, Montgomery tells us, Mr. HENRY SAVAGE "married Elizabeth Nevin, the Laird of Monkroddin's eldest daughter, niece to the first Viscountess Montgomery, and cousin-german of her Ladyship's daughter, MRS. SAVAGE, of Portaferry. Since which time," he adds, "the said SAVAGE families have been good friends, and Protestants, only the

---

[1] The history of the Echlin family has been recently re-written, with admirable care and exactness, by the present representative of the family, the Rev. J. R. Echlin, M.A., of Ardquin, Co. Down.
[2] Hill : *Montgomery Manuscripts*, pp. 81, 82, footnote.

Henry Savage, Esq., of Ardkeen, born A.D. 1588; died A.D. 1655.

said HENRY did not put himself out of the Roman communion, but did read our Bibles; and on his deathbed, bid be assured that he would die in the faith of being saved by the merits and mediation of Jesus Christ only—he not hindering any of his offspring to be Protestants."

MR. HENRY SAVAGE'S younger brother, RICHARD SAVAGE, married another daughter of the Laird of Monkroddin. The Laird's name was Thomas Nevin. Montgomery calls his family "an ancient worshipful family." Monkroddin was near Irvine, in Scotland. One of the sisters of the first Lady Montgomery had married "Andrew Nevin, second Laird of Monkredding, or Monkroddin, in the parish of Kilwinning." In his notes to the *Montgomery Manuscripts*, Mr. Hill writes:—"Although the Monkredding estate was small, consisting only of 700 acres adjoining the village of Kilwinning, its lairds were kinsmen of the Earls of Eglinton, and appear to have been engaged in several confidential matters connected with the Eglinton family. In 1581, Andrew Nevin, the second laird and father of Thomas, witnessed an obligation from Margaret Maxwell, Lady Giffyn, and Duncan Foster of Killmoir, her spouse, to the third Earl of Eglinton. He also witnessed a bond given by the same Earl in 1582, relating to a marriage contract between Robert Master of Setoun and Margaret Montgomerie the Earl's daughter. In 1583, Monkredding was one of the witnesses to an obligation of Muir of Caldwell to surrender certain papers to Agnes Montgomerie, Lady Sempill.—Paterson: *Parishes and Families of Ayrshire*, vol. ii., p. 253. Fraser: *Memorials*, vol. ii., pp. 221, 224. Thomas Nevin, of Ballycopland, parish of Donaghadee, obtained a grant of denization in May, 1617.—*Calendar of Patent Rolls*, James I., p. 326. This gentleman appears to have returned to the family estate in Ayrshire, where he died about 1651. His will, dated on the 22nd of January in that year, is preserved in Dublin, although it was written in Scotland. In this document he mentions his lands in Ireland, and his son 'Mr. Hew, in Ireland,'—*MS. Notes of Rob. S. Nicholson, Esq.* On coming to the Ards, it is certain that the Nevins first settled in the parish of Donaghadee, where their descendants continued in possession of considerable landed property until late in the eighteenth century. In 1771, the lands known as the two *Ballymacrewses* were held by David and John Nevin, and had previously been in possession of Benjamin Nevin, probably their father. Besides this property, John Nevin held a part of Ballyvester, and David a part of Cannyreagh, in the same parish. In 1775, John and William Nevin held extensive house property in Donaghadee, including 'the water-corn mill and windmill.'—*MSS. in possession of Daniel Delacherois, Esq., Donaghadee*."[1]

---

[1] Hill: *Montgomery Manuscripts*, pp. 53, 54, footnote.

Mrs. Elizabeth Savage, *née* Nevin, was still living in 1655.

In A.D. 1634, Mr. Henry Savage, of Ardkeen, was appointed High Sheriff of the County of Down.

Henry Savage, Esq., of Ardkeen, born A.D. 1588; died A.D. 1655.

Mr. Henry Savage is mentioned by Montgomery first on the list of those whose servants attended the funeral of the 1st Viscount Montgomery in September, 1636, and also as one of the Esquires who took part in the procession. The Viscount died in May, 1636. His body was embalmed, and his funeral took place in the September following. "The solemnity was performed with all the pomp that the rules of heraldry would admit and decency did require." William Montgomery gives a minute account of it, which, as it illustrates the state of society in the Ards in the first half of the 17th century, and contains references to several of the leading families of the neighbourhood, we shall take the liberty of quoting extensively :—

"His corpse being embalmed and rolled in wax searcloths was close coffined, (no more now Lord or Montgomery) was locked up in a turrett till a week before its interment, at which time (being in September the said last mentioned year), it was carried privately by night a mile out of town [Newtown Ards], and in a large tent laid in state, and attended with the formalities of wax candles, friends and servants, till the day of the procession on foot from the said tent to the Church. The persons who made up the procession were all clothed in blacks (called in Scotland dueil weeds from this word dueil, but burrowed from the French, signifying mourning), and were seen in the following order, which the reader may please to peruse, if he doe not already know well enough the manner of burying Viscounts, which is, viz.—Imprimis, 2 conductors (with black truncheons) named Thomas Kenedy and John Lockart, both of Comerer—2dly, poor men (the oldest could be had) called salys (*i.e.* almsmen) in gowns, to the number of 76, the year current of his late Lordship's age, walking two and two, with their black staves.—3dly, the servants of Gentlemen, Esquires, Knights, Barons, Viscounts, and Earles, hereafter named, viz., by two's as they went.

"Hy. Savage, of Ardkeen	... 1	Hugh Kennedy, of Greengraves ...	1
		Rt. Barclay, Dean of Clogher ... 2	
Robert Adair, of Ballymenagh	... 1	Sir Wm. Murray, Kt. and Bart. ...	1
Archd. Edminston, of Duntreth	... 2	Mr. Jo. Alexander	1
Sir Jos. Cunningham, Kt. ...	... 1	Sir Edw. Trever	2
Jo. Shaw, of Greenock, Esq.	... 1	Sir Wm. Semple, Kt.	2
Geo. Montgomery, Esq. ...	... 2	Charles Alexander	1
Sir Anthy. Alexander, Kt. ...	.. 1	N. Montgomery, Esq., of Langshaw	1

186   THE SAVAGES OF THE ARDS.

<small>HENRY SAVAGE, ESQ., OF ARDKEEN, born A.D. 1588; died A.D. 1655.</small>

The Lord Alexander	 2	PAT. SAVAGE, OF PORTAFERRY, ESQ.	5
The Lord Viscount Claneboy	... 3	Sir James Montgomery, Kt.	... 6
Sir Wm. Stewart, Kt. and Bart.	... 5	The Lord Montgomery, the Earle's son	2

"The Earle of Eglinton ... 5

"Besides the attendants on the two Lordships' bodies.

"4th, Then marched the standard borne by Lt. Robert Montgomery.

"5th, After it followed the servants to the second Viscount, the chief mourner, viz.—

"John Boyd, Henry Purfrey, Hugh Montgomery, of Grange, Jun., William Catherwood, Hugh Montgomery, of Newtown, Edw. Johnston, of Greengraves, Mr. Samuel Row, James Fairbairn.

"6th, Next came the servants of the defunct—

. . . . . .

"7th, In the 7th space came two trumpeters fitly equipped, sounding the death march.

"8th, Walked the horse of mourning, led by the chief groom, Jo. Kennedy, and one footman.

"9th, In the next place went the Divines, neither Doctors nor Dignitaries— Mr. James Mirk, Mr. Js. Blair, Portpatrick, Mr. William Forbes, Mr. Hugh Nevin, Mr. James Montgomery.

"10th, Then came the Gentlemen and Esquires, who were mourners, viz.—

"Jo. Cunningham, of Newtown,	Hugh Montgomery, of Derrybrosk,
James Lenox,	RICHARD SAVAGE,[1]
James Cunningham, of Gortrie,	William Melville,

Water Hows Crymble, of Donaghadee,

Tho. Kenedy, of Pingwherry,	Jo. Gordon, of Pingwherry, sen.,
James Edminston,	Mr. Jo. Echlin, of Ardquin,[2]
Mr. William Cunningham, of the Rash,	Hu. Kennedy, of Drumawhay,
Malcom Dormont,	William Montgomery, of Ballyhaft,
Thomas Nevin, of Monkroddin, jun.,	Hugh Echlin,
James Melvill, Esq.,	Lieut. Thomas Melvill,
John Crawford,	Mr. William Adair,
Andrew Cunningham, of Drumfad,	Jo. Gordon, of Aghlain, jun.,
Pat. Muir, of Aughneil,	William Burley, Gent.,
Thomas Boyd, of Whitehouse,	Mr. William Stewart,
Hugh Hamill, of Roughwood,	Robert Adair, of Ballymenagh,

---

[1] Brother of HENRY SAVAGE, of Ardkeen.
[2] Son of Robert Echlin, Bishop of Down and Connor.

Henry Savage, of Ardkeen, Esq.,   Arch. Edminston, of Duntreth, Esq.,
Thomas Nevin, of do. [*i.e.* Ardkeen] sen.,[1]   Mr. John Trevor,
William Montgomery, of Briggend,   Alex. Lecky, of Lecky,
Mr. Marcus Trevor,   Hugh Kenedy, of Girvan Mains.

"11th, In this place went together the late Lord's Phisitians, viz., Hugh M'Mullin, practitioner, and Patrick Maxwell, Dr. in physic, and next after them came—

"12th, Alexander Colvill, Dr. in Divinity, Robert Barclay, Dean of Clogher.

"13th, Then there walked Knights and Noblemen's sons, mourners, viz.—
Sir Jas. Conningham, Kt.

Sir William Semple, Kt., the Lord Semple's son,   Sir Wm. Murray, Kt. & Bart.,
Mr. Charles Alexander,   Mr. John Alexander,
Sir James Erskin, Kt. & Privy Counsellor,   Sir Ed. Trevor, Kt. & Privy Counsellor.

"14th, Went Mr. Robert Montgomery, Clerk, the Curate in Newtown, alone.

"15th, Dr. Henry Leslie, Lord Bishop of Down and Connor, who preached the funeral sermon.

"16th, Then followed the great banner, advanced by William Montgomery, of Ballyskeogh.

"17th, Neile Montgomery, of Langshaw, Esq., bore the cushion with a Viscount's coronet on it, and a circolet about it.

"18th, Athlone Pursuivant-at-Arms, appeared marching by himself, and presenting to view the spurs, gauntlet, helm and crest.

"19th, Then the defunct's Gentleman Usher, named Jo. Hamil, walked bareheaded next before the King at Arms.

"20th, Ulster King at Arms carried the sword, target or shield armorial.

"21st, Then was drawn (by six led horses, cloathed in black) the hearse, environed with a circolet mounted on the carriage of a coach, supported with posts or pillars, under which was laid the coffin, inclosing the remains of that late worthy Viscount, covered with a velvet pall, and on it pinned taffeta escutchions of his Lordship's own, and his matches coat's armorial, and elegys of the best sort also affixed thereto. The hearse on each side being accompanied by six men, with single banner rolls without; and even in rank with them went six footmen belonging to his late Lordship and his three sons, each having a black battoun in his right hand.

"22d, Next immediately after the hearse followed now the Rt. Hon. Hugh, 2nd Lord Viscount Montgomery, of the Great Ardes, the chiefest mourner; after him walked Sir Jas. Montgomery, George Montgomery, and PAT. SAVAGE aforesaid, as next chiefest mourners (I dare say it), both in hearts and habits.

[1] Mr. HENRY SAVAGE's father-in-law, then evidently residing with his son-in-law, at Ardkeen Castle.

HENRY SAVAGE, ESQ., OF ARDKEEN, born A.D. 1588; died A.D. 1655.

"23d, Then walked the Viscount Claneboy and the Earl of Eglinton together; the Lord Alexander and the Lord Montgomery together; John M'Dowal, of Garthland, and the Baron of Howth's son; —— St. Lawrence, Esq., and Sir William Stewart, Knight, Bart., and Privy Counsellor, in one rank. All these, as chief mourners, who were attended by some of their own servants, appointed to wait on them and be near their persons; six men, also covered with long black cloaks, marching by two and two, in the servants' rear, a great mixed multitude following and going about the herse at decent distance; only all the women in black, and those who had taffeta scarfs and hoods of that colour, went next the six men in cloaks. The great bell then in the west end of the Church tolling all the while that the procession was coming from the tent.

"24th, And now, all being orderly entered and seated, and the coffin placed before the pulpit, and the service ended, the Lord Bishop preached a learned, pious and elegant sermon (which I have seen in print long ago, from which I might have borrowed some memories if I had it now). This done, and the corpse moved to the upper end of the chancel, was (after the office for the dead performed) there inhumed. The Church pulpit and chancel being circoled with black baze, and stuck with scutchions and pencils [pencels] of the defunct and his matches, at due distances; the whole edifice thoroughly illuminated by wax candles and torches. The full obsequys were thus ended.

"Divers elegant elegys and epitaphs were made by Newtown School (as was their grateful duty) and others on his Lordship's death, as encomiums of his life (whose love to the learned was eminent). . . .

"This funerall was extraordinarily great and costly; all the noblemen and noblemen's sons, and the gentry which came from Scotland, and the knights, gentry, and heralds, with their retinue, and the rest which came from Farmanagh, Tirowen, Donnegall, Armagh, and Antrim (which was no smal number), with the attendants of all these mourners, and their horses, besides the phisitians, divines, and bishop; and their servants, etc., were all entertained to the full, in meat, drink, lodging, and other accommodations. The better sort of them in the Viscount's house, and the residue in the town, where wine (because there was no excise or new impost) was plenty at his Lordship's expense; the atcheivements (alone) costing above 65l. at the lowest rate that they could be bought by Sir James Montgomery, who was one of the executors to the late Lord his father's last will and testament."

Such is a vivid picture of the life and society in the Ards in which the members of the SAVAGE families moved at this period.

"In 1636, a commission was issued to inquire into defects supposed to exist in all titles to estates, and to prepare an act of Parliament for remedying the same." In 1637 (12 Charles I.), all his lands were confirmed to MR. HENRY SAVAGE, of Ardkeen. "A grant in virtue of the said commission and for the fine of £10 10/- to HENRY SAVAGE, Esq., and his heirs, of the Manor, Castle, town and lands of Ardkyne. The towns and lands also of about 20 more lands (all particularly named;) and amongst them the rent of 12s. English and suit of courts out of the Castle, towns and lands of Ballygalgett and Kirkestown. The Estates were created the Manor of Arkyne, with power to hold a Court Baron; to impark 300 acres, with free warren, park and chase, to enjoy all waifs and strays, &c. This grant is dated 8 March, 1637."[1]

In 1639, Mr. HENRY SAVAGE was appointed by Hugh, Lord Viscount Montgomery, one of the Trustees to a Deed dated 6th October of that year. "It was found by Inquisition (*Down, No. 109, Car. 1*) that Hugh, lord viscount Montgomery, by deed, dated the 6th of October, 1639, granted to Sir James Montgomery, of Rosemount, Kt., PATRICK SAVAGE OF PORTAFERRY, HENRY SAVAGE OF ARKIN, William Shaw of Newtowne, and John Montgomery of Ballycreboy, Esqs., the manor of Downbreaklyn, and all the towns, lands, and hereditaments of Ballymilagh (now Mealough), Ballyknockbreda, Ballycarny (now Ballycairne), Ballydowneagh (now Duneight, Parish of Blaris), Ballyclogher (now Clogher), Ballyaghlisk (now Ballyaglis, Parish of Drumbeg), Lisnegnoe (now Lisnoe, Parish of Blaris), and that part of Ballylessan containing 140 acres, in the possession of George Montgomery of Drumfaddy. The printed abstract of the Inquisition in the Calendar does not state the trusts of the above deed; but an original copy of the latter, found among the family papers at Donaghadee, contains additional details."[2]

The rebellion and massacre of 1641 left the Ards untouched. The Ards, indeed, was the only district in the County of Down into which the sword of the insurgents failed to penetrate. "In less than a week after the commencement of the rebellion, the insurgents had possession of the counties of Tyrone, Monaghan, Longford, Leitrim, Fermanagh, Cavan, Donegal, Derry, and nearly all Armagh and Down. The district of Ards was the only portion of Down which was happily free from pillage and massacre, although the inhabitants there, on the first breaking forth of the rebellion, hardly hoped to escape the doom of other places. Refugees from other districts of Down, and

---

[1] Extracted from some MS. notes lent by COL. HENRY J. SAVAGE, the present representative of the Ardkeen family.
[2] Hill: *Montgomery Manuscripts*, p. 94, footnote.

HENRY SAVAGE, ESQ., OF ARDKEEN, born A.D. 1588; died A.D. 1655.

also from the adjoining counties, crowded thither, from among whom the second Viscount and his brother Sir James Montgomery of Rosemount collected a considerable force."[1]

But though the inhabitants of the Ards were thus secure from the ferocity of the Irish, those of them who still remained members of the Roman Catholic Church ran considerable risk from the zeal of the Scottish Covenanters. Probably the most influential of the Roman Catholics in the Ards at the time was Mr. HENRY SAVAGE, of Ardkeen; and William Montgomery, in his *Incidental Remembrances of the Two Ancient Families of the Savages*, informs us that HENRY SAVAGE needed special protection from the Government and from the Covenanting Protestants :—"In all the fermentation raised by the Covenant teachers," he writes, "against the peaceable Irish papists in the Lower Ards, yet Sir James Montgomery still protected them, and procured the Lord Conway's order, dated Decr. 1642, that only bonds should be taken of HENRY SAVAGE, of ARCHIN, Esq., for the delivery of the arms in his house at any time when called for, and the rest of the Papists to be disarmed, which privilege Sir James got confirmed and enlarged on another occasion, and there was need and reason for granting that safeguard, because of the unruly Scottish mob and common soldiers, who would make the pretence of searching for arms and amunition an opportunity to quarrel and plunder. . . . He [Mr. HENRY SAVAGE] was (by marriage)," he continues, "next cousin to our 2nd Visc^{t.} and to Sir James Montg^{y.} and that was related also to some of his reg^{t.} officers, to whom he was kind, and hospitable to the rest; yet all this did not release the fear he had of the vulgar people and the inferior officers, whereof the 3d Viscount and Sir James, at the league in Armagh, signed an order, dated the 22^d August, 1644, directed to Quartermaster John Hamill, prohibiting all persons whatsoever to give any disturbance to the person of HENRY SAVAGE aforesaid, or to his wife, children, servants, tenants, houses, or goods, and requiring restitution to be made if anything hath been seized or taken from him or them, as all persons concerned should answer for disobeying this their order, requiring and ordering the officers and soldiers to give assistance for recovery of anything so taken, and to protect him and his aforesaid from such injuries; for granting which Sir James was complained of and made to answer (and other trivial dust was raised against him) before Sir Robert Meredith, Sir Robert King and Sir John Clotworthy, comm^{rs.} of Parliament, for these parts of Ireland, Anno. 1646. Thus worth is attended with envy and obloquy—such malice had the Covenanters against them both."[2]

---

[1] Hill: *Montgomery Manuscripts*, p. 151, footnote.
[2] *Montgomery Manuscripts*, Early Edition, pp. 283-4. Printed at the *News-Letter* Office (Belfast), 1830.

William Montgomery gives a pleasing picture of the social aspect of the Ards in 1648:—

"In these cloudy times, our s^d Visct. appeared in his lustre, by going with a great train of attendance and the convoy of his troops to Mellifont (S^r. Js. M. his uncle, making a figure suitable to himself,) and there his L^oP wedded the Honble Mary, eldest sister of Henry, Ld Visc^t. Moor, Sr J. M. assisting to have her La^P's marriage portion of £3000 secured by bonds of the staple, w^h her brother (the Ld Moor) gave for the same; and there was need of the best security, for his L^oP's estate was entailed, and himself but tenant for life. This was done in the month of Decr. 1648. When his L^oP returned with his Lady and her sister and two of her younger brothers, &c.; the reception at Newtown was great as military appearance and good cheer could make it, and their entertainment suitable. For divers days, the Ladies had the pleasure to see several Gent^m. on horseback, with lances at their thighs, running at full career at glove and ring, for the scarf, ring and gloves w^h her Ladyship had set forth (on the 1st day of that solemnity) as prizes for the 1, 2 and 3 best runners (a sight never beheld by any of the Ladies or any of the attendants before that time). These exercises continued for two other days, matches for mastery being made among the Gent^n runners themselves, and the wagers were mostly bestowed on a supper and good wine; other days there were horse races made to entertain her Ladyship's brothers, who were always guests at the consumption of the winnings. Among these cavaliers, Capt^. Geo. Montgomery (his L^oP's uncle) bore away more prizes than all the rest, and to shew his good horsemanship (for he had in his travels learned to manage them) he broke his lance against the garden wall at high speed, and wheeled his horse upon his hinder feet, and rode back curveting and troting to the great admiration of fearfull ladies and all the other beholders. I," adds William Montgomery, "was then at Newtown school, and was a diligent spectator."[1]

MR. HENRY SAVAGE was appointed by Mr. Hugh Nevin, Vicar of Donaghadee, &c., one of the "overseers" of his will, dated 12th October, 1652. He (Hugh Nevin) appoints his "brother (-in-law), Tho. Maly to be an overseer," and also nominates as overseers and assistants of his family his "beloved friends and kinsmen, Sir Robert Adair, MR. HENDRIE SAVADGE, Mr. William Schaw of Newtowne, and Captain William Howstowne, and Captain James Mc Gill, and I hope the right honourable the lord of Ardes will give his assistance. I shall likewise desire my good friends, Hugh Montgomerie of Granguch (Gransheogh), John Montgomery of Ballie Pollie, Mathew Haslett, and Robert Callewell, to be assisting to the above-named overseers."[2]

HENRY SAVAGE, ESQ., OF ARDKEEN, born A.D. 1588; died A.D. 1655.

---
[1] Hill: *Montgomery Manuscripts*, p. 177.   [2] Notes to Hill's *Montgomery Manuscripts*.

MR. HENRY SAVAGE, of Ardkeen, died after a protracted illness. William Montgomery thus describes his character and his opinions:—"This Gentleman was loyal and moderate in his Romish religion, and read the Holy Scriptures, and, on his death bed, (whereon he lay long,) assured me that he trusted for salvation only to the merits and mediation of Jesus Christ. He kept no images in his house, nor used no beads at his prayers, (that ever I could see or hear of,) and he said if he had any such images in picture, he would meditate on but not worship them. He used to say that invocation of saints was needless, (although it were supposed they heard or knew our wants,) because he was sure his Saviour was God all sufficient, and our intercessor as man and priest."

His will, dated 31st August, 1655, commences with these words:—"I bequeath my soul to God my Maker, hoping through the merits of Jesus Christ my Saviour to be made partaker of life everlasting." To his eldest son and heir, Mr. JOHN SAVAGE, he bequeathed the Castle and Townland of Ardkeen, with the corn-mill situated thereon, the townlands of Tullomoyle, Ballyward and Lisbane, with the mill situated thereon, Cookstown, the chief rents and chiefries out of the townlands of Ballygalget, Ballycranemore (apparently), Kirkestone, Irishtown, Ratalla, and Ballycranebeg; the Castle of Scetrick, and all the islands in Lough Coyne (Strangford Lough) belonging to him; and a third part of the townland of Imovally during the life natural of Catherine Savage, *alias* Haddow, &c., which he had bought from the said Catherine Savage.

To his second son, HUGH SAVAGE, he bequeathed the townlands of Irishtown and Balligolnye, which he had bought from "Rolland Savadge the younger."[1]

To his third and fourth sons, JAMES SAVAGE and RICHARD SAVAGE, he bequeathed the rights, &c., of the lands which he held of the Lords Claneboy and Montgomery.

To his wife, ELIZABETH SAVAGE, *née* Nevin, he left all the towns, lands, and premises above-mentioned during her viduity. And the following affords us rather a vivid picture of the extent of the old Castle of Ardkeen at the time. If she should marry again, she was to have only a third part of his own proper inheritance for life, *together with the whole houses on the south side of the Court at the Castle of Ardkine, or otherwise the third part of all his houses at the said Castle*, at her option.

He mentions also his daughters Joan and Elizabeth, and a Mary Savage and her sister Aliso Oge Savage. And he appoints "the Rt. Hon. my

---

[1] The son of Roland Savage, of Ballygalget Castle.

singular good friend Lord Viscount Montgomery of Ardes, my wel-beloved friends Lt. Col. Hugh Coghran,[1] Capt. W. Maxwell, Capt. Hugh M'Gill,[2] and Patrick Savage of Ballygalgott, to be overseers to my last will." He had issue,

HENRY SAVAGE, ESQ., OF ARDKEEN, born A.D. 1588; died A.D. 1655.

  I. JOHN.
  II. Hugh.
  III. James.
  IV. Richard.
    I. Joan, married to Lt. Col. Hugh Cochrane, of Ferguslie, near Paisley, who served under Gustavus Adolphus, King of Sweden, and all through the Civil War in Ireland, from 1641 to 1652. (His brother, William Cochrane, became Earl of Dundonald.) She had issue,
      1. JOHN COCHRANE, of FERGUSLIE, who married Barbara, daughter of James Hamilton, a merchant of Glasgow, and died without issue prior to 1697.
      2. WILLIAM COCHRANE, *successor to his brother at* FERGUSLIE, who married Bethia, daughter of William Blair, of Auchinvale.
        1. Grizzel Cochrane, married to Mr. Robert Millar, Minister of Ochiltree, who was "outed" in 1662, and died in 168-.
        2. Margaret Cochrane, married to John Hamilton, of Barr, Parish of Lochwinnoch.
        3. Euphemia Cochrane, married, in 1688, to Archibald Stewart, of Newtown.
  II. Elizabeth.

MR. HENRY SAVAGE, of Ardkeen, died in 1655, and was buried, in accordance with the wish expressed in his Will, in the ancient parish church of Ardkeen, under the shelter of Ardkeen Castle Hill, where the dust of so many of his kinsmen reposes. He was succeeded by his eldest son,

XIV.—JOHN SAVAGE, ESQ., OF ARDKEEN, HIGH SHERIFF OF THE COUNTY OF DOWN (BORN ABOUT 1634, temp. Charles I.; DIED IN 1699, temp. William III.).

JOHN SAVAGE, ESQ., OF ARDKEEN, who died A.D. 1699.

MR. JOHN SAVAGE was probably educated along with his kinsfolk the SAVAGES of Portaferry and William Montgomery (author of the *Montgomery Manuscripts*) at Newtown School; for says Montgomery—in his *Incidental Remembrances of the Two Ancient Families of the Savages*,—"At Rosemount I found my cousin HUGH SAVAGE, of Portaferry, in May 1644, and his two sisters. The women were taught vocal and instrumental music by Thomas Naule, adduced to that end, and they had a schoolmaster to other purposes, and we had for our teacher

---

[1] Lt. Col. Hugh Cochrane had married his elder daughter, JOAN SAVAGE.
[2] To Captain Hugh M'Gill further reference will be made hereafter.

JOHN SAVAGE, Esq., OF ARDKEEN, who died A.D. 1699.

Mr. Alexander Boid (and Master of the liberal Arts, who had travelled into France, as Tutor to Mr. Eclin of Ardquin's sons); we had *divers sons of* HENRY SAVAGE [of Ardkeen] *aforesaid*,[1] our cousins, at school with us, and we the males were removed to the great school of Newtown, Mr. Boid having the oversight of my cousins, the SAVAGES, and me."

At the time of his father HENRY's death, JOHN SAVAGE was of full age and unmarried.

There is a "Funeral Entry" on record in Ulster's Office, Dublin Castle, which is signed by JOHN SAVAGE, the son of MR. HENRY SAVAGE [of Ardkeen].[2]

In 1663, MR. JOHN SAVAGE, of Ardkeen, was appointed High Sheriff of the County of Down.

In this year, on the 15th September, the 3d Viscount Montgomery died, and at his funeral (which was conducted with great pomp and solemnity), Wm. Montgomery tells us MR. JOHN SAVAGE, of Ardkeen, was one of the pall-bearers—

"19, The coffin, covered with a deep velvet, fringed pale, and above it was laid the defunct's naked sword and scabbard by it and his gauntlet, and on the sides were taffety scutcheons, and underneath

"20, The corners and sides of the pall by—Andw. Monro, Esq., Jo. SAVAGE, of Ardkeen, Esq., 2 Sr. Jo. Skffington, Barts., Sr Edw Chichester, Kt. Sr. Robt Monro, Gentn., Major Garrett Moore, Capt. Hu. Shaw, Capt Hu. M'Gill, Capt. J. Lessly, Capt. Hu. Montgomery."

MR. JOHN SAVAGE, whom Montgomery calls his "cousin," is also mentioned amongst the gentlemen whose servants attended the funeral—

"And next to the Earle walked

"23, The Honbl Jas. Montgomery, his uncle, and Henry Monty his brother, Willm Monty of Rosemount, Esq. his uncle, and Geo. Montgomery aforesd. his grand uncle.—24, HUGH SAVAGE, of Portiferry, ESQ. the defunct's cousin-german. They [qu. *then ?*] followed by two and two the servants of the persons undernamed; of the Earle's six, of his brother's two, of his uncle Garret now aforesd one, of his uncle Jas one, of his grand uncle Geo. one, of his uncle Wm two, of *cousin* JOHN SAVAGE aforesd one, of the Major-Genl Monroe one, of all 16; those were on the outsides, and many followed us (who were nearest the Earle) in long black cloaks, wh they hired in Belfast for that service."[3]

[1] In an Inquisition recording the death of HENRY SAVAGE, of Ardkeen, dated 19 Car. II. (1667-8), the name of only one son, JOHN, is mentioned as *then* living.

[2] MS. note in possession of Mr. F. W. F. Savage.

[3] As an illustration of the condition of the country at this time, we quote the following interesting account by William Montgomery of his rapid ride from Newtown Ards to Kilkenny and back to Dublin, in September, 1663, with the news of his noble relative's death :—

SAVAGE OF ARDKEEN, MAIN LINE.

In 1669, MR. JOHN SAVAGE, with 167 others, was restored to his estate as an "Innocent Protestant" by the Commissioners under the Act of Settlement. [JOHN SAVAGE, ESQ., OF ARDKEEN, who died A.D. 1699.]

MR. JOHN SAVAGE, it would appear, married a daughter of Thomas Clarke, Esq., of Dromintine, Co. Down (eldest son of Sir Thomas Clarke, Kt., of Dromintine, Co. Down). His wife's christian-name we have been unable to ascertain.

"In the claim (No. 2087) of HUGH SAVAGE, of Ardkeen, of a chief-rent of 30/- out of the lands of Ballygalget, it is stated that JOHN SAVAGE, late of Ardkeen, was son and heir of HENRY SAVAGE, and that HUGH SAVAGE (the claimant) was son and heir of JOHN SAVAGE.[1]

It is probably the same MR. JOHN SAVAGE, of Ardkeen, who is mentioned in the following extract from an "Agreement for Partition of the Jointure Lands between the Representatives of the Five Uncles of James, Earl of Clanbrassil, referred to at p. 146 of *The Hamilton MSS.*, and dated 1697:—

"Debts with which the above Lands are charged, being five properties:—

JOHN SAVAGE, Esq.,	£90
Widow Wood,	50
Mrs. Richardson,	100
John Robinson's Executors,	100
Fairly of Ballydowne,	200 "

"The 16th day [of September, 1663], before it was light, I took horse for Dublin, and met Capt. Hu. Montgomery at Dundalk; he had gone fm Newtown on the 12th day early, because of his Lop's hopeless condition, and was bringing Dr. Fitzwilliams, which being now needless, the Dr. returned when he thought fit. I rode on well mounted, and was with the Countess about 8 o'clock that night, and left her in tears, I sympathising with her good Lap. The 17th I left town as soon as I could sod the roads, and went to the D[uke of Ormonde] at Kilkenny before night (and ere he had heard the sad news from any other). . . I returned a great part of the way on the 18th, and came to Dublin the 19th day."—Hill's *Montgomery Manuscripts*, pp. 241-3.

[1] MS. note of Mr. G. F. Barry, in possession of Mr. F. W. E. Savage. Mr. Barry's note also includes the following data concerning the Clarke family:—

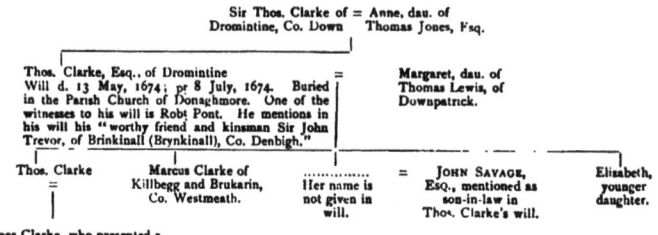

```
                    Sir Thos. Clarke of = Anne, dau. of
                    Dromintine, Co. Down  Thomas Jones, Esq.
        ┌──────────────────────────┴──────────────────────────┐
Thos. Clarke, Esq., of Dromintine          = Margaret, dau. of
Will d. 13 May, 1674; pr 8 July, 1674. Buried   Thomas Lewis, of
in the Parish Church of Donaghmore. One of the  Downpatrick.
witnesses to his will is Robt Pont. He mentions in
his will his "worthy friend and kinsman Sir John
Trevor, of Brinkinall (Brynkinall), Co. Denbigh."
   ┌──────────┬──────────────────┬──────────────┬──────────────┐
Thos. Clarke  Marcus Clarke of   ............  = JOHN SAVAGE,   Elisabeth,
    =         Killbegg and Brukarin,  Her name is   ESQ., mentioned as  younger
              Co. Westmeath.    not given in   son-in-law in    daughter.
                                will.          Thos. Clarke's will.
James Clarke, who presented a
claim (No. 2525) at Chichester Ho., 1700.
Henry Savage was agent and witness to the Claim.
```

John Savage, Esq., of Ardkeen, who died A.D. 1699.

And again the name appears in the list of the Mortgagees on the Countess's Jointure Lands—

"John Savage, Esq., of Ballydowne,.........£80 0 0"

Mr. John Savage, of Ardkeen, had issue,

I. Hugh, of whom presently as heir to his father, and representative of the Savages of Ardkeen.

II. John, who is mentioned in the will of his elder brother, Captain Hugh Savage, of Ardkeen, who entails on him, in case he should survive, and on his heirs male, failing issue of his own sons, the Ardkeen estate.

III. Philip. (Qy.—Could this be the Right Hon. Philip Savage, Chancellor of the Exchequer in the Irish Parliament, whose daughter and heiress was married to Sir Arthur Acheson, ancestor of the Earls of Gosford; who was the subject of one of Walter Savage Landor's *Imaginary Conversations;* and who was buried in St. Audoen's Church, Dublin, in 1717?)[1]

I. Sarah, married to Patrick Savage, Esq., of Ballygalget.

Mr. John Savage, of Ardkeen, died in 1699. He was succeeded by his eldest son,

Capt. Hugh Savage, of Ardkeen, who died A.D. 1723.

XV.—HUGH SAVAGE, ESQ., OF ARDKEEN, A CAPTAIN IN THE ARMY OF KING WILLIAM III. (DIED A.D. 1723, temp. George I.).

During the struggle between the partizans of William III. and James II. different members of the Savage family took different sides. Mr. Hugh Savage, of Ardkeen, joined the army of William. He fought at the Battle of the Boyne, July 1, 1690, and was there wounded. According to family tradition he lost a leg there; but this appears improbable, for he is stated to have fought again, under Ginkel, at the battle of Aughrim, on the 12th July of the following year, and to have been again wounded in the latter engagement.

Concerning the members of the Savage family who fought on the side of James, Mr. D'Alton writes as follows:—"Besides Captain Roland [Savage] there are in the Army List [of James II.], in Col. Cormack O'Neill's infantry, Edmund Savage, a lieutenant, and Henry Savage, an ensign. Captain Roland represented Newry in King James's Parliament, and in the Inquisition for his attainder was described as of Portaferry and Newry, in Down. Within which county were also outlawed Patrick and Henry Savage of Ballygalget, Thomas and Hugh of Dromode, James of Ballyspurge, Hugh of Ballydawes, Lucas of Dunhunk, and John and James Savage of Rock." In 1702, he adds, Patrick

---

[1] We observe that a query as to the parentage of Philip Savage, Chancellor of the Exchequer, printed in *Notes and Queries* many years ago, was never answered.

Savage, of Portaferry, purchased "part of the confiscations of Captain Rowland Savage, 'with the freshwater lough thereto pertaining.' The Hollow Swordes Blades Company also purchased his estate of Dromardin, in the Ardes. At the Court of Claims Patrick Savage, a minor, sought, and was in part allowed, a remainder in tail under settlements of 1685 in said Roland's estates; while HUGH SAVAGE, *as son and heir of* JOHN SAVAGE [of Ardkeen], was allowed a chiefry *out of certain lands of the same forfeiting proprietor;* as was another Patrick Savage, to a certain extent, a mortgage charged upon same; and John M'Cormick and Dame Elizabeth Ponsonby claimed and were allowed charges on other premises of Roland."[1]

CAPT. HUGH SAVAGE, OF ARDKEEN, who died A.D. 1723.

The chief-rent which CAPTAIN HUGH SAVAGE, as son and heir of JOHN SAVAGE, of Ardkeen, claimed, was one of 30/- out of the lands of Ballygalget, late the estate of Roland and John Savage, who had been attainted. These lands of Ballygalget passed (as we shall presently see), at CAPTAIN HUGH SAVAGE's death, to his second son, PHILIP SAVAGE, ancestor of the ROCK SAVAGE (Ballygalget) family, now the representatives of the ARDKEEN family in the male line.

CAPTAIN HUGH SAVAGE was one of the "innocent proprietors" restored to his estates after the Revolution. The decree is dated February 27, 1701.

It was in the lifetime of CAPTAIN HUGH SAVAGE, of Ardkeen, that William Montgomery put together his "*Incidental Remembrances of the Two Ancient Families of the Savages in the Lower Half Barony called the Little Ards. Collected out of my narratives of the lives of the three first Lord Viscounts Montgomery of the Great Ards, and of the Honble. Sir James Montgomery of Rosemount, Knight, and out of relation of my own acts and sufferings. Written and attested this St. Taffy's day, Ano. Domine 1700.*"[2]

"When," Mr. Hill tells us, "William Montgomery wrote his *Incidentall Remembrances of the two Ancient Families of the Savages*, he sent a copy to PATRICK, of Portaferry, the then representative of that branch, and a copy to CAPTAIN HUGH SAVAGE, the representative of the Ardkeen branch. The Manuscript copy sent to PATRICK SAVAGE is now [1869] in the possession of Mrs. Sinclair, the author's great-great-great-granddaughter, and on it Wm. Montgomery has made the following entry, at the end :—'The like of ye sd Remembrances is sent to Captn Hugh Savadge of Ardkin transcribed by Abraham Holm — lett all this be printed.'"[3]

---

[1] See *King James's Army List.*
[2] The Editor was indebted for his first perusal of a copy of this now very scarce book to the kindness of the Rev. Classon Porter, of Ballygally Castle, Co. Antrim.
[3] Hill: *Montgomery Manuscripts*, vol. i., p. 237, footnote.

CAPT. HUGH SAVAGE, OF ARDKEEN, who died A.D. 1723.

In the year 1701, Montgomery dedicated also to his "Kinsman Patrick Savage of Portneferry, Esq.," *A Description of the Barony called the Ards.*

This seems the most appropriate place to give extracts from these two interesting MSS., and so much of them may be quoted as will best illustrate the condition of the Ards in CAPTAIN HUGH SAVAGE's lifetime, and exhibit the traditions and facts concerning the SAVAGE family and its branches in the possession of the neighbours and kinsmen of their representatives at the close of the 17th, and the beginning of the 18th, century; the more particular references to the PORTAFERRY branch being reserved for the article in which we shall treat of the PORTAFERRY SAVAGES hereafter.

THE CASTLES OF ARDKEEN, BALLYGALGET, KIRKISTONE, AND SCETRICK.

"The old Castle of Archin (when built none can tell me)[1] stands on an eminent hill, (fortified after the Danish manner of forts, and perhaps thence called Archin—*i.e.*, the head of the Ards)[2] is almost environed by Loughcone; and Ballygetgit [Ballygalget], another Castle in view of, and about a mile and a half from, Archin, stands in the middle between it and Kirkistown, *alias* Eren Castle, later built and near the sea; the lands of both these two other castles were belonging (by deeds from Archin family) and built by Rowland, a cadett of Archin. I say the owners of said three Castles belonging to all of one blood, and by occupying by their tenants the full breadth of the said frontiers, could not but be (as thus posted, each Castle within sight of the other two) a notable outguard to the Lords of the Litle Ards, whose lands (and the Bishop's and the lands of Castlebuoy, long ago the possession of the Knights Hospitallers of St. John's of Jerusalem), lie within them, and are surrounded by the sea; so that, long running risks, the SAVAGES were convinced that castles of stones were necessary to save castles of bones from being broken.

"[The ARDKEEN family] hath another [Castle], as they called Sketrick,[3] the oldest (as is said) of them all.[4] . . . Both are very tenable for war (if fortified and repaired). Of whose family a cadet called Rowland (an officer of

---

[1] We know, however, that it was built prior to A.D. 1180. *Vide ante*, p. 122.
[2] We know that this etymology is wrong. *Vide ante*, p. 122.
[3] Sketrick Castle is described by Bishop Reeves (*Ecclesiastical Antiquities*) as "one of the largest of the Anglo-Norman Castles that remain [in that district]. . . . Skatrick Island," he writes, "which possesses the ruins of a very fine Anglo-Norman Castle, though joined to the town of Ballydown, in Killinchy, by a causeway, is not mentioned among them [the Castles of Dufferin], because it has, by some strange allocation, been assigned to the Barony of the Ards." . . . It is mentioned in the *Annals of Ireland* at the year 1470, and by the name of Sgathdeirge. Its dimensions are as follows:—height, 57 feet; length, 51 feet; breadth, 27 feet; thickness of walls, 4½ feet.
[4] It could hardly be older than Ardkeen Castle, which, as we have seen, was in existence in 1180.

SAVAGE OF ARDKEEN, MAIN LINE.

the Queen's army against the Irish). He, since K. James's[1] entry into England, built the two Castles of Ballygalgit and Kirkiston, *alias* Erew,[2] being high square piles, as are usual in Ireland, and gave the same (with lands adjoining) to his two sons. . . .

"About these castles are divers Irish popish householders, but inconsiderable), being mingled with Brittish and Protestants. . . .

"Kirkestown Castle aforesd, (which, wth B.gallgott and Quintin Bay, are the only ones in repair in this half barrony), whose garden-walls are washed with a pleasant fresh lough near the sea, and opposite to ye [North (?)][3] rock. James M'Gill of Ballymonestragh, Esqr., improved this place very much, by building garden walls and houses, and repairing in and about. He purchased ye same, and some lands adjoyning, from ye grandson of ye sd Rouland: and hath also built a wind miln there, whh is seen farr off at sea, and serves in day-time in good steade as a land-mark for saylors to avoyd the north and south rocks, whh are noted in all mapps for the misfortunes that ships, especially foreigners, have had on them in stormy and dark weather: so that it were to be wished that a lighthouse were to be erected and maintained there."

THE FAMILY OF SAVAGE.

In the following words William Montgomery introduces his *Description* of the Ards territories of the SAVAGE families, which, at the date at which he wrote, were reported, he says, to be "*much above four hundred years standing in Ireland.*" (They had been, as a matter of fact, above *five hundred* years in occupation of their prominent position in Ireland when he wrote—about A.D. 1700):—"The lower half barony [of the Ards] was planted by a colony and recruits of the English not long after De Courcy pierced into those parts of Ulster and sacked Down Patrick. The chief name and commander of that colony was SAVAGE, who with the assistance of ye Russels, Fitzsymonds,[4] Audleys, Jordans, and Welshes, &c., in Lecahill, and of the Whyts and others in the county of Antrim, many of which familys depended on and were (as ye Smiths and M'Gowans) fosterers or followers of the SAVAGES); they have hitherto kept their ground in the little Ards agt. all ye incursions of the Oneils and divers clanns their vassalls: altho' the York and Lancastrian broils drew many of their people to take ye part the[y] best wished to, which was the Yorke side."[5] . . .

---
[1] King James I.
[2] Same as "Eren," p. 198.
[3] There is a blank in the MS.
[4] The FitzSimonses, as we have already stated, were, according to Mr. Hill, a branch of the SAVAGES, being descended from a *Simon* Savage.
[5] *Incidental Remembrances of the Two Ancient Families of the Savages, &c.*

CAPT. HUGH SAVAGE, OF ARDKEEN, who died A.D. 1723.

The SAVAGES OF THE ARDS, he adds, "have always been a stout and warlike people, loyal to ye crown of England; who, however they might have had some few civill broils amongst themselves, on account of ye Tannestry custom,[1] when they were out of fear of ye O'Neills, and so become, as many noble English families in Leinster, Mounster, and Connaught, too much addicted to ye Irish customs, fewds, and exactions; yet of a long time past, and now, they are as much civilized as the Brittish (perhaps the more since having married with those nations); and doo live decently and conformably to ye Church re-established by law, and enjoy good houses, orchards, and enclosed fields, wh^h they improve, and hold all the possession they had at ye entry of King James as aforesaid, except Kirkestown, also Erew, and the lands adjoyning before mentioned, wh^h nevertheless of ye s^d purchase made thereof, doth pay chief rent to ye Castle of Ardkin, and doth suite to the Courts Leet and Barron of ye Mannor thereof, the said Henry haveing taken out letters patents, pursuant to ye Comⁿ of Grace for remedy of defective titles, granted by King Charles ye Martir of glorious memory."

THE SURNAME "SAVAGE," AND THE SAVAGE ARMS.

"The late MR. SAVAGE,[2] his ancestor, *imo*, July A^o 1573, by his Latin charter to Denis Smith, wrote himself *Patricius filius et heras Rowland defuncte suæ, nationis principalis & signes;* his subscription to that deed, Patrick Savage; and the same Patrick, the 17th of the said month and year, in a bond made to Phelimy Smith, the 15th of the said Q. Eliz., subscribes Pat. Savage; and his successor, the late Patrick, and his said son Hugh, wrote their sirnames, Savadge. Item, Henry of Archeen, in a deed dated 15th Jacobi (whereof I saw the counterpart), made to Rowland of Ballygalgot, his sirname is spelled Savadge; also in another deed from the said Henry, himself writes Savadge; item, 6th Junii, A^o 1641, Edmund Duff of Derri[3] and Margaret his wife (he was grand uncle to the present Mr. Savage of Portaferry) subscribes their names Savadge; but both Portaferry and Archeen now write Savage. The Frenchmen of that name write Sauvage (this word sounding after their pronunciation, as if we should write it Sovage), which they acknowledge to be an adjective noun, or word to signify a wild creature.[4] Now, may I not think that the Eng^d and Irel^d people of this sirname brought themselves from

---
[1] The Irish custom of electing a Chief from among the members of the Sept or Tribe irrespective of primogeniture.
[2] Of Portaferry.
[3] Edmund Duff Savage (*dark* Edmund), of Derry, in the Ards.
[4] Not the meaning of the original surname. *Vide ante*, p. 6.

the French, and also from the ancient English way (which last was to write Salvage, that likewise imports wild or untamed) to shelter themselves under the similitude of the French word afores^d, lest, if at all understood by the vulgar, or that they brought in the letter D to make the sirname vary from both the other ways of spelling it, to shun the imputation of wildness imposed on them by the said French and ancient English way of writing it. However it be, I may say that there needs no tergiversation on that account; because many brave men think it no disgrace to be of the sirname of Wildman, for perhaps it was given so at first, when sirnames came to be in frequent use and vogue, from the representation of such alike untamed, uncloathed man depicted in their shield of arms, and thus the Deburgos, Fitzursulas, and in many others obtained their sirnames, which yet adhere to their offspring.

"This I am sure of, that our Savadges their Lyons Rampant are as wild and untamed like (being in that positure, and armed and langued Gules), and are seldomer if ever reclaimable from their ferity, as the wildest man that ever ran frantic and naked out of doors to the woods and mountains."[1]

In A.D. 1717, CAPTAIN HUGH SAVAGE, of Ardkeen, was appointed one of James Montgomery's trustees for the sale of the Rosemount estate. "On the 23rd November, 1717, articles were agreed on between James Montgomery and his trustees for the sale of the Rosemount estate. These trustees were HUGH SAVAGE, of Ardkeen, Hugh Maxwell of Rowbane, Robert Hamill of Ballyatwood, and John Montgomery of Cregboy, in the county of Down, Esq^rs.; and Henry Dalway of Marshall's Towne, in the County of the towne of Carrickfergus, Esqr. James Montgomery was induced to sell Rosemount because he was indebted several persons in several sums of money amounting to Three Thousand one hundred pounds and upwards, which debt in a short time with the interest accruing thereon, would sink the estate; for preventing whereof, and making provision for himself, and raising portions for his children, the owner agreed to surrender it into the hands of his trustees. —(*MS. preserved at Grey Abbey.*)"[2]

Harris informs us that the old dwelling-house within the precincts of Ardkeen Castle was thrown down by CAPTAIN HUGH SAVAGE, and that he built a new dwelling-house lower down on the slopes of the Castle Hill. This seat (Ardkeen), he says, "was originally a dwelling-house enclosed within a Rampart, and standing boldly over the lake on a pretty high Hill. But this situation being found inconvenient on account of its great exposure to the

---

[1] *Incidental Remembrances of the Two Ancient Families of the Savages, &c.* (Ed. 1830.)
[2] Hill: *Montgomery Manuscripts*, vol. i., p. 420.

CAPT. HUGH SAVAGE, OF ARDKEEN, who died A.D. 1723.

storms, the late HUGH SAVAGE, Esq., demolished the House, and erected a new one lower down on the shore of a little narrow bay formed here by the Lough, called the Dorn, perhaps from some resemblance to the haft of a sword, which the word signifies in Irish." The House was not really built on the shores of the Dorn, but on the slope of the Castle Hill to the east.

Some portion of the ancient Castle must have been left, for according to the recollection (in 1877) of MRS. ARMSTRONG, daughter of the REV. HENRY SAVAGE, OF GLASTRY, and great-great-granddaughter of CAPTAIN HUGH SAVAGE, it had been stated to her, in her girlhood, that her father, when a child, was sleeping within the Castle during a violent storm, when the alarm was given that a portion

Last remaining fragment of the ancient CASTLE OF ARDKEEN, on the summit of Ardkeen Castle Hill (1884).

of it was beginning to totter, and he was carried out—probably down to the new dwelling-house.[1] The REV. HENRY SAVAGE was born in 1772, probably about fifty years after the erection of the new house. It is quite possible that the Keep was still standing, and habitable, when he was a little child; but Mr. Arthur Nugent, who was living in MR. SAVAGE's lifetime, thinks that every vestige of the Castle except the girdle of walls, about three feet high, which were suffered to remain till comparatively recent times, must have vanished at an earlier period. The story, however, was certainly told to MRS. ARMSTRONG, and we believe her informant was her aunt, Miss Mary Savage, the REV. HENRY SAVAGE's sister.

CAPTAIN HUGH SAVAGE married Lucy, daughter of Thomas Lucas, Esq., of Castle Shane, in the County of Monaghan, and widow of Captain Poyntz. She died 13th November, 1751, and her will is dated 31st August, 1751, and

---
[1] See *Life and Letters of Edmund J. Armstrong* (Longmans), p. 446, footnote.

proved 26th November of the same year. "In the early part of the 17th century," writes Sir Bernard Burke, "several members of the Lucas family emigrated from England, and settled in the sister island, where their descendants still remain, in the counties of Clare, Cork, King's County, and Monaghan. In the last they acquired, partly by purchase and partly by royal grant, considerable estates, which were erected into a manor by patent of Charles II., 1683, to be called the manor of Castle Shane, and the principal part of which has ever since continued in the family."

CAPT. HUGH SAVAGE, OF ARDKEEN, who died A.D. 1723.

CAPTAIN HUGH SAVAGE'S will is dated 31st July, 1723, and it was proved the 29th of January, 1724. When it was written he was in failing health—"sick of body, but of perfect and sound memory." He bequeaths "My soul to God my Maker, hoping by the merits and bitter passion of his D^r son my Saviour to be made partaker of his heavenly kingdom." He speaks of his "worldly goods though little, yet more than he deserves." He bequeaths to "my dear wife the third part of all my real estate during her life, and all my chattels;" to his eldest son, FRANCIS SAVAGE, everything, entailed to his (FRANCIS's) tenth son lawfully begotten, and heirs male lawfully begotten; failing such heirs male, to his *second son*, PHILIP SAVAGE (afterwards of Ballygalget, Rock Savage), and *his* heirs male lawfully begotten; failing PHILIP and such heirs lawfully begotten, to his *third* son, CHARLES SAVAGE, and his heirs male lawfully begotten; failing these, to his fourth son, LUCAS SAVAGE, and his heirs male lawfully begotten; failing these, to his brother, JOHN SAVAGE, should he be living, and to his heirs male, &c.; and failing these, to a ROBERT SAVAGE, of the City of Dublin, gentleman, and his heirs male, &c.[1]

---

[1] Of this Robert Savage we have no certain knowledge. There is a record of a marriage between Robert Savage, of Dublin, gent., and of Knockclough, Co. Sligo, and Susannah, daughter of Captain Francis King, by Magdalen his wife, on the 28th Feb., 1713; and the following letter may be read in connection with it:—

Copy of a Letter from LIEUTENANT SAVAGE, R.N., *to* SIR JOHN BOSCAWEN SAVAGE, K.C.B., &c. *(Lent to the Editor, in 1886, by Mrs. Clara English, granddaughter of Sir J. B. Savage.)*

"Lieutenant Savage, Royal Navy, presents his compliments, and has the honour to acknowledge Major-General Sir John Savage's letter of the 26th ultimo, and in reply Mr. Savage begs to assure Sir John Savage, that, whatever enquiries have been made, arose from a vain and idle pursuit alone. Being a younger scion of the family, Mr. Savage was desirous to ascertain from which branch he was lineally descended—the Portaferry, Lords of the little Ardes, or the Ardkeen, styled in Irish 'Slut na Seneschal,' the offspring of the Seneschal, originally the same family who settled in the County Down in 1177 under John de Courcy.

"In Mr. Savage's great-grandfather's will (Robert Savage, who died in 1736, and who married into the Lord Kingston's family), he styles John Moore of Drumbanagher, Armagh, *Uncle*—then it would appear from that (his having married Catherine, 4th daughter of Patrick Savage of Portaferry) we were descendants of that family, although Mr. Savage has always understood *Ardkeen*, and that his grandfather Francis, of Rock Savage, Co. Sligo—who died in 1772—was the last named in the entail.

It is perfectly clear, from the terms of this will, that CAPTAIN HUGH SAVAGE was determined, as far as his power extended, that the Ardkeen estate should never pass out of the male line of his descendants, as ultimately it unfortunately did.

The lands of Ballygalget, Ballybraniken, and Ballyspurge were not to pass to his eldest son, FRANCIS. He leaves Ballygalget, &c., in the hands of his executrix (his wife) and of her two brothers, Francis and Edward Lucas, Esqrs., to be sold, if need be, for the purpose of raising the portions of his younger children.[1] He mentions his daughters Mary and Lucy. He mentions also a natural son, by name John Savage.

CAPTAIN HUGH SAVAGE, of Ardkeen, by his wife Lucy Savage (*née* Lucas), had issue,

I. FRANCIS, of whom presently as successor to his father, and representative of the family at Ardkeen.

II. PHILIP, of ROCK SAVAGE (Ballygalget),[2] born 1696; married, *1st*, Jane, daughter of Balthaser Cramer, Esq., of Ballyfoile, in the Co. of Kilkenny, High Sheriff, Co. Kilkenny, 1683, and had issue,

   1. Hugh, born June 24, 1725.
   2. John, born July 4, 1726.
   3. Marmaduke-Coghill, 52nd Light Infantry; born Nov. 3, 1728; married Hannah, daughter of Thomas James Brotherton, Esq., of Hereford, and died in 1780, having had, with other issue, JOHN-BOSCAWEN (afterwards SIR JOHN BOSCAWEN SAVAGE, K.C.B., K.C.H., of ROCK SAVAGE—BALLYGALGET), who, on the death of his cousin, FRANCIS SAVAGE, Esq., OF ARDKEEN AND HOLLYMOUNT, in 1823, became the representative of the ARDKEEN family in the male line, and of whom hereafter as representative of the ARDKEEN family.

"By Sir John Savage favouring Mr. Savage with any information relating to the family Pedigree, which it is his intention when completed to have registered in the Herald's Office Ireland, he will feel much obliged, and Mr. Savage begs leave to add that he has never seen or heard of the advertisement relative to any property left by a person of that name, but should he meet with it, or hear anything relating thereto, he will have much pleasure in communicating it to Sir John Savage.

"Coston, Lowestoffe [*sic*]

"Suffolk, October, 17th, 1838."

The Catherine Savage, mentioned in the above letter, who married John Moore, Esq., M.P., of Drumbanagher, is stated to have been either aunt or sister of Richard Savage, of Portaferry.

[1] Ballygalget (Rock Savage) became the property and residence of his second son, PHILIP SAVAGE, and his descendants.

[2] For a full account of PHILIP SAVAGE, Esq., and his descendants, see hereafter under "SAVAGE OF ROCK SAVAGE (BALLYGALGET)." To make the genealogy clear, we give the *names* of his descendants in this place, but without details.

4. FRANCIS, of GLASTRY, in the Ards,[1] High Sheriff of the County Down, 1791; born 1733; married his first cousin Mary, third daughter of FRANCIS SAVAGE, ESQ., of Ardkeen, and granddaughter of CAPTAIN HUGH SAVAGE, of Ardkeen, and by her had issue,

[CAPT. HUGH SAVAGE, OF ARDKEEN, who died A.D. 1723. [SAVAGE OF GLASTRY.]]

    Francis, of Newcastle, Co. Down; born Dec., 1757; married Elizabeth, daughter of Arthur Atkinson, Esq., and died in 1803, having had issue,

        Francis, an officer in the 89th Regt. Foot; born 1786; married Miss Selina Ann Boyd, and died, 1827, having had issue,

            Francis-Charles, who died in 1826.
            Elizabeth-Charlotte.
            Charlotte-Selina.

        Charles, Lt. Col. H.M. Indian Forces; born 1787; died, unmarried, 1876.

        Henry, of Frindsbury, Kent, Captain Royal Marine Artillery, J.P., &c.; born 1797; married Miss Mary Perry, and died without issue, 1879.

        Elizabeth.
        Mary.

    Charles, born 1759; died unmarried, 1780.

    HENRY, Incumbent of Ardkeen, previously in the army, *who succeeded his father at* GLASTRY; born 1772; married Anne, daughter of Edward M'Guckin, Esq., by whom he had issue,

        FRANCIS, J.P., Barrister-at-Law, *who succeeded his father at* GLASTRY; born 1800; married Eliza, daughter of George Watts, Esq., and died without issue.

        Raymond, born 1803; married Eliza, daughter of John Scott, Esq., and died without issue.

        EDWARD, of GLASTRY, *successor to his brother* FRANCIS; born 1810; married, 1845, Mary, daughter of John Willington, Esq., J.P., of

---

[1] For a fuller account of FRANCIS SAVAGE, Esq., of Glastry, and his descendants, see hereafter under "SAVAGE OF GLASTRY."

Killoskehane, Co. Tipperary, and died, 1849, having had issue,
- Emily, who died in infancy.
- SARAH-JANE-ANNE, *heiress to her father;* born 1845; died, unmarried, 1867.

William, born 1812.
Mary.
Rose, who died in infancy.
JANE, *who, on the death of her niece* MISS S. J. A. SAVAGE, *became the representative of her brother,* EDWARD SAVAGE, Esq., of GLASTRY; born 1801; married Edmund John Armstrong, Esq., and had issue,
- Henry-Savage Armstrong, born 1840; died in infancy.
- Edmund-John Armstrong, the Poet; born 1841; died, unmarried, 1865.
- GEORGE-FRANCIS ARMSTRONG, M.A., D.Lit., F.R.U.I.; born 1845; married Marie Elizabeth, daughter of Rev. John Wrixon, M.A., and has issue,
  - FRANCIS-NESBITT-SAVAGE ARMSTRONG, born 1880.
  - John-Raymond-Savage Armstrong, born 1882.
  - Arabella-Guendolen-Savage Armstrong.
- Annie-Eliza Armstrong, married to Captain W. T. Croft, and has had issue,
  - Edmund-Armstrong Croft.
  - Arthur-William Croft.
  - Ethel Croft, who died in infancy.
  - Hilda-Frances Croft, who died in infancy.

Rose, who died unmarried.
Emily, who died in infancy.
Anne, born 1805; died, unmarried, 1879.
Mary Ann, born 1762; died unmarried.

5. HENRY, of ROCK SAVAGE, Major 16th Foot, High Sheriff of the County of Down; married Jane, daughter and co-

SAVAGE OF ARDKEEN, MAIN LINE.

heiress of —— Hamilton, Esq., and died without issue, 1797.

6. Charles, Major 51st Regt. of Foot; married Amelia, daughter of —— Lushington, Esq., and died without issue, August 8, 1801.

7. Edward, died unmarried.

8. James, born 1739; married Mary Anne, daughter of —— Galway, Esq., and died, 1803, having had issue,

    HENRY, who died young, 1808.

1. Lucy, born 1727; died 1729.
2. Jane, born 1730.
3. Lucy, of Nunsbridge; born 1731; died 1809, aged 78 years.

MR. PHILIP SAVAGE, of ROCK SAVAGE (Ballygalget), married, *2ndly*, Jane, 4th daughter of John Echlin, Esq., and had issue,

1. Philip, of Nunsbridge, born August 20, 1742; died 1790.
2. Robert, born 1745; died at the age of 9 years.
1. Rose, died in infancy.
2. Mary, born 1752; married John Mahallom, Esq., of Ballynacnamee. (?)

III. Charles, born 1702; died without issue in 1740; buried in Ardkeen Church.[1]

IV. Lucas, of Lissize, Co. Down; married Anne, daughter of Robert Ross, Esq., and widow of James Wallace, Esq. His will is dated 20th September, 1753; proved 18th September, 1755. He died, 1755, having had issue,

1. Ross, of Lissize.
1. Lucy.
2. Anne, married to Archibald Moore, Esq., and had issue,
    Anne Moore.
    Esther Moore.
    Elizabeth Moore.

I. Lucy, married to JOHN REILLY, ESQ., of SCARVAGH, in the County of Down, by whom she had issue,

CAPT. HUGH SAVAGE OF ARDKEEN, who died A.D. 1723.

---

[1] Inside the ruins of the old Church of Ardkeen, on a recumbent slab, is the following inscription. (It is at the *western* end of the slab, and is to be read as the reader faces the west):—

    Here Lyeth The BoDy of Mr. CHARLES
    Savage of Ardkeen who depart[d]
    this life on the 22[d] day of October
    in the year of our Lord 1740
    and in the 38 year of his age.

CAPT. HUGH SAVAGE OF ARDKEEN, who died A.D. 1723.

1. JOHN REILLY, Esq., of SCARVAGH; married, 1773, Jane, daughter and co-heiress of Colonel W. Lushington, of Sittingbourne, Co. Kent, and had, with other issue,

 JOHN-LUSHINGTON REILLY, ESQ., of SCARVAGH, who had, with other issue,

  JOHN-TEMPLE REILLY, Esq., of SCARVAGH.

 William-Edmond Reilly, who married and had issue.

 James-Miles Reilly, who married Emilia, 2nd daughter of Rev. Hugh Montgomery, of Grey Abbey, and granddaughter of the 1st Viscount Bangor, and had, with other issue,

  Sir Francis-Savage Reilly, K.C.M.G., Q.C.; born 4th February, 1825; died, unmarried, 27th August, 1883.[1]

  Brigadier-General William-Edmond-Moyses Reilly, C.B., Director of Artillery and Stores (1884), born 13th January, 1827.

II. Mary, married to Francis Lucas, Esq., of Grenan, second brother of EDWARD LUCAS, Esq., of CASTLESHANE, Co. Monaghan.

III. Anne.

CAPTAIN HUGH SAVAGE, of Ardkeen, died in 1723. He was succeeded by his eldest son,

---

[1] *Sir Francis Savage Reilly.*—The following obituary notice of Sir Francis Savage Reilly appeared in the *Morning Post* of Tuesday, August 28, 1883:—"We regret to announce that Sir Francis Savage Reilly, K.C.M.G., Q.C., the eminent Parliamentary draughtsman, and Counsel to the Speaker of the House of Commons, died at Bournemouth, after a brief illness, yesterday. Sir Francis Reilly was born in 1825, and was the son of Mr. James Miles Reilly, Barrister-at-Law, of Cloan Eaven, Co. Down, Ireland, and only brother of Brigadier-General W. E. M. Reilly, C.B., R.A., who was with him at the time of his death. Sir Francis was educated at Trinity College, Dublin, where he graduated and obtained a foundation scholarship and other honours. He was called to the Bar in Lincoln's Inn in 1851. As a Parliamentary draughtsmen he for many years had a leading practice, and filled many important public offices. He was assessor to the Marquis of Salisbury and Lord Cairns in the London, Chatham, and Dover Railway arbitration, and he assisted the Duke of Richmond and Gordon in a similar way in the Surrey and Sussex Railway arbitration. He was next appointed assessor to Lord Cairns in the memorable Albert Life Assurance Company Arbitration, and he was also assessor to Lord Westbury and Lord Romilly while they were arbitrators in winding up the 45 assurance companies which were absorbed in the European Life Assurance Company. On the death of Lord Romilly he was made sole arbitrator, with leave to appeal to the Court of Chancery; but none of his decisions were set aside, and the excessively complicated proceedings were brought to a speedy termination under his direction. Early in 1882, Sir Francis was made a Bencher of Lincoln's Inn, and appointed Counsel to the Speaker of the House of Commons. In April last year, on the joint recommendation of Earl Granville and the Earl of Kimberley, he was made a K.C.M.G., chiefly on account of the important

XVI.—FRANCIS SAVAGE, ESQ., OF ARDKEEN, HIGH-SHERIFF OF THE COUNTY OF DOWN, DIED 1770, temp. George III.).

FRANCIS SAVAGE, ESQ., OF ARDKEEN, who died A.D. 1770.

MR. FRANCIS SAVAGE, of Ardkeen, was named, we presume, after his paternal grandfather, Francis Lucas, Esq., of Castle Shane, and thus the christian-name *Francis*, which occurs so frequently in the ARDKEEN family, was brought into use amongst them.

In 1723 (the year of his father's death) MR. FRANCIS SAVAGE married his cousin Mary, daughter of Edward Lucas, Esq., of Castle Shane, in the Co. of Monaghan,[1] by Elizabeth, daughter of Thomas Smyth, Esq., of Drumcree.[2] (The marriage licence is dated Feb. 1, 1723.)

In the year 1732 Mr. FRANCIS SAVAGE was High Sheriff of Downshire.

On the 21st of February, 1760, the French, under Admiral Thurot, attacked and plundered Carrickfergus, and carried off the Mayor of the town and some of the principal inhabitants. Volunteer companies and Militia at once marched

---

professional services which he had rendered to the Colonial Office, and more especially to the Foreign Office, during the 20 years in which he was their draughtsman and adviser. Besides preparing and advising under many important Orders in Council regulating British jurisdiction in the Ottoman dominions, China and Japan, and other countries, he acted as legal adviser in the San Juan and the Mosquito Coast arbitration, and in the affairs of Cyprus, of the Western Pacific, of Egypt, and in matters connected with the Suez Canal Company. He was also for many years consulting counsel to the Veterinary Department of the Privy Council, and in that capacity had to deal with the cattle plague, and the intricate ramifications of the Orders in Council connected with it. He was one of the original members of the Statute Law Commission, under whose supervision the admirable index to the Statutes of the realm has been prepared and published; and down to the time of his death he was one of the most active members of the Commission. Sir Francis recently purchased an estate at Coombe, near Kingston-on-Thames, intending to reside within an easy distance of the House of Commons, but the disease which had occasionally prostrated him during the past few years attacked him again about a fortnight ago. Internal hemorrhage set in, and the best medical skill unfortunately proved of no avail. Sir Francis was never married, but he leaves a few relatives and a large circle of friends, to whom his death at the early age of 58 years, and so soon after he had gained his well-won honours, will be a grief."

[1] *Vide ante*, p. 202.

[2] Family of SMYTH OF DRUMCREE:—

LINEAGE. THOMAS SMYTH, Esq., of Drumcree, Captain in the Army, son (by Elizabeth his wife, daughter of Sir Robert Hawkesworth, of Hawkesworth) of Captain Ralph Smyth, who died in 1684, and brother of William Smyth, Bishop of Kilmore and Ardagh, ancestor of the Gaybrook and Barbavilla families, married Elizabeth Hatfield, and had, with other issue, a son and heir,

WILLIAM SMYTH, Esq., of Drumcree; married Mary King, an heiress, niece and ward of Dr. King, Archbishop of Dublin, and by her was father, with other children, of an eldest son,

THOMAS SMYTH, Esq., of Drumcree, who married, 1st, his cousin Alice, daughter of Thomas Nugent, Esq., of Clonlost, by whom he had a son, WILLIAM, his heir; he married, 2ndly, Miss Purefoy; and, 3rdly, Martha Hutchinson, daughter of the Archdeacon of Down and Connor, by whom he had a son, Thomas-Hutchinson, ancestor of the family of Ballynegall." (*See* Burke: *Landed Gentry*.)

2 E

FRANCIS SAVAGE, ESQ., OF ARD-KEEN, who died A.D. 1770.

to the coast to guard the counties of Down and Antrim against any attacks of the enemy, and Mr. FRANCIS SAVAGE was Colonel-Commandant of the Ards Regiment of Volunteers. The following allusion to him appears in a "History of Belfast," printed by George Berwick in 1817:—

"List of Volunteer companies and Militia that marched to oppose the French, set down in the order of time in which each respective corps arrived from Friday the 22nd to Tuesday the 26th Feb., 1760. Those marked (X) did not accept of pay from the town of Belfast.

. . .

"County of Down.

"Saintfield, Henry Savage, Esq.,[1] lieut. (James Stevenson's Regt).[2]

"Ards Regiment—FRANCIS SAVAGE, Esq., Col.-Commandant; arrived on Monday at noon, divided into three companies [numbering 220 men] raised at Portaferry, Grey Abbey, and Ballywalter; and same day marched to Bangor to guard the coast."[3]

---

[1] This was HENRY SAVAGE, of Prospect, near Saintfield. See hereafter under "SAVAGE OF PROSPECT."

[2] This was James Stevenson, of Killyleagh, M.P., who married Anne, daughter of Lt.-Gen. Nicholas Price, of Hollymount, Co. Down.

[3] The following account of the movements of the Volunteer Regiments on this occasion appeared in an able series of articles by Mr. Richard Lilburn, printed in the *Belfast Weekly News* in 1886, entitled "Chapters in the History of Orangeism:"—

"COUNTY DOWN.

"LORD HILLSBOROUGH'S REGIMENT.—Purdy's Burn, 195 men, commanded by Captain James Wilson (for his father, Hill Wilson, Esq., appointed Paymaster to the King's forces on that occasion), Lieutenants Alexander Legg and Thomas Stewart, arrived in Belfast on Friday morning, well armed, being the first considerable body that came in; entered forthwith on duty, and continued so till the French sailed.

"Castlereagh, 80 men, commanded by Captain Thomas Pottinger, arrived same day.

"Hillsborough, 184 men, commanded by Lieutenant Daniel Hull, arrived same day.

"LORD RAWDON'S REGIMENT, UNDER HIS LORDSHIP'S COMMAND.—Moira, 135 men, his Lordship's company, commanded by Captain Stothard, arrived on Friday. Dromore, two companies, 183 men, commanded by Captains Coslet Stothard and James Waddell, guarded the French prisoners to Banbridge, and arrived in Belfast on Saturday. 60 armed with back swords and pikes. Gilford, 90 men, one-half armed with guns, commanded by Captain Acheson Johnston, arrived on Saturday. Waringstown, 60 men, commanded by Captain Samuel Waring, arrived on Sunday; and on same day the Magheralin force, 30 men, commanded by Captain Charles Douglas.

"COLONEL WARD'S REGIMENT.—In the absence of Bernard Ward, Esq., colonel, attending Parliament, Lieutenant-Colonel John Echlin commanded. The forces of Downpatrick, Castleward, Bangor, Newtown, the Ards, Lecale, and Gillhall arrived on Saturday, numbering 350 men, accompanied by Captains Henry Waring, Charles Echlin, Steele Hawthorne, David Caddell, and John Magill, with lieutenants and ensigns to each company. The Waringsford company, numbering 50 men, arrived same day, and was attached to Colonel Ward's regiment.

Harris, in *The Ancient and Present State of the County of Down*, published in 1744, thus describes the Little Ards and the SAVAGE Castles as they were in the lifetime of MR. FRANCIS SAVAGE, of Ardkeen:—"The Tract of Country North and South of *Portaferry* from North of *Kirkistown* to *Quintin Bay Point* is usually called *the little Ardes*, to distinguish it from *the great Ardes*, that extend Northward from their Bounds to *Donaghadee*. As this part of the Country has been often the Seat of War between the *Irish* Septs and the *Savages*, whose Estate it antiently was, and a good part of it still is, we may expect to see several Castles in it; of which, besides the Castle of *Portaferry* before mentioned, there are three yet remaining on the Coast, as *Quintin Bay Castle*, lying two Miles South of *Portaferry*, an inconsiderable place called *Tara*; *Newcastle*, standing boldly over the sea on a Neck of Land, three Miles East of *Portaferry*; and *Kirkistown* Castle, near four Miles North East of the same Place. *Kirkistown* is an *English* Castle, surrounded by a high Wall strongly built, and containing within the Circuit of it a good Dwelling House of Mrs. Lucy Magil, now the widow Savage. . . .

"The Coast from *Ballyhenry* Bay bears N.E., and is uneven, having in it several little Bays, and some inconsiderable Islands, among which there is one pretty large off *Ardchin*, which is employed as a Horse-park by the Family of the *Savages* [of Ardkeen]."

FRANCIS SAVAGE, ESQ., OF ARDKEEN, who died A.D. 1770.

"COLONEL JAMES STEVENSON'S REGIMENT.—The colonel being at Parliament, Lieutenant-Colonel Robert Blackwood held command, and arrived in Belfast on Saturday, at the head of 167 men, from Killyleagh.

"Cumber and Ballymeen, three companies, 135 men, arrived on Friday afternoon, commanded by Captains Robert Gillespie, James Patterson, and Robert Kyle.

"Cumber, Captain John White and 47 men arrived on Saturday.

"Seaforde, Colonel Mathew Forde and 144 men arrived same day.

"Saintfield, Lieutenant Henry Savage and 50 men arrived same day.

"THE ARDS REGIMENT.—Colonel Francis Savage, commanding, arrived at noon on Monday, at the head of three companies numbering 220 men, raised at Portaferry, Greyabbey, and Ballywalter, and same day marched to Bangor to guard the coast.

"Newtown, Captain Arthur Kennedy arrived on Friday forenoon at the head of 85 men.

"Hollywood, Captain James Hamilton arrived same day, at two o'clock in the afternoon, with 80 men.

"Donaghadee Volunteers, Captain Hugh Boyd arrived on Saturday at the head of 133 men, and on Monday marched with several other companies to guard the coast between Holywood and Donaghadee.

"Downpatrick Volunteers, three companies numbering 130 men, commanded by Captains John Trotter, Charles Johnston, and William Hamilton, arrived on Saturday.

"Newry Volunteers, Captain Thomas Braddock arrived same morning on horseback at the head of 30 men.

"The total strength of the army of Down was 2,579 men."

FRANCIS SAVAGE, ESQ., OF ARD-KEEN, who died A.D. 1770.

Harris's lists of the Co. Down families at different periods in the history of the County are also interesting, not only as showing the social state of Downshire, but also as illustrating the antiquity and stability of the SAVAGES in particular:—" Under him [De Courcey] settled there the *SAVAGES, Whites, Riddells, Sandals, Poers, Chamberlanes, Stokes's, Mandevilles, Jordans, Stantons, Logans, Passelewes, Russels, Audleys, Coplands,* and *Martells,* and perhaps the *Fitz-Simons's, Crowleys,* and *Bensons.* The principal Gentlemen here in Queen *Elizabeth's* Time were Sir *Nich. Bagnal,* Sir *Henry Bagnal,* Sir *Hugh M'Genis,* Sir *Owen M'Neal Oge,* SAVAGE, *Fitz-Simons, Dowdal, Cormac O Neal, Iver Roe M'Genis, Bryan Orten O Neal, John White* of the Dufferin, *M'Cartan,* the *Bensons, Russels, Jordans, Audleys,* and *Mandevilles.* These Families are for the most part extinguished, partly by Civil Wars and Rebellions, and partly by the course of Nature, and at present the Chief Names are SAVAGE, *Southwell, Rawdon, Hill, Magill, Ward, Needham, Waring, Maxwell, Price, Mountgomery, Echlin, Stephenson, Bayly, West, Ross, Hamilton, Isaak, Blackwood, Ford, Fortescue, Kennedy, Matthews, Hall, Wallis, Johnson, Close, Lambert, Bateman, Douglass, Hunter, Wilson, Reily,* &c., &c., &c."[1]

The will of MR. FRANCIS SAVAGE, of Ardkeen, is dated 14th July, 1770. It was proved on the 7th September of that year. In it he states that by the will of his late brother, Mr. CHARLES SAVAGE (who had died in or about the month of November, 1740), he had a power of dividing among his daughters the real estate of which he (CHARLES SAVAGE) had died seized, being only a fee-farm rent issuing out of the town and lands of Ballyspurge, in the Barony of Ards, and Co. of Down, with the issues and profits thereof which had since accrued, and also the net remainder of his personal estate, with the interest the same had yielded at his death. But this chief rent of Ballyspurge, he says, having been formerly part of his family estate, he has been, and is, desirous to repurchase and transmit the same entire to his son CHARLES. And he bequeaths certain sums of money to his son-in-law and daughter, Edward and Elizabeth Lucas, of Castle Shane; to his son-in-law and daughter, FRANCIS and MARY SAVAGE (afterwards of GLASTRY); and to his unmarried daughter, Hester Savage, conditionally on their having conveyed their portions of the Chief Rent of Ballyspurge to his son and heir CHARLES. Of course no mention whatever is made in this will of the Ardkeen estate, which had been entailed in the male line with so much care and precaution by his father, CAPTAIN HUGH SAVAGE.

[1] *The Antient and Present State of the County of Down.* Dublin: Printed by A. Reilly, for Edward Exshaw, at the Bible on Cork-hill. M,DCC,XLIV.

SAVAGE OF ARDKEEN, MAIN LINE.

Mr. FRANCIS SAVAGE, of Ardkeen, by his wife, Mary Savage (*née* Lucas, who died in January, 1785, at the age of 84, and was buried in the Church of Ardkeen), had issue,

    I. CHARLES, of whom presently as successor to his father at Ardkeen.

    II. Francis, who married Jane —— (who died on the 14th of March, 1797, aged 22 years).

    I. Elizabeth, married to her cousin, EDWARD LUCAS, ESQ., of CASTLE SHANE, M.P. for Co. Monaghan, by whom she had, with other issue,

        1. FRANCIS LUCAS, Esq., of CASTLE SHANE, who died, without issue, in 1789.

        2. CHARLES LUCAS, Esq., of CASTLE SHANE, Barrister-at-Law; married, *1st*, in 1786, Sarah, eldest daughter of Sir James Hamilton, Knt., of Monaghan; and, *2ndly*, Louisa, daughter of —— Evatt, Esq., of Mount Louise. By the former he left at his decease an only child and successor,

The Rt. Hon. EDWARD LUCAS, of CASTLE SHANE, Co. Monaghan, J.P., High Sheriff 1817, M.P. for Co. Monaghan 1834-41, and Under-Secretary of State for Ireland 1841-46, sworn of the Privy Council there 1845; born 27th of Sept., 1787; married Anne, 2nd daughter of William Ruxton, Esq., of Ardee House, Co. Louth, M.P. for Ardee, and had issue,

Francis Lucas, Esq., formerly Lieut. 46th Regt., who died, unmarried, in 1846.

EDWARD-WILLIAM Lucas, Esq., D.L. and J.P., formerly Lieut. 88th Regt., born in 1819.

Fitzherbert-Dacre Lucas, Esq., married, 24th May, 1852, Laura Adelaide, only child of Lieut.-Col. John Lucy Scudamore, of Kent Church Court, Co. Hereford, and had issue by her (who married, *2ndly*, J. Donegan, Esq., of Cork), Edward Scudamore Lucas, born in 1853. Mr. F. D. Lucas died on the 30th of Sept., 1857, from a wound received at Lucknow the previous day, when, as for four months previously, during the Indian Mutiny, he had acted as a Volunteer.

Charles-Pierrepont Lucas, Capt. Bengal N. I., born in 1825.

Gould-Arthur Lucas, late Capt. 73d Regt., subsequently R.M. of Lower Ucomanzi, Natal; born in 1829; married, in 1857, Christabella, daughter of William Allen, Esq., of Liscongill, Co. Cork.

Catherine-Anne Lucas, married, in 1852, to Samuel Fitzherbert Filgate, Esq., J.P., of Hillsborough, Co. Down.

Anna-Isabella Lucas.

Isabella-Florinda Lucas.

3. Edward Lucas, in Holy Orders, who married Elizabeth Anne, daughter of Theophilus Clements, Esq., of Rathkenny, and was father of Theophilus Edward Lucas, who took the name of CLEMENTS. (*See* Burke: *Landed Gentry*.)

II. Hester, who died, unmarried, on the 22nd of November, 1799, and was buried in Ardkeen Church on the 24th of the same month.

III. Mary, born in 1733; married to her first-cousin, FRANCIS SAVAGE, Esq., of GLASTRY, High Sheriff of the Co. Down, 1791 (4th son, and *2nd that survived with issue*, of PHILIP SAVAGE, Esq., of ROCK SAVAGE, Ballygalget, 2nd son of CAPTAIN HUGH SAVAGE, of ARDKEEN). She died on the 9th of September, 1778, aged 45 years, having had issue as given above. (*See* Children of Capt. Hugh Savage, of Ardkeen, GLASTRY Branch, above; also, hereafter, "SAVAGE OF GLASTRY.")

MR. FRANCIS SAVAGE, of Ardkeen, died in July, 1770, and was buried in the Church of Ardkeen on the 21st of July, 1770. He was succeeded by his only son,

XVII.—CHARLES SAVAGE, ESQ., OF ARDKEEN, HIGH SHERIFF OF THE COUNTY OF DOWN (BORN A.D. 1746, temp. George II.; DIED A.D. 1779, temp. George III.).

Mr. CHARLES SAVAGE, of Ardkeen, was born in 1746. He married, *1st*, on the 24th of January, 1769, Anne, daughter of Cromwell Price, Esq., of Hollymount, near Downpatrick, Co. Down,[1] by his wife Mary, daughter of Hugh (Montgomery) Willoughby, Esq., of Carrow (she died in July, 1775); and, *2ndly*,

---

[1] Family of PRICE OF SAINTFIELD:—

NICHOLAS PRICE, Esq., of Hollymount, Co. Down, who married Catherine, daughter of James Hamilton, Esq., M.P., and widow of Vere Essex Cromwell, Earl of Ardglass, had a son,

in 1777, Catherine, daughter of John Leonard, Esq., of Brownstown, Co. Kildare. (The marriage licence is dated 9th July, 1777.)

Mr. CHARLES SAVAGE, of Ardkeen, was High Sheriff of the Co. of Down in 1770.

CHARLES SAVAGE, ESQ., OF ARDKEEN, born A.D. 1746; died A.D. 1779.

Mr. CHARLES SAVAGE, by his wife Anne Savage (née Price), had issue,
I. FRANCIS, of whom presently as successor to his father at Ardkeen.
II. Cromwell, who died without issue.
  I. Mary-Anne, married, 6th October, 1795, to WILLIAM EVANS MORRIS BAYLY, Esq., of NORELANDS, Co. Kilkenny, J.P. and D.L., High Sheriff of the County of Kilkenny in 1802,[1] by whom she had issue,

LIEUT.-GENERAL NICHOLAS PRICE, who married Dorcas, 4th daughter of Roger West, Esq., of The Rock, Co. Wicklow, and had issue,
JAMES, who married Frances, natural daughter of Lord Herbert, of Cherbury, and had two daughters, Catherine, married, 1st, to John Savage, Esq., of Portaferry, and 2ndly, 13th January, 1738, to Edward Baillie, D.D., Dean of Clonfert; and Dorcas, married to Dr. Whittle, of Lisburn.
CROMWELL, High Sheriff of the County Down 1781, M.P. for Downpatrick; married, 1st, Margaret, daughter of —— Anderson, Esq., of Belfast, and by her (who died 1741) had a son, Nicholas-Tichborne, born 1725, who died young; and two daughters, Elizabeth, married, 1743, to Roger MacNeal, Esq., of Tinesk; and Dorcas. He married, 2ndly, Mary, daughter of the late Hugh Montgomery Willoughby, Esq., of Carrow, and by her had a daughter, *Anne, married to Charles Savage, Esq., of Ardkeen.*
NICHOLAS, of SAINTFIELD, M.P. for Lisburn; married, 1st, Mary, daughter of Francis, 1st Lord Conway, of Ragley, Co. Warwick, by whom he had a son, FRANCIS; and, 2ndly, 1732, Maria, daughter of the Hon. Col. Alexander Mackenzie, 2nd son of the 4th Earl of Seaforth, by whom he had also issue.
Sophia, died, unmarried, October, 1720.
Margaret, married, May, 1718, to Rowland Savage, Esq., of Portaferry.
Anne, married to James Stevenson, Esq., of Killyleagh, M.P.

[1] FAMILY OF BAYLY OF NORELANDS :—
LINEAGE. JOHN BAYLY, Esq., who married Miss Bernard, had, with other children, a son,
JOHN BAYLY, Esq., who married Miss Strettell, of Ballitore, and, with daughters, left two sons, CLAYTON and Robert.
The Elder,
CLAYTON Bayly, Esq., of Norelands, married, in 1771, Mary, daughter of Sir William Morris, Bart., of Kilcreen, Co. Kilkenny, and had issue,
  I. WILLIAM-EVANS-MORRIS, of Norelands.
  II. John, who married a daughter of Admiral Sir Digby Dent, and died in 1822, leaving issue, Robert, Clayton, Caroline, Sophia, and Berri.
  I. Margaret, married to Lieut.-General Sir James Kearney.
  II. Mary, who died unmarried.
The Son and Heir,
WILLIAM-Evans-Morris Bayly, Esq., of Norelands, J.P., D.L., High Sheriff 1802; born 4 May, 1774; married, 6 October, 1795, Mary Anne, only daughter of CHARLES SAVAGE, Esq., of Ardkeen, Co. Down, and had issue, as in the text.—*See* Burke : *Landed Gentry* (Early Editions).

Charles Savage, Esq., of Ardkeen, born A.D. 1746; died A.D. 1779.

1. CLAYTON BAYLY, who assumed the surname and arms of SAVAGE, by Royal Sign Manual, dated 17th October, 1837, in compliance with the will of his maternal uncle, FRANCIS SAVAGE, Esq., of Ardkeen and Hollymount, and of whom presently as heir to his uncle, FRANCIS SAVAGE, of Ardkeen.
2. William-M. Bayly, Esq., of Annamult, Co. Kilkenny, born August, 1801; married, 17th October, 1836, the Hon. Anne Maxwell, 3d daughter of Henry, 6th Baron Farnham, and died Sept., 1840, leaving issue,
   William-Cromwell Bayly.
   Anne Bayly.
   Isabella-Sarah Bayly.
1. Mary-Anne Bayly, married, in 1828, to HENRY MEREDYTH, Esq., only son of SIR HENRY MEREDYTH, Bart., of Carlandstown, Co. Meath, who succeeded his father as 4th Baronet in 1859, and by whom she had issue one son,
   HENRY-WILLIAM MEREDYTH, 5th Baronet, J.P. and D.L.; born 1829; married, 12th April, 1862, Harriet Anne, elder daughter of the Rev. William Le Poer Trench (*See* "Clancarty, Earl of," Burke's *Peerage and Baronetage*), and had issue,
   HENRY-BAYLY MEREDYTH, born 1863.
   William-Clayton Meredyth, born 1865.

Mr. CHARLES SAVAGE, of Ardkeen, died at York on the 18th of August, 1779. He was succeeded by his elder son,

XVIII.—FRANCIS SAVAGE, ESQ., OF ARDKEEN AND OF HOLLYMOUNT, IN THE CO. OF DOWN, M.P. FOR THE CO. OF DOWN, HIGH SHERIFF OF THE CO. OF DOWN (BORN 1769, temp. George III.; DIED 19TH SEPT., 1823, temp. George IV.).

Francis Savage, Esq., of Ardkeen and Hollymount, born A.D. 1769; died A.D. 1823.

Mr. FRANCIS SAVAGE, of Ardkeen and Hollymount, born in 1769, inherited the House and Demesne of Hollymount from the Price family, through his mother.

The Demesne of Hollymount is situated a short distance from Downpatrick, in the Barony of Lecale, the old territory of the SAVAGE family. It is interesting as having been the temporary residence of the celebrated Mrs. Delany (the friend of Swift), whose husband, when Dean of Down, rented it from the family of Price. It is described in some of her letters, written there and preserved in the work known as *The Life and Correspondence of Mrs. Delany.*

Writing from Hollymount to Mrs. Dewes, on the 11th of June, 1745, Mrs. Delany thus speaks of it:—"This is really a sweet place, the house *ordinary*, but is well enough for a *summer house*.[1] Two rooms below, that is a small parlour and drawing-room, and within the drawing-room a little room in which there is a bed, but the Dean makes it his closet. Above stairs four pretty good bed-chambers and a great many conveniences for the servants. I have a closet to my bed-chamber, the window of which looks upon a fine lake *inhabited by swans*, beyond it and on each side are pretty hills, some covered with wood and others with cattle. On the side of one of the hills is a gentleman's house with a pigeon-house belonging to it, that embellishes the prospect very much. About half-a-mile off is a pretty wood which formerly was enriched with very fine oaks and several other forest trees (it covers a hill of about twenty acres); it is now only a thicket of the young shoots from *their venerable stocks*, but it is very thick, and has the finest carpeting of violets, primroses, and meadow-sweet, with innumerable inferior shrubs and weeds, which make such *a mass of colouring* as is delightful. But thorny and dangerous are the paths, for with these sweets are interwoven *treacherous nettles and outrageous brambles!* but the Dean has undertaken to clear away those usurpers, and has already made some progress: it is called Wood Island, though it is no more than a peninsula; the large lake that almost surrounds it is often covered with threescore couple of swans at a time. On the other side of the lake are various slopes [?] and on the side of one of them the town of Down. The ruins of the old cathedral are on an eminence just opposite to Wood Island, from whence I have taken a drawing. D. D. [Dr. Delany, Dean of Down] is making a path round the wood large enough to drive a coach; in some places it is so thick as to make it gloomy in the brightest day; in other places a view of the lake opens, and most of the trees are embroidered with woodbine and the '*flaunting eglantine.*' Four extraordinary seats are *already made*, one in an oak, the other three in ash-trees. This afternoon we proposed spending some hours there, but the rain drove us back again; on the beach of the lake are a great many pretty cockle shells,[2] which will not be neglected when the weather will permit me to go to it."[3]

FRANCIS SAVAGE, ESQ., OF ARDKEEN AND HOLLYMOUNT, born A.D. 1769; died A.D. 1823.

---

[1] It must have been afterwards enlarged.

[2] "*Query*—Freshwater mussels?"—(Note by the Editor of the *Memoirs*.)

[3] *Life and Correspondence of Mrs. Delany*, vol. ii., pp. 360, 361. In a letter of the 21st June, of the same year, to the same correspondent, Mrs. Delany briefly describes the old Cathedral of Down, as it then appeared, and gives an account of some of her rambles in the woods of Hollymount:—"Wednesday I went to Down with the Dean, and whilst he was visiting the poor, walked round the ruins of the cathedral, which has been a fine Gothic building; it is situated on an eminence just above the town, and commands an extensive view of mountains and lakes. I was called from my attention on this venerable

Francis Savage Esq., of Ardkeen and Hollymount, born A.D. 1769; died A.D. 1823.

Some years ago the little Demesne, with its thick and venerable woods, presented a very picturesque appearance, but many of the trees within recent years have been again felled, and the beauty of the old place has been impaired accordingly.

Mr. FRANCIS SAVAGE resided chiefly at Hollymount, and his withdrawal from his ancestral home at Ardkeen no doubt tended to hasten the decay of the House by Strangford Lough.

We find Mr. FRANCIS SAVAGE mentioned in 1796, along with two other members of the SAVAGE family, as one of the Grand Jury that endeavoured to repress the seditious movements which began to manifest themselves in that year even in the County of Down, and which culminated two years later in the Rebellion of '98. "At the Summer Assizes in 1796," writes Mr. Lilburn (*Belfast Weekly News*, Feb, 26, 1887), "the country being in a very disturbed state, owing to the rebellious movements of the people, the Grand Jury of Down resolved to exert themselves to preserve the peace of the country and enforce due obedience to the law. The resolution was subscribed by Daniel Mussenden, Sheriff; FRANCIS SAVAGE [of Ardkeen], foreman; Sir John Blackwood, Bart.; Hon. Robert Ward; J. Reilly; David Kerr; Richard Magennis; Matthew Fforde; Nicholas Price; PATRICK SAVAGE [of Portaferry]; J. W. Maxwell; Arthur Johnston; Savage Hall; Rainey Maxwell; Arthur Annesley; Holt Waring; Gawn Hamilton; Robert Waddell; George Mathews; Thomas Dowglas; John C. Gordon; Thomas Lane; FRANCIS SAVAGE [of Glastry]; Thomas Waring."

ruin, by the bell that rang for prayers, after which we went home, and as soon as dinner was over we walked to Wood Island, where the Dean amused himself with his workmen, and I at my work under the shelter of a young oak, in which D. D. has made a very snug seat. When he had discharged his labourers we set forward for adventures; and as bold as Don Quixote, he undertook, armed with a stout cane instead of a lance, and I (with my shepherdess's crook) followed intrepid, to penetrate the thickest part of the wood, where human foot *had not trod, I believe, for ages*. After magnanimously combating brakes, briars, and fern of *enormous size* and thickness, we accomplished the arduous task, and were well rewarded during our toil by finding many pretty spots enamelled and perfumed with variety of sweet flowers, particularly the *woodbine and wild rose*, which grow here in great abundance. We came home as weary and warm as we used to do frequently at Calwich, and enjoyed the refreshment of an easy seat, and the pleasure of talking over our toils, as you and I and our dear brother have often done there, and we hope we may often again."—(Pp. 363, 364.)

The Delanys did not remain long in the Co. Down, and one misses the references to the families and social life of the county which one would expect to find in the gossip of the Correspondence. The principal persons of the neighbourhood to whom allusion is made are the Baylys; Mr. Hall; Mr. Ward, a country curate; Mr. Johnston (agent, that is, rent-collector, to the Dean); Mr. Cornabée, a Frenchman by birth, who had a living in the neighbourhood; Mr. Matthews and his family; and the then Sheriff of the County. Mrs. Delany intimates that the duties of the Parish had been shamefully neglected by the Dean's predecessor.

Mr. Savage entered the Irish House of Commons, as member for the County of Down, in 1794, being elected on the 2nd of January of that year, *vice* the Rt. Hon. Arthur Hill, created Marquis of Downshire, supported by the then powerful interest of the Downshire family. In 1798 (January 8) he was re-elected, along with the Rt. Hon. Robert Stewart, Viscount Castlereagh, and he sat as member for the County in the Parliament of the United Kingdom after the Union till 1812. He took a prominent place in Lord Downshire's party in the Irish Parliament in opposition to the Union. On the night of the 15th of January, 1800, he seconded an amendment to the Address, proposed by Sir Lawrence Parsons, which led to an anxious debate. The incident is described in a letter, written during the progress of the debate, by Mr. Henry Alexander to the Rt. Hon. Thomas Pelham, since printed in the *Cornwallis Correspondence*, and is mentioned by Lord Cornwallis, the Lord Lieutenant, in his letter to the Duke of Portland written the following day. As the letters contain references to several celebrated names, and as the event was a momentous one, some passages from them may be here quoted:—

FRANCIS SAVAGE, ESQ., OF ARD- KEEN AND HOLLYMOUNT, born A.D. 1769; died A.D. 1823.

"Henry Alexander, Esq., to the Right Hon. Thos. Pelham.
"Jan. 15, 1800.
"My dear Mr. Pelham,

"Dublin is much and seriously, although I think, at present, not mischievously agitated. Our Parliament adjourns after the Militia business is disposed of. Grattan, I hear, is to be introduced at or after 12 to-night,[1] until which period the debate is to be prolonged. I pity from my soul Lord Castlereagh, but he shall have something more than helpless pity from me,—but he has a phalanx of mischievous talent, and a host of passion, folly, corruption, and enthusiasm to contend with. The Catholics yesterday came to some absurd resolutions. To-morrow the Guild of Merchants meets, and the day after, I understand, they are to communicate all rights to the Catholics. Grattan has, you know, the confidence of 40,000 pikemen. The passions of the Bar and many of the country gentlemen give them a favourable accolade—men will believe what they wish, and we shall have hot work. However, we are upon the whole stronger than last year. I believe the Minister stronger in point of votes—but with Ponsonby, Grattan, Burke, Plunket, &c., to agitate the mob, and Foster and *Parnell to obstruct public business*,[2] much is to be laboured.

"I leave my letter open for contingencies.

"I am (at four o'clock), yours truly, H. Alexander.

"Going to the Lords at nine. Sir L. Parsons has moved an amendment to the Address, or that part of it stating the existing unity of the Kingdom as it actually exists, and adding that the assertion of our birthrights to legislative independence to your Parliament in '82 contained sentiments which we are now called on to repeat. The speech was founded on all the injuries for 600 years sustained by Ireland, the necessity of meeting

[1] "He was elected for Wicklow borough; and Lord Castlereagh, Jan. 10, informed Mr. King that Grattan had paid 2400*l*. for this seat."—(Note by the Editor of the *Cornwallis Correspondence*.)

[2] A peculiar talent, which seems to have run in the blood.

FRANCIS SAVAGE, ESQ., OF ARDKEEN AND HOLLYMOUNT, born A.D. 1769; died A.D. 1823.

a packed Parliament before the packing was completed, of crushing the coiled snake before it made its leap, talked something of petty Scotch and English politicians, and figuratively of a puny miner capable of blasting the work of giants—*ob. invidiam.* He was seconded by SAVAGE, member for the County of Down.

"Lord Castlereagh, rising to reply, gave the Speaker an opportunity of creating a laugh by asking if the noble Lord meant to second the Baronet. Lord Castlereagh replied in a very manly style, prophesied that the seceders from Parliament would soon feel they owed a momentary co-operation to motives that would die away. And he has chosen, like a man, rather to throw the glove than pick it up.

"As I know not how I may be useful, I return, and

"10 at night."

"Yours again,
"H. ALEXANDER."

"Marquis Cornwallis to the Duke of Portland.
"[Private.]
"Thursday, Jan. 16, 1800.

"My dear Lord,

"The House divided at 10 o'clock this morning, after a sitting of eighteen hours, on an amendment to the Address, deprecating the discussion of Union. It was moved by Sir Lawrence Parsons, and seconded by Mr. SAVAGE, Lord Downshire's member for the County of Down. The Ayes were 96, the Noes 138; majority 42, which, considering the number of our vacancies, and some disappointments, I consider to be a satisfactory issue to our first contest.

"I have, &c.,
"CORNWALLIS."[1]

Mr. FRANCIS SAVAGE, of Ardkeen and Hollymount, married, *1st*, Jane, daughter of James Crawford, Esq., fourth son of James Crawford, Esq., of Crawfordsburn, Co. Down, and by her had issue an only child,

I. MARY-ANNE, who was married, on the 9th of May, 1814, to Mathew Forde, Esq., of Seaforde, Co. Down, and of Coolgreany, Co. Wexford (born 1785), J.P. and D.L. for the Co. Down, Col. of the Royal North Down Militia, High Sheriff 1820, and M.P. for the Co. Down from 1821 to 1826, eldest son of Mathew Forde, Esq., of Seaforde and Coolgreany, High Sheriff for Co. Down 1803, by Catherine, eldest daughter of the Right Hon. William Brownlow, of Lurgan, M.P. for the Co. Armagh. She died without issue.

Mr. SAVAGE married, *2ndly*, on the 19th of May, 1806 (the marriage licence is dated 17th May, 1806), the Lady Harriet Butler, 3d daughter of Henry Thomas, 2nd Earl of Carrick, by whom he had no issue.

In 1819, Mr. FRANCIS SAVAGE was High Sheriff of Downshire.

---

[1] *Cornwallis Correspondence.* By Charles Ross, Esq. Vol. iii., pp. 161-163.

MR. FRANCIS SAVAGE died on the 19th September, 1823, leaving no surviving issue. By his will (proved, 1823) he left all his property to his widow, the LADY HARRIET SAVAGE, for life; and after her death his estate was to pass to his nephew, CLAYTON BAYLY, Esq., eldest son of his only sister, MARY ANNE SAVAGE, by her husband, William Evans Morris Bayly, Esq., of Norelands, Co. Kilkenny (*see above*, children of CHARLES SAVAGE, ESQ., of Ardkeen), conditionally on his assuming the name and arms of SAVAGE. In 1829, LADY HARRIET SAVAGE married Col. Mathew Forde, of Seaforde and Coolgreany (whose first wife had been her first husband's daughter by his first marriage, as we have seen). Under a decree of the Court of Chancery in 1837, the manor of Ardkeen was sold to the late Mr. Harrison, of Belfast, for the sum of £85,000. It is now (1887) the property of Captain Harrison, of Holywood, Co. Down. An arrangement was effected between LADY HARRIET and MR. CLAYTON BAYLY, by which the latter entered into possession of the property on the payment to her of an annuity of £1,500 a-year for life;[1] and Mr. CLAYTON BAYLY, by Royal Sign Manual, dated 17th October, 1837, assumed the name and arms of SAVAGE. Mr. CLAYTON BAYLY SAVAGE (who married, 26th Feb., 1821, Isabella Jane Octavia, 2nd and younger daughter of Mathew Forde, Esq., of Seaforde and Coolgreany, by Catherine, eldest daughter of the Right Hon. William Brownlow, of Lurgan, M.P. for the Co. Armagh) died without issue; and the proceeds of the sale of the Ardkeen Estate, together with Hollymount House and Lands, passed to his paternal relatives, the members of the family of the Meredyths, Baronets, of Carlandstown.

On the death of MR. FRANCIS SAVAGE, of Ardkeen and Hollymount (Sept. 19th, 1823), the representation of the ARDKEEN family in the male line passed to the heir male of PHILIP SAVAGE, Esq., of ROCK SAVAGE (BALLYGALGET), second son of CAPTAIN HUGH SAVAGE, of ARDKEEN—*i.e.*, to the said PHILIP SAVAGE's grandson, and CAPTAIN HUGH SAVAGE's great-grandson,—the only surviving son of MARMADUKE COGHILL SAVAGE, Esq., viz., to

XIX.—MAJOR-GENERAL SIR JOHN BOSCAWEN SAVAGE, OF ROCK SAVAGE (BALLYGALGET), CO. OF DOWN, K.C.B., K.C.H., COLONEL-COMMANDANT AND DEPUTY-ADJUTANT-GENERAL ROYAL MARINES (BORN 23 February, 1760, temp. George II.; DIED 8 March, 1843, temp. Victoria).

SIR JOHN BOSCAWEN SAVAGE led a rather remarkable life, took part in some of the most brilliant naval battles of the most stirring period of our history, and attained considerable distinction. He was born at Hereford,

---
[1] Lady Harriet Forde died at St. Leonards-on-Sea, 25th July, 1865. See Burke's *Peerage, &c.*

SIR JOHN BOS-
CAWEN SAVAGE,
OF ROCK SAVAGE,
born A.D. 1760;
died A.D. 1843.

23rd February, 1760. His Commission as Ensign in the 91st Foot is dated 5th December, 1762. It had been obtained for his elder brother, and on the death of the latter, in infancy, it was transferred to him at the early age of two years. His Commission as Ensign in the 48th Foot bears date 1st September, 1771. In the year 1772, being then only twelve years of age, he mounted guard in Dublin Castle; in the following year, being then but thirteen years of age, he was engaged, as an Ensign in the same regiment, in quelling a Negro insurrection in Tobago; and at the age of fifteen he fought a duel with his own Colonel. The following narrative of his life is drawn from an obituary notice of SIR JOHN SAVAGE which appeared in the *United Service Magazine* in 1843, and from some other publications:—

"This veteran officer, who died at his residence on Woolwich Common, on March 8, 1843, was descended from an ancient family of that name settled at Ardquin [Ardkeen], Co. Down, Ireland, for many centuries, and at a very early age entered the army; his first commission bears date December 5, 1762, in the 91st Regt. of Foot. He exchanged to the 48th Regt. of Foot in 1773 [1], and was employed in the West Indies (Island of Tobago) during the rebellion of the Negroes there; he afterwards returned to England, and sold out of the army in 1776. In January, 1777, he obtained a Second Lieutenant's commission in the Marines,[1] was promoted to First Lieutenant shortly afterwards; Captain April 24, 1795; Major, August 15, 1805; Lieut.-Col. in the Army, Jan. 1, 1812; ditto in the corps of Marines, March 24, 1815; Colonel and Commandant of

---

[1] He was at this time a lithe, active, quick-witted youth, full of joviality and animal spirits. "One day my grandfather," writes one of his grandsons, "having come on shore in a hired boat, with a party of officers, from the ship they were serving in, was left last in getting out of the boat, and his companions ran away, leaving him to pay the boatman. This he appeared in no hurry to do, and the boatman, a big fellow, having expressed his determination to have his money or thrash my grandfather, the latter challenged him to fight, and, a crowd having speedily collected, just before hostilities should commence, my grandfather said to the boatman that he wished just to put one question to him before they began, and, on the boatman signifying that he was ready to hear it, he asked him 'whether he had ever heard of the copper-bottomed ships in the Navy, and how much faster they could sail than the other ships?' and continued, 'Well, you know, I'm copper-bottomed, and you may catch me if you can,' and ran off, to the great amusement of the bystanders at the discomfited and enraged boatman." A portrait in chalks of Sir John at this period, taken in Marine uniform, proves him to have been a handsome and singularly bright-faced lad. The large blue eyes are full of intelligence, courage, and mischievous fun; and the fair oval face is well set-off by his light wavy long hair, powdered (apparently) after the fashion of the times.

"At another time a party going on shore determined to play him a trick and leave him behind, and they got away all right and put up the mast intending to sail ashore; but Savage, becoming aware of their departure, ran to the stern gallery, and as the boat passed under it jumped thence on to the mast, upsetting the boat and giving his friends a thorough ducking."

the Chatham Division, June 20, 1825.[1] He was appointed Deputy Adjutant General, March 17, 1831; promoted to Major-General, and removed from the serving corps to the Unattached List, Jan. 10, 1837.

SIR JOHN BOS-
CAWEN SAVAGE,
OF ROCK SAVAGE,
born A.D. 1760;
died A.D. 1843.

"SIR JOHN embarked on board H.M.S. Princess Amelia, 1778, and was transferred to H.M.S. Bedford, 74 guns, in 1779, and sailed in the fleet under the command of Sir George Rodney to the relief of Gibraltar; on the passage to which fortress a convoy, consisting of one line-of-battle ship and frigates, was captured. The above fleet also fell in with the Spanish fleet on Jan. 16, 1780, under the command of Don Juan De Langara, brought them to action, captured six sail of the line, drove two line-of-battle ships on shore, and then proceeded and relieved Gibraltar. On her return to England, the Bedford captured a French line-of-battle ship and frigate.

"In 1782, CAPTAIN SAVAGE sailed to the West Indies, on board H.M.S. Dolphin, and returned to England the following year.

"During the peace he was employed on board several ships, and at his divisional headquarters, in the usual routine of military duties.

"At the breaking out of the Revolutionary War with France he embarked on board the Niger, and in that frigate narrowly escaped shipwreck on the coast of Holland in a dreadful hurricane.[2]

---

[1] Some time about 1818 he fought another duel, with a Major someone, of the Marines, with whom he had had a dispute about bringing his dog "Bingo" into the ante-room of the Mess at Woolwich. Both officers were either put on half-pay or removed from the service; but both were speedily reinstated, the Major through interest, and Savage in consequence of his services.

[2] In the following characteristic letter to his wife, he describes this great storm, in which the *Niger* so nearly perished :—

"Niger, at the Nore, March 13th, 1793.

"We arrived here this day, and am glad to have it in my power once more to address my Dearest Sophy, a thing, I assure you, at one time never expected. But I will in some measure endeavour to relate our situation. We sailed on the 27th of last month from the Nore, with a convoy for the Texel and Elbe, and on the first of this it came on to blow, in consequence of which I, as usual, was obliged to go to bed, where I lay untill the 3d without having either eat or drunk anything except a little Tea. All this time the Gale had been increasing, and about 6 o'clock in the morning of that day, a sea struck the ship in a most violent manner, which broke my scuttle and filled my bed full of water. I was asleep at the time, and on being awoke in that manner concluded the ship had foundered. My bed and bedding were so wet it was impossible to lay on them, and I was so extremely ill I could scarcely stand. I fortunately had my cloak and great coat in my Trunk, which were dry. I therefore rol'd myself up in them and went into Mainwaring's cabin, where I lay down on the sopha. I was in this situation, almost perished with cold, and sick to death, untill 12 o'clock, at which time Harriss came and wish'd me much to get up and endeavour to eat something. Upon my telling him I was not able to get up, let alone eat, he said, 'Why, all your Messmates are in the Gunroom.' I express'd my surprise at their *all* being there, when he reply'd, 'Probably, Savage, you do not know your situation, but it is expected that the ship will be on shore in a very short time, and it is determined, as soon as the people, who are nearly worn out, get a little refreshment, to cut away the masts, throw the guns overboard, and let the anchors

SIR JOHN BOS-
CAWEN SAVAGE,
OF ROCK SAVAGE,
born A.D. 1760;
died A.D. 1843.

"In 1795, he embarked on board H.M.S. Orion, 74, under command of Captain Saumarez (afterwards Admiral Lord de Saumarez), joined the Squadron under the command of Sir John Jervis, 1797, and was, on the 14th Feb. of that year, engaged with the Spanish fleet off Cape St. Vincent, where four sail of the line were captured."[1] He was subsequently employed in blockading Cadiz

go, as the only hope left of saving our lives.' This, you may be assur'd, was dreadful intelligence, but I had no reason to doubt it. Poor Harriss's [condition] too plainly prov'd the truth of his assertions. I reflected on my miserable situation, and for the first time in my life most seriously wish'd myself unmarried. I form'd ten thousand ideas what would become of you after I was gone, but could not think of one that offer'd the least comfort. I look'd back on every material transaction of my life, and was happy in finding that I had ever done to the utmost of my power to assist my fellow creatures, therefore nothing on that head lay heavy on my conscience, and the only pang I felt was that of parting from you and my Dear Boy, particularly as my circumstances were in such a derang'd state, and I had not a friend in the world whom I could rely on to assist you. I therefore most fervently recommended you both to the protection of my Maker, and, sustain'd by the idea that He would not desert you, and that you would yet live to see many happy days, I, with a degree of calmness which brought with it none of those horrors so frequently attendant on the approach of Death, resigned myself to whatever fate might attend me.

"I then got up and found all my Messmates sitting round the Table with a large piece of Boil'd Beef, without either Table Cloth or plates, and every one of them cutting and eating in the most voracious wild manner I ever saw. I was recommended to follow their example, as it would probably be the last refreshment we should have for some time, that every exertion would be expected from us, as an example to the people, and that without some kind of sustenance it was impossible we could even assist ourselves. This was fair argument, and, however extraordinary it may appear, I eat very hearty and drank a strong glass of Grog. I then ventured to enquire into the real state of the ship, and soon found the information given me by Harriss was too true. We were then in fifteen fathoms water; some were of opinion the ship would ride by her anchor, others differ'd and had not a hope. Just at this time all Hands were call'd on Deck to put the dreadful determination in force. Such a sea I declare I never in my life saw, and as for myself—I had not the most distant idea, had we anchor'd, that it was possible for the ship to have lasted 10 minutes, and the consequence of her parting the cables would have been that every soul must have perish'd. At this time there was an opening in a Black Cloud to the windward which, we flatter'd ourselves, would turn out to our advantage, and it pleas'd God it should be so, for the wind came a little in our favour, and we were enabled to set a Double Reef'd Fore-Sail, by which means we the next evening got safe to an anchor at Cuxhaven. This, my dearest Sophy, I shall ever consider a wonderful preservation, and I assure you I shall with reverence remember the 3d of March during the remainder of my life. We continued at Cuxhaven untill the 8th, when we sail'd with a convoy for this place, but on the 10th we were as near as it was possible being cast away on the Long Sand Head (Patten will tell you where it is), but fortunately got into Margate Roads in the evening, and sailed the next day for the Nore. I forgot to tell you in the first Gale we parted company with the Nimble cutter, and as she has not been heard of since we much fear she founder'd and all on board perish'd. Thus, my dear Sophy, you see you have had more than one chance of losing your Husband, a circumstance which at this period might have been fortunate, it scarcely being in his power to render you or himself a service."

[1] The *Orion* did brilliant service in this great battle:—

"Captain Troubridge, in the Culloden, led the van of the leading column, and, passing slowly through the line, poured two tremendous broad-sides, double-shotted, into the enemy's three-deckers; the other ships followed, opening a dreadful fire on the right and left as they passed through. No sooner had he crossed the enemy's line than Troubridge tacked again, and, followed by the Blenheim,

until June, 1798. In 1797, during the blockade, Capt. Saumarez resolved to make a desperate effort to cut out the enemy's gunboats. "Having in his own mind no doubt that the affair would be both desperate and bloody," writes Sir John Ross, in his *Memoirs and Correspondence of Lord De Saumarez,* "he selected those officers and men who were unmarried for the service, a list of whom he sent to the First Lieutenant with the necessary orders to prepare the boats. This list being exhibited in the ward-room, CAPTAIN (now MAJOR-GENERAL SIR JOHN) SAVAGE of the Marines had the mortification to see his name was omitted, while those of the two subalterns of that distinguished corps were inserted. This gallant officer, who had been a sharer with his heroic chief in several actions, felt hurt that he was not chosen on this glorious occasion; and, having ventured respectfully to express his feelings, was sent for to the cabin, where he was addressed by his commander in the following terms:—'Captain Savage, don't imagine that your name is left out in this list because I have not a high opinion of your zeal and intrepidity. I well know that you would be foremost in the assault; but I am also well aware that this is a desperate enterprise; many will fall; and if you should be one, who is to support your wife and family? The case is different with me, and my duty is to obey. Perhaps if Lord St. Vincent knew what I do, he would not send us; but it does not become me *now* to make any observation. However, aware as I am of the consequences, I cannot conscientiously order you to accompany me, under the conviction that your valuable life would thereby be sacrificed.'

SIR JOHN BOS-CAWEN SAVAGE, OF ROCK SAVAGE, born A.D. 1760; died A.D. 1843.

Prince George, *Orion,* and Irresistible, engaged in close combat the weather division of the enemy, which had been separated from the rest of the fleet. He thus succeeded in engaging the enemy, who were loosely scattered, and still struggling in disorderly array, in close combat, before they had time to form in regular order of battle. By a vigorous cannonade these ships drove the nine Spanish vessels which had been cut off to leeward, so as to prevent their taking any part in the engagement which followed. The Spanish admiral upon this endeavoured to regain the lost part of his fleet, and was wearing round the rear of the British line, when Commodore Nelson, who was in the sternmost ship, perceiving his design, disregarded his orders, stood directly towards him, and precipitated himself into the very middle of the hostile squadron. . . . While Nelson and Collingwood were thus precipitating themselves with unexampled hardihood into the centre of the enemy's squadron on the larboard, the other column of the fleet, headed by Sir John Jarvis in the Victory, of 100 guns, was also engaged in the most gallant and successful manner; though, from being the van on the starboard tack, by which the enemy's line was pierced, they were the rear on the larboard, where Nelson had begun his furious attack. The Victory, passing under the stern of the Salvador del Mundo, followed by the Barfleur, Admiral Waldegrave, poured the most destructive broadsides into that huge three-decker, which surrendered and was secured, having been previously silenced by the *Orion,* Captain Saumarez. These ships, moving on, engaged in succession the Santissima Trinidada, whose tremendous fire from her four decks seemed to threaten destruction to every lesser opponent which approached her. At length, after having been most gallantly fought by Jarvis and Collingwood, she struck to Captain, now Lord de Saumarez, in the *Orion.*"—Alison: *Hist. of Europe,* vol. iv., pp. 15-17.

SIR JOHN BOS-
CAWEN SAVAGE,
OF ROCK SAVAGE,
born A.D. 1760;
died A.D. 1843.

The entreaties of CAPTAIN SAVAGE were in vain. He beheld with mixed feelings of disappointment, gratitude, and admiration his humane and heroic commander leave his ship at the head of the enterprise with that smile on his sunny countenance which denoted a full determination to face every danger. But the boats had not proceeded far before a storm arose directly from the land, against which they could make no way, and it was with some difficulty they regained the ships. It was afterwards ascertained from various sources that these gun-vessels had been moored in that position with riveted chains, having no person on board them, in order to tempt an attack; and that the plan was to let the boats take possession, and then open a destructive fire from the batteries, which were kept several nights lined with troops for the purpose. Had not a merciful interposition of Providence prevented the advance of the boats, there can be no doubt that many, if not all, the lives of the assailants would have been sacrificed. We shall leave the feelings of Earl St. Vincent when the truth came out, as well as those of CAPTAIN SAVAGE and all concerned, to the imagination of the reader."[1]

After these events (we again quote the *United Service Gazette*) CAPTAIN SAVAGE "was placed under the orders of Sir Horatio Nelson, up the Mediterranean. On the 1st Aug., 1798, Nelson engaged the French fleet off the mouth of the Nile, when eleven sail of the line and two frigates were taken and destroyed."

Before going into action, Sir James Saumarez, who was commanding the *Orion*, having addressed the officers and ship's crew, turned round to CAPTAIN SAVAGE, who was the Captain commanding the Marines on board, and said to him, "Now, Captain Savage, will you say a few words to your men?" CAPTAIN SAVAGE, turning to the Marines, addressed them thus:—"My lads, do you see that land there? Well, that's 'the Land of Egypt,' and if you don't fight like devils, you'll d—d soon be in 'the House of Bondage.'"[2]

"About the middle of the action," writes Sir John Ross, "Sir James [Saumarez] received a wound from a splinter, or rather the sheave from the

---

[1] *Memoirs and Correspondence of Admiral Lord de Saumarez, from Original Papers in possession of the Family.* By Sir John Ross, C.B., K.S.A., K.C.S., F.R.A.S., Captain in the Royal Navy (Bentley, 1838), vol. i., p. 186, *et seq*.

[2] "The squadron advanced to the attack at half-past six in the afternoon. . . . When the British fleet came within range, they were received with a steady fire from the broadsides of all the vessels and the batteries on the island. It fell right, and with terrible severity, on the bows of the leading ships; but, without returning a shot, they bore directly down upon the enemy. Captain Foley led the way in the Goliah, outsailing the Zealous, under Captain Hood, which for some time disputed the post of honour with him; and when he reached the van of the enemy's line, he steered between the outermost ship and the shoal, so as to interpose between the French fleet and the shore. In ten

heel of the spare top-mast on the booms, which, after killing Mr. Baird, the Clerk, and wounding Mr. Miells, a midshipman, mortally, struck him on the thigh and side, when he fell into the arms of CAPTAIN SAVAGE, who conducted him under the half-deck, where he soon recovered from the shock it gave him."[1] Subsequently in the course of the action SIR JOHN SAVAGE was himself severely wounded. "A round shot passed between his arm and his side as he was holding up his sword, and severely contused him." He refused, however, to allow his name to appear in the list of the wounded.[2] He used to tell afterwards that as another English Ship passed under the stern of the *Orion*, he was speaking to the Captain of Marines on board, when the latter was cut in two by a round shot.[3]

SIR JOHN BOS-
CAWEN SAVAGE,
OF ROCK SAVAGE,
born A.D. 1760;
died A.D. 1843.

---

minutes he shot away the masts of the Conquerant; while the Zealous, which immediately followed, in the same time totally disabled the Guerrier. The other ships in the column—viz., the *Orion*, Audacious, and Theseus—followed in their order, still inside the French line [between it and the shore]; while Nelson in the Vanguard, at the head of six ships—viz., the Minotaur, Defiance, Belerophon, Majestic, Swiftsure, and Alexander—passed along the French line on the outside, and cast anchor by the stern opposite their respective opponents."—Alison : *Hist. of Europe*, vol. iv., p. 190.

[1] *Memoirs, &c., of Admiral Lord de Saumarez*, vol. i., p. 221.

[2] The following is the medical certificate of his having received a wound at the Battle of the Nile—a wound which used to trouble him in after life :—

"Tortworth Court, Gloucestershire, March 14th, 1799.

"I do hereby certify that John Boscawen Savage, Esq., late Captain of Marines on board H.M.S. Orion, did receive a very severe contusion in his left arm and side on Board His Majesty's ship Orion, then commanded by Sir Jas. Saumarez, on the night of First August, 1798, being then in action with the French Fleet off the mouth of the Nile.

"And I do further certify that his name was omitted in the list of killed and wounded by his own particular desire, and contrary to my opinion.
(Signed)
"WM. NEPECKER,
"Late Surgeon of H.M.S. Orion."

[3] The following certificate of Sir John Savage's services in the *Orion* was written in 1818 by Sir James Saumarez :—

"These are to certify that Lt.-Colonel J. B. Savage was Captain of the Royal Marines on board His Majesty's ship the Orion under my Command from the year 1796 to the year 1798, and was present in the Victory of the 14th of February under the Earl of St. Vincent, and of the Nile under Lord Nelson; in both which Actions he acquitted himself as a brave and gallant Officer, and on all occasions most highly to my satisfaction both as an Officer and a Gentleman.

"Given at Guernsey the 3d Day of Feby. 1818.
(Signed)
"J. SAUMAREZ."

MR. F. W. E. Savage, Sir JOHN's grandson, preserves an interesting memorial of his grandfather's service in this ship—a water-colour sketch of the quarter-deck of the *Orion* made by SIR JOHN himself at Gibraltar in 1798. Some engravings from sketches by him of the Battle of the Nile are in the possession of his granddaughter, Mrs. English, daughter of the late Lieut.-General Henry Savage.

Sir John Boscawen Savage, of Rock Savage, born A.D. 1760; died A.D. 1843.

The *Magazine* continues, "After the prizes had been secured at Lisbon he returned to England in Nov. 1798. In 1801, he embarked on board the Ganges, 74, joined the Baltic fleet, and this ship was second to Lord Nelson in all the action off Copenhagen, April 2, 1801, when six sail of the line and all the other vessels opposed were captured. He joined Lord St. Vincent's fleet off Brest, sailed for Jamaica, and remained there until Nov., 1803, when he returned to England.

"Sir John was made a K.C.B.[1] and K.C.H. for his services, and was in the receipt of a Good Service Pension of £300 per annum. He also received a reward from the Patriotic Fund during the war.

"The following are the names of the ships at the capture or destruction of which Sir John was present :—

	Guns.		Guns.
Gupuscaio	64	Phœnix	74
Monario	74	Princessa	74
Diligente	74	St. Juan	74
St. Domingo	74	St. Eugino	75
Prothero	64	St. Joseph	112
Salvador del Mundo	120	St. Nicholas	80
St. Judro	74	L'Orient	120
Le Franklin	84	Le Timoleon	84
Le Tonnant	84	Le Guerrier	74
Le Conquérant	74	Le Spartiate	74
L' Aquilon	74	Le Sovereign Peuple	74
Le Herony	74	Le Numen	74

exclusive of the whole Danish fleet in the action off Copenhagen, besides frigates and many other smaller vessels of war."

In 1809, he was made a Freeman of Hereford (with which neighbourhood his mother's family were connected), "in consideration of his gallant behaviour in the different actions between the English and the French and Spanish fleets off the Nile and off Cape St. Vincent."[2]

Sir John Savage married, on the 30th of Oct., 1786, at Alverstoke, Hants, Sophia, eldest daughter of Lieutenant William Cock, Royal Navy (who was

---

[1] Having been previously made a C.B.

[2] After the form of oath occur the words—"John Boscawen Savage, Esq., late Captain, now Major, in the Royal Marines, in consideration of his gallant behaviour in the different actions between the English and the French and Spanish Fleets off the Nile and off Cape St. Vincent. He was admitted 30th Oct., 1809."

lost at sea), and of Elizabeth Ward his wife, and first cousin of George Ward, Esq., of Northwood Park, Isle of Wight, and of Plumer Ward, the novelist, author of *Tremaine*, *De Vere*, &c., who was father of Sir Henry George Ward, Secretary of the Admiralty, afterwards Lord High Commissioner of the Ionian Islands, and finally Governor of Bombay.

In 1808, on the death (in his minority) of his first cousin, HENRY SAVAGE, of ROCK SAVAGE (Ballygalget), SIR JOHN succeeded to ROCK SAVAGE HOUSE and the BALLYGALGET estate with the exception of Nunsbridge, in accordance with the will of his uncle, HENRY SAVAGE, Esq., of ROCK SAVAGE; and in 1809, on the death of his aunt, Miss Lucy Savage, daughter of PHILIP SAVAGE, Esq., of ROCK SAVAGE, Nunsbridge also fell into his possession as heir-at-law. He used subsequently to pay occasional visits to the Ards, and at such times was generally a guest at GLASTRY HOUSE, where he was ever welcome at social gatherings on account of his geniality and kindliness, his stirring narratives, and brilliant sallies and repartees. But, having been so much on foreign service, and being little enamoured of Irish country-life, he found the family mansion at ROCK SAVAGE an incumbrance, and the story goes that, being on one occasion in company with some gentlemen in the Ards, he gave vent to his impatience at the trouble and expense it imposed upon him, and declared, with more impetuosity than prudence, that he would "sell it to the first bidder for 100 stivers." One of the company present at once offered to buy it; the mansion was sold, and the purchaser out of its materials built a row of houses in the main street of Portaferry.[1]

In his later years SIR JOHN SAVAGE resided at Woolwich, at first in a small house near the Common called Mill Hill Cottage.[2] He was a general favourite in the neighbourhood, and it is said that no one would ever disturb

---

[1] *See* hereafter under "SAVAGE OF ROCK SAVAGE (*Ballygalget—Later Line*)."

[2] This house stood in a walled-in garden, and its appearance and dimensions caused him perhaps some irritation, and on one occasion, in inviting the then Lord Downshire down to lunch with him, he headed his letter "*Rat-Trap Hall*, near the Common." Lord Downshire came, and, having arrived at the Common, began to inquire for *Rat-Trap Hall*, which, of course, nobody had ever heard of. Driven to extremities his Lordship entered the Barrack Tavern, and pursued his inquiries there, as elsewhere, in vain. "Then, where does *Sir John Savage* live?"—"Oh, *Sir John Savage* lives close by, but *his* house is called *Mill Hill Cottage*."

To an earlier date belongs the following speech by Sir John, at a banquet, in response to a toast, badly reported in the *Morning Post*, April, 1832:—

"The Chairman (Sir W. Burnett) proposed 'The Health of Col. Savage of the Royal Marines,' who was one of the distinguished visitors who had honoured them with his company that day.

"Dr. Quarrier hoped it would not be forgotten in drinking this toast that Col. Savage was now the oldest officer in His Majesty's service.

"The toast was drunk with considerable applause.

SIR JOHN BOS-
CAWEN SAVAGE,
OF ROCK SAVAGE,
born A.D. 1760;
died A.D. 1843.

his old liver-and-white spaniel "Chance" (so called because it was a foundling) as it lay across the pathway opposite the house he last occupied on the Common, but that every man, for love of its master, stepped out of its way with the reverence of a Turk. William IV., then Duke of Clarence and Lord High Admiral, whom he had known in earlier years, continued his friend, and was the recipient of invitations to Mill Hill Cottage. Introducing SIR JOHN on one occasion to the Princess Charlotte, he asked him to tell her stories of his fighting days. After the Duke had ascended the throne, he honoured SIR JOHN, amongst other things, with the right of entrée at his levées;[1] and finally offered him a Baronetcy, which, not considering himself well enough off, he wisely declined.

His tall, straight, manly figure preserved its erect soldierly carriage to the last, and in his 83rd year he would jump across a ditch that divided the Common from the pathway opposite his house rather than take the longer way round. He contracted a fatal illness from standing with his back to the boiler of a Thames steamer on his way to London, and getting chilled afterwards by the winter air; and, having lain for a considerable time on a sick-bed, he died at Woolwich Common on the 8th of March, 1843, in his 84th year. He had lived in the reigns of five successive English Sovereigns.[2] On the 12th of June in the same year, his widow died at nearly the same age.

"Col. Savage felt proud at the unexpected honour paid to him. The Veteran soldier proceeded to explain the circumstance of his entering the army when he was but an infant, and his subsequent career, with the characteristic pith and brevity of a soldier's speech, to the great amusement and applause of his audience. He stated that his father, having a family to provide for out of a soldier's means, had purchased for him a commission which fell vacant at the memorable siege of Belleisle in 1761(2), trusting to the Regiment to do his (Colonel Savage's) duty until he should be able to do it for himself. At seven years of age he was in America, and at eleven he saw some rough work in one of our West India Islands, when His Majesty's troops were engaged against the Mutineer negroes. A good many of the troops fell in open fight, some were ate, some roasted—and God knows what besides. It was then considered time to think something about his education, and he was sent to England for that purpose. He was now certainly the oldest officer in the service. He had been in the Marines since the year 1777, and that was fifty-five years. During that time he could assure them he had done his work. He had been in several general actions, been often wounded, and been at the taking of thirty of the enemy's line-of-battle ships *in fair fight*—not merely hawling down pennants in port, but *in fair fight*. He was now the oldest officer in the King's Service, and hoped he should long continue so. (*Much laughter and applause.*)"

[1] The old Entrée-Card is still preserved. The story is told that, finding Sir John Savage in a place reserved for privileged persons, and not recognising him, an officious person in authority politely reminded him that "this place is reserved for only those who are *attached* to his Majesty." "Yes," replied Sir John, "and there is nobody more *attached* to his Majesty than I am."

[2] In the *Belfast Herald* of the time appeared the following notice of him:—"In the obituary we mentioned the death of Major-General Sir John Boscawen Savage, K.C.B., K.C.H. Most of our readers are well aware that the Family of Savage settled in this country with Sir John De Courcy in the 12th century. They had summons to Parliament as Barons Savage of the Ards so

His portrait, painted at the expense of the officers of the Corps, hangs in the Royal Marines' Mess-room at Chatham. It is a copy, but not a successful one, of an excellent likeness on ivory.

Sir John and Lady Savage were both buried in a vault in the Churchyard of the Parish Church of Woolwich.[1]

Sir John Boscawen Savage, of Rock Savage, born A.D. 1760; died A.D. 1843.

---

early as the 48th Edward 3rd in 1374, and for many years after. One branch of this Family settled at Portaferry, where it remains to this day, although the present worthy possessor assumed the name of Nugent on succeeding to the Estate of a maternal ancestor, and his eldest son is at present High Sheriff. Another branch settled at Ardkeen, a few miles north of Portaferry, where Sir Robert Savage in the year 1342 was about to build a castle for defence against his troublesome neighbours, the O'Neils, when his son and heir, Sir Henry, said, 'A castle of bones is better than a castle of stones—Ille celebratior qui non minus fortiter quam facile dixit, nolle castro saxorum sed potius ossium confidere.' From this Sir Henry the subject of our present memoir was lineally descended. The direct male line of Ardkeen terminated on the death without male issue of the late Francis Savage, of Hollymount, who represented this county in Parliament from 1793 to 1812, when he resigned. Sir John was the eldest son of Marmaduke Coghill, son of Philip Savage, of Ballygalget, or Rock Savage, who was the 2nd son of Hugh, of Ardkeen, who died in 1722."

The following curious but touching tribute of gratitude to Sir John Savage, for some forgotten act of generosity very characteristic of him, was found amongst his papers after his death:—

(*Addressed on outside*)—"John B. Savage, Esq., Capt. Marines, Portsmouth."

(*Inside*)— "TO THE GENEROUS FRIEND OF L. P., SIXTEEN YEARS DECEASED.

"If gratitude sincere can value give
To this poor trifle which you now receive,
Accept it—a memento of that friend
Who ne'er forgot your friendship to life's end.
Your Purse was his—and could my prayers prevail,
This purse no generous impulse e'er should fail.

"A small offering of gratitude from L. P. March, 1798."

[1] Their monument bears the following inscription:—

"Sacred to the Memory of
"Major-General Sir John Boscawen Savage,
"Knight-Commander of the Most Honourable Military Order of the Bath,
"Knight-Commander of the Royal Hanoverian Guelphic Order,
"Late Colonel-Commandant and Deputy Adjutant General, Royal Marines.
"He served his country faithfully for nearly Seventy Years,
"And was actively employed during the Brightest Period of its Naval Annals,
"Having been present at the Actions off Cape S*t.* Vincent, 16th Jan*y.* 1780, and 14th Feb*y.* 1797,
"At the Battle of the Nile 1st August, 1798,
"And at Copenhagen 2nd April, 1801.
"He died March 8th, 1843, aged 83 years.
"Also of
"Dame Sophia Savage,
"Relict of the above,
"Who died June 12th, 1843, aged 82 years.
"Their remains lie interred in a Vault in the Burial Ground of this Church."

SIR JOHN BOSCAWEN SAVAGE, by his wife, Sophia Savage (née Cock), had issue,
   I. A son, who died in infancy (?).
  II. HENRY-JOHN, of whom presently as heir to ROCK SAVAGE (Ballygalget), and representative of the ARDKEEN family.
 III. John-Morris, Colonel Royal Artillery, born at Portsmouth, England, 1796; married, Nov. 16, 1826, at Rochester, Kent, Mary Anne, daughter of William Hillier, Esq., R.N. Colonel John Morris Savage was educated at the R. M. Academy, Woolwich; entered the Royal Artillery as 2nd Lieut., July 7, 1817; 1st Lieut. Royal Horse Artillery; 2nd Captain and Adjutant 9th Battalion Royal Artillery; Deputy Assistant Inspector of Studies R. M. Academy, Woolwich; commanded Royal Artillery, Pigeon House Fort, Dublin, and afterwards at Kingston, Canada. After having served about 38 years in the Royal Artillery, Colonel Savage retired from the army in 1855. He then settled at Sault Ste. Marie in the Algoma district in Canada, and served the Civil Government of Canada as first Registrar of the District of Algoma. He died on the 11th Oct., 1876, aged 80. The following obituary notice of him is extracted from the *Belfast News-Letter* of Nov. 13, 1876:—
"Colonel John Morris Savage, who died in Canada on October last, was the second and last surviving son of the late Major-General Sir John Boscawen Savage, K.C.B., of Ballygalget, in the County of Down, who was the representative of the very ancient Anglo-Norman family of SAVAGE, settled in that County since the reign of Henry II., the Portaferry branch of which is at present represented by Colonel Andrew Nugent, of Portaferry, who commands the Scots Greys. Colonel Savage was born in 1796, and entered the Royal Artillery in 1818, and retired in 1855. He was, after the death of his father in 1843, conjointly with his late brother, Mr. Francis James Saumarez Savage, who died in 1864, owner of the small properties of Priestown and Nunsbridge, but they were afterwards sold; and his elder brother, the late Lieutenant - General Savage, Royal Engineers, having sold the Ballygalget property to his kinsman, Major Nugent, the last remnants of the possessions of the SAVAGES of ARDKEEN, Co. Down, thus passed from their hands." Colonel Savage, by his wife, Mary Anne Savage (née Hillier), who died at Sault Ste. Marie, Canada, Nov. 12, 1876, aged 76 years, left issue,
       1. John-Morris, 2nd Captain Royal Artillery, born 1829. He

was educated at the Royal Military Academy, Woolwich; entered the Royal Artillery as 2nd Lieut., 18th Dec., 1847; married, Feb. 7, 1854, Mary Louisa, 2nd daughter of Theophilus Richards, Esq., of Birmingham; served in the Crimea, distinguishing himself gallantly in the defence of the Quarry Pit in front of the Redan on the 18th June, 1855; and died of cholera in the Crimea, 24th June, 1855, aged 26 years, leaving issue an only child,

Sir John Boscawen Savage, of Rock Savage, born A.D. 1760; died A.D. 1843.

Francis-Forbes, in Holy Orders, born in 1855, who is married and has issue.

2. Harry-Boscawen, late Major Royal Marine Artillery; born 20th Aug., 1836; educated at the Royal Marine College, Portsmouth; appointed 2nd Lieut. Royal Marine Artillery, 30th Dec., 1853; served throughout the China War of 1856–59, including the Bombardment of Canton, capture of the Forts in the river, and was landed for the protection of the Batteries; blockade of the river, landing before bombardment and capture of Canton; expedition to the North, and capture of the Forts at the mouth of the Peiho River in 1858, and operations there; also the campaign of 1860 (medal with three clasps). Retired on full pay with rank of Lieut.-Colonel, Oct. 2, 1879. Colonel Harry Boscawen Savage married, 20th Oct., 1874, at Christ Church, Lancaster Gate, Emily Maria, only daughter of the late Joseph Collyer, Esq., of Bedford Square, London, and of Castlebury, near Ware, Herts, and has issue,

Morris-Boscawen, born on the 14th of March, 1879.
Marian-Alicia.
Jane-Ada.

3. Philip-Charles-Coffin, born on the 5th Feb., 1838; educated at the Royal Military College, Sandhurst; entered the service as Ensign Royal Canadian Rifles, 20th July, 1855; Lieut., 19th Feb., 1858; Captain $h. p.$ on disbandment of that Regt., 1st April, 1870; Captain 2nd Batt. 7th Foot, 1873; exchanged to 2nd Batt. 64th Foot, 1880; retired on pension with hon. rank of Major from 64th Foot, 9th June, 1880; gazetted hon. rank of Lieut.-Colonel, 1st July, 1881.

4. Edmund-Sandilands, born 7th April, 1839; educated at the Royal Military College, Sandhurst; entered the service as Ensign 17th Foot, July 2, 1858; Lieut., 9th Nov., 1861; exchanged to 3rd West Indian Regt., 1870; Captain *h. p.* on disbandment of that Regt., 29th June, 1870; Captain 63rd Foot, 1871; placed on *h. p.* 23rd May, 1877; Captain 2nd West India Regt., 1880; retired with hon. rank of Major from 2nd West India Regt., with pension, 9th June, 1880; gazetted Hon. Lieut.-Colonel, 1st July, 1881. Lt.-Col. E. S. Savage married, in 1864, Elizabeth, daughter of Major-General Rae, R.M., and has issue.

5. Frederick-Marmaduke, who died without issue.
6. Charles.

1. Marianne, married, *1st*, to Robert Miller, Esq., who died without issue; and, *2ndly*, to W. F. L. Gompertz, Esq., M.R.C.S.L., who died without issue.

2. Jane-Anne, married, Aug. 7th, 1852, to Henry Mawdsley, Esq., only surviving son of Thomas Woods Mawdsley, Esq., of Liverpool, and has issue,

> Henry Mawdsley, born 2nd Oct., 1860.
> John-Herbert Mawdsley, born 10th May, 1862.
> Emily Mawdsley.
> Fanny Mawdsley.
> Marianne Mawdsley.

3. Emma, married to Berkeley Small, Esq., of Toronto, Canada West, and died without issue.

IV. Francis-James-Saumarez, born at Portsmouth on the 18th of January, 1800, named after his godfather, Admiral Lord de Saumarez, the gallant Captain of the *Orion*, under whom his father had so often fought. At the age of five years he entirely lost his hearing and, for some time, his speech and sight, owing to a fever.[1] He had been destined for the Royal Navy, and was to have gone to

---

[1] The fever was brought on in the following way:—His father's soldier-servant, in whose charge he had been placed, going to drink with some of his comrades, left him alone, to fly his kite, on Southsea Common. The Common was cut up with deep holes, dug, when the French invasion was feared, to prevent the enemy using their cavalry if they should land. The child, whilst flying his kite, tumbled into one of these holes, which was full of water, and afterwards fell asleep in his wet clothes.

sea under the auspices of his godfather.[1] Mr. F. J. S. Savage married, on the 16th of April, 1833, at St. Margaret's Church, Rochester, Kent, Susannah Jane, 2nd and youngest surviving daughter of the Rev. William Eveleigh, LL.D., Vicar of Aylesford and Lamberhurst, Kent, by his wife Susannah, 6th, but 3rd surviving, daughter of the Rev. James Harwood, M.A., Vicar of Dartford, Kent, by his wife Rebecca, daughter of Thomas Chase, Esq., of Bromley, Kent.[2] Mrs. F. J. S. Savage was niece of the Rev. John Eveleigh, D.D., Provost of Oriel, Prebendary of Rochester, and Rector of Purleigh, in Essex. She died at River, near Dover, Kent, on the 1st of May, 1858, in her 52nd year, and was buried in Buckland Churchyard on the 5th of May, 1858. Mr. Francis James Saumarez Savage died suddenly, of apoplexy, at his residence at Southampton, on the 14th of March, 1864. He was buried in the Cemetery near Southampton.[3] By his wife, Susannah Jane Savage (*née* Eveleigh), Mr. F. J. S. Savage left issue an only child,

    1. Francis-William-Eveleigh, born on the 13th of July, 1834, at Rochester, Kent; educated at the Royal Military Academy, Woolwich; entered the Royal Artillery, as 2nd Lieutenant,

SIR JOHN BOSCAWEN SAVAGE, OF ROCK SAVAGE, born A.D. 1760; died A.D. 1843.

---

[1] Presenting his godson with a gold watch, Lord De Saumarez writes the following note to Sir John Boscawen Savage, on the 21st July, 1830:—

"My dear Sir,

"I herewith have the pleasure to send the watch I promised for my godson, and request his acceptance of it, in the recollection of its coming from one who has his happiness and welfare sincerely at heart.

"With very kind regards to Mrs. Savage and your son,

"I remain, my dear Sir,

"Yours most truly,

"Naval Club, Bond Street,   "J. SAUMAREZ.

"21st July, 1830."

[2] Eveleigh, West Eveleigh, Clyst St. Lawrence, and Holcombe in Ottery, Co. Devon; and Eveleigh-De Moleyns, Ventry Baron. Harwood, of Hagbourn and Streatley, Co. Berks, and Crickheath and Tern, Co. Salop; and Berwick, Baron.—*See Appendices.*

[3] The following is a copy of the Inscription on Mr. F. J. S. Savage's tomb, in the Cemetery near Southampton:—

In Memory of
Francis James Saumarez Savage,
Esquire,
Youngest son of the late
Major-General
Sir John Boscawen Savage, K.C.B., K.C.H.,
Died March 14, 1864,
Aged 64 years.

22nd December, 1852; 1st Lieutenant 17th February, 1854; was subsequently, at his own request, appointed Cornet 13th Light Dragoons, 23rd November, 1855, whilst serving in the V. 32. Pr. Howitzer Battery in the Crimea; Lieutenant, 9th October, 1857; and retired, 16th Aug. 1859, by sale of his Commission. Was appointed Captain in the Northamptonshire and Rutland Militia, August 23, 1860; resigned April 6, 1863. Mr. F. W. E. Savage served with the Royal Artillery in the Crimean Campaign in 1855, including the Battle of the Tchernaya, and the Siege and fall of Sebastopol (Medal and Clasp and Turkish Medal).

I. Sophia, who was born in 1791, and died in infancy.

SIR JOHN BOSCAWEN SAVAGE was succeeded at Ballygalget (Rock Savage), and in the representation of the ARDKEEN family, by his eldest surviving son,

XX.—LIEUTENANT-GENERAL HENRY JOHN SAVAGE, OF BALLYGALGET (ROCK SAVAGE), CO. DOWN, COLONEL-COMMANDANT ROYAL ENGINEERS (BORN 19TH JUNE, 1792, temp. George III.; DIED 7TH FEB. 1866, temp. Victoria).

LIEUTENANT-GENERAL HENRY JOHN SAVAGE was born at Portsmouth, on the 19th June, 1792. At the age of 14 (October, 1806) he passed his examination for a cadetship at the Royal Military Academy, Woolwich, where he joined, after having been three months at Marlow (where the 60 junior Cadets were then quartered). In 1808, he was offered a commission in the Royal Artillery, which he declined, preferring to obtain one later in the Royal Engineers. On the 30th September, 1809, he was gazetted 2nd Lieut. in the corps of Royal Engineers, and joined for duty at Portsmouth, under the command of General Evelegh, R.E. In 1811, LIEUT. SAVAGE was ordered to Jersey, where he had charge of numerous coast defences then in progress, and was appointed extra A.D.C. to the Governor, Sir George Don. On the 22nd October, 1813, at Jersey, he married his first wife, Eliza, daughter of John Dolbel, Esq., of Colomberie, Jersey, a niece of Sir Thomas Le Breton, Bailiff of that island, a lady, like himself, of Norman descent.[1] A few days later, having received sudden orders to proceed to the Peninsula, he left Jersey for Portsmouth, where he embarked on board the *Lord Beresford* for Spain. He was employed

---

[1] One of her sisters was married to the late Cæsar Hawkins, Esq., Sergeant-Surgeon to the Queen (she died 1858); another to the late Admiral Vernon.

in the Peninsula and in Southern France, under Sir Arthur Wellesley, from November, 1813, to the end of the war, including the investment of Bayonne and repulse of the sortie from that town.[1] He was one of the R.E. officers employed in February, 1813, in constructing, at Socon, the bridge of boats across the Adour, over which a great part of the British Army passed into France. Subsequently he marched with his men across France, and embarked at St. Malo. He was again employed in Jersey from 1814 to 1817. In December, 1815, he was promoted to the rank of Captain, and, being placed on half-pay on the reduction of the army, which took place after the Peace, continued to reside in the Island of Jersey for several years. In 1825, he was ordered to Lyme Regis, Dorsetshire, where he was stationed until 1827, during which time he superintended the construction of the Cobb Pier. On leaving Lyme Regis a number of the inhabitants subscribed and

LIEUT.-GENERAL HENRY JOHN SAVAGE, born A.D. 1792; died A.D. 1866.

[1] Before Bayonne he narrowly escaped being taken prisoner one day when he had been out by himself reconnoitring the enemy's position. He was chased by a picket of French Dragoons. In his flight he came to two roads. Not knowing his way, he wisely left the choice of roads to his horse. One road, as it turned out, led to the French camp, the other to the English. His horse took him safe to the English camp.

The following letter, written by General (then Lieutenant) Savage to his mother, while in the lines before Bayonne, during the Siege, and immediately after the Sortie, has been kindly placed at our disposal by his son, Col. H. J. Savage:—

"Bouron, near Bayonne,
"April 15th, 1814, 7 o'clock evening.

"My dearest Mother,

"As by the time you receive this you no doubt will have heard that the French have made a most vigorous sortie from Bayonne, I write these few lines just to tell you that I have, thank God, escaped. About two hours before daybreak yesterday morning, I was woke by a very heavy firing. I immediately mounted, and with Tinling went up to the front, and remained together during the whole of the action, which, it being for the first two hours *dark*, was beautifully grand, shot and shells flying in all directions, and several houses in flames. At first they gained a little ground and took some prisoners, among whom, I am sorry to say, was Sir J. Hope, who, in the dark, mistook some French advancing to be our Guards retiring, and went forward to rally, when, unfortunately, his horse was killed under him, and himself and an aide-de-camp, who was wounded, were taken prisoners. Poor General Hay was killed, and Generals Stopford and Bradford wound[ed.] The Guards are the principal sufferers, having lost 13 officers and nearly five hundred men. Our who[le] loss, I suppose, cannot be less than eight or nine hundred. The cavalry suffered equally. Having been on a working party since three o'clock this morn. intrenching a churchyard close [to] the citadel, under a heavy fire, I am so tired I cannot say more. They killed and wounded some of my men, but missed me. I shall write more fully by the next Packet. The siege *will not take place*. The battering train which was ordered up is countermanded. We have received the glorious news from Paris, and sent it in to the Governor of Bayonne, who believes it, and regrets having made the sortie. An armistice is expected to take place every hour. We have had no firing this morning. With most affectionate love to my dearest Father, Brother, Uncle, and Aunt, ever believe me your most affectionate son,

"H. J. SAVAGE."

LIEUT.-GENERAL HENRY JOHN SAVAGE, born A.D. 1798; died A.D. 1866.

presented him with a handsome silver Cup. He was employed in Canada from 1827 to 1829. In 1829, his first wife died at sea, on passage home from Canada, and was buried at Halifax, Nova Scotia. CAPTAIN SAVAGE was Resident Engineer in Charge at Pembroke from 1829 to 1837. He there superintended the erection of a loading wharf at Hobbs Point, Milford Haven. Four diving bells were used in carrying on this work. An account of the method employed in the construction of the Wharf, with drawings to illustrate the same, by CAPTAIN SAVAGE, was published in the 1st Vol. R. E. Corps Papers (1837). He was promoted Brevet-Major, 10th Jan., 1837; in which year he was ordered to the Mauritius, where he held the appointment of Commanding Royal Engineer till 1843. While in the Colony he also performed the duties of Surveyor General, Civil Engineer, and Surveyor of Roads and Bridges. In 1840, at Port Louis, Mauritius, MAJOR SAVAGE married his 2nd wife, Clara Eleonore, eldest daughter of C. A. E. Mylius, Esq., Civil Service, and granddaughter of Baron Ernest Henry von Mylius, of Ehrengreif Castle, Westphalia, Knight of the Holy Roman Empire.[1] MAJOR SAVAGE proceeded to Dublin in 1843, and was C.R.E., Dublin District, till 1846.[2] On 22nd May, 1845, he was promoted to the rank of Lieut.-Colonel. From 1846 to 1848 he was employed at Gibraltar. In 1848 he proceeded to Halifax, Nova Scotia, and held the appointment of C.R.E. there until 1854. On leaving Halifax the Mayor and Corporation presented him with an address.[3] On 21st March, 1854, he was promoted to the rank of Colonel. On arriving in England in that year, COLONEL SAVAGE was appointed C.R.E., Chatham District, and remained there until 1857, when he embarked for Gibraltar, having been appointed Com. R.E. there, which was his last command. He was promoted to the rank of Major-General at the end of 1858, and, returning to England early in 1859, proceeded with his family to Jersey. In 1860, the "Good Service" Pension of £100 per annum for distinguished and meritorious service was conferred on him. In 1862, he was promoted to the rank of LIEUT.-

---

[1] Titles conferred upon him by Joseph II. of Germany, in 1767. See Appendices to this volume.

[2] In Dublin he superintended works of improvement in the proximity of the Royal Barracks, and used to describe the condition of the neighbourhood of the Royal Barracks, Dublin, previous to the clearing away of the old slums, and the scenes witnessed there at that time, as appalling. Soldiers used frequently to be found lying naked in the streets, having been made drunk, and then stripped and robbed, in the houses of the degraded populace.

[3] The Mayor and Corporation of Halifax also applied to the Dep.-Adj.-Genl. Royal Engineers for a renewal of his command at that station, which, however, could not be granted, being against the rules of the service.

GENERAL, and appointed Colonel-Commandant Royal Engineers. In 1858, GENERAL SAVAGE sold the Ballygalget (Rock Savage) property to his kinsman, Major Nugent (now of Strangford). He resided during the latter years of his life at St. Helier's, Jersey, where he died on the 7th of February, 1866, in the 74th year of his age. He was buried in St. Saviour's cemetery, in that Island.[1]

LIEUT.-GENERAL HENRY JOHN SAVAGE, born A.D. 1792; died A.D. 1866.

LIEUT.-GENERAL SAVAGE, by his 1st wife, Eliza Savage (*née* Dolbel), had issue,

I. HENRY-JOHN, of whom presently as successor to his father, and representative of the ARDKEEN family.

II. William, born at St. Helier's, Jersey, in 1822; educated at the Royal Military College, Sandhurst; entered the Army as 2nd Lieut. 21st Royal N. B. Fusiliers, 7th Aug., 1840, and was promoted to 1st Lieut. in the same Regiment. Subsequently he exchanged to the 3rd West India Regiment, and died at Sierra Leone, unmarried, on the 5th of October, 1854.

I. Eliza-Sophia, born at St. Helier's, Jersey; married, at the Mauritius, 21st July, 1842, to Lieut. George Bayly, 35th Regiment, afterwards Brevet-Major and Staff-Officer of Pensioners,[2] and has had issue,

1. George-Cecil Bayly, Bt.-Major Royal Artillery, Paymaster Duke of Cornwall's Light Infantry; born June 5, 1843, at Mauritius; served in the Afghan Campaign, 1879.
2. Henry-Charles-Nesham Bayly, born January 3, 1846, at Mauritius; died at Mauritius, April 18, 1847.
3. Edward-Henry Bayly, Commander R.N., born December 1, 1849, at Trim, Co. Meath; served in the early part of the Ashanti War, under Commander Commerell, in H.M.S. "Rattlesnake."

---

[1] The following is the inscription on General Savage's tomb in the churchyard of St. Saviour's, Jersey:—

To the memory of
Henry John Savage,
Lt.-General, Col. Commandant
Royal Engineers,
who
Departed this life 7th Feby., 1866,
Aged 73 years.

"Who shall separate us from the love of Christ?"—Romans viii., xxxv. verse.

[2] Major Bayly died at Woolwich in 1865.

4. Charles-Algernon Bayly, born at Dublin, February 26, 1852.
5. Alfred-William-Lambart Bayly, Captain (1885) Bombay Staff Corps, born at Paisley, February 18, 1856; served in the Afghan War in 1879–80, and was present at the defence of Candahar and in the battle of Candahar (Medal with Clasp); served subsequently at Suakin; and has served in Burmah on Staff as Deputy-Assistant Adjutant and Quarter-Master General.

II. Sophia-Caroline, born at St. Helier's, Jersey; married, at the Mauritius, in Jan., 1841, to Lieut. John Graham M'Kerlie, R.E., now (1888) Colonel Sir John Graham M'Kerlie, K.C.B. (civil), for some years Chairman of Her Majesty's Board of Works, Ireland, and has had issue,
1. Robert M'Kerlie, born in 1856.
1. Sophia-Caroline M'Kerlie, born in 1847; died in 1848.
2. Helen-Graham M'Kerlie.

III. Penrose-Anne, born at St. Helier's, Jersey; married, at Dublin, August 20, 1844, to Lieut. George-Frederick Macdonald, 16th Regiment, who was appointed Staff-Officer of Pensioners at Toronto, 7 April, 1863, and is now Colonel (retired), son of General George Macdonald, Colonel of the 16th Foot; and has had issue,
1. George Macdonald, born in 1845; died in 1855.
2. Edward Macdonald, born in 1846; died in 1878.
3. James Macdonald, born in 1853; died in 1858.
4. Henry Macdonald, born in 1857; died young.
5. George Macdonald, born in 1864.
6. Frederick Macdonald, born in 1867.
7. A son, born in 1868.
1. Caroline Macdonald, married, 10th April, 1877, at St. Mary's Church, Beverley, Yorkshire, to Robert Hill, Esq., of Thornton Hall, Yorkshire.
2. Clara Macdonald, married to Robert Walton, Esq.
3. Sophy Macdonald, married to Frederick Whitmore, Esq.
4. Georgina Macdonald, married to Samuel Marriott, Esq.,
5. Flora Macdonald, married to William Dick, Esq.
6. Alice Macdonald, married to Charles Brookes, Esq.
7. Edith Macdonald, born in 1863; died in 1884.
8. Eva Macdonald, died, unmarried, in 1868.

IV. Harriet-Frances, born at Lyme Regis, Dorsetshire.

By his 2nd wife, Clara Eleonore Savage (*née* Mylius), LIEUT.-GENERAL SAVAGE had issue,

    I. Clara-Jane, born at Port Louis, Mauritius; married, at Rochester, 1867, to Lieut. (now Major) Thomas English, Royal Engineers, and has had issue,
- 1. Thomas-Mylius-Savage English, born in 1868.
- 2. Henry-Boscawen-De-Heyn English, born in 1869; died at Hawley, Kent, in 1883.
- 3. Douglas-Arthur-Watkins English, born in 1870.

    II. Gertrude-Emily, born at Gibraltar; married, at Rochester, 1874, to Lieut. (now Captain) John Richmond Jekyll, late Royal Marine Light Infantry, and has had issue,
- 1. John-Joseph-Savage Jekyll, born 1876; died the same year.
- 2. A son, born 1883; died in infancy.
- 1. Doris-Gertrude-Cecily-Mary Jekyll.
- 2. Clara-Millicent Jekyll.

    III. Mary-Emma-Griffith, born at Halifax, Nova Scotia; married, at Bombay, 1872, to Lieut. (now Captain) M. H. Gregson, Royal Engineers, and has had issue,
- 1. Henry-Guy-Fulljames-Savage Gregson, born in 1872.
- 2. Geoffrey-Kirkes Gregson, born in 1881.
- 1. Violet-Mary Gregson, born in 1876; died in 1886.
- 2. Hazel Gregson, born in 1877; died the same year.

    IV. Caroline-Eleonore-Augusta, born at Halifax, Nova Scotia; married, at Rochester, 1871, to Lieut. (now Captain) George Robert Rollo Savage, Royal Engineers, third and only surviving son of the late Henry Savage, Esq., of Ardglass, Co. Down (*see hereafter under* "SAVAGE OF PROSPECT"), and has had issue,
- 1. Lily Savage.
- 2. Kathleen Savage.

    V. Eugenia-Isabel-Clara, born at Brompton, Kent.

    VI. Annie-Eliza-Charlotte-Maria, born at Gibraltar.

    VII. Alice-Maud-Beatrice, born at St. Helier's, Jersey.

LIEUTENANT-GENERAL HENRY JOHN SAVAGE, of Ballygalget, was succeeded in the representation of the ARDKEEN family by his elder and only surviving son,

XXI.—COLONEL HENRY JOHN SAVAGE.

Colonel Henry John Savage, born A.D. 1816.

COLONEL HENRY JOHN SAVAGE was born in Jersey, on the 1st of August, 1816. He was educated at the Royal Military College, Sandhurst, and, having duly qualified for his Commission, was gazetted Ensign in the 91st Regiment on the 5th of June, 1835. Served in South Africa against the Boers, beyond the Orange River, in 1845, and again at the Cape of Good Hope, in the Kafir Wars, in 1846, 1847, and 1853. From 1858 to 1863 served with his regiment in India, and in 1858 attained the rank of Major in the 91st Regiment. In February, 1859, received an official letter of thanks from Major-General Sir Hugh Rose (afterwards Lord Strathnairn) for the coöperation of the Left Wing of the 91st Regiment, under his command, with the Field Force in India, in pursuit of the Rebels of the Mutiny. In the April following commanded Field Detachments of Artillery, Cavalry, and Infantry against Rebels in the Nagpore Province; and in 1860 was gazetted Lieut.-Colonel in the Army. He subsequently, as senior officer, commanded the 91st Regt. in India; exchanged, as a Major and Bt. Lieut.-Colonel, 28th October, 1864, to 84th York and Lancaster Regt.; and, after serving in the army nearly 32 years, retired on full pay as Major, 84th, with the rank of Colonel, on the 9th March, 1867.

In 1849, COLONEL SAVAGE married Isabel, only child of the late Colonel Ward by his wife Harriet, daughter of the late Colonel Francis Tidy, C.B., 24th Regt.,[1] by whom he has had issue,

---

[1] ALEXANDER, 2nd Duke of Gordon, by his marriage (in 1706) with Lady Henrietta Mordaunt, daughter of the celebrated general, Charles, Earl of Peterborough and Mordaunt, had issue,
    I. COSMO-GEORGE, *s.* his father.
    II. Adam, a Gen. in the army, and Commander-in-Chief of the Forces in Scotland; married, 2nd Sept., 1767, Jane, daughter of John Drummond, Esq., and widow of James, 2nd Duke of Atholl, and died in 1801.
    I. Anne, married William, Earl of Aberdeen; and died 25 June, 1791.
    II. Betty, married the Rev. John Skelly, and had issue, Capt. Gordon Skelly, R.N.; Francis, Skelly, Col. in the Army; and two daughters, Katherine Skelly, married to Charles Grey, Esq., of Morwick; and Henrietta Skelly, who married the Rev. Thomas-Holmes Tidy, and had issue, Gordon-Skelly-Holmes Tidy, deceased; Francis-Skelly-Holmes Tidy, Col. 24th Regt., C.B., who commanded the 14th Regt. at Waterloo, and who married Martha, daughter of the Right Hon. Judge Pindar, and had issue,
        1. Thomas-Holmes Tidy, Colonel in the Army, married Catherine, daughter of Gen. Maister, and had issue;
        2. Gordon-Skelly, late Capt. 48th Regt., deceased;
        3. Francis-Grey, late Lieut. 13th Light Infantry, deceased;
        1. Harriet, who married Lieut.-Col. Ward, 91st Regt., and died 11th Oct., 1873, leaving issue, *Isabel, married to Colonel H. J. Savage.*—(*See* Burke: *Peerage*, &c., "Huntly, Marquess.")

I. HENRY-CHARLES, Captain 80th (South Staffordshire) Regt., born at Fort Beaufort, on the borders of Kafirland, South Africa, 29th July, 1854. Served with the Right Wing of the 80th Regt. in Perak during the operations in the Malay Peninsula against the natives for the murder of Mr. Birch, the British Resident. Was present throughout the whole of the Zulu War. Served in the Right Attack against the Chief Sekukuni, under Colonel Rowlands, in 1878, and was present at the attack and capture of Sekukuni's stronghold, under Sir Garnet Wolseley, in 1879. Just before the War commenced, was Acting District Adjutant to Colonel Pearson, who afterwards commanded the troops shut up in Etsowe, and for nine months was District Paymaster at Lydenburg during the First Sekukuni Campaign, and frequently in charge of ammunition escorts from Lydenburg to Fort Weeber. (Medal and Clasp for campaigns of 1878 and 1879.) Captain Savage married, 22nd Nov., 1883, Florence, daughter of Robert Edwards, Esq., C.E., son of William Edwards, Esq., of Isicoad Holt, Flintshire. COLONEL HENRY JOHN SAVAGE, born A.D. 1816.

II. Arthur-Raymond-Boscawen, Lieut. Royal Artillery, born at Rochester, Kent, on the 7th of August, 1868.

I. Isabel-Harriet, who died in 1852, aged 2 years.

II. Isabel-Ada, born at Corfu, Ionian Islands.

III. Florence, born at Kamptee, India; married on the 20th of November, 1879, to Lieutenant J. O. English, Royal Artillery, and has issue,

    1. Stephen-Savage English, born at Southsea, Hants, 17th of March, 1885.

        1. Florence-Maud-Isabel English.

KNOCKDHU, Co. Down, site of BALLYGALGET CASTLE and ROCK SAVAGE HOUSE.

CHAPTER IV.

SAVAGE OF ARDKEEN *(continued).*—SAVAGE OF BALLYGALGET,
EARLIER LINE.

SAVAGE OF
BALLYGALGET—
EARLIER LINE.

TWO separate branches of the SAVAGES OF ARDKEEN have been styled at different eras "of BALLYGALGET." The earlier family of the SAVAGES OF BALLYGALGET was founded by ROLAND SAVAGE, son of JAMES SAVAGE (otherwise FERDOROUGH M'JENIACKE), and grandson of SIR ROLAND SAVAGE, of Lecale, last Seneschal of Ulster of the SAVAGE kindred. He was called " ROWLAND SAVAGE FITZJAMES, of Ballygalgatt." To this ROLAND SAVAGE, as we have seen, was granted the wardship of his nephew, HENRY SAVAGE, of Ardkeen, chief of the Ardkeen family, during the latter's minority. In A.D. 1602, ROLAND SAVAGE, whom Montgomery describes as "a cadet of Ardkeen," and who, he informs us, had been "an Officer of Queen Elizabeth's army against the Irish," was pensioned for good service to the Queen.[1] Under his nephew, HENRY SAVAGE, of Ardkeen, ROLAND SAVAGE of Ballygalget held the lands of Ballygalget, Rathallowe, Ballycranymore, Irishtowne, *alias* Ballygealagh, the quarter of Ballysporte called

---

[1] See *Calendar of State Papers*, James I.

SAVAGE OF ARDKEEN, BALLYGALGET BRANCH.

Knockrewell (?), together with five islands in Loughcone (Strangford Lough), called Islandroman, Islandroe, Partane, and the two Monashes. (*See* Inquisitions, Down, No. 102, Car. 1.) He married Catherine Magennis, daughter of Hugh Magennis, of the family of Iveagh. "Since the entry of King James into England" (1603), writes Montgomery, ROLAND SAVAGE "built the Castles of Ballygalget and Kirkistone, and gave the same with the adjacent lands to two of his sons." "The lands of both these two other castles," says Montgomery again, "were belonging to (by deeds from the Archin family), and built by, Rowland, a cadet of Archin." Of the Castle of Ballygalget we have already given a description from Montgomery.[1] It stood on a hill known as Knockdhu, near a little fresh-water lough, which has been drained in recent years; and it was within sight of both the Castle of Ardkeen and the Castle of Kirkistone, while not far from it was Castlebui, or Castleboy,[2] the ancient

ROLAND SAVAGE, ESQ., OF BALLYGALGET, who died A.D. 1640.

---
[1] *Vide ante*, p. 198.
[2] CASTLEBOY.—The following account of this interesting Castle we extract from Father M'Laverty's valuable work on *The Diocese of Down and Connor*:—"'The lands of Castleboy, otherwise Johnstown, which formerly belonged to the Hospitallers (Reeves' Eccl. Antiq.), consist of nine townlands, containing 1,358 acres. In the townland of Castleboy there remains a small portion of the castle standing, and a few perches to the N.W. the ruins of the chapel, measuring sixty-three by twenty-one feet. The east window was a triplet of lancet compartments. On the north and south sides were lancet windows, about six feet removed from the west angles. There were entrances on the north and south sides, about twenty-six feet from the west end. A small lancet window was in the west wall, about six feet from the floor. A cemetery surrounded the building, but the ground is now cultivated up to the very walls.' This was the Commandery or Preceptory of the Ards belonging to the Knights of the Military Order of St. John of Jerusalem (now called Knights of Malta), an order which professed the rule of St. Augustine, and was instituted to protect the Christians of the Holy Land and pilgrims going to Jerusalem. The order had in Ireland two Grand Priories, Wexford and Kilmainham; the latter was the more important; its ruins were employed to build the Royal Military Hospital, which stands on the site of the Grand Priory. The only Commandery or Preceptory which the order possessed in the diocese of Down and Connor was that of Castleboy, or St. John's of the Ards, but it had the rectories of Ballytrustan, Rathmullan, with the chapelry of St. John's Point, Ballyminestra, Carncastle, St. John's of Carrickfergus, Ballywalter, near Doagh, and Ballyrashane, and extensive landed possessions. . . . These [landed possessions] were grants which the several Anglo-Norman lords had conferred on the Hospitallers. The Commandery of Castleboy was founded in the twelfth century by Hugh de Lacy, Earl of Ulster. . . . An Inquisition held at Ardquin, July 4, 1605, found that at the suppression of monasteries, 'John Rawson, Knight, Prior of the late Priory or hospital of St. John of Jerusalem, in Ireland, was seized in fee in right of said priory, of the preceptory and manor of St. John of the Ards in Little Ardes in the foresaid county, of an old castle in the village of St. Johnston, otherwise Castleboy, the Townland of St. Johnston, otherwise Castleboy aforesaid, Drumardan, Balliadams, otherwise Adamstown, and Ballinucholl in Little Ardes, being members of the foresaid manor and preceptory.' Then follow a list of rectories and advowsons belonging to the preceptory, which, with all its possessions, was afterwards granted by the Crown to Sir James Montgomery. The site and manor passed afterwards into the possession of the Echlin family." . . . Father

ROLAND SAVAGE, ESQ., OF BALLYGALGET, who died A.D. 1640. stronghold of the Knights of the Military Order of St. John of Jerusalem, better known as the Knights of Malta. "Near the site of Shankill, or Ballygalget Church," writes the Rev. Father O'Laverty, "once stood the Castle of Ballygalget, called also Rock Savage, which was built in the reign of James I. by Roland Savage of Ardkeen, who served against the Irish in the wars of Queen Elizabeth."[1] This Church of Shankill (Old Church) stood, according to Bishop Reeves, "on the highground of Knockdoo, otherwise Rock Savage, and about a furlong north of the Roman Catholic Chapel."[2] The following inquisition respecting the townland of Ballymartin, parcel of the manor of Ballydreene, or Islandmaghie, was taken in the year 1617:— "COUNTY OF DOWN.—*Tullomkill*, 18*th October*, 15*th year James* 1*st.*—The townland of Ballymartin, *alias* Ballymartynagh, is, and anciently hath been, parcell of the manor of Ballydreene, *alias* Islandmaghie, and the inheritance of the Bishop of Down, &c. Merryman, late Bishop of Down, was seised of the said manor of Ballydreene, in right of his said Bishoprick, and was also seised, as of fee, of the townland of Ballymartyn, as part of the said manor. The sept or family called Slutt M'Henry Keyes, did lately expulse and disseize the said Bishop out of the whole manor aforesaid, in tyme of war and rebellion. One ROWLAND SAVAGE, of Ballygalgett, some tyme entered upon and possessed the said manor of Ballydreene, *alias* Islandmaghie, as tenant or farmer to the then Bishop of Downe, and did also hold the towneland of Ballymartin, *alias* Ballymartynagh, and did pay for the said lands, yearly, the rent of £4, for the space of three years together, to one Rob. Hamston, late Bishop of Downe, and did also give to the said Bishop a horse valued at £20, for or in the name of a fine or income for a lease of the said lands for three years."[3] ROLAND SAVAGE, of Ballygalget, died on the 10th of February, 1640. In his will, which he made in that year, he directs that he shall be buried in the Parish Church of Ardkeen. He mentions his "wife, *alias* Cath. Magennis." To his eldest son, "ROLLAND, and his heirs," he bequeaths "Ballygalgott;" to his second son,

---

O'Laverty adds in a footnote :—"The people of Castleboy have a tradition that an ecclesiastic, whom they call 'John of Jerusalem,' when going to the Holy Land, directed their forefathers not to pay tithes until he should return, and they ascribed the exemption of the parish from tithes to the circumstance that he never did return. This is a curious mixture of fact and fable; the legend seems to refer to John Rawson, Knight, the last Prior of the Order of St. John of Jerusalem in Ireland, while the exemption seems to arise from the circumstance that both lands and tithes having been granted to the Montgomeries the tithes merged into rent."—*Diocese of Down and Connor, Ancient and Modern.* By J. O'Laverty, P.P., M.R.I.A. Vol. i., pp. 91–6.

[1] *Diocese of Down and Connor*, vol. i, p. 91.
[2] Vide *Ecclesiastical Antiquities*, &c.
[3] *Hamilton Manuscripts.* Edited by T. K. Lowry, Esq., LL.D. *Appendix*, p. l.

JOHN, and his heirs, Kirkistone; to his third son, PATRICK, he bequeaths Ballyrusselly, Ballygarvegan, Ballyhenry, which he held of PATRICK SAVAGE, of Portaferry, Esq., and Kirkubbin, which he held of James, Lord Viscount Claneboye; Knockmiller,[1] Quintin Bay, Ballymartyr (?), Quarter townland of Tullanacrissi, &c., which he held of Dualtagh Smith, Margaret Russel his mother, and Daniel Gruome Smith, and PATRICK SAVAGE, of Portaferry. He mentions also Ballyspurge. Allusion is made to Henry Savage of Ballyfunaragh, and to Patrick his son and heir. To his own third son, PATRICK, he bequeaths his "silver cupps and his harpe." He refers also to his eldest daughter Elizabeth, his youngest daughter Mary, his former wife's daughter Rose Savage, and his daughter Erothlin Oge Savage; and as "overseers of his last will and testament," he appoints his "right trusted and well beloved friend James Lord Viscount Clandeboye, and James Hamilton Maistor of Claneboy." By his wife, Catherine Savage (née Magennis), ROLAND SAVAGE had issue,

 I. ROLAND, of whom presently as representative of the SAVAGES OF BALLYGALGET—EARLIER LINE.

 II. JOHN, OF KIRKISTONE CASTLE. (*See below, under* "SAVAGE OF KIRKISTONE CASTLE.")

 III. PATRICK, OF BALLYSPURGE, to whom his father granted, 18th August, 1634, a mortgage which he had on part of the Portaferry estate, consisting of the town and lands of Ballyrussely, Ballygarvegan, and Ballyhenry. (Will appearing on Inquisition, dated 3 June, 1649.) He died on the 11th of June, 1649, leaving issue,

  1. JOHN SAVAGE, OF BALLYSPURGE, who was succeeded by

   PATRICK SAVAGE, OF BALLYSPURGE (*pro nepos*), to whom Ballyspurge and Ballyvranigan (?) had been left by his grandfather's will. (Inq. at Downpatrick, 9 April, 1662.)

 I. Elizabeth.
 II. Erothlin.
 III. Mary.

Mr. ROLAND SAVAGE, of Ballygalget, dying, as we have seen, on the 10th of February, 1640, was succeeded by his eldest son,

ROLAND SAVAGE, Esq., of Ballygalget (to whom his father had granted the lands of Ballycranymore). He married Margaret Russell (who was living and endowed with premises, 9th April, 1662), and had issue,

---

[1] Qy. Knockeveile?

I. JAMES, who appears to have died young.
II. Roland, who died without issue.
III. PATRICK, of whom presently as successor to his father at Ballygalget.

Capt. ROLAND SAVAGE, of Ballygalget, died on the 10th of February, 1645. (*See* Inq. Down, No. 16, Car. 1.) He was succeeded by his son,

PATRICK SAVAGE, Esq., of Ballygalget, to whom his father had given Ballygalget and Ballycranymore, and on whose issue by his wife, Jane Dobbin, he settled Ballyspurge. MR. PATRICK SAVAGE, of Ballygalget, proved the will of his deceased uncle, Patrick Savage, Esq., of Ballyspurge, who died in 1649. He married Jane, daughter of —— Dobbin, Esq., and had issue,

I. ROLAND, of whom presently as successor to his father at Ballygalget.
II. James, of Ballyspurge, who was outlawed as one of the adherents of James II.
III. Patrick, designated "of Ballygalget," outlawed as an adherent of James II.
IV. Henry, designated "of Ballygalget," outlawed as an adherent of James II.

Mr. PATRICK SAVAGE, of Ballygalget, was succeeded by his eldest son,

ROLAND SAVAGE, Esq., of Ballygalget, a Captain in King James II.'s Irish Army, in the regiment known as Sir Neill O'Neill's Dragoons, M.P. for Newry in King James II.'s Parliament in 1689. On the 10th April, 1690, King James II. issued a commission for applotting £20,000 per month on personal estates and the benefit of trade and traffic, "according to the ancient custom of this kingdom used in time of danger." Of this tax he appointed assessors in the several counties; and we find the names of ROLAND SAVAGE and JOHN SAVAGE amongst the assessors for the County of Down.—"*For the County Down:* The High Sheriff *pro temp.*, Phelim Magenis, Murtagh Magenis, ROWLAND SAVAGE, JOHN SAVAGE, John M'Artan, and Toole O'Neill. Their applotment, £2,011.14.3 for three months."[1] The following extract from Reid's *History of the Presbyterian Church in Ireland* (quoted in the notes to *The Hamilton MSS.*, p. 143) describes the operations of a CAPTAIN SAVAGE at this time in the cause of James II. and in connection with the County of Down. We have not been able to identify this CAPTAIN SAVAGE as ROLAND of Ballygalget, but it is probable that he was the same man. At any rate, the picture of the state of affairs in the County Down at the period is worth preserving in this place. Dr. Reid, after having related some of the more remarkable incidents of the Siege of Derry, which was then proceeding, continues thus:—

"In the meantime the Protestants of Down made a vigorous attempt to preserve their properties from being plundered by the Romanist soldiery. The protections which

---

[1] See Dalton's *King James's Army List*, p. 35.

many of them had received from Tyrconnel and General Hamilton were disregarded by the military, especially by the regiment of Magennis, of Iveagh, whose companies, composed of rude and half-civilised natives from the mountains of Mourne, were stationed in the several towns. Their unauthorised and oppressive exactions were, for a time, borne in silence; the people having few arms, and being destitute of a leader. But hearing that Captain Henry Hunter had escaped from Antrim, where he had been confined for nearly three weeks, and had reached Donaghadee with the view of passing over into Scotland, they had recourse to this experienced officer for counsel and assistance. He immediately abandoned his design of leaving the kingdom, placed himself at the head of the Protestants who had arms, and marched towards Newtownards, which the company of Captain Con Magennis were just preparing to plunder. On the 15th of April he attacked this party at a place called Kinningbourne, about two miles from the town; and having made prisoners of the greater number, he drove them out of that district. On the same day he dispersed a second party of this obnoxious regiment, stationed at Comber, and rescued that town also from their exactions. Thence, with an increased number of adherents, he proceeded to the Ards, where another large detachment from the same regiment, having crossed over at Strangford from the head-quarters at Downpatrick, were engaged in plundering the unprotected Protestants of that barony. These he likewise defeated; and compelled them to retreat across the ferry in such haste, that they left behind them in Portaferry all their plunder, together with several vessels laden with grain which they had seized not long before. So soon as intelligence of these proceedings reached Carrickfergus, Lieutenant-Colonel Mark Talbot, the Governor, at the head of a small body of a hundred musketeers, marched towards Newtownards; but hearing of the dispersion of the detachment in the Ards, and the increasing number of the Protestants who had risen in arms, he hastily retreated to his quarters. From Portaferry Hunter returned to Comber, where he received repeated messages from Sir Robert Maxwell, then residing in the Castle of Killyleagh, urging him to assist in expelling CAPTAIN SAVAGE'S company, who had been recently quartered upon the inhabitants of that town, and had threatened to take possession of the Castle. Hunter accordingly marched during the night to Killyleagh, and entered it at daybreak; and, having surprised and disarmed the entire company, he sent the captain and lieutenant prisoners to Portaferry to be shipped to England or the Isle of Man. Magennis, irritated by these repeated discomfitures, and especially at the disgraceful capture of the company under SAVAGE, proceeded with a considerable force from Downpatrick towards Killyleagh, with the view of rescuing his officers and men, and checking the further progress of Hunter. But the latter was on the alert, and boldly advanced against him. Both parties met at the Quoile Bridge, and after a smart skirmish, Magennis was compelled to abandon Downpatrick, and retreat over the strand to Dundrum, leaving the Protestants in possession of that district. Hunter secured a small piece of ordnance, which he placed in Killyleagh Castle, and proceeded to Downpatrick, where he liberated all persons confined for political offences. Among the prisoners released from the gaol of Downpatrick, Hunter mentions in particular 'a very aged clergyman, called Mr. Maxwell, of Phenybrogue.' By these unexpected successes the people of Down experienced a seasonable relief from the exactions of the soldiery; the embargo which had been laid on vessels in the seaport towns of that county was removed, and many persons from the remote parts of the province effected their escape into the sister kingdoms; the garrison in Derry were encouraged by the intelligence of these proceedings,

CAPTAIN ROLAND SAVAGE, OF BALLYGALGET, living A.D. 1701.

2 K

CAPTAIN ROLAND SAVAGE, OF BALLYGALGET, living A.D. 1701.

and greater leniency and moderation were thenceforth observed by the Romanist authorities in other places, lest a similar spirit of revolt should be excited. . . . But these triumphs of the Protestants were of short duration." "In 'Leslie's *Answer to King,*' p. 155 *et seq.*, he relates these events with a strong bias against both Hunter and the Protestants. He represents Sir Robert Maxwell as sending one John Stuart, an apothecary in Downpatrick, to invite CAPTAIN SAVAGE and his company to take up their quarters in Killileagh, to protect the town against Hunter and his rabble, as he calls the Protestants; and then, as despatching one Gawn Irwin twice to Hunter, urging him to attack SAVAGE, who was betrayed, he alleges, by Sir Robert. He palliates the severities of the Romanists, and greatly underrates the losses of the Protestants; but, at the same time, he deems it of importance to inform us that part of Colonel Mark Talbot's wig was shot off his head by a bullet from the Castle of Killileagh, while pursuing the enemy." . . . .

ROLAND SAVAGE and many of his kinsmen who had devoted themselves to King James's service were attainted by King William. "In the Inquisition for his attainder," writes Mr. D'Alton, CAPTAIN ROLAND SAVAGE "was described as of Portaferry and Newry, in Down." "Besides this CAPTAIN ROLAND," he also writes, "there are in the Army List, in Col. Cormack O'Neill's infantry, Edmund Savage, a lieutenant, and Henry Savage, an ensign." Within Down County "were also outlawed Patrick and Henry Savage of Ballygalget, Thomas and Hugh of Dromode, James of Ballyspurge, Hugh of Ballydawes, Lucas of Dunhunk, and John and James Savage of Rock. . . . PATRICK SAVAGE, of Portaferry," he continues, claimed "part of the confiscations of CAPTAIN ROWLAND SAVAGE, with 'the freshwater lough thereto belonging.' The Hollow Swordes Blades Company also purchased his estate of Dromardin in the Ards. At the Court of Claims, PATRICK SAVAGE, a minor, sought and was in part allowed a remainder in tail under settlements of 1685 in said ROLAND's estates, while HUGH SAVAGE,[1] as son and heir of JOHN SAVAGE, was allowed a chiefry out of certain lands of the same forfeiting proprietor; as was another Patrick Savage, to a certain extent, a mortgage charged upon same; and John M'Cormick and Dame Elizabeth Ponsonby claimed and were allowed charges on other premises of ROLAND."[2]

With the attainder of CAPTAIN ROLAND SAVAGE and his near kinsmen the earlier line of Ballygalget was swept out of its possessions in the Ards, and it would be very difficult to trace the history of the various descendants

---

[1] Evidently CAPTAIN HUGH SAVAGE, of ARDKEEN.
[2] See *Illustrations, Historical and Genealogical, of King James's Irish Army List* (1689). By John D'Alton, Dublin, 1855. In the Reports of Record Commission, Roll. 2 Anne, p. 389, we find the following:—"61. Patrick Savage, of Portaferry, Esq., 16th June, 1703. Consideration £56. All their right and interest in, to, and out of, the lands of Ballyfuneragh [Ballyfindon], 119 A., 3 Roods, 16 Per., the freshwater Lough thereto belonging. Bar. Ards, Co. Down—the estate of Rowland Savage attainted. Inrolled 22 September, 1703."

of the outlawed proprietors. The chiefry of Ballygalget, however, remained, as we have seen, in the hands of the lords of the Manor of Ardkeen; and we have found allusion made to Ballygalget, and wishes expressed concerning it, in the will of CAPTAIN HUGH SAVAGE, the representative of the Ardkeen main line, who had taken the side of King William in the civil war, and had been wounded at the Battles of the Boyne and Aughrim. Ballygalget became the property and place of residence of CAPTAIN HUGH SAVAGE'S second son, PHILIP SAVAGE, known subsequently as PHILIP SAVAGE, Esq., of ROCK SAVAGE, the founder of the Later Line of the SAVAGES OF BALLYGALGET. (*See hereafter* "SAVAGE OF ROCK SAVAGE—BALLYGALGET, LATER LINE.")[1]

[1] In the old Church of Ardkeen there is a recumbent slab bearing an inscription to the memory of one of the Savages of Ballygalget who died in 1681, but which of them it has proved impossible up to the present to determine, so much of the inscription has been obliterated by time and exposure. It runs, however, as far as we can trace it, thus:—

    HERE LYETH THE BODY OF
    PE SAVAGE, ESQ.
    LATE OF BALEGALGET
    WHO DEPARTED THE 14 DAY
    FEB., 1681, AND OF EAR II
    CRE NTWO

It is possible that the "PE" of the christian-name is a wrong reading for KE, and that the christian-name is really PATRIKE (Patrick). If so, this would be probably the Patrick of Ballygalget whom we have assumed to be father of Capt. Roland, the last inheritor of Ballygalget of that line. The concluding portion of the inscription is almost completely illegible, and perfectly unintelligible.

KIRKISTONE CASTLE, formerly the seat of the SAVAGES OF KIRKISTONE.

CHAPTER V.

SAVAGE OF ARDKEEN *(continued)*.—SAVAGE OF KIRKISTONE CASTLE.

ROLAND SAVAGE, Esq., OF BALLY-GALGET, FOUNDER OF THE KIRKI-STONE BRANCH.

ROLAND SAVAGE, Queen Elizabeth's officer, uncle of HENRY SAVAGE, of ARDKEEN CASTLE, built, as we have seen, in the early years of the reign of James I., the Castles of Ballygalget and Kirkistone. The latter (which, with its lands, he held under the Chief of Ardkeen) he left to his second son, JOHN SAVAGE. The first of the KIRKISTONE line, therefore, was

JOHN SAVAGE, Esq., OF KIRKISTONE, who died A.D. 1641.

JOHN SAVAGE, Esq., of Kirkistone Castle. He received a grant of Rathallowe from his father. He subsequently mortgaged it to HENRY SAVAGE, of Ardkeen. On the 6th May, 1614, he had 30 acres of Rathallowe. Mr. JOHN SAVAGE, of Kirkistone, married Katherine, sister of Touell O'Neill, of Balladrantagh, Co. Antrim (deed dated 23 April, 1639), and by her had issue,

I. PATRICK, of whom presently as successor to his father at Kirkistone.

II. JAMES, of whom presently as successor to his brother at Kirkistone.

Mr. JOHN SAVAGE died on the 11th of May, 1641. (*See* Inquisitions, Down, No. 103, Car. I.) He was succeeded by his elder son,

PATRICK SAVAGE, ESQ., OF KIRKISTONE, born A.D. 1638.

PATRICK SAVAGE, Esq., of Kirkistone, born in 1638 (see Inq.). He married, but died without issue, in 1660 (?). He was succeeded at Kirkistone by his brother,

JAMES SAVAGE, ESQ., OF KIRKISTONE, born A.D. 1640.

JAMES SAVAGE, Esq., of Kirkistone, born in 1640. (He was twenty years of age in 1660.—*See* Inquisitions.) According to Montgomery, "the son of John

Savage," who must have been this JAMES SAVAGE, sold Kirkistone to Capt. James McGill, of Ballymonestragh. "James McGill, of Ballymonestragh," Montgomery writes, "improved the place very much. He purchased the same and some lands adjoining from ye grandson of ye s^d Rowland." Notwithstanding this sale, Mr. JAMES SAVAGE seems to have been succeeded at Kirkistone by his son, or grandson,

JAMES SAVAGE, ESQ., OF KIRKISTONE, born A.D. 1640.

WILLIAM SAVAGE, Esq., of Kirkistone, High Sheriff of the County of Down in 1731, who married Lucy, eldest daughter of Hugh McGill, Esq., killed by a cannon-ball, at the siege of Athlone, in 1690,[1] and granddaughter of the above-

WILLIAM SAVAGE, ESQ., OF KIRKISTONE, living in A.D. 1731.

---

[1] We take the liberty of extracting a lengthy footnote from Mr. Hill's *Montgomery Manuscripts*, showing the relationships of the SAVAGES of KIRKISTONE Castle with the McGill family. Some of the Memoranda quoted in it are a striking and touching illustration of the stirring times in which they were written. The phonetic spelling, representing the Ards Ayrshire pronunciation of certain words, is also noteworthy.—" Captain James McGill married Jean, daughter of Alexander Bailie, of Inishargy, and by her had several children. Their mother carefully recorded their names and the dates of their births in [an] old family Bible . . . which she bequeathed to her second daughter Mary, who married William Montgomery. The author calls Mary 'eldest daughter' of Captain James McGill, but according to her mother's account in the following record she was the second. Mrs. Jane McGill mentions also the names of such of her children as died before her, and the manner of their deaths:—

'Memorandam—Sarah McGill was born on the 23 of desember being Setterday about 5 o'clock in the eftenoune, 1648.

'Mem^r.—Mary McGill was borne the last of november at 3 in the morning on Seterday 1649.

'Mem^r.—Elessabeth McGill was borne on the 15 day of agust on frayday 1651.

'Mem^r.—Margratt McGill was borne on the 19 of June 1653 att 6 in the morning.

'Meme^r.—hugh McGill was borne on the 21 Septtember 1655 on frayday att 7 in the morning.

'Meme^r.—Jeane McGill was borne on the sixth day of octtober 1657 on teusday.

'Meme^r.—Kettreine McGill was borne the 8 day of September 1658 frayday at 11 a clok.

'Meme^r.—William McGill was borne on the 13 day of Jeanuerie 1660 on monday morning.

'Mem^r.—2 Kettreine was borne on the 20 october 1662 on teusday morning.

'Meme^r.—The 2 Jeane McGill was borne 2 day of June 1664 on munday at ten a clok in the morning.

'Meme^r.—Anne McGill was borne on the 7 day of June 1665 on teusday in the eftenoun.

'Meme^r.—Jeames McGill was borne on the 6 day of apryll 1669 on teusday in the efternoon.

'Meme^r.—Kettreine McGill 3 was borne on the forth of may 1672 on munday att night.

'Meme^r.—That my deire husband deparrted this Lyff on the 26 of Jully 1683.

'Meme^r.—That my deire son Jeams McGill was murdred att Portglenone bridge with the barbrous Ierisse on the 7 day of apryll 1689, he being just tuintie yeare ould the night befor his death. I brought his bons hom in a box and lead them by his father.

[James M'Gill served under Lieutenant-Colonel Shaw, who had charge of the trenches at Portglenone, and who, being attacked on the 7th of April by a superior force of the Irish, was obliged to retreat after a gallant resistance, in which several of his officers and men were slain.]

'Meme^r.—That my deire sone hugh McGill was killed with a connone ball at the sedge of Achlone on the nynteine of Jullie 1690 he being in his thartie fyrst yeare of his edge.

'JEANE McGILL.'

WILLIAM SAVAGE, ESQ., OF KIRKISTONE, living in A.D. 1731.

mentioned Captain James McGill. It was probably through this marriage that Kirkistone Castle passed once more, temporarily, into the possession of the SAVAGE family. In 1731, WILLIAM SAVAGE was godfather, with Archdeacon Usher, to Elizabeth Montgomery (born Sept. 29, 1731), daughter of William Montgomery, Esq., by his second wife, Elizabeth, daughter of Mr. Samuel Hill, whose grandfather was Treasurer of Ireland during the Commonwealth. Of MR. WILLIAM SAVAGE, the Rev. Father O'Laverty writes—" The last possessor

[The death of Hugh McGill at Athlone is noticed by Storey as having occurred on Sunday, the 20th of July, 1690. 'That day,' says he, 'one captain Mackgill, a voluntier, was killed at one battery with a cannon shot from the castle.'—*Impartial History of the Affairs of Ireland*, p. 102. His death is also noticed by a brother officer, D. Campbell, in a letter addressed to Sir Arthur Rawdon, and written from *Carricknosure* (Carrick-on-Suir) on the 24th, four days after its occurrence. 'The lieutenant-general,' says the writer, 'broke ground and lost but about 14 men; the enemy raised a battery, and poor unfortunate Hugh McGill would needs go to see it, tho' dissuaded from it by every one; his arm and shoulder were shot from him by a cannon shot, of which he immediately fell dead, and not much lamented, because everyone condemned his going thither.'—*Rawdon Papers*, pp. 327, 328.]

'Memorandom—That my deir mother margrat mertteine depearted this Lyff on the 11 of november 1671.

'Memorandom—That my deir fether allexander Baellie depearted this Lyff on the tharteine of September 1682 . . . of Inshargie.

'Memorandom—That my deir brother eduard Beallie of ringdifference [Ringdufferin] pearted this lyff on the 25 of November 1682.

'Memorandom—That my deir sister-in-law eleissabeth dumbare depearted this lyff on the seventh of agust 1683.

'JEAN M^cGILL.

'Memerandom—That my deir brother, John Beallie of inshargie pearted this lyff on the thread of may 1687.

'Memorandom—That my deir sister-in-Lau Sarah Leix pearted this Lyff.

'Memorandom—That my sone hugh's first chyld Lucy McGill was borne on the thred day of november 1685 in Casseell balfore in the countie of fermanach.

'Memarandom—That my sone hughs 2 doughter Isabella was borne on the eleven day of Januerie 1686 in belinester in the countie of down decd.

'Memorandom—That my sone hughs thred doughter Lettishia was born on the tenth of May 1688 in belinester in the countie of doun : she is dead.

'Memerandom—That my sone hugh McGill's fourth doughter Jean McGill was borne on the 27 Jullie 1690 in belinester in the countie of doun eight days after her fa[ther] was killed at Athlone.

'Jeane McGill of bellinesters Book which I promissed to my doughter Mary att my death.

'Jeane McGill off bellinester ought this book.

'This book I leave to my deer doughter Montgomrie of Grenchoch as witnes my hand,

'JEAN M^cGILL.'"

Montgomery Manuscripts, pp. 361-2.

of Kirkistone Castle of the race of the SAVAGES was WILLIAM SAVAGE, who, when Sheriff of the County of Down in 1731, distinguished himself in discovering and reporting to the Castle [at Dublin] the number of friars in the friary of Drumnacoyle." The following is Father O'Laverty's poetic account of this incident, which is curiously associated with another old Castle of the SAVAGES in their ancient territory of Lecale:—"About the year 1750, the Dominicans [then under the ban of Government] removed to Moneyscalp, in the parish of Kilcoo. In the townland of Drumnaquoil, in a field belonging to James Laverty, which adjoins the road that there forms the boundary between the townlands of Drumnaquoil and Dunturk, is the site of the friary of Drumnaquoil, which was the 'locus refugii' of the Franciscans of Down, the site of whose monastery is now occupied by the Protestant Parish Church of Downpatrick. I have been unable to find out the date at which the Franciscans located themselves there; but a legend told by the people accounts for the selection of that secluded spot. They say that when the friars were at prayer in Rome, a vision of a lady in white warned them to build a friary where they would hear the sound of three bells ringing. The friars, wearied and footsore, sat down one day before the gate of SAVAGE's Castle in Drumaroad, to rest themselves, for they had searched all Ireland through for the promised sign, when at last their hearts were gladdened by the long-expected chimes surging across the valley from the lonely hill-side of Drumnaquoil. Some would say, perhaps, that it was less owing to the influence of the vision than to the hope of escaping the priest-hunters that the friars came to that mountain solitude; but the eyes of the Government were upon them even there." The duty of reporting their presence and encroachments lay with the Sheriff of the County, and WILLIAM SAVAGE of Kirkistone did not shirk his responsibilities. Father O'Laverty quotes the following document, with WILLIAM SAVAGE'S signature affixed, which is preserved in the Public Record Office, Dublin:—

"To the Right Honourable the Lords' Committee, appointed to inquire into the present state of Popery in the Kingdom of Ireland.

"In obedience to your lordships' order, bearing date the 6th day of the instant November, to me directed, as sheriff of the County of Down, requiring me to return unto your lordships an account of what reputed nunneries or fryaries, and what number of fryaries, are within the said County of Down, and what number of fryars or nuns are reputed to be in the same respectively.

"I do hereby humbly certify unto your lordships that, after the strictest inquiries, I can find there is but one reputed fryary in the said County of Down, kept at a place called Drumnacoyle, in the said county, within eight miles of

256   THE SAVAGES OF THE ARDS.

WILLIAM SAVAGE, ESQ., OF KIRKISTONE, living in A.D. 1731.

Rathfriland, in which there is commonly reputed to be nine fryars. And that there is not in the said County of Down any reputed nunnery, nor any nuns.

"Dated at Kirkistowne, the nineteenth day of November, one thousand seven hundred and thirty-one.

"WM. SAVAGE."

Mr. WILLIAM SAVAGE, therefore, was living at Kirkistone Castle in 1731, about twenty-five years after the completion of the *Montgomery MSS.*

KIRKISTONE CASTLE in 1884.

Kirkistone Castle is the property of the Montgomeries of Grey Abbey, and within the memory of persons now living it was occupied by some ladies of the Montgomery family. At the time we write, however, it has gone to decay. The fine old Keep is bound round with vamps of iron, and its walls bulge dangerously. Its only inhabitants are cattle, pigs, and jackdaws. The large square courtyard, of great dimensions, still remains, with its high walls and its strong circular towers. The ruins are amongst the most imposing in the Ards, and are often visited by travellers from distant countries. They stand not far from the sea, in the midst of level green fields, and the summit of the Keep commands extensive views of the hilly country of the Barony, the indented coast-line, and the wide Channel. The Keep is also a conspicuous object from many spots in the district.[1]

---

[1] The Castle has been preserved with laudable care by the Montgomery family, and some years ago it was in the charge of a farmer, Mr. James Kelly, who, strangely enough, traced his descent maternally to the Ballygalget Savages, thus:—Alice Savage, of Ballygalget, ran off with Mitchell M'Cormick, of Corney, mate of a ship. They went to England to be married. James Kelly, of Ballyfinderagh, married Isabella M'Cormick, daughter of the foregoing. James Kelly, keeper of Kirkistone Castle (aged 45 in 1884), is son of this James Kelly and Isabella M'Cormick. Alice M'Cormick (*née* Savage) lived to the age of 92, and died in James Kelly's childhood. He remembered her and her brother, Mr. James Savage, whom he recollected visiting at his father's house when he was very young, and making a money present to him and his brother for the purchase of clothes. Mrs. Alice M'Cormick died about the year 1839. She was probably born, therefore, about the year 1747. She was possibly a daughter of one of the descendants of the Earlier Ballygalget Line.

Ruins of the old Church of Ardkeen, burial-place of the SAVAGES OF ARDKEEN CASTLE.

CHAPTER VI.

SAVAGE OF ARDKEEN *(continued)*.—SAVAGE OF BALLYGALGET
(ROCK SAVAGE)—LATER LINE.

THE branch of ARDKEEN (the representative of which in the male line, COLONEL HENRY JOHN SAVAGE, is now also the representative of the male line of the ARDKEEN house) was established at Ballygalget by PHILIP SAVAGE, Esq., second son of CAPTAIN HUGH SAVAGE, of ARDKEEN CASTLE, early in the 18th century. {SAVAGE OF BALLYGALGET (ROCK SAVAGE).}

We have seen that by the will of CAPTAIN HUGH SAVAGE, of ARDKEEN, while the ARDKEEN estates generally were to devolve upon his eldest son, FRANCIS, the lands of Ballygalget, Ballybranigan, and Ballyspurge were not to pass to him. They were left in the hands of his Executrix (his widow) and her two brothers, Francis and Edward Lucas, to be sold, *if need were*, for the purpose of raising the portions of his younger children. By what subsequent arrangement we are not aware, but, as a matter of fact,

PHILIP SAVAGE, ESQ., OF BALLY-GALGET (ROCK SAVAGE), born A.D. 1696; died A.D. 1780.

the lands of Ballygalget became the property of CAPTAIN HUGH SAVAGE'S second son, PHILIP SAVAGE.[1]

MR. PHILIP SAVAGE settled at Ballygalget, where was erected, near the site of the old Ballygalget Castle, the mansion known as ROCK SAVAGE HOUSE. This mansion was prettily situated on the side of Knockdhu Hill, not far from a little lake (since drained[2]) which used to be covered with wild-fowl, and its demesne, as described by those who remember it, was a picturesque feature in the landscape, with plantations, hedge-rows, and fine garden. The interior of the House was remarkable for its handsome wood-work, its doors, wainscoting, &c., being made of beautiful Spanish mahogany, said to have been "royalties" washed up on the shores of the SAVAGE lands in the Ards from time to time from the wrecks of mahogany-ships, formerly but too frequent on the dangerous Downshire coast.

The old Church of Knockdhu, or Shankill, was situated on the side of Knockdhu Hill, behind the demesne-wall of Ballygalget, and there many of the Ballygalget Family were buried. When the graveyard was disused, the farmers whose forefathers had also been interred there carried the earth of their old family-graves thence to Ardkeen.

The Rev. J. O'Laverty, P.P., in his account of *The Diocese of Down and Connor*, from which we have already quoted, mentions the interesting fact that at a time when the Roman Catholics were oppressed, the Savages of Ballygalget, though themselves Protestants, granted them the use of a small house on their lands for the purposes of worship.

We now enter more fully into the history of the ROCK SAVAGE (BALLYGALGET) Family.

MR. PHILIP SAVAGE, of Rock Savage (Ballygalget), born in 1696, married, *1st*, Jane, daughter of Balthasar Cramer, Esq., of Ballyfoile, in the Co. of Kilkenny, High Sheriff of Co. Kilkenny in 1683,[3] by Sarah, daughter of Lieut. Col. Oliver Jones, and niece of Hester Lady Coghill, wife of Sir John Coghill,

---

[1] Among the papers preserved at Portaferry House is a lease, dated July 26, 1724, for a year of Ballygalget, Francis Lucas, Edward Lucas, and Mrs. Lucy Savage (widow of Captain Hugh Savage, of Ardkeen) of the 1st part, Francis Savage (of Ardkeen, no doubt) of the 2nd part, and Philip Savage of the 3rd part. There is also a Lease and Mortgage of part of Ballygalget for £400—Philip Savage to Lucy Savage (his mother).

[2] By the late John Echlin, Esq., of Rhuban (Echlinville).

[3] FAMILY OF CRAMER.

According to Sir Bernard Burke *(Landed Gentry)*, "The founder of the family" of Cramer "in Ireland was TOBIAS VON CRAMER *or* KRAMER, of Lower Germany: in the reign of James I. he settled in Ireland, and was made a free denizen, 28th May, 1639. He was father of BALTHAZAR CRAMER, Esq., who left issue two sons, TOBIAS and JOHN, and two daughters. The elder son,

LL.D., Master-in-Chancery in Ireland, and ancestress of the present Sir Joscelyn Coghill, Bart. (*see* Burke's *Peerage and Baronetage* under "COGHILL," and *Landed Gentry* under "CRAMER OF RATHMORE"), by whom he had issue,

PHILIP SAVAGE, ESQ., OF BALLY-GALGET (ROCK SAVAGE), born A.D. 1696; died A.D. 1780.

I. HUGH, born on the 24th of June, 1725; died, unmarried, at Haverford West, April 23, 1799.
II. John, a Lieut. in 9th Regt. of Foot, born July 4, 1726; drowned on his passage to England with a recruiting party.
III. Marmaduke-Coghill (named after his cousin, Marmaduke Coghill, LL.D., Judge of the Prerogative Court, Chancellor of the Exchequer (Ireland), M.P. for the University of Dublin, eldest son of Sir John Coghill, LL.D., Master-in-Chancery in Ireland), born on the 3rd of Nov., 1728; entered the Army as Ensign 37th Foot, 30th Aug., 1756; became Lieutenant in the same Regiment 30th Sept., 1757; was a Lieutenant in the 75th Regiment in 1760–62; and was appointed to the 52nd Regiment 19th Feb., 1766. He is mentioned in the Army List of 1780 as Lieutenant of one of the six companies stationed at Plymouth of the thirty-six Independent Companies of Invalids, the date of his appointment October 6, 1779. He married Hannah, daughter of Thomas James Brotherton, Esq., of Hereford, and died at Hereford, in 1780, aged 52 years. The following epitaph by his friends and former companions, intended to be placed on a marble monument in the Cathedral Church of Hereford (which, however, was never erected, owing to an order that no more monuments were to be set up there on account of the foundations having given way), describes a distinctly-marked character:—

"TO THE MEMORY OF MARMADUKE COGHILL SAVAGE, ESQ.

"He was descended from an ancient Family in the Kingdom of Ireland, and devoted himself to a Military life, wherein, tho' not fortunate

---

TOBIAS CRAMER, Esq., had assigned to him, for his services under CROMWELL, the lands of Ballyfoile, which were afterwards confirmed by patent under the Act of Settlement. He was Sheriff of Dublin, 1653, and High Sheriff, Co. Kilkenny, 1669. By Mary, his wife, he had two sons and two daughters, BALTHAZAR, of whom presently; Tobias; Hester, the wife of Sir John Coghill, Bart.; Deborah, wife of Arthur Webb., Esq. The elder son,

BALTHASAR CRAMER, Esq., of Ballyfoile, Co. Kilkenny, born in Dublin 1644, High Sheriff, Co. Kilkenny, 1683, married, *1st*, Elizabeth, widow of Dr. Hugh Drysdale, who died without issue; and, *2ndly*, Sarah, daughter of Lieut.-Col. Oliver Jones, and by her had, with other issue,

1. OLIVER, married Hester, daughter of Sir John Coghill, and by her was ancestor of the present Sir John Joscelyn Coghill, Bart.
2. AMBROSE, of whom presently.
3. *Jane, wife of Philip Savage, Esq., of Rock Savage.*

[margin: PHILIP SAVAGE, ESQ., OF BALLY-ALGET (ROCK SAVAGE), born .D. 1696; died .D. 1780.]

enough to rise to a superior command, he displayed a perfect knowledge of the Profession he had adopted. He was a Gentleman of real honour and constant integrity, open and unreserved in his disposition, sincere in his professions, and zealous in his attachments. He was a pleasant, steady, and confidential friend, possessed strong distinguishing sense, which in a various life he had applied to the study of mankind, and a conversation happily adorned with much genuine wit and great originality of expression, which rendered him frequently an instructive, always an entertaining, companion. His friends, who best knew his worth, will most lament his loss; but even his most distant and casual acquaintances will not refuse to drop a tear over his grave."[1]

---

[1] The following old Song, by an unknown author, while it reflects the manners of the time in which he lived, farther illustrates some phases of the character of MARMADUKE COGHILL SAVAGE:—

SONG

Commemorating Lieut. Marmaduke Savage's Passage to Quebec with the 10th Regt. in 1767, on his way to join his own Regt., the 52nd.

1

On the third day of June, in the year sixty-seven,
The Tenth in three transports sailed out of Crookhaven,
All jovial and hearty, like soldiers so valiant,
And Commodore Hall was quite Top and Top-gallant.
　　Tol de rol.

2

The Major commanded on board the Carnarvon,
A ship near as large as the town of Dungarvan,
Which carried the women, and baggage so weighty
Of officers seventeen and men three times eighty.
　　Tol de rol.

3

A notion prevailed in this jolly division,
They'd ne'er see Quebeck till they spent their provision;
So down they all sat and fell eating and drinking,
And made their heads swim to prevent them from sinking.
　　Tol de rol.

4

Of all jolly fellows the first to be reckon'd
Was MARMADUKE SAVAGE of the fifty-second,
And he at the Bottle was such a gay shover,
That before he left land he was near half-seas over.
　　Tol de rol.

5

The next jolly fellows were Basset and Vatas,
Fitzgerald and Thomson, and Blacky the fat man;
Montgomery and Parsons, with Crampton and Halley,
Thwaits, Edwards, and Vernon, Jump, Shaw, Green and Kelly.
　　Tol de rol.

Mr. Marmaduke Coghill Savage, by his wife Hannah (*née* Brotherton), left issue,

    1. A son, who died in infancy.

    2. JOHN BOSCAWEN, Major-General, K.C.B. & K.C.H., of whom hereafter as successor to his first cousin, HENRY SAVAGE, a minor, at Rock Savage (Ballygalget), and who, on the death

marginal note: PHILIP SAVAGE, ESQ., OF BALLYGALGET (ROCK SAVAGE), born A.D. 1696; died A.D. 1780.

    6
Blacky was mellow, and Thomson was rosy,
Parsons was rocky, and Shaw he was Boozy;
For they were as happy as Ducks in a shower;
And thus they went on at near nine knots *three hours*.
    Tol de rol.

    7
But vain is the courage of fresh-water sailors,
The next day they look'd like a parcel of Taylors,
And tho' the King's Birthday the glass was neglected,
Ev'n Compton and SAVAGE for once look'd dejected.
    Tol de rol.

    8
Sure never were men in so dire a condition,
Poor Shaw for a groat would have sold his commission;
While Edwards and Vernon, Jump, Thwaits, and Kelly,
Were pictures of Jonas just from the Whale's Belly.
    Tol de rol.

    9
So sick were our heroes, that not an old stager
Could get upon deck for three days but the Major,
And he look'd so round as he sat with his wraps on,
The sailors mistook him oft times for the capstan.
    Tol de rol.

    10
Then Hall, Moore, and Shirley, the lads of the Navy,
Went down with a how-d'ye-do and God save ye;
Alas, brother-soldiers, what brought you on ship-board,
Rouse up, or by Neptune we'll tip you the whipcord.
    Tol de rol.

    11
Then some from their Ca*bb*ins, and some from their Tickings,
Got up on deck and fell foul of the chickens.
"Hiloa Bucks!" cries Blacky, "I think you are at it,"
Then fell on his Buttocks and cried out "*Odd rat it.*"
    Tol de rol.

    12
The storm being over, these jolly brave fellows
Recovered their Spirits and laughed at the Billows;
Thwaits swore a whole volley, and offered to back it,
That he'd swim to America in a cork Jacket.
    Tol de rol.

PHILIP SAVAGE, ESQ., OF BALLY-GALGET (ROCK SAVAGE), born A.D. 1696; died A.D. 1780.

of FRANCIS SAVAGE, Esq., of ARDKEEN and HOLLYMOUNT, in 1823, became the representative in the male line of the ARDKEEN Family. (*Vide ante*, p. 221.)

1. Jane, married to J. Lenox, Esq., and had issue,

William-John Lenox, appointed to the India Office, 12th August, 1805; made Assistant Clerk in the Public Department, 30th July, 1822; transferred with the same rank to the Revenue Department, 23rd June, 1823; placed in special charge of the Public Department, 25th April, 1826, which appointment he held until 21st June, 1828, when he retired as an Assistant Clerk. Mr. Lenox went to sea as a Volunteer in his early life in the same ship as that in which his uncle, Sir John

13
Now Jump, grown a sailor, made use of such hard words,
His right was his Starboard, and his left was his Larboard;
While SAVAGE, still using the soldierlike terms of war,
Tacking called wheeling, fore and aft front and rear.
Tol de rol.

14
At length a sad sameness made all days look like one day,
And only for prayers they had ne'er known Sunday;
But Montgom'ry the Chaplain, like a good Vicar,
Took care of their souls, their meat, and their liquor.
Tol de rol.

15
Such was their Piety, such was their Boozing,
That in nine Weeks, of Wine they drank ninety-one dozen,
Of Rum, Shrub, and Brandy good fifty-eight gallons,
And eighty-six dozen of Porter to Balance.
Tol de rol.

16
At length out of spirits, and out of Provision,
They arrived at Point Levi in doleful condition,
But the sight of Quebeck soon with courage renewed them,
And the Spirit of Wolfe, as they landed, review'd them.
But the sight of Quebeck, &c.
And the Spirit of Wolfe, &c.

By reference to the Army Lists of 1767 and '68 we find that Basset was the Major of the 10th Foot; Vatas, evidently Capt. Vatass; Blacky, Lieut. Blackmore; and Compton, misspelt for C*r*ampton, also a Lieut.; Halley, probably meant for Hely, another Lieut.; and Vernо*n*, for Vernо*n*, an Ensign; Jump, probably the nickname of Ensign Marcus Anthony Tuite; Shaw*e*'s name, also an Ensign, is wrongly spelt Shaw; and there were two Montgomerys in the Regt., one named John, an Ensign, and the other James, the Chaplain.

SAVAGE OF ARDKEEN, LATER BALLYGALGET BRANCH. 263

        Boscawen Savage, was then serving as an officer of Marines.[1] He died about the year 1830.

PHILIP SAVAGE, ESQ., OF BALLYGALGET (ROCK SAVAGE), born A.D. 1696; died A.D. 1780.

IV. FRANCIS, of GLASTRY, High Sheriff of the Co. Down, born Aug. 30, 1733; married, 1756, his first cousin Mary, third daughter of FRANCIS SAVAGE, Esq., of ARDKEEN, and granddaughter of CAPTAIN HUGH SAVAGE, of ARDKEEN. (*Vide ante, under* FRANCIS SAVAGE, ESQ., OF ARDKEEN, *and hereafter, under* SAVAGE OF GLASTRY.)

V. HENRY, of whom presently as successor to his father at Rock Savage (Ballygalget).

VI. Charles, a Major in the 51st Regiment of Foot, born in 1737; married Amelia, 3rd daughter of William Lushington, Esq., Lieut.-Col. of Dragoons, youngest son of Stephen Lushington, Esq., of Sittingbourne, Co. Kent (who died on the 26th of June, 1786. Mrs. Charles Savage died on the 3rd of September, 1806). During the Rebellion of 1798, Major Charles Savage, it is stated, was three times down on his knees in the lawn of Ballygalget to be shot by the Rebels, and was three times liberated. He died without issue, at Rock Savage, on the 8th of August, 1801, aged 64 years, and was buried in the Rock Savage family-vault at Ardkeen, on the 15th of August, 1801.

VII. Edward, who died, unmarried, at Rock Savage, aged 20 years.

VIII. James, of Mount Ross,[2] born on the 15th of October, 1740; married, on the 30th of September, 1794, Mary Anne, daughter of —— Galway, Esq.; and died at Mount Ross, on the 18th of May, 1803, aged 64, leaving issue,

    HENRY (HARRY), of whom hereafter as heir to his uncle HENRY at Rock Savage (Ballygalget).

I. Lucy, who was born on the 6th of August, 1727, and died of small-pox in 1729, aged 2½ years.

II. Jane (Jenny), who was born on the 1st Jan., 1730, and died unmarried.

III. Lucy (a second of that name), of Nunsbridge, who was born on the 12th of Feb., 1731, and died in 1809, aged 78 years.

MR. PHILIP SAVAGE, of Rock Savage, married, *2ndly*, in 1741 (?), Jane, fourth daughter of John Echlin, Esq., of Priestown, by his wife Jane Echlin, daughter

---

[1] Sir John Savage used to say of him that during some naval action "Billy was below, nursing the cat."

[2] The House of Mount Ross, now in the possession of farmers, stands in a rather imposing and lofty situation some distance from Ballygalget—a solidly-built white house with two wings.

PHILIP SAVAGE, ESQ., OF BALLY-GALGET (ROCK SAVAGE), born A.D. 1696; died A.D. 1780.

of the Rev. John Echlin, Vicar of St. Mary's, Drogheda, of the PRIESTOWN branch of the family of ECHLIN OF ARDQUIN AND ECHLINVILLE, Co. Down,[1] and by her (who died on the 20th of Sept., 1781, aged 76 years, and who was buried in the Rock Savage family-vault at Ardkeen) had issue,

I. Philip, of Nunsbridge, born in 1742, to whom his father left the property of Nunsbridge.[2] He died on the 8th of May, 1790, aged 48 years, and was buried in the Rock Savage family-vault at Ardkeen.

[1] The father and mother of Mrs. PHILIP SAVAGE (*née* Jane Echlin), of Rock Savage, are interred in the Chancel of Ardkeen Church, where a recumbent slab still bears the following inscription:—
"Here lyeth the Body of
John Echlin of Priestown
who departed this life
the 4th Septr 1714
aged 45 years.
And also Jane Echlin his wife
who departed this life
25 of November, 1742, aged
67 years."

The following genealogical account of the Priestown Echlins is extracted from the *Echlin Memoirs*, by the Rev. J. R. Echlin, of Ardquin:—

"ROBERT ECHLIN, of Portaferry, married Euphemia (as is supposed, the fourth daughter of Bishop Echlin) *after* 1635, and by her had a son,

"JOHN ECHLIN, described in Trin. Col. Reg. as '*Colonus*,'—wife unknown. He had issue,

"1. David Echlin, described as 'of Priestown,' born before 1680, and died in 1767.

"2. Rev. John Echlin, Vicar of St. Mary's, Drogheda, born about 1680. He married Elizabeth Bomford, and died without issue in 1763, aged 83. He left a legacy to *his niece Jane, wife of Philip Savage, of Rock Savage*. In a letter to this J. E. from John Echlin, of Thomastown (son of the Rev. Robert Echlin), dated 1760, he is addressed as '*Cousin*.'

"1. Jane Echlin, married John Echlin, and had issue,
   1. Elizabeth Echlin, who married Robert Parkinson.
   2. Mary Echlin, who married Thomas Parkinson.
   3. Anne Echlin, who married Lawrence Bomford.
   4. *Jane Echlin, who married Philip Savage, of Rock Savage.* Jane Echlin's mother, by will dated 1742, left to her the sub-lease of Priestown, held under the See of Down by the Ardquin Echlins.

"2. Euphemia Echlin, married to Robert Kelly, of Killough. With two sons, who died unmarried, and a daughter, Alice, who married a Mr. Cooper, they had a daughter, Mary, who married Abraham Kettlewell, of the Co. Meath, and another daughter, Jane, who married Edward Molyneux. Mary Kettlewell's granddaughter, Anne Hathorn, marrying Jane Molyneux's son James, the issue of such marriage was
Echlin Molyneux, Q.C., of Walcot, Bray, Co. Wicklow, Esq.

"3. Elizabeth, married Hugh Johnston, of Rademon, Co. Down. They had issue two daughters, Esther, who married —— Pollock, and Sarah.

"4. Esther Echlin, who married John Jelly, of Rathmullen, Killough, Co. Down."

[2] NUNSBRIDGE.—"Philip Savage, of Rock Savage, left a will dated July 9th, 1773, and bequeathed to his son, Philip Savage, and his heirs, all those pieces or parcels of the s^d town and lands of Bally-

II. Robert, born on the 12th of March, 1745; died at Ballygalget (Rock Savage), aged 9 years.

I. Rose, who died in infancy.

II. Mary, born in 1752;[1] married to John Mahallom, Esq., of Ballymacnamee (in the Ards, Co. Down), and had issue,

1. Maria Mahallom.

[margin: PHILIP SAVAGE, ESQ., OF BALLY-GALGET (ROCK SAVAGE), born A.D. 1696; died A.D. 1780.]

By the second marriage of MR. PHILIP SAVAGE, of Rock Savage, the Echlin property of Priestown, lying along the shores of Lough Strangford, between Ardkeen and Portaferry, passed into the possession of the BALLYGALGET (ROCK SAVAGE) family. "Jane Savage's mother," writes the Rev. John R. Echlin in the *Echlin Memoirs*—*i.e.*, Jane Echlin, wife of John Echlin, Esq., and eldest daughter of John Echlin, Esq., of Priestown—"by will dated 1742, left to her the sub-lease of Priestown, held under the See of Down by the Ardquin Echlins." By a codicil to his will, dated 24th Feb., 1779, Mr. PHILIP SAVAGE made the following direction:—"I, Philip Savage, above and within named, do make this further codicil to my will—vizt., I direct that on the death of my wife the sum of £100, part of the principal sum of £300 due by Mr. Echlin in my will mentioned, shall be paid to my son Philip, and that the residue of that money, together with the purchase-money of my Lease of Priestown

---

galget, in the Co. of Down, then commonly called and known by the names and descriptions of 'The Shot and Timothy Parks,' wherein he had lately built a Maltkiln, house and effects, and which said premises were afterwards called and known as 'Nunsbridge.' The s^d Philip Savage afterwards duly made and published two several Codicils to his s^d Will, bearing date respectively on or about the 27th day of February, 1777, and 4th day of March, 1779, but did not thereby revoke or in any manner alter the s^d devise and bequest hereinbefore mentioned; and, having shortly afterwards died, his s^d Will and Codicils were duly proved, and Probate thereof granted forth of the Prerogative Court of Ireland to his sons, Francis Savage [of Glastry], James Savage, and the s^d Philip Savage the younger, the Executors therein named, on or about the 15th day of November, 1781.

"On the death of Henry Savage, in the year 1808 (the only son of James Savage, and grandson of Philip, senior), the Ballygalget estate, with the exception of Nunsbridge, became vested in Sir John B. Savage, under the Will of his uncle, Henry Savage, and on the death of Lucy Savage, in 1809, intestate and unmarried (one of the daughters of Philip Savage, senior, and aunt of Sir John B. Savage), Nunsbridge, which she held possession of till her death, fell into the possession of Sir John B. Savage as her heir-at-law."—(*Copy of a paper in the possession of Mr. F. W. E. Savage.*)

The Property and House of Nunsbridge took their name from the bridge called "Nun's Bridge," a little south-west of the ruins of Castleboy, near which the dwelling was erected. Why the bridge was called "Nun's" Bridge is not known. Traces of the garden of Nunsbridge House still remain.

[1] This date is doubtful. It is also doubtful whether this Miss Mary Savage was the daughter of Jane Savage (*née* Cramer) or of Jane Savage (*née* Echlin). In a MS. note by Miss Mary Mahallom, formerly in possession of Mrs. E. J. Armstrong (Miss Jane Savage, of Glastry), Miss Mahallom states that her mother was daughter of Jane Echlin; but in the same note she gives 1732 as the date of her own mother's birth. We have not been able to clear up the difficulty.

2 M

PHILIP SAVAGE, Esq., OF BALLYGALGET (ROCK SAVAGE), born A.D. 1696; died A.D. 1780.

(which lease I order to be sold on her death), shall be equally divided among all our children, share and share alike."[1] Mr. PHILIP SAVAGE died on the 27th of October, 1780, aged 83 years, and was buried in the vault of the BALLYGALGET (ROCK SAVAGE) family at Ardkeen. He was succeeded at Ballygalget (Rock Savage) by his fifth son,[2]

MAJOR HENRY SAVAGE, OF BALLYGALGET (ROCK SAVAGE), born A.D. 1735; died A.D. 1797.

HENRY SAVAGE, Esq., of Rock Savage (Ballygalget), Major in the 16th Foot, High Sheriff of the County of Down, born in 1735. MAJOR HENRY SAVAGE, of Rock Savage, entered the army 15th October, 1759; was Lieutenant 37th Foot, Jan. 8, 1768; Captain, April 15, 1774; Major in the 16th Foot, April 28, 1781. He married Jane, daughter and co-heiress of —— Hamilton, Esq. By his will, dated 4th Nov., 1797, MAJOR HENRY SAVAGE left his estate in trust for his wife, JANE SAVAGE,[3] for her natural life; then in trust for the use and behoof of his infant nephew, HENRY SAVAGE, son of his brother James Savage, and the heirs male of his body lawfully begotten; and, in case of the death of his said nephew without issue male, then in trust, &c., for the second son of his said brother, James Savage, and his heirs male; and, in default of such issue, for the use of the third, fourth, fifth, and all and every other son and sons of his said brother James, and their heirs male, &c.; and, in default of such, then in trust for his nephew, JOHN BOSCAWEN SAVAGE, Captain of Marines, and his issue male in same manner; and, in default of such like male issue, &c., of JOHN BOSCAWEN SAVAGE, then for the use and behoof of his brother, FRANCIS SAVAGE (of GLASTRY), and his heirs, &c. He left his sister, Lucy Savage, a legacy, "for her kindness and attention" to him; and he appointed

---

[1] Priestown became the property of SIR J. B. SAVAGE on the death of his first cousin HENRY. "In the year 1843 Priestown was sold by the SAVAGE FAMILY to James Warnock, of Portaferry, Esq., on whose death it became the property of his brother, John Warnock, of Ballywhite House, Portaferry, Esq., the present possessor."—*Note to* APPENDIX II. *of the Echlin Memoirs*, p. 63, by the Rev. J. R. Echlin, of Ardquin. (Second Edition.)

[2] Why Mr. PHILIP SAVAGE, of ROCK SAVAGE, in his will, should have passed over his three older surviving sons, HUGH, MARMADUKE, and FRANCIS of GLASTRY, in favour of his fifth son HENRY, does not transpire. Stories are certainly told of the wild ways of his sons when young lads; for example, it is recorded that they used to ride through the Ards, bent on frolics that were not always welcome to the country-folk, and that a common cry of the villagers as they saw them galloping towards their houses was, "Get in, girls, get in; here come the Ballygalgets!" But such escapades, the result of animal spirits, in an age famous for frolics and practical jokes, could hardly account for an act of such apparent severity on the part of their father.

[3] A mural tablet was erected to the memory of MAJOR HENRY SAVAGE, of ROCK SAVAGE, near the vault in Old Ardkeen Church, in which his remains, and afterwards those of his widow, were deposited. Subsequently the family removed the tablet to the New Church of Ardkeen, near Kirkistone, when the old one was about to be deserted. It now hangs on the south wall of the little chancel of the New Church.

his brother, James Savage, and Thomas Savage of Portaferry, his executors. MAJOR HENRY SAVAGE, of Rock Savage, died without issue, on the 6th of November, 1797, aged 62. He was succeeded at Ballygalget (Rock Savage), in accordance with the terms of his will, by his nephew (the only child of James Savage, Esq., of Mount Ross),

HENRY (HARRY) SAVAGE, of Rock Savage (Ballygalget), born on the 11th of March, 1797. "On the death of James Savage, his widow and little son HARRY removed to Ballygalget."[1] HENRY SAVAGE, of Rock Savage, died on the 12th of November, 1808, aged 11 years, of an illness which he brought home with him from Armagh School in 1807, and he was buried in the November of that year.[2] He was succeeded (in accordance with the terms of the will of his uncle, MAJOR HENRY SAVAGE, of Rock Savage) by his first cousin,

---

[1] MS. statement of the late Miss Maria Mahallom, of Ballymacnamee, granddaughter of PHILIP SAVAGE, Esq., of Rock Savage.

[2] The following is the inscription on the mural tablet erected in Ballyphilip Church, Portaferry (north wall of nave), to the memory of James E. Savage, of Rock Savage, his widow Mary Anne Savage, and his son HARRY SAVAGE, of Rock Savage :—

To the Memory of
James E. Savage, Esq.,
Son of Philip Savage, of Rock Savage, in the County of Down, Esqr.
Born at Rock Savage on the 15th Oct., 1740; married to Mary A. Galway, the 30th Sep., 1794.
And after an illness of four months and eighteen days, to which
he submitted with the most Christian resignation,
Died Wednesday, the 18th May, 1803.
Also
Harry Savage,
his son, who was born on the 11th March, 1797;
His opening virtues promised much, and the improvement of his mind was beyond his years,
But it pleased God to afflict him with a long and grievous indisposition
which his anxious parent observed upon his return from
Armagh School for Christmas Vacation
on the 14th of December, 1807,
And which terminated his existence in this life,
and all her hopes on this side of Eternity,
on the 12th of November, 1808.
Also
Mary Anne Savage,
Born on the 9th of June, 1774,
So long a widowed wife and childless mother,
Whom it pleased God to call from this trial of her fortitude and submission
upon Easter Monday, the 28th day of March, 1842.
Her hope for herself and for those she loved was, that,
after this painful life ended, they might
dwell together in life everlasting,
thro' Jesus Christ our Lord.

SIR J. B. SAVAGE, K.C.B., &c., OF BALLYGALGET (ROCK SAVAGE).

JOHN BOSCAWEN SAVAGE, of Rock Savage (Ballygalget), only surviving son of Marmaduke Coghill Savage, and eventually the representative in the male line of the ARDKEEN Family. (*Vide ante, under* ARDKEEN, *main line*, p. 221.)

ROCK SAVAGE HOUSE (BALLYGALGET).

SIR JOHN BOSCAWEN SAVAGE came into possession of the Ballygalget property when he was 48 years of age. He had not been born in Ireland, had not resided there, had led a soldier's life literally from his childhood, and had taken part in the most brilliant events of English history in a time of exceptional glories and triumphs. For one of such experiences the life of an Irish country gentleman had little charm. His occasional visits to the Ards were, on the whole, irksome to him, and the maintenance of the family-mansion, which he did not care to occupy, was a burthen. It is said (as we have already mentioned) that in a moment of irritation—aroused, it is said, by the demand for the absurd tax known as the "window-tax"—he declared before a company of friends and acquaintances in the Ards that he would sell the House for a ridiculously small sum of money. He sold it, against the earnest remonstrances of his kinsman, Mr. NUGENT, OF PORTAFERRY. The House was forthwith pulled down, and out of the materials a row of houses two stories in height was built at Portaferry, where they still stand. One of these houses is the Hotel kept by Mr. James Elliott.[1] The fine Spanish mahogany woodwork (of the doors, &c.) is said to have been sent to London and there sold. The furniture was auctioned, and some of it was purchased by the late Mr. Bernard Ward, of Vianstown, Co. Down. One of the old Chippendale mahogany tables, and some other pieces of furniture (also in mahogany), passed to Mr. Bernard Ward's grandson, Mr. John Echlin Ward, who now has them. The lake which adorned the demesne, as has been already stated, was drained by the late Mr. John Echlin, of Echlinville; the trees were cut down; and eventually, as we have seen, Ballygalget was sold by SIR JOHN SAVAGE'S eldest son, the late LIEUT.-GENERAL HENRY JOHN SAVAGE, Royal Engineers, to his kinsman, Major Andrew Nugent (Savage), of Strangford; and Priestown and Nunsbridge by his two younger sons, the late Col. John Morris Savage, Royal Artillery, and the late Mr. Francis James Saumarez Savage, respectively, to Mr. James Warnock, of Portaferry, and the Rev. Mr. Bullick, Incumbent of Ardkeen. The lands around the site of Rock Savage House are now held by a farmer named Smith, doubtless one of that old English family of Smiths so frequently mentioned in historical records as "dependents of the SAVAGES" in the Ards.

[1] In the summer of 1884, Mr. G. F. Armstrong discovered in the neighbouring garden the remains of a mantel-piece which was well-known to have belonged to Rock Savage House, and a portion of which is now in his possession.

GLASTRY HOUSE, Co. Down, formerly seat of the SAVAGES OF GLASTRY.

CHAPTER VII.

SAVAGE OF ARDKEEN *(continued)*.—SAVAGE OF GLASTRY.

THE GLASTRY FAMILY of SAVAGE was founded by FRANCIS SAVAGE, fourth son, and second that survived with issue, of PHILIP SAVAGE, of Ballygalget (Rock Savage), and grandson of CAPTAIN HUGH SAVAGE, of ARDKEEN (ob. 1723); and, like the ROCK SAVAGE family, the GLASTRY family have ever since held the position of a distinct branch of the ARDKEEN SAVAGES.

SAVAGE OF GLASTRY.

The SAVAGES OF GLASTRY have always been regarded as doubly Ardkeen, Mr. FRANCIS SAVAGE having married his first cousin, MARY SAVAGE, third daughter of FRANCIS SAVAGE, Esq., of Ardkeen, and, like himself, grandchild of the above-named CAPTAIN HUGH SAVAGE, of Ardkeen. They assumed a prominence in the Ards not only on account of this double descent, paternally and maternally, from ARDKEEN, but from the fact that when the representatives of the ARDKEEN main line and of the BALLYGALGET line ceased to reside in

SAVAGE OF GLASTRY.

the district, and after the demolition of Rock Savage House, they became the sole representatives of the ARDKEEN family residing in the Ards, and around them the traditional feeling of the neighbourhood rallied as around the heads of the House.

The old House of Glastry stands in its grounds in a slightly elevated position some distance from the highroad leading from Kirkcubbin to Ballyhalbert. It is a large, but odd-looking, structure, the back portion of it being considerably higher than the front, its original design never having been fully carried out.

FRANCIS SAVAGE, ESQ., OF GLASTRY, born A.D. 1733; died A.D. 1808.

FRANCIS SAVAGE, Esq., of Glastry, High Sheriff of the County of Down, third son (but second son surviving with issue) of PHILIP SAVAGE, Esq., of BALLYGALGET (ROCK SAVAGE), by his 1st wife, Jane, daughter of Balthazar Cramer, Esq., of Ballyfoile, Co. Kilkenny, High Sheriff, Co. Kilkenny, 1683 (*vide ante*, p. 263), and grandson of CAPTAIN HUGH SAVAGE, of Ardkeen, was born on the 30th of August, 1733. He held for a time an appointment in His Majesty's Customs at Belfast. In 1791 he was High Sheriff of the County of Down, and resided during his tenure of the Shrievalty at Turf Lodge, County Down. Besides Glastry House and lands, he was owner of several of the islands in Strangford Lough, and of the lands of Ballyferis, in the Great Ards, County of Down, and was lessee of the impropriate tithes of Ballyhalbert (St. Andrew's), Innishargie, and Whitechurch, in the Ards. Failing his nephew HARRY SAVAGE, and his brother MARMADUKE and his issue, he was left, as we have seen, by the will of his brother, MAJOR HENRY SAVAGE, of Rock Savage, next heir to the Ballygalget (Rock Savage) property. He is also referred to in the will of his uncle and father-in-law, FRANCIS SAVAGE, of Ardkeen; and we have seen that he was appointed one of the executors of the will of his father, PHILIP SAVAGE, of Rock Savage. In 1756 he married his first cousin, Mary, third daughter of FRANCIS SAVAGE, Esq., of Ardkeen, a lady who is stated to have been very beautiful; and by her had issue,

I. Francis, of Newcastle, Co. Down, born in December, 1757; married Elizabeth, daughter of Arthur Atkinson, Esq., of Mullertown, Mourne, Co. Down, and died at Newtownards on the 28th of November, 1803, having had issue,

1. Francis, an Officer in the 89th Foot, born at Newcastle, Co. Down, 8th Dec., 1786; married, 23rd Feb., 1807, Selina-Ann, daughter of —— Boyd, Esq. (She was born at Newry, Co. Down, 1787, and died at Quinlon, in the East Indies, 26th June, 1817.) Mr. Francis Savage died at Aleppo, near Madras, 13th Oct., 1827, having had issue,

Francis-Charles, an Officer in India, born at the Cape of Good Hope, 7th Jan., 1808 ; died, unmarried, at the Cape of Good Hope, 1826, aged 18.

Elizabeth-Charlotte, married to the Rev. Mr. Wilson, and went to America, where she died, leaving issue.

Charlotte-Selina, born at Madras, 19th December, 1813 ; married, April, 1834, to Mr. Hugh Graham, of Belfast, and died, leaving issue.

FRANCIS SAVAGE, ESQ., OF GLASTRY, born A.D. 1733; died A.D. 1808.

2. Charles, Major, retired (1883) with hon. rank of Lieut.-Colonel, H.E.I.C. Army (Bengal), born in 1787 ; died, without issue, in London, on the 28th of April, 1876, in his 89th year, leaving his property to his brother Henry.

3. Henry, of Frindsbury, near Rochester, Kent, Captain Royal Marine Artillery, in the Commission of the Peace for the Co. of Kent, born in 1797; married Mary-Anne, eldest daughter, by his 2nd wife, of John Perry, Esq., of Moor Hall, Essex; and died at Frindsbury, without issue, 27th Feb., 1879, aged 82. The following obituary notice of him appeared in one of the local Kent newspapers, in 1879 :—" DEATH OF CAPTAIN SAVAGE, J.P.—We regret to learn that the illness of Capt. Savage, to which we alluded last week, terminated fatally on Thursday morning last. Gradually declining health and the increasing infirmities of very advanced years, had for some time prevented Capt. Savage from discharging his public duties as a Justice of the Peace for the County and in other capacities. He will perhaps be best remembered locally as the active and first Captain of the 19th Kent Rifle Volunteers, a corps which, under his judicious command, attained a position of eminence in the County. During his long residence in this neighbourhood [Rochester], his uniformly considerate conduct and unassuming manners won for him an amount of respect which it falls to the lot of few men to enjoy. His benevolent and liberal disposition was constantly exhibited in acts of charity, and especially to all movements connected with the development of the Church. He was especially open-handed in his assistance towards the erection and endowment of the new church at Upnor, with which his

FRANCIS SAVAGE,
ESQ., OF GLASTRY,
born A.D. 1733;
died A.D. 1808.

name must ever remain associated. He supplemented the liberal donation of the late T. H. Day, Esq., of £555 towards the building of that church, by a most munificent contribution; and to the handsome donation of the late Mrs. Day, of £500 towards its endowment, he added the large sum of £1,500. During the past year he gave a further sum of £2,000 on the erection of the parsonage-house and laying out of its grounds on the site given by the Ecclesiastical Commissioners, besides leaving the sum of £500, the interest of which is to be applied to a repairing fund. . . . By the death of Captain Savage the neighbourhood has experienced an irreparable loss, and his memory will no doubt be long cherished in the minds of many of its residents. He was in his 83rd year."

1. Elizabeth, who died, unmarried, on the 21st June, 1823.
2. Mary, who died, unmarried, at Portaferry.

II. Charles, born in Dec., 1759; died, unmarried, while a student of Trinity College, Dublin, at Passage, Co. Waterford, Oct., 1780, aged 21.[1]

[1] The following verses, preserved by his niece, Mrs. Edmund John Armstrong (Miss Jane Savage, of Glastry), were written by young Charles Savage on leaving his home in search of health:—

LINES

Composed by the late CHARLES SAVAGE. 1780.

Ah! what avails the vain attempt of Skill
　　Against the shaft which Fate unerring aims?
We must resign us to High Heaven's will,
　　And yield submission to Death's early claims.
Torn from my friends, a wanderer I fly
　　The gloomy prospect of bleak Winter's reign.
How I'd prefer my own tempestuous sky,
　　And wish to die upon my native plain!
There [gentle friends] would consolation give,
　　And soothe the pain which fell disorders send,
Allay my sorrows while ordained to live,
　　And close my eyes when all my troubles end.

To which may be subjoined the following

LINES,

Suggested by the foregoing, and written years after. By the Rev. HENRY SAVAGE, of GLASTRY (his younger brother).

Yes, hapless youth, adorned with every grace
　　That early virtue, innate truth could give!
Thy fate with thy deserts did not keep pace,
　　Nor saved thee who alone deserved to live.

III. HENRY, of whom presently as successor to his father at Glastry.

I. Mary-Anne, who died at an advanced age, about the year 1827.[1]

MR. FRANCIS SAVAGE, of Glastry, died on the 23rd of March, 1808, and was interred in the family-vault under the Old Church of Ardkeen. He was succeeded at Glastry by his only surviving son,

HENRY SAVAGE, of Glastry, B.A., T.C.D., in Holy Orders, in the Commission of the Peace for the Co. of Down, born on the 15th of May, 1772.[2] His first sermon was preached at Bangor, Co. Down, on the 24th of November,

Margin notes: FRANCIS SAVAGE, ESQ., OF GLASTRY, born A.D. 1733; died A.D. 1808. REV. HENRY SAVAGE, OF GLASTRY, born A.D. 1772; died A.D. 1815.

> Most true it is that men of talents rare,
> Men who, like thee, in every branch can shine—
> In council, science, politics, and war,
> And sweetly-flowing beauties of the Nine,
> 'Gainst these implacable, unerring still,
> Too cruel Fate her direful arrow aims;
> Like thee they must "obey High Heaven's will,
> And yield submission to Death's early claims."

[1] Miss Mary-Anne Savage resided, during the later years of her life, at Donaghadee, Co. Down. A letter, written on "Jan. 20th," some time subsequent to 1821, and addressed to her favourite niece, Miss Jane Savage, of Glastry (afterwards Mrs. E. J. Armstrong, who is said to have borne a strong resemblance to her), is still preserved, with a lock of her dark-brown hair, streaked with grey, folded in it. Evidently this letter was written very shortly before her death. It contains references to several members of the Glastry family-circle then living.

[2] The following letter, giving us a glimpse of social life in Ulster a hundred years ago, was written by the Rev. HENRY SAVAGE, of Glastry, when he was a child of only 8 years of age, and addressed to his aunt, Miss Mary Savage, at Rock Savage. It gives her an account of some private theatricals which he had witnessed, in 1780, at Shane's Castle (Lord O'Neill's), where he had been a guest along with his parents. The "Mt. Pottinger" whence it was dated is now a populous district of Belfast, but was then a gentleman's place, and was probably rented at the time by Mr. FRANCIS SAVAGE, of Glastry. (*See* Burke's *Peerage*, &c., "Pottinger of Mt. Pottinger.")

"My dear Aunt, "Mt. Pottinger, 30th 1780.

I do not know what apology to make for not writing to you before this; by Tom. I have been a second time: at Shanescastle. and the play was the Merchant of Venice. there was no play-bills printed for the last time they were, they went to England and everywhere; but I will try to recolect the characters and write one for you.

Duke of Venice,	M! C. O'Niel.	pretty well.
Anthonio,	M! S! John O'Niel.	the same.
Bassanio,	M! D. Dunkin.	the same.
Gratanio,	M! Blaford [?]	the same.
Lorenzo,	M! O'Niel.	Not very well.
Shylock,	M! M! Lang.	Capital.
Lancaulet,	M! Rice.	the same.
Gollo [Gobbo],	M! Dunkin.	pretty well.
Portia,	Mrs. O Niel,	pretty well.
Nerrissa,	Miss Bristow,	very ill.
Jessica,	Miss F. Bristow,	the same.

REV. HENRY SAVAGE, OF GLASTRY, born A.D. 1772; died A.D. 1815.

1793, when he was only in his 22nd year.[1] What appears to be the first sermon he preached in the Old Church of Ardkeen was delivered there on the 9th of February, 1794. The REV. HENRY SAVAGE was appointed to the Incumbency of Ardkeen, through his family influence, in the latter year. He married, in 1799, Anne, daughter of Edward M'Guckin, Esq., and had issue,

I. FRANCIS, of whom presently as successor to his father at Glastry.

II. Raymond, born in Glastry House, on Whit Sunday, the 21st of May, 1809; married Eliza, daughter of John Scott, Esq., of Cork. (She died on the 15th Oct., 1840.[2]) Mr. Raymond Savage was killed by a

	CATHERINE & PRETRUC		[Paper torn]
	Petruchio,	Mr O'Niel,	Capita
	Baptisto,	Mr D. Dunkin	pret
	Taylor	Mr St. John O'Niel	Capita
	Servant to Peruchio		Mr Dunk
[Paper torn]		O'Niel	the same
	ine		

Adieu,
my dear Aunt,
H. SAVAGE"

[1] The MS. is in the possession of his grandson, Mr. G. F. Armstrong.

[2] The following stanzas on the death of his wife, who predeceased him by just one year, were found amongst the papers of Mr. Raymond Savage, and after his death were apparently printed (with a rather hyperbolical introduction) in an American journal of the time :—

TO MY WIFE.

Remember thee, my lost One?—Yes,
  So long as life and memory last;
Though dead, I could not love thee less,
  Or cherish less the blissful past.

Oh no, my love, though I should roam
  From clime to clime, from sea to sea,
I'll still recall our once sweet home,
  Where my affections rest with thee!

'Tis vain that destiny thus strives
  A love like mine to change or break;
From death it greater strength derives,
  And trials more devotion wake.

How oft, as in the "stilly night,"
  I look to Heaven, thy home on high,
Then gaze upon the moon's soft light,
  And trust you look through it on me!

fall from his horse while riding alone through a forest near Snow Port, in North America. His body was found, with his horse standing near it. He died on the 6th of October, 1841, without issue.

REV. HENRY SAVAGE, OF GLASTRY, born A.D. 1772; died A.D. 1815.

III. Edward, who died in infancy, and was interred in the Glastry family-vault at Ardkeen.
IV. EDWARD, of whom presently as successor to his brother FRANCIS.
V. William, born in Glastry House, on the 19th of January, 1812.
I. Mary, "born at Belfast, on the 6th of February (Ash Wednesday), 1799 nine, and baptised by the Revd. Jacob Stewart, deceased."[1]
II. Rose, who died in infancy, and was interred in the Glastry family-vault at Ardkeen.
III. JANE (married to Edmund John Armstrong, Esq.[2]), of whom presently

> That thought endears each lucid ray,
>   And makes new beauties to my eye,
> For then thy angel-spirit may
>   Be echoing to my lonely sigh.
>
> Remember thee, my lost One?—Yes,
>   The sun may cease to rise and set,
> The seas their stated limits pass,
>   Ere I shall thee one hour forget.
>
> Thy gentle image ever dwells
>   The sad, sad inmate of my breast,
> Though it each darkening cloud expels,
>   And soothes to hope and peace and rest.
>
> To it I turn when worldly things
>   And worldly men my scorn excite;
> In lieu of hate mild pity springs,
>   Sole promptings of thy spirit bright.
>
> Then let thy sainted spirit pray
>   That when life ceases in this heart,
> My soul to Heaven may wing its way,
>   With thee united, ne'er to part.
>
>   By the late Raymond Savage to the
>   memory of his beloved Wife.

[1] Extract from the Register of Baptisms in Ardkeen Church, believed to be in the handwriting of her father.

[2] Mr. Edmund John Armstrong was third surviving son of John Armstrong, Esq., J.P., of the old and famous Border family of the Armstrongs of Mangerton Castle and Gilknock Hall, in Liddesdale, celebrated in the Border Ballads and in the tales of Sir Walter Scott, the principal branches of which in Ireland are now represented by the Rev. Sir Edmund Frederick Armstrong, Bart., of Gallen, Capt. Carteret Andrew Armstrong, of Garry Castle, and William Bigoe Armstrong, Esq., of Castle Iver, King's County, all descended from the Cavalier Officer, Andrew Armstrong, who settled in

REV. HENRY SAVAGE, OF GLASTRY, born A.D. 1772; died A.D. 1815.

as successor to her niece, Miss SARAH J. A. SAVAGE, in the representation of the SAVAGES OF GLASTRY.

IV. Anne, born at Portaferry, on the 11th of May, 1805; died, unmarried, at Douglas, Isle of Man, February, 1879, and was buried in the cemetery of Kirkbradden.

Fermanagh in the reign of James I., not many years after the treacherous murder of John Armstrong, of Gilknock Hall, and the breaking up of the Armstrong Clan, by James V. of Scotland.—(*See* Burke's *Peerage and Baronetage, Landed Gentry*, &c.) The Armstrongs were of the old Scandinavian race of the North of England, and passed over the Border and settled in Liddesdale at an early period, and there became very powerful. Official documents show that the heads of the Armstrong family on the Borders could, in 1528, muster 3,000 horsemen. Mr. John Armstrong, born in 1751, married three times, and by his first wife had no surviving issue. He married, *2ndly*, Miss Blair, of Blairmount, Co. Antrim, and had issue that survived, one daughter, Elizabeth, who died young. He married, *3rdly*, Thomasine, daughter of Thomas Tucker, Esq., of Moynalty, Co. Meath (who was for a time, we believe, heir-presumptive to the estates of the Whaley family, the town-mansion of which family, in St. Stephen's Green, Dublin, is now the Catholic "University College;" and whose ancestor, the Rev. Thomas Tucker, in Oct., 1692-3, was presented to the United Rectories of Killbeg and Robertstown and the Rectory of Moynalty, Co. Meath, by King William III., in recognition of services rendered by him to that monarch. Mrs. John Armstrong was niece also of Miss Thomasine Tucker, married to Rev. Henry Brooke, Rector of Kinawley, uncle of the celebrated Henry Brooke, author of *Gustavus Vasa, The Fool of Quality*, &c.—*see* Burke's *Landed Gentry*, under "Brooke of Dromavana,"—and sister of Mrs. Boswell, wife of Alexander Boswell, Esq.—Boswells, Lords Auchinleck.) Through an intermarriage with the Lockhart family, Mr. Armstrong we find, became connected, in a distant way, with Sir Walter Scott. (See *Life and Letters of Edmund J. Armstrong*.) By his wife, Thomasine Armstrong (*née* Tucker), Mr. Armstrong had issue, with other children, who died young,

I. ALEXANDER-BOSWELL, of whom presently as successor to his father.

II. Montagu-Augustine, Resident Justice of the Peace at Port Elizabeth, Cape of Good Hope; born in March, 1802; married Miss Oxholm, of an eminent Danish family, and died December 4th, 1883, at King Williamstown, Cape of Good Hope, having had issue,

1. Montagu, who married, and died, leaving issue, a Son.
    1. Alexina, married to the late Dr. Peters, of King Williamstown, Cape of Good Hope, and has issue.

III. *Edmund-John, born August 12, 1804; married, in 1839, Jane, third daughter, and last to survive, of the Rev. Henry Savage, of GLASTRY, and had issue as in the text above.*

IV. John-Echlin, in Holy Orders, D.D., LL.D., Vicar of Llanstadwell, Pembrokeshire, on whom the Board of Trinity College, Dublin, conferred the Hon. Degree of Doctor-of-Divinity, in recognition of his zealous efforts and remarkable success as a controversialist; born 1806; married, *1st*, Juliet, daughter of Henry Bolton, Esq., and had issue,

1. Henry, who died in infancy.

He married, *2ndly*, Henrietta, daughter of J. Mathew, Esq., and died, without surviving issue, in 1873.

V. George-Fleming, who went as a missionary to Tasmania, and there died of fever, unmarried, in his 22nd year.

I. Thomasine-Margaret, born 6th July, 1786; married, 3rd February, 1809, to her cousin, JOHN ECHLIN, ESQ., OF ECHLINVILLE AND ARDQUIN, Co. Down, J.P. and D.L. for the County of Down, and High Sheriff of the County in 1827 (the families of Armstrong and Echlin were closely related by common descent from the Flemings, Lords Slane), and had issue,

V. Rose (a second of that name), born at Portaferry, on the 17th of April, 1807. She accompanied her brother Raymond to America, and there died unmarried.

VI. Emily, twin with her brother EDWARD, born in Glastry House on the 8th of December, 1810; died in infancy on the 1st of June, 1814, and was interred in the Glastry family-vault at Ardkeen.

The REVEREND HENRY SAVAGE, of Glastry, died on the 4th of May, 1815, aged 42 years. A letter on his case, from Dr. James Hamilton, of Edinburgh, addressed to his physician in the Ards, and preserved among the papers of his

REV. HENRY SAVAGE, OF GLASTRY, born A.D. 1772; died A.D. 1815.

1. John Echlin, born 28th January, 1810; died 4th March of same year.
2. JOHN-ROBERT ECHLIN, of Ardquin, Co. Down, M.A., and J.P. for the Co. of Down, present representative of the family of ECHLIN OF ARDQUIN; born 15th July, 1811; married, *1st*, Jane, 3rd daughter of James Pedder, Esq., of Ashton Lodge (now Ashton Park), Lancashire, and had issue one son, John Pedder Echlin, born 1837, died 1838. He married, *2ndly*, 1841, Mary Anne, 2nd daughter of Ford North Esq., of the Oaks, Ambleside, Westmoreland, and by her had issue,

   JOHN-GODFREY ECHLIN, born 5th April, 1843; married, 1870, Anna Medicis, elder daughter of the Rev. John Wrixon, Vicar of Malone, Co. Antrim (by Annabella, his wife, daughter of the late Rear-Admiral John Dawson), and sister of Marie Elizabeth, wife of George Francis Armstrong, Esq. (*refer to text*), and has issue.

   Frederic Echlin, born 14th March, 1844, Commander Royal Navy; married, 1885, Lily, daughter of Thomas Kerr, Esq., C.M.G., Governor of the Falkland Islands, and has issue.

   Alfred-Ford Echlin, in Holy Orders; born 27th September, 1849; married, 1876, Miss Isabel G. Barrat, and died, leaving issue one Son.

   Edith-Althea Echlin, married, 1869, to the Rev. George Henry Joy, D.D., and has issue.

   Thomasine Echlin, married, 1877, to the late Rev. George Read, M.A., and has had issue.

   The Rev. J. R. Echlin married, *3rdly*, 1878, Henriette Wilhelmine Louise Margarethe, eldest daughter of Richard Von Oertzen, late of Crobnitz, Upper Lusatia, Germany.

3. George-Fleming Echlin, born 27th June, 1812; married Harriet Georgina, daughter of Colonel Johnston, of Bundoran, and died January, 1869, leaving issue.
4. Charles, born 11th May, 1820; married Miss E. Farrell, and has issue.

1. Elizabeth Echlin, married to Rev. James Gerahty, formerly Rector of Donaghendry, Co. Tyrone, and died, 1877, leaving issue.
2. Hester-Jane Echlin, married to the Rev. Charles Ward, Rector of Kilwaughter, Co. Antrim, son of Bernard Ward, Esq., of Vianstown, Co. Down, and died, 1877, leaving issue one Daughter.
3. Thomasine-Margaret Echlin, married to John Auchinleck Ward, Esq., son of Bernard Ward, Esq., of Vianstown, Co. Down, and died, leaving issue.
4. Jane Echlin, married to the Rev. John Going, Rector of Hawkchurch, Devon, and has issue.
5. Margaretta-Watson-Jane-Colville Echlin, married, 1845, to Alexander Cranston, Esq., and died without issue, 1849.

REV. HENRY SAVAGE, OF GLASTRY, born A.D. 1772; died A.D. 1815.

daughter, the late Mrs. E. J. Armstrong, suggests grave doubts as to whether his early death was not, in great measure, the result of the excessive bleeding and other absurd treatment to which he had been subjected by his medical advisers in Ireland. He was interred (as was also his widow, who died on the 7th of May, 1828) in the Glastry family-vault at Ardkeen, where the monumental altar-shaped tomb outside, and close to, the south wall of the ruined Church, is a conspicuous object from the Portaferry coach-road as it skirts the old Ardkeen deer-park. He was succeeded at Glastry by his eldest son,

FRANCIS SAVAGE, Esq., of Glastry, Barrister-at-Law, in the Commission of the Peace for the County of Down, for some time Resident Magistrate at

6. Harriet Echlin, married to Henry Perceval, Esq., and has issue.—(*See* Burke's *Landed Gentry*, under "Echlin of Ardquin;" and *Genealogical Memoirs of the Echlins of Pittadro*, by the Rev. J. R. Echlin, M.A.)

II. Martha-Jane, died, unmarried, 1881, aged 89 years.

III. Sarah-Douglas, died at Echlinville, Co. Down, unmarried, in 18—.

Mr. John Armstrong died in 1820, aged 69 years.

The Eldest Son,

ALEXANDER BOSWELL ARMSTRONG, Lieutenant-Colonel in the Army, served as Lieutenant 21st Royal North British Fusiliers, at the capture of Genoa in 1814, and subsequently in the American War, including the capture of Washington, attack before Baltimore, 13th September, 1814, and on New Orleans, 8th January, 1815, where he was wounded and taken prisoner. At the conclusion of the Great War, in 1815, he was one of the numerous officers of His Majesty's forces placed on half-pay. Joining the Cape Mounted Rifles, he was present when Graham's Town was attacked by about ten thousand Kafirs, 22nd April, 1819, who were repulsed with great slaughter by three hundred men under the command of Colonel Wiltshire. Commanded in the Kat River Settlement during the Kafir War of 1834-35, and was thanked in General Orders for his defence of that locality against an attack of Kafirs on the 19th February, 1835. Served also throughout the whole of the Kafir War of 1846-47, and was present at the attack on the Amatola, 16th April, 1846, and two subsequent days' engagement (Medal). He was well known in the early history of Cape Colony, where the old military post of Fort Armstrong still bears his name. Lieut.-Col. Armstrong became subsequently a Civil Magistrate at the Cape of Good Hope. He married Mary, daughter of the Rev. John Frazer, of Co. Waterford, and had issue,

I. JOHN-OSBORNE, of whom presently.

II. Alexander-Thomas, Major-General in the Army, Lieut.-Col. 10th Bengal Lancers, born 1826, served in the Campaign of the Punjaub; was present at the Siege of Mooltan; served in the Abyssinian Expedition in 1867 (Medals); died at Chepstow, Monmouthshire, on the 18th of December, 1879, unmarried.

I. Sarah, married to Major-General George Stone, Royal Artillery, and died, having had issue,
  1. George Stone, Lieut. Royal Engineers.
  1. Arthur Stone.

II. Henrietta, married to Wyndham Knight, Esq., of Bilting House, Kent, eldest son of Edward Knight, Esq., of Godmersham Park, Kent, and Chawton, Hants, and has issue,
  1. Edward Knight, who is married and has issue.
  1. Mary Knight.—(*See* Burke's *Landed Gentry*, under "KNIGHT OF GODMERSHAM.")

III. Mary, married to Major Charles J. Lindam, late Rifle Brigade, afterwards of the Royal Body

Ballyshannon, Co. of Donegal, born in 1800; married Eliza, daughter of Mr. George Watts, of Dublin (who married, 2*ndly*, Mr. Nixon, of Riverview, Co. Tipperary); died at Holywood, Co. Down, without issue, on the 8th of October, 1842; and was interred in the Glastry family-vault at Ardkeen. He was succeeded by his elder surviving brother,

FRANCIS SAVAGE, ESQ., OF GLASTRY, born A.D. 1800; died A.D. 1842.

EDWARD SAVAGE, Esq., of Glastry, afterwards of The Copse, Co. Wicklow, twin with his sister Emily, born in Glastry House on the 8th of December, 1810;

EDWARD SAVAGE, ESQ., OF GLASTRY, born A.D. 1810; died A.D. 1849.

> Guard, son of the late Lieut.-Col. Lindam, Hanoverian Legion, of the Danish family of that name.* (Major C. J. Lindam served in the 10th Foot in the Sutlej Campaign of 1845-6, and was severely wounded (lost a leg) at the Battle of Sobraon—Medal. Served also four years as Paymaster in the Rifle Brigade in British Caffraria, including the Kafir War, 1846-7—Medal. For some time he was Deputy-Governor of Milbank Prison. From the 19th of May, 1854, he was one of H.M.'s Body Guard of the Honourable Corps of Gentlemen-at-Arms, from which he retired in the year 1876.) Major and Mrs. Lindam have had issue,
> 1. Charles Lindam.
> 2. John Lindam, in Holy Orders.
> 3. Robert Lindam.
> 1. Minnie Lindam, married to the Rev. F. Sparks, and has issue.
> 2. Mary Lindam.

Lieut.-Col. Alexander Boswell Armstrong died in 1863.

The Eldest Son,

JOHN OSBORNE ARMSTRONG, C.B., Major-General in the Army, born 1819, entered the army as Ensign in the 91st Foot; afterwards served with great distinction in the Cape Mounted Rifles against the Boers and Kafirs; "was present at the attack on the Amatola in April, 1846; served on the staff of Major-General Somerset during the war of that year as Field-Adjutant, and subsequently as Aide-de-Camp, and was present at the action of the Gwanga. Commanded three squadrons of the Cape Mounted Rifles, under Sir Harry Smith, against the rebel Boers over the Orange River, and was in the action at Boem Plaats, August, 1848, where he was severely wounded, and had his horse shot under him (Brevet of Major). Was selected by Sir Harry Smith to form and command a corps of Irregular Horse ('Armstrong's Horse') during the war of 1852-53, and was several times mentioned in General Orders, having commanded detachments in various successful affairs against the enemy (Brevet of Lieut.-Col. and Medal). His commissions bore date as follow:—Ensign, October 28, 1837; Lieutenant, February 7, 1840; Captain, January 8, 1847; Brevet-Major, December 22, 1848; Brevet Lieutenant-Colonel, May 23, 1853; Brevet-Colonel, November 28, 1854; Major, October 8, 1861; and Major-General, July 6, 1867."—(See *Army and Navy Gazette*, July 4, 1874.) Received a

---

* The following is from a letter written to the *Times* by the Dean of Winchester, on the death of the late Col. Lindam:—"Lieutenant-Col. Lindam received his commission in the 2nd Light Infantry of the German Legion in the year 1810. He was sent out at once to Portugal, where he joined the allies under Wellington, who were lying in the lines of Torres Vedras. He served through the murderous Battle of Albuera, and was one of those who stood triumphant on the fatal Hill. Of the Brigade of the Light Infantry to which he was attached nine hundred out of fifteen hundred were either wounded or killed. He then followed Wellington's victorious march through N.W. Spain, and was present at most of the fighting, including the taking of San Sebastian. At the close of the Peninsular War, in 1814, he embarked at Toulouse with the British Infantry (the cavalry were marched through France) and came home. The 'Hundred Days' now followed, and his regiment was ordered to Belgium, where he was once more under the command of Wellington. At the Battle of Waterloo he was severely wounded in the defence of Hougomont. He was carried insensible to the rear, and was unconscious till long after the battle was over. He was brought home, and for two years it was thought unlikely his constitution could recover from the wound, and so, to save his purchase money, he was induced in 1817 to sell out. For his services in the Peninsula and at Waterloo he received the rank of Lieut.-Col., and was created a Knight of the Royal Hanoverian Guelphic Order. (Peninsular and Waterloo Medal.)"

EDWARD SAVAGE, Esq., of GLASTRY, born A.D. 1810; died A.D. 1849. married, 4th February, 1845, Mary, daughter of John Willington, Esq., J.P., of Killoskehane Castle, Co. Tipperary, granddaughter of John Willington, Esq., of Killoskehane, J.P. and D.L., High Sheriff of the Co. Tipperary, and of Alicia, daughter of Jonathan Willington, Esq., of Castle Willington, and niece of the Viscountess Monck. (*See* Burke's *Landed Gentry*, under "Willington of Castle Willington," and Burke's *Peerage and Baronetage*, under "Viscount Monck.")[1] In the lifetime of MR. EDWARD SAVAGE, Glastry House and lands were sold, and he went to reside first at The Copse, Valley of Clara, Co. Wicklow, and

---

Good Service Pension, &c. Major-General Armstrong married Ellen Constance, daughter of the late Lieut.-Col. D'Arcy, by whom he had issue,
 I. JOHN-EDWARD-LOVELL, of whom presently as successor to his father.
 II. JOHN-CECIL, of whom presently as successor to his brother.
 I. May.
 II. Ethel.
 III. A daughter, who died in infancy.
Major-General Armstrong died at his residence, Stoulgrove House, near Chepstow, Monmouthshire, on the 28th of June, 1874, and was buried in Tidenham Churchyard (where his own child and his brother, Major-General Alexander-Thomas Armstrong, are also interred).
 The Eldest Son,
 LIEUTENANT JOHN EDWARD LOVELL ARMSTRONG, born 8th January, 1865, was educated at Wellington College, and at Sandhurst, and was gazetted to the 2nd Battalion Hampshire Regt., 20th October, 1883. He served in the campaign in Burmah, in 1885-6. Died at Mandalay, 29th January, 1886, from the effects of two bullet-wounds received in an encounter with Dacoits at Segaing Fort on the 8th of the same month. He was succeeded by his only surviving brother,
 JOHN-CECIL ARMSTRONG.

[1] FAMILY OF WILLINGTON:—
 "The family of WILLINGTON is of great antiquity, and it is recorded by Sir William Dugdale (*Monasticum Anglicanum*, tom. ii., p. 280) that this family were, at a very early period, benefactors of the Priory of Restors, in Derbyshire, and many of their benefactions are contained in the confirmation charter of King Henry III. It also appears that, in 1279, John, Archbishop of Canterbury, confirmed to the Priory the 'Church of Wilinton,' the gift of Nicholas, Lord of Wilinton. An heiress of this house married into the family of Fynderne, of which an heiress again intermarried with Harpur, and according to the Visitations of Derbyshire, 1569 and 1611, and Harleian MS., 1093, fol. 76 and 77, the arms were quartered with Harpur and Findern in Swarkstone Church and Sir John Harpur's house at Swarkstone.
 "The family emigrated at so early a date into Gloucestershire that we know but little of those at 'Willington,' in Derbyshire, beyond what is stated in the pedigrees and what is contained in the book mentioned above, and in some other remaining MSS. in the British Museum and elsewhere. They settled at Sandhurst, temp. King John. In the reign of Edward III. John de Willington, and after him Ralph de Willington, his son, were summoned to Parliament as barons of the realm.
 "This family flourished in Gloucestershire and Devon for many centuries, where, through female heirship, they are now represented by the Chichesters and Bassetts. A junior branch of the male line settled, temp. Henry VII., in Warwickshire, where they had lands at Barcheston, Hurley, and Whatsley. Of the Barcheston Willingtons there are several co-representatives through female heirship, viz., Charles Holte Bracebridge, Esq., of Atherstone Hall, the Marquess of Anglesey, the Earl of Denbigh, &c.
 "The Hurley Hall branch is now extinct in the direct male line, but is at present represented

afterwards at Clifton, Somersetshire. By his wife, Mary Savage (*née* Willington), MR. EDWARD SAVAGE had issue,

I. Emily, who died in infancy, and was buried in the Old Churchyard of Monkstown, Co. Dublin.

---

by the Willingtons of Fen End House, Hampden-in-Arden, Co. Warwick, and the Willingtons of Castlewillington, Co. Tipperary. In the female line it is also represented by the Jowetts of Wichnor Park, and the Floyers of Hints. The Rev. John Willington, Vicar of Edgeley, and J. Waldyve Willington, Esq., F.R.H.S., of Castlewillington, are the surviving male representatives. In the Histories of Gloucestershire (Sir Robert Atkyns and Rudder) there are, under articles 'Sandhurst' and 'Yate,' accounts of the family, as well as in Risdon's 'Survey of Devon,' p. 317, and in other histories of the same county. In the Records of the British Museum there are numerous references to the family, and documentary evidence is also to be found there of the ancient precedence and importance of this ancient family. A good pedigree appears under article 'Atherington,' in Sir William Pole's 'Devon,' p. 422. The Willingtons of Gloucestershire are identical, having seats in both counties. Sir William Dugdale (Dr. Thomas's ed.) has also a pedigree commencing about temp. Henry VI., tracing them into Gloucestershire, and continuing them to the time of the publication of this edition. The Willingtons of Ireland are an offshoot from the Hurley branch. In the Visitation of Warwickshire, 1619, there is mention made of two members of that family, one of whom is mentioned as *vivens in Hibernia*, and another as having died in that country. In the Tamworth Parish Register there is a memorandum stating that 'In 1598, on the 30th day of April, Robert, Earl of Essex, went from Drayton-Basset towards Ireland with a host of men to make warre againste the earl of Tyroone, an Irishman,' and it is therefore supposed that George and John Willington, uncle and nephew, who are mentioned as being then in Ireland, joined the Earl of Essex in his expedition, and eventually became the founders of the Irish branches of the Willington family. The earliest mention made of this family in this country is 'John Willington, of Killeens, in the barony of Stradbally, Queen's Co.,' whose will is dated 10 September, 1658, and a branch which settled at Ballymoney, in the King's Co. Charles Willington, of Ballymoney, whose will is dated 28 April, 1721, mentions James Willington, of Killoskehane, Co. Tipperary, as 'his brother,' and it would appear, therefore, that the family mentioned below derived its origin from a younger son of the Ballymoney family."

JOHN WILLINGTON, Esq., 3rd son of Thomas Willington, Esq., of Hurley Hall, by Alice, his wife, daughter of John Willington, Esq., of Whately, died in Ireland, and is considered to have been grandfather of

JAMES WILLINGTON, Esq., of Killoskehane Castle, who married Mary Carden, and died 6 February, 1730, at the advanced age of 104 years, having had issue,

JOHN, of whom presently.

JONATHAN, ancestor of the Castlewillington branch, of which we have hereafter to treat.

The eldest son,

JOHN WILLINGTON, Esq., of Killoskehane Castle, Co Tipperary, married Mary, daughter of Richard Eyre, Esq., of Eyrecourt Castle, Co. Galway, by whom he left issue,

James, who died unmarried, November, 1754.

John, of whom presently.

Jonathan, of Rapla, Co. Tipperary; married Miss Disney, by whom he had three sons, all of whom died unmarried. He died, 1818, and was buried in Gloucester Cathedral.

Mr. Willington died, January, 1767, and was succeeded by his 2nd son,

JOHN Willington, Esq., J.P. and D.L., of Killoskehane Castle, who married, *1st*, 23 October, 1767, Alicia, daughter of Jonathan Willington, Esq., of Castlewillington, by whom he left issue,

JOHN, of whom presently.

EDWARD SAVAGE, ESQ., OF GLASTRY, born A.D. 1810; died A.D. 1849.

II. SARAH-JANE-ANNE, of whom presently as heiress to her father, and his successor in the representation of the SAVAGES OF GLASTRY.

MR. and MRS. EDWARD SAVAGE both died of cholera, within a few days of each other, at Clifton, Gloucestershire, and were buried in the graveyard of Clifton. It was the constantly-expressed wish of Mr. EDWARD SAVAGE that, failing issue of his own, the Glastry family property (or what was left of it) should pass to the eldest surviving son of his own second surviving sister, JANE, wife of Edmund John Armstrong, Esq.; and, before the birth of his daughter, MISS SARAH J. A. SAVAGE, he had constituted his nephew, Edmund Armstrong, the Poet (then a

---

Jonathan, Major in the Army, died unmarried; will dated 15 November, 1835.
James, Captain in the Army; served in the Peninsular War; died unmarried.
Mary, married, 1787, to George Bennett, Esq., of Richmond House, Templemore.
Elizabeth, married, 1789, to John Shelton, Esq., of Rosmore, Co. Limerick.
Priscilla, who died, unmarried.
Alicia, married to Ringrose Drew, Esq., of Drew's Court, Co. Limerick, and died 11 June, 1868.
Mr. Willington married, 2ndly, 1785, Bridget, daughter of Theobald Butler, Esq., of Knockra Castle, and by her had further issue,
    Theobald, who married Miss Woods, by whom he had issue a son and daughter, viz.,
        Richard, Major 77th Regiment, who married Miss Rose, by whom he left issue. This gentleman served with distinction throughout the Crimean Campaign, and died at Murree, in India, 1 September, 1868, aged 36.
        Maria, married to the Rev. George Chute, M A., Vicar of Drayton-in-Hales, Salop.
    Richard, late Colonel of the 84th Regiment.
    Bridget, married to the Hon. Charles Monck, and was mother of the present Lord Viscount Monck.
Mr. Willington served as High Sheriff two successive years.
His eldest son,
    JOHN WILLINGTON, Esq., of Killoskehane, J.P., married, 23 January, 1815, Sarah, daughter of Christopher Ormsby, Esq., of Dublin, and had issue,
        JOHN-JAMES, of whom presently.
        Ormsby, born 26 October, 1816; died, unmarried, 1855.
        Jonathan, born 20th June, 1821; died unmarried.
        Jane-Anne, died unmarried.
        Alicia, married, 1 July, 1843, to John, eldest son of the late James Willington, Esq., of Castlewillington, Co. Tipperary, and had (with other issue) a son, JAMES WALDYVE WILLINGTON, Esq., now of Castlewillington, the present representative of this branch.
        Mary, married 4 February, 1845, to Edward, son of the Rev. Henry Savage, of Glastry, Co. Down, and had an only daughter, Sarah-Jane-Anne, who died, unmarried, in her 21st year.
        Sarah, died, unmarried, October, 1847.
        Elizabeth, died unmarried.
Mr. Willington died, 15 April, 1835, and was succeeded by his eldest son,
    JOHN JAMES WILLINGTON, of Killoskehane Castle; born, 26 November, 1815; died, unmarried, January, 1862, whereupon this branch became extinct in the direct male line, and Mr. Willington was succeeded by his nephew,
    JAMES WALDYVE Willington, Esq., of Castlewillington, Co. Tipperary; born, 15 July, 1846.—(*See* Burke's *Landed Gentry.*)

little child, to whom he was greatly attached), his heir and representative. After the birth of his daughter SARAH, he made a will, naming her his heiress; but, if she should not attain the age of 21, his estate was to devolve upon his brother-in-law, Edmund John Armstrong, Esq., husband of his sister JANE, and father of his nephew Edmund; his intention being to preserve the little that remained of the Glastry property, and the representation of the SAVAGES OF GLASTRY, in the line of his sister, Mrs. ARMSTRONG. MR. EDWARD SAVAGE, dying at Clifton, Gloucestershire, on the 8th of October, 1849, was succeeded by his only surviving daughter,

Edward Savage, Esq., of Glastry, born A.D. 1810; died A.D. 1849.

SARAH JANE ANNE SAVAGE, heiress of the Glastry property (now reduced to very small proportions), and representative of the SAVAGES OF GLASTRY, born Dec., 1845. After her father's death, MISS SARAH SAVAGE was made a Ward of Court. Attaining the age of 21, she made a will, carrying out the spirit of her father's original intentions as far as was then possible, and leaving as her joint-heirs her uncle-by-marriage, Edmund John Armstrong, Esq., her aunt, JANE ARMSTRONG (second surviving daughter of the REV. HENRY SAVAGE, of Glastry), and her two surviving first-cousins, GEORGE FRANCIS ARMSTRONG and Annie Eliza Armstrong, only surviving children of the above-named Edmund and JANE ARMSTRONG. MISS SARAH J. A. SAVAGE died at Kingstown, Co. Dublin, on the 11th of September, 1867, and was buried in the same grave with her sister Emily and her cousin Edmund Armstrong, in the Old Churchyard of Monkstown, in the same County. She was succeeded in the representation of the SAVAGES OF GLASTRY by her aunt,

Miss Sarah J. A. Savage, born A.D. 1845; died A.D. 1867.

MRS. EDMUND JOHN ARMSTRONG (née JANE SAVAGE), third daughter, and last that survived, of the REV. HENRY SAVAGE, of Glastry, born at Nun's Quarter, near Kirkcubbin, Co. Down, on the 30th of July, 1801; married at Holywood Church, Co. Down, 23rd Oct., 1839, to Edmund John Armstrong, Esq., son of John Armstrong, Esq., J.P. (*see footnote, p.* 275), and brother of Mrs. Echlin, of Echlinville, and had issue,

Mrs. Edmund John Armstrong [Miss Jane Savage, of Glastry], born A.D. 1801; died A.D. 1880.

I. Henry-Savage Armstrong, born on the 30th of July, 1840; died in infancy.

II. Edmund-John Armstrong, the Poet, author of *The Prisoner of Mount Saint Michael, Ovoca,* &c., born in Mornington House, Dublin, on the 23rd of July, 1841. After having commenced his University course in Trinity College, Dublin, Edmund Armstrong, owing to a neglected cold and excessive physical exertion, ruptured a blood-vessel in the spring of 1860. He retired for his health to the Island of Jersey. In the spring of 1861, his health being restored, he made a long walking-tour in France, in company with his younger brother; recommenced his studies at Dublin University; was elected President of the University Philosophical Society in the summer of 1864; won the highest prizes of that association and of the Historical Society; and in the following autumn delivered an Inaugural Address as President of the Philosophical Society, which attracted much attention; but almost immediately afterwards he was attacked by a severe congestion of the lungs, to the effects of which he succumbed. He died, unmarried, on the 24th of February, 1865, aged 23. He was buried in the same grave with his cousins Emily and SARAH SAVAGE in the Old Churchyard at Monkstown, his funeral being attended by deputations from the Historical and Philosophical Societies, a large number of his fellow-students, and eminent men of his University and City. A selection from his *Poetical Works* was soon afterwards published as a Memorial of him by the Historical and Philosophical Societies of Dublin University in 1865, and a New and Enlarged Edition of his *Poetical Works*, his *Life and Letters*, and his *Essays and Sketches*, in three volumes, in 1879. His genius and his works attracted the attention and won the praise of many of the leading intellects of his time, including the late Charles Kingsley, Sir Henry Taylor, author of *Philip Van Artevelde*, Sir Arthur Helps, Dean Milman, Professor Craik, and Mons. De Ste.-Beuve. Ste-Beuve predicted that he would take his place, along with Keats, in the small group of English poets of precocious genius who died young, and that "his young star would continue to shine before the eyes of all students of English poetry;" and the *Edinburgh Review* concluded a eulogistic article on his character and his works with the words, " His life was a poem."[1]

---

[1] The following extracts are from a sketch of Edmund Armstrong, written by Professor E. Dowden, LL.D., of Trinity College, Dublin, author of *Shakspere: His Mind and Art*, &c., and published in the *Dictionary of National Biography:*—"ARMSTRONG, EDMUND JOHN (1841-1865), a poet who died in early manhood, was born in Dublin, 23rd July, 1841. As a boy he was distinguished by his adventurous spirit, romantic temper united with humour and love of frolic, and his passionate delight in music and literature. Long rambles among the Dublin and Wicklow mountains gave inspiration and colour to his verse. At the age of 17-18 his religious faith yielded before turbulent moods of scepticism. . . . In 1859 he entered Trinity College, Dublin, distinguishing himself highly by his compositions in Greek and Latin verse. Immoderate work and intellectual excitement in the spring of 1860 were followed by severe illness; a blood-vessel in the lung was burst, and the lung seriously injured. A summer of convalescence was spent in Wicklow, and then he found it possible to trace back his way towards Christian beliefs. He wintered, 1860-61, in Jersey—a joyous and fruitful season for him, during which much was seen, felt, and thought. Here began a long correspondence

III. GEORGE FRANCIS ARMSTRONG, M.A. *(stip. con.)*, Dublin University; Doctor-of-Literature *(honoris causâ)*, Queen's University in Ireland; Fellow of the Royal University of Ireland; Professor of History and English Literature, Queen's College, Cork; formerly Professor in the Queen's University; Author of *Poems: Lyrical and Dramatic; Ugone: A Tragedy; The Tragedy of Israel* (A Trilogy); *A Garland from Greece; Stories of Wicklow; Mephistopheles in Broadcloth*, &c. (*see* "Men of the Time"); born on the 5th of May, 1845; married, on the 24th of April, 1879, Marie Elizabeth, younger daughter of the late Rev. John Wrixon, M.A., Vicar of Malone, Co. Antrim (youngest son of Captain John Wrixon, 5th Dragoon Guards, of

MRS. EDMUND JOHN ARMSTRONG (MISS JANE SAVAGE, OF GLASTRY), born A.D. 1801; died A.D. 1880.

on religious questions with a friend as yet unseen, Mr. G. A. Chadwick [now Dean of Armagh]. Having returned from a delightful visit to Brittany, he left Jersey reluctantly in mid-summer, 1861, and spent the warmer months of the year in Ireland. On the approach of winter he again resorted to Jersey, now accompanied by a younger brother, G. F. Armstrong (since Professor of English Literature, Queen's College, Cork). In April, 1862, the brothers started for Normandy, thence visited Paris, and once more returned to Jersey, to bid it a final farewell. Armstrong had now sufficiently recovered to accept a tutorship in the North of Ireland. During his vacation (summer of 1862) he walked much among the Wicklow mountains, and was engaged in writing his poems *The Dargle* and *Glandalough*. In October, 1862, now looking forward to the clerical profession, he continued his college course. In April, 1863, he read before the Undergraduate Philosophical Society an essay on Shelley, designed partly as a recantation of his earlier anti-Christian opinions. In May of the same year he was rapidly producing his longest poem, *The Prisoner of Mount St. Michael*, a romantic tale of passion and crime in blank verse, the landscape and local colour having been furnished by Armstrong's wanderings in France. This was followed by the idyllic poem *Ovoca*, partly dramatic, partly narrative in form. In October, 1863, he came into residence at Trinity College, Dublin, and attracted much attention by his speeches delivered before the Historical Society, and essays read before the Undergraduate Philosophical Society. Of this latter Society he was elected President, and in October, 1864, delivered his opening address, 'On Essayists and Essay-writing.' In the winter his health broke down, and he went to reside at Kingstown, where, after an illness of several weeks, he died, 24th Feb., 1865. He was buried at Monkstown, Co. Dublin. As a memorial of his genius, his college and other friends published the volume, 'Poems by the late Edmund J. Armstrong' (Moxon, 1865). It includes the two longer poems named above, with many lyrical pieces which show much ardour of imagination and mastery of verse. A short memoir by Mr. Chadwick is prefixed. His poems appeared in a new edition, with many added pieces, edited by G. F. Armstrong, in 1877 ('The Poetical Works of Edmund J. Armstrong.' Longmans, Green & Co.). At the same time, and by the same publishers, was issued a volume of his prose ('Essays and Sketches by Edmund J. Armstrong, edited by G. F. Armstrong'), including essays on Coleridge, Shelley, Goethe's Mephistopheles, E. A. Poe, Essayists and Essay-writing, &c. In the 'Life and Letters of Edmund J. Armstrong, edited by G. F. Armstrong' (1877), a portrait is given. An article on Armstrong, by Sir Henry Taylor, appeared in the *Edinburgh Review*, July, 1878."—*Dictionary of National Biography*, edited by Leslie Stephen, vol. ii. (London: Smith, Elder & Co.) See also *Cabinet of Irish Literature* (Blackie & Sons), vol. iv.; *The Household Library of Ireland's Poets*: Ed. by G. D. Connolly (New York); *Edinburgh Review*, vol. ii.; *Life and Letters of Edmund J. Armstrong* (Longmans & Co.); *Correspondence of Sir Henry Taylor* (Longmans & Co.), &c.

MRS. EDMUND JOHN ARMSTRONG [MISS JANE SAVAGE, OF GLASTRY), born A.D. 1801; died A.D. 1880.

Blossomfort, Co. Cork—Blossomfort branch of the family of Wrixon-Becher, Baronets—by Maria his wife, daughter of Col. Bentley, Royal Engineers), and his wife Anne Arabella Wrixon (youngest and last surviving daughter of the late Rear-Admiral John Dawson, of Carrickfergus, Co. Antrim—Dawson of Moyola Park, Co. Londonderry—by his wife Medicis, eldest daughter of the Rev. Alexander Clotworthy Downing—Downing of Rowsgift and Bellaghy, Co. Londonderry. —*See* Burke's *Extinct Baronetage*, under "Downing," and Burke's *Landed Gentry*, under "Fullerton of Ballintoy"). By his wife, Marie Elizabeth (*née* Wrixon), Mr. G. F. ARMSTRONG has issue,

    1. FRANCIS-NESBITT-SAVAGE ARMSTRONG, born in Dublin on the 5th of July, 1880.
    2. John-Raymond-Savage Armstrong, born in Dublin on the 13th of May, 1882.
    1. Arabella-Guendolen-Savage Armstrong, born at Bray, Co. Wicklow.

I. Annie-Eliza Armstrong, married, in 1869, to Captain William T. Croft, late 14th (Prince of Wales's Own) Regt. (served in the New Zealand War, 1863-4—including the Skirmish of Pokeno. Mentioned in despatches. Medal), and has had issue,

    1. Edmund-Armstrong Croft, born at The Heath, Fairlight, Sussex, May 15, 1874.
    2. Arthur-William Croft, born at Richmond Hill, Surrey, Aug. 27, 1879.
    1. Ethel Croft, born at Fermoy, Co. Cork, Aug. 24, 1870; died at Kingstown, Co. Dublin, Dec. 1870, and was buried beside her uncle Edmund Armstrong, and her cousins Emily and SARAH J. A. SAVAGE, in the Old Churchyard of Monkstown, Co. Dublin.
    2. Hilda-Frances, born at Tower Hill, Glanmire, Co. Cork, 13th July, 1875; died at Richmond Hill, Surrey, Jan. 4th, 1880, and was buried in Richmond Hill Cemetery.

MRS. ARMSTRONG died at the residence of her son-in-law, Captain W. T. Croft, at Richmond Hill, Surrey, on the 3rd of January, 1880, and was buried with her husband, and beside her son Edmund and her nieces Emily and SARAH J. A. SAVAGE, at Monkstown, Co. Dublin. Her only surviving son and her representative, and representative also of his uncle, EDWARD SAVAGE, Esq., of Glastry, is the above-named GEORGE FRANCIS ARMSTRONG.

Tomb of the Savages of Glastry, outside the Old Church of Ardkeen.

CHAPTER VIII.

SAVAGE OF ARDKEEN *(continued)*.—MONUMENTS, EPITAPHS, ETC.,

OF THE ARDKEEN FAMILY IN THE ARDS.

THE paucity of imposing monuments of the SAVAGES OF THE ARDS, as compared with those of their English kinsfolk in Cheshire, Worcestershire, and Gloucestershire, is to be accounted for to some extent by the extremely unsettled state in which Ulster continued during the six earlier centuries of their history in that province, and partly, perhaps, by the traditional and hereditary simplicity and directness of the Ulster branches, which found such memorable expression in the 14th century from the lips of HENRY, LORD SAVAGE, who refused to erect stone structures even as places of defence. But, however this may be, sepulchral monuments of the SAVAGES of Ardkeen and Portaferry are not numerous, and where they are extant, they are of the plainest kind.

The old Church of St. Mary of Ardkeen (figured at the head of Chapter VI. of this work), became, as we have said, the burial-place of the SAVAGES OF ARDKEEN CASTLE, and the flags that bore the names of members of the SAVAGE family who had been interred in the vaults beneath, paved, at one time, nearly the entire Church.

The Old Church of Ardkeen. The Church of Ardkeen, formerly styled "Ecclesia Sanctæ Mariæ de Ardkene," is of great antiquity. The advowson of the parish belonged to the Earldom of Ulster, and passed thus to the Crown. "In the inquisition taken after the death of William De Burgo, Earl of Ulster, the church is called 'Arwoghun,' and the profits thereout, which, by an old extent, were valued at £20 a-year, are returned as reduced to 100s. in consequence of the war of the Logans." We have record of the presentation of Thomas de Breda to the Church of Ardkeen by the Crown in 1347, and of Thomas Cuthbert in 1386. "In 1609 it was annexed, by Charter of James I., to the prebend of St. Andrew's, under the name of Earchin."[1] Father O'Laverty writes:—"The ruins of a Protestant Church, which replaced the ancient Catholic structure, stand within the old cemetery on the shore of a little creek called the Dorn (the haft of the sword). The Martyrology of Donegal places at September 8th the festival of St. Fionntain of Ard Caoin."

The Church, under the name of "Earchin," was reported in 1621 to be in ruins. It was subsequently restored; but it does not appear to have been used for divine service for many years. In the Parish Register occurs an entry by the then Parish Clerk, stating that divine service was held on August 16, 1761, in the Church, for the first time since the usurpition (*sic*) of Oliver Cromwell.[2] Thenceforward it continued to be, as it had been of old, the house of worship in which assembled, Sunday after Sunday, successive generations of the SAVAGES and their neighbours and dependants. One of the last of the Incumbents of Ardkeen who officiated in the Old Church was himself a member of the ARDKEEN family—the REV. HENRY SAVAGE, of GLASTRY,[3] whose family-tomb, standing against the outer side of the south wall of the building, is a prominent feature of the desolate churchyard.

One of the REV. HENRY SAVAGE'S successors, the late Rev. Mr. Bullick, "whose zeal for the welfare and advancement of that church of which he was for many years a minister"—(we quote the words of his epitaph)—seems to have prompted him, in ecclesiastical matters, to works rather of destruction than of conservation, succeeded in turning the ancient structure into a melancholy ruin. Whether he had tried his "'prentice hand" first upon the Dwelling-House at Ardkeen (he had hoped, it is said, to have discovered hidden treasure there, but "was rewarded only by finding a bottle of wine in the cellar"), or whether

---

[1] Bishop Reeves: *Ecclesiastical Antiquities*, &c., p. 21.

[2] We are indebted for this interesting item of history to the present Rector of the Parish, the Rev. Hugh Stowell.

[3] *Vide ante*, p. 273.

the ruin of the spiritual house suggested the effacement of the temporal, we THE OLD CHURCH OF ARDKEEN. do not know; but what we do know is, that the people of the neighbourhood so reverenced both buildings that the memory of the Rev. Mr. Bullick is cherished with but scant affection in the Little Ards.[1] To counterbalance in some degree his works of demolition, a small new Parochial Church was erected under Mr. Bullick's auspices, in a lofty and exposed position, not very far from Kirkistone. When it became known to the members of the ARDKEEN connection, then living no longer in the Ards, that the ancient structure was about to be abandoned to the winds and the rain, they caused two mural tablets of the BALLYGALGET (ROCK SAVAGE) and GLASTRY families to be removed from it and set up in the New Church; but the recumbent slabs could hardly be removed, and they were suffered to remain where they were. The falling in of the roof of the Church, and the growth of weeds and grasses, have hidden most of the slabs from view, and on several of those from which the earth has been recently scraped, the inscriptions are almost worn away.

When, in 1884, the present writer visited the Old Church, in the hope of copying the once numerous epitaphs of the SAVAGE family, he found the interior of the ruins a piteous sight indeed; for, amidst the piles of *débris* of the fallen roof the rabbits had made their burrows, and, going deeper and deeper and dashing back the earth as they advanced, had thrown up quantities of human bones from the graves beneath.

In the absence of the heads of the ARDKEEN family and its branches from the neighbourhood, the Churchyard, ill-protected by any surrounding wall, was itself also for a time suffered to fall into an appalling state of disorder and neglect, the cattle from the fields roaming over it, and the pigs rooting in the graves; but, thanks, we believe, chiefly to Mr. Arthur (Savage) Nugent, a strong high wall was at last built round it, and something of its former look of decency was restored.

Underneath the Church are the vaults of the SAVAGE family, in which, or VAULTS OF THE SAVAGES OF beside which, are laid also several of the Echlins of Ardquin and Echlinville, ARDKEEN. their connections and neighbours. How old these vaults are it seems impossible to ascertain; but their antiquity must be very considerable.

Mr. Arthur Nugent (to whom the compilers of this work are indebted for much information respecting the facts and traditions of the SAVAGE family in the Ards) mentions that one Charles Coulter, the sexton of the Old Church, and caretaker of the Park and Place for the late Col. Forde, of Seaforde (who,

---

[1] We have already seen that the Rev. Mr. Bullick levelled the remnant of the old walls of the Castle, which Time and HUGH SAVAGE of ARDKEEN had spared.

2 P

it will be remembered, married LADY HARRIET SAVAGE, widow of the last FRANCIS SAVAGE, of Ardkeen and Hollymount), told him that the last time the vaults were opened (probably for the reception of the remains of that very FRANCIS SAVAGE, of Ardkeen and Hollymount), he had been inside them, and had counted nine leaden coffins in a vault under the chancel. Mr. Arthur Nugent had subsequently an opportunity of seeing the interior of the vaults himself. When on a visit to his brother at Portaferry, he heard that some miscreants had succeeded in breaking a hole down to the foundations of the old structure, and had got access to the vaults, evidently in the hope of finding something valuable there to plunder. Accompanied by his brother, Major Nugent, of Strangford Lodge, he proceeded to Ardkeen. Both gentlemen crept into a vault by means of the narrow passage that had been dug to it. Several coffins were distinguishable in a wonderful state of preservation, with the cloth and fragments of velvet palls upon them, but no lead. The impression produced was, that the burials of the ARDKEEN family had been costly and magnificent. They did not remain long enough to make a strict examination of the plan or form of the vault itself, but withdrew from the melancholy charnel-house saddened by the sights they had witnessed there.

Charles Murray, of Portaferry, who was born on the Ardkeen estate close by, and who often, as a child, played about the Castle Hill and in the ancient burial-ground, informs the present writer that he well remembers the hole leading down to the vaults, through which, when a boy, he had himself crept, and describes what he saw within, adding nothing, however, to the facts communicated by Mr. Nugent.

The ancient burial-place of the SAVAGES OF BALLYGALGET seems to have been at Knockdoo, beside Rock Savage, at a spot which appears to be identical with the *Sithe* mentioned in *The Ecclesiastical Taxation of Down, Connor and Dromore*, so ably edited by Bishop Reeves, who writes of it as follows:—" In the townland of Ballygalget, on a high ground at Knockdoo, otherwise Rock Savage, and about a furlong north of the Roman Catholic Chapel, is a spot called 'Shankill,' where traces of a building, measuring 36 by 16 feet, exist in a long-disused burying-ground, which was once enclosed by an irregular cashel, of about forty yards diameter." Here, it is said, the SAVAGES OF BALLYGALGET had a private chapel, and here many of them are interred.

When the old burial-ground at Knockdoo was closed up, the peasants of the neighbourhood, as we have before mentioned, carried the earth of their old family-graves thence to Ardkeen, so that they might be buried in the same dust as their kindred.

SAVAGE OF ARDKEEN—MONUMENTS, ETC.

The following are the inscriptions relating to the SAVAGE family now visible and legible in and about the Old Church of Ardkeen.

The oldest, apparently, of the epitaphs bears date 1681, and records the death, as we have conjectured, of PATRICK SAVAGE, Esq., of Ballygalget. But the slab that occupies the chief place, the centre of the Chancel, under the altar (when *was* an altar), bears the date 1687, six years later. In 1884 the name of the person whose burial it was intended to record was so effaced as to baffle all attempts to decipher it. But this stone, occupying the principal place in the church, had commemorated, one would suppose, a member of the House of Ardkeen.

Commencing with this central flag of the chancel, we shall give the other inscriptions in their relation to it.

Centre of Chancel, under Altar—

> HERE
> LYETH THE
> BODY OF
> . . . .
> WHO DIED THE [27?] OF
> MARCH IN THE 48 YEAR OF
> HIS AGE 1687.

Next the above, on the left (or north) side of it *(in capital letters)*—

> Here lyeth the Body of
> [John] Echlin of Priestown
> who departed this life
> the 4th of September 1714
> aged 45 years.
> And also Jane Echlin his wife
> who departed this Life
> 25 of November 1742 aged
> 67 years.[1]

To the left of the preceding, again in the Chancel *(in capital letters)*—

> Here Lyeth the Body of
> [PATRIC]*Y*E Savage, Esq.,
> Late of Balegalget
> who departed the 14 day
> Feb. 1681 and of EAR II
> CRE & NTWO

This inscription, which was much effaced in 1884, concludes with a series of letters which, as we have stated, are hardly legible and wholly unintelligible.

---

[1] This Jane Echlin was mother of Mrs. Philip Savage, of Ballygalget (Rock Savage).

[PATRICK] SAVAGE OF BALLYGALGET.

A comparison of dates leads to the conclusion that the christian-name must have been "Patricke."[1]

It is a pity that something could not be done to preserve this and other inscriptions in the Old Church from further effacement. A comparatively small sum of money, spent under the guidance of some person experienced in such matters, would render the Church and its ancient contents a very interesting relic.

FRANCIS SAVAGE, ESQ., OF GLASTRY, AND MAJOR HENRY SAVAGE, OF ROCK SAVAGE.

Two mural tablets to which we have alluded, one belonging to the GLASTRY family and one to the ROCK SAVAGE, originally hung on the Chancel-walls. The marks of both are still traceable. That to the memory of FRANCIS SAVAGE, of Glastry, hung to the left; that to the memory of MAJOR HENRY SAVAGE and his widow to the right. Both were removed, as we have described, by the ROCK SAVAGE (BALLYGALGET) and GLASTRY families to the New Parish-Church of Ardkeen about the close of the year 1845. There they are now to be seen on the south Chancel-wall. The inscriptions upon them are as follow:—

FRANCIS SAVAGE, ESQ., OF GLASTRY.

On the Tablet to the Memory of FRANCIS SAVAGE, of Glastry (known as "*Old* Frank Savage")—

> Here lye the Remains of Francis Savage,
> Esq., of Glastry, Fourth son of Philip
> Savage, Esqr of Rock Savage. He died
> in March 1808, aged 76
> And of Mary his wife third daughter
> of Francis Savage, Esqr of Ardkeen
> She died in September 1778, aged 45
> in Beauty she was excelled by very few
> by none in goodness and gentleness
>
> Also of Charles Savage, their son
> He died in 1780 aged 21. For Literature
> he was in Trinity College an ornament
> and to human nature for sound sense
> and goodness of heart.[2]

MAJOR HENRY SAVAGE, OF ROCK SAVAGE (BALLYGALGET).

On the Tablet to the Memory of MAJOR HENRY SAVAGE, of Rock Savage (Ballygalget), and his widow—

---

[1] *Vide ante*, p. 272.

[2] The obvious fact that the removal of this and Major Henry Savage's tablet from the Old Church of Ardkeen, where their remains *do* lie, to the New Church, near Kirkistone, where they do *not*, should have been recorded on or beside these monuments in their present position, was amusingly demonstrated by the remark of a well-known local "character" in the Ards, who, on entering the New Church with a companion, one day, pointed to Mr. Francis Savage's tablet, and exclaimed, "The first thing I read when I come into this Church is a *lee* (a lie). That stone there says, '*Here* lies Francis Savage, of Glastry.' Now that's a *lee*, for Francis Savage, of Glastry, lies at Ardkeen."

SAVAGE OF ARDKEEN—MONUMENTS, ETC.

MAJOR HENRY SAVAGE, OF ROCK SAVAGE (BALLYGALGET).

Near this place[1]
are deposited the Remains of
Henry Savage, Esqr of Rock Savage
late Major in the 16th Regt of Foot
after having distinguished himself in the service of his country
both in the German and American Wars
He returned to fulfil the Social duties of Domestic life.
He was a just Magistrate, steady Friend
and most excellent husband.
As a Tribute to his many virtues
and as a Testimony of true affection
This monument is erected by his afflicted widow
He departed this Life
the 6th of November, 1797, aged 62 years.

Likewise the remains of Jane his widow
in whom Benevolence and Sincerity
were conspicuously united.
She died at Bristol Hot Wells on the
12th June, 1799, aged 57, sincerely regretted
by her relatives for those Virtues
which constitute a
Friend & a Christian.

On revisiting the Old Church in the summer of 1886, the present writer found the inscriptions even more effaced than two years previously, while some of the stones that had been visible in 1884 were deeply imbedded in rubbish. One stone, however, not apparent in 1884, had been partly stripped of its covering. It recorded the death of young CHARLES SAVAGE, of Ardkeen, who died in 1740. It is inside the Church, in the aisle, south side, and the inscription is to be read as the reader faces the west— [CHARLES SAVAGE, OF ARDKEEN, who died A.D. 1740.]

Here lyeth The Body of Mr CHARLEs
SAVAGE of Ardkeen who departed
this life on the 22d day of October
in the year of our Lord 1740
and in the 38 year of his age.

Outside the Church, at the north corner of the Chancel-wall, is the vault of the SAVAGES OF ROCK SAVAGE (Ballygalget). A recumbent grave-stone bears the following inscription:— [VAULT OF THE SAVAGES OF ROCK SAVAGE (BALLYGALGET).]

Here lyeth the body of PHILIP SAVAGE, Esq.
late of Rock Savage, who departed this life the 27th
day of October, 1780 Aged 83 years Also of JANE
SAVAGE his wife who died the 20th September

---

[1] "This place" refers, of course, to the wall of the Old Church at Ardkeen.

1781 Aged 76 years Here likewise lieth Remains of PHILIP SAVAGE late of Nunsbridge, Esq., their son who died the 8th May, 1790 Aged 48 years. Here Also lieth the Remains of Charles SAVAGE Late Major in the 51st Reg! of Foot who died the 8th of August, 1801 Aged 64 years Here also lieth Remains of Lucy SAVAGE of Nunsbridge Second Daughter of the late Philip Savage of Rock Savage Esq. She departed this life 3d April 1809 aged 78 years.

In the graveyard, nearer the gate, on another recumbent slab, is an inscription to the memory of several members of the family of the SAVAGES who resided at Cloughy—

Mingled with their native dust rest underneath the Remains of Mr Henry Savage of Cloughy who Departed this life March 12th in the year of our Lord 1771 aged 65 years & of his Son Captn Jas Savage who Depd this Life July 12th in the year of our Lord 1789 aged 45 years
Here also lie the remains of his son Patrick Savage who departed this life the 16th day of February, 1802 aged 56 years.

There is only one more monument of the SAVAGE family at present visible at Ardkeen. It is the altar-tomb, above described, of the SAVAGES OF GLASTRY. The following is a copy of the inscription it bears:—

Here lieth the Remains of the Revd Henry Savage of Glastry who departed this life the 4th May, 1815, aged 42 years. Also Rose and Edward two of his children who died infants. Likewise his daughter Emily who died the 1st June, 1814 aged 3 years. And also of Anne Savage otherwise M'Guckin his wife who departed this life on the 7th of May, 1828, aged 50 years. And likewise of his oldest son Francis Savage of Glastry Esq who departed this life in Holywood the 18th October, 1842, aged 42 years.

On the eastern side of the tomb is the following inscription:—

> Erected
> By
> The Revd Henry Savage.

A curious and weird story attaches to this monument of the SAVAGES OF GLASTRY. One morning, between twenty and thirty years ago, a labourer, passing by the Church in the dim light of early dawn, was startled by hearing a human cry proceeding from the tomb. Appalled by the ghostly sound, he hurried away; but, soon afterwards meeting one of his neighbours, he communicated the fact and his fears to the latter, and the two men, plucking up courage, stole into the graveyard. On approaching the grave, they both heard faint cries issuing from it. Venturing still nearer, they perceived that the top slab of the tomb had been moved back. They went forward and looked in, and there they beheld a little babe lying in the inside. The slab must have been wrenched aside in the night-time, and by more than one person, for it is of great weight. The child, a female infant, was lifted out, and taken away to the Poorhouse at Downpatrick. A woman was subsequently arrested on suspicion of having exposed it; but, no evidence against her being forthcoming, she was discharged. The child was carefully brought up at the Downpatrick Union, and, in memory of the place in which she had been discovered, was christened "Mary *Tomb*." She is now a respectable young woman at service somewhere in the County of Down.

Some superstitious dread, it seems, had prevented the people of the neighbourhood from restoring the stone to its former position. It remained as it had been wrenched from its bed for over twenty years. When, at the end of that time, a grandson of MR. SAVAGE, of Glastry, visited the spot, the stone, under his superintendence, was forced back into its place, but not until it had been seen that a member of the family had been the first to put a hand to it. Directions being left to have it cemented, and the tomb put into proper order, workmen some time afterwards proceeded from Portaferry to execute the commission. To their astonishment they found the slab again shifted back to the position in which it had been when the infant lay there. This time, however, it was carefully and successfully sealed in its proper place. When the same member of the GLASTRY family visited the graveyard two years later, a young self-sown hawthorn-tree was observed to have begun to shoot its sprays from within the tomb. It was remarked that hawthorn is the emblem of *hope*, and that the omen in relation to the SAVAGES OF ARDKEEN should be regarded as a good one.

Ruins of Portaferry Castle, ancient stronghold of the SAVAGES OF PORTAFERRY.

CHAPTER IX.

SAVAGE (NOW NUGENT) OF PORTAFERRY.

THE DIVISION OF THE UPPER ARDS BETWEEN ROLAND AND RAYMOND SAVAGE in A.D. 1559-1

WE have seen that in A.D. 1536 RAYMOND SAVAGE, Chieftain of his sept, son of SIR ROLAND SAVAGE, of Lecale, and of Mawlyn in the County of Antrim, KNT. (last Seneschal of Ulster of the SAVAGE name), was confirmed by the Lord Deputy Grey in the chieftainship and superiority of his sept in the territory of the SAVAGES otherwise called Lecale; and that in A.D. 1559, contention having arisen between RAYMOND SAVAGE and his kinsman ROLAND SAVAGE for the chieftainship and superiority of their sept in the Ards, a division of towns and territories in the Ards was made between them by the Lord Deputy Sir William Fitzwilliam and the Council, RAYMOND being allotted ARDKEEN and the townlands which have since constituted the ARDKEEN estates, and ROLAND PORTAFERRY and the townlands which have since constituted the PORTAFERRY estates. As RAYMOND was eldest surviving son and representative of SIR ROLAND SAVAGE, it would seem natural that he should have succeeded to the chieftainship and superiority of the SAVAGES in Antrim, where also Sir ROLAND had been the leader, and that his lordship should thus have extended over Lecale, part of Antrim, and about half the barony now known as the Upper Ards,—that is to say, over fully three-fourths of the territories then remaining to the SAVAGE family.

The Division of the Upper Ards between Roland and Raymond Savage in A.D. 1559.

Now, as the division of the towns and territories in the Ards was *probably* determined mainly *by possession at the time*, it is presumable that in some way or another ROLAND SAVAGE at this period (A.D. 1559) had been in possession—though in *disputed* possession—of the southern portion of the Upper Ards (or that about Portaferry), while RAYMOND was in possession—though in *disputed* possession—of the northern part of the Upper Ards (or that about Ardkeen). Each claimed the "inheritance and chieftainship of their nation," and each in his contention was evidently supported by a large number of his kinsmen. ROLAND, however, was clearly not a son of SIR ROLAND SAVAGE, of Lecale, and his possessions, in whatever way they had come into his hands—whether by *tanist* custom or by direct inheritance—were much smaller and less valuable than those which RAYMOND possessed, or should have inherited, as the son and heir of SIR ROLAND. The decision of the Lord Deputy and Council in 1559 left each claimant "Chieftain of his nation and freeholders" in about half the entire portion of the Ards then tenanted by their kinsfolk. But RAYMOND had been already recognised as Chieftain "of his nation" in Lecale, and, as we have just said, as son and heir of SIR ROLAND, would have been heir to the supremacy of his "nation" in Antrim besides.

The questions arise, how had ROLAND SAVAGE, of Portaferry, before the year 1559, come into (disputed) possession of so much of the Upper Ards as was confirmed to him in that year, and on what grounds did he lay claim to the portion then apparently in (disputed) possession of RAYMOND, Lord of Ardkeen and of Lecale, and in that year confirmed to the latter?

We have found no documentary mention of any "Lord of the Little Ards" *so styled* at this time; nor (as far as we have yet been able to ascertain) were the Ards spoken of prior to this period as the possession of any Lord distinct from the existing Chief of the entire sept of the SAVAGES in Down and Antrim. From 1559 onwards, the Chief of the PORTAFERRY branch was undoubtedly Principal of his nation *within his own territories in the* Little Ards, just as the Chief of the ARDKEEN branch was Principal of *his* nation *within the limits of the ARDKEEN estates in the* Little Ards.

When, in the year 1539, Lord Leonard Grey had seized the Castles of the Lord of Lecale in *Lecale*, he states that he proceeded to the Ards and seized several Castles there. Nothing is stated to lead us to infer that the Chieftain of the Ards was any other at that moment than the then existing Lord of

THE DIVISION OF THE UPPER ARDS BETWEEN ROLAND AND RAYMOND SAVAGE in A.D. 1559.

Lecale. This seems to be the interpretation put upon the words of Lord Leonard Grey by Mr. Bagwell in his excellent *History of Ireland under the Tudors*, and it is evidently also Mr. Bagwell's interpretation of facts, for he writes:—" Lecale in Down [in 1574-5] had been partially, but only partially, peopled by the exertions of Essex. Ards was little better, less owing to Sir Thomas Smith than to the natural tendencies of its old English inhabitants, *whose chief* EDMOND [*i.e.* RAYMOND] SAVAGE was received into protection."

Whose *son*, then, was the ROLAND SAVAGE of 1559 who disputed with RAYMOND the supremacy of the Ards?

To this question our researches hitherto have not enabled us to give any conclusive answer. Farther research may lead to the discovery of his parentage and lineage, and unravel an old mystery, but for the present it must remain, we fear, undetermined. Indeed, Montgomery, who was strongly prejudiced in favour of the seniority of PORTAFERRY, seems to have been entirely ignorant on this point, while he traces back the lineage of ARDKEEN to "the SENESCHAL" —that is, SIR ROLAND, of Lecale.

We have seen a copy of some notes of the late Sir William Betham, Ulster King-of-Arms, on the PORTAFERRY and ARDKEEN pedigrees, but they are manifestly inaccurate in both cases, and his own commentary proves that he had no confidence in them. " The above statement," he writes, " is compiled from records, and correctly states the facts of the *existence* of the different individuals of the Portaferry family . . . but their precise descent is not certain." He places, apparently, as the immediate predecessor of ROLAND SAVAGE (of 1559), " PATRICK SAVAGE, Seneschal, or Chief Judge, of Ulster, 1493." Now, the Seneschal of Ulster in 1493 was SIR ROLAND SAVAGE of Lecale, father of RAYMOND SAVAGE of Lecale, and the Portaferry family are *not* the " race of the Seneschal." And he places JENKIN (*a-Bui*) SAVAGE (father of HENRY SAVAGE, of ARDKEEN) directly under " BRIAN LE SAVAGE," whereas, as well as we can discover from the Inquisitions, &c., this JENKIN (or JANICO) was the son of JAMES FERDOROUGH SAVAGE, brother of EDMOND (*i.e.*, RAYMOND), surnamed FERDOROUGH *Mac Seneschal*, and no BRIAN LE SAVAGE is found mentioned in any authentic records we have ever seen.

The probable true account of the matter appears to us to be this:—That ROLAND, descended undoubtedly from a common ancestor with RAYMOND, had, during the struggles of the latter against English and Irish alike to retain his extensive and valuable territory in the fertile plains of Lecale, risen to eminence and power in the Ards, where he may have *inherited* considerable estates; and had, either by *tanist* custom or by the mere force of circumstances, come to be regarded, and to regard himself, as chief of his "nation" *there;* that THE DIVISION OF THE UPPER ARDS BETWEEN ROLAND AND RAYMOND SAVAGE in A.D. 1559. RAYMOND, when his grasp of Lecale was beginning to relax, had resolved to make good his supremacy in the Ards, and, on that supremacy being disputed by his powerful kinsman and the latter's followers, had at last appealed to the sword; that both leaders, finding the warfare which followed unpalatable and destructive, agreed to pray the Crown to arbitrate between them; and that, by the decision of the Crown, the two houses of ARDKEEN and PORTAFERRY were then placed on that independent footing on which they remained ever afterwards—PORTAFERRY, without doubt, getting the best of the bargain.

It is remarkable enough that ROLAND should have borne precisely the same christian-name as RAYMOND's father. It is quite within the range of probability that he may have been named after Sir ROLAND, and nothing is more likely than that the rival claimants for the supremacy of the Ards were first-cousins.

Sir Bernard Burke also seems to have failed to discover the name of the father of ROLAND SAVAGE, of Portaferry, of 1559, and he accordingly commences the PORTAFERRY pedigree at the latter date, acknowledging at the same time the great antiquity of the PORTAFERRY family. "From the extreme scarcity of records in Ireland," he writes, "it is impossible at this remote period to determine, without liability to error, which is the senior branch of the family, that of PORTAFERRY or ARDKEEN CASTLE. . . . However," he adds, "the mutual mention of one another, the exact coincidence of the armorial bearings and the christian-names of the respective progenitors, may be received as presumptive evidence in favour of a common ancestry as far back as the twelfth century." And Sir W. Betham, in a letter in the possession of Mr. F. W. E. Savage, addressed to Albert Woods, Esq., College of Arms, London, in November, 1843, says, "ARDKEEN is said to have been the elder branch, but that is disputed by the PORTAFERRY branch. They are both very ancient estates, but the exact period of separation I cannot exactly say—I believe in the 13th century."

All the results of our present researches have tended to show that many of the known leaders and chiefs of the family from the earliest times were in the direct line of the ARDKEEN ancestry; but the title "LORD SAVAGE" was certainly borne by chiefs of the PORTAFERRY branch *after* the year 1559. We shall, however, conclude in the cautious and kindly words of William Montgomery, writing nearly two hundred years ago:—"Neither will I assert anything which may make discord among these good friends, or may savour of partiality in myself." Both branches may be well proud of their long common line of powerful and distinguished ancestors. If the ARDKEEN branch were the elder, the PORTAFERRY branch has been the more fortunate and the more

THE DIVISION OF THE UPPER ARDS BETWEEN ROLAND AND RAYMOND SAVAGE in A.D. 1559.

tenacious of the ancestral lands; and, while the numerous members of one branch may take a justifiable pride in the successes and distinctions of the other, it must be some kind of satisfaction to the members of the ARDKEEN family, that, though *they* have recently parted with the last remnant of their Ulster estates, the race of the LORDS SAVAGE of Ulster have still a worthy representative residing in the ARDS in the person of LIEUT.-GENERAL ANDREW NUGENT, now lord of the old Manor of PORTAFERRY.[1]

A daughter of PORTAFERRY, named CECILIA SAVAGE (*Irish*, SHEELY), was married, according to Montgomery, to one of the Earls of Antrim, and "the [late] Marquis" of Antrim, he adds, "called those of this family *cousins*." The *Ulster Journal of Archæology* explains this passage as follows :—" The Earls of Antrim coveted alliance with the SAVAGES, and one of them married CECILIA SAVAGE. She married, not an *Earl* of Antrim, but John Macdonnell, surnamed Cathanach, who was great-grandfather of the 1st Earl of Antrim."[2] "On the formal surrender of the Kingdom of the Isles, in 1476," writes Mr. Hill in his admirable work *The Macdonnells of Antrim*, "there came a third company of settlers, more numerous probably than any of the two preceding. But the largest number arrived during the closing years of the fifteenth century, and immediately after the execution of Sir John Cahanagh. This leader of the Clan Ian Vohr had married CECILIA SAVAGE, a daughter of the chieftain of that great family seated at Portaferry, in the County Down, and by her had four sons, two of whom

---

[1] Montgomery, it must be confessed, does not throw very much light on this question of seniority. He gives us to understand that the Chiefs of the SAVAGE family, "in grants from themselves, were stiled," as far back as Queen Elizabeth's time, "Lords of the Little Ards, and *principales suæ nationis*;" and he adds, "I have seen a letter from the Lord Depty Chichester, to Savage of Portaferry, directed thus, viz., ———," unfortunately omitting the address to which he wished to call attention. Elsewhere, however, he states simply, "I have a letter from the Ld Deputy Chichester, stileing on of them Ld in the direction thereof to him." The following tradition, which is preserved amongst the old people of Portaferry, has evidently grown out of the contest for precedence and possession of the Little Ards between the Lords of PORTAFERRY and ARDKEEN :—" At one time there was a dispute between the members of the family as to which was the rightful owner of the Portaferry Estate, and it was decided in the Courts in Dublin that whichever of the two claimants, travelling from Dublin, should reach the Castle of Portaferry first, should be considered the rightful owner. Both started at the same moment from Dublin Castle on horseback. When they arrived in the County Down they separated. One went direct to Strangford; but the other, knowing (or believing) that there was no boat at Strangford, made at once for Comber, thinking to cross the strand there and ride down to Portaferry by the eastern shore of the Lough. Arrived at Strangford, the first was for a moment checked by finding that there was no boat there to be had; but he immediately jumped into the water, swam the terribly strong Ferry, and reached the Castle. Meanwhile, the other had found, on arriving at Comber, that the tide was in, and, being consequently obliged to ride round by Newtown Ards, reached Portaferry Castle only to find that his rival kinsman had been in possession of it hours before him."

[2] Vol. ix., p. 247.

escaped from the massacre in which their father and brothers lost their lives. The elder of these two, Alexander, now represented the *Clandonnell South* [the Macdonnells of Isla and Cantire], whilst the younger, Angus, settled finally in the island of Sunda, and became there the founder of a numerous and powerful family.[1]

The Division of the Upper Ards between Roland and Raymond Savage in A.D. 1559.

In the absence of fuller information, we must content ourselves with following the example of Sir Bernard Burke, and commence the separate history of the PORTAFERRY branch of the SAVAGES with

I.—ROLAND, LORD SAVAGE, OF PORTAFERRY (LIVING prior to 1559; DIED 12th February, 1572).

Roland, Lord Savage, who died in A.D. 1572.

The Lord Deputy Fitzwilliam and the Council, in 1559, dividing the Upper Ards between ROLAND and RAYMOND SAVAGE, ordered and adjudged, as we have seen, that "ROWLAND SAVAGE" should be Captain of his Nation and freeholders, having rightful inheritance in the lands of Ballyncontowne, Tullagharnan, Bally-dowe, Tewesities, Ballentonragh, Ballynbentlyng, Ballyngrenagh, Ballyfannor, Ballywored, Tolnecrewe, Ballywlake, Ballywarter, Tolocraffeere, Knockavillar, Ballyharvan, and other lands.

A letter, of the supposed date of 1562 (quoted in the *Ulster Archæological Society's Journal*, vol. ix., p. 177[2]), written to the Earl of Essex by "RAWELYN" (ROLAND) SAVAGE, throws some light upon the position of the head of the PORTA-FERRY branch a few years after the division of the Upper Ards between the rival chieftains of the race:—

"To the Rt. Hon.' the Earle of Sussex,
Lieut. Gen. of Ireland.

"Hit may please your honor, for that Mr. Brereton and also Alexander M'Randall boye are here at present, that in so much your honor's poor supplyent, RAWELYN SAVAGE, chief of his nation, is a neyghbour and borderer unto them, that your honor would move them, yea, and require them to shewe their friendship unto him, and that they wold nether ayde nor assist such as be or shall be hynderers and evyll doers unto hym, but shall mayntayn him for the apprehension and punishinge of them . . . [3] to justice so that they may be brought to answer for their evyll . . . [3] and that he maye have your honor's lycence to kepe such as shall owebé [*obey*] the Quene's majesty and your honor, for the better defence of himself and his countrey. And this in the way of justice."

---

[1] Hill: *Macdonnells of Antrim*, p. 35.
[2] Bibl. Cotton. vesp. F. xii. p. 29.
[3] The MS. has evidently been found illegible.

ROLAND, LORD SAVAGE, who died in A.D. 1572.

This ROLAND SAVAGE, styled LORD SAVAGE, was reported as able to muster in the service of the Crown 30 horse and 60 foot.

In a communication from the Lords Justices and Council to Queen Elizabeth, sent from Dublin Castle on the 27th of November, 1567, a letter was enclosed from Captains Pers and Malbie to the Lord Deputy Sydney, dated Carrickfergus, October 6, in which they state that in the midst of the troubles caused by Sir Brian M'Felim O'Neill, "LORD SAVAGE's followers are drawn from him into Lecale."—October 6, 1567.—" 28. II. Captains Pers and Malbie to the Lord Deputy Sydney.—Sir Bryan M'Felim would provide no cess beeves. They have taken up beeves in the Dufferin, of Turlough Oge M'Con Moyle by force. Alister Oge and his brother Carragh, Rory Oge M'Quillan, and old M'Quillan slack as to cess. LORD SAVAGE's followers are drawn from him into Lecale. . . . Soldiers sick of Irish ague and delirious."[1]

In an old map of "Hibernia," dated 1567, a copy of which is printed in the *State Paper Calendars* of Henry VIII.'s reign, a castle is depicted near the entrance of "Strangford Haven," and beside it appear the words "Sovage Castel." No name but that of SAVAGE appears from the mouth of Strangford Lough to the "Bay of Cragfergus," *i.e.* the Lough of Belfast. In another, but evidently later one, in the same *Calendars*, we find the name "Sauadg" written across the district south of the Blackstaff river in the Ards.

Just a year before LORD SAVAGE's death, viz., in 1571, Campion, in his *History of Ireland*, wrote :—" English gentlemen of longest continuance in Ireland are the race of those which at this day, either in great poverty or perill, doe keepe the properties of their ancestors' lands in Vlster, being then companions to Courcy the Conqueror and Earl of that part. These are the SAVAGES, Iordans, FitzSymonds, Chamberlanes, Russels, Bensons, Audleys, Whites, FitzVrailyes, now degenerate, and called in Irish Macmahon, the Beare's son."

ROLAND, LORD SAVAGE, died at Portaferry (according to Sir Bernard Burke) on the 12th of February, 1572, leaving issue,

I. PATRICK, his heir.
II. Roland, of Derry (in the Little Ards), whose son, PATRICK SAVAGE, Esq., was father of two sons, JOHN and Robert. The elder,
JOHN SAVAGE, Esq., of Ballyvarley, married and had issue,
PATRICK, of whom hereafter as heir to Portaferry.
Francis.
JAMES, who succeeded his nephew at Portaferry.

[1] *Cal. State Papers, Ireland*, 1509-1573, p. 350.

Hugh, ancestor, according to Sir B. Burke, of the families of SAVAGE OF KNOCKADOO, Co. Sligo, and SAVAGE of BALLY- MADUN, Co. Dublin. *(See Appendices.)* ROLAND, LORD SAVAGE, who died in A.D. 1572.

Margaret, married to Hugh Trevor, Esq., and had issue, Andrew Trevor, John Trevor, and Mary Trevor (who married Edward Trevor).

III. Edmund (or Edward), of Coney.
IV. Richard, who died without issue.
V. James.

ROLAND, LORD SAVAGE, of Portaferry, was succeeded by his eldest son,

II.—PATRICK, LORD SAVAGE, OF PORTAFERRY (BORN A.D. 1535, temp. Henry VIII.). PATRICK, LORD SAVAGE, born A.D. 1535.

PATRICK, LORD SAVAGE, OF PORTAFERRY, was 37 years of age at the death of his father ROLAND, whom he succeeded in 1572.

Sydney, in his account of the state of Ulster in 1575, gives a dreary description of the northern province at that period, but no portion of the north seemed to promise better than the Ards, and the more hopeful condition of that district he ascribes to the existence there of the SAVAGES and their followers. Much of Lecale, he says, is waste, but it is mending. Dufferin, or White's country, all waste and desolate. "The *Ards much impoverished, but in good hope of recovery; for that there are many freeholders of English race, of ancient habiting there.* County of *Clandeboy* utterly disinhabited. Town of *Knockfergus* much decayed and impoverished, no ploughs going at all where before were many; and great store of kine and cattle belonging to the town now few or none left; church and houses, saving castles, burned, the inhabitants fled, not above five householders of any countenance left remaining. The *Glynnes* and the *Route*, possessed by the Scots, now governed by Sorley Boy."

Marshal Bagenal, in his Description of Ulster, written in 1586, thus speaks of the Little Ards and the LORD SAVAGE:—"Little Ardes lieth on the North side of the River of Strangford, a fertile champion country. It is the inheritance of the LORD SAVAGE, who hath now for certain yeares farmed the same to Captain Peirs. There are besides dwellinge here certeine ancient freeholders of the SAVAGES and Smithes, able to muster amongst them all some 30 horsemen and 60 footemen. They are often harrowed and spoyled by them of Clandeboye, with whom the borders of their lands do joyne. Great Ardes is that countrey which was undertaken by Mr. Smithe; it is almost an island, a champion and fertile land, and now possessed by Sir Con M'Neill Oig O'Nele, who hath planted there Neil M'Brian Ferto, with sundrey of his owne surname, but the aancient

PATRICK, LORD SAVAGE, born A.D. 1535.

dwellers there are the Ogilmers, a rich and strong sept of people, alwaies followers of the Neils of Clandeboy. The force of the enhabitantes nowe dwellinge here is 60 horsemen and 300 footemen."

The old English family of Smith, mentioned above, held Quintin Castle under the Lords of Portaferry.

Spenser, in the character of Irenæus, in his *View of the State of Ireland*, written before 1596, but not published till 1633, thus alludes to the SAVAGE family and the Ards :—"[Bruce] wasted Belfast, Green-Castle, Kelles, Belturbet, Castletowne, Newton, and many other very good towns and strong holdes; he rooted out the noble families of the Audlies, Talbotts, Tuchets, Chamberlaines, Maundevills, and the SAVAGES out of the Ardes, though of the Lo. SAVAGE there remaineth yet an heire, that is now a poor gentleman of very mean condition, yet dwelling in the Ardes."

QUINTIN CASTLE (restored), held by the Smiths under the SAVAGES OF PORTAFERRY, now owned by the Anketell family.

In A.D. 1594, Captain Pers, according to the State Papers, "fermeth the Little Ards of the Lo. SAVAGE."

At this time the SAVAGES seem to have been the only English family in all that district that retained any of their ancient possessions. This is clear from the well-known map, a copy of which is published in the *State Paper Calendars*, entitled "Ortelius' Improved or New Map of Ireland, wherein are inserted all the Principal Irish Families of Irish and English Extraction who possessed that Kingdom at the commencement of the Seventeenth Century." In this map the whole of the peninsula south of N. T. Ards is marked "Ardes," and the name "Savages" is boldly written across it.

About this time, as a consequence of the constant warfare and disturbances in Ulster, the Ards seem to have fallen into a state of comparative desolation and decay. This was no doubt grossly exaggerated by the Irish satirist O'Daly, when he wrote—

> "Ardh-Uladh, destitute, starving,
> A district without delight, without mass,
> Where the son of SAVAGE, the English hangman,
> Slaughters barnacles with a mallet."[1]

But, even allowing for the hostility and asperity of O'Daly, there is nothing improbable in the assertion that the country was at this time poor.

At the date A.D. 1599, Dymmock, in his *Treatise of Ireland* (written about 1600),[2] includes LORD SAVAGE's followers amongst the Ulster forces who took part in Tyrone's rebellion, though the chiefs of the SAVAGES were loyal to the Crown—

"A Perticuler of the Rebell Forces of Horse and Foote Ordinarilye imployed in the Rebellion, 28 April, 1599 :—

"In the Province of Vlster
. . .
"LORD SAVADG of litle Ardes,
foote   horse
30   10."

This statement the Editor of Dymmock (the Rev. Richard Butler) elucidates in a note by a quotation from Moryson :—" Lord Savage.—Those of Lecale and the Little Ards held for the Queen, but, overcome by Tyrone, were forced to give way to him to tyrannize in their countries. (Moryson, p. 32.)"

PATRICK, LORD SAVAGE, of Portaferry, married Anne Plunket, and died on the 31st of Dec., 1603-4; and, according to Sir Bernard Burke, he "left two sons,"

---

[1] *Tribes of Ireland.*—We have found another rendering of the lines in a MS. letter of the late John O'Donovan to the Superintendent of the Ordnance Survey, Phœnix Park, Dublin, dated "Newtown-Ards, May 7, 1834," and preserved in the Library of the Royal Irish Academy :—

"The inhabitants of the Ards seem much more comfortable now than when Angus of the Satires visited them in the reign of Elizabeth. . . .
[*Here follow some lines in Irish.*]
"The Ards of Uladth, scarce and starving,
A country without happiness, without religion,
Where SAVAGE, the foreign hangman,
Scrapes off the limpets with his knife" [dagger].

[2] Dymmock's *Treatise of Ireland.* Published for the Irish Archæological Society from a MS. in the British Museum, with Notes by Rev. Richard Butler, A.B., M.R.I.A. (Trim.)

PATRICK, LORD SAVAGE, born A.D. 1535.

ROLAND, who succeeded his father at Portaferry.
PATRICK, who succeeded his brother ROLAND at Portaferry.
William Montgomery states that the latter son, PATRICK, "was reported to be the 17th son, and succeeded to the Manor of Portaferry (by virtue of ancient deeds of feofm! in taile) for want of heirs male by his brethern." ROLAND, however, whether the *eldest* of the seventeen sons or the eldest living at his father's death, became next owner of Portaferry. PATRICK, LORD SAVAGE, of Portaferry, therefore, dying 31st December, 1603-4, was succeeded by,

ROLAND, LORD SAVAGE, who died in A.D. 1619.

III.—ROLAND, LORD SAVAGE, OF PORTAFERRY (LIVING A.D. 1603, temp. James I.; DIED June 25, 1619, temp. ditto).

Of this ROLAND, LORD SAVAGE, of Portaferry, Montgomery writes:— "The Lord Deputy Chichester would have had the said Pat's immediate predecessor and brother, called ROWLAND, to marry his niece, but Russell of Rathmullen (as is reported) made him drunk, and then wedded MR. SAVAGE to his own daughter, by whom the said ROWLAND had one daughter, who was married to one O'Hara, a Gentleman in the county of Antrim." The "Russell of Rathmullen" here alluded to must have been George Russell, the son of Christopher Russell, who founded the branch of the Russell family known as the "Russells of Rathmullen." LORD SAVAGE married Rose Russell, on the 20th of April, 1604. The O'Haras were a family of Irish origin, maternally descended from an Irish King of Munster, and into their hands passed the SAVAGE lands about Lough Guille. The O'Hara who married LORD SAVAGE's daughter was Charles O'Hara, who died in 1639.

At A.D. 1606 the State Papers have the following entry:—"(Lord Deputy —May 20, 1606—to Attorney or Solicitor-General for Ireland). Warrant for a fiat of a grant of a weekly market every Thursday at Portaferry to ROWLAND SAVAGE, Esq."—(ROLAND, it is to be observed, is here not styled LORD SAVAGE.)

A grant of a Ferry at Strangford to the SAVAGES is believed to have been made or confirmed also about this time by James I.

ROLAND SAVAGE, of Portaferry, married (as we have seen) Rose Russell, of Rathmullen, by whom he had issue,

  A Daughter, married to Charles O'Hara, of Co. Antrim, who died in 1639.

ROLAND SAVAGE, of Portaferry, styled LORD SAVAGE (the last of the family, it would seem, who was so designated), died on the 25th of June, 1619, and was succeeded by his brother,

IV.—CAPTAIN PATRICK SAVAGE, OF PORTAFERRY (LIVING A.D. 1603, temp. James I.; DIED A.D. 1644, temp. Charles I.).

To CAPTAIN PATRICK SAVAGE, and to the state of the Ards in his lifetime, we have frequent and interesting allusions in the *Montgomery Manuscripts*:—

"In or about the said year, 1623," says Montgomery, "the said Viscount [Montgomery] married his daughter Jane to PAT. SAVAGE, Esq., whose predecessor by charters from Queen Elizabeth, and formerly (as I am credibly informed), was stiled, and in their deeds of lands they named themselves, Lords of the Little Ards, and principals of their nation. . . .

"This Patrick was reported to be the 17th son, and succeeded to the Manor of Portaferry (by virtue of ancient deeds of feofm! in taile) for want of heirs male of his brethren. He was the first Protestant of his family, through the said Viscount's [Montgomery's] care to instruct him, giving him also (as I am credibly informed) above six hundred pounds stl. as a marriage portion, which was a great sum in those days.

"He was captain of a troop, A.D. 1641, in the regiment of horse under the command of his bro:-in-law, the 2nd Viscount Montgomery; and the said Jane,[1] dying in Anno 1643, himself also departed this life in or about the beginning of March, 1644, leaving orphants only two daughters, and HUGH, his 9th son (so he was, as the said HUGH himself told me), to the care of Sir James Montgomery, their mother's brother (who performed that part with fidelity and love), to their great advantage, compounding their debts, and paying them out of the rents (which then were high); for he waved the benefit of the wardship he had of the said HUGH's estate and person, and bred them all at Rosemount (his own house), though a widower, according to their qualities, till harvest, 1649, that O. C.'s [Oliver Cromwell's] army triumphing over us all, obliged himself and son to go to Scotland and leave them at Portaferry aforesaid.[2]

The following is Montgomery's account of the condition of Portaferry in the lifetime of CAPTAIN PATRICK SAVAGE:—

"The said Sir James, his sister Jane being married to PATRICK SAVAGE aforesaid, he found his estate much in debt, and not one stone-walled house in Portaferry, 'till that match (as was credibly informed me), only some fishermen's cabins, and the old Castle near it out of repair, nor any such mills as now are, and very little grain to employ one, that county being much wasted, 'till the Viscount's plantation, which was not suffered to spread into the Little Ards till their own greater was furnished with inhabitants, and no trade by

---

[1] Mrs. Jane Savage, *née* Montgomery.
[2] *Incidental Remembrances of the Two Ancient Families of the Savages*, &c.

sea, nor as convenience for it, before the said year 1623. Therefore the said Viscount employed his 2nd son, the said Sir James, to settle his brother and sister SAVAGE's affairs, for themselves remained with the Viscount at Newtown above 18 months, till a long but low house was built for them, and olitory garden was put in order, where they lived about two years. In the meantime the said Sir James was setting and leting the lands and laying out tenements to the best advantage, but the freeholders and followers (who were mostly degenerate old English or mere Irish) were obstinate, and would not renew their deeds nor alter their holdings from their own way. And besides these misbehaviours they cosheered[1] much upon MR. SAVAGE, who bore with them in these customs in which he was fostered; so that his debts encreased, and he was persuaded to go with his family to the Isle of Man, to live privately but plentifully, yet much cheaper than at home, and so be rid of cosheerers, and to stay to [two] years at least in Peeltown, 'till Sir James should improve his estate in rents, and build for him a house befitting his quality, and should bring in freeholders to submit to him. During this recess Sir James put the most stubborn and refractory to the law, to make them examples, for there were flaws in their deeds, and their titles were defective, sealing leases of ejectment against them, whereby they were overcome and submitted, some paying fines; and encreasing rents, to be paid in money, besides the usual duties and services; and obliging them to the English way of living, habit, and building. Others of them he brought to stoop to their lure, partly by threats to take the severity of the law against them, partly by conferences and gentle speeches, showing also kindness to those he found willing to support their landlords.

"The most effectual course he took was to get wastes filled with British planters on the lands, and builders of stone houses in the town (whose example taught the natives husbandry and industry), and to cause build mills on the loughs, tying the tenants to grind and pay the 16 grain as toll, or thertage (commonly called moultre), and other helps for reparations; which achievements soon brought plenty at home and traffic from abroad, and merchandise-ware to the town.

"And afterwards he brought matters to fuller settlement and prosperity, by encouragement of which monied men had from his passing two patents to remedy MR. SAVAGE's defective titles, thereby ascertaining his royalties and customary profits, both at sea and land. But the last effect came not fully to pass till *Caroli primi* that the last of these patents were passed.[2] . . .

---

[1] The Irish custom of the younger members and followers of a family living on its Chief.
[2] For copies of these Patents see Appendices to this volume.

"Sir James (during MR. SAVAGE'S stay in the Island) repaired the old Castle by roofing and flooring it, and by striking out longer lights with freestone window-cases, and also building (and joining to it) a fair slated stone house, as may be seen, with the SAVAGES' and MONTGOMERYS' arms above the door thereof.[1] . . . The aforesaid buildings being made, Sir James sent for MR. SAVAGE (who had run in debt among the merry Manxmen); but now he came home and lived splendidly like himself, and better for the helps of additional portions given by the first Visct. Montgomery to discharge debts compounded in his absence."

CAPTAIN PATRICK SAVAGE, OF PORTAFERRY, who died in A.D. 1644.

Of the troop of which PATRICK SAVAGE was Captain in 1641 he seems to have been deprived not long afterwards; but it was restored to him again in 1643, and this favour, like so many other advantages, he appears to have owed to Sir James Montgomery, who interceded on his behalf with Ormonde. Mr. Hill, in the footnotes to the *Montgomery Manuscripts*, prints the following letter from Sir James to Ormonde, written at Rosemount on the 9th of December, 1641. It is doubly interesting on account of a reference it contains to a manifest recognition of kinship with the SAVAGES OF THE ARDS by the then EARL RIVERS (SAVAGE, OF ROCK SAVAGE, CHESHIRE.) The letter runs as follows:—

"My Lord, one of the three troopes under the command of my Lord Montgomery hath been long in debate. One Captain Bruffe had a commission from your Lop. procured upon a mistake that the troope was voyde upon the death of my brother (the second Viscount), but he has never gotten possession of it, nor has he been in this kingdome these nyne months past, and is now (as I am informed) in England. One Sergeant-Major Crawford had ane other commission from the Earle of Leister. And he has notwithstanding neglected the service, and has taken on to be a leiftennant collonell in the service in Scotland to go into England. Mr. PATRICK SAVADGE, OF PORTAFERRY, a gentleman of worth, and one of whose fidelitie I dare assovr yor Lop., has for the most part mentained that troope, and had my Lord Montgomerie's good will of it, but was borne out of it by Crawford's commission. But he now haveing taken on in Scotland, and divers of his officers mynded to follow him, my Lord Montgomery is desyrous to conferre the troope upon MR. SAVADGE, *who was also by former letters recommended unto yor Honor by the Earle Rivers out of England.* I doe therefore entreate your Lop. to send by this

---

[1] Of the stone bearing these arms Mr. Arthur Nugent writes:—"When my father was adding to his house [the present 'Portaferry House'], he took a stone having the Savage and Montgomery arms on it [from the Castle] and placed it on the main wall at the back of Portaferry House, but unfortunately it is so high up that no one can see it without a long ladder." See next Chapter.

bearer a new commission to MR. SAVADGE, with a *non obstant* of the two former commissions, and power to him to choose his officers to the approbation of his Lop. And lykewise in regard to his Lop. had some cloathes wh came from England that he intended for Crawford if he had attended the service and done his dutty, but now that he runnes this course, he thinks it not fitt that he should have them. And in truth MR. SAVADGE only does deserve them, for he was at the greatest charge for maintning yt troope, and therefore (for his better discharge) desyres yor Lop. will be pleased to send him also ane order by this bearer to deliver the same to MR. SAVADGE."

CAPTAIN PATRICK SAVAGE, of Portaferry, married, as we have seen, in 1623, Jean, daughter of the 1st Viscount Montgomery, and by her, who died in 1647, had issue (with eight sons who died in his lifetime),

I. HUGH, of whom presently as successor to his father at Portaferry.
I. Jane.
II. Elizabeth, co-heiress to her brother, married to George Wilton, Esq., of Gaulstown, Co. Westmeath.
III. Sarah, co-heiress to her brother, married, *1st*, to Sir Bryan O'Neill, of Bakerstown, Bart., "so created for his gallantry at Edgehill," and had issue. Lady O'Neill was married, *2ndly*, to Richard Rich, Esq.

CAPTAIN PATRICK SAVAGE died about the beginning of March, 1644, and was succeeded by his son,

V.—HUGH SAVAGE, ESQ., OF PORTAFERRY (BORN A.D. 1629, temp. Charles I.; DIED A.D. 1683, temp. Charles II.).

Of this MR. HUGH SAVAGE Montgomery has left us many pleasant reminiscences. The passages in which he speaks of his education have been already quoted in connection with JOHN SAVAGE, ESQ., OF ARDKEEN.[1]

"Soon after Benburb fight," adds Montgomery, "June, Anno 1646, my cousin HUGH, and his sister and myself, were removed to Carrickfergus, they to be under their Aunt the 2nd Viscountess Montgy's care; for she lived there with her 2nd husband, Majr Genl Robt Monro, and we were put to school under Sir George Leslie (the Bp of Down's brother), having the said Mr. Boid, with my said cousin HUGH and me, as our tutor. . . .

"There are some other instances (partly spoken of before) of Sir J. M. kindness to the children of the said PATRICK SAVAGE, viz., their education at Rosemount and elsewhere aforesaid, his preserving safe and leaving to his

---

[1] *Vide ante*, pp. 193-4.

nephew, the said HUGH (the only surviving son of the said PATRICK), all his parchments and papers, and by using the benefit of the Wardship (which he waved as aforesaid), and by his codicil annexed to his will Anno 1648 (when Monck[1] obliged him to render himself in London), declaring he did not intend to affect that estate as Ex^r to Lt Barry, but thereby to awe his nephew to do brotherly duty to his sisters, and have respective regard and kindness for the family of Rosemount; which intimation made me freely give up to the said HUGH all his father's bonds for the debt due to the said Barry; and for the same ends I have endeavoured and shewn my love and respects to the present MR. SAVAGE[2] and his late father at BALLYVARLEY.[3] . . .

HUGH SAVAGE, ESQ., OF PORTA- FERRY, born A.D. 1609; died A.D. 1683.

"The said HUGH being educated at Rosemount, Newtown, and Carrickfergus with me (as if we were two b^{rs}), his love and trust to me was such that he boarded himself with me in Rosemount many years, wherein his affairs were set to rights. . . .

"This HUGH was a nimble, active man, and witty in his repartees, delighting in tennis and such like stirring exercises, by which taking cold the sciatica seized him many years, and made him lame till his death. He was greatly beloved, particularly by our said Vis^t Montgomery and all the branches of his Lo^p's family. Coll. Vere Cromwell, late Earl of Ardglass, coveted his conversation, which he many times afforded to them; but all could not remove his melancholy, because his lameness and pain always much disheartened him, for he could not ride (for a long while) but on a side saddle, nor walk with ease but on a plain floor."

There is one other interesting reminiscence of this HUGH SAVAGE in the *Montgomery Manuscripts* which Montgomery did not copy into his *Incidental Remembrances* of the SAVAGES :—" Now before I leave this brief account of him [*i.e.* of the First Viscount Montgomery], I take the liberty to relate one instance of favour to him from the Royal Martyr, viz.—His Majesty went to shoot at the Butts; necessaries were brought; the King desires Mr. Montgomery to try one of his bows, and he shot three or four ends with his Majesty so well that he said, 'Mr. Montgomery, that bow fitts your hand, take them and a quiver of arrows for your use.' I was told this by my father, who carefully preserved them, and divers times (in my sight) used them at Rosemount, charging me to do likewise. They were left to his nephew SAVAGE'S care,

---

[1] General Monck.

[2] This was PATRICK SAVAGE of DERRY, afterwards of PORTAFERRY.

[3] This was JOHN SAVAGE of BALLYVARLEY, father of the above-named Patrick, son of Patrick Savage, Esq., who was grandson of ROLAND SAVAGE, LORD OF THE LITTLE ARDS.

Hugh Savage, Esq., of Portaferry, born A.D. 1609; died A.D. 1683.

Ao. 1649, who restored them to me on my return; the bow was too strong for me, and he using it, it broke in his hands. One half of it was desired and made a staff for the old Countess of Strevling [Stirling] when she was entertained here by her daughter, the 2nd Viscountess Montgomery, at Mount Alexander House."

The name of MR. HUGH SAVAGE appears amongst those of the "Gentlemen Freeholders or Relations" who attended the funeral of the 3d Viscount Montgomery, in Montgomery's account of the funeral-procession, as "MR. HUGH SAVAGE of *Carnesure*," and Mr. Hill tells us in a footnote that he "resided for a time at Carnasure, near Comber."

MR. HUGH SAVAGE, of Portaferry, died unmarried, Montgomery tells us, at his sister Wilton's House in Gaulstown, in the County of Westmeath, on the 10th of February, 1683, and was buried in the chancel of Killucan Church. He was succeeded in the representation of the PORTAFERRY family by his cousin,

Patrick Savage, Esq., of Portaferry, born A.D. 1642; died A.D. 1724.

VI.—PATRICK SAVAGE, ESQ., OF PORTAFERRY, HIGH SHERIFF OF THE COUNTY OF DOWN (BORN A.D. 1642, temp. Charles I.; DIED A.D. 1724, temp. George I.).

This Mr. PATRICK SAVAGE, of Derry (a townland in the Parish of Portaferry), was son of John Savage, Esq., of Ballyvarley, who was son of PATRICK SAVAGE, Esq., who was son of ROLAND SAVAGE, of Derry, who was 2nd surviving son of ROLAND, LORD SAVAGE (first of the Portaferry line mentioned in Sir B. Burke's pedigree), who died in 1572.

Montgomery tells us that MR. HUGH SAVAGE's "encumbered estate came by virtue of the said feofm! to his nearest kinsman and a cater of his own, PATRICK SAVAGE, who deservedly now enjoys it, he having by his prudent management recovered it out of great incumbrances, especially to Mr. Maxwell, of £500 sterling, and to the said HUGH's sister, to whom he gave by accord £800 sterling, and brought the said estate to great improvements of rents and buildings."[1]

To this PATRICK SAVAGE it was that William Montgomery dedicated his "Description of the Barony called the ARDS: Anno Domi Christi, 1701." To him also he addressed the following letter, when sending him his *Remembrances of the Two Ancient Families of the Savages*, a copy of which, it will be remembered, was at the same time sent to his other cousin, CAPTAIN HUGH SAVAGE, OF ARDKEEN :—

---

[1] *Incidental Remembrances of the Two Ancient Families of the Savages*, &c.

"S^r.

"ACCORDING to my promise, I send to you all the foregoing Remembrancers (worth your notice) which are any where scattered in my writings, that they may obtain a room in your *escritoiri* [*sic*], to be a vindication that I have writ nothing for my posterity's perusal which may disgust your family, if I should be aspersed so to have done. The paper on every leaf is attested by the first letters of my name and sirname, as I usually subscribe them in letters: miss eve [*sic*] and the whole ten pages is transcribed from my original, and now compared with me by Mr. Rob Walker, schoolmaster in your town,
"And is presented by,
"S
"Your affect^e Friend and Servt

"For Patrick Savadge of   "WILL. MONTGOMERY.
"Portaferry, Esqre."   "(*A true copy from the Original.*)"

PATRICK SAVAGE, ESQ., OF PORTAFERRY, born A.D 1642; died A.D. 1724.

From Montgomery's two MSS. we have already quoted the principal passages that refer to the Ardkeen branch of the SAVAGES, and to their lands, castles, &c. We shall now give similar passages which refer to those of the Portaferry branch during the lifetime of PATRICK SAVAGE OF PORTAFERRY and of HUGH SAVAGE OF ARDKEEN.

THE ARDS, AND PORTAFERRY AND ITS NEIGHBOURHOOD, A.D. 1701.

"The barony of Ards is thick and well peopled, being about seventeen miles long and three broade, except between Gray Abbey and Ballywalter, where it is narrowest. It is separated (on the south end thereof) from ye barony of Lecahill by a great and swift flux and reflux of the sea (thence called Stronfoord River) a muskett shott over. In w^h, neare ye Ards side, under an hill (by the Irish) called Bankmore, there is a whirlpool or eddy of the returning or incoming tides, called (by the Scotts) the Rowting Well (from the sound it makes sometimes in calme weather) near to which, if small boats come, they will be sucked in and swallowed up, except about full sea, when the water is smelt and even; a great vessel, with top sailes and a good gale, doth hardly pass through it, without being laid about, yet we have not heard of one boat or person lost by it, for sailers and fishermen shun that place.

"From thence, in a mile, stands the Thursday mercat town of Portneferry, where store of great barques belonging to it doo anchor, and at half ebb ly dry; hence, and from the daily passage to ye other land, perhaps the town was so called. Here was a wooden Kay, which one of the proprietors pulled up, selling the timber for building of Drogheda bridge (is reported), because Kildare's family had got the custom-house fixed at his town of Strongfoord.

"About half a quarter of a league up ye river, great shipps may saile to a cape (or lands end) at the entry of Logh Coan, which, from an hill that extends its taile in the s^d river, is called Ballyhendry point, giving under

PATRICK SAVAGE ESQ., OF PORTA- FERRY, born A.D 1642; died A.D. 1724.

shelter thereof a spacious place to ride in at anchor, safe from ye north and east wind's fury.

"Some miners offered to ye late Mr Savadge to find good coales in ye bank above this place, but want of money and encouragement hath hindered the tryall thereof. . . . .

"The said Little Ards, next Lecahill, sends (every winter) great store of good wheate, beare, oats and barley to Dublin and elswher; and all the eastern coast thereof (from whence Scotland and the Isle of Man are seen, and is but four hours sailing distant) abounds with fishes, as herrings, in harvest, also codd, ling, mackerel, barins, lythes, blockans, lobsters, crabs, gray lords (which are near as big as codds), whiteing, haddocks, plaice and large dogg fish, &c., and hath good cattle especially sheep w^h (feeding often on ye sea oare), keep whollsome and fatt all ye winter and spring time; within the said land are many fresh loughs, in which are store of pike and eeles, duck, teel, widgeon and swans. It is supposed that the ducks and widgeons have brought into these loughs and turff pitts of the spawn of these pikes on their feathers, because in many places no stream runs into or from those waters, to bring that fish therein.

"The hills, whereof some be craggy and full of furzes and heath, and the corn and pasture fields, afford partridge, quails, curlew and plover, of both sorts, and abundance of hares and some store of rabbits and no want of foxes.

"The whole territory doth much want fewell, for with great pains they make it of bogg mudd, clapped together and formed with hands, and turned often to dry in the sun; but the gentry supply their parlours and lodging rather with coals from England or Scotland."

CASTLES OF PORTAFERRY, QUINTIN BAY, AND NEWCASTLE.

"The Lord's Castle is that of Portnoferry, the largest old pile of them all, and he hath a fair slated house built A^o 1635, by ye care of Sr James Montgomery added thereunto, for the reputed Lord (and so call him) being Patrick, who marryed a daughter of ye first Ld Visc^t Montgomery of the great Ards. . . . .

"There is likewise on the eastern shore (one league from ye s^d Barr) Cottins bay, als. Quintin Bay Castle, w^h commands ye bay that is capable to receive a bark of forty tonns burthen. Sr James Montgomery of Rosemount purchased the same, and lands adjoining thereunto, from Dualtagh Smith, a depender on ye Savadges of Portneferry, in whose mannor it is: and ye s^d Sr James roofed and floored ye castle, and made freestone window cases, &c. therin: and built ye baron, and flankers, and kitchen walls contiguous; all w^h

SAVAGE (NOW NUGENT) OF PORTAFERRY.

Wm Montgomery, Esq. and his son James (joyning in ye sale) sold unto Mr George Ross who lives at Carney, part of the premises.

"Near it is a ruined pile called Newcastle, formerly belonging unto ——, another dependant of Portneferry, which wth diverse lands adjoining, now doth belong to James Hamilton of Bangor, Esq."

[margin: PATRICK SAVAGE, ESQ., OF PORTAFERRY, born A.D. 1642; died A.D. 1724.]

In 1684, MR. PATRICK SAVAGE was High Sheriff of the County of Down.

In 1702, he purchased part of the confiscations of CAPTAIN ROLAND SAVAGE,[1] styled of Portaferry and Newry, with the fresh-water lough thereto belonging.[2] Mr. PATRICK SAVAGE, by his wife Mary ——, had issue,

I. Patrick, who died on the 13th of June, 1712, aged 25, and was buried in the Portaferry family-vault at Templecraney Church.

II. Roland, who died on the 13th of May, 1723, aged 35, and was buried in the Portaferry family-vault at Templecraney Church. He married, in May, 1718, Margaret, daughter of Nicholas Price, Esq.,[3] of Saintfield, Co. Down, and by her (who died April, 1721, aged 27) had issue,

1. Dorcas, who died unmarried.
2. Catherine, married on the 10th of September, 1740, to ROGER HALL, Esq., of NARROW WATER, Co. Down, and had issue,
    SAVAGE HALL, Esq., of NARROW WATER.
    Dorcas Hall, married to Francis Carleton, Esq.
    Anne Hall, married to PATRICK SAVAGE, Esq., of PORTAFERRY.
    Catherine Hall, married to James Moore, Esq.
    Sophia Hall, married to Richard Ainsworth, Esq.

---

[1] Captain Roland Savage, of Ballygalget.

[2] *See* D'Alton: *King James's Army List.*

[3] FAMILY OF PRICE.—The following account of the family of PRICE OF SAINTFIELD, between which and the SAVAGES there have been several intermarriages, we extract from Burke's *Landed Gentry:*—

NICHOLAS PRICE, Esq., of Hollymount, Co. Down, who *m.* Catherine, dau. of James Hamilton, Esq., M.P., and widow of Vere Essex Cromwell, Earl of Ardglass, had a son,

"LIEUT.-GEN. NICHOLAS PRICE, who *m.* Dorcas, 4th dau. of Roger West, Esq., of the Rock, Co. Wicklow, and had issue,

JAMES, who *m.* Frances, natural dau. of Lord Herbert of Cherbury, and had two daus. · Catherine, *m.* 1st, to John Savage, Esq., of Portaferry, and 2ndly, 13 Jan., 1738, to Edward Baillie, D.D., Dean of Ardfert; and Dorcas, *m.* to Dr. Whittle, of Lisburn.

CROMWELL, M.P. for Downpatrick, *m.*, 1st, Margaret, dau. of Mr. Anderson, of Belfast, and by her (who *d.* 1741) had a son, Nicholas Tichborne, *b.* 1725, who *d.* young; and two daus., Elizabeth, *m.* 1743, to Roger MacNeal, Esq., of Tinesk; and Dorcas. He *m.* 2ndly, Mary, dau. of the late Hugh Willoughby, Esq., of Carrow.

III. Francis, who died on the 8th of January, 1722, aged 25, and was buried in the Portaferry family-vault at Templecraney Church.

IV. EDWARD, of whom presently as heir to his father at Portaferry.

I. Catherine, married to John Moore, Esq., of Drumbanagher, M.P. for Armagh.

MR. PATRICK SAVAGE, of Portaferry, died on the 13th of Sept., 1724, aged 82, and was succeeded by his fourth son,

VII.—EDWARD SAVAGE, ESQ., OF PORTAFERRY (BORN A.D. 1702, temp. Anne; DIED 18th March, 1725, temp. George I.).

Mr. EDWARD SAVAGE, of Portaferry, died unmarried, on the 18th of March, 1725, aged 23 years, and was buried at Portaferry. He was succeeded by his uncle,

NICHOLAS,
Sophia, *d.*, *unm.*, Oct., 1720.
Margaret, *m.*, May, 1718, to Rowland Savage, Esq., of Portaferry.
Anne, *m.* to James Stevenson, Esq., of Killeleagh, M.P.
" The 3rd son,
"NICHOLAS PRICE, Esq., of Saintfield, M.P. for Lisburn, *m.* 1st, Mary, dau. of Francis, 1st Lord Conway, of Ragley, Co. Warwick, by whom he had a son, FRANCIS; and 2ndly, 1732, Maria, dau. of the Hon. Col. Alexander Mackenzie, 2nd son of the 4th Earl of Seaforth, by whom he had also issue. He *d.* 1742, and was *s.* by his son,
"FRANCIS PRICE, Esq., of Saintfield, many years M.P. for Lisburn, who *m.* Charity, dau. of Matthew Forde, Esq., of Seaforde, Co. Down, and *d.* 1794, having had issue,
NICHOLAS, of Saintfield House.
Christian-Arabella, *m.* to William Hoey, Esq., of Dunganstown, Co. Wicklow.
Harriet-Jane. Mary, *d.* young.
" The only son,
"NICHOLAS PRICE, Esq., of Saintfield House, J.P. and D.L., High Sheriff 1801, *b.* 1 Oct., 1754; *m.* Nov., 1779, Lady Sarah Pratt, dau. of Charles, 1st Earl of Camden, and by her (who *d.* 7 April, 1817) had one dau.
ELIZABETH-ANNE, *m.* to James Blackwood, Esq., of Strangford, Co. Down (a descendant of the BLACKWOODS *of Ballyleidy*), and had issue,
1. Nicholas, *b.* 1805; *d.* 1819.
2. JAMES-CHARLES, of Saintfield House.
3. William-Robert-Arthur, *b.* 22 Jan., 1813; *m.* 1st May, 1843, Anna Eliza, 2nd dau. of the Rev. W. Jex Blake, of Swanton Abbots, Norfolk, and had one dau., Anna Maria Frances. He *m.* 2ndly, Henrietta, dau. of George Kenyon, Esq., of Cefn, Co. Denbigh.
4. Townley, *b.* 5 Jan., 1815; *m.* 1st Feb., 1841, Maria Catherine, eldest dau. of the Rev. W. Jex Blake; and 2ndly, Anna, eldest dau. of the Hon. & Rev. Henry Ward, and has issue. He *m.* 3dly, Sarah, dau. of Hugh Lyle, Esq., of Knocktarna, Co. Derry, and has issue.
5. Richard, *b.* 12 May, 1818; lieut.-col. royal art.; *m.* Anne, 2nd dau. of Lieut.-Col. Wade, of Clonabraney, Co. Meath, and has issue.

VIII.—JAMES SAVAGE, ESQ., OF PORTAFERRY.

Mr. JAMES SAVAGE was 2nd surviving son of JOHN SAVAGE, Esq., of Ballyvarley, son of PATRICK SAVAGE, Esq., son of ROLAND, LORD SAVAGE, who died in 1572.

MR. JAMES SAVAGE married Mabel, daughter of Edmund Magee, Esq., of Lisburn, Co. Antrim. He had issue,

I. JOHN, of whom presently as successor to his father at Portaferry.
II. ANDREW, of whom hereafter as successor to his brother at Portaferry.

Mr. JAMES SAVAGE, of Portaferry, was succeeded by his elder son,

IX.—JOHN SAVAGE, ESQ., OF PORTAFERRY.

MR. JOHN SAVAGE married Catherine, daughter of —— Savage, Esq., and had issue,

I. JAMES, who died young.

MR. JOHN SAVAGE, of Portaferry, was succeeded by his brother,

X.—ANDREW SAVAGE, ESQ., OF PORTAFERRY (LIVING IN A.D. 1730).

MR. ANDREW SAVAGE, of Portaferry, an officer in the Spanish Army, had been a Roman Catholic, but became a Protestant. He married Margaret, sister and co-heiress of John Nugent, Esq., Lieut.-Governor of Tortola and the Virgin Isles (who died without issue), and daughter of Andrew Nugent, Esq., of Dysert, by his wife the Lady Catherine Nugent, 2nd daughter and co-heiress of Thomas, 18th Baron Delvin, 4th Earl of Westmeath;[1] and by her had issue,

    1. Sarah, *d.* young.   2. Mary-Georgiana.
    3. Sarah-Elizabeth, *m.* to the Rev. Henry Archdall, 4th son of Edward Archdall, Esq., of Castle Archdall, Co. Fermanagh, and has issue.
    4. Elizabeth-Catherine, *m.* Oct., 1841, to Rev. Alexander Orr, and has issue.

    "The eldest surviving son,

    "JAMES-CHARLES PRICE, Esq., of Saintfield House, High Sheriff of the Co. Down, 1859, *b.* 17 June, 1807; *m.* 18 March, 1841, Ann Margaret, eldest dau. of Patrick Savage, Esq., of Portaferry, Major 26th Foot, and has issue,

    I. NICHOLAS, *b.* 11 June, 1842.
    II. James-Nugent, *b.* 15 Oct., 1844.
    III. William-Charles, *b.* 17 Oct., 1845; *d.* 5 Nov., 1845.
    IV. Francis-William, *b.* 27 Dec., 1847.
    I. Harriet-Anna, *d.* 17 Jan., 1847.
    II. Elizabeth-Dorcas.
    III. Catherine-Anne."

[1] Thomas, 18th Baron Delvin, 4th earl [of Westmeath], a colonel in the army of James II., and outlawed in consequence in 1691; but being one of the hostages exchanged for the observance of the

ANDREW SAVAGE, ESQ., OF PORTAFERRY, living in A.D. 1730.

I. PATRICK, of whom presently as successor to his father at Portaferry. MR. ANDREW SAVAGE, of Portaferry, was succeeded by his son,

PATRICK SAVAGE, ESQ., OF PORTAFERRY, who died in A.D. 1797.

XI.—PATRICK SAVAGE, ESQ., OF PORTAFERRY, HIGH SHERIFF OF THE CO. OF DOWN (DIED A.D. 1797, temp. George III.).

In MR. PATRICK SAVAGE's time the celebrated traveller Arthur Young visited Portaferry, and we cannot do better than quote his account of his visit, which is particularly interesting as throwing light on the condition and prosperity of the Little Ards during the latter half of the 18th century:—

"Reached Portaferry, the town and seat of PATRICK SAVAGE, Esq., who took every means of procuring me information concerning the neighbourhood. . . . The plentifulness of the country about Portaferry, Strangford, &c., is very great: this will appear from the following circumstances, as well as the register of butchers' meat and common poultry elsewhere inserted :—Pidgeons, 2s. a dozen; rabbits, 4d. a couple. The fish are, turbot, 4s., sole, 10d. a pair; bret and haddock, 1d. each; lobsters, 5s. a dozen; oysters, 19d. a hundred; John dory, garnet; whiting, 4d. a dozen; mackarel, mullet, partridges, and quails in plenty. Wild ducks, 10d. to 1s., widgeon, 6d. a couple; barnacle, 10d. each; teal, 6d. a couple, plover, 3d.

"The country is in general beautiful, but particularly so about the straights that lead into Strangford Loch. From MR. SAVAGE's door the view has great

---

articles of Limerick, the outlawry was reversed, and he was restored to his estates and honours. His lordship *m.* Margaret, only dau. of John, Lord Bellew, by whom he had (with two sons, Christopher, Lord Delvin, who *d. unm.* at Bath, 12 April, 1752, and John, who *d. unm.* in 1725) two daus. and coheiresses, viz.,

I. LADY MARY NUGENT, who *m.* Francis, 21st Lord Athenry, and had several children.
II. LADY CATHERINE NUGENT, *m.* to Andrew Nugent, Esq., of Dysert, and had issue,
    1. Lavallin, of Dysert and Tullaughan, who claimed the barony of Delvin in 1799, but *d. s. p.*
    2. John, lieut.-governor of Tortola and the Virgin Isles ; *d. s. p.*
    3. Patrick-Anthony, capt. in the army ; *d. unm.* in 1785.
    1. *Margaret*, *m. to ANDREW SAVAGE, Esq., of PORTAFERRY, Co. Down*, and had a son and successor, PATRICK SAVAGE, who *m.* in 1765, Anne, dau. of Roger Hall, Esq., of Narrow Water, and had a son and heir,
        ANDREW SAVAGE, Esq., of PORTAFERRY, who assumed the surname of NUGENT on inheriting a portion of Governor Nugent's fortune, and claimed the barony of Delvin in 1814. He *m.* 13 June, 1800, Selina, dau. of Thomas, 1st Viscount de Vesci, and had, with other issue, a son and heir,
            JOHN SAVAGE, who *m.* 29 April, 1833, Catherine, dau. of John, 2nd Viscount de Vesci, and *d.* in 1857, having had issue.—*See* Burke's *Peerage and Baronetage*, under WESTMEATH, Earls of.

variety. To the left are tracts of hilly grounds, between which the sea appears, and the vast chain of mountains in the Isle of Man distinctly seen. In front the hills rise in a beautiful outline, and a round hill projects like a promontory into the streights, and under it the town amidst groups of trees; the scene is cheerful of itself, but rendered doubly so by the ships and herring-boats sailing in and out. To the right the view is crowned by the mountains of Mourne, which, wherever seen, are of a character particularly bold, and even terrific. The shores of the Loch behind MR. SAVAGE'S are bold ground, abounding with numerous pleasing landscapes; the opposite coast, consisting of the woods and improvements of Castle-Ward, is a fine country.

PATRICK SAVAGE, ESQ., OF PORTAFERRY, who died in A.D. 1797.

KEEP OF PORTAFERRY CASTLE, from the gardens of PORTAFERRY HOUSE.

"July 30th, crossed the streights in MR. SAVAGE'S boat, and breakfasted with Mr. Ainsworth, Collector of the Customs; he gave the following particulars of the barony of Lecale, of the husbandry of which I had often heard as something better than common."[1]

MR. PATRICK SAVAGE married, in 1765, Anne, daughter of ROGER HALL, ESQ., OF NARROW WATER,[2] Co. Down, and by her had issue,

---

[1] Arthur Young, Esq., F.R.S.—*Tour in Ireland*, &c., made in the years 1776, 1777, 1778, and brought down to 1779.

[2] FAMILY OF HALL OF NARROW WATER.—Of the family of HALL OF NARROW WATER, so closely allied by marriage to the SAVAGES, Sir Bernard Burke gives the following account:—

"This family is of English extraction. WILLIAM HALL settled in Ireland in the 17th century, and *d.* at Red Bay, co. Antrim, 1640; his son,

"FRANCIS HALL, Esq., of Mount Hall, co. Down, *m.* Mary, dau. of Judge Lyndon, and had issue, ROGER, Edward (*see* HALL *of Mairwarra*), Alexander Trevor, and a dau., Fridswid, *m.* 1681, to Chichester Fortescue, Esq., of Dromiskin. The eldest son,

"ROGER HALL, ESQ., of Mount Hall, *m.* 1686, Christian, dau. of Sir Toby Poyntz, of Acton, co. Armagh, and had issue, TOBY, his heir; Roger; and Rose, *m.* 1708, to Richard Close, Esq. The son and heir,

PATRICK SAVAGE, ESQ., OF PORTAFERRY, who died in A.D. 1797.

I. ANDREW, of whom presently as successor to his father at Portaferry.
II. Patrick-Nugent, Major, 26th Foot, who married Harriet, daughter of the Rev. Henry Sandiford, and had issue,
    1. Henry, born in 1810, who married, and settled in Australia.
    2. Andrew, born in 1811, Captain Marine Artillery. He served through the Carlist War in Sir De Lacy Evans's legion.
    1. Ann-Margaret, born in 1807; married, 1841, to JAMES CHARLES PRICE, ESQ., OF SAINTFIELD.
    2. Harriett.
III. Roger-Hall, Capt. R.N., who died unmarried.
IV. John-Lavallin, who died unmarried.
V. William, in Holy Orders, Rector of Shinrone, King's Co., who married

"TOBY HALL, Esq., of Mount Hall, *m.* 1712, Margaret, dau. of the Hon. Robert Fitzgerald, and sister of the 19th Earl of Kildare, and by her (who *d.* 8 Dec., 1758) he left at his decease, 4 May, 1734, two daus., Christian and Elizabeth, and one son,
  "ROGER HALL, Esq., of Mount Hall, who *m.* 10 Sept., 1740, Catherine, only dau. of Rowland Savage, Esq., of Portaferry, and had issue, SAVAGE, his heir; Dorcas, *m.* to Francis Carleton, Esq.; Anne, *m.* to Patrick Savage, Esq., of Portaferry; Catherine, *m.* 1765, to the Right Hon. William Brownlow, M.P.; Elizabeth, *m.* to James Moore, Esq.; Sophia, *m.* to Richard Ainsworth, Esq. The son and heir,
  "SAVAGE HALL, Esq., of Narrow Water, *b.* 1763; *m.* 1786, Elizabeth, 4th dau. of John Madden, Esq., of Hilton, co. Monaghan, and by her (who *d.* 1801) had issue,
  I. ROGER, his heir, of Narrow Water.
  II. Savage, in Holy Orders, Rector of Loughall; *b.* 1798; *m.* 1831, Anne, eldest dau. of the late William-James O'Brien, Esq., of co. Clare, and *d.* 1851, leaving issue,
    1. Savage, 89th regt., *b.* 1834.
    2. William-James, royal artillery, *b.* 1835; *m.* Dec. 1863, Elizabeth-Theodosia-Catherine, 2nd dau. of the late Rev. W.-B.-Forde, of Seaforde, co. Down, and by her (who *d.* May, 1866) has issue, Roger, *b.* 4 Nov., 1864, and William-Charles, *b.* May, 1866.
    3. Roger, *b.* 1840.
    1. Margaret-Barbara, *m.* 1858, to Wm. Orme, Esq., of Owenmore, co. Mayo.
    2. Elizabeth-Grace, *m.* 1860, to Major H.-C. Moore.
    3. Annette.   4. Alice.   5. Emily, *d.* 1865.
  III. SAMUEL-MADDEN, now of Narrow Water.
  I. Anne, *m.* to Trevor Corry, Esq., of Newry, and *d.* 1852.
  II. Catherine, *m.* to Capt. Nowlan, deceased.
  III. Elizabeth, *m.* to the Rev. W.-B.-Savage, *d.* 1867.
  IV. Jane, *m.* to the Rev. Sir Hunt-Johnson Walsh, Bart.
"The eldest son,
  "ROGER HALL, Esq., of Narrow Water, J.P. and D.L., High Sheriff, co. Armagh, 1815, and for Down, 1816; *b.* 6 Nov., 1791; *m.* 10 Nov., 1812, Barbara, 4th dau. of Patrick Savage, Esq., of Portaferry, co. Down. He *d.* 20 Sept., 1864, and his wife *d.* June, 1853. He was succeeded by his brother,
  "SAMUEL-MADDEN-FRANCIS HALL, Esq., of Narrow Water, co. Down, J.P. and D.L., late Major 75th regt.; *b.* 1800; *m.* 24 Sept., 1845, Anne-Margaret, youngest dau. of the late Andrew-Savage Nugent, Esq., of Portaferry."

Elizabeth, daughter of SAVAGE HALL, ESQ., OF NARROW WATER, Co. Down, and had issue,
   1. Patrick.
   2. Roger.
   3. Andrew.
   4. John.
   1. Elizabeth.
   2. Anne.
   3. Margaret.
  I. Barbara, married, 10th Nov., 1812, to ROGER HALL, ESQ., OF NARROW WATER, J.P. and D.L., High Sheriff, Co. Armagh, 1815, and for Down, 1816.
  II. Dorcas-Sophia.

MR. PATRICK SAVAGE died on the 7th of March, 1797. He was succeeded by his eldest son,

XII.—ANDREW (SAVAGE) NUGENT, ESQ., HIGH SHERIFF OF THE CO. DOWN, LIEUTENANT-COLONEL OF THE NORTH DOWN MILITIA (BORN A.D. 1770, temp. George III.; DIED A.D. 1846, temp. Queen Victoria).

Mr. ANDREW SAVAGE, who was born on the 3rd of June, 1770, on inheriting a portion of the fortune of his maternal grand-uncle, Governor Nugent *(see above)*, assumed the name of NUGENT, and claimed the Barony of Delvin in 1814.

In 1803, he was High Sheriff of Downshire.

He married, on the 13th of June, 1800, Selina, youngest daughter of Thomas Vesey, 1st Viscount de Vesci, by his wife, Selina Elizabeth, eldest daughter and co-heiress of the Right Hon. Sir Arthur Brooke, Bart., of Colebrooke, Co. Fermanagh, and had issue,

  I. PATRICK-JOHN, his heir and successor at Portaferry.
  II. Thomas-Vesey, born in 1807; married Frances, eldest daughter of Sir James M. Stronge, Bart., of Tynan Abbey, and has had issue,
     1. Andrew-Robert, who was born on the 22nd of June, 1836, and died in October, 1856.
     2. Edmund-Henry-Stuart, who was born on the 26th of Jan., 1849.
     1. Isabella-Frances.
     2. Selina-Frances, married to E. Wingfield Verner, Esq., son of Sir William Verner, Bart.
  III. Andrew, of The Lodge, Strangford, Co. Down, a Major in the Army, late 36th Regt., J.P. and D.L. for Co. Down, High Sheriff, 1867;

ANDREW (SAVAGE) NUGENT, ESQ., OF PORTAFERRY, born A.D. 1770; died A.D. 1846.

born on the 28th of May, 1809; married, on the 4th of Oct., 1841, Harriet-Margaret, 2nd daughter of Henry, 6th Lord Farnham, and widow of Edward Southwell, Viscount Bangor, and has had issue,

1. Walter-Andrew, Lieut. R.E., born 28th Dec., 1846; died 1870.
   1. Harriet-Annette-Catherine, married, Feb., 1863, to Henry Head, Esq., M.D., of Fitzwilliam Square, Dublin, and has issue.
   2. Miriam-Dora.

IV. Arthur, born in Dec., 1810; married, *1st*, Charlotte, only daughter of Major-Gen. Brooke, of Colebrooke, Co. Fermanagh, brother of Sir Henry Brooke, Bart., and by her, who died 1870, had issue,

1. Selina, who died on the 5th of Nov., 1871.

He married, *2ndly*, Isabella, 2nd daughter of John Tisdall, Esq., of Charlefort, Co. Meath.

V. Charles-Lavallin-William, a Major-General in the Army, formerly 58th Regt.; born in 1815; married Charlotte-Alicia, daughter of the late Major-Gen. Pitt; and died at Southsea, in 1884, having had issue,

1. Charles, R.E., who died in 1879.
2. George, Capt. Royal Artillery.
3. Arthur, Capt. 54th Foot.
4. William.
5. Rowland, Lieut. R.N.
6. Thomas.
7. Raymond, R.N.
1. Amy, married to Lieut. F. Laye, R.N.
2. Edith.
3. Mabel.

I. Selina-Elizabeth, married to the late SIR JAMES MATTHEW STRONGE, 3rd BART. of TYNAN ABBEY, Co. Armagh; M.P. for that Co.; Lieut. in the 5th Dragoon Guards; subsequently Hon. Col. of the Royal Tyrone Fusiliers.

II. Anne-Margaret, married, in Sept., 1845, to SAMUEL MADDEN FRANCIS HALL, Esq., of NARROW WATER, late Major 75th Regt.

LIEUT.-COL. ANDREW NUGENT died on the 2nd of February, 1846.[1] He was succeeded by his eldest son,

---

[1] The following amusing local ballad associated with Lt.-Col. Savage's (Nugent's) name, and illustrating the local feeling and manners of Portaferry in the early years of the present century, may as well be preserved here. It appeared in some local newspaper of the day:—

XIII.—PATRICK JOHN NUGENT, ESQ., OF PORTAFERRY, LIEUT.-COL. OF THE NORTH DOWN MILITIA, HIGH SHERIFF OF THE CO. OF DOWN, &C. (DIED A.D. 1857, temp. Queen Victoria).

LIEUT.-COL. PATRICK JOHN NUGENT, of Portaferry, married, on the 29th of April, 1833, his cousin Catherine, daughter of John, 2nd Viscount de Vesci, by his wife, Frances Letitia, daughter of the Right Hon. William Brownlow, of Lurgan,[1] by whom he had issue,

I. ANDREW, now of Portaferry.

II. John-Vesey, Lieut.-Col. late 51st Foot, born on the 16th of July, 1837. Served with the 51st Light Infantry in the N.W. Frontier of India Campaign, 1865—Umboyla Expedition; Jowaki Expedition, 1877 (Medal with Clasp); Afghan War, 1878-9-80; assault and capture of Ali Musjid; advance to the relief of Shurpur; operations in the

---

"THE LAUNCH.

"On Monday last was launched at Portaferry a remarkably stout and elegant brig, burthen about 180 tons. She went off in handsome style, and, from the nature of the descent, with gradually increasing velocity, till she plunged safely into the dock. The day being fine, a very numerous and respectable body of spectators had assembled on the occasion, who were much gratified by the novelty and grandeur of the exhibition, and the success attending it. She is named the *Andrew Savage*, in compliment to COLONEL SAVAGE.

"The following lines were hastily written on the occasion:—

"Behold th' auspicious day arise!
   What crowds together hie!
To clear the launch all hands now strive,
   And tools incessant ply.

"At length each dagger driven askew,
   The eager hum arose;
Then loud the deaf'ning clamour grew,
   With cries there 'off she goes.'

"Huzza! she goes, glad Cuan hears,
   The christening-bottle flies;
The *Andrew Savage* hail,—three cheers
   In echoing plaudits rise.

"Stupendous sight! Art's wondrous frame,
   Majestic borne along;
In chorus strain, the loud acclaim,
   The hills and shores prolong.

"The subject element to gain,
   She plies each sliding block;
And, hast'ning o'er the slippery plain,
   Bounds clear into the dock.

"To bear the stately buoyant brig,
   His arms kind Neptune lends;
While Amphitrite, in her *new* gig,
   Well pleased the scene attends.

"Fair fabric! fair Lough Cuan's pride!
   Success thy course attend.
Where'er thou roam, securely glide,
   Whilst winds and waves befriend.

"And never as yon *gig machine*,
   Nep's whelming power fear;
But safely borne o'er *gulphs marine*,
   His friendly trident rear.

"Portaferry, January 28 [1811]."—(Copied from an old scrap-book of the late Mrs. Thomasine Echlin, of Echlinville, in the possession of her nephew, Mr. G. F. Armstrong.)

[1] John, 2nd Viscount de Vesci, *b.* 15 Feb., 1771; *m.* 25 Aug., 1800, Frances Letitia, dau. of the Right Hon. William Brownlow, of Lurgan, by whom (who *d.* 6 June, 1840) he had issue,

LIEUT.-COL. PATRICK JOHN NUGENT, OF PORTAFERRY, who died in A.D. 1857.

Hisarak Valley. (Mentioned in despatches, Medal with Clasp, Brevet of Major.) Lieut.-Col. Nugent married, on the 19th of Jan., 1886, Emily Georgiana, eldest daughter of the late Herbert Langham, Esq., of Cotterbrook Park, Nottinghamshire.

III. Arthur-Vesey, late 17th Regt., born on the 2nd of March, 1841.

I. Frances-Isabella, married in April, 1862, to Capt. George Barrington Price, Scots Greys.

LIEUT.-COL. PATRICK JOHN NUGENT died in November, 1857. He was succeeded by his eldest son,

LIEUT.-GENERAL ANDREW NUGENT OF PORTAFERRY, born A.D. 1834.

XIV.—LIEUTENANT-GENERAL ANDREW NUGENT, OF PORTAFERRY, J.P. AND D.L., LATE LT.-COL. COMMANDING ROYAL SCOTS GREYS (BORN A.D. 1834, temp. William IV.).

LIEUT.-GENERAL ANDREW NUGENT, present representative in the male line of the SAVAGES OF PORTAFERRY, was born on the 30th of March, 1834. He served with the Scots Greys in the Eastern Campaign of 1854-55, including the Battle of Balaklava (in which he took part in the Charge of the Heavy Brigade under General Scarlett),[1] Inkerman, and Tchernaya, and the Siege and Fall of Sebastopol (Medal with three Clasps, and Turkish Medal).

THOMAS, present Viscount.

William-John, *b.* 12 Aug., 1806; *m.* in July, 1837, Isabella Elizabeth, dau. of the Rev. Francis Brownlow and Lady Catherine Brabazon his wife, sister of the 9th Earl of Meath, and *d.* 3 Aug., 1863.

Catherine, m. 30 April, 1833, to her cousin Patrick John Nugent, Esq., of Portaferry House, co. Down, claimant of the Barony of Delvin, who d. in 1857.—See Burke: *Peerage and Baronetage,* under DE VESCI, VISCOUNT.

[1] "The Greys were led by Colonel Darby Griffith, and the two squadron leaders who followed him were Major Clarke on the right and Captain Williams on the left. Handley, Hunter, Buchanan, and Sutherland were the four troop leaders of the regiment; the adjutant was Lieutenant Miller; the serre-files were Boyd, Nugent, and Lenox Prendergast. And to them, though he did not then hold the Queen's Commission, I add the name of John Wilson, now a cornet and the acting adjutant of the regiment, for he took a signal part in the fight."—Kinglake: *Invasion of the Crimea,* vol. v., p. 117, Cabinet Ed. (1877).

Ruins of the Old Cathedral of Downpatrick, ancient burial-place of the SAVAGES OF PORTAFERRY.

CHAPTER X.

SAVAGE OF PORTAFERRY *(continued)*.—RELICS, EPITAPHS, ETC.

THE SHRINE OF ST. PATRICK'S HAND.

THE SAVAGES OF PORTAFERRY were for a time the possessors and guardians of the remarkable and interesting relic known as *The Shrine of St. Patrick's Hand.* Of the history of this relic and its association with the SAVAGE family, the Rev. Father O'Laverty, than whom there could hardly be a better authority on such a subject, writes as follows:—

THE SHRINE OF ST. PATRICK'S HAND.

"Father M'Aleenan, when parish priest of Portaferry, having understood that some Protestant gentlemen were desirous of purchasing for the Museum of the Royal Irish Academy the Shrine of St. Patrick's Hand, which was at that time in the possession of Miss M'Henry, of Carrstown, directed the attention of the bishop and clergy to the matter, and obtained from them a commission to purchase it for the diocese. Father M'Aleenan succeeded in purchasing it for £10. The following is the substance of the interesting account of that reliquary in Miss Cusack's *Life of St. Patrick*, which is principally supplied by Mr. J. W. Hanna[1]:—It is probable that the hand and

---

[1] Mr. J. W. Hanna was an able and industrious antiquarian, the results of whose researches, contributed to the *Ulster Archaeological Society's Journal* and other publications, are of great value to all who desire to master the history of Ulster.

THE SHRINE OF ST. PATRICK'S HAND.

arm were placed in the present shrine by Cardinal Vivian in 1186, when he translated the relics. Nothing farther is known of it until it came into the possession of Magennis, of Castlewellan, possibly from some of the Magennises who were at various times Abbots of Down. In the early part of the eighteenth [17th] century, George Russell, of Rathmullan, married one of the Magennises, and the relic passed into the possession of their only child Rose, who married ROWLAND SAVAGE. Upon the failure of male issue, the Portaferry estate, and with it the relic, passed to another branch of the SAVAGES, one of whom, on becoming a Protestant, gave it into the custody of the Rev. James Teggart, then parish priest of the Ards. After Father Teggart's death, about 1765, Mr. SAVAGE, of Portaferry, handed it over to the guardianship of Mr. M'Henry, of Carrstown, in the custody of whose family it remained until it passed into that of the Bishops of Down and Connor. The tradition of its transmission, as told to Father M'Aleenan by Mrs. Crangle, of Carrstown, is as follows:—When Down Cathedral was plundered, Magennis saved the reliquary, which passed, on the marriage of his daughter, to Carr, of Carrstown, or Ballyedock. After the death of Magennis' daughter, Carr married one of the SAVAGES, who, surviving him, bequeathed the reliquary to her own relations, the SAVAGES, and they retained it until MR. SAVAGE, the [grand]father of the late COLONEL NUGENT, on becoming a Protestant, gave it to Father Teggart. It passed on his death into the possession of his niece, who was his housekeeper. She, however, knowing that Mr. M'Henry, of Carrstown, was maternally descended from the Carrs, and consequently a relative of the Carr who once possessed it, gave it to him, and thus it passed into the custody of the M'Henrys."

Mr. Arthur Nugent gives a more particular account of the manner in which the reliquary passed out of the hands of his family, as follows:—A curious old reliquary called "St. Patrick's Hand" was in possession of the PORTAFERRY SAVAGES at one time, and up to 1842, as well as Mr. Nugent can recollect, was retained in trust by a farmer on the estate, named M'Ennery. He, having lost his farm, took it to the late COL. NUGENT, of Portaferry, in Mr. Arthur Nugent's presence, saying, "Here, your Honour, I surrender into your *hands* St. Patrick's *hand*, which me and my forebearers have held in trust for the SAVAGES OF PORTAFERRY for several generations." Col. Nugent replied, "I won't be bothered with it; for, if I take it into my house, all the beggars in the country will be at my door." When Mr. Arthur Nugent followed M'Ennery out of the door, the latter said to him, "Here, Mr. Arthur, take it yourself." But he refused, fearing that his father would be displeased. He immediately, however, wrote to the late Dr. Dawson, the then Dean of St. Patrick's, who was a noted antiquarian. The Dean replied, "Give the man £25. At the same time, I don't believe it to be anything connected with Ireland; but in my opinion it is the relic of St. Fillan, the Patron Saint of Robert Bruce, who usually carried it at the head of his army, and it is well known that Edward Bruce brought this relic over to Ireland, where it was lost." This was the Dean's idea of the Hand, and in the Museum at Edinburgh the Curator told Mr. Nugent they had (which he saw) all the relics of the Saint except the Hand. Before Mr. Nugent could get possession of the reliquary, the Priest heard of what he was about, sent in for it, and gave poor old M'Ennery only £7 for it.[1] Mr. Nugent believes it came into the SAVAGE family from the old family of Russell, of Killough, by marriage. Still, his father knew nothing of its history, except (which all the country knew) that the M'Ennery family held it in trust for the CASTLE family (*i.e.* the SAVAGES OF PORTAFERRY CASTLE). . . . . It is long since a particle of bone has been inside it. It contains now nothing but a small bit of yew. Mr. Nugent's own idea is, as to the SAVAGE family, that during the period of the penal laws, when they turned Protestants, the SAVAGES got rid of the reliquary for fear of losing their estates. He thinks that it was most likely his great-grandfather who parted with it. He had been a Captain in the Spanish army, and had turned Protestant to claim the Estate.[2]

THE SHRINE OF ST. PATRICK'S HAND.

Father O'Laverty describes the reliquary thus:—"The Shrine is silver, and of antique workmanship; it represents the hand and arm of an ecclesiastic of rank, covered with an embroidered sleeve, and wearing a jewelled glove. It stands 1 foot 3½ inches high, but there is no inscription except I. H. S., so that it is difficult to estimate its probable age. The reliquary was opened in 1856 by Dr. Denvir. It contained a piece of wood of the yew-tree, about nine inches long, which was bored lengthwise with a hole sufficiently large to receive the wrist-bone of a human arm. The wood was smeared over at both ends with wax, obviously the remains of the seals which had authenticated the relic. The wood appears to have been intended as a receptacle for the bone, for the purpose of preserving it in its place, and preventing it from rubbing against the outer case. When it was examined by Dr. Denvir no portion of the bone remained. It had probably been dissolved by the water

---

[1] The Rev. Father O'Laverty (as quoted above) says £10. However, old M'Ennery (rest his soul!) was the poorer, through the transaction, by at least £15.

[2] Substance of a letter to the Editor from Arthur Nugent, Esq., of Quintin Lodge, Leamington, dated Oct. 21, 1886.

THE SHRINE OF ST. PATRICK'S HAND.

which persons were in the habit of pouring through the shrine, in order that they might wash sores with it, in hopes of obtaining thereby a miraculous cure. About the commencement of this century, the shrine was despoiled of some of the Irish diamonds, with which it was studded, by one of the M'Henrys, in order to bring them with her, as a protection against any misfortune, when she was removing to Ballymena with her husband, a carpenter, named Richard Colly, or Collins. It is not unlikely that they are still in the neighbourhood of Ballymena. The late Dr. Denvir had the lost Irish diamonds replaced with new stones, and the shrine completely repaired by the late Mr. Donegan, of Dublin, who, out of devotion to the Apostle of Ireland, refused to charge for his work. Dr. Denvir intended to have inserted under a large crystal, which ornaments the back of the hand, a portion of the relics of St. Patrick which he obtained from the Cardinal of St. Mark's Church, in Rome, where a portion of the relics, which were carried to Rome by Cardinal Vivian, are preserved. The Shrine of St. Patrick's Hand is now deposited among the archives of Down and Connor, which are under the special custody of the bishop."[1]

MONUMENTS, EPITAPHS, &C., IN THE ARDS, OF THE SAVAGES (NOW NUGENTS) OF PORTAFERRY.

THE ANCIENT BURIAL-PLACE OF THE SAVAGES OF PORTAFERRY.

The old burial-place of the SAVAGES OF PORTAFERRY was the ancient Cathedral of Downpatrick, figured at the head of this section of our history.[2] It may have contained monuments of the family now no longer in existence, and the

---

[1] *Diocese of Down and Connor:* by the Rev. J. O'Laverty, P.P., M.R.I.A. Vol. i., pp. 71-73 (footnotes).

In the possession of the Savages of Dunturk, Co. Down (no doubt in some remote way connected with the SAVAGES OF THE ARDS), it appears that there was formerly another relic of the Patron Saint of Ireland, viz., "The Shrine of St. Patrick's Jaw-Bone." Of this relic we may quote Father O'Laverty's account, which is as follows:—"The Most Rev. Dr. Dorrian has also a silver reliquary, which he purchased from a family named Cullen, who resided in the parish of Derriaghy, Co. Antrim, at the base of Collin mountain. It consists of a silver box, or shrine, inclosing a human jaw-bone, in a perfect state, but now only retaining one double tooth. It had formerly five, three of which were given to members of the family when emigrating to America, and the fourth was deposited under the altar of Derriaghy Chapel by the parish priest, when the chapel was rebuilt in 1797. The outer case is of antique appearance, fitted with a lid, and has a hall-mark of some early date impressed upon it. The bone is that of a male of rather large size. The family believed that it was the jaw-bone of St. Patrick, and a tradition to that effect has been handed down for generations. The great-grandmother of the old men the Cullens, who sold it to the Bishop, bought it from her relatives, the Savages of Dunturk, in the County of Down. Formerly water, in which the bone was immersed, was administered to persons afflicted with epilepsy. See *Ulster Journal of Archæology*, vol. ii., which contains drawings of both the shrines."—*Diocese of Down and Connor*, footnote, pp. 73-4.

[2] From a water-colour drawing in the possession of Arthur Nugent, Esq., of Quintin Lodge, Leamington, by Mr. Nugent's kindness photographed specially for the above engraving.

vandalism that destroyed the old Cathedral and pulled down the venerable Round Tower was not likely to spare the effigies of an Anglo-Norman Knight or the epitaph of an Ulster Baron; but no known traces of any important family-monument of the SAVAGES are to be found either in Lecale or in the Ards.

On the demolition of the Cathedral and Round Tower (at the dictation, it is said, of the Lord Downshire of the day), in 1795 (?), the bones of the SAVAGES OF PORTAFERRY buried there were removed by the heads of the Family then living to the ancient church of Templecraney, close to the front-entrance of Portaferry demesne, and were there deposited in a family-vault specially built for their reception.[1] At Templecraney, in the old churchyard of Ballytrustan, and in the new churchyard of Ballyphilip, are to be found such monuments as are now known to exist of the SAVAGES OF PORTAFERRY.

We copy some of the principal epitaphs.

At Templecraney, on a large mural slab, inserted in the inner side of the chancel-wall of the now ruined and ivy-grown Church, over the family-vault, is the following inscription:—

<blockquote>
Vnder neath
Lyeth ye bodies of Pat^(k)
Savage of Portferry Esqr who
Departed the life the 13 day of
Septr 1724 aged 82 years ∞
& of his four sons c^d viz of Pat^k
Savage eldest son who dyed
ye 13 of June 1712 aged 25 of
Fran Savage Esqr Third son w
ho Dyed ye 8 of Janu 1722 Aged
25 ∞ of Row^d Savage Esqr Seco
nd son who Dyed May ye 23 ∞
1725 Aged 35 years of Marg^t
Savage Alias Price wife to s^d ∞
Row^d who Dyed April 1721 aged
27 of Dorcas Daugh^r to s^d Row^d
& Marg^t & of Edward Savage
Esqr who Dyed March ye 18
1725 Aged 23 years.
</blockquote>

At Ballytrustan, in the graveyard, outside the old ruined chancel of the Church, on an altar-shaped tomb, is the following:—

---

[1] In 1846, when this vault was opened for the interment of the late Mr. Andrew (Savage) Nugent, of Portaferry, there was within it a great heap of bones (some very large) and many skulls. Evidently the box which had contained them had rotted, and fallen to pieces.

Erected
By her children to the memory of their beloved
Mother Catherine Ann Savage of Portaferry
who departed this life 21st May 1837 aged 69
Thomas Savage her husband who departed this
Life 30th May 1803 aged 48
Rosalinda Savage her daughter who departed
This Life 11th Aug. 1817 aged 25
Roland Savage who departed this Life 21 April
1821 (?), aged 65 Brother of Thos. Savage
Patrick Thomas Savage her son who departed
this life 11th (?) December 1853 aged 59 years
Jane Savage her daughter who departed this
Life 17th June 1855 aged 64 years
Lucy Savage her daughter who departed this
Life the 8th May 1856 aged 65 years.

To the right of the foregoing, on a recumbent slab (in capital letters), is the following:—

Here lyeth the Dr
Body of M[rs] Catherine
Sauage wife to M[r] Thomas
Savage of Barr Hal[l]. who
Departed this life April the
20th 1759 aged 36 years.
As also lyeth Here the
Bodys of his Daughter
Cath. & her son Edward who
Departed this life all young.

Above the foregoing, on a marble tablet set in the wall (outside) of the ruined Chancel, is this very odd epitaph:—

Beneath the tomb lyeth y[e] Dr. Body of
Mrs. Cath. Sauage who was indowed
with all the virtues goodness goodhumour
& sweetness that ever woman was
The best of wives & a most
tender & affet[e] Mother ready on
all occasions to relieve y[e] distressed
who has now left Hir Dr Husban.
    To morn
& His Mighty loss deplor
She that was once so Dr to
    Him is now no more
O Death before you kill another
Fair & wise & good as she
Time shall throw a dart at thee.[1]

---

[1] Deciphered and copied with the kind assistance of Mr. James Shanks, of Ballyfoundra, Aug., 1886. The last three lines will be recognised as an imperfect quotation from Ben Jonson's well-known *Epitaph on the Countess of Pembroke*.

SAVAGE OF PORTAFERRY (continued)—RELICS, EPITAPHS, &c.

The Savages of Barr Hall branched from the SAVAGES OF PORTAFERRY, but we have not been able to ascertain at what time. A small house known as "Bar Hall" still stands at the head of Bar Hall Bay, the most southern of the inlets of the Ards. {THE SAVAGES OF BARR HALL.}

In the graveyard of Ballyphilip Church, Portaferry, facing the roadway, on an erect marble tombstone, in a railed-in enclosure, is the following inscription :— {EPITAPH AT BALLYPHILIP.}

In
Loving Memory
of the
Honourable Catherine Nugent
Born 19th June, 1802
Died 27th February, 1882.
Looking unto Jesus.
Erected by her children.

The Arms of SAVAGE OF PORTAFERRY, with those of Montgomery, were, as William Montgomery states, set in the walls of the Old Castle of Portaferry early in the seventeenth century. Mr. Arthur Nugent informs us that the stone with these Arms was subsequently removed by his own father, on the decay of the ancient Castle and the enlargement of Portaferry House (now the seat of the PORTAFERRY family), and was placed in the wall at the back of the House, facing the kitchen-yard, and under the staircase window, but unfortunately so high up as not to be well seen except with the aid of a very long ladder. {ARMS OF SAVAGE AND MONTGOMERY AT PORTAFERRY HOUSE.}

The Arms of NUGENT are emblazoned in the new Cathedral of Downpatrick; but those of SAVAGE have been, up to the present time, unaccountably omitted. {ARMS OF NUGENT IN DOWN CATHEDRAL.}

Ruins of Templecraney Church, later burial-place of the SAVAGES OF PORTAFERRY, with part of the pleasure-grounds of PORTAFERRY HOUSE.

CHAPTER XI.

PROSPECT BRANCH OF THE SAVAGES OF THE ARDS.

SAVAGE OF PROSPECT.

HENRY SAVAGE E.-Q., OF PROS- PECT, born A.D. 1743; died A.D. 1805.

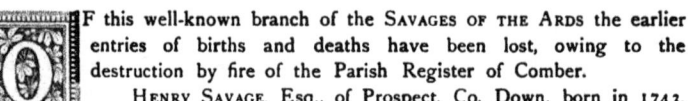

OF this well-known branch of the SAVAGES OF THE ARDS the earlier entries of births and deaths have been lost, owing to the destruction by fire of the Parish Register of Comber.

HENRY SAVAGE, Esq., of Prospect, Co. Down, born in 1743, was a Lieutenant in the Saintfield Regiment of Volunteers (James Stevenson's Regt.) which marched with the other Volunteer Regiments to oppose the French in February, 1760. He had landed property in the Ards and some near Comber. He entailed his property of Ballylone on the eldest son of his third son, Henry Savage, afterwards of Ardglass. An entry in his note-book, in 1798, states "this day the rebels demanded arms of me." He married Grace, granddaughter of the Hon. Susan Gillespie, who was wife of Hugh Gillespie, Esq., of Cherry Vale, Co. Down, and daughter of the third Baron Rollo, and aunt of the distinguished General, Sir Robert

Rollo Gillespie, K.C.B., whose statue stands in the Square of Comber;[1] and by her had issue, HENRY SAVAGE, ESQ., OF PROSPECT, born A.D. 1743; died A.D. 1805.

I. PATRICK, of whom presently as representative of the SAVAGES OF PROSPECT.

II. George, Captain 12th Light Dragoons, who married Anna Sophia, daughter of the late Col. Halcott, and had issue,

 1. Anna, married to the late Col. Robert-Clifford Lloyd, 68th Light Infantry, son of the Rev. Bartholomew Lloyd, Provost of Trinity College, Dublin, and has had issue,

  Charles-Dalton-Clifford Lloyd, Barrister-at-Law, Lieut.-Governor of the Mauritius, born on the 15th of Jan., 1847. Mr. Clifford Lloyd (who distinguished himself by his firmness and ability in connection with the troubles in Ireland consequent upon the Land League agitation) married Isabella Sabine, daughter of the late Captain Sabine Browne, and granddaughter of the late Admiral Sir John Gordon Bremer, K.C.B.

  Humphrey-Clifford Lloyd, born on the 22nd of June, 1848.

---

[1] FAMILY OF GILLESPIE.—The following is extracted from a printed sketch of the life of Major-Gen. Sir Robert Rollo Gillespie, by Percy Boyd, dedicated to the Marquis of Londonderry, G.C.B.:—

"The family of General Gillespie was of Scottish extraction. His grandfather, Hugh Gillespie, or Gilleaspick, one of the Lochow branch of the Campbell family, being involved in the troubles of 1715, removed from Scotland at about that period, and, taking refuge on the opposite coast of Ireland, settled at Cherry Vale, a retired situation on an arm of Lough Cone, a few miles from Comber, then the property of Montgomery, Earl of Mount Alexander. To this retreat he was followed by his brother-in-law, Robert, Lord Rollo, who, with his relative Lord Balfour of Burleigh, Lord Lovat, and some other Jacobites, sojourned there during part of the ensuing winter. Mr. Gillespie was married to the Honourable Susan Rollo, daughter of Andrew, third Lord Rollo, by the Honourable Margaret Balfour, daughter of James, Lord Burleigh. The progenitor of the Rollo family, according to Douglas, was a near relative of the Duke of Normandy, afterwards William the Conqueror, with whom he came to England, and settled in Scotland in 1130 [?], in the reign of King David the First. To him and other members of his family were granted the lands of Duncruit and the barony of Bannockburn. The Rollo family afterwards became connected by marriage with some of the noblest families in Scotland, those of Montrose, Strathallen, and Argyle. Robert, the eldest son of Hugh Gillespie, was married to Miss Baillie, of Innishargie, in the County of Down, a lady of highly respectable family; and their only child, the future General, was born at Comber, on the 21st of January, 1766, in that house still in the possession of his family."

After a brilliant and striking career, Sir Rollo Gillespie was killed at the assault on the fortress of Kalunga, in India, Oct., 1814, his last words being, "One shot more for the honour of Down!" His monument in the square of Comber consists of a handsome pedestal surmounted with a statue, erected by his countrymen and companions in 1845. There is also a statue of him in St. Paul's Cathedral, London, which was voted by both Houses of Parliament.

HENRY SAVAGE,
ESQ., OF PROS-
PECT; born A.D.
1743; died A.D.
1805.

Arthur-Clifford Lloyd, Major 45th, Sherwood Foresters. Wilford-Neville Lloyd, Captain Royal Artillery, born on the 15th of Sept., 1855. Served with distinction through the Zulu Campaign, having been mentioned in several despatches. Was present at the Battle of El Teb; and was entrusted with the honour of carrying home and presenting to her Majesty the standard of the Mahdi captured at Tokar.[1]

Grace Lloyd, married to Maurice Cross, Esq., late Judge of the Small Cause Court, Madras, India.

Lily Lloyd, married to Captain Ferdinand Beauclerk, R.E., of Ardglass Castle, Co. Down.[2]

III. Henry, of Ardglass, born in 1792; married, in 1841, Jane, daughter of William Lawley, Esq., of Leegomery, Shropshire, and died in 1860, having had issue,

---

[1] "TROPHY FROM TOKAR.—Lieutenant Wilford Lloyd, of the I Battery of the B Brigade Royal Horse Artillery, left Aldershot on Wednesday morning for Windsor Castle, in order to present the Mahdi's standard, captured by the British troops at the relief of Tokar, to the Queen. Lieutenant Wilford Lloyd, who is a relative of Mr. Clifford Lloyd, received permission to accompany the army in the Soudan, and on his return home, towards the expiration of his leave, was commissioned by General Graham to convey the trophy to her Majesty. The gallant officer, who has already seen considerable active service, left Trinkitat on the 5th of March, travelling viâ Cairo and Alexandria to Venice (where he was detained in quarantine five days), and thence to London, where he arrived on Sunday. Lieutenant Lloyd, wearing the blue and gold uniform of his corps, arrived at Windsor about noon, and immediately proceeded with the flag to the palace. The standard, which is about two and a-half yards long and two yards wide, is composed of red and yellow silk. On one side is an Arabic inscription to the effect that it was presented by the Mahdi to the Governor of Tokar, and on the other a text from the Koran—'There is no God but God, and Mahomet is his prophet. Every one professes the knowledge of God.' The Queen, accompanied by Princess Beatrice, received Lieutenant Lloyd in the corridor after luncheon. The gallant officer, who was introduced by General Sir H. F. Ponsonby, presented the flag, on behalf of General Graham, to her Majesty, who was greatly interested in the trophy. Lieutenant Lloyd was included in the Queen's dinner party."—*Irish Times*, March 28, 1884.

[2] FAMILY OF BEAUCLERK, OF ARDGLASS CASTLE.—We extract the following from Burke's *Landed Gentry*:—" Aubrey William Beauclerk, Esq., of Ardglass Castle, and St. Leonard's Lodge, *b.* 20 Feb., 1801; was eldest son of Charles-George Beauclerk, Esq., of St. Leonard's Forest, Sussex, by Emily-Charlotte his wife, dau. of William Ogilvie, Esq., and grandson of Topham Beauclerk, Esq. (son of Lord Sydney Beauclerk, Vice-Chamberlain to the King, by Mary his wife, dau. of Thomas Norris, Esq., of Speke, and grandson of Charles, 1st Duke of St. Albans, by Diana, his wife, dau. and heir of Aubrey de Vere, 20th Earl of Oxford). He *m.* 1st., 13 Feb. 1834, Ida, 3d dau. of Sir Charles-Forster Goring, Bart; and 2ndly, 7 Dec., 1840, Rose-Matilda, dau. of Joshua Robinson, Esq., of Kew Green; by the former of whom (who *d.* 23 April, 1839), he had issue, AUBREY DE VERE, now of Ardglass; Ida, *d.* young; Diana-Arabella, *d.* 1855; and Augusta, *m.* 4 Jan. 1866, to Thomas E. Howe, Esq.; and by the latter he had two daus., Louisa-Catherine and Isabella-Julia, *m.* 19 Oct. 1867, to George Palatiano, Esq., M.D. Major Beauclerk, formerly M P. for East Surrey, *d.* 1 Feb. 1854."

1. Henry-Kyle-Gillespie, Lieut. 15th Regt., born in 1843; died, in China, in 1878.
2. William-Lawley, who died in 1860, aged 14 years.
3. George-Robert-Rollo, Captain Royal Engineers; served in Afghanistan; married Caroline Eleonore Augusta, daughter of the late LIEUT.-GEN. HENRY JOHN SAVAGE, of BALLYGALGET (ROCK SAVAGE), Co. Down, Col. Commandant Royal Engineers (representative of the SAVAGES OF ARDKEEN— *Vide ante*, p. 241), and has issue,
   Lilly.
   Kathleen.
   1. Mary.

I. Jane, married to James Nixon, Esq., of Prospect, Co. Fermanagh, and had issue,
1. A son, who died in infancy.
2. A son, who died in infancy.
3. James Nixon.
4. William Nixon.
1. Grace Nixon, married to John Dawson, Esq.
2. Margaret Nixon, married to W. Murdock, Esq.
3. Eleanor Nixon.
4. Jane Nixon, died unmarried.
5. Padina Nixon, died unmarried.
6. Georgina Nixon, married to the Rev. R. Wolesley.
7. Martha Nixon, who died unmarried.
8. Ann Nixon, who died unmarried.
9. Henrietta Nixon, who died unmarried.

II. Grace, married to Thomas Cottnam, Esq., of Minore, Co. Monaghan, and died without issue.

III. Henrietta-Eliza, married to William Johnston, Esq., of Brookvale, Co. Monaghan, and had issue,
1. William-Henry Johnston.
1. Jane Johnston.
2. Grace Johnston; and three other Daughters.

MR. HENRY SAVAGE, of PROSPECT, died in 1805. He was succeeded by his son, PATRICK SAVAGE, Esq. (who inherited property near Comber), born in 1784; gazetted to a Cornetcy 9th Light Dragoons, 1801; Major 24th Light Dragoons, 1814; Lieut.-Col. in the Army, 27th May, 1825; sold his commission in 1836,

Lt.-Col. Patrick Savage, born in A.D. 1784.

having been brought into the 13th Light Dragoons as a Major from half-pay of the disbanded 24th Light Dragoons, for that purpose. In 1807 he served with the British army in the assault on Buenos Ayres. On his voyage homeward he was shipwrecked in Mount's Bay, and was thanked by the War Office for his courage in saving life on that occasion. LIEUT.-COLONEL SAVAGE served throughout the Peninsular War, and was present in many engagements with the enemy, and was wounded in an action near Molinas. In 1817, while in India, he was with the 24th Light Dragoons in the Punjaub campaign under the Marquis of Hastings, and was present in many engagements. Lieut.-Colonel Savage married, May, 1828, Charlotte, daughter of Edward Miller, Esq., of Ballycastle, Co. Antrim, by Mary, daughter of Charles O'Neill, Esq. (of the Feevagh branch of the O'Neills of Clannaboy), and had issue,

  I. HENRY, of whom presently as representative of the SAVAGES OF PROSPECT.

  II. George, Major 37th Regt.; married, in 1861, Isabella, daughter of —— Hamilton, Esq., and died in 1869 at head-quarters of his Regt. in India, having had issue,

    1. WILLIAM HENRY SAVAGE, of whom presently as representative of the SAVAGES OF PROSPECT.

    1. Charlotte.

  III. Alexander-Edward, born in 1832; married Fanny, daughter of —— Macdonald, Esq., and died in 1883, having had issue 13 children.

  IV. Patrick, born in 1836.

  I. Grace-Charlotte-Gillespie, born in 1835; married, in 1855, to the Right Honourable John Young, P.C., J.P., D.L., of Galgorm Castle, Co. Antrim, and died 1876, having had issue,

    1. William-Robert Young, born in 1856.
    2. Patrick-Savage Young, born in 1858; married, in 1883, Florence, youngest daughter of Sir Charles Lanyon, of The Abbey, Whitehouse, Co. Antrim.
    3. Henry-George Young, born in 1870.
    4. John-William-Alexander Young, born in 1873.
    5. George-Charles-Gillespie Young, born in 1876.
    1. Annie-Charlotte-Maria Young.
    2. Maria Young.
    3. Grace-Cottnam-Gillespie Young.
    4. Charlotte-Elizabeth-Rose Young.
    5. Rose-Maude Young.

SAVAGE OF PROSPECT.

   6. Jane-Henrietta Young.
   7. Ethel-Margaret Young.
 II. Maria, born in 1831; died in 1858, unmarried.
 III. Charlotte-Jane-Henrietta, born in 1841; married, in 1872, to John Villiers Ryan, Esq.; and died in India, without issue, in 1874.

LIEUT.-COLONEL PATRICK SAVAGE died in Jersey. He was succeeded by his eldest son,

 CAPTAIN HENRY SAVAGE, Royal Engineers, who married Emily, daughter of —— Jollie, Esq., of Quebec, and had issue,
  I. Alice, married to the Vicomte de Coux, of Tarbes, France, and has issue.

CAPTAIN HENRY SAVAGE was succeeded in the representation of the SAVAGES OF PROSPECT in the male line by his nephew,

 WILLIAM-HENRY SAVAGE, Esq., 1st Ghoorkahs, H.M. Indian Army, born in 1862.

Marginalia: LT.-COL. PATRICK SAVAGE, born in A.D. 1784. CAPT. HENRY SAVAGE, R.E. W. H. SAVAGE, ESQ., born in A.D. 1862.

Carrickfergus Castle.

CHAPTER XII.

THE SAVAGE FAMILY AT CARRICKFERGUS.

THE CASTLE OF CARRICKFERGUS.

THE Castle of Carrickfergus, built by the Anglo-Norman conquerors of Ulster about the close of the 12th century, was the stronghold of the North, and long continued to be a fortress of great importance to England and to the Ulster Englishry. Round it grew up a thriving town, which underwent many vicissitudes of fortune, being frequently attacked and several times burnt by the Irish; and the Town became the centre of the County of Carrickfergus.

The Castle, as it appeared in 1567, was thus described by Clarkson in that year:—"The building of the said Castle on the south part is three towers, viz., the gate-house tower in the middle thereof, which is the entry at a drawbridge over a dry moat, and in said tower is a prison and porter-lodge, and over the same a fair lodging, called the Constable's lodging; and in the curtain tower between the gate-house and west tower in the corner, being divers squares, called Cradyfergus, is a fair and comely building, a chapel and divers houses of office on the ground, and above the great chamber and the lord's lodging, all which is now in great decaie as well as the converture,

---

[1] We have drawn most of our information concerning the SAVAGE family in connection with Carrickfergus from M'Skimin's excellent historical account of that interesting town.

being lead, also in timber and glass, and without help and reparation it will soon come to utter ruin."

The Manors conferred by Edward III. upon the famous SIR ROBERT SAVAGE, in 1341, in reward for his services in crushing the rebellious Mandeville, &c., stretched from the Bann and the shores of Lough Neagh to within a comparatively short distance of Carrickfergus walls; and the proximity of their possessions, the prominence of their family, and the martial duties of many of their chiefs as Seneschals and Wardens of the English Marches, brought the SAVAGES frequently into contact with the life, and involved them in the fortunes, of Carrickfergus during several centuries subsequently.

It would be extremely difficult, if not impossible, with the scanty documents at our disposal, to trace the history of the branches of the Family that were most closely identified with the Town and Castle of Carrickfergus; and for the present we must content ourselves with little more than noting those persons of the SAVAGE name who from time to time held the three important offices of Constable of the Castle, Sheriff of Carrickfergus, and Mayor of Carrickfergus; and certain incidents recorded in the chronicles of the Town, with which the SAVAGES were associated.

"The Constable," writes M'Skimin, "was always a person of high rank and trust, as appears from the following account of those that held the office. Until the reign of Edward IV., he was (save in the minority of the heir) always nominated by the Earls of Ulster, the castle being part of their hereditary possessions. Edward, Earl of March and Ulster, son and heir of Richard Plantagenet, Duke of York, ascending the throne by the title of Edward IV., the Earldom of Ulster devolved to the Crown. (Records, Rolls Office, Dublin.)

"Several important privileges were formerly attached to this office. 1568, the Charter of Elizabeth declares that by reason of 'this office' he [the Constable] is a freeman of the Corporation, and the Mayors were always sworn into office before him or his deputy. It also appears from our records that he received the King's share of the customs of this port, and that he and his warders (20 Englishmen) had annually 100 cows grazed free by the Corporation. He had also the best fish out of each fishing-boat that arrived from time to time within our liberties, by the title of the 'tythe of fish.' *(Records of Carrickfergus.)* This fish continued to be taken by the military officer commanding here so late as 1755, when the custom was abolished through the exertions of Henry Ellis, Esq."[1]

---

[1] M'Skimin: *History of Carrickfergus* (1829), p. 160.

A.D. 1327. "In this year John de Athye was appointed Constable, with a salary of 100 marks, at which time a writ was directed to ROBERT SAVAGE, to deliver Bryan Fitz-Henry O'Neill then in his custody, for the security of the peace, to the said Constable, to be kept in this castle till further orders. We have seen already that the Bryan Fitz-Henry O'Neill here alluded to had been a prisoner of SIR ROBERT SAVAGE, first Seneschal of the name of whom we have found mention, and had probably been taken prisoner by SIR ROBERT in one of his many conflicts with the Irish.

A.D. 1340. In this year EDWARD SAVAGE (probably *Edmund* SAVAGE, who was Seneschal of Ulster and Warden of the Marches in the reign of Richard II.) and William Mercer are mentioned as having been Constables of Carrickfergus Castle.

A.D. 1375. The King, Edward III. (as we have already seen), granted in this year to Jeffrey Scolmaistre of Cragfergus and ROBERT SAVAGE the office of Controller of the great as well as the small customs in the ports of Cragfergus, Culrath, and Down, to hold during the King's pleasure.—49 Ed. III., 1375.[1]

A.D. 1389, Oct. 14. Robert Lang was appointed Constable. But in the same year Lang's grant was revoked, and a mandate was sent to Lang, EDMUND SAVAGE, and William Meuve, to deliver the keys to Sir Gilbert de Malshel, nominated to the office. The EDMUND SAVAGE here alluded to was either the above-named Seneschal of Ulster or son of EDMUND the Seneschal of Ulster and Warden of the Marches, who was himself granted the Liberties of Ulster by King Henry V. in 1418. And it would seem that it was in his capacity of Seneschal of Ulster that he was entrusted, along with Lang and Meuve, with the custody of the keys of the principal fortress of the country, for the defence of which he was responsible.

A.D. 1402. "The King (Henry IV.) granted letters to ROBERT SAVAGE and Thomas Sutton, burgesses of the town of Carrickfergus, to send two weys of corn as well for the necessity of the Bishop of Connor as their own. 6 March, 3 Henry IV.[2]

A.D. 1404. In this year, as we have previously described, the SAVAGES slew Corby M'Gilmore in the Church of the Friars Minors at Carrickfergus, in revenge for his treacherous murder of their kinsmen.

A.D. 1550. In this year, in a Map of the town which is preserved, "the town appears protected on the north and west by a broad trench or wet

---

[1] *Patent and Close Rolls.*
[2] *Patent and Close Rolls of the Court of Chancery.*

Cragfergus
A Churche
A Travers
The towne ditche
The rampier
A bridg to bee drawn upp
A Watch house
A ward house
A watch house
The old gatehouse
Stephenson
Dobed
Cindell
wilss
Great Patricke
A Water Mill not in working
A Sluce with a gate for to stop the wrack of sea going by the Mill wheel.
At this place may be made a great pond for water which will Skowre the Haven from wrackes and saye a channell in the same Haven.
Patrick Savage
Barry Vdes
The macleone
[?]
The ground works of the Castell
A Peer to bee made where the foundations almost taller being with it fith [?]

ditch, and without any regular streets, consisting chiefly of a number of castellated mansions called by the names of their respective owners, among which are those of Sendall, Russel, and SAVAGE, families who arrived here with John de Courcy."[1] One of the Castles is named on the map as that of PATRICK SAVAGE. It is pretty evidently the Castle Savage which William Montgomery in 1701 describes as being "now ye Custom house in Carrickfergus." (Montgomery adds, "and MR. SAVAGE of Anacloy now hath freehold tenem^ts in that town.")

The following are the persons of the SAVAGE name who are recorded as having held the offices of Sheriff and Mayor of Carrickfergus :—

A.D. 1571. Patrick Savage, Junior (probably the son of Patrick Savage whose Castle is depicted on the Map of 1550), *Sheriff*.
A.D. 1578. Mychaell Savadge, *Sheriff*.*
A.D. 1581. John Savadge, *Sheriff*.[2]*
A.D. 1585. Mychaell Savadge, *Sheriff*.*
A.D. 1587. John Savadge, *Mayor*.[2]*
A.D. 1590. William Savadge, *Sheriff*.
A.D. 1593. M. Savadge, *Mayor*.*
A.D. 1594. John Savadge, *Mayor*.[2]*
A.D. 1598. John Savadge, *Mayor*.[2]*
A.D. 1604. John Savadge, *Mayor*.[2]*

According to M'Skimin's account, this John Savage is the same John Savage that held the office of Mayor in 1587. M'Skimin tells us that in 1600 he "possessed considerable property in the Middle Division [of Carrickfergus], extending from the Town to the Commons."

A.D. 1621. James Savadge, *Sheriff*.
He died in this year.
A.D. 1622. Robert Savadge, *Sheriff*.
A.D. 1640. Robert Savadge, *Sheriff*.
A.D. 1641. Mychaell Savadge, *Sheriff*.

---

[1] M'Skimin: *History of Carrickfergus*.

[2] M'Skimin states that this John Savage "was a lineal descendant of a person of that name who arrived here with John de Courcy."

* M'Skimin states (p. 33)—"In April [of 1576] we find the following notice in our records. In this same Court *Mykill Savidg*, *John Savidg*, with others, were fyned for neglecting their duty in not answering to assist the Maior, being misused in the streate by Captain Looyd and his soldiours."—It is remarkable that, notwithstanding this, Michael and John Savage were elected to the highest offices in Carrickfergus immediately afterwards, and many times in succession.

A.D. 1643. Patrick Fitzjames Savadge, *Sheriff*. M'Skimin states that it is recorded that "the said Pat. FitzJames Savadge and William Bashforde, by the generall consent of the Maire, Bench and Comons, were chosen and elected Sheriffs for the succeeding year, in regarde they were very diligent this year in their office, and for that they were very expert in these times of distractions."

A.D. 1645. John Savadge, *Sheriff*.

The following extracts throw some light on the property acquired by the SAVAGE family at Carrickfergus :—

A.D. 1595. "1595, 7th July, *Mr. John Savadge* Maior, Richard Thomas and John Dier, Sheriffs, yt was ordered and agreed by the consent of the hole assemblie, that all such persons whiche shoulde hereafter be admitted to the Liberties and Freedome of this corporacon before suche tyme as there weare a devesian made unto the freemen of Suche Landes as by her Majesties Grant and letter appointinge So to be devided amongst them bearinge date at Nonsuche the 15th October, 1594, That then they and everie of them So made free, if they shall clame or desire to have such proportion of landes as other freemen of ther like qualities Should have allotted unto them, that then they are to pay Suche Somes of mony as other the freemen have alredie payd in their Sutts [suits] for obtainynge the Same as the chardges thereof appearethe in Recorde."

Amongst the names of persons to whom what is called the first division of lands was made, with the sum granted by each to defray the expenses of the agents sent to London and Dublin, appear—

Whole Shares.

John Savadg	£2
Mychaell Savadg	£2

Quarter Shares.

George Savadg	10/-
John Savadg, Oge	10/-

In A.D. 1600, amongst the castles and houses in Carrickfergus those of JOHN SAVAGE and JAMES SAVAGE are mentioned.

"In 1603, lands were again allotted to the Corporation," amongst others to the following persons who paid the sums annexed to their names :—

THE SAVAGE FAMILY AT CARRICKFERGUS.

Number of Quarter Shares.

Willm. Savidg	...	...	...	...	2
John Savadg	...	...	...	...	4
George Savadg	...	...	...	...	1
James Savadg	...	...	...	...	2

Savage Property at Carrickfergus.

A.D. 1606. "Oct. 28th, 1606, it was agreed that the lands west of Woodburn river, below the Knockagh, should be divided; for which purpose they were laid out into ten lots, eight of which contained four alderman's whole shares, each; the others three like shares each. The great lots varied from 66 to 68 perches in breadth, extending from the sea to the base of the Knockagh hill." Amongst other names appear the following:—

Number of Quarter Shares.

Sir Arthur Chichester	...	...	...	4	
John Savadg	...	...	...	...	4	Landes
George Savadg	...	...	...	1	above
William Savadg	...	...	...	2	Woodburn
James Savadg	...	...	...	...	2	Landes.

In 1666, and again in 1672, we find a James Savage discharging the humble duties of "sword-bearer" at Carrickfergus; but, as far as we have been able to discover, the name SAVAGE does not appear in connection with any important office there subsequent to the year 1643. *James Savage, "Sword-Bearer."*

In 1701 (as we have quoted already), Montgomery informs us that "Mr. Savage of Anacloy now hath freehold tenem[ts] in that town." Anacloy is between Crossgar and Downpatrick, in the Co. of Down, which suggests a connection (evidently implied by Montgomery) between Carrickfergus and the main stock of the SAVAGES then flourishing in the Ards. *Mr. Savage of Anacloy, A.D. 1701.*

In M'Skimin's History we find the name in comparatively recent times identified with only very minor offices. "About 1670," he tells us, "some persons of the family" of John Savage, Mayor of Carrickfergus in 1587 (who, according to M'Skimin, "was a lineal descendant of a person of that name who arrived here with John de Courcy"), "removed to Rostrevor. The last male descendant at Carrickfergus was Patrick Savage, shoemaker, who sold off houses in the town and lands in the North-East Division to Henry M'Gee." There are still (1886) some of the *name* occupying very humble positions in the town. *Humble Descendants.*

APPENDICES

APPENDICES.

APPENDIX I.

SAVAGE AND VERNON.

(From Lysons' *Magna Britannia*, vol. 2, p. 648.)

```
Richard de Vernon
of Shipbrooke, Co.
Chester, one of Hugh ─┬─
Lupus's Barons        │
    │
    2                 │
    │                 │
    ├─────────────────┤
    │                 │
    3                 │
    │                 │
    ├─────────────────┤
    │                 │
    4                 │
                      │
┌─────────┬───────────┴──────────────────────────┐
2d son    Warin Vernon          Anda, dau. and co-heir of
Ralph, Rector of   5th Baron ──┬── the Baron of Wichmalbank
Hanwell,                       │
   had                         │
an illegitimate son  Warin S. P.    Margaret    Anda           Rose
   Sir Ralph = Mary daur                        married Wm     married
He lived to the │ of Lord Dacre                 Stafford       John Littlebury (?)
age of 150
   │
   │
Sir Ralph Vernon ─── Agnes daur              Sir Richard ─── ...
                   of Richard                slain at the
                   Damory 1325               battle of Shrewsbury
                   no male issue
         ▼
              Sir Richard ── ...          Sir Ralph ── ...
              Vernon who died             Vernon of
              in France                   Shipbrooke
                    │                         │
                    │         Ralph Vernon ── ...
An only daughter
married to Sir Ralph Folshurst
                        Dorothy        =   Sir John Savage K.G.
                        only child and heir  who was slain at the siege of Boulogne, 1492.
                        In consequence of this marriage the family of Savage inherited Shipbrooke.
```

APPENDIX II.

SAVAGE AND DRAYCOTE.

**DRAYCOTE OF PAGNESLEY—
TOTMONSLOW HUNDRED.**

Arms—Or fretty Gules, on a canton argent [Azure?] a cross patonce Azure [Argent?].
Crest—A dragon's head erased.

Sir Roger Draycote of Pagnesley, Co. Stafford, Kt. 4 E. 4. = Agnes, daur of Sir Roger Aston, Kt., of Tixall, Co. Stafford.

Roger Draycote, Esqr = Catherine, daut of John Savage, of Maxfield, Co. Chester, Esq.
18 E. 4.

—*Heraldic Visn of Staff.*, Part 2, Vol. 2, Page iii.

APPENDIX III.

SAVAGE AND SOMERSET.

"SOMERSET, EARL AND MARQUESE OF WORCESTER.

"HAVING, in my discourse of Henry, Duke of Somerset (who lost his life in 3 E. 4), sufficiently manifested that he left no other issue than one natural son called Charles, begotten on Joan Hill, his Paramour, I shall now take notice in what I have seen memorable of the same Charles and his descendents. This Charles being a person of great parts, arrived to very high advancements in those times wherein he lived as well in Honour as Estate: for in the 1st of Hen. 7th, being then a Kt. so much did that prudent Prince discern of his abilities, that he constituted him one of his Privy Council, and in 2d of Heny 7th made him Constable of Helmsley Castle, in com. Ebor. In 3 Heny 7th he was Admiral of the King's Fleet, then at sea. So likewise in 4th Heny 7th, being also first Vice Chamberlain, and after Chamberlain of the King's Household. Which eminent favours were doubtless in the chief furtherances to his marriage with Elizabeth, the sole daughter and Heir to William Herbert, Earl of Huntington, by reason whereof he bore the title of Lord Herbert: and in 19 Heny 7th was by the same appelation made constable of Payne Castle with the territory of Elwell in Wales. In 20 Heny 7th he was made Constable of Montgomery Castle, and in 1st Henry 8th he had summonds to those Parliaments then held, by the name of Charles Somerset de Herbert, Chevalier. Being then Lord Chamberlain to King Heny 7th, he continued in the same office to King Heny the 8th, upon his coming to the Crown, and was made choice for one of his Privy Council, in the 1st year of his reign, as also Constable of Montgomeryshire Castle. The same year likewise he had a grant of the Constableship of the Castle of Ruthyn in North Wales, being also made Sheriff of Glamorganshire, and Governor of the Castles of Caerdiffe, Cowbridge, and Nethe. In 2d Heny 8th he was again made Constable of Pain Castle. In 5 Heny 8th, upon the King's expedition into France, which was in June, He followed him thither with 6,000 foote, where he had the command of that part of the Army which sat down on the east side Therouene, upon the siege of that city, whence the first approaches were made thereto: and gave a great defeat to a strong party of the Enemy which sallied out on that side where he lay. Whereupon the French reported him slain by mistake, the Master of the Ordinance being then killed, by a Bullet shot the first night into his Tent. Therouene being in a short time gained, and the English Army marching to Tournay, he lead the rear thereoff thither, and encamped on the West part of the Town. Meriting therefor so highly for these his heroick adventures, and exemplary vallour, upon the 1st of Feby next ensuing he was made Lord Chamberlain of the King's Household for life, and by reason of his noble descent and near alliance to the King in blood, which the patent itself doeth impart, was upon the day following, it being the Festival of the Blessed Virgin's Purification, advanced to the dignity of an Earl by the Title of Earl of Worcester, his solemn creation being performed at the

APPENDIX III. 349

Archbishop's Palace at Lambeth the same day. After which, before that end of the year, he attended the Lady Mary, the King's Sister, upon her Coronation at St. Dennis in France by the King's special appointment. And in 9th Heny 8th, upon that overture made by the Emperour Maximilian, for rendering his Imperial dignity to King Henry, and that he would come in person into England, was sent with Dr. Cuthbert Tunstall unto him into Flanders. In 10th Henry 8th he was imployed into France with the Bishop of Ely for confirming the Articles of Peace betwixt King Henry and the French. Whereupon the city of Tourney was rendered, and the Princess Mary, the King's daughter, betrothed to the Dolphin. At the taking of which City, having formerly been, he would not suffer the Marshall de Chastillon to enter with Banners displayed, because it was not gained by conquest. In 12th Henry 8, by agreement made by King Henry and Francis the First of France, for an interview betwixt Guisnes and Ardres, he was joined with Monsieur de Castellon to lay out the ground for those Triumphs, which were then to be made there. And in 13th Henry 8th imployed together with the Bishop of Ely to mediate a Peace betwixt the Emperor and the King of France. Before the end of which year, upon the attainder of the Duke of Buckingham, he obtained a Grant in general tail of the Manor of Ealding in Kent, with the advowson of the Church, then in the Crown, by reason thereoff. To his first wife he married Elizath, daur and Heir of William, Earl of Huntington, as hath been already observed, and by her had Henry, his son and successor, as also a daur called Elizabeth, married to Sir John Savage, Knight. To his second wife Elizabeth, daughter of Thomas Lord la Warr, by whom he had issue Sir Charles Somerset, Knt, and Mary, a daur, married to Lord Grey de Wilton. And to his third wife Eleanore, daur of Edward, Lord Dudley, but by her he had no issue. By his Testament dated 21st Martii, 1524, 15 Henry 8th, bearing then the title of the Earl of Worcester, Lord Herbert Gower and Chepstowe, and Chamberlain to the King, being then Kt of the Moste Noble Order of the Garter. He bequeathed his body to be buried in the Church of our Lady and St. George, within the Castle of Windsor, by his 1st Wife in his Chapel of our Ladie, where his Tomb was then made by the consent and agreement of the Dean and Canons of the same place, at such time as he founded a Priest to say Masses daily and perpetually there, and to pray to God for his Soul, and for the soul of Elizabeth his first Wife, His own, her friends' and Mother's Souls, and all other. Appointing that in case he should depart this life in London, Railoo [?], or near the River Thames, that his body should be brought by water to the said Chh of Windsor, as possibly as might be without pomp or great charge of torches, herse, wax, or great Dinner, or clothing, but only for them that must needs be had, that is to say, twenty Men of his own servants, to bear every Man a Torch, and to have clothing, and the Bier and the Herse to be covered with black Cloth, and his body under the same with a White Cross upon it. Also that no Month's-minde dinner should be kept for him, but only an obit of one hundred Masses to be said for him at Windsor or other places where his Executors should appoint. He also bequeathed to Eleanore his wife six hundred marks in plate. To his son Henry all his Harneys, Artillery, and Habilaments of war, except the Harneys for his own body, which he gave to his son George. And his said son Henry All his robes of Estate and Robes of Parliament, with his Mantle, Gown, and Hood of the Order of the Garter, and departing this life 17 Henry 8th, was buried in the before specified Chapel, where his Monument yet remaineth."

—See *The Baronage of England*, by William Dugdale, Tome 2d, page 293.

APPENDIX IV.

FUNERAL OF SIR JOHN SAVAGE, OF CLIFTON, KNT.
OBIIT JAN. 24, 1597–98.

From the *Macclesfield Parish Magazine*, September, 1887.

"TRANSCRIPT OF THE PARISH REGISTERS—*continued*.

"THE record of the burial of Sir John Savage (January 24, 1597-98) appeared in the portion of Registers printed last month. The following interesting and detailed account of the funeral is preserved in Harleian MS., 2, 129. We are enabled to print it here by the kindness of Mr. R. J. W. Davison, who has transcribed the original.

"'The order of the funerals of diver's p'sons in Cheshier Lancashier and North Wales by Randle Holme of Chester deputy to the office of Armes and his sonne Randle Holme Junr.

- - - Smyth S^r W^m brereton's man	A Trompiter wth a banner of his Armes on Silke Soundinge a dolefull note.		Then his gentlemen retayners in Clokes 2 & 2 in like maner wth handkerchafes at the ceremony passinge by dowinge duty with lowe curtesie.
[*The margin has been cut into in binding, and the Christian names or parts of them are sometimes wanting.*]		- - 1 Dutton - - th Aston	
Jo. Bepworth Rand barlow	Tow yeomen in black cotes for Conductors wth black staves in on hand and a white Handkerchafe in the other; theis are to kisse & p'sent their staves to the heyre as no longer officers		Then his Guydon in regard he was leiftenant borne by a gent' in a cloke & his asistant somtyme traylinge it wth his cotes & mottoe to shew he had byn a captaine & leader as well of horse as foote.
	So many poore in gownes as he was yeares of Age wch was 74; but there was 80 in all to goe 2 and 2 orderly to gether in eich of their hands a pencell (?) with his creast or other crestes: some with lions paw for Savage others the unicorn head on for daniers some wth beares head for bostock some wth boares head for Vernon on the other side the year of our Lord wch pencells (?) are to be delivered to the heyre and after are to be placed about the hearse in the chappell where the body lyeth.	Alex. Cotes Rich Brereton Jo. Powell	Then his word or motto carried by a gent' in a black cloke whereby in word he was reputed & knowne before, to be offred. Then his spurs guilt also carried by a gent': to shew the (*sic*) were wone in service for his prince & cuntrey to be offred. Then his gauntlets silvered carried also by a gent' in a cloke shewing by stroke of hand he did defend his knighthood his prince and cuntrey to be offred.
- Robinson	Then an other Trumpiter wth a ban'er as before dolfully soundinge.	Tho Ridiard Jo Frodsham	Then his crest healme mantle & pendents carried by a gent' also. Whereby he was knowne in feild when his face was uncovered and showen, wth his assistant to carry, to be offred.
Ed Williams - ra Farmer	Then 2 yeomen for Conductors to his servants wth black staves in their hands and handkerchafes in the other.		
- - m Mynsule	Then the Cullers or great Ensigne to be carried and sometyme trayled by an able & tall yeoman in a black cote and at deliveringe of the ceremonies to wrap himselper (? *himselfe*) in it or it be delivered & layd downe: in regard he had served for his prince in defence of his cuntry and for the sayd good service was k^{ted} in the field.	Jo. Ardren	Then his Sword and Targett carried by a gent' in a cloke to show wth the same he fought for his cuntreys good and wth the shield for his owne defence the sword to be drawn at ceremony in p'sentinge & put up again & to be delivered wth a kisse & the target also.
	Then his howsold servants 2 & 2 & other retayners in cotes & clokes to have eich man his handkercheff in his hand some 3 yards betwene each cople all passinge by at the ceremony reverently making obeisance.	Tho. Aston Esqr.	Then his cote of armes carried by a gent' or Esqr of blood: signifyinge that therby in field he was knowne when face and corpes were unshon.
			Then the preacher phisicion & herald
- ik Flecher	Then a square banner of his quarteringes in mettall in representation he was her maities Leiftenant & genrall of his cuntrey to be borne by a tall gent' in a black cloke; for that he dyed Leiftenant of the county Palatine & of the city of Chester.	Leigh Savage Davenport 2 Tatton Rafe Rydiard	Then the maior of Maclesfeild Tho. Leigh Esqr. wth him Tho Savage Rand Davenport of Henbury Wm Davenport of Bromall & Wm Tatton in p'sentation of all the rest. [*In the right hand margin are the words,* "*This should be after.*"] Then his gent' usher bareheaded before the Coch with the body on.

APPENDICES IV. & V.

	Then the coch horses in black wth Armes on—also the body covered wth velvett, on the same.	Wm Heath	Then his great horse covered wth black bagges or cloth to the heeles wth armes thereon on eich side & head led by the gentle groom of his stable but to pass by at the church dore.
	Then the Queristers and Singinge men in order in white serpluses to singe alonge to the grave side & stand there duringe the Sermon and to singe at the Interment of the body.		Escutions on both sides & ends wth both his ladyes Impaled—on either side the body a foot man in black bareheaded, at every end of a coch a ban'er Roule carried by a gent' in clokes . . . . (? *seventh*) Savage & bostock, 8. Savage & Somerset, 9. Savage & Rosse, 10. Savage & Cotgrave (? *Colgrave*), theis are also all to be delivered to the heyre.
	Then the Chaplins and Ministers to make curtesie & goe to the grave side.		
Hawarden . . et Pickring . . br Whitby	The Steward of his howse clarke of kitchen & other officers of houshould in their degrees wth white staves wch at the ceremony they are to surrender in respect of their offices to kisse the stafe & deliver it.		
	Then the gentlemen of blood & alliance 2 & 2 in clokes.	Jo. Savage Esqr.	Then the principall mourner alone wth gowne & hood close.
			Then his children and sonnes in law.
Ed ball A Aston Jo. Payne Jo. Brereton Jo. Massy Jo. Savage	Then his 6 baner roules of descent one after an other that his howse hath mached withall borne by 9 gent' of blood in clokes the first wth Savage & Walkington 2 Savage and Daniers Impaled 3 S^r Jo. Savage & Swynerton 4 Savage and brereton of brereton 5 Savage—& Stanley 6 Savage K^t of Garter that mar' the h. of Sr Rafe Vernon Lo of Shoprale : this to be offred up at the ceremony to the heyre.	Molyneux Cholmley Bulkley Salisbury Worberton Savage	Then his 4 assistants in gownes & hoods not close beinge 4 Knightes Sr Rich Molynex, Sr Hugh Cholmley, Sr Rich Bulkley, Sir Robt Salisbury, Peter Worberton Esq Edw Savage Esqr.
			Then the . . . (?) of his blood in black.
			Then frends and well willers, then tenants & others
Willm Aldersey Alderman	Then An Alderman of Chester in gowne & hood to carry a playne white staff in regard he was maior & leiftenant for the citty of Chester & dyed in his maioralty this is to be by him broken and throne into the grave or vault wth the corpes but *not delivered.		to stand all in order till the body be disloged from the coch then to be borne by gent' of blood in order so entringe the church then a place to be rayled with formes about the corpes duringe the sermon tyme & thos that carry banners to be placed all about the body.
	[* *because this office did not descend to the heir.*] Then an Esqr or K^t wth an other white staffe tipp^d wth gould in regard he was Leiftenant and sheriff of Shier wch also to be broke and throne into the vault wth him to be in a cloke.		the sermon ended the herald to draw up the cheif mourner to the Communion Table and eich with his atchevement to delive it to him. the herald bringing them up, the Trompetts soundinge dolfully all while, then the mourners in their places to make obesance as the (*they*) came, then to goe downe agayn & bury the body the queristers singing a requiem, the body Interred the Tow Trompetts to sownd up aloud & so returne homward as they came.
Tho. Mynsule	Then his penon of Armes wth crest & motto carried by a gent' of blood & offered to the heyre.		
Rog. Harlston	Then a gent' in black to traile his lance made black with a small banner at end to be delivered as of right at ceremony beinge he is redy to supply his fathers magnanimity & virtue.		

"1597. 'This is a coppy of the funerall of Sr John Savage K^t Leiftenant of the County & Citty of Chester buried at Macclesfield 24 January 1597. 40 Q. Eliz. The funerall worke came to lvij^li. x^s. viij^d.'"

APPENDIX V.

SAVAGE MONUMENTS AT MACCLESFIELD.

AS our descriptions of the Savage Monuments at Macclesfield have been drawn from various and rather antiquated sources, and probably contain, therefore, some unavoidable inaccuracies, we think we may take the liberty of quoting the following passages from an account of them by a more recent observer on the spot, Mr. J. A. Finney, author of the excellent and interesting little work, *Notes on the Antiquities of Macclesfield* (Brown & Son, Printers, 50, Mill Street, Macclesfield). We cannot, however, hold either ourselves or the author responsible for certain of the Latin inscriptions, which, in passing from copyist to copyist, have no doubt become considerably less classical than they were even in the originals, and are indeed frequently quite shocking.

"The most interesting monument in St. Michael's Church, Macclesfield, is the one on the south side of the chancel. It is a splendid altar-tomb of alabaster, on which are the recumbent figures of a 'Knight and his Ladye.' The knight's feet rest on a dog. In the lady's head-dress, which is extremely rich, the letters I.H.S. are frequently repeated. The knight's represents Sir John Savage, and the lady's Katherine, his wife, daughter of Thomas, first Lord Stanley, of Knowsley, parents of Archbishop Savage, who founded the adjoining chapel. This Sir John Savage served the office of Mayor of Chester, and died 11 Henry VII., aged 73 years.

"Eight coats of arms (illegible at the time the celebrated Cheshire historian, Ormerod, visited this church, 1818), formerly painted and gilt, at the sides of this interesting tomb, are preserved in the Harl. MSS., taken about 250 years ago, where a rude drawing of the tomb is given.

"I have been at some pains to discover the site this monument occupied previous to the rebuilding of the chancel; but as the old plan of the church is not now to be found, and having good authority for knowing that it formerly stood on the north side of the old church (to which side it was intended to be restored in the new), I, with others interested in the matter, conjecture that the site would be on the left hand as you enter under the tower, and very probably the vault containing their remains would be found about the same place, as the Savage Chapel was not founded until the year 1501.

"The date of this tomb 1495.

"Several monuments which formerly existed in this church previous to the rebuilding have disappeared, for we find the Harl. MS. says:—'Upon the north side of the church kneeleth a man and a woman in these Coates armour, with the inscription under (Arms, Two Coats). The first quarterly, 1, Savage 2, Vernon 3, Bostock 4. Gules a chevron argent, between three martlets of the second (Qy., A. Bagot's Coat). The second coat, lozenge or and gules, a bond ermine (Qy., one for Da La Zouch).' 'Orate, pro bona statu Edmundi Savage, fundatoris hujus fenestræ (qui in eversione Edinburie et Leith miles. Constitutibus [?] fuit anno R. R. Illustrissimi, R. Henrici octavi trigesimo septimo, necnon de villa de Makelesfild suffectus major anno Edwardi sexti primo) et d'næ Marie uxoris [?] et antea nuptæ Rogero Leigh armigero.'

"In a window, the following coat for Distellegh Sable, on a bend gules coticed with two bendlets, dancette of the second, three swans, or quartering sable a bend argent between two owls of the second. There are also various notices of escutcheons of the Savages, and inscriptions too imperfect to be given at length, commemorating Sir John Savage and Katharine, his wife, daughter of Thomas, Lord Stanley, and sister of Thomas, first Earl of Derby, and requesting, in one place, intercession for Thomas, Earl of Derby, and George, Lord Strange, his son. And in another the same for Sir John Savage, knight, and Katharine, his wife, sister of the said Earl, and for Thomas, Archbishop of York. 'Qui istam capellam [?] fund verunt;' apparently alluding to the Savage Chapel.

"Adjoining the church of St. Michael, Macclesfield, on the south side, is the

CHAPEL OF ARCHBISHOP SAVAGE

(now called Earl Rivers' Chapel).

"This is supposed to be the only remains of a college for secular priests, founded in the year 1501 by Thomas Savage, a native of Macclesfield, youngest son of Sir John Savage, the fourth knight of Clifton, and Katharine, sister of Thomas Stanley, Earl of Derby.

"He was bred a Doctor of Laws in the University of Cambridge, and appointed to the See of Rochester in the year 1492, thence translated to London in 1497, and afterwards made Archbishop of York in 1501. He died at York on September 12th, 1507. His body lies buried in the north side of the choir of York Minster, where a fine perpendicular Gothic altar and effigy of the archbishop now marks the spot. Round the top of the floriated arch, over the monument, are inserted at intervals between the foliage the words—

'Doctor—Savage—Rochester—London—York—Thomas Dalby.'

The names of the places refer to the different Sees he occupied. The name—Thomas Dalby—is supposed to refer to the mason who erected the tomb. The heart of Archbishop Savage was interred in the vault of his chapel in Macclesfield, under the site of the altar, which was standing at that time. The remains of this venerable building, even in its present ruinous state, bespeaks its ancient grandeur. This may readily be imagined when we reflect that the large eastern window of five lights, as well as the two smaller windows at each side of the altar recess, were formerly filled with stained glass, which very probably would be removed (Qy. where to?) at the time the monument to Earl Rivers was put up in the place the altar formerly occupied, which we learn was of pure white marble. This, together with the splendid fittings of gold and silver plate, and the beautifully sculptured niches, filled with figures of rare workmanship, and other decorations of this noble chapel, must have formed a *coup d'œil* very imposing, and especially at the stated times when Archbishop Savage would officiate there. Fancy depicts the long line of chorister boys attached to the Free Grammar School, the clergy of the church, with the archbishop following in procession from the sacristy of the Old Church down the middle aisle, and from thence through the doorway (now built up) which formerly communicated with the church, into the Savage Chapel, to celebrate the divine office.

"I have simply given this short description of its former appearance in order that a comparison might be drawn from its present aspect, which is neglected in the extreme, and which a very trifling expense, compared with the interest attached to such venerable remains, would make it a place worthy of a visit of the great, and an ornament to the town, as well as its antiquarian value, and also as a work of art.

"The entrance to this chapel is by the western door, under a turret or tower of three stories. Over the door is a projecting or Oriel window, on the lower part of which are carved the arms of England, placed between those of the See of York, impaling arg. a pale lozengy sable (Savage ancient) on the left hand ; and the coat of Savage quartered with those of Archbishop Savage's successive Sees on the right. The entrance is enriched with various other shields and Gothic ornaments. The oldest monument in the chapel is the one nearest the eastern end on the south side, under a lofty Gothic arch with canopied crockets, and a rich finial. The outer wall is pierced below the arch into a window, consisting of eight trefoil-headed lights, filled with stained glass, under which is an altar-tomb, in niches at the side of which are three male and three female figures, the centre niche being occupied by an armorial shield, supported by angels.

"On the tomb repose two figures, life-size, executed in alabaster. The knight is habited in plate armour, and has a collar of S.S. round his neck, with a jewel dependant. The countenance expresses great age ; his head rests on his helmet and his feet on a dog, which lolls out its tongue as if in blandishment. The lady has a close head-dress and a small lap-dog. Under her head is a pillow supported by angels.

"In 1584 this important inscription was visible on the arch :—

"'Sir Iohn Savage, which was made knight in the wars of —— which died the 25th day of July, in the year MCCCCCXXVIII, and Lady Elizabeth his wife dau. to —— which Lady Elizabeth died the —— day of —— anno domini ——.'

"The transcriber, or Sir Peter Leycester, has committed a slight error in the date of Sir John's death. His widow married Sir John Brereton, of the Shocklach branch, who was beheaded for matters touching Queen Anne, wife of Henry VIII.

"At the west end of the chapel, on the left hand as you enter, is a large mural monument consisting of an altar-tomb, on which are the figures of an armed knight and his lady, and of a female sitting at his feet. Over them is a circular arch, on front of which are two pillars terminating in pyramids. The arch is surmounted with two figures, and the arms and supporters of Savage. Within the arch are three tablets, the first of which is inscribed—

"'Memoriam sacrum viri clarissimi prudentissimi piissimig, D. Joannis Savagi, equitis arati, antiquæ Savagorum gente oriundi, de tota republica Cestriensi et Hamptoniensi optime meriti 5to Decemb. anno 1597, ætat 74, in dolorem consanguineoru et honorum omnium vita functi. Thomas Savagus miles et baronettus, majore filio nepos, in uxorem duxit Elizabetham filia' Thomæ baronis Darcie de Chich, prima' et per eam favore principis indulgentiore existens sorti thalami et affinitati cineri in successione proximus isti honori, pietatis orgo singularis, hoc posuit monumentum.'

"The other tablets contain Latin verses.

"On the opposite side, at the east end, is a large mural monument occupying the recess where the altar formerly stood.

"The erection of this monument caused the blocking up of the large eastern window, and also the two smaller windows on each side of the altar recess.

"Above a large altar-tomb is a recumbent figure in a flowing robe and a large wig, under a canopy supported by four marble Corinthian pillars, over which are the arms and crest of Savage, with the supporters, a falcon billed or, and a unicorn arg. Over the pillars are also the earl's arms, impaled . . . . . . with those of his wives. . . . .

"This tomb was erected in the month of September, 1696.

"Near this monument is an ancient gravestone, ornamented, says Ormerod (1818), with a decorated cross and various carvings, but now almost obliterated. One of the Rosicrucian brethren who visited this church in November, 1869, along with other gentlemen connected with that society, thought he

could trace the likeness of a monk carved on one part of the stone, with his hand pointing upwards.
The inscription round the edge has ages since been obliterated. In the church notes of A.D. 1514,
(Harl. MSS.) is a drawing of this tombstone. The cross there appears bottonie and fixed in the ground,
and has a wreath suspended on a cross beam at its junction with the centre; lower down, a shield
charged with a heart is fixed to it; on the right of it are skulls and cross-bones, and to the left an ecclesiastic standing praying before the cross, and below his feet a book. Round the sides were—

'HIC JACET. CORPVS. dni. GEORGI SAVAGE.
QVI OBIT. DIE. MENSIS. 1552.'

Ormerod adds—'Quy. whether this was not George Savage, rector of Davenham, and father of Bishop
Bonner.'

"Continuing our notice of the monuments in Archbishop Savage's Chapel, Macclesfield, we remark
on the north side two altar-tombs, placed under obtuse gothic arches, which formerly were open to the
church as well as the chapel (these are now partitioned off from the church by a series of glass windows).
On the first is the recumbent alabaster figure of a warrior in plate armour, his head resting on his helmet
and his feet on a dog, a chain being around its neck. The countenance is very aged. In the centre
niche of the tomb below is a coat much defaced impaling Savage ancient.

"On the second is another recumbent alabaster figure of a warrior in plate armour. The face has
a much more youthful expression than the last. His collar is composed of S.S., and the belts for the
sword and dagger are richly studded; his head rests on a helmet with the family crest, and his feet on
a lion.

"In niches at the side of the altar-tomb below are figures of angels supporting blank shields. Over
the arches are mouldings ornamented with crockets and finials, and the arms of Savage placed between
two unicorns' heads. No dates are given, nor any inscription to define which of the Savages they
represent, unless we suppose the elder figure to be that of Sir John Savage, the ninth earl [?] of that name,
who was buried here in 1615, and the other, Sir Thomas, his son, who died in 1635, of whom we find
'Sir Thomas Savage, of Rock Savage, was by the charter of James the First, January 19th, 1624,
appointed First High Steward for life of the borough of Congleton.' He married, in 1602, Elizabeth,
eldest daughter and co-heir of Thomas, Lord Darcy, afterwards Earl Rivers, and by her had issue seven
sons and six daughters. In 1626 he was created Viscount Savage by Charles the First. In 1634 he
filled the office of Chancellor of the Queen's court at Westminster, and died the following year at
London, from whence his remains were removed to Macclesfield, resting on its way to interment in the
Old Chapel then standing on the old bridge in Congleton. We read there was paid for a horse-load of
wine from Chester, carried by Thomas Thorley, 4s. 4d., for the entertainment of the company attending
Lord Savage's corpse, after which it was removed to the burying-place of the family, attached to St.
Michael's Church, Macclesfield, and on the same day (December, 16th, 1635), the Lady Mary Savage,
his mother, was also buried, as appears by the register of St. Michael's Church.

"In the north-east angle is a board to which are affixed some brasses, which have apparently been
removed from the wall below, formerly enclosed within the altar rails. This is shown in the floor of
the chapel here, the space being still left open where they were fixed as an enclosure for the altar.

"I must here notice that this brass anciently represented a MAN and a WOMAN—Roger Legh,
third possessor of Ridge (or what we now call Ridge Hill, Sutton), and Elizabeth, his wife; but the
figure of Roger is removed (Quy. where to). The brass originally represented Roger Legh and
Elizabeth, his wife, with their seven sons and six daughters, soliciting an indulgence from the Pope
(Innocent VIII., it is thought), who is depicted at the altar in the act of granting their petition. Under
the last-mentioned figure is this inscription :—

"'The pardon for saying v' paternosters and 5 aves, and a credo, is XXVI. thousand years
and XXVI. days of pardon.'

"On another brass is the following inscription in Latin :—

"'ORA PRO ANIMABUS ROJER LEGH ET ELIZABETH UXORIS SUAE, QUI QUIDEM ROJERUS OBIT. IIIIth DIE
NOVEMBRIS ANNO DOMINI MVCVI. ELIZABETH VERO OBIT, Vth DIE OCTOBRIS, ANNO DOMINI MCCCCLXXXIX.
QUORUM ANIMABUS PROPITIETUR DEUS.'

"In Burroughs' 'View of Popery,' the engraving is given different to this, showing that there is a
probability of the present brass being only a substitute for the original, as the words, or rather letters,
are placed in a different manner. Thus—

"'ORATE P'A'N' BUS ROJERI LEGH ET ELIZABETH UX' IS SUE, QUI QUID'M ROJERUS OBIT. IIIIth DIE
NOVEMBRIS A'D'NI M'T'VIo ELIZABETH VERO OBIT. Vth DIE OCTOBRIS A'D'NI MCCCCLXXXIX. QUOR A' IAB' P'
PICIETUR D:'

"The label from the man's mouth is defaced, but in Harl. MSS.—
'IN DIE JODICII LIBERA NOS DOMINI.'
"From the woman's:—
' A' DAMPNAC 'S 'E P'PETUA LIBNOS D'NE.'
"Under the figure of the Pope:—
'THE P'DON FOR SAYING V PATOR NOST' V AVE S AND A CRED IS XXVI. THOUSAND YERES AND XXVI. DAYES OF PARDON.'

"There were formerly, even in my recollection, several pieces of ancient armour belonging to the different members of the Savage family in this chapel, which at their deaths would be deposited on their several tombs; but they have gradually—I will not say decayed, but, through not being properly cared for, dwindled down to two small fragments (Qy. where are they gone to?).

. . . .

"The inscriptions on the monuments in this chapel appear in Ormerod's time to have been readable, but the last half century has dealt so hardly with them that they are now in some cases only partially legible, whilst the beautiful tombs themselves are fast going to decay, which if allowed to continue, Macclesfield will lose a gem of antiquity, which it would be difficult to find such another in the whole county of Cheshire. I have no doubt that if ever the walls come to be renovated some choice relics of stonework and other decorations would be brought to light that few are aware of. Let us hope that some of the descendants of this noble family may take an interest in the building, and save this splendid relic of bygone ages from further decay, which I am sure would redound to their honour, and Macclesfield would have cause to rejoice that a monument so interesting, both in its antiquarian and historic value, was saved from further ruin."

To these extracts we may add the following from a letter from the present Vicar of Macclesfield, addressed to Mr. Francis W. Savage, of Springfield, in August, 1887:—

"There is *no lettering whatever* on the head-dress of the effigy of Lady Elizabeth in the Savage Chapel.

"The monument restored by Lord Derby is in the chancel of the Church, and *not* in the Savage Chapel. It is an altar-tomb with two effigies, viz., Sir John Savage and Lady *Catherine* his wife. She was, I believe, the daughter of the 1st Lord Stanley.

"There is some lettering in the meshes of Lady *Catherine's* head-dress, viz., in alternate meshes, 'I.H.S.' and 'K.'"

APPENDIX VI.

SAVAGE AND BABINGTON.

(DERBYSHIRE.)

IN *Materials Illustrative of the History of Henry VII.* we find, dated February 17, 1489, an abstract of a curious and interesting Licence connected with the SAVAGE family and with Derbyshire, but in which the Savages mentioned bear, strange to say, two Christian names (Ralph and Arnold) that seem to identify them with the *Kent* branch.

We cannot at present investigate the origin and history of this Licence; but we quote it not only because it is connected with the SAVAGES in Derbyshire, and for the curious illustration it affords of the religious feeling and habits of the time, but because of the striking coincidence of the linking in it of the two names, BABINGTON and SAVAGE, which, read by the light of subsequent events, is a ghastly association. The Licence is as follows:—

Feb. 17, 1489. "Licence to John Babyngton, Knt., and Ralph Savage, to found a perpetual chantry for one secular chaplain in honour of Christ and the Virgin, at the altar of our Lady, in the parish of St. Helen of North Wynfield, co. Derby, in the diocese of Coventry and Lichfield, to pray for the good estate of the king, the queen, prince Arthur the king's first-born, & the said John Babyngton and Ralph Savage, & for the soul of Arnold Savage; with mortmain licence to receive an annuity of viii. marks for the monastery of the Holy Family, Lenton, co. Notts. Given at Westminster E. pt. 18 Pet. m. 15(17)."

Just a century after this Licence was granted, viz., in 1586, Anthony Babington, a gentleman of Derbyshire, and George Savage, an English gentleman, and an exile, who had served as a soldier in the Spanish army in the Netherlands, zealous Roman Catholics, true to the faith of their forefathers, were hanged, and drawn, and quartered for having conspired with the priest Ballard and others to do away with the great Protestant Queen Elizabeth, and restore to freedom her Catholic captive, Mary, Queen of Scots; a conspiracy remarkable in history as having precipitated the execution of the latter Queen.

APPENDIX VII.

SAVAGE, STANLEY, AND BROOKE.
BROOKE OF HASLER.

Arms—A cross engrailed, per pale sable and gules, in the dexter quarter an annulet of the last.

Sir Richard Stafford of Pipe in co. Suff. = Mawde daur & coheir of Sir Wm Caumville of Clifton, co. Staff.

Mawde daur & heir = Sir Thos Ardern of Elford Co. Staff Kt

Sir John Ardern Kt = Mawde, daur of Pilkington (her name was Margaret)

Mawde daur & heir = Thomas Stanley, 2d son of Sir John Stanley, Kt Lieut of Ireland

*Sir John Stanley of Elford Esq =

| Margorie = Willm Staunton from her the Brookes of Haseler | Anne = Christopher Savage of Elmley Castle | Elizabeth or Maude = Wm Fere or Ferrers |

Christopher Savage son & heir

APPENDIX VIII.

SAVAGE OF CARDINGTON, BEDFORDSHIRE.

John Savage of Whaddon Coun. Bucks, Captaine of a Company = Amy ...

Sarah his 2nd wif relict of Alderman Smythes of London, daur of Mr. Sewestor = Sir Arthur Savage of Cardington Co. Bedfd Knight and owner of the Castell of Reban in the County of Kildare in Ireland obt 13 March Ano 1633 = Jane daur of Thomas Stafford, of Tattenhow in the Coun. Bucks Esq., 1st wife

Jane 1 wife of Francis Ewar of Bucknell Co. Oxon.

Sir Thomas Savage of Cardington & Castell of Rabon son & heir lieuing Ao 1634 = Dowglas dau. of Sir Thomas Snagg of Maston-Morton Co Bedford Knight

John 2
Henry 3
William 4
Edmund 5

Francis Savage only son & heire aged about Ao. 1634 9 years

Dowglas
Thomas Sauage.

—From *The Visitations of Bedfordshire*, Annis Domini 1566, 1582, and 1634. Edited by F. A. Blaydes.

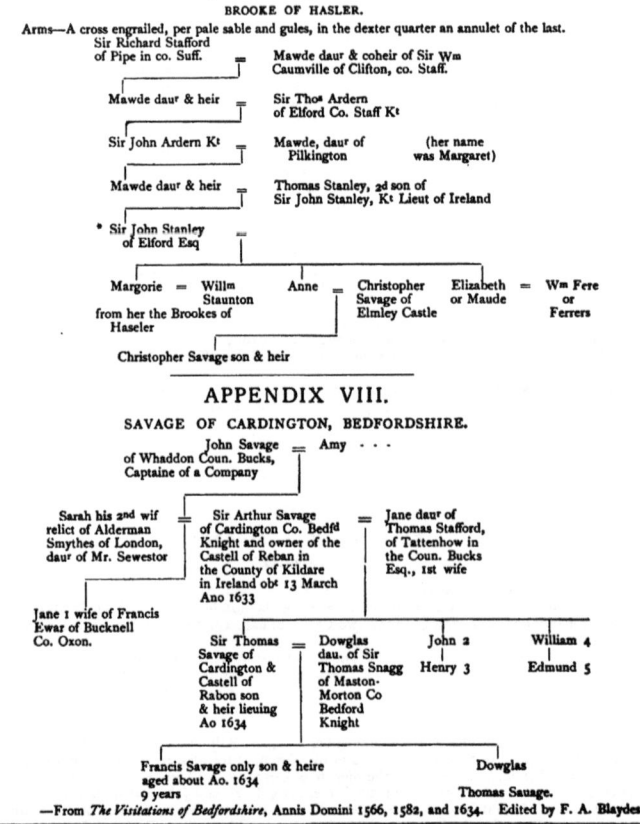

* This John was the last of his race of the Elford line, his only son, John Stanley, having been accidentally killed by a blow from a tennis-ball, when a youth. His post mortem inquest was taken in 1510 1st Hen. VIII., and it was found that the said John Stanley died the 21st of Novr last Past with out heirs male, and that Christopher Savage, son & heir of Anne, one of the daurs and heirs of the said John, Margary daur & heir of Anne, who was daur & heir of Margery, another daur of the said John, and Elisabeth late wife of William Fere (Ferrers), another daur & heir of the said John, where his next heirs. And the said Christopher Savage was aged 12 & the said Margery 7, & the said Elisabeth 40 years old, at the date of the Inquisition. Of these daus & coheirs Anne was wife of Christopher Savage Elmley Castle, co. Worcester, Margery wife of Wm Staunton. Elizm Ferrers, in several Pedigrees, and notably in Visn Warwcks, is called Maude, & made wife of Sir John Ferres, son & heir of Sir Thos Ferrers of Tamworth.—From *The Heraldic Visitations of Staffordshire in 1614 & 1663-64.* Part 2, vol. 2, page 56. 1884.

APPENDIX IX.

SAVAGE OF ELMLEY CASTLE.
GRANT OF ELMLEY CASTLE TO CHRISTOPHER SAVAGE BY HENRY VIII.

THE following original document, in Latin, is in the possession of Francis Walker Savage, Esq., of Springfield :—

"Charter from Sir William Herbert, Knight, on behalf of the Serene and excellent Prince King Henry the VIII. in the XXXVI yere of his Reigne. Grants to Christopher Savage and the heirs of the said Christopher the Manor and Castle of Elmley, with all its Members, in the County of Worcester, &c., &c. Very important Charter, with signature *and pretty seal of Sir William Herbert, Knt.*, dated VI. day of November, in the 36 yere of King Henry VIII. 1544."

APPENDIX X.

THE WORCESTERSHIRE BRANCHES OF THE SAVAGES.
EXTRACTS FROM NASH'S "HISTORY OF WORCESTERSHIRE."

ANN, daughter of William Sheldon of Beoley, esquire, and wife first of Francis Savage of Elmley Castle, and afterwards of Anthony Daston, of Dumbleton, in Gloucestershire, esqrs., was owner of Broadway-great farm, and left it equally between her two sons, Walter and Anthony Savage.

Walter's son inherited his possessions, but Anthony's son sold his to lord-keeper Coventry.

Mr. Savage now enjoys some lands descended to him from Annie, heir of William Sheldon; and an estate at Middle Hill, which formerly belonged to Mr. Taylor, afterwards to Robert Surman, whose daughter sold it to Mr. Dukes, of whom Mr. Savage purchased.

Mr. Savage is building a very handsome house on his estate at Middle Hill.

The chief landholders at this time are Geo.-Will'm, earl of Coventry, sir Edward Winnington, bart., and George Savage, esquire.—vol. 1. p. 144.

By the attainder and death of the unfortunate Edward Plantagenet, earl of Warwick, 15 Henry VII., heir-general of the Beauchamp family, this manor of Little Comberton fell to the crown, and was granted by King Henry VIII. to John Dudley, viscount Lisle, afterwards duke of Northumberland, by whom it was conveyed to George Willoughby. Thomas the son of George Willoughby conveyed it, 9 Eliz., to his relation John Hunks. It afterwards came to Mr. William Savage, and the estate passed from him to others; but the royalty remains with the Savages of Elmley Castle.—vol. 1. p. 273.

NETHERTON, another hamlet of this parish, lying near Elmley Castle, is an antient manor formerly belonging to the priory, now to the dean and chapter of Worcester. 3 Edw. VI. this manor, together with the court leet, court baron, and perquisites of court, etc., was granted by the dean and chapter with licence from the king, to Thomas Savage, esq., in fee farm to him and his heirs for ever, under the yearly rent of 20l. 8s. 2d, the tithe corn, and six quarters of wheat and six of barley.—vol. 1. p. 293.

Mr. Clifton had afterwards an estate in Doverdale, which now belongs to Mr. James Newnham. The Savages of Elmley Castle have for some time been lords of the Manor, although they are not possessed of any land in the parish.—vol. 1. p. 293.

ELDERSFIELD CHURCH.—On another stone, Christopher Savage, gent, and Elinor his wife. He died 1 Feb. 1704, aged 66. She, 2 Jan. 1717, aged 73. And Christopher Savage died 22 Feb. 1681, aged 80, and 10 months.

On the outside wall in the church-yard is a monument in memory of Thomas and Margaret Savage, son and daughter of Henry Savage,[*] gent, by Elizabeth, his wife. He died Aug. 26, aged 43 weeks three days; She, August 30, aged 2 years 54 days, 1698.—vol. 1. p. 374.

Elmley Castle falling into the king's hands upon the attainder of the Earl of Warwick, the castle was destroyed, and the manor 36 Henry VIII. granted by the King to Mr. Christopher Savage, a

---

[*] "Henry Savage, son of Francis Savage, was born of a genteel family at Dobs Hill, in this parish, admitted Commoner of Baliol College 1621, aged 17; proceeded A.B. 1625. In the beginning of the Rebellion he travelled into France with William, Lord Sandys (whose sister Mary he afterwards married); was elected master of Baliol College, May 20, 1660; and the year following was created D.D. After the Restoration he became king's chaplain, prebendary of Gloucester, 1665, and rector of Bladon, near Woodstock; died 2 June, 1672; and was buried in the chapel of Baliol College, next below the steps leading to the altar, being the first that was known to be buried there. (Wood's *Athenæ*, Oxon., vol. ii., 499; and Huddesford's *Life of Anthony Wood*, vol. i., p. 143.) He wrote an imperfect History of his College, intituled "Balioferguus," printed at Oxford, 1668, 4to."

gentleman descended from a worthy family in Cheshire, who since their settlement in this county have been dignified with the highest offices, and remarkable for their hospitality.*

The estate continued in the Savages, till Thomas Savage, Esq., dying without issue male in the year 1742, gave it to his daughters, one of whom married Thomas Coventry, esq., the other William Byrche, LL.D., and Chancellor of Worcester. After some litigation matters were in the year 1743 finally settled by act of parliament, and the estate in fee went to Thomas Byrche, son of Dr. Byrche, by the eldest daughter of Thomas Savage, Esq., of Elmley-castle, which Byrche assumed the name of Savage, and dying in the year 1776, without issue, left his estate to his widow Dorothy, second daughter of Thomas Kynnersley, esq., for life, afterwards to Robert Clavering, eldest son of Robert Clavering, esq., by Jane, youngest sister of the said Thomas Byrche Savage ; on failure of issue by him to Thomas Perrott, son of John Perrott, esq., by Elizabeth, eldest sister of the said Thomas Byrche Savage. On failure of issue by him to Jane, eldest daughter of the said Robert Clavering ; and on failure of issue by her, to Mary, daughter of the said John Perrott ; and on failure of issue by her, to his own right heirs for ever.

The chauntry of Elmley, founded by the pious Guy Beauchamp, earl of Warwick, at the dissolution of religious houses, 37 Henry VIII., was given by the king to Sir Philip Hoby, by the name of the advowson of the church of Elmley, and the advowson of the free chapel of St. Mary, of Elmley, together with the yearly rent of 20l., parcel of the possessions of the chantry and free chapel issuing out of the manor of Wickham, alias Childs-Wickham, and all that manor of Naunton, parcel of the church of that chantry. After Sir Philiph Hoby left this county this chantry became the property of Mr. Langston, and from him came to Mrs. Catherine Savage, daughter of Mr. Richard Daston, a family of great antiquity at Broadway, in the county of Gloucester.

The rectory of Elmley-castle was granted to the Bishop of Worcester, 4 Eliz., being part of the exchange then made.

5 Eliz. it contained 57 families, Nov. 68, according to the return made to Bishop North, at his primary visitation, A.D. 1776. It pays to the land tax at 4s. in the pound, 148l. 6s. 8d.; to the poor in the year 1775, 60l.

In the Parliamentary survey taken about the year 1647, Thomas Savage, esq., is said to hold for three lives of the bishop of Worcester the rectory, and impropriate parsonage of Elmley-castle, and all messuages, lands, tenements, glebe lands, tythes, pensions, oblations, rents, services, and hereditaments in the parish of Elmley and Kersey, at the yearly rent of 20l. ; the improved rent, supposed then to be about 65l.—vol. 1. p. 383.

We are indebted for the following extracts to the kindness of Mr. Richard Savage, of Stratford-upon-Avon—

From Nash's Worcestershire, Vol. I.

P. 255.—*Little Comberton.*—" Little Comberton Manor belonged to Wm Savage (after 9 Eliz^h) and passed from him to others, but the royalty remains with the Savages of Elmley Castle."

P. 273.—*Netherton.*—" 3 Edw. VI. This manor together with the court leet, court barron and perquisites of Court, &c., was granted to the Dean & Chapter with licence from the King to Thos. Savage, Esq., in fee farm to him and his heirs for ever under the yearly rent of £20 - 8 - 2, the tithe corn, & six quarters of wheat & six of barley."

P. 293.—*Doverdale.*—" The Savages of Elmley Castle have for some time been lords of the Manor, although they are not possessed of any lands in the Parish."

P. 374.—*Eldersfield.*—On another stone Xtopher Savage, gent., and Eleanor his wife. He died 1 Feby. 1704, aged 66. She 2nd of Jany., 1717, aged 73. Xtopher Savage died 22 Feb 1681 aged 80 & 10 months. On the outside walls of the Churchyard is a monument in memory of Thomas and Margaret Savage, son & daughter of Henry Savage, gent., by Elizth his wife. He died Augt 26th aged 43 weeks and 3 days. She Augt 30 aged 2 years and 54 days, 1698.

P. 291.—*Dormston Church.*—Anciently appropriated to the Priory of Shedley.

From Nash's Worcestershire, Vol. II.

P. 10.—*Ingleborough.*—In the small south aisle or rather a small chapel built by the Savages of Bag End in Dormston, a canopy supported by black marble pillars under which is a cumbent statue of a man in armour, his sword girt about him, booted and spurred, over him a shield 6 lions rampant sable, crest

---

* " During the civil wars, Thomas Savage, of Elmley-castle, esq., was a zealous Royalist, and compounded for his estate with the Parliament for 1,487l."

a horse's head. As the whole chapel is ready to fall I have thought proper to engrave the monument before it is broken to pieces. The inscription is as follows:—" Here resteth the body of John Savage of Egroke [?] Esq., in hope of a glorious resurrection, who had by his three wives six sones and four daughters. He was in commission of the peace and high sheriff of the county. He departed this life Dec! 22 Anno Dom. 1621. Anno ætatis 52 Beati mortui in Domino."

A small monument Sheldon imp. Savage. "Near to this monument erected by her loving husband for a memorial of her, lieth the body of Frances the wife of John Sheldon of Newberry, gent, who departed this life Jan. 23d. an. Do. 1690. In her life &c."

On the same wall—

" Here lieth the body of Hester Savage, dau! of Robert Savage of Dormston, gent., by Dorothy his wife who departed this life 17 an. Do. 1638, March." Savage impaling 3 bars.

" Here lieth the body of Dorothy the wife of Robert Savage of Bag End in the county of Worcester, gent., and eldest dau of John Stanford of Abbots' Sangford [?] (Salford) in the county of Warwick, Esq., who departed this life Octo. 18 anno 1715. Ætatis 38."

P. 83.—*Lenchwicke.*—" Richard Andrews had lands in Lenchwick called Twyford which he aliened to Richard Savage 34 Henry VIII. and Ralph Savage to Wm Spooner 1 Ed^d VI."

P. 123.—*Malvern.*—" The Priory was granted 36 Henry VIII to Wm Pennocke, who alienated it to John Knotsford, Serjeant-at-arms, whose daughter Ann married William Savage of the family of Rock Savage in the county of Chester, from whom by inheritance it come to Thomas Savage, Esq., of Elmley Castle in this county."

P. 131.—*Jesus Chapel.*—Account of two windows in the Chapel.—John Savage being one of the figures represented bearing a palm branch lifted up to heaven with an inscription. A violent storm blew this window down soon after 1720. An ignorant glazier misplaced the panes.

P. 427.—*Tredington.*—Tidelminton with Admiscote (which I take to be the same as Edmundscote) which (was ?) afterwards the lands of Richard Pacy and by licence of Wm Bishop of Worcester A.D. 1366 alienated to the Monastery of Evesham, in Oxfordshire, and after the dissolution 36 Hen. VIII. granted to Wm Ingram and Anthony Foslord. From Ingram they passed to John Hungerford. From him to Henry Bird 8 Elizth & after to the Savages.

APPENDIX XI.

SAVAGE OF DORMSTON.

We are indebted for the following also to Mr. R. Savage, of Stratford-upon-Avon—

From the Stock and Bradley Registers.

Marr^d 1634, Nov. 6. Robert Savage of Dormston and Dorothy Dyson of this Parish.
Mar^d 1673, Nov. 20. Nicholas Cotterell of Abbot's Morton and Elizth Savage of Bradley.
1680, May 13. Mr. John Sheldone and Mrs. Francis Savage of Aberton.

Do. Church Lench Reg^{rs}.

Marr. 1694, Sept. 4. Mr. Robert Savage of Dormston to Mrs. Dorothy Stanford of Salford.

APPENDIX XII.

WARWICKSHIRE BRANCHES OF THE SAVAGES.

(Kindly contributed by Mr. R. Savage of Stratford-upon-Avon)—

SAVAGES AT STRATFORD-UPON-AVON.

ABSTRACTS of Wills and Notes of Proceedings, various, Courts of Law, &c., connected with the Town of Stratford-upon-Avon, collected by Clarence Hopper, 1866. In Shakespeare's Place Library:—

Miscell. Chancery B.A. 1605–1655.
Underhill & Savage.

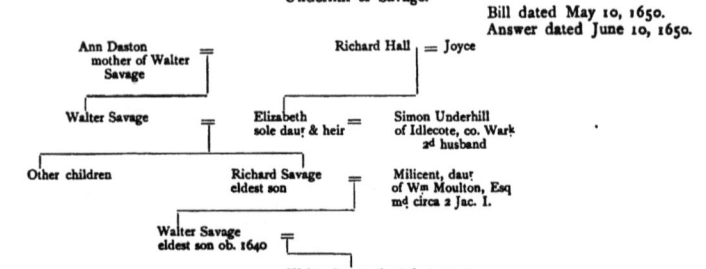

Bill dated May 10, 1650.
Answer dated June 10, 1650.

```
Ann Daston                              Richard Hall = Joyce
mother of Walter =
Savage
   │                                           │
Walter Savage =   Elizabeth        =   Simon Underhill
                  sole daur & heir      of Idlecote, co. Wark
                                        2d husband
   │                   │
Other children    Richard Savage   =   Milicent, daur
                  eldest son            of Wm Moulton, Esq
                       │                md circa 2 Jac. I.
                  Walter Savage
                  eldest son ob. 1640
                       │
              Walter Savage the deft. æt 11 at
              his father's death, & 21 at date of suit.
```

These proceedings show that about 64 years ago Richd Hall, of Idlecote, in right of his wife Joice, was seized, by deed of feoffment, of the parcels of land in Stratford by the name of Square Meadow, West Meadow, and a little meadow adjoining. Underhill bargained with Thomas Nash of Stratford on the 6th of Jan for the sale of the said land, three closes for £340.

Records Guild Accounts (Stratford). Master's Accounts.

1468–69. Fines Thomas Savage, Tachbrooke Malory, and Matilda his wife.
1469–70. Fines John Savage of Kynton, and Alice his wife.

APPENDIX XIII.

SAVAGE OF TETBURY.

EXTRACTS FROM THE PARISH REGISTER OF TETBURY.

(From LEE's *History of Tetbury*.)

1626. July 13, Francis, s. of Francis Savage, gent., bap.
1627. October 4, Mary, d. of Charles Savage, bap.
1628. April 24, Lucy, d. of Francis Savage, bap.
1629. November 5, John, s. of Charles Savage, bap.
1630. August 5, John, s. of Francis Savage, gent., bap.
1633. October 17, William, s. of Francis Savage, bap.
1635. September 10, Ann, d. of Francis Savage, gent., bap.
1636. July 8, Francis Savage, bur.
       December 29, Frances, d. of Francis Savage, bap.
1638. August 10, Frances Savage, bur.
       February 19, Thomas, s. of Francis Savage, bap.

APPENDIX XIII.

1640. April 7, Thomas, s. of Francis Savage, bap.
1649. September 27, M! Anthony Ashfield and M!ˢ Mary Savage, mar.
1650. September 20, Mary, d. of Anthony Ashfield, bap.
1651. December 19, Francis, s. of John Savage, bap.
Jan. 18, M! Joseph Norwent and M!ˢ Mary Savage, mar
1653. April 17, Elizabeth, d. of Joseph Norwent, bap.
November 23, John, s. of John Savage, born.
1655. April 23, Mary, d. of M! William Savage, born.
May 25, Mary, d. of M! William Savage, bur.
1656. October 5, Charles, s. of William Savage, born.
1657. July 31, Elizabeth, d. of John Savage, born.
January 4, Mary, wife of M! Joseph Norwent, bur.
1658. July 28, William, s. of William Savage, born.
1659. September 24, Mary, d. of John Savage, born.
1660. May 22, George, s. of M! William Savage, bap.
August 12, Jane, d. of John Savage, born.
August 12, Ann, d. of John Savage, born.
September 13, M!ˢ Ann Savage, bur.
December 21, Jane, d. of M! John Savage, bap.
1661. November 21, Ann, d. of William Savage, gent.
January 16, Katherine, d. of John Savage, gent., bap.
1662. February 21, Thomas Savage and Elizabeth Hall, mar.
1663. October 8, William, s. of John Savage, gent., bap.
October 15, Richard, s. of William Savage, gent , bap.
October 17, Richard, s. of William Savage, bur.
November 19, Elizabeth, d. of Thomas Savage, bap.
February 2, Elizabeth, wife of M! Charles Savage, bur.
1665. June 22, Charles, s. of John Savage, gent.
January 11, John, s. of Thomas Savage, bap.
1666. July 20, Abington, d. of William Savage, gent., bap.
August 6, Susannah, d. of John Savage, gent., bap.
August 21, Susannah, d. of John Savage, bur.
September 13, Abington, d. of W. Savage, bur.
November 1, Charles, s. of John Savage, gent., bur.
January 1, Mary, wife of William Savage, gent., bur.
1667. December 15, Thomas, s. of Thomas Savage, bap.
1668. April 16, Thomas Savage, bur.
May 1, Jane, d. of M! John Savage, bap.
1669. November 19, Ann, d. of M! John Savage, bap.
1671. March 8, M! Francis Savage, sen., bur.
1672. December 8, Jane, d. of John Savage, gent., bap.
1675. November 25, Elizabeth, d. of John Savage, bap.
1676. April 25, Barbara, d. of M! William Savage, bap.
1678. March 25, Barbara, d. of M! William Savage, bap.
April 1, Margaret, d. of John Savage, bap.
May 7, Katherine, d. of M! William Savage, bap.
1679. December 10, Elizabeth Savage, born.
1681. July 30, Thomas, son of John Savage, bap.
October 3, William Savage, Esq., bur.
1683. September 8, M! John Savage, bur.
1684. January 17th, Hannah, d. of John Savage, bap.
May 6, Mary, d. of M! Francis Savage, bap.
September 4, M! Anthony Savage, bur.
January 1, M! William Savage and M!ˢ Hues, mar.
1686. September 7, Dorothy, d. of M! Francis Savage, bap.
1687. February 15, Katherine, d. of M! Francis Savage, bap.
1689. June 13, Ann, d of Francis Savage, Gent., bap.
March 10, William Savage, Gent., bur.
1690. November 21, Susanna, d. of M! Francis Savage, bap.

1691. May 16, John Savage, bur.
  October 23, William, s. of M! Francis Savage, bap.
1692. February 20, Charles, s. of Francis Savage, bap.
1693. June 26, Sarah, d. of John Savage, bap.
1694. May 7, Walter, s. of Francis Savage, bap.
1696. October 20, Ann, d. of M! Francis Savage, bap.
  January 11, Daniel Johnstone and Jane Savage, mar.
1698. April 9, Charles, s. of Francis Savage, bap.
1702. October 16, Mary, d. of Francis Savage, junr., bap.
  October 17, M! Francis Savage's wife, bur.
1703. March 24, Mary, d. of Widow Savage, bur.
1706. June 13, Nathaniel Body and Katherine Savage, mar.
1708. April 16, Elizabeth, d. of Francis Savage, bap.
  July 1, M! John King and M!̄ Elizabeth Savage, mar.
1709. October 5, John, s. of Thomas Savage, bap.
1711. February 24, Mary, d. of Thomas Savage, bap.
1713. September 14, Eleanor, d. of Francis Savage [?].
  October 6, Widow Savage, bur.
1715. April 28, Francis, s. of Francis Savage, bap.
1716. January 16, Thomas, s. of Thomas Savage, bap.
1719. November 8, William, s. of Thomas Savage, bap.
1722. February 22, Charles, s. of Thomas Savage, bap.
1724. January 19, M!̄ Dorothy Savage, bur.
  July 16, Charles, s. of Thomas Savage, born.
1728. February 26, Thomas, s. of Thomas Savage, bur.
1730. March 1, Michael Manning and Mary Savage, mar.
1735. August 16, Thomas, s. of John Savage, bap.
  November 5, Thomas, s. of John Savage, bur.
1738. March 29, Jane, wife of John Savage, bur.
1740. April 19, M! Francis Savage, bur.
1744. March 24, Elizabeth, d. of John Savage, bap.
1745. December 26, Elizabeth, wife of Charles Savage, bur.
1749. March 18, Sarah, d. of John Savage, bap.
1750. April 16, M! Charles Savage, bur.
1751. January 13, M!̄ Mary Savage, bur.
1753. March 17, Abigail, relict of M! Fr. Savage, bur.
1759. August 27, Thomas Oatridge and Ann Savage, mar.
1762. January 7, John Boulton and Alice Savage, mar.
1763. May 8, Thomas, s. of William Savage, bap.
  August 10, M!̄ Eleanor Savage, bur.
1764. January 20, John Savage and Jane Parker, mar.
1765. January 21, Mary, d. of John Savage, bap.
1766. September 28, William, s. of John Savage, bap.
1767. April 30, Elizabeth, wife of John Savage, bur.
  May 31, John, s. of James Savage, bap.
  July 23, Sarah, wife of M! William Savage, bur.
1769. October 20, Francis Savage, bur.
1770. April 5, Theodore, s. of James Savage, bur.
  August 28, John, s. of James Savage, bap.
1771. April 28, Elizabeth, d. of John Savage, junr., bap.
  August 24, Edward Hill and Elizabeth Savage, mar.
1772. December 22, M! John Savage, bur.
1775. October 19, M! William Savage, bur., aged 84.
1777. Nov. 18, M!̄ Elizabeth Savage, bur, aged 69.
1779. July 26, Thomas Savage and Sarah Hill, mar.
1787. August 6, John Savage, junr., bur.
1790. February 24, Francis, s. of Rev John Savage and Charlotte his wife, bap.
1797. September 29, James Savage, bur.
1803. March 26, Rev. John Savage, Rector of Beverstone, bur.

1815. November 2nd, Mrs Jane Savage, widow, aged 88, bur.
1827. March 20, Jane Savage, bur.
1836. January 26, John Claxton Savage, aged 23, bur.
1842. February 12, Maria Savage, bur.
1845. July 1, John Savage, aged 65, bur.
1846. September 18, Charlotte Savage, aged 92, bur.
1847. August 31, Charlotte Savage, aged 71, bur.
1852. October 7, Sarah Savage, aged 87, bur.

APPENDIX XIV.

DORSETSHIRE BRANCH—SAVAGE OF BLOXWORTH.

Extracts from the Parish Registers. The Registers begin 1579.

BAPTISMS.

Agnes, daughter of George Savage, gent., and Mary ——, 1588.
William, 1590, Richard, 1591, Elizabeth, 1594, George, 1596, Margery, 1597, George, 1600, sons and daughters of ditto.
Giles, son of George Savage, gent., and Mary, 1603. Mary, 1606, Patronil, 1608, Mabel, 1610, daughters of ditto.
Mary, daughter of Will. and Alice Savage, 1612.
Jane, daughter of John Savage, gent., and Mary, 1613.
George, son of Will. Savage, esq., and Joan, 1636.
Mary, daughter of Richard Savage, gent., and Mary, 1663.
William, son of ditto, 1664.
Richard, son of Richard Savage, gent., and Mary ——, 1668.
Page, son of George Savage, esq., and Anne, 1668.
Elizabeth, daughter of Tho. and Eliz. Savage, 1676.
John, son of George Savage, esq., and Anne, 1672.
Galen, son of George Savage, gent., and Anne, 1678.
Mary, daughter of W. Savage, esq., and Grace, 1688.
Will, son of ditto, 1687.

MARRIAGES.

Roger Dalley, gent., and Agnes Savage, 1626.
John Savage and Edith Williams, 1647.
Alexander ..... and Mrs Jone Savage, 1652.
Richard Savage, gent., and Mary Savage, 1662.

BURIALS.

Petronel, wife of Will. Savage, sen., gent., 1602.
William Savage, sen., gent., 1610.
Mary, wife of George Savage, gent., 1638.
William Savage, esq., 1649.
William, son of George Savage, gent., 1654.
Dorothy, daughter of George Savage, esq., of Deane, and Anne, his wife, 1655.
Alice, daughter of George Savage, esq., and Anne ——, 1657.
William Savage, sen., 1660.
John, son of George Savage, esq., 1663.
Mary, wife of Richard Savage, gent., 1668.
George Savage, gent., aged 74, 1677.
Sir George Savage, 1683.
John Savage, rector, 1697.
John, son of Sir George Savage, 1601 (sic).
Mr Jonadab Savage, 1710.

THE RECTORY.

The antient patron was the abbot of Cerne; the modern the Savages and Trenchards, lords of the manor.

PATRONS.	RECTORS.
Richard Savage of Piddle Hynton.	William Savage, inst. 8 May, 1548p.
William Savage.	Austin Green, inst. 4 July, 1558q.
William Savage.	Robert Welstead, inst. 6 Sept., 1597q.
	John Savage occurs 1651.
George & Philippa Trenchard.	John Savage, also rector of Turner's Piddle, inst. 9 June, 1698, on the death of Savageq.

p. First Fruits Office.   q. Dean of Sarum's Register.

APPENDIX XV.

SAVAGE FAMILY IN OXFORDSHIRE.

(Kindly placed at our disposal by Mr. R. Savage, of Stratford)—

From the *Visitation of the County of Oxford*.

1566. William Harvey.
1574. Richard Lee.
1634. John Philpott and Wm Riley.

together with the gatherings of Oxfordshire collected by Richard Lee in 1574.

Savage of Clanfield, p. 157.—Arms, Argent, on a fess azure between three pheons sable three roses or (Savage) impaling gules a chevron erminois between three lions' heads erased or, on a chief barry nebulee argent and purple, a pale azure, charged with a pelican argent, all within a bordure of the third charged with ten hurts (Fox).

To Walter Savage of Clanfield in the hundred of Bampton in comit. Oxoniæ, July 16, Ano 1574.

William Savadge of Tatchbroke, com. Warwick, gent., married and had issue Thom. Savadge.

Thomas Savadge of Barford Com. Warw., sone and heire of Will., married and no issue.

Robert Savadge, sone and heire after ye sayd Thom. married to his 2d wife Anne daug. to William Atkynson of . . . . . . Com. Warw., and by her had issue Walter and others (Word.).

Walter Savage of Clanfield, com. Oxon., gent., 2d sone to Thom., married Anne, daughter to Michaell ffor of Chacombe, com. Northt., gent., wyddowe to John Edmonds of Doddington, in the Countye of Oxford, gent., who hath no yssue by her as yet (1566).

Washerton, Co. Warwick, Regist. —

Marr.

1742. Sep. 14. Charles Savage of Bishops Tachbrooke and Anne Eyres of St. Nicholas in Warwick.—Lic.

Will of Richd Savage of Tachbrooke Episc. co. War. gent. (Somerset Hs.)

1682. Dec. 20. Richard Savage of Tachbrooke, Episc. co. Warwick, gent., made his will, which was proved 3 Decr. 1684, and registd in "Hare" fol. 167.

He desired to be interred at the discretion of his Exzes. To his eldest son William Savage of Tachbrooke all the corn on his estate there. To his grandson William Savage the younger, his free land in Hampton Lucy, in the occupation of William Higgins and Henry Aliband : but the said William is to pay out of the sd premises £50 to his younger brother Richard Savage. To Mary Savage, testator's wife, all the interest in the lands of his son-in-law John Chebsey of Ladbrooke, co. Warwick, in trust for daughter Ester wife of the said John Chebsey. Said wife and dau. Sarah Savage to be joint executrixes ; to whom all household goods, &c., equally divided. Forty shillings to the poor of Tachbrooke. Son in law William Randle, of Preston, co. Warwick, and Joseph Trebell, Vicar of Tachbrooke, overseers, to each of whom forty shillings.

The mark of Richard Savage.

Witnessed by William Trebell, Joseph Commander, and Mary Walton.

An Indenture, dated 8 April, 1602, between Thomas Savage of Tachebrooke, Epis. in Co. War. yeoman 1st pt. Richard Lane, Stratford-on-Avon, gent. ; Richard Vennar, Wellesbourne Mountford, yeoman, and William Savage, son and heir apparent of the said Thomas Savage, 2nd part. John

Savage, second son of Thos. Savage, 3rd part. Settlement of lands in Bishops Tachbrook, Alveston and Tiddington on the marriage of Wm Savage with Alice Faulkner, Tiddington, widow. Recites a deed dated 10 Octr., 1595, whereby it appears Thos. S., the father, had lands in Bps. Tachbrook, Bradwell, Alveston, Tiddington, Barton and Leamington.

From above deed and Alveston with Tiddington Registers I frame the following pedigree :—

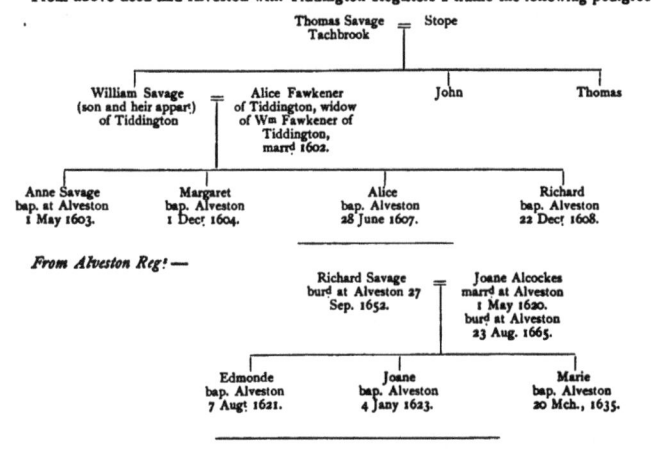

```
                        Thomas Savage = Stope
                         Tachbrook
    ┌──────────────────────┬─────────────────┬─────────┬─────────┐
William Savage    =   Alice Fawkener        John        Thomas
(son and heir appart)  of Tiddington, widow
of Tiddington          of Wm Fawkener of
                       Tiddington,
                       marrd 1602.
    ┌─────────────┬─────────────┬─────────────┐
Anne Savage    Margaret       Alice          Richard
bap. at Alveston bap. Alveston bap. Alveston bap. Alveston
1 May 1603.    1 Decr. 1604.  28 June 1607.  22 Decr. 1608.
```

From Alveston Regr.:—

```
              Richard Savage      =   Joane Alcockes
              burd at Alveston 27     marrd at Alveston
              Sep. 1652.              1 May 1620.
                                      burd at Alveston
                                      23 Aug. 1665.
       ┌──────────────────┬──────────────────┐
    Edmonde              Joane              Marie
    bap. Alveston        bap. Alveston       bap. Alveston
    7 Augt 1621.         4 Jany 1623.        20 Mch., 1635.
```

APPENDIX XVI.

IRISH "PEDIGREES" OF THE SAVAGES OF THE ARDS.

AN old *soi-disant* pedigree of the SAVAGE family, written in the Irish language, formerly in the possession of the late Sir William Betham, Ulster King-of-Arms, states that the earliest of the SAVAGE name to settle in Ulster were two brothers, William and Richard, "sons-in-law of Sir George (?) Grey, of Kent, ancestor of the Earls of Kent." They and a Knight named Russell, also a companion-in-arms of De Courcy, and a scion of the English house of Russell, now represented by the Duke of Bedford (*see* Russell of Killough in *Burke's Landed Gentry*), married three sisters (according to this Irish "pedigree"), daughters of the above-named Grey. The Irish "pedigree" is full of errors. Neither the name of Sir George Grey nor that of Richard Savage have we found in any contemporary authentic records.

The following also purports to be the translation of an Irish "pedigree" of the SAVAGES OF ARDKEEN. Some familiar names occur in it; but we have failed to make head or tail of it as a *pedigree* :—

"The Genealogy of Savage of Ardkeen in Ulster.

"Jenkin boy Savage son of Bri son of Jenkin Boy son of Edmond son of Jenkin Oge that is the Seneschal of the King, son of Robert, son of Edmond Oge son of Edmun Oge Mor son of Henry son of Sir Robert the Great Savage that is the first man who came to that country of that family."

APPENDIX XVII.

ALLUSION TO THE SAVAGES OF THE ARDS BY SIR THOMAS SMITH, QUEEN ELIZABETH'S SECRETARY.

FROM a "Tract by Sir Thomas Smith on the Colonisation of the Ards in County of Down."— (Printed in 1572):—

"Muche more than that whiche Strangbowe wonne remayneth not at this day ciuile in Irelande; but many parcels have been wonne by the English men therein without the King's forces, whiche eyther by the occasions afore rehersed were lost, or els for lack of inward policy degenerated, as great countries in Munster, by the Geraldines and Butlers; In Conalt, by the Burges; In Meth, by Nogent; In Vlster, sometimes by Lacy, Earl of Lincolne, after him by Mortimer; yea, a great part of the Arde was and is possessed by the SAUAGES, in whose ofspring, which at this time hold it, save the name, remayneth nothing English, with diverse other parcelles, which, for shortness sake, I let passe."—(Given by the Rev. G. Hill, in an Appendix to his *Macdonnells of Antrim*.)

APPENDIX XVIII.

FERDOROUGH [RAYMOND] SAVAGE, OF ARDKEEN.

From the Carte Papers, vol. LV., p. 76. (*Copy kindly placed at our disposal by Charles H. Brett, Esq., of Belfast.*)

"Jerome Brett to Fitzwilliam.

"Jan. 8, 1574-5.

"RIGHT honorable and my synguler good L. yn awnser off my letters sent the xth off Decembr. last past I receved none, nor yet is my messyng[r] retñed wherrfore I suppose he is ether slayne or taken emong the wode kerne. Beinge eftsones tolde to trouble yo[us] L. as well to sygnyffye what lately hathe beffallen, as also of my successe sence my ffyrst lettrs sent. Imedyate aft[s] the Ẁche S[r] Bryan mackeffelim & I fell to conclusyon ffor Inhabytinge off the ards to her ma[ties] vse, as hemselffe knoweth, theropon he brought xxxt[i]ij of his Create vnd[r] my mẽye, the daye was apointed ffor our metinge to the end the contract myght be sett down yn wrytinge. In the meane beffell to hem that Ẁche is hapened, the consyderacyon whereoff standethe in yo[us] wysedom to consyd[r] so sudenlye hit chawnsed & yn suche secret man[?] yt was p[r]tended as all the Create was scatered & spoyled er I culd recou[r] one bullocke. In his rowme is vpstarte Neele mackebrian fferto yn power I suppose about iij[e] men who acompaned w[th] s[r]ten Scottes made ij or iij attemptes to spoile the lytle ardes, but being p[r]vented (tho w[th] greate watche & charge by reason my companye ar not manye) ys nowe ffallen ffor a tyme at peace w[ch] givethe [some reaste,

tho lytle assurance,	yo[ur] L.
for Neal fertoo to be at	knowethe theyre peace
lyssal by me pardoned	notw[th]standinge I hope
or to be sent to lym' to kepe	to passe this wint[r]
Little Ards. The erle hath only	p[r]telye by shewe & the
to do with the rober of vlster.	more by pollecye &

yet not otherwise then manlye & ffor the honor off her ma[te] The cause that makes hem Quyet ys yn hope upon good & sufficient pledges I shuld p[r]sure at yo[us] L. hands the lebertye off Kyldouffe Ogyllmerre; ffor whom when he was yn hande w[th] S[r] Bryan I wrote my lett[r]s to the LL. off the honorable Cownsell of Ingland; and ffor as muche as he is nowe yn yo[us] L. mercye & the best warant to Inhabyte theardes, yff yt myght please yo[r] L. the rather at my humble sute to consyd[r] off this mosyon And yff yt shalbe thought not meete or necessarye yet that I maye be his gaoylour at Arkyne Castell wher ffor his salve kepinge I will importune my lyffe, I shalbe the more Quyet ffor the gretest power that neele fferto hath is his bretherene.

"Iff yt myght stande w[th] yo[us] L. likinge to assyst me w[th] any men I will pseu[e] as I have begon w[ch] is to s[r]ve paynffully & not to starte any weye. the more pte of my Company ar gon, flled ffor ffeare & ffor no want the s[r]vice ffalletthe to cowardlye myndes very desperat, they be yn other bands mayntened contrarye to all m[r]shall lawe deptinge w[th] wepon & armor, so here I remayne acompanied w[th] s[r]ten gentlemen off [Qy. no?] name or power but Mr. Storys who is both wise and valyant, w[th] them & they w[the] me I p[r]tende to contynewe (And yet not ffolyshelye) but to the honor off her ma[te] ffor as myche as this axyon extendethe the ffurderance off her mat^{ies} s^rvice & comon ffor all men as vnto yo^{us} L. yt is very well knowen tho to others (havinge no good liking to Imbrace yt) hit is but held a matter desperat & p^rvatt, wher in thruthe yt settethe fforthe the avavncment off her hyghnes revennewe, hit openethe the meane & hyghe weye to refforme all Irelande as well as this countreye. And ffynally hit will cut off her mat^{tes} Inordynat chargis sustened yerlye; Iff yt will please yo^a L. to lett me have one C men off her mat^{es} retenewe, I will maynteyne them as horsemen and axe alowance but ffor ffotemen & they shall alweis lye at Castell rewe Comb^r. or at holywode redye to attend upon yo^{us} L. Iff this maye not pswade, but taken ffor a pollecye to Inhabyte the Ardes, allow yt (and yet in truthe yt is not so ment) the northe shalbe new^s be refformed vyntyll the Ardes be Inhabyted, whereby yt may be the nurse & ffeder off som armye to anker yt one ffor startinge Iorneis gevethe rather to syvell Inhabytant Import^s shemt then anoyance to the Iryshery & ffugytant. This told I am wth yo^{us} L. ffor that at yo^{us} hands & yn yo^{us} tyme I toke my excasyon wyshinge wth my herte yo^u were the p^rncypall or cheffe ptaker yn this axyon and then spedely shuld ensue good successyon, ffor god doth blesse yt, hit is not my power that can deffende yt, I am wth the cowntrye & my owne men not above cxx vc hathe ffayled me, the northe was nev^r so brouken. Iff by ffayle off supplye hit be my life must make the sacraffice, gods will be ffulfilled I am resolved.

"My good L. I have been many tymes myche dysquyeted wth o^a common bludd succour off Inglyshe mens bludd, ffardorowe Savage the Sencyall sonne so named and now of late came to my countrey to be entertayned (I meane the countreye wheroff I have gov^rment) ffor xij horsemen & xl kerne sayinge that he was ffrom my L. off essex & offred me many curtezyes bewaylinge that my Companye was not grett^r wch was lacrime crokedilis [?], as yn end hit shewed yt selffe, ffor by kyllinge off whyte Browne & others he hathe receved suche entrance as it is very harde to kepe hem from bytinge of such shepe; ffor testymonye on the vij of January he came ov^s the loughe by bote with xxvj kerne and sent abowte s^xten horsemen & belodged hem selffe & his men yn Sundrye avaunctagis tyll all most the mornyng then he caused soudenlye the praye off the towne to be reysed supposinge that I wold as I have to oughten don have been the ffyrst man that shuld have rescued the preye but as yt hapened and as they were bewreyed by Mr. Storyes & his men lyinge yn theyr barke who shot off a ffaucon whereat they were all amased & then seid the came to have some of my kerne to make a praye, & so ffrom one sale to a nother, as I have taken hem & tho the matter and his murderous ententyon be aparent as well by proffe as by confessyon, yet I have not pceded to any excecusyon vntyll yor L. pleass³ be furd^r knowen, he hathe yo^a L. pdon once alreadye ffor all offences (treyson to the p^rinces pson and coynyng off money excepted) the murdering of browne & whyte ffor that yt was off mallyce p^rtensed is treason against the pson of her Ma^{te} by the Statute 10 H. 7. then is his pdon not in force. he hathe synce and off very late comytted sund^rye ffelonys & treasons as yn aydinge & receivinge off S^r bryans men that were hurt by the Inglyshe host. As yn takinge p^sson^{rs} & releasinge them yn makinge peace and warre wch wthout warrant he can not do. he receved Patricke hazard a notorios treytor & a murderer & lett hem at leb^rtye whom I have taken yn hand respectinge yor L. pleass³ as well ffor the one as the other, this delaye I make not as Ignorant off my comyssyon ffor by the one & the other I maye put them to dethe wth out respect off levinge or the pson; I meane by the comyssyon receved ffro yor L. dated the xxiiij off July yn the xvj yere off her mat^{es} reygne, and the comyssyon dated the xxix off Septembr yn the xiiij yere off her mat^{es} reygne grawnted fforthe to Sr Thomas Smythe & to Thomas his sonne; most humbly takinge my leve ffrom the Castell off Arkyne this viij^t off January.

"Yo^{us} honors most humblye to comand
"JHEROM BRETT.

"Even as & whylst I was wrytinge my lett^r at mednyght soudenly slypt patricke hazard his ffote owte off Irons & lept out the Castell off Arkyne suche a lepe as yff he had ben condemned I had ffor his dethe as leve have given hem that lepe as the gallows, yet he ded yt, I ment no severe punyshemt yff he cold have put me good suretyes.

"I praye yo^{us} L. yff I may not have kylduffe ogylmerre upon my kepinge I may receve yo^{us} conffortable lett^{rs} ffor hem, to ffeede his ffrendes this wynt^r & yor L. ffrendeshep to Sr Bryan yff yt be meit he shall com fforthe, & that he maye by yor honor knowe I have ben ernest ffor hem.

"To the right honorable my singuler goode Lorde Sr Willm ffytzwillm knyght lorde deputye off her mat^{es} realme off Irlonde.

"JERROME BRETTS le^re
Rec^t at Tryme the xviijth
of January 1574 by
his messenger."

APPENDIX XIX.

CONFIRMATORY GRANT OF PORTAFERRY MANOR TO PATRICK SAVAGE BY CHARLES I.

The following copy of Charles I.'s Confirmatory Grant of PORTAFERRY MANOR to PATRICK SAVAGE has been kindly given to us by Lt.-General Nugent, of Portaferry. A Confirmatory Grant of ARDKEEN MANOR to HENRY SAVAGE, in pretty similar terms, was also made by the same Monarch.

"CHARLES by the Grace of God of England Scotland France and Ireland King Defender of the Faith and soforth To all to whom these our present Letters shall come Greeting Know ye that we for and in consideration of the true faithfull and acceptable service by our beloved subject Patrick Savage, of Portforrie in the County of Downe Esqre and his ancestors to us and our Crown before this time multiplicitly impended and as the said Patrick with greater study to the like services for the future to us and our Crown may be prompted to yield and that he may be better able to persovoro [persevere] and proceed in transacting the same of our special Grace and of our certain knowledge and meer motion by the advice and consent of our well beloved and faithfull Cousin and Counsellor Henry viscount Falkland our General Deputy of our s^d Kingdom of Ireland and according to the tonor and effect of our cortain Lotters with our proper hand signed and undor our signott bearing date at our Pallace of Westminster the 7th day of august in the second year of our Reign of England Scotland France and Ireland and now in the Rolls of our Chancory in our s^d Kingdom of Ireland Inrolled have given and granted and confirmed and by these presents for us our heirs and successors we do give and grant and confirm unto the said Patrick Savage his Heirs and assigns the manor Town and Lands of Portforry otherwise Ballymurphye, Tollenocreeny otherwise Creggroddan, Ballynorolack Ballytollenerussally Ballotollobrood Balledorry Ballycoroge Ballyhearly Ballyhenry Ballyconton Ballotowshilly Ballenotawrogh Ballofowner Ballewarrod otherwise Tallenegore and Ballymniske otherwise Ballyvickenishe with their appurtonances all and singular which are situate lying and being in the County of Downe afores^d the three quarters of Parsonhall Ballycollals Ballynycoll the quarter of land of Carrownomallot the Quarter of Land of Carrynopolle parcell of Ballocarrocke othorwise Ballocorroge the s^d lands of Carrownoglearogh parcoll of Ballyderry the said lands of Carrownobrillogh parcoll of Balvicknishe, the s^d lands of Ballycame the quarter of Ardkeaghan parcoll of Ballynowlack the said quartor of Banckmore parcoll of Ballytollaboord afores^d and the stable quartor parcoll of Ballotolloboor and the quarter of land called Torrogonill otherwise Toradonill parcoll of Towshilly afores^d and the town and Lands of Ballogarvigan in the Little Ardes all which are seituate lying and being in the County of Downe afores^d and all other Castles manors Lands Tenements and hereditaments with all their rights members and appurtenances of which the said Patrick Savage on the 7th day of aug^t in the said 2nd year of our Reign was seized or of which he was then reputed seized or of right ought to be seized or of which the issues and profits of the same Patrick Savage then were answered and paid as of his Inheritance and also all and singular Castles messuages Tofts mills houses cottages buildings structures Barns stables Pidgeon houses Garden places Orchards Gardons Lands Tenements Hereditaments meadows pastures Commons Demesne Lands wasts Brambles Bryers Turbarys and mountain Lands moores marshes as well sweet as salt woods underwoods waters watercourses pools standing waters Lakes Piscarrys Fishings and the soil and foundation of the same covered with water mineralls warrons Tythes of Garbage Grass Grain and hay wooll Flax Hemp and Lambs and all the Lands Tythable whatsoever and all other Tythes whatsoever as well greater as lesser of whatsoever kind nature or species and the profitts commodities and suits stocks mulcts Rents reversions and services Rent charges Rents seek and services as well free as customary works of tennants Farms Fees of farms annuitys Knights fees wards marriages Escheats Reliefes Herriotts fines amercements Estovers and Commons of Estovers customs Rights jurisdictions Franchises Libertys Immunities Exemptions priviledges advantages emoluments and hereditaments whatsoever with all their appurtenances Rights and members of whatsoever kind nature or species they are or by whatever names the said premisses above by these presents granted are known deemed or taken or to any part or parts parcell or parcells of the same in anywise belonging appertaining incident or appendant or as members parts or parcells of the same premisses or of any of them ever or att any time heretofore were had known used accepted or reputed and also all and singular reversion and reversions remainder and remainders whatsoever of all and singular the premises above by these presents before granted and every parcell thereof dependant or expectant of in or upon any house or houses Grant or Grants demise or demises whatsoever for term of life lives or years or in fee taile or orŵise of the premises above by these presents before granted or of any parcell thereof heretofore being made or granted of Record or not of Record and all and singular Rents and annuall profitts whatsoever reserved upon any demises of the premisses above by these presents before granted and of every parcell thereof and all and singular the premises above by these presents before granted and every parcell thereof with all their rights members and appurtenances whatsoever as fully freely and intirely and in as ample and beneficiall manner and form as all and singular the same to our hands or to the hands of any of our Progenitors or ancestors Kings or Queens of England by reason or pretext of any exchange or acquisition or of any gift or grant or confirmation or by reason or pretext of any Act of Parliament or of any Acts of Parliament or by reason or pretext of any surrender or dissolution or release of any abbey monastery Priory or house of religion or by reason of any attainder forfeiture or escheat or in right of our Crown or of our antient right or by any legall manner right or title recited or not recited have come or ought to come or in our hands now are or ought to be or happen to be or happen and all our right title and interest of and in the Premisses saving always and out of this our Grant to us our heirs and successors altogether excepted and reserved our Royall composition and expedition to Riseings by and upon the premisses and every parcell thereof heretofore established or hereafter to be established and assessed and all sums of money by reason of our said composition or expedition to riseings to us our heirs and successors due or payable or to be due or payable and moreover we will and of our like speciall grace and of our certain knowledge and meer motion for us our heirs and successors We do grant to the said Patrick Savage his heirs and assignes that they and every of them shall have and hold and shall and may have and hold one free markett at Portferry aforesaid every Thursday for ever to be held as fully freely and intirely and in as ample manner and form as the said markett at any time heretofore was held and used and the said markett to the said Patrick Savage his heirs and assignes for us our heirs and successors We do give grant and confirm by these presents not only all and every our reight title claime and interest whatsoever of and in the said market together with all and singular customs Libertys and free customs priviledges Tolls Toll Books Jurisdictions profitts fines amercements and all other perquisites and commoditys whatsoever of in and out of the said markett growing renewing coming or arising or to the said markett belonging Incidont or in anywise appendant AND FURTHER of our speciall Bountifull Grace and of our certain knowledge and meer motion we have given granted and confirmed and by these presents for us our Heirs and successors we do give grant and confirm to the s^d Patrick Savage his heirs and assignes the customs or annuall payments following anciently due and payable to witt nine pence sterling in England for every Horse Cattle Ox or Cow brought to Portferry aforesaid entred to be transported or sold in or near Portferry aforesaid or to the Port or Harbors of the same and out of every Hogshead of wine or aqua vite brought from parts without or beyond seas ten quarts when the said Hogsheads shall be discharged or landed upon land or any part of the said Lands of the said Patrick Savage above granted or mentioned to be granted and also out of every Hide entred to be transported or sold in or near the said Town of Portferry one penny sterling and also out of every Horse Cattle Ox or Cow sold in the said markett four pence sterling in England and out of every young beast or merchandize or commodity sold in the said markett or Town of the price of two shillings one penny sterling and also two fatt cows two Barrells of ale anciently due payable and issueing from and out of the town and Lands of Ballyfondragh otherwise Ballyfoneragh Ballyoranagan and Donevley in the County of Downe aforesaid at the Feast of the nativity of our Lord yearly and also all and singular suits and services of the inhabitants and tenants of the town of Karney and Granagh and all other suiters whatsoever to the Court of the Mannor of Portferry aforesaid anciently belonging and of right accustomed and also the chief rent of six shillings and eight pence and two meders of Butter and one fat sheep issueing and payable from and out of the said quarter of Banckmore and the suits and services to the Court of the mannor of Portferry aforesaid from the tenants of the Quarter of Land of Banckmore in the Coy of Downe aforesaid to the said mannor anciently belonging or of right accustomed AND FURTHER of our speciall bountifull Grace and of our certain knowledge and meer motion we do Grant and give Licence to the said Patrick Savage his heirs and assigns that they and every of them may have and hold and shall have and hold one Court Leet or view of Frank pledge anciently held and used within the mannor of Portferry aforesaid and all things to the Court Leet or view of Frank pledge belonging in and within the said mannor to be held before any seneschall or seneschalls by the said Patrick Savage his Heirs or assignes appointed or constituted twice in every year at the days and times heretofore used and accustomed and the said Court Leet or view of Frank pledge with all things which to the Court Leet or view of Frank pledge belong to the said Patrick Savage his heirs and assignes by these presents being Willing that the said seneschall and seneschalls from time to time may have enjoy and execute and every of them may have enjoy and execute full power authority and Jurisdiction in the same Court Leet or view of Frank pledge to enquire of all Felonys Deceipts Trespasses purprestures nusances and of all and all manner of offences causes and matters whatsoever which in the Court Leet or view of Frank pledge ought and used to be enquired of according to the custom of our said Kingdom of Ireland happening or arising in or within the precincts of the mannor of Portferry aforesaid and every parcell

APPENDIX XIX.

thereof and also to do execute and ordain in the same Court all other things whatsoever which in the Court Leet or view of Frank pledge can ought or used to be done ordained or executed by the Laws and customs of our said Kingdom of Ireland AND FURTHER we will and by these presents for us our Heirs and successors we do grant and give Lycence to the said Patrick Savage his heirs and assignes that they and every of them shall and may have and hold in and within the precincts and limits of the mannor of Portferry aforesaid one Court in the nature of a Court Baron there anciently held and used to enquire hear determine and do all and singular such things and matters in the same manner and form which and as in any Court Baron within our Kingdom of England and within our said Kingdom of Ireland ought or used to be enquired heard determined and done to be held before the Seneschall or Seneschalls by the said Patrick Savage his heirs and assignes or any of them from time to time to be named and constituted and before the free suiters to the Court of the said mannor of Portferry respectively and in the same Court to hold Pleas of all and singular actions Trespasses covenants accounts contracts Detinue Debts and Demands whatsoever which in Debt or damage shall not exceed the sume of forty shillings of current money of Ireland within the premisses above by these presents before granted and Limitts and Bounds of the same happening and arising and the said Court Baron with all things to the same belonging for us our Heirs and successors we do Grant and confirm unto the said Patrick Savage his heirs and successors for ever We will moreover that he the s^d Patrick Savage his Heirs and successors and every of them to his and their own proper use and behoofe may have and receive and from time to time may and shall have receive collect and levy all and singular profitts and amercements fines commoditys advantages and emoluments whatsoever to such Court belonging or appertaining or in the same to be forfeited taxed or imposed or in any manner thereout issueing or arising without any account for the same to us our Heirs or successors to be paid or made AND FURTHER of our speciall bountifull Grace and out of our certain knowledge and meer motion we do give and grant to the said Patrick Savage his heirs and assignes that they and every of them from henceforth for ever shall have hold and enjoy and shall and may have hold and enjoy all and singular Goods and chattels waived and forfeited and all and singular Goods and chattels of Felons and fugitives Felons de se and wrecks of the sea arising or accrueing within any part parcell or Creeks or caves of the said premisses in as ample manner and forme as is found by Inquisition by virtue of a commission under the Great seal of Ireland taken the 20th day of September in the year of our Lord one thousand six hundred and twenty seven by the said Patrick Savage and his ancestors all and singular the said Goods and chattels of felons and fugitives felons de se and wrecks of the sea and other the premisses have had and enjoyed so that the same Patrick Savage his heirs and assigns by themselves or by their Bailiffes or Servants Bailiffe or Servant all the said Goods Chattles waiffes Forfeitures Goods and Chattles of felons and fugitives felons de se and wrecks of the sea may levy have possess and receive to his and their proper use and behoofe without the molestation or hindrance of us our Heirs or Successors or other officers or ministers of us our Heirs or Successors and without any account or any other thing for the same to us our Heirs or Successors or to any other person to be rendered or made as fully freely and intirely as at any time heretofore they have been levied collected had or possessed by the said Patrick Savage or any of his ancestors whatsoever AND FURTHER of our speciall bountifull Grace and of our certain knowledge and meer motion we will and by these presents for us our Heirs and successors We do grant and licence give unto the said Patrick Savage his heirs and assigns that they and every of them may have and enjoy and shall and may have hold and enjoy within all and singular the said manor Towns villages Hamlets Lands Tenem^{ts} Hereditam^{ts} and other the premises above by these presents before granted or mentioned to be granted and every parcel thereof free warren Park and free Chase and all that to a free warren Park and free Chase belong or appertain to keep Hares Rabbits Deer Pheasants and Partridges and all other animals which to a free warren Park and free Chase do belong as fully freely and intirely as at any time heretofore was used had or enjoyed so that no person shall enter into the said Towns Lands Tenem^{ts} Hereditam^{ts} and other the premisses by these presents mentioned to be granted or any parcel thereof to hunt or chase in the same or anything there to take which to a free warren or chase belongeth without the Licence of the said Patrick Savage his heirs or assigns under the penalty against malefactors in Chases Parks or warrens ordained and constituted and that it shall be lawful to the same Patrick Savage his heirs and assigns as much of the premisses as they shall please from time to time with Pales Hedges and ditches to include and a Park thereof to make To HAVE hold and enjoy the said manor of Portferry with the appurtenances and all and singular the Towns Villages Hamlets Lands Tenem^{ts} Hereditam^{ts} Chief rents annual payments customs Debts priviledges franchises suites and services marketts Courts Leet or view of Frank pledge Courts Baron Goods and chattles of Felons Fugitives Felons de se and wrecks of the sea free warren Chase and Park and all and singular other the premisses above by these presents before granted or mentioned to be granted and every parcel thereof with all and singular their rights members and appurtenances unto the said Patrick Savage his heirs and assigns to the sole and proper use and behoof of him the said Patrick Savage his heirs and assigns for ever to be held of us our Heirs and successors in Chief by Knights service Yielding thereout and the said Patrick to grant out of the premisses yearly unto us our Heirs and successors of our said Kingdom of Ireland to wit to the hands of the Vice Treasurer or General Receiver of us our Heirs or successors of our said Kingdom of Ireland for the time being forty shillings sterling current money of England at the Feast of Easter and Saint Michael the Archangel by equal portions annually to be paid AND FURTHER of our like special Grace and of our certain knowledge and meer motion by the assent and advice aforesaid and according to the tenor and effect of our Letters above mentioned we have given and granted and by these presents for us our Heirs and successors we do give grant and confirm unto the s^d Patrick Savage his Heirs and assigns full Licence power and authority that they and every of them may have and hold and shall and may have and hold one Fair in or at the Town of Portferry every 25th day of July and for the same day and the day next following to continue annually to be held for ever unless the said 25th day of July shall happen or be in the Lords day or on Saturday in which case we will and by these presents for us our heirs and successors we give Licence unto the said Patrick Savage his heirs and assigns that they and every of them from henceforth for ever annually may have and hold and shall and may have and hold the said Fair in or at the same town of Portferry afores^d on monday then next ensueing for the same day and the day next following to continue there annually to be held for ever together with a Court of Pyepowder to be held during the same Fair and with all customs Libertys and free usages Priviledges Tolls markets Houses Jurisdictions Profits commoditys Fines amercements and other perquisites whatsoever of in or out of the said Fair and Court growing renewing or arising or to such Fair and Court respectively belonging incident or in anywise appendent yet during the said Fair shall not be to the nusance of any other neighboring Fair Giving also and for us our heirs and successors granting unto the said Patrick Savage his heirs and assigns one free Toll Book in every market and Fair aforesaid by him the said Patrick Savage his Heirs and assigns or his or their Deputy or Deputys for ever to use and keep and due Fees of all Entrys there to be received AND FURTHER of our special bountiful Grace and of our certain knowledge and meer motion We will and by these presents for us our Heirs and successors we do grant unto the said Patrick Savage his heirs and assigns that we our Heirs and successors for ever annually and from time to time shall exonerate and acquit and keep indemnified not only the said Patrick Savage his Heirs and assigns and every of them but also the said manor messuages Lands Tenements Hereditaments and all and singular other the premisses above by these presents mentioned to be Granted and every part and parcell thereof with all and singular their rights members and appurtenances against us our heirs and successors of and from all and all manner of intrusions Corrodys Rents Fees annuitys pensions portions sums of money and all things whatsoever of or for the premisses above by these presents before granted or any parcell thereof to us due or payable or thereupon to us charged or to be charged except of the Rent to us our Heirs and successors by these presents reserved and the sums of money to us due for our Royall composition and riseings as above reserved PROVIDED ALLWAYS that these our Letters Patents or anything in the same contained shall not in anywise extend or be construed to preclude or exclude us our heirs or successors from any reliefe of Primier Seizin or Livery nor of any Fine or composition for Livery or Primier seisin nor of any Fine for alienation nor of any Intrusion or mesne profitts to us due by reason of the custody of the said Patrick Savage or of any of his predecessors or for not sueing Livery of the premises or any parcell thereof nor of any Fine or value or forfeiture marriage nor of any other Debt or demand to our Court of Wards and Liverys belonging by reason of any alienation Intrusion primier Seisin custody default of Livery or removing our hands But that we our heirs and successors may have and enjoy the whole and intire benefitt of every such Livery Primier Seisin Fine for alienation Intrusion and all mesne profitts whatsoever to us due or to us our Heirs or successors hereafter to be due by reason of such default of Livery Primier Seisin alienation Intrusion default of Livery and to remove our hands from the premisses and the value or forfeiture of marriage of the said Patrick or other person whatsoever in such ample and beneficial manner and form as if these our Letters Pattents had not at all been made Willing moreover and by these presents firmly commanding by Injoyning the Treasurer Chancellor and Barons of our Exchequer and to all and singular Receivers auditors and other officers and ministers of us our heirs and successors of our said kingdom of Ireland for the time being that they and every of them without any other writt or Warrant from us our Heirs or successors in any manner to be sued or prosecuted the full intire and due manifest allowance and exoneration of and from all and all manner of corrodys Rents Fees annuitys Pentions Portions sumes of money and all things whatsoever except of the Rent aforesaid services Tenures compositions Riseings arrearages and other the premisses in these Pattents above as is aforesaid excepted and reserved to the said Patrick Savage his heirs and assigns doing and from time to time they shall cause to be done and that these our Letters Pattents or the

APPENDIX XIX.

Inrolment of the same shall be as well to the said Treasurer Chancellor and Barons of our said Exchequer as to all and singular Receivers auditors and other officers and ministers of us our Heirs and successors whatsoever for the time being a sufficient warrant and discharge in this behalfe AND FURTHER of our speciall more abundant Grace and of our certain knowledge and meer motion we will and by these presents for us our heirs and successors We do grant unto the said Patrick Savage his heirs and assigns that they and every of them may use these our Letters Pattents or by manner of confirmation or by manner of a new Grant according to their Liberty and will and that these our Letters Pattents or the Inrollment of the same shall be in all things and by all things firm good valid sufficient and effectuall in the law against us our Heirs and successors as in all our Courts as elsewhere within our said Kingdome of Ireland or elsewhere wheresoever without any confirmation Licence or Toleration from us our heirs and successors hereafter to the said Patrick Savage his heirs and assignes to be procured or obtained notwithstanding the ill naming or ill reciting of the said mannor Houses messuages Lands Tenements Hereditaments and other the premisses above by these presents recited or any parcell thereof and notwithstanding that an office or Inquisition or Inquisitions of the premisses or any parcell thereof by which our Title ought to be found before the perfection of these our Letters Pattents are not at all found taken or returned and notwithstanding the not naming or ill naming not reciting or ill reciting of any Town village Hamlet Parish Place or County in which the said premisses or any parcell thereof do or does lye or are or is and notwithstanding the not reciting or ill reciting or the not naming any demise or demises for terme of life lives or years or in fee taile or of other the premisses or of any parcell thereof made to any person or persons being of Record and not of Record And notwithstanding any other defect of the certainty or computation or Declaration of the true annual value of the premisses or of any parcell thereof or the annual rent reserved of or upon the premisses or of or upon any parcell thereof And notwithstanding any other defects in not naming or not rightly naming any Tennants farmers or occupants of the premisses or of any parcell thereof and notwithstanding the Statute in the Parliament of the Lord Henry the sixth late King of England our ancestor at Westminster made and published in the eighteenth year of his Reign and afterwards in this our Kingdom of Ireland (among other things) by authority of Parliament established and confirmed and notwithstanding any other defects in not naming or in not rightly naming the nature kind species Quantity or Quality of the premisses or of any parcell thereof or in not reciting our title and notwithstanding any Restriction Prohibition or Provision by our most dear Father the late King James of most happy memory or by our Privy Council or of our said Father in our said Kingdom of England to the contrary of the premisses at any time heretofore made published or provided or any other statute act ordinance Restriction or provision or any other cause or matter whatsoever in evacuation oneration or annihilation of these our Letters Patents in anywise notwithstanding We will also and by these presents for us our Heirs and successors we give and grant unto the said Patrick Savage that he may and shall have these our Letters Patents under our great seal of Ireland in due manner made and sealed without any Fine great or small for the same to us in our Hannaper or elsewhere to our use to be rendered paid or made so that express mention of the true value of the same or of the certainty of the premisses or any of them or of other Gifts or Grants by us or any of our Progenitors to the same Patrick Savage heretofore made in these presents are not at all made any statute act ordinance or provision or any other thing cause or matter to the contrary of the premisses made in anywise notwithstanding IN TESTIMONY OF WHICH THING these our Letters we have caused to be made Patents WITNESS our aforesaid Deputy General of our Kingdom of Ireland at Dublin the fourteenth day of January in the 3rd year of our reign.

"KING & KING

"Inrolled in my office the 24th May 1628.
"WM CROFTON
"Exd by J. KING
" Inrolled in the roll of Patents of the Chancery of the 3rd year of Charles by me JAMES NEWMAN Clerk in the Office of the Master of the Rolls."

APPENDIX XX.
SECOND CONFIRMATORY GRANT OF PORTAFERRY BY CHARLES I.

We are indebted also to Lieut.-General Nugent for the following.

"CHARLES by the Grace of God of England Scotland France and Ireland King defender of the faith and so forth To all to whom these our present Letters shall come Greeting Know ye that we of our special Grace and from our certain knowledge and mere motion likewise by the advice assent and consent of our very faithful and well beloved Counsellor Thomas Viscount Wentworth our deputy General of our said Kingdom of Ireland and president of our Council established in the Northern parts of our said Kingdom of England and one of our Commissioners according to the intention and effect of our Commission under our Great seal of our said Kingdom of Ireland bearing date at Dublin the 7th day of September in the twelfth year of our Reign as well for and in consideration of a fine or sum of £21 of good and lawful money of England by our well beloved hereinafter named subject Patrick Savage Esqre before the sealing of these our letters Patent at the receipt of our Exchequer of our said Kingdom of Ireland well and faithfully paid for our use which said fine or sum of £21 is due to us and payable by virtue of a certain order composition agreement and concord made between our said Commissioners and the said Patrick Savage Esqre as for and in consideration of the Rents services reservations and duties in these presents by virtue of the Commission composition and agreement aforesaid reserved or mentioned to be reserved Have given granted bargained sold released and confirmed and by these presents for us our Heirs and successors Do give grant bargain sell release and confirm to the aforesaid Patrick Savage Esqre his heirs and assigns All the manors Castles towns and Lands of Portferry otherwise Ballymurphy and also all the towns villages Hamlets Lands tenements and Heredits of Tolloneereeir otherwise Criggroddan Ballyblake otherwise Ballyblack Ballytollynerussally Ballytollebrood Ballyderry Ballyorock Ballehorly Ballyhenry Ballycontow Ballytewshilly Ballenetauragh Ballyfoner Ballywored otherwise Tollenegore Ballymekinsh otherwise Ballyvickerish and Ballicott otherwise Ballynicott and also the quarters of Parson Hall a quarter of the land of Carrownemallott a quarter of the land of Carrownepoll otherwise Carrniepoll reputed parcel of Ballycoroke otherwise Ballycoroge aforesd quarter of the land of Carrownegleragh reputed parcel of Ballyderry aforesd quarter of the land of Barrowbrienkeagh reputed parcel of Ballyvicknisse, three quarters of the land of Ballycarne a quarter of Ardkeaghan reputed parcel of Ballyneolacke aforesaid a Quarter of the land of Bankmore reputed parcel of Ballytollebroode aforesaid Leseable quarter reputed parcel of Ballybroode aforesaid a Quarter called Torregoorill otherwise Torradorrill reputed parcell of Ballytewshilly aforesaid and also the towns lands tenements and Hereditaments of Ballytollecarnan otherwise Tollecarnan and the half of the town and lands of Kintagh and the half of the town and lands of Carrowdressagh and three parts of the town and lands of [   ] and third part of the quarter of Ballyoranigan And also all the towns villages or Hamlets lands tenements and Hereditaments of Ballygarvigan And also one Island called Islandcorr reputed parcel of Ballytollebrood aforesd and one Island called Islandballyhenry reputed parcel of Ballyhenry afsd and also one watermill in or near Karny and also all the lands tenements and Hereditaments now or late in the tenure or occupation of the said Patrick Savage his tenants or farmers about three acres of Land in or near the town and land of Knockmiller and Karney aforesaid next adjoining to the said mill and one other water mill in or near Granagh together with 6 acres of the land of Ballydocke next to the said mill of Granagh and the yearly rents chief rents issuing thereout to wit two Beeves annually out of the town and lands of Ballyheneragh and out of five half quarters of Ballycranigan and 6s/8d of the money of England annually out of the town and lands of Dunnevally and ten shillings of the money of England annually out of the town and lands of Ballydocke and twelve pence of the money of England annually out of the town and lands of Grannagh and suit of Court out of the towns villages hamlets and lands of Karney and the half town of Knockmiller and out of the half town and lands of Ballymartin orWise Quintonbay and also one Court leet and Court in the nature of Court Baron within all the premises and with all the profits issuing out of the same and all things and Estrays within the premises and wreck of the sea within any of the aforesaid Lands and free warren and park within same all which premises are situate lying and being in the little Ards in the County of Down with all other Lands tenements rights and hereditaments to the premises or any part or parcel thereof belonging or with the same occupied or enjoyed or used or reputed as part parcel or member of the premises Also all and singular the manors Castles messuages mills Lands Tenements watercourses fishings fisheries Pidgeon houses rents services Bogs moors marshes as well fresh as salt meadows feedings pastures lands commons and commons Estovers turbary moss mountain Royalties mines quarries warrens reliefs Herriotts perquisites Courts of view of frank pledge and all things to courts leets and of view of Frank pledge belonging Court Barons Fairs markets Tolls

Tollbooks Customs rights Jurisdictions franchises liberties privileges immunities advantages easements profits commodities Emoluments and all hereditaments whatsoever as well spiritual as temporal of whatever kind nature or species they are to the aforesaid premises above by these presents granted released or confirmed or mentioned to be before granted released or confirmed or to any parcel thereof belonging incident or appertaining or taken reputed or known as part parcel or member of the premises or any parcel thereof or with the said premises or with any parcel thereof used occupied or enjoyed and our reversion and reversions remainder and remainders whatsoever of all and singular the premises depending expectant upon any Grant or Grants Lease or Leases for term or terms of years or life or lives or in fee or by way of entail and all and singular the rents services and reservations upon the same premises respectively reserved or payable AND FURTHER of our mere special grace and from our certain knowledge and mere motion we do for us our Heirs and successors give grant release and confirm to the aforesaid Patrick Savage Esq⁻ᵉ his heirs and assigns for ever all and singular the before recited premises and all and every parcel thereof with all and singular their rights members and appurts whatsoever and our whole and entire right claim estate and Interest whatsoever of and in all and singular the premises and every parcel thereof as fully freely and entirely and in as ample and beneficial a manner and form as all and singular the said premises and every parcel thereof now is or are or ought to be in our hands or used to be or were in the hands or possession of any of our forefathers or ancestors or of any tenant occupier or farmer or any other person whatsoever whether above recited or not recited or badly recited or by whatsoever name right or title they may have been ever or at any time heretofore recited or not recited being of record or not of record all advowsons rights patronages or presentations to all or any churches Rectories vicariges and other Ecclesiastical benefices within the premises always excepting reserving and saving to us our Heirs and successors our Royal composition and expedition to war (Anglice) risings out and general hostings whenever they may become due and remain established in or upon the premises and all tenth parts sums rations aforesaid composition and expedition to war established To HAVE enjoy and hold our aforesaid manors Castles towns villages Hamlets Lands tenements and Hereditaments whatsoever and other all and singular the premises by these presents granted released or confirmed or mentioned to be granted released or confirmed with all and singular their entire rights members and appurts to the aforesaid Patrick Savage Esq his heirs and assigns to the sole and proper benefit and use of the said Patrick Savage his Heirs and assigns for ever To HOLD to us our Heirs and successors in capite by Knight service Yielding thereout annually to us our Heirs and successors at the receipt of our Exchequer of our said Kingdom of Ireland for the time being the sum of £8 good and lawful money of England at two yearly terms to wit at the feast of Easter and Lent [?] Michael the Archangel to be paid by equal portions annually AND FURTHER our more special grace and from our certain knowledge and mere motion likewise by the advice and assent aforesaid and for the considerations aforesaid and by virtue of the Commission before mentioned we have remitted released and quit claim and by these presents for us our Heirs and successors we do remit release and quit claim to the said Patrick Savage Esq his Heirs and assigns all and singular the conditions and also all and singular the covenants and articles and all other conditions covenants agreements and commands which in any former letters patent of the premises above mentioned or any of them or any parcel thereof made to the said Patrick Savage or any other person or persons whatsoever and all the right and title forfeiture and re-entry which we our Heirs or successors have had shall have or ought to have of in or to all and singular the premises above mentioned or any parcel thereof by reason or pretext of any condition or conditions Covenant or covenants contained in any former letters Patent of the premises above mentioned or any of them or any parcel thereof by reason of the violation or nonperformance of any condition whatever or otherwise howsoever or in what way soever and all forfeited Estates of the said Patrick Savage or of any other person or persons whose Estate or Estates in the premises above mentioned or any parcel thereof the said Patrick Savage or any person or persons for his use or in trust for him lately had or now has or pretends to have for the nonperformance or violation of any condition or conditions or otherwise howsoever and also all losses forfeitures or penalties recognizances or [   ] actions and demands whatsoever by reason of the violation or nonperformance of any condition or conditions whatsoever of all and every the right title claim Estate Interest and demand whatsoever and all and every our right title claim Estate Interest and demand whatsoever of and in all and singular the above mentioned premises and every parcel or part thereof AND FURTHER our further especial Grace and from our certain knowledge and mere motion with advice assent and consent aforesaid for and in consideration aforesaid and by virtue of the Commission above mentioned we have granted and by these presents for us our Heirs and successors We do grant that we our Heirs and successors yearly and from time to time for ever will exonerate acquit and keep indemnified as well the aforesaid Patrick Savage Esq⁻ᵉ his heirs exors admors assigns feoffees and tenants and every of them respectively as all the aforesaid manors castles messuages towns villages Hamlets lands tenements and hereditaments and other all and singular the before ment^d premises above by these presents released confirmed or granted or mentioned to be released confirmed or Granted and every parcel thereof with all their entire rights members and appurt^s against us our Heirs and successors of and from all suits and arrears of rent intrusions transgressions ingressions alienations fines mesne rates Corrodies fees agreements annuities pensions portions 20th parts 10th parts sums conditions provisions conventions restrictions pains penalties compositions reservations concords agreements mandates instructions and articles and from all limitations and Recognizances obligations and other services whatsoever and forfeitures of the same and every of them and of and from all and all manner of suits actions complaints duties and demands whatsoever of out of upon or for the before mentioned premises to the aforesaid Patrick Savage by these presents released confirmed or granted in or within the premises or any of them or any parcel thereof to us our Heirs and successors due payable growing arising accruing or to be paid or performed or henceforward against us our heirs or successors imposed or to be imposed as well as from alienations wardships marriages intrusions or ingressions after the death of any of our tenants and all mesne profits by reason of any intrusion alienation biesnes prime seisin and from all other things whatsoever which now are or shall be imposed in the disposition supervision of our Court of Wards and [   ] and besides from the rents tenure services and burthens above in these presents to us our Heirs and successors for the premises reserved or intended to be reserved and besides from our said royal composition and expedition to war aforesaid if they should and might be established in manner and form aforesaid in and upon the aforesaid premises without any exemption or exoneration therefrom AND FURTHER of our more especial Grace and from our certain knowledge and mere motion We will and by these presents for us our Heirs and Successors We do grant that these our letters Patent or the Enrolement of the same and all and every article clause sentence and word expressed in the same shall be in all things and thro all things firm valid and effectual in Law any Statute act ordinance instruction or provision or any other thing cause or matter whatsoever notwithstanding WE ALSO will &c^o that which is herein expressed to be for ever IN TESTIMONY OF WHICH we have caused these our letters to be made Patent WITNESS our Deputy Lieutenant General of our Kingdom called Ireland at Dublin the 15th day of March in the 13th Year of our Reign.

"R. WOGAN, Dep^y Keeper of the Rolls."

APPENDIX XXI.

DOCUMENTS RELATING TO BALLYGALGET PRESERVED AT PORTAFERRY HOUSE.

I.—1st Charles I., July 14th, 1638. Patent to Rowland Savage, Gentleman, of several lands in the County of Down.

II.—9th Aug., 1638. Will of Rowland Savage.

III.—Lease for a year and conveyance of Ballygalgett, &c., in Trust, 15th Jan., 1685. Patrick Savage, Gentleman, to Robert Savage, Gent., and others.

IV.—16th Jan., 3d Anne, 1703. Exemplification of a recovery suffered of the lands of Ballygalget and Ballybranagan. Patrick Savage.

V.—8th June, 1710. Lease for a year. Patrick Savage to Hugh Savage.

VI.—Feb., 1710.   Do.   do.

VII.—31st July, 1723. Will and Probate of Hugh Savage.

VIII.—26th July, 1724. Lease for a year of Ballygalet. Francis Lucas, Edward Lucas, and Mrs. Lucy Savage, 1st part; Francis Savage, 2nd part; Philip Savage, 3rd part.

IX.—Lease and Mortgage of part of Ballygalet for £400. Philip Savage to Lucy Savage.

X.—18th Aug., 1733. Assignment of Mortgage, 1724. Lucy Savage, 1st part; Philip Savage, 2nd part; Charles Echlin, 3rd part.

XI.—Will and Codicils of Philip Savage. Will dated 9th July, 1773; 1st Codicil, 27th Feb., 1777; 2nd Codicil, 4th March, 1779; Probate, 15th Nov., 1781.

XII.—Lease dated 1st Nov., 1781. Francis Savage, James Savage, and Philip Savage, Esq^{rs.} Trustees of Philip Savage, Esq., deceased, to Henry Savage, Esq.

XIII.—Will and Codicil of Henry Savage, Esq., dated 1797; Probate 16th Dec., 1797.

XIV.—Nov., 1798. Mortgage. To Francis Turnly, Esq., James Holmes, James Trail Kennedy, Merchant, Ex^{rs} of H. Savage.

XV.—Will of Francis Turnly, Esq. Probate, April, 1801.
XVI.—July, 1805. Assignment of Mortgage. John Turnly, Esq., 1st part; Catherine Turnly, widow, 2nd part; William Maxwell Wilson, 3rd part.
XVII.—July, 1805. Deed of Trust. William M. Wilson to Andrew Savage, Esq., and M. A. Savage, Guardians of Henry Savage, a Minor.
XVIII.—Will of Mary Anne Savage, dated 1838; Probate, August, 1847.
XIX.—Dec., 1856. Assignment of Mortgage for £1,000, late currency in the town and lands of Ballygalget, in the Co. of Down. John Riddel, Esq., 1st part; Guy Stone Wilson, Esq., 2nd part; Col. Savage, 3rd part; Lenox Drennan, Esq., 4th part.

APPENDIX XXII.

PRIESTOWN PROPERTY.
Copy Codicil of Philip Savage of Ballygalget's Will.

"24th Feb$^{ry.}$ 1779.

"I PHILIP SAVAGE above and within named Do make this further Codicil to my Will vizt I direct that on the death of my wife the sum of £100 Part of the principal sum of £300 due by Mr. Echlin in my will mentioned shall be paid to my son Philip, and that the residue of that money together with the Purchase money of my Lease of Priesttown (which Lease I order to be sold on her death) shall be then equally divided among all our children share and share alike. Witness my hand and seal this [   ] day of [   ] Seventeen Hundred and Seventy nine 1779.

"Signed Sealed and Published as a Codicil in pursuance of
"A. B.
"C. D.
"E. F.

"P. S. (seal)

"This Formula of attestation is sufficient here, as this Codicil relates only to personal estate."

APPENDIX XXIII.

"MARCH BETWEEN B.GELGET AND DRUMARDEN.

"MARCH on the East side of B.gelget Lough be run from the little Bog in or adjoining to Ballywhollert as then marked out—untill it comes in a straight line to the big stone opposite to Pa^{tk} Obrien's house on the other side of the Lough—and then drawing another line from said stone to the South side of Obrien's house be the March of Drumarden and B.gelget—and that all land or water lying to the North of said line, be for ever deem'd Drumarden and belong to Echlinville, and all land and water to the South of said line, be for ever deemed B.gelget.

"Award dated 24 March 1737.
"Witness C. ECHLIN
"ALLEX^R HAMILTON

"Awarded by ROB^T ROSS
&
"THO^S NEVIN."

APPENDIX XXIV.

MAJOR-GEN. SIR JOHN BOSCAWEN SAVAGE, K.C.B., K.C.H.

A SILVER SALVER, presented to Sir. J. B. Savage, now in the possession of his grandson and representative, Col. Henry J. Savage, bears the following inscription:—

"Presented
to Colonel J. B. Savage
by his friends
of the Chatham Division of the Royal Marines
as a small token of their esteem
on his quitting the Command of that Division
when appointed Dep^{ty} Adjutant General.
March 17, 1831."

John Boscawen Savage was gazetted a K.C.B., 25th October, 1839.

APPENDIX XXV.
SAVAGE AND COCK.

THE Cock family was one of old standing in Devonshire. Lieut. Cock, R.N., father of Lady Savage (wife of Sir John Boscawen Savage, K.C.B., K.C.H.), died at sea on the 24th of March, 1766, in the 46th year of his age. It seems doubtful whether he was killed by pirates or drowned. The following inscription on a tombstone at Fremington, Co. Devon, records simply his death "at sea":—

In Memory
of William Cock son of Lieut^{nt}
William Cock and Eliza his wife
of this Parish, who died ye 12th
day of October, 1749, aged 14 days
Also of Mrs. Mary Cock, mother
of the above Lieut^{nt} Cock who died
the 7th of May, 1753, aged 64 years.
And of the said Lieut^{nt} William Cock
who died at sea the 24th of March
1766, in the 46th year of his age
Also of Eliza Ward mother to
the above Mrs. Eliza Cock who died
[*obliterated*] of March, 1766, aged 71 years.

The pedigree of the Cocks of Plymouth appears in Heralds' College down to the last Visitation of Devon in 1620; but it is short, giving only four generations.

The canton with anchor on the shield of the family is interesting on account of its historical association, having been granted to Capt. Cock for his gallant naval services to his country. There is a notice of him in a Book of Worthies of Devon, at Heralds' College, of the date 1701. He was the only person of note that lost his life in the attack on the Spanish Armada, and it is not known whether he was buried at sea or on land.

ARMS OF COCK.

Certificate of Marriage of William Cock and Elizabeth Ward at Gibraltar.

"Gibraltar, October y^e 24th 1747, O.S.

"These are to certifie, Whom it may concern, that Mr. Willm Cock and Elizabeth Ward were Lawfully married by me according to the prescribed form of the Church of England the Day and year above Written, as Witness my Hand.

"EDMUND BAXTER,
"Chaplain to the Garrison."

APPENDIX XXVI.
SAVAGE AND NUGENT.

IT is said that when Mr. Savage, of Portaferry, announced to the famous Lord Norbury his intention of assuming the name NUGENT instead of his own ancient patronymic of SAVAGE, Lord Norbury remarked, "Well, I'd rather be an *old Savage* than a *new gent*." When a man gets a reputation for wit, he is sure of being made responsible for more witticisms than he has ever uttered. The *bon-mot* in question has also been attributed to Archbishop Whately. The author of it is quite as likely to have been some member of the SAVAGE family who was displeased at the abandonment of the old and distinguished family-name. It should be remembered, however, that the name NUGENT is itself an old and distinguished one.

3 C

APPENDIX XXVII.
LIEUT.-GENERAL HENRY JOHN SAVAGE.
His Nomination for a Cadetship.

"HIS nomination for a Cadetship was obtained by the Protestant Duke of Norfolk in the following manner:—His father, John B. Savage, then a Captain of Marines, went one day to see the Duke (who was his old friend and schoolfellow, if a connection did not also exist on his mother's side) at his house in St. James' Square, to ask him if he would get a nomination for his boy. The Duke told him to go over to the Ordnance Office and try, but J. B. S. replied he had just come from there and it was useless his going again, as he was always put off with fair words. The Duke said, 'Wait here, Savage, and I'll go and see what I can do;' which he did, and brought back the nomination in his pocket and gave it to him. The boy afterwards went with his aunt, Mrs. Fenwick, his mother's sister, to stay at Arundel Castle, and there was an amusing account of the celebrated owls in the Keep in one of her letters to her sister or brother-in-law."—*(MS. note of Mr. F. W. E. Savage.)*

Address Presented to him by the Corporation of Halifax, N.S.
From the *Halifax* (Nova Scotia) *Morning Chronicle*, June 22, 1854:—
"Address to Col. Savage, R.E.

"His Worship the Mayor, accompanied by the Recorder and a number of the Aldermen, called at the Waverley House, on Wednesday, 21st inst., and presented Colonel Savage, R.E., with the following address, which had been unanimously agreed to by the City Council, on his departure from this Garrison for England, after a period of six years' service:—

"Address.
"City of Halifax, Nova Scotia, June 19, 1854.

"Sir,—The Mayor and Aldermen of the City of Halifax have great pleasure in conveying to you the high sense they entertain of your conduct while resident here for several years as the Head of the Royal Engineer Department.

"Whenever public business has brought you in communication with the City authorities you have acted with unvarying courtesy, and while you have carefully guarded the military property under your charge, your urbanity and obliging disposition towards the City have been fully evinced.

"The zeal and activity with which, on occasions of fires, you and the men under your directions have given aid, entitle you to our sincere gratitude. We regret that you are about to leave this station, but trust that happiness may attend yourself, your lady, and family, wherever Providence may direct your course.

"For and on behalf of the City Council,
"HENRY PRYOR, Mayor.
"To Colonel Henry J. Savage, Royal Engineers.
"To which the Colonel made a most feeling reply (extempore), to the following effect:—
"Reply.

"Mr. Mayor and Gentlemen,—It is with mingled feelings of pleasure and pain I rise to address you,—pleasure in having gained during a long residence in this city your good opinion, and pain at parting from the many kind friends I am about to leave. Permit me, gentlemen, to express my gratitude for the very flattering and kind manner in which you have been pleased in your address to notice my conduct during the time I held the command of the Royal Engineer Department in Nova Scotia. I assure you it ever was my endeavour to preserve the interest and property of Her Majesty committed to my charge; and it is truly gratifying to me to learn that in so doing my conduct has met with your approbation. Allow me to assure you, after a long service of forty-four years, at various stations abroad and at home, I never left one with such regret as Halifax. I take with me an addition to my family of two dear children, born in this city (Bluenoses), who will, I am confident, from constantly hearing their parents speak in praise of its inhabitants, be proud of being natives of Nova Scotia. They may again return, and will, I am sure, be most kindly received.

"For your kind good wishes for the health and happiness of Mrs. Savage, my family, and myself, accept our united thanks,—most sincerely do we wish you all the same. Adieu. God bless you!"

Addenda to p. 241.

Mr. Thomas Mylius Savage English was gazetted a 2nd Lieutenant in The Cameronians (Scottish Rifles), March 14, 1888.

Major John Richmond Jekyll died of typhoid fever at Brisbane, Queensland, while Governor of H.M. Gaol there, January 31, 1888.

APPENDIX XXVIII.

SAVAGE AND VON MYLIUS.

[*Translation.*]

"WE Joseph the Second, by the Grace of God Roman Emperor elected, at all times and always August King of Germany and of Jerusalem, Co-regent, heir and successor of the Throne and Kingdom of Hungary, Bohemia, Dalmatia, Croatia, Sclavonia, Archduke of Austria, Duke of Burgundy, Lorrain, Stiria, Carinthia, Carniola,—Grand-duke of Tuscany, Grand-prince of Transylvania, Margrave of Moravia, Duke of Brabant, Limburg, Lutzemburg, Guelderland, Wirtemburg, the high and the low Silesia, of Milan, Mantua, Parma, Placentia, and Guastalla, of Calabria, Bar, Montferrat and Teschen; Prince of Swabia, and Charleville, Prince and Count of Hapsburg, Flanders, Tyrol, Hainault, Kiburg, Goritz, Grandisca,—Margrave of the Holy Roman Empire, of Burgan, high and low Lusatia, Pont à Mousson, Nomeny, Count of Namur, Provence, Vaudemont, Blankenburg, Zutphen, Saarwerden, Salm, Blankinstein, Lord of the Vandal March, Mechlin, &c.

"Be it known to all men that we and our successors to the Holy Roman Empire, and by this letter make known to all men, through the height of the Roman Imperial dignity in which the Lord hath placed us, according to his paternal Providence, be already ornaments by many noble families and illustrious subjects. [*There seems to be something defective in the translation.*] We are nevertheless the more inclined to elevate to higher dignity and protect with Our Imperial favours, the names and families of those who as well as their ancestors have distinguished themselves above others in Our service, and that of the Holy Empire, by their faithful attachment and honourable conduct to the end that many others may be equally exalted and encouraged by such honourable rewards to the pursuit of good conduct and to the practice of noble and honourable actions.

"When it was humbly stated to Us by the actual privy Counsellor of the Duke of Wirtemburg, and Ambassador to the Circle of Swabia, ERNEST HENRY VON MYLIUS, dear and faithful to us and to the Empire, that his grandfather and father had been in the service of the Prince Elector of Saxonia as Counsellor of appeal, that the brother of his grandfather was privy Counsellor Royal of Prussia and Auditor General, and also that a great part of his family had been esteemed and considered equal to nobles at that time so that a certain MYLIUS of Gradenfield had signed the instrument of peace of Westphalia, and the dissolution of the Diet in the year sixteen hundred and fifty-four, as an Imperial Counsellor and also as a Counsellor of the King of Denmark and the Court of Oldenburg; but especially that himself had been from his youth so distinguished in the sciences that he obtained the grades of Licenciate, and after having finished his studies he occupied the place of tutor to the honourable Prince of Wirtemburg during several years; he has afterwards applied to the Court of the Duke of Wirtemburg, in whose service he has been employed twenty-two years as Counsellor of the Regency and privy Counsellor of the Regency, and privy Counsellor of the Embassy, and afterwards, particularly in the cause of the last war having rendered important and useful services to Us and our ancestors and most severe Diet of the Circle of Swabia, and they have been greatly multiplied recently in the Diet of Swabia which lately took place, and we now feel disposed, in consideration of his particular merits, described above with regard to Us, as to elevate him with clemency to the order of a Knight of the Holy Roman Empire, to which very great favour he offers himself with the most humble thankfulness, to rever[*e*] during his life-time, which he always may, can, and shall do.

"Consequently from motives proceeding from Our Imperial sentiment, We have from Our deliberate judgment good counsel and correct knowledge granted to the said ERNEST HENRY VON MYLIUS the Imperial favour, and have elevated established and considered worthy by Our own Imperial desire him and his heirs, born in lawful wedlock, and the heirs of their heirs of both sexes, descending from his family to the dignity of Knight of the Holy Roman Empire, and have joined, conjoined, and enabled him to appear in the [   ] society and community of other persons of the Nobility as if they were descended from that rank, and should have four ancestors paternal and four maternal.

"We do that, We elevate, place, and consider worthy also of the title of Knight in the Holy Roman Empire, by the perfection of the Roman Imperial power. We think, state, and will that in all and everything honourable relating to or becoming a Knight, actions and affairs spiritual and temporal, they may be considered, held, honoured, esteemed and acknowledged for such; that to this effect they enjoy all and every favour, honour, dignity, seat, note, advantage, liberty, rights and privileges, and that they be admitted to any holy place, Cathedral, Chapel, high and low functions and fiefs spiritual and temporal, observing the customs and statutes established and observed in each of them; and to tourney with all other nobles, knights and feudatories, and other persons of nobility, of high birth and faithful to

APPENDIX XXVIII.

us and the Roman Empire, and enjoy the right and all other jurisdictions and rights, pronounce sentences and issue writs, and they shall be in force, complete an[d] receivable.

"Afterwards, and in order the better to remember this our Imperial favour, We have granted to ERNEST HENRY VON MYLIUS, Knight of the Holy Roman Empire, and to his heirs, born in lawful wedlock, and to the heirs of their heirs of both sexes, the following arms suited to a Knight, and have graciously imparted and permitted the privilege of wearing them for ever :—

"A shield divided in an oblique direction, laid over with a gules cross-beam ; in the upper silver field, on which are seen three standing gules roses with green leaves, and in the lower golden field a sable half wheel of a mill: upon the shield repose two open noble tournament helmets, which are azure coloured, gules lined, gold crowned and surrounded with jewels ;—the first of which on the right is hung over with gules and golden ornaments, and the other one on the left with sable and gold ornaments. Above the one in front appears a golden griffin seeing inwards, and holding in his two claws a lighted silver lantern ; but above the one behind appears an eagle's wing, the upper part of which is silvered, the lower part gilted [sic] and overlaid with the gules cross-beam already described in the shield. In this manner the arms are painted in their proper colours in the middle of Our Imperial and gracious letter.

"In consequence We grant concede and permit ERNEST HENRY VON MYLIUS, Knight of the Holy Roman Empire, his heirs in lawful wedlock, and his successors of both sexes, the right and power to wear, employ, and make use of the Arms of nobility above described, in all and everything, actions and affairs noble and honourable, in sport, or seriously in quarrel, assault, battle, fight, tournament, struggle, game of chivalry, in the field of battle, tilt, banners, tints, insignes, seals, jewels, tomb-stones, drawings, and on every occasion and purpose, for their honour and necessity, will, and good pleasure.

"But besides, for the better attestation of Our Imperial and Royal favour, We have graciously granted and permitted ERNEST HENRY VON MYLIUS, Knight of the Holy Roman Empire, and his heirs born in lawful wedlock of both sexes, that henceforth they ought and may at all times call or name themselves, and write to Us and Our successors in the Roman Empire, so [?] their chanceries, and others and to each other in all their discourses, writings, actions and affairs, MYLIUS BARON D'EHRENGRIEF, Knight of the Holy Roman Empire, and also add all the legal titles they may then possess or those they may afterwards acquire, and which ought and may be also named, entitled and written to all and every one.

"We command and ordain all and every Prince, Electors Princes, spiritual and temporal, Prelates, Counts, Barons, Knights, Vassals, high Bailiffs, Curators, Administrators, Judges of Domain, Country Justices, Mayors, Burgomasters, Judges, Counsellors, Persons skilled in Heraldry, Heralds, Under-Heralds, Citizens and Parishioners, and all other faithful subjects of whatever dignity, rank or condition, to us and the Empire, seriously and firmly by this letter, and it is Our will that they acknowledge, favour, and consider worthy ERNEST HENRY VON MYLIUS, BARON D'EHRENGRIEF, Knight of the Holy Roman Empire, his lawful heirs born in lawful wedlock, and the heirs of their heirs descending from both sexes, for ever as Ours and the Empire well bred companions of fiefs and tournaments, and of the nobility, and not withhold our aforesaid Imperial and Royal favours, honours, dignities, liberties, rights and privileges, their elevation to the nobility of the Holy Roman Empire, the Armorial bearings of Knights, ornaments of the crest, and name, nor lead in error, but as aforesaid, let them peaceably celebrate and enjoy of them, and do nothing contrary to these presents, nor permit other, in any way or manner whatever, if they wish to avoid Our severe displeasure and that of the Empire, and punishment, and besides to be condemned to a fine of fifty marcs of fine gold, which every one who shall have acted maliciously against what has been above ordained will be obliged to pay immediately one half to Us and the other half to ERNEST HENRY VON MYLIUS, BARON D'EHRENGRIEF, Knight of the Holy Roman Empire, and his lawful heirs and successors who may be offended thereby, though harmless and inoffensive to Us and the Holy Roman Empire, and all other Rights and Privileges.

"In witness Hereof this letter, sealed with Our Imperial seal attached hereto, given at Vienna the twenty-eighth day of the month of July in the year of our Lord one thousand seven hundred and sixty-seven, and in the Fourth year of Our Reign.

"JOSEPH
"Yst Prince of the Empire Coloredo.
"*Ad mandatum Sac: Cæs:*
"*Majestatis propriorum*
"FRANZ GEORGE VON LEYKAM."

APPENDIX XXIX.

SAVAGE AND EVELEIGH.

FAMILY OF EVELEIGH, OF EVELEIGH DOWN, HANTS, WESTER EVELEIGH, CLIST ST. LAWRENCE, AND HOLCOMBE IN OTTERY, CO. DEVON.—The family of Eveleigh is one of remote antiquity. The Eveleighs (*leigh*, a meadow near a wood) are apparently of the West Saxon race, who, under Cedric their King, established themselves in the South and West of England. There is little doubt that they landed at Southampton Water in one of the many incursions that the Saxons made on the British coast, and established themselves there. In the changes that occurred many centuries after, some of the family became vassals of a Norman follower of William (de Hoghton), and afterwards of John of Ghent, and followed the Lancastrian side. Previously to this a branch migrated to Devon, though probably some intercourse still existed between them.

The Hampshire branch spell their name after the old fashion, viz., *Evelegh*. No significance can be attached to this difference of spelling at a time when the manner of spelling surnames was of such little consequence.

Their first settlement appears to have been at Eveleigh (Eveleigh Down), now situated in the civil parish of Houghton, ecclesiastical parish of All Saints, Diocese of Winchester, in a detached part of the hundred of Buddlesgate, County of Southamptonshire—half-a-mile from Broughton Drove, the boundary between the parishes of Houghton and Broughton, half-a-mile from the Roman road from Old Sarum to Winchester and one mile from the river Test, eleven miles from the City of Salisbury, and seventy from London.

It is now, and has been within the oldest memory, a "Homestead" belonging to "Houghton Manor Farm," the whole containing 437 acres, and is the property of the Ecclesiastical Commissioners. The homestead consists of two tenements, now occupied by Farm Servants.

The Parish of Houghton contains 2,672¼ acres. No person in this or the neighbouring parishes now bears the name of Eveleigh.

Eveleigh Down was broken up and brought into tillage in the year 1790, and contained about 220 acres, which, together with the woods (30 acres), form part of Houghton Manor Farm (187 acres), total of the Manor, 437 acres.

In the last century it was the property of Lord Rivers (a descendant in the female line of the Savages, Earls Rivers). At that time no building existed on the estate except the Keeper's house in one of the woods—"Hare Warren."

Lord Rivers's successor, Mr. Townsend, built the two tenements.

Wester Eveleigh Farm, 207 acres, now called "Dymonds," is situated in a detached part of the parish of Farringdon and hundred of East Budleigh, in the County of Devon, about one mile from Honiton Clist, on the Road to Bishop's Clist, at the foot of a slight declivity and where the road crosses a tributary of the River Clist, on the right hand side abutting the road, the dwelling House facing towards Bishop's Clist, the farm buildings in rear next the brook.

The present House bears date 1676, initials R.B.

No person bearing the name of Eveleigh now resides in the parish of Farringdon (301 persons).

The College of Arms was instituted by Richard III., on the 2nd March, 1483, in the first year of his reign, but the arms of Eveleigh were borne long before that period; by whom granted is not known.

John Eveleigh, of Wester Eveleigh, Co. Devon, the representative of the Family in that county, married Margaret Churchill, daughter of John Churchill, of Brokwell (now Buckerell), in the same county. This marriage appears to have taken place about the year 1489, soon after the Battle of Bosworth. His eldest son was Thomas—other issue not mentioned.

The Family appears to have finally left the ancestral home, probably through political causes, as no further mention is made of their residing at Wester Eveleigh again.

This Thomas, then of Clyst St. Lawrence, married Thomazin More, daughter of Myghele More of the same place (a "More" lived at Sudbury in the time of Queen Elizabeth). His eldest son was John —other issue unmentioned.

APPENDIX XXIX.

This John Eveleigh (living 1564), of Holcombe, a locality still existing and marked also in Speed's map of 1610, in the parish of Ottery St. Mary (present population 3,973. To this day the Eveleighs are more numerous in this parish than any other in Devon—30 persons in number), married, first, Alys Collyns, daughter of Henry Collyns—evidently a mésalliance. His children by her were Robert, Elizabeth, and Margaret. Robert does not appear to have married, but his sister Elizabeth married Richard Calmadge,[1] gent., and his youngest sister, Margaret, William Lentall (Lenthall),[2] of Monkton, gent.—now Monkaton in the parish of Pinchawes (Pinhoe) in the hundred of Wonford. He married "en secondes noces" Jone Sowthcott, one of a numerous family, and daughter of John Sowthcott, Esq., of Bovey Tracey, Co. Devon, and her issue were George, Rycharde, John, Nicholas, Thomas, Mary and Margarett—curiously enough the two youngest daughters of both wives were named Margaret.

Margaret, the youngest daughter by 2nd wife, was 1st wife of Sir William Sandys, of Northbourne, Kent; and the 4th son (3rd by 2nd wife), John Eveleigh, M.A., Proctor of Exeter College, 1590, and Principal of Hart Hall, Oxford, 1591, died in 1604, leaving by Prudence, his wife, daughter of Robert Burnes, M.D., sometime Fellow of Merton College, Oxford, a son, the Very Rev. John Eveleigh, of Blackhall and Coplands Meade, Co. Oxford, Dean of Ross, whose daughter and co-heiress, Jane Eveleigh, married Col. Frederick William Mullins, of Burnham, M.P.

Of this marriage there was a son, from whom descends the present Family of Eveleigh-De Moleyns. (*See* Ventry, Baron. Burke's *Peerage*.)

Arms—Per pale, or and sable, two chevrons interchanged between 3 griffins passant. Crest—A demi-griffin per pale or and sable.

PEDIGREE OF EVELEIGH FAMILY.

EVELEIGH.
Johannes Evelinge, Artium Magister et Proctor, Fellow of Exeter College, Oxford.
John Eveleigh (temp. 2 Elisabeth)=Margaret, daughter of John Churchill, of Brokwell, Co. Devon, of Wester Eveleigh, near Exeter, J.P. | (now Buckerell).

Thomas Eveleigh, of Clist=Thomasine, daughter of Michael Moore, of Clist St Lawrence.
St. Lawrence

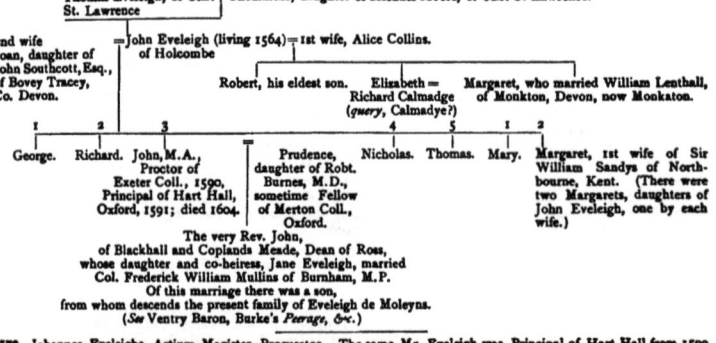

2nd wife =John Eveleigh (living 1564)= 1st wife, Alice Collins.
Joan, daughter of   of Holcombe
John Southcott, Esq.,
of Bovey Tracey,   Robert, his eldest son.   Elizabeth =   Margaret, who married William Lenthall,
Co. Devon.   Richard Calmadge   of Monkton, Devon, now Monkaton.
                                                  (*query*, Calmadye?)

1   2   3   4   5   1   2
George. Richard. John, M.A.,   Prudence,   Nicholas. Thomas. Mary. Margaret, 1st wife of Sir
                  Proctor of   daughter of Robt.   William Sandys of North-
                  Exeter Coll., 1590, Burnes, M.D.,   bourne, Kent. (There were
                  Principal of Hart Hall, sometime Fellow   two Margaretts, daughters of
                  Oxford, 1591; died 1604. of Merton Coll.,   John Eveleigh, one by each
                                    Oxford.   wife.)
                  The very Rev. John,
                  of Blackhall and Coplands Meade, Dean of Ross,
                  whose daughter and co-heiress, Jane Eveleigh, married
                  Col. Frederick William Mullins of Burnham, M.P.
                  Of this marriage there was a son,
                  from whom descends the present family of Eveleigh de Moleyns.
                  (*See* Ventry Baron, Burke's *Peerage*, &c.)

1578. Johannes Eveleighe, Artium Magister, Procurator. The same Mr. Eveleigh was Principal of Hart Hall from 1599 to 1604; Proctor in 1590. (From MS. Catalogue of Fellows of Exeter Coll.)—*See above*.
1680. Edward Eveleigh, Seneschalis or Bailiff of Exeter.
1674. John Eveleigh, M.A. the same year, afterwards Rector of South Sidenham and Vicar of Lamerton, Devonshire. (From MS. Catalogue of Fellows of Exeter Coll.)
1702. Johannes Eveleigh de Ottery Divæ Mariæ, admissus Maii 18, Mag⁰ Verman Burs Mag⁰ Rous Tutore. (From MS. Catalogue of Fellows of Exeter Coll.)
1719. Anne, daughter of William Eveleigh, Esq., of Holcombe, Ottery St. Mary, Devon, and wife of John Leigh, Esq., of Northcourt (I. of W.), died in this year.—(From Burke's *Genealogical and Heraldic History of the Commons of Great Britain and Ireland*—1838.)
John Eveleigh, Lieut. R.N., 16 May, 1809.—*See* Navy List.
John Eveleigh, Capt. R.N., 29 March, 1810.— do.

---

[1] Query—Calmadye?
[2] The Rt. Hon. William Lenthall, Speaker of the Long Parliament, was of this Family. (*See* Lenthall of Bessels Leigh. Burke's *Landed Gentry*.)

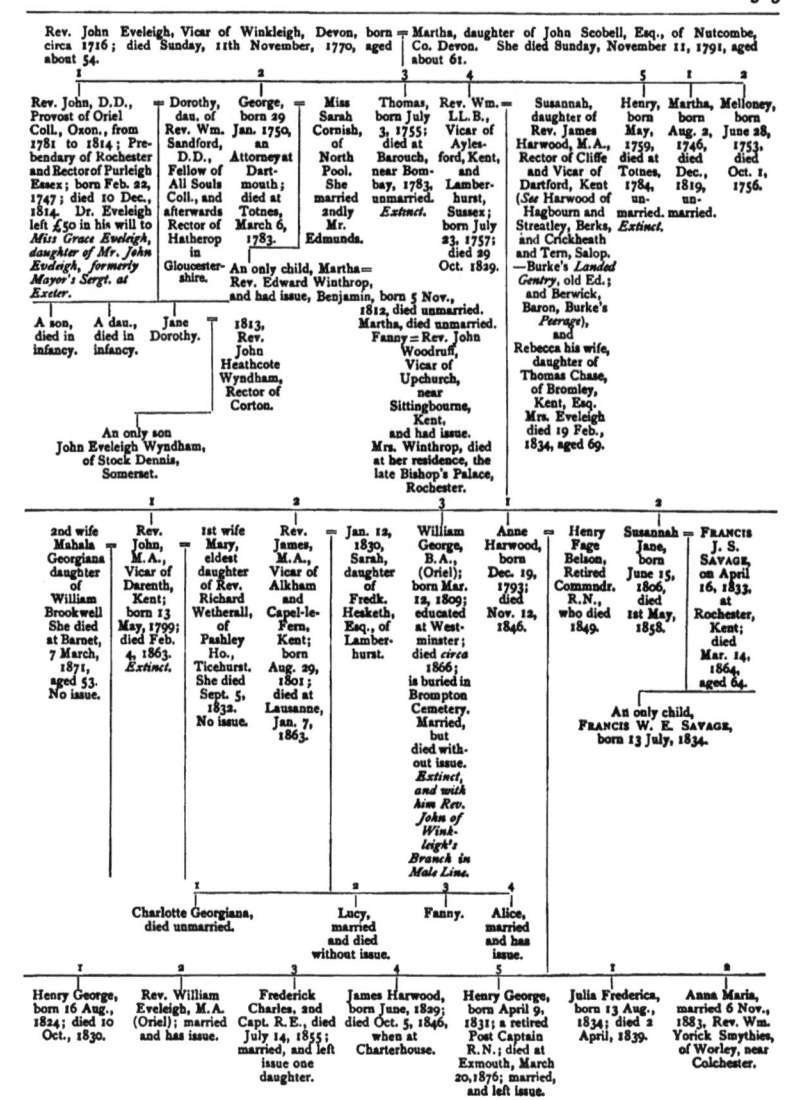

APPENDIX XXIX.

Rev. John Eveleigh, Vicar of Winkleigh, Devon, born circa 1716; died Sunday, 11th November, 1770, aged about 54. = **Martha**, daughter of John Scobell, Esq., of Nutcombe, Co. Devon. She died Sunday, November 11, 1791, aged about 61.

1. Rev. John, D.D., Provost of Oriel Coll., Oxon., from 1781 to 1814; Prebendary of Rochester and Rector of Purleigh Essex; born Feb. 22, 1747; died 10 Dec., 1814. Dr. Eveleigh left £50 in his will to *Miss Grace Eveleigh, daughter of Mr. John Eveleigh, formerly Mayor's Sergt. at Exeter.* = **Dorothy**, dau. of Rev. Wm. Sandford, D.D., Fellow of All Souls Coll., and afterwards Rector of Hatherop in Gloucestershire.

2. George, born 29 Jan. 1750, an Attorney at Dartmouth; died at Totnes, March 6, 1783.

3. Miss Sarah Cornish, of North Pool. She married 2ndly Mr. Edmunds.

4. Thomas, born July 3, 1755; died at Barouch, near Bombay, 1783. Lambert. She *Extinct.* married unmarried.

5. Rev. Wm. LL.B., Vicar of Aylesford, Kent, Lamberhurst, Sussex; born July 23, 1757; died 29 Oct. 1829. = **Susannah**, daughter of Rev. James Harwood, M.A., Rector of Cliffe and Vicar of Dartford, Kent (*See Harwood of Hagbourn and Streatley, Berks, and Crickheath and Tern, Salop.*—Burke's *Landed Gentry*, old Ed.; and Berwick, Baron, Burke's *Peerage*), and Rebecca his wife, daughter of Thomas Chase, of Bromley, Kent, Esq. Mrs. Eveleigh died 19 Feb., 1834, aged 69.

1. Henry, born May, 1759, died at Totnes, 1784, unmarried. *Extinct.*

2. Martha, born Aug. 2, 1746, died Dec., 1819, married.

1. Melloney, born June 28, 1753, died Oct. 1, 1756.

A son, died in infancy. | A dau., died in infancy. | Jane Dorothy. = **1813, Rev. John Heathcote Wyndham**, Rector of Corton.

An only son **John Eveleigh Wyndham**, of Stock Dennis, Somerset.

An only child, Martha = Rev. Edward Winthrop, and had issue, Benjamin, born 5 Nov., 1812, died unmarried. Martha, died unmarried. Fanny = Rev. John Woodruff, Vicar of Upchurch, near Sittingbourne, Kent, and had issue. Mrs. Winthrop, died at her residence, the late Bishop's Palace, Rochester.

2nd wife Mahala Georgiana daughter of William Brookwell. She died at Barnet, 7 March, 1871, aged 53. No issue. = **1. Rev. John, M.A.**, Vicar of Darenth, Kent; born 13 May, 1799; died Feb. 4, 1863. *Extinct.* = **1st wife Mary**, eldest daughter of Rev. Richard Wetherall, of Pashley Ho., Ticehurst. She died Sept. 5, 1832. No issue.

2. Rev. James, M.A., Vicar of Alkham and Capel-le-Fern, Kent; born Aug. 29, 1801; died at Lausanne, Jan. 7, 1863.

= Jan. 12, 1830, **Sarah**, daughter of Fredk. Hesketh, Esq., of Lamberhurst.

3. William George, B.A., (Oriel); born Mar. 12, 1809; educated at Westminster; died circa 1866; is buried in Brompton Cemetery. Married, but died without issue. *Extinct, and with him Rev. John of Winkleigh's Branch in Male Line.*

Anne Harwood, born Dec. 19, 1793; died Nov. 12, 1846. = **Henry Fage Belson**, Retired Commndr. R.N., who died 1849.

2. Susannah Jane, born June 15, 1806, died 1st May, 1858. = **Francis J. S. Savage**, on April 16, 1833, at Rochester, Kent; died Mar. 14, 1864, aged 64.

An only child, **Francis W. E. Savage**, born 13 July, 1834.

---

1. Charlotte Georgiana, died unmarried. | **2. Lucy**, married and died without issue. | **3. Fanny.** | **4. Alice**, married and has issue.

---

1. Henry George, born 16 Aug., 1824; died 10 Oct., 1830.

2. Rev. William Eveleigh, M.A. (Oriel); married and has issue.

3. Frederick Charles, 2nd Capt. R.E., died July 14, 1855; married, and left issue one daughter.

4. James Harwood, born June, 1839; died Oct. 5, 1846, when at Charterhouse.

5. Henry George, born April 9, 1831; a retired Post Captain R.N.; died at Exmouth, March 20, 1876; married, and left issue.

1. Julia Frederica, born 13 Aug., 1834; died 2 April, 1839.

2. Anna Maria, married 6 Nov., 1883, Rev. Wm. Yorick Smythies, of Worley, near Colchester.

FRANCIS JAMES SAUMAREZ SAVAGE.

Addendum to p. 235.—In Mr. F. J. S. Savage's will (which, however, he left unexecuted) occurred the following remarkable direction—"It is my desire that my body remains unburied until after it has been opened and the cause of death fully ascertained, for the benefit of medical science."

The loss of his hearing in childhood (owing to the accident mentioned in the text) made it impossible for Mr. F. J. S. Savage to enter the Navy, for which he had been destined; but his excellent natural ability, the special adaptability of his mind to details, his industry, and the thoroughness with which he always pursued his inquiries into any subject that he took up, would have enabled him to succeed in almost any profession, could he have been trained for any.

APPENDIX XXX.
SAVAGE OF GLASTRY.

Addendum to p. 278.—

AFTER the death of the Rev. Henry Savage, of Glastry, and the coming of age of his eldest son, Francis, of Glastry, his widow and younger children went to reside at Lagan Vale, near Belfast, then a large suburban house standing in wooded grounds; and there Mrs. Savage died.

APPENDIX XXXI.
SAVAGE OF KNOCKADOO, CO. SLIGO, AND SAVAGE OF BALLYMADUN, CO. DUBLIN.

SAVAGE OF KNOCKADOO.—This family, according to Sir Bernard Burke (*see General Armory*, p. 900), was "a branch of SAVAGE OF PORTAFERRY; descended from HUGH SAVAGE, Esq., of the City of Dublin, third son of JOHN SAVAGE, Esq., of Ballyvarley, Co. Down, great-grandson of ROWLAND SAVAGE, Esq., of the Little Ards, who died at Portaferry in 1552." And Sir Bernard adds—"The REV. ROBERT SAVAGE, of Knockadoo, and Lukesland House, Co. Devon, died 1841, leaving his sisters his co-heirs." And their Arms, he tells us, were the same as those of Portaferry.

SAVAGE OF BALLYMADUN.—This family, Sir Bernard Burke tells us, was in its turn descended from PORTAFERRY through the KNOCKADOO branch. "FRANCIS SAVAGE, Esq., of Ballymadun," he writes, "was eldest son of REV. CHRISTOPHER KINGSBOROUGH SAVAGE, who was eldest son of FRANCIS SAVAGE, Esq., of Knockadoo.

APPENDIX XXXII.
AMERICAN BRANCHES.

WE have seen a Genealogy of the Family of John Savage, of Upper Middletown (now Cromwell), Connecticut, United States of America, which family claims descent from the Savages of Cheshire. This John Savage "was married at Hartford, Conn., February 10, 1652, to Elizabeth Dubbin. He removed to Upper Middletown (now Cromwell), Conn., and became a freeholder in May, 1654. His lands are recorded March 22nd, 1657, vol. i, p. 25. He died, May 6th, 1685, and his will, made Nov. 22nd, 1684, is in the Probate Records at Hartford. He left a large landed estate to his family. He was often called upon by the town in various stations. He appears to have settled in Upper Middletown as his first location in the colony, and was the first of the name in the colony." He had, by his wife Elizabeth (*née* Dubbin), eleven children. Amongst his living descendants in the United States are (in 1888) the following :—The Hon. Judge Albert R. Savage, of Lewiston, Maine; Mrs. Sarah Corey St. Lawrence, of Day, Saratoga, Co. New York ; the Rev. George Slocum Folger Savage, D.D., of Chicago, Ill., Secretary of the Chicago Theological Seminary, &c.; Charles Casse Savage, New York City, author of *Illustrated Biography* (1852), *The World, Geographical, Historical, and Statistical* (1853), &c.; Mrs. Jane Crane Forbes; Hiram Francis Savage, of South Glens Falls, N.Y.; Mrs. Sarah Elizabeth Hinze; Mrs. Julie Frances Clark, of Middleborough, Mass.; Amasa Savage, of East Galway, Saratoga, Co. N.Y.; John Henry Savage; George Pruden Savage; Watson Lewis Savage, now a practising physician in New York City, and director of the New Gymnasium of the Berkeley Lyceum Association; James Francis Savage, of Boston, Mass.; Charles Wesley Savage, LL.B., of Lowell, Mass.; Julius B. Savage, of Southington, Conn.; Cornelius Savage, of New York City; Henry Burnham Savage, a practising physician in New York City; Mrs. Kate Louise O'Brien; Alexander Duncan Savage, of New York City; Thomas Rutherford Savage, a physician, connected with the Michigan Asylum for the Insane at Kalamazov, Mich.; and Lyman Bayley Savage.

APPENDIX XXXIII.
MISCELLANEOUS REFERENCES.

A.D. 1401.—Johannes Savage, Prior of Wymundham. *See Gesta Abbatum Monasterii Sancti Albani*, p. 480.

3 Jany, 1446.—"Know all men by these presents that I Margaret daughter of Thomas de Rupe have granted, &c., to Edmund, son of David Pyll, one messuage in the burgage of Kinsale, which messuage lies between that of *John son of Thomas Sawage* on the west to the messuage of Fynne O'Myhygane on the east, in length from the common street on the south to the land of the heirs of Alicie de Rupe on the north. To hold of the chief lords of the fee. Given at Kinsale 3 Jany 24 Hen. VI. Witnesses, Sir Henry Glassane, Vicar of Kinsale, William and Edmund sons of Maurice de Rupe, Dionisius o'Ronane, Sir John Ragnald, and others." Seal (R.)

From *Materials Illustrative of the Reign of Henry VII.*, vol. i.

A D. 1485, 21st Sept.—Thomas, the King's trusty and well-beloved chaplain, Thomas Savage, doctor of laws, of the office of Chancellor of the Earldom of the Marshes.—(*P.* 507.)

A.D. 1486.—Lease for seven years to Sir John Savage, Junior, of very extensive lands, mines, water-mills, fisheries in the High Peak, including "the whole of the demesne land called le Castel Flattes, in the field of Castleton;" mills and meadows in Ashbourne, &c.—(*P.* 332.)

A.D. 1486, 18th Feb.—Commission to the King's uncle, Jaspar, Duke of Bedford, Thomas Savage, Chancellor of the Earldom of March, Owen Pole, Clk., Edmund Mountforth, Knt., James Baskervyle, Knt., Morgan John Philip, Hugh Huntley, Thomas Morgan of Gloucester, and John Leighton, Esq., to hear and determine all causes, plaints, &c., amongst [?] tenants, farmers, and inhabitants of the Earldom of March, in Wales, and the marches thereof, &c., &c.

A.D. 1486, Feb. 25.—Grant to Sir John Savage, Senior, in consideration of his good and faithful service in the King's last victorious battle, of the office of keeper of the parkes of Halton and Norwode, parcel of the duchy of Lancaster; to hold for the term of his life, with the accustomed wages and fees thereunto belonging.—(*P.* 605.)

A.D. 1486, March 7.—Grant, in tail male, to John Savage, the younger, Knt. (in consideration of his having largely exposed himself, with a crowd of his kinsmen, servants, and friends, as volunteers in the King's service, in the battle against the King's great adversary Ric. III., the late pretended King of England; and also in consideration of other services rendered, alway with anxious solicitude during prosperity as well as adversity), of the castle, manor, and lordship of Gresley and Kymbley or Kymberley, Co. Notts.; the manor and lordship of Ilkeston, and a coal mine in Ilkeyston *alias* Ekylston, Co. Derby, forfeited by John Zouche, Knt., Lord Zouche; also of the manors and lordships of Elmeton and Holmesfield, Co. Derb.; and Grandly and Sutton, Co. Notts.; Shepeshed, Co. Leic.; and 22s. rent in the town of Leicester; also of the manors and lordships of Sutton Hubybunderell *alias* Hopbudler or Hopbulder, Watton *alias* Wotton, Corston, and Eudunburnell, or Eudenburnell, or Eudonburnell, or Eudeburnell, Co. Salop, forfeited by Francis Lovell, Knt., Viscount Lovell, under an act of the Parl. held at Westminster 7 Nov. last.—(*P.* 865.)

A.D. 1486, 19 July.—Grant to Lawrence Savage, son of Sir John Savage, Senior, of an annuity of 20 marks, during the King's pleasure, out of the issues and profits of the High Peak, in Co. Derby.—(*P.* 507.)

About same date.—Robert Savage, master of the King's barge.

Sept. 19, 1488.—Christopher Savage, son of Sir John Savage, Knt. (in consideration of true and faithful service done, "as well for the repressing of oure rebelles as otherwise"), of the offices of steward and master of the game at Fekneham and parker of the same forest, Co. Worcester, and of all offices within the said forest in the King's gift.

Same date.—Do. to James Savage, son of Sir John Savage, the elder, Knt. (in consideration of true and faithful service done unto us in our late victorious journey and feld) of the office of keeper of the park of Baskewode, co. Notts.

Same date.—Do. to Edward Savage, son of Sir John Savage, the elder, of the offices of bailiff and parker of the Lordships of Hatfield and Thorne.—(*P.* 10.)

From *Calendars of State Papers.*

Temp. Henry VIII.—John de Sauvaige, Lord of Schaubeke, President of Flanders, also Chancellor of Brabant and Burgundy.

2 Henry VIII., 20 July.—Sir John Carn [?] to be bailiff and parker of Hatfield and Thorne, Yorkshire, which Edward, son of John Savage, Sen., holds by patent of 19 Sept., 1 Henry VII.

A.D. 1513, 25 Sept.—Knights made at Tourayne (Tournay), in the Church after the King came to Mass, under his banner in the Church, 25 Dec., 5th year of his reign,— . . . Sir John Savage.

A.D. 1514.—Marriage of the Princess Mary. Names of the Englishmen which were sent in ambassade to the French King, before the Queen's landing, and other gentlemen in their company:— The Earl of Worcester, Lord Chamberlain; the Lord of St. John's, Thos. Docwra, and the Dean of Windsor, Doctor West. Ambassadors:—The Lord Herbert, son of the Earl of Worcester; Sir John Savage; Sir ——; Sir Christopher Garneys; Sir ——; Clarenceux King of Arms.

May, 1520.—Grants. . . . . Anth. Savage, of Elmeley, *alias* of Hanley, Worc. Pardon for the homicide of John Pauncefote, of Hasfeld, Glouc., justice of the peace in co. Glouc. Westm. 6 May. —*Pat.* 12 *Hen. VIII.*, p. l. m. 23.

Christ., s. & h. of Christopher Savage & Anne his wife, d. and one of the heirs of John Stanley & Geo. Savage, clk. Livery of lands in Chepyng-Campden, Buryton, Westington, Aston-under-Edge, Ulington, & Norton-under-Edge, Glouc., whereof the said George Savage was enfeoffed to the use of the said C. Savage, sen., and of the reversions of all possessions now held for life by Thomas Savage & Arnold Savage of the inheritance of the said Christopher the son in co. Chester, to the annual value of 8*l.* *Del.* Westm., 14 May 12 Hen. VIII.—S. B. *Pat.* p. 2., m. l.

Vol. XLII., p. 288.

A.D. 1567, Feb. 18.—Minute of letter to Sir John Savage, Sir Hugh Cholmley, and Sir Laurence Smith, to vew and muster all the levies at the port of Chester.

DITTO, p. 292.

A.D. 1567, May 29.—Chester. Sir John Savage, Sir Laurence Smith, and Sir Hugh Cholmondley to the Council. Have borrowed certain sums of money for the purpose of sending soldiers into Ireland, for repayment of which they request a sufficient remittance. Inclosing 1st account of money borrowed of certain merchants and others of Chester for the purpose of transporting soldiers to Ireland.

Vol. XLIII., p. 294.

A.D. 1567, June.—Some account of the charges for transporting 250 soldiers from Chester to Ireland by order of Sir John Savage, Sir L. Smyth, and Sir H. Cholmondley, and of sums advanced for payment of the same.

Vol. LVIII., p. 344.

A.D. 1569, Sept.—Certified of Sir John Savage, Sir Hugh Cholmley, and others of the furniture of horses, armour and weapons, and of general musters of the whole county of Chester.

Vol. LX, p. 354.

A.D. 1569, Dec. 10.—Sir John Savage to the Council. The declaration has been zealously subscribed by the Justices of Chester out of duty to the Queen, by whom is opened to us the plain path of virtue to our eternal salvation. Incloses 1st Declaration by the Justices of Chester of their submission to the Act of Parliament for uniformity of Common Prayer.

Vol. LXIX., p. 377.

A.D. 1570, May 26.—Roke [*Rock*] Savage. Sir John Savage to the Earl of Leicester. Sends the certificates of the musters of Leicestershire.

From *The Annals of Lock Ct.*

A.D. 1577.—Robert Savage—*i.e.* the Sub-Sheriff of the Co. Sligo, was killed, and six of his people along with him, by Mac Donnchadha.

The Ardkeen Succession.

"Jenkin Savage [Janico-a-bui] died seized of the Castle of Ardkine, &c., as well as of the 4 towns or townlands to the same castle belonging, viz., Town called Ardkine, Ballyshane, Ballycrane, Ballyculter. That Roland Savage after the death of s^d Jenkin took charge of all the premises until the taking of the Inquisition (Inq. C.R.O. taken at Ballykacomer, 3 Feb., 1 James I.)"—*MS. Note by G. F. Barry, Esq., in possession of F. W. E. Savage, Esq.*

A.D. 1660, June (?)—Certificate for Arthur Savage. For the Prebend of Carlisle, by the death of Fred Tunstall. Annexing Certificate by Dr. Guy Carleton [Dean of Carlisle] and four others, in favour of Petitioner.

Petition.—Thomas Savage, B.D., rector of Sutton-Bonnington, Co. Notts, for the Deanery of Lichfield. Adhered to the Church throughout the late times. Annexing Certificate by Drs. Gilbert Sheldon, Rob. Sanderson, and George Morley in favour of Thomas Savage, formerly of Magdalen College, Oxford.

John Savage, D.D., Rector of Clothill, Notts, "from his ready wit styled the Aristippus of the day." Query, *date and parentage?*

A.D. 1641. (Ireland). Valentine Savage, Deputy-Clerk of the Crown.

The Rev. Samuel Morton Savage. Query, *date and parentage?*

Ballygalget (Earlier) Line and the Portaferry Family.

Patrick Savage, of Ballygalget, who is a party to a Deed, 25 Nov. 1670, is called *cousin-german* of John Savage of Ballyvarley, Co. Down, who was ancestor of the Savages of Portaferry.

A.D. 1671.—Philip Savage, Prothonotary (Ireland).

A D. 1693.—Capt. Robert Savage mentioned in Calendar of Treasury Papers as "late Provost Marshal in Ireland."

A.D. 1695.—Rt. Hon. Philip Savage, Chancellor of the Exchequer, Ireland. Patent dated Sept. 13, 1695.

SAVAGE OF ARDKEEN.—Patrick Savage of Maghernely, Co. Armagh, by will proved in 1732, leaves "his dearly beloved cousin," Francis Savage, of Ardkeen, his interest in his lease of Maghernely. He had a brother Robert.

Capt. Patrick Savage, of Corgery, who married Catherine [Magennis?], 22 May, 1725, mentions his cousin, Francis Savage, of Ardkeen, and his dearly beloved brother, Col. Daniel Magenis.

SAVAGE OF BELGOOLY, CO. CORK.—We have been favoured with some information about the above family, which claims descent from Ardkeen; but have been unable to obtain sufficient details to work out the genealogy. The following letter, addressed by the late Sir W. Betham, Ulster King-of-Arms, to the late Dr. Savage, R.A., furnishes a few facts of family history :—

"DUBLIN CASTLE,
"Feb. 20th [18]53.

"Sir,—I have directed a sketch of the arms of your family to be made. The Crest you sent me points out the Savages of Ardkin as your ancestors.

"I have a pedigree up to your great-grandfather, Johnson Savage, of Belgooly, in Co. Cork, whose son, Johnson Savage, was one of the sufferers in the Black Hole of Calcutta, and was married to Amy, daughter of —— Edwards, by ——, daughter of —— Raymond, of the Co. Kerry.

"We have very full pedigrees of the Savages of the North of Ireland, who were amongst the most ancient and noble families there. One was a Peer of Parliament by the title of Lord Savage of the Ards.
"I am, Sir, your obedient Servant,
"To Dr. Savage, R.A." "W. BETHAM.

According to the family papers, &c., the Johnson Savage, of Belgooly, referred to in this letter by Sir William Betham, was in the army, and married the daughter of a Scotch laird named Ainsworth. He quarrelled with his Colonel (the Colonel being stepfather to his wife), sent him a challenge, and was placed under arrest. He sold out in order to fight the Colonel, but the latter was ordered suddenly abroad. He left five sons, viz., the above-named Johnson Savage, Junior, and four brothers. The four brothers went to America. The eldest son, Johnson Savage (Junior), entered the army, as his father did before him; went to India, and there married a rich wife, and came home very wealthy, so much so that he was called "The Golden Bird." Horses, hounds, and boon companions, however, ultimately reduced him to very straitened circumstances. By his 2nd wife, Amy Savage (*née* Edwards), he had three sons and two daughters. One of his grandsons was the late Dr. Savage, who was for 30 years attached to the Royal Artillery, Medical Department, and whose sons and present representatives are Major Johnson W. Savage, R E., and the Rev. Mr. Savage, Vicar of Woodnesborough, Sandwich.

APPENDIX XXXIII.

Extract from a work on Freemasonry. Printed in Belfast, 1818.—Page 112.—
"AHIMAN REZON
"OR
"CONSTITUTION OF FREE MASONRY.

"Thomas Savage, earl of Rivers, having succeeded the earl of St. Alban's in the office of Grand Master, in June 1666, Sir Christopher Wren was appointed Deputy under his lordship, and distinguished himself more than any of his predecessors in office, in promoting the prosperity of the few lodges which occasionally met at this time; particularly the old lodge of St. Paul's, now the lodge of Antiquity, which he patronised upwards of 18 years. The honours which this celebrated character afterwards received in the Society, are evident proofs of the unfeigned attachment of the Fraternity toward him."

From *The London Gazette*, Sat., Oct. 28, 1809.
"Admiral's Office, Oct. 25/9.
"This day, in pursuance of the King's pleasure, the following flag-officers of his Majesty's fleet were promoted, viz. :—

"Vice-Admirals of the White, H. Savage, Esq.; B. S. Rowley, Esq.; Sir R. Bicherton, Bart.; G. Bowen, Esq., to be Vice-Admirals of the Red."

Messrs. Marcus Ward & Co. have called our attention to the emblazoning of the Savage Arms, as possibly representing Cheshire, on the Common Seal of the Borough of Warrington—*Argent, six lioncels sable.* "The shield is placed between two flags, in saltire, viz., that bearing the arms of the Duchy of Lancashire, and that bearing the arms of Cheshire. In place of crest is a scroll inscribed Anno Decimo *Victoria Regina.* The Scroll, supported by Sword and Sceptre in saltire,—a laurel-wreath hanging upon the upper portion of Scroll."

SAVAGE OF BLOXWORTH.—We are probably wrong in our conjecture that the ancestor of this branch of the SAVAGE family was *tenth* son of Sir John Savage, "Senior," who died in 1495. There are three pedigrees of the SAVAGE family in the British Museum (Harl. MS. 1505, Harl. MS. 2187, and Harl. MS. 1535), in all which this Richard Savage is *sixth* son. In the pedigree, Harl. MS. 2187, though placed sixth, the figure 8 also is written against his name. It has been suggested also that it was not this Sir Richard, but his son, who was the first owner of Bloxworth. The dates make it perhaps improbable, but, we think, not impossible. The descent of the Bloxworth Savages from Rock Savage (Cheshire) is well established, and unquestioned.

HUGH SAVAGE, commonly called "OLD ROCK."—Montgomery writes:—"Upon a design of surprising the Duke of Ormond and the Castle of Dublin, one Maj[r] Blood, who was in the plott, went through the North of Ireland privately, and in like manner conferring divers Presbyterian Ministers to engage them and to learn what assistance they w[d] lend to a cause on foot for God's glory (so he called the rebellion he was hatching) and their profit, they being now ejected by the B[ps] and not suffered to preach. Our Earl had some small notice of this, but no description of the man. The Duke had more perfect intelligence, and sent for his Lo[p] giving him a character of Blood, and where and with whom he had been, and desired to have him apprehended; his Lo[p], therefore, sent Mr. Hugh Savage (one of the Gents. of his troop) called commonly Old Rock (because it is supposed he is descended of the family of Rock Savage), and with him the Duke's warrants and his own order to take such and such out of his s[d] troop, which then lay at Newtown, and to search for Blood, who escaped very narrowly." To this passage the Rev. Mr. Hill appends the following note:—"The gentleman mentioned in the text was probably father-in-law of Colonel Hugh Cochran"—*i.e.*, CAPTAIN HUGH SAVAGE, of Ardkeen, who died in 1723. But if so, it is strange that Montgomery, who frequently mentions HUGH SAVAGE, of Ardkeen, and sends him a copy of his *Incidental Remembrances of the Two Ancient Families of the Savages*, should not have identified him as such. Our own impression is, that "Old Rock" must have been some descendant of Sir Arthur Savage of Rhebane.